Crisp, comprehensive, packed with unusual insights, and refreshing in style, Hexham's book is invaluable for anyone wishing to understand the recent religious resurgence that has caught so many educated people by surprise, and shown up their tone deafness about all that is happening.

—Os Guinness, author of *The Case for Civility*

As Pope Benedict constantly reminds us, Christians today face a new situation where other religious traditions once more challenge Christian belief just as they did in the days of the apostles. This book helps us understand our non-Christian neighbors and as such is a valuable tool for all Catholic educators.

—Henry Rosenbaum, SAC Former Director of Education for the Roman Catholic Diocese of Calgary

This is not the conventional or predictable textbook on world religions. As a good teacher, Irving Hexham is not afraid to offer the kind of opinion or insight that is bound to provoke discussion and debate. This book is the fruit of many years of trying to encourage university students to engage meaningfully with the study of religion and is borne out of great experience.

—Gerald J. Pillay, Vice-Chancellor (President) and Rector, Liverpool Hope University

This textbook-type tour of world religions, spiced with personal close-ups, fully merits a place on thoughtful Christians' bookshelves. Informal and informative, learned, wise, chatty, and sometimes provocative, it is a very impressive performance.

—J. I. Packer, Professor of Theology, Regent College

My former colleague from Regent College days, and long-time friend, Irving Hexham has written an absolutely fascinating book on world religions which reflects a balance and level of scholarship rarely found in introductory works. Therefore, I enthusiastically endorse this book.

—Bruce Waltke, Professor of Old Testament, Knox Theological Seminary

Irving Hexham writes that "bland approaches [to the study of religion] produce bland students." Irving Hexham is not bland, and by combining authoritative knowledge of the world's religions with a keen eye for current events, he has given us a textbook that will not produce bland students. Instead it will produce students who know about religion and who know how religious people the world over relate to the crucial issues of the day.

—Terry C. Muck, Dean and Professor of Mission and World Religion, E. Stanley Jones School of World Mission and Evangelism, Asbury Theological Seminary

Irving Hexham is well known to his many readers through his publications on religious studies, both as a general field of research, as well as represented in various movements, both local and worldwide. In *Understanding World Religions*, his provocative work, especially on African and also Indian religious views, is worth the price of the volume. We need to examine these often neglected areas of study.

—Gary R. Habermas, Distinguished Research Professor and Chair of the Department of Philosophy and Theology, Liberty University

Often it is just scholars who take real interest in world religions and new religious movements. The only time most of us lift our heads is when we hear of some tragic event that shows us other people believe differently than we do. But this is the world we live in and Irving Hexham's book is a resource that brings clarity to this vast world of religious beliefs. This book needs to be read and kept available on the bookshelf of every Christian leader.

—Carson Pue, President, Arrow Leadership

Honestly, if you would have told me 25 years ago that I'd need a resource that would help me understand world religions, I'd probably have rolled my eyes and said, "I have no plans to be a missionary." [Today] we live in a very different culture, post-Christian America, and developing an understanding of other world religions is essential. *Understanding World Religions* by Irving Hexham is pitched just right for most of us. It has the feel of a fascinating and almost uncensored sit-down conversation with a brilliant storytelling world religion expert.

—Mark Howell, Pastor of Communities at Canyon Ridge Christian Church in Las Vegas, Nevada. www.markhowelllive.com.

Irving Hexham's *Understanding World Religions* is outstanding. We recommend this book with no reservations.

—Robin A. Bruce, UK Apologetics
http://www.ukapologetics.net/11/hexham.htm

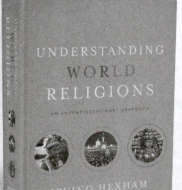

UNDERSTANDING WORLD RELIGIONS

AN INTERDISCIPLINARY APPROACH

IRVING HEXHAM

ZONDERVAN ACADEMIC

ZONDERVAN ACADEMIC

Understanding World Religions
Copyright © 2011 by Irving Hexham

Requests for information should be addressed to:
Zondervan, 3900 Sparks Dr. SE, *Grand Rapids, Michigan* 49546

ISBN 978-0-310-31448-6 (ebook)

This edition: ISBN 978-0-310-59846-6

Library of Congress Cataloging-in-Publication Data

Hexham, Irving.
    Understanding world religions / Irving Hexham.
    p. cm.
    Includes bibliographical references (p. 477). and index.
    ISBN 978-0-310-25944-2 (hardcover, printed) 1. Religions—Textbooks. I. Title.
BL80.3.H49 2011
200—dc22
                                                             2010013103

Cover design: Christopher Tobias
Cover photography: Kazuyoshi Nomachi/© Aidar Ayazbayev/www.123.rf.com
Interior design: Publication Services, Inc.

Printed in the United States of America

21 22 23 24 25 26 /TRM/ 25 24 23 22 21 20 19 18 17 16 15 14 13 12 11 10 9 8 7 6 5 4 3

CONTENTS

ACKNOWLEDGMENTS

FOR A BOOK LIKE THIS, THE MOST APPROPRIATE PLACE TO BEGIN IN ACKNOWLEDGING ALL THE help I have received over the years is with my entrance to Lancaster University in 1967. Therefore, I must begin by thanking Colin Lyas for accepting a former gas fitter into a degree program even though I did not fit the normal category of incoming students straight out of an English grammar school. Next, I need to thank the excellent religious studies professors who taught me at Lancaster, beginning with Ninian Smart, Edward Conze, Adrian Cunningham, Bob Morgan, James Richardson, Stuart Mews, and James Dickie (Yaqub Zaki). The education provided by the department at Lancaster was second to none. Clark Pinnock and Francis Schaeffer also deserve mentioning for encouraging me to go to university in the first place. Their recognition of my academic potential and real support changed my life from that of a manual worker to a scholar.

After leaving Lancaster, I went to the University of Bristol, where I studied with two excellent Africanists, Fred Welbourn and Kenneth Ingham, to whom I owe a great deal. Fred taught me to understand African thought and encouraged my interest in new religious movements, while Kenneth insisted that I become a competent historian. Later G. C. "Pipin" Oosthuizen and Hans-Jürgen Becken deepened my knowledge of African religion, as did Gerald Pillay and the Right Reverend Londa Shembe. More recently, Ulrich van der Heyden also played an important role in encouraging my study of religion in both Africa and Germany.

Michael Hahn of the University of Marburg is to be thanked for kindly allowing me to sit in on his graduate course on Buddhism at the University of Calgary and for later proving to be a true friend. So too Tony Barber deserves thanks for his friendship and insights into Chinese religion and culture. Niri Pillay and her mother also provided vivid insights into the Hindu tradition. Samerah Barett and Nastaran Naskhi need to be thanked, alongside my former neighbor Ishmael Bavasah, for correcting my understanding of Islamic culture. Samerah took time out of her busy schedule in law school to carefully read and comment on my chapters on Islam, which I appreciate. So too did Gordon Nickle and David M. Williams, who graciously corrected any academic errors they found in the text. Katrine Brix provided scholarly comments on my chapter on Christianity, while Trevor Watts and Kristen also looked it over and gave their views as Christian readers. Henry Srebrnik advised with the chapter on Judaism, and I also benefited from regular conversations with my colleagues Eliezer Segal, Leslie Kawamura, and Elizabeth Rohlman.

My thanks go to both the staff at Research Services of the University of Calgary and the Social Sciences Research Council of Canada for their generous support of my research over many years. Without them I would have produced far less. In particular the grants I received to visit Africa and Europe helped greatly with this book.

Finally, I must thank a host of students from numerous religious traditions who took my courses at the University of Calgary. They both inspired me and corrected my misunderstandings of their traditions.

This book is dedicated to my wife Karla Poewe.

INTRODUCTION

ABOUT THIS BOOK

Why on earth would anyone write yet another introduction to world religions? In the course of writing this book I have asked myself this question many times. The reason is, however, fairly simple. I was dissatisfied with existing religious studies texts, which tend to be rather antiseptic works written on the basis of a 1960s *Star Trek* form of cultural relativism that is, frankly, dull. Like Captain Kirk and his crew, their authors appear to feel mandated to observe religious traditions without offering criticisms of any except Christianity. Such an approach attempts to present "the facts" as neutrally as possible, but it fails to stimulate discussion or challenge the prejudices of students about real issues.

Therefore, I attempt to go beyond mere description to introduce students to the type of controversy that I believe lies at the heart of all healthy academic pursuits. My book aims to be like Rodney Stark's one-time best-selling *Sociology* (1992), which presents theories and issues in the context of real academic disputes. It also takes its cue from Walter Kaufmann's equally stimulating *Religion in Four Dimensions* (1976). The rationale behind this approach is that one ought to draw students into the study of religion and religions by addressing issues that capture their imaginations.

When my *Concise Dictionary of Religion* first appeared in 1993, various reviewers praised it for its objectivity in reporting basic information. Nevertheless, some reviewers worried that it was "opinionated," that after giving the facts, I sometimes gave my opinion. William M. Johnston saw the logic of my approach as a teaching technique when he wrote, "More than most reference book writers, Hexham fans controversy ... this introduction to persons and concepts sparkles, particularly in classroom use. No other glossary combines range, incisiveness and outspokenness so dexterously ... This glossary shows how a reference work can voice dissent without sacrificing rigor."

I believe that while individuals who belong to different religions may be good people, the teachings of some religious groups may be evil. Therefore, papering over controversial issues simply opens the door for critics like Christopher Hitchens, the author of *God Is Not Great* (2007), and groups such as the Freedom from Religion Foundation, who fault scholars of religion for their lack of common sense. One may strongly disagree with Hitchens and his colleagues, such as Oxford professor Richard Dawkins,[1] the author of *The God Delusion* (2006), who together form a group of highly critical writers promoting what is

---

1. For information on Dawkins see his website: http://richarddawkins.net/.

often called the "new atheism,"[2] but one cannot deny that they make some interesting points.

From experience, I know that students are far more likely to take an issue seriously and become fascinated by a topic if they are presented with different opinions that challenge their way of thinking or the work of other academics. Bland approaches produce bland students. Therefore, when I present controversial topics or points of view that are normally ignored by introductory texts, I am not necessarily presenting my own views. What I am doing is presenting ideas and arguments that I believe will stimulate debate and draw students into serious discussions about the study of religion.

For example, in chapter 9 I present various arguments about the origins of Indian, or what I call "yogic," religions, which are related to the Indus Valley civilization, and I raise issues surrounding the Aryan invasions. Then, in chapter 10 I introduce Nirad C. Chaudhuri's ideas about the development of the Hindu tradition. Not everyone will agree with what is said here; Chaudhuri is an important commentator who makes a convincing argument that deserves attention even though some people regard his work as controversial. By presenting the Hindu tradition in this way, I intend for students to be stimulated to find out more and to seriously study the issues involved.

Therefore, while some people will disagree with the ideas and arguments, the way they are presented allows professors and students alike to enter into meaningful debates. In this way the book is a teaching tool rather than a set text that preserves a received tradition.

Another area where some readers will feel disquiet is in my discussions of various modern thinkers at the end of each main section that outlines a major religious tradition. For example, my treatment of Gandhi as a contrarian will surprise many readers and annoy some. Others will complain that I spend far too little time discussing Gandhi's personal religious beliefs and far too much time on his views about imperialism and cultural issues. My approach is intended to make people see beyond stereotypes. What I hope to achieve is a presentation that makes the reader want to read what Gandhi, and the others I discuss, actually said and that develops in the reader a fascination with these important and, each in their own way, fascinating people.

As a student of Ninian Smart (1927–2001), I place great value on understanding a religion as it is understood by its practitioners. To borrow Smart's words, I believe the student of religion must learn to "walk in anther person's moccasins," or, to put it another way, "see the world through the interpretive lenses, or tinted glasses, worn by true believers."

My other mentors include Edward Conze (1904–1979), James Dickie (or Yaqub Zaki, to give him his Arabic name), Kenneth Ingham, and Fred Welbourn (1912–1986)—all of whom took very different approaches to the study of religion and never avoided controversy. I also admire, among others, the work of Walter Kaufmann (1921–1980) and Karl Popper (1902–1994), to whom I owe an intellectual debt. From all of these people I learned that "understanding precedes criticism," which expresses the spirit of this book.

The book is divided into four parts: (1) "Studying Religion," (2) "African Traditions," (3) "The Yogic Tradition," including Hindu religions and Buddhism, and (4) "The

---

2. "The New Atheism," *Wired*, November 2006.

Abramic Tradition," which includes Christianity, Judaism, and Islam; these are followed by a short conclusion reflecting on Christian approaches to other religious traditions. Each part deals with a major religious tradition and some of its manifestations. These sections are designed to provide basic information about various religions in an engaging way. Thus, the last chapter dealing with each major religion focuses on one particular individual. In this way students are given insights into the work of people who embrace specific religious traditions, and they are helped to see that very often such people adopt positions that seem contradictory to outsiders. This is done to help students grasp the complexity of religious life and recognize that engagement with an individual's life and work brings with it the realization that religious beliefs are never as neat and clear-cut as they appear in most textbooks.

Initially I had planned to make each part and each section within it identical. As a result I intended to produce a uniform manuscript which allows students to compare the history, teachings, and practices of each major religious tradition with those of other traditions systematically. As I wrote the book, I found that this neat scheme did not work. Religions and religious traditions are different. Each is unique. Therefore, a different approach was demanded for each tradition if I hoped to capture its essence in a few short chapters. As a result the book lacks the obvious cohesion of the earlier plan but is, I believe, more authentic and useful to the student of religions.

Some readers will no doubt find the inclusion of footnotes tiresome and inappropriate for an introductory textbook. Although I can understand this reaction, I believe it is wrong. Therefore, I compromised by providing footnotes—and at times there are a lot of them—only for those sections and arguments where serious questions exist about the claims I make. In this way I provide professors and students with a means of checking things out for themselves and seeing why I say the things I do on controversial or little-known topics.

Similarly, maps were used only when they added to the text and dealt with unfamiliar issues. Therefore, there are no biblical maps which are easily found in other books. The pictures also were chosen in the hope that they will communicate something of the ethos of a religion in a particular time and place. As a result they are rather eclectic and not the standard glossy photo. Hopefully they make the book interesting and are informative.

Other readers may be surprised that I have retained the essentially Christian designations of dates, "BC" and "AD," instead of the increasingly popular "Common Era" or "CE" and "BCE." This is because the "Common Era" is common to Jews and Christians but still excludes Buddhists, Hindus, and Muslims. It is therefore a very misleading term. For this reason I prefer the traditional Western usage to a modern innovation which does not even have the saving grace that it supposedly developed in a homogeneous society.

In conclusion, I hope that this book will stimulate debate and encourage a new generation of students to become involved in the study of religion and religious traditions.

PART 1

STUDYING RELIGION

CHAPTER 1

INTRODUCTORY ISSUES IN THE STUDY OF RELIGION

WHAT IS RELIGION?

Most people have a clear idea of what they mean by *religion* and can usually identify religious behavior when they see it. Nevertheless, when we have to define religion, we soon discover that the task is quite difficult, because religion is manifested in many different ways in our world. Thus, while for most people religion involves a belief in God, this is not true for certain forms of Buddhism. Indeed, to the educated Buddhist, God is quite unimportant.

Yet for many peasants living in Buddhist countries, the role of gods in their daily lives is important. Therefore, a distinction has to be made between Buddhism as a great tradition[1] and the many little traditions embedded in a predominantly Buddhist culture. The educated Buddhist does not seek God, but his peasant neighbor, while acknowledging the importance of Buddhism for liberation, does worship various gods.

Because of the difficulties created by movements, such as Buddhism, that are

Photo 1.1 This small side shrine is part of a larger Buddhist temple. From the arrangement, flowers, and fruit, it is clear that the Buddha receives veneration from his followers. But the Buddha is a man, not a god. So what makes Buddhism a religion?

---

1. See, e.g., Robert Redfield, *Peasant Society and Culture: An Anthropological Approach to Civilization* (Chicago: Univ. of Chicago Press, 1956), 70–104.

clearly religious, many students turn to experts for a definitive definition of religion. What they find is a bewildering series of definitions. For example, sociologist Émile Durkheim (1858–1917) defined religion as "a unified system of beliefs and practices relative to sacred things, that is to say, things set apart and forbidden—beliefs and practices which unite into one single moral community called a Church, all those who adhere to them."[2]

Photo 1.2 Max Müller is generally known as "the father of religious studies." Although he concentrated his work on the religions of India, he had wide interests and an appreciation for African and other religious traditions neglected by later scholars.

Another author who is often cited for his definition of religion is the philosopher Immanuel Kant (1724–1804), who defined religion as "the recognition of all duties as divine commands."[3] Similarly, Max Müller (1823–1900), whom many regard as the true founder of religious studies,[4] gave a twofold definition of religion as "a body of doctrines handed down by tradition, or in canonical books, and containing all that constitutes the faith of Jew, Christian, or Hindu" and as "a faculty of faith ... which distinguishes man from animals."[5]

Reflecting on these and many similar definitions of religion, one soon sees that most of them reflect both the complexity of the subject and the interests of the person making the definition. Thus Durkheim writes as a sociologist, Kant as a philosopher, and Müller as a historian-linguist influenced by theological discussions.

NINIAN SMART'S MODEL FOR IDENTIFYING RELIGION

It was for this and related reasons that Ninian Smart, who founded the first religious studies department in Britain, proposed that serious students of religion abandon the quest for a clear definition in favor of a workable model, or guide, which would allow the student to identify religion and religions as they are observed in daily life. Instead of defining religion theoretically, Smart argued, we ought to call something a religion when it conforms to

2. Émile Durkheim, *The Elementary Forms of the Religious Life* (London: Allen and Unwin, 1915; fifth impression, 1964), 47.

3. Immanuel Kant, *Critique of Practical Reason*, trans. Lewis White Beck (New York: Liberal Arts Press, 1956), 134.

4. Eric J. Sharpe, *Comparative Religion: A History* (London: Duckworth, 1975), 35–38.

5. Max Müller, *Introduction to the Science of Religion* (London: Longmans, Green, 1873), 16–17.

certain general characteristics found in similar phenomena which we also call religions. We can say we are in the presence of a religion, he suggested, when we discover

> a set of institutionalized *rituals*, identified with a *tradition* and expressing and/or evoking *sacral* sentiments directed at a *divine* or *trans-divine* focus seen in the context of the human *phenomenological* environment and at least partially described by *myths* or by myths and *doctrines*.[6]

Each of the key terms in this model for identifying religion can be discussed at great length. All we will do here is briefly discuss their key characteristics. First of all, when we attempt to study a religion, or religions, all we can really do is look at their institutional manifestations. We can observe behavior, but we can never really know what goes on in a person's head. Therefore, for practical purposes, studying religion means studying religious institutions or institutions identified as religious. This means the study of religion is the study of religious movements which are observable within society and therefore are a form of social movement.

The next question is whether a movement is religious or secular. Many secular movements appear religious. For example, a crowd at a hockey game or watching American football often acts in ways that look like those of a religious group. But although some people argue that such actions are "religious at heart," there is a big difference between a secular and a religious gathering. Political parties, the fans mobbing rock stars, and the veneration of nationalist leaders all have similarities to religion, but none are religious in themselves. Therefore, they need to be excluded from our study.

This is why the other characteristics indicated by Smart are important. Let us begin by considering ritual behavior. Rituals are repetitive behavior fixed by tradition. In the study of religion they are, as Smart says, "traditional religious behavior or actions." Probably the most obvious form of ritual is the Roman Catholic Mass, which contains a lot of color, carefully ordered actions, a fixed order of words, particular smells, and what is in many ways a carefully orchestrated theatrical performance. In other religious traditions, things like pilgrimage to Mecca, for Muslims, or sacrifices and ritual bathing, for Hindus, are good examples of ritual action.

Some religious traditions, especially those associated with religious movements such as the Protestant Reformation, react strongly against what they call "dead rituals." Such groups fail to recognize their own ritual actions while identifying the rituals of other religious movements as somehow unspiritual or

Photo 1.3 Ninian Smart at a conference in Washington, D.C., shortly before his death. He pioneered modern religious studies at Lancaster University, in England, before moving to the University of Santa Barbara in the U.S.

---

6. Ninian Smart, "Towards a Definition of Religion," unpublished paper, Lancaster University, 1970. Cf. Ninian Smart, *The World's Religions* (Engelwood Cliffs, N.J.: Prentice-Hall, 1989), 10–21.

false. For example, the Plymouth Brethren strongly reject rituals like those of the Catholic Mass or High Anglican services on theological grounds. Yet, in fact, their own services have many rituals, even though the participants usually fail to recognize them as rituals. The very order and arrangement of the Brethren service actually make it a ritual action. Consequently, rituals need to be understood in terms of the convictions of the worshipers and the relationship between them and the divine, or, as Smart argues in some cases, the "trans-divine."

Seeing ritual in this way, one can argue that a football game is a ritual act, but not a religious one. And yet very clearly the divine, or trans-divine, element is missing. This is why, Smart insists, religious rituals need to be "identified with a tradition." Traditions are those things that add meaning to action. For students, probably the best example of a tradition is the act of graduation after they complete their degree. On such occasions people dress up in peculiar clothes, make speeches, and do all sorts of unusual things. While cynics might say that such actions are a waste of time, they serve a useful purpose. They remind people that the awarding of a degree conveys certain privileges and responsibilities that gain their validity from the fact that they are not some new, fly-by-night invention. Tradition assures the student that their degree is valid because the institution awarding it has stood the test of time. Thus a degree from Harvard University is immediately recognized because of the tradition associated with Harvard, while one from Upper Backwoods College may have little value.

Smart then notes that these institutions, and the rituals and traditions associated with them, have an impact upon the people involved. This he describes as "expressing and/or evoking *sacral* sentiments." In other words, participating in religious activities within the framework of a traditional institution not only expresses a certain commitment to spiritual

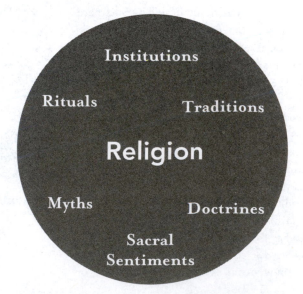

Figure 1.1 Ninian Smart's suggestion about recognizing a religion. When all of these features are found together in society, then we are probably dealing with a religion.

values but often has the remarkable effect of creating or evoking a sense of the sacred in the worshiper and sometimes even in people who simply attend the ceremony without really intending to worship.

This sense of the sacred, Smart explains, is "directed at a *divine* or *trans-divine* focus." That is, the participant directs their feeling of worship, awe, and respect toward either the divine or something beyond the divine. By "the divine" he means God, gods, or, as in the case of Buddhism, something beyond or at least separate from the divine. This latter option Smart identifies as the "trans-divine focus," a term for such things as Nirvana in Buddhism, or the veneration of ancestors in African and other primal traditions.

Next, Smart reminds his readers that religion takes place within "the human *phenomenological* environment," by which he means the totality of human social life and individual experience within which religion exists.

Finally, Smart raises the important point that religious people describe their beliefs and practices in terms of myths, or, as he says, "myths and doctrines." Here it is important to understand what Smart means by *myth*. For many people a myth is a story that is simply untrue. Essentially, this is the way the German theologian Rudolf Bultmann (1884–1976) used *myth* when he developed his theories about the necessity of what he called "demythologising," which he believed was necessary to make the New Testament acceptable to the modern world. In Bultmann's view the New Testament is a product of a prescientific age, many of whose stories, such as accounts of miracles, are therefore unacceptable to people living in an age of science. Therefore, in his view, these stories need to be reinterpreted to explain what they really mean in terms of their message and not regarded as literal accounts of what happened. In other words, Bultmann says that the stories he identifies as myths in the New Testament are simply untrue.

Photo 1.4 Mircea Eliade portrayed on a Moldovan postage stamp, which shows the esteem in which he is held in the land of his birth.

On the other hand, some religious writers in the tradition of Mircea Eliade (1907–1986), Joseph Campbell (1904–1987), and Carl Gustav Jung (1875–1961) define myth as some sort of special story containing unique insights into religious truth, archaic insights often lost to humans living in industrial societies. The task of the

Photo 1.5 Mircea Eliade in discussion with graduate students—date unknown.

scholar is to probe these myths to get at their inner truths. The problem with this view is not that it represents myths as untrue but that it represents them as in some sense containing a supertruth not located in any other type of story.

Against these two extremes stands the anthropological understanding of myth, which appears to be close to Smart's view. Initially developed by Bronislaw Malinowski (1884–1942), who reacted to abstract theorizing by nineteenth-century writers about the meaning of myth, the anthropological approach looks at myths in terms of their function in society.[7] This definition emphasizes that a myth is any story which affects the way people live. It is not necessarily either unhistorical, as Eliade tends to argue, or historical. Rather, a story which becomes a myth can be true or false, historical or unhistorical, fact or fiction. What is important is not some special feature of the story itself but the *function* which it serves in the life of an individual, a group, or a whole society.

Myths, in the anthropological understanding, enable members of different societies and subgroups within societies to make sense of their lives and their world. As anthropologist John Middleton puts it, "a myth is a statement about society and man's place in it and in the surrounding universe … Myths and cosmological notions are concerned with the relationship of a people with other peoples, with nature and with the supernatural."[8] The importance of a myth lies not in its particular qualities as a story but in the use made of it. When a story acts upon the imagination of an individual or group in such a powerful way that it begins to shape their lives, molding their thoughts and directing their actions, then that story has become a myth. Thus what makes a story a myth is not its content, as the rationalists thought, but the way the story takes on a life of its own in the thought of an individual or an entire society. Once accepted, a myth can be used to ennoble the past, explain the present, and hold out hope for the future. It gives individual and social life meaning and direction. This ability to guide action distinguishes myths from legends, folk tales, and other stories. In short, myths have the power to change lives and shape societies.

However one defines myth, the success of a myth depends upon people accepting and acting upon what they consider to be its message. Nevertheless, most people who act upon what they consider to be the message contained in a myth do so because they believe it is true. In other words, they accept the story as true before it becomes a myth in their lives. Questions of historic, philosophic, or any other form of verifiable truth are therefore important in the creation and maintenance of mythologies. In fact, such questions often precede the acceptance of myths. What matters is not simply the power of myths to inspire belief and to enable believers to make sense of their experiences but the prior belief that the story is true.

Smart also points out that while all religions have their own mythic cores, the myths of a single religion often appear to conflict with one another or with the teachings of the group. For example, the Hebrew Bible makes it very clear that there is only one God. Yet Jesus spoke and acted in such a way that he appeared to accrue to himself certain powers

---

7. I have developed aspects of this argument in various papers and books, including Irving Hexham and Karla Poewe, *New Religions as Global Cultures* (Boulder, Colo.: Westview, 1997), 79–98.

8. John Middleton, ed., *Myth and Cosmos* (New York: Natural History Press, 1967), x.

and attributes that belong to God alone. For his early Jewish followers such statements and actions created a crisis of understanding. If there is only one God, how could Jesus possibly do and say things that only God can do and say? Similarly, in Buddhism there seem to be contradictory stories about the nature of the Buddha, about whether he has one or many bodies, and about how these bodies, some of which are spiritual, relate to each other. There are also questions about how many Buddhas there actually are and how they relate to the man known to history as the Buddha.

Questions like these gave rise to the development of Christian doctrine and Buddhist philosophizing. Within both religions, and indeed within all other major religious traditions, the sometimes apparently contradictory nature of mythic stories creates the need to develop doctrine. Doctrines are articulate expressions of logical reasoning applied to the bedrock mythic substructure found in all religions. In doctrines, theologians and philosophers attempt to show how the stories cohere despite apparent contradictions.

SOME OBJECTIONS TO SMART'S VIEWS

Helpful as Smart's definition is, some scholars have identified weaknesses in its articulation. They point out that while it is an excellent description of religion in practice, it remains essentially descriptive. Hence, while it is very useful for identifying religions, it does little to help us generate hypotheses or theories about religion. They also note that throughout history the devout in all religious traditions have complained that some people go through the motions of piety without really internalizing the tradition itself. As a result we can find nominal members of any given religion. But, it is claimed, Smart failed to distinguish between genuine commitment and mere conformity to a social norm.

Finally, some people are deeply committed to ontological values and say they are part of a great religious tradition yet do not readily identify themselves with religious institutions. Smart's definition concentrates on societal manifestations of religion within institutions and ignores individuals who remain outside these institutions, even though these people may represent a sizable segment of a population. Objections such as these give rise to what we may call the ontological understanding of religion, which attempts to see beyond the appearances.

THE ONTOLOGICAL UNDERSTANDING OF RELIGION

Because of the weaknesses of an institutional definition of religion, Fred Welbourn and others have countered Smart's view by arguing that it simply does not fit the reality of religion in traditional societies like those of Africa. Welbourn, for example, suggested that while most members of the African group known as the Baganda used the Arabic word *dini* to describe religion as practiced by Arabs, Europeans, and African converts, they used another word, *kusamira*, to refer to their traditional religion. For them, the essence of traditional religious practices was *kusamira*, which involves one's entire way of life. Thus, Welbourn sympathized with Paul Tillich's characterization of religion as "ultimate concern." Although the use of a model like Smart's allows the scholar to identify the externals of religious observance, Welbourn and Tillich argue, it often fails to fully capture the essence of religion, which involves the totality of personal existence.[9]

The argument against seeing religion as a way of life is that it is too inclusive to be of any value to scholars. If, as Tillich argues, everyone has an ultimate concern, how can anyone study such a vague concept? Likewise, if all of life is religion, what is not religious? And how can we ever talk about religion as an identifiable aspect of reality? The answer of people like Tillich and Welbourn was that perhaps we should recognize that religious institutions must be studied as institutions and not as a special category of institution labeled "religious."[10] Once this is done, Welbourn argued, we must recognize that in an ontological sense all institutions can have a religious dimension. Therefore, to thoroughly study religion we must consider both the institutional forms of piety and ontological commitments.

Many scholars object that the ontological approach to religion results in a definition of religion that includes everything. Welbourn counters that unless we are prepared to include ontological definitions we can never really understand the religion of the Baganda, Islam, or even certain forms of Christianity.[11] To reinforce his point he cites the example of some Marxist students he encountered when he was a student at Cambridge in the 1930s. These people, he notes, were not intellectual Marxists but ontological believers. Their commitment to Marxism was as total as his own to Christianity or that of the Baganda to their traditional way of life.

Photo 1.6 Paul Tillich, one of the pioneers of existential theology. He fled Nazi Germany to teach in the U.S., where he made his reputation as an original thinker. Key to Tillich's understanding of religion is the concept of "ultimate concern." This he based on the biblical concept of idolatry, asserting that whatever a person makes the most important thing in their life expresses their true religious faith. If someone claims to be a Christian but their life revolves around their family or some other created thing, and not God, they are an idolater.

We can, he suggests, say that these commitments are examples of "pseudo-religion," but such a judgment, in his view, does an injustice to both the facts and the people involved in such movements.[12] Religion, Welbourn argues, should be viewed in terms of each person's implicit ontological commitments, what really motivates them in their day-to-day lives, rather than in terms of explicit religiosity, with its "unimportant institutional rituals."

Welbourn also argues that while it is easy to recognize myths and rituals, once they have ceased to function as living realities, we are rarely aware of our own myths and ritu-

9. Fred B. Welbourn, "Towards Eliminating the Concept of Religion," unpublished paper given at the Colloquium on the Concept of Religion, Lancaster University, 15–18 December 1969; cf. Paul Tillich, *Systematic Theology* (Chicago: Univ. of Chicago Press, 1973; first published 1951), 1:12–15.

10. Welbourn, "Towards Eliminating the Concept of Religion," 13.

11. Ibid., 13–14.

12. Ibid., 7–8.

als. For example, no one in sixteenth-century Tudor England would have regarded stories about King Arthur as a myth. King Arthur was a reality, and stories about him legitimated the Tudor dynasty. Today, however, we can see that these highly religious stories are fictions that served a political and religious function by providing a basis for rituals that reinforced the dynasty's claim to power. "But," Welbourn asks, "do we see myths that motivate ourselves and our contemporaries? Do we reflect on the way the rituals of our society maintain a specific social order?" In his view we do not, but instead tend to concentrate on myths and rituals of the past that have lost their power. Using examples like King Arthur, Welbourn argues that the most powerful myths and rituals are those we fail to recognize as such. The task of scholars of religion, then, is to explore modern society in search of living examples of myths and rituals, to study *implicit* as well as *explicit* expressions of religion.

Photo 1.7 Fred Welbourn, who pioneered the modern study of African religions. In developing his theories, which are similar to those of Paul Tillich, he argued that rather than concentrating on texts, scholars of religion need to "get their hands dirty" by observing what actually goes on in religious communities. Therefore, he sought to apply anthropological methods within the context of religious studies.

DOOYEWEERD: GROUND MOTIVES AND FAITH COMMUNITIES

Another approach to study of religion is found in the writings of the Dutch philosopher Herman Dooyeweerd (1894–1977). Outlining his understanding of religion in his theoretical text *A New Critique of Theoretical Thought*,[13] Dooyeweerd opts for a philosophical, ontological definition. He argues that religion is "the innate impulse of human selfhood to direct itself toward the *true* or toward a *pretended* absolute Origin of all temporal diversity of meaning, which it finds focused concentrically in itself." He then adds, "As the absolutely central sphere of human existence, religion transcends all modal aspects of temporal reality, *the aspect of faith included . . . religion is absolute self-surrender*."[14]

Thus for Dooyeweerd, as for Tillich and Welbourn, religion involves each individual's basic ontological commitment, or ultimate concern, which enables them to function as a human being. Unlike Tillich and Welbourn, however, Dooyeweerd immediately admits the weakness of his all-encompassing definition and agrees with the critics of ontological definitions that any attempt to abstract the purely religious from other aspects of existence will inevitably ignore some aspects of religion and distort other aspects.

Dooyeweerd then suggests ways in which religion can be meaningfully, though not exhaustively, studied. In doing so, he recognizes the importance of institutional analysis and allows for an academic study of religious movements and institutions that is distinct from the study of ontological commitments. He suggests that when we study religion we need to recognize that it plays a vital role in the integration of individual personality, even though

---

13. Herman Dooyeweerd, *A New Critique of Theoretical Thought* (Amsterdam: H. J. Paris, 1953).
14. Ibid., 57–58.

Photo 1.8 Herman Dooyeweerd was a Dutch Christian philosopher who developed the ideas of Abraham Kuyper in relation to the philosophy of law. This led him to spend a lot of time pondering the nature of religion. As a result he developed ideas similar to those of Welbourn and Tillich.

we cannot fully grasp the essence of religion at a personal level. To attempt to grasp an individual's ontological commitments, he claims, is futile. Therefore, while we cannot precisely identify an individual's ontological commitments, their ultimate concerns, we can identify such concerns historically and socially when they are expressed by groups of individuals living in community. In this way Dooyeweerd seems to be coming close to the views of Smart while at the same time paying attention to the complex issues of commitment. "A religious community," Dooyeweerd argues, "is maintained by a common spirit, which as a *dynamis*, as a central motive power, is active in the concentration-point of human existence." This spirit of community, he claims, works through what he calls a religious ground idea or ground motive, which gives content to the entire life and thought of a society. Thus it can be seen in the historical development of human societies, where it takes on particular forms that are historically determined.[15]

These insights lead Dooyeweerd to argue that the ultimate ontological commitments of individuals find expression historically and socially in various religious or faith communities that can be studied. Having recognized this, he argues, we must also recognize that because individuals are often born and raised in a faith community and die in it, the commitments expressed in the community are capable of molding both individual members and the community as a whole. By studying these communities, then, it is possible to study the ontological commitments of their members. In this way, Dooyeweerd appears to combine the institutional and ontological definitions of religion while seeking to overcome common objections to both.

EXPLICIT OR IMPLICIT RELIGION

Social and cultural anthropologists often argue that what people do is more important than what they say. That is, implicit beliefs find expression in behavior and are as much a subject for study as explicit statements made by individuals about their beliefs. Most Christians, however, think of religion in terms of explicit beliefs and creedal statements, which

15. Ibid., 61.

Methods for the study of religion

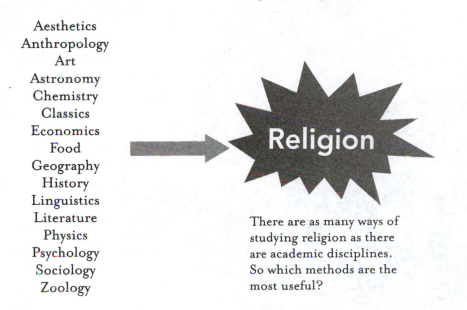

Aesthetics
Anthropology
Art
Astronomy
Chemistry
Classics
Economics
Food
Geography
History
Linguistics
Literature
Physics
Psychology
Sociology
Zoology

Religion

There are as many ways of studying religion as there are academic disciplines. So which methods are the most useful?

Figure 1.2 Because religion is a living entity, the academic field of religion is much like African studies, women's studies, and a host of other scholarly enterprises that study a multifaceted social reality. Therefore, it can be legitimately studied from many different perspectives.

are usually taken at face value. Thus theology is based on the analysis of beliefs as they are found in the Bible, devotional works, and books of theology. Theologians are trained to read texts, which they then interpret according to established exegetical techniques.

From experience it is clear that people trained in theological and other literary disciplines often find it very difficult to appreciate the methods of social scientists. Therefore, it is not surprising that when theologians discuss "sociology" they tend to think of it in terms of the highly philosophical work of figures like Karl Marx (1818–1883), Max Weber (1864–1920), and Peter L. Berger (1929–).[16] Rarely does one find a theologian engaging in serious dialogue with sociologists like Charles Glock (1924–),[17] Rodney Stark (1934–),[18] or Reginald Bibby (1943–),[19] whose work is based on survey research, statistical analysis, and empirical observations. Similarly, although such a thing as theological anthropology[20] exists, few Christians are seriously engaged in social anthropology

16. Cf. Charles Villa-Vicencio, *Trapped in Apartheid: A Socio-Theological History of the English-Speaking Churches* (Maryknoll, N.Y.: Orbis, 1988).

17. Charles Y. Glock and Rodney Stark, *Religion and Society in Tension* (Chicago: Rand McNally, 1965).

18. Rodney Stark and William Sims Bainbridge, *The Future of Religion: Secularization, Revival and Cult Formation* (Berkeley: Univ. of California Press, 1985).

19. Reginald Bibby, *Fragmented Gods: The Poverty and Potential of Religion in Canada* (Toronto: Irvin, 1987).

20. See, e.g., Charles H. Kraft, *Christianity in Culture* (Maryknoll, N.Y.: Orbis, 1979), for one of the better examples of this genre.

Photo 1.9 Karl Marx (left) and his close collaborator Friedrich Engels. This bronze monument was erected during the cold war by the German Democratic Republic (GDR) in a park near Alexanderplatz in former East Berlin. Unlike many other monuments from that period, it has survived. For the GDR, Marxism was a pseudoreligion, as the German film *Goodbye Lenin* brilliantly shows. Yet although most Americans have no problem rejecting Marxism as a political philosophy, the ideas of Marx play an important role in theories about the origins and nature of religion.

as an academic discipline. Occasionally the works of an anthropologist like Mary Douglas (1921 – 2007) may catch the imagination of a theologian, but generally little or no effort is made by theologians, or people trained in classical religious studies, to engage in or understand the discipline except for apologetic purposes.

One exception to this general picture of disciplinary apartheid is the Annual Conference on Implicit Religion, organized by Welbourn's student, Dr. Edward Bailey. For almost thirty years he has encouraged the production of numerous papers and books examining what he calls "implicit religion." By this he means the actual practices and beliefs of people as discovered by others through careful observation of their actions and not simply by taking their words at face value. Bailey argues that it is important to observe what people actually do, not simply analyze what they say.[21] By observing their actions, the way they live, he claims, it is possible to get at the nature of people's actual ontological commitments, that is, to detect their "implicit religion." Today, several British universities offer courses in the area. Both MA and PhD degrees are available on the topic of implicit religion, although the notion has not really caught on in North America.

OPERATIONALIZING DEFINITIONS OF RELIGION

Frustrated by the problem of finding a usable definition of religion, one that meets the practical needs of scholars engaged in empirical research, Rodney Stark and William Sims Bainbridge have argued for an institutional definition. They rejected all ontological defi-

---

21. Information on this group can be obtained from Dr. Edward Bailey, The Rectory, Winterbourne, Nr. Bristol, England.

nitions on the grounds that meaningful empirical research, based on archival evidence or fieldwork, demands a clear definition that distinguishes religion from other forms of social life.[22] Therefore, they defined religions as "*human organizations primarily engaged in providing general compensators based on supernatural assumptions.*"[23] Later, they refined their theory[24] to define religion in terms of "*systems* of general compensators based on supernatural assumptions" (emphasis added).[25]

Using this definition, Stark and Bainbridge provide their readers with five dimensions of "*religiousness.*"[26] These dimensions are based on a scale devised by Stark and Glock[27] and are not unlike the indicators of religion proposed by Ninian Smart.[28] Stark and Bainbridge describe these factors as *belief, practice, experience, knowledge,* and *consequences.* They then claim that by studying these dimensions of social institutions and movements, scholars are able to measure and examine religion from a variety of perspectives that allow them to generate hypotheses and create usable research instruments.

To many people this definition appears reductionist because of the use of the term "general compensators." Stark and Bainbridge are at pains to point out that this is not the case. They are not proposing a crude deprivation model of religion. Rather, they carefully explain, they use the terms to refer to clearly religious expectations such as the "promise of a triumph over death."[29] Subsequently, in a series of books like *For the Glory of God,*[30] Stark has attempted to show how his theories work by providing many complex examples.

It should be noted that while Stark and Bainbridge's understanding of religion excludes certain types of ontological definition such as Tillich's description of an ultimate concern and Welbourn's analysis of individual commitments,

Photo 1.10 Rodney Stark, who is arguably the leading sociologist of religion in the U.S. Stark described this photo as "ugly," and in truth it does not do him justice. His various books offer challenging definitions of religion, of various religious groups such as cults and sects, and of new religious movements. Central to Stark's concerns is a desire to move the study of religion away from vague generalizations toward operational definitions that clearly distinguish between different forms of religious organization.

22. Stark and Bainbridge, *The Future of Religion,* 3–8.
23. Ibid., 8.
24. Rodney Stark and William Sims Bainbridge, *A Theory of Religions* (New York: Peter Lang, 1987).
25. Ibid., 39.
26. Ibid., 9–10.
27. Rodney Stark and Charles Y. Glock, *American Piety* (Berkeley: Univ. of California Press, 1968).
28. Ninian Smart, *Worldviews* (New York: Charles Scribner's Sons, 1983), 7–8.
29. Stark and Bainbridge *The Future of Religion,* 37.
30. Rodney Stark, *For the Glory of God* (Princeton: Princeton Univ. Press, 2003).

it includes the type of ontological commitment discussed by Dooyeweerd.[31] More importantly, however, Stark and Bainbridge show that by utilizing their definition it is possible to construct testable hypotheses, general theories, and definite research programs, which enliven the study of religion.

RELIGIOUS STUDIES: FIELD OR DISCIPLINE

One very popular approach within religious studies is to argue that there is a particular method that sets off study of religion from other forms of academic discipline. It is claimed that religious studies itself is a discipline, because it possesses a unique way of approaching its subject. In this sense religious studies is seen as analogous to anthropology, economics, geography, history, sociology, or any other academic discipline. Such an approach was promoted by Mircea Eliade and his disciples as well as many other religious studies scholars influenced by the idea that there is something peculiar to religion that demands a unique method if it is to be studied meaningfully.

By contrast, Ninian Smart, Fred Welbourn, Rodney Stark, and many other students of religion argue that religious studies is a field and not a discipline. On this view, religious studies is like African studies, Asian studies, women's studies, or any other form of scholarship that takes a multifaceted social reality as its central focus. They argue that, as with other forms of area studies, religion can, and must, be studied using a multiplicity of meth-

---

31. Stark and Bainbridge, *The Future of Religion*, 51–53.

Practical methods for the study of religion

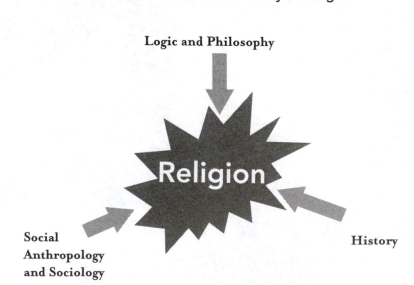

Figure 1.3 Practical approaches to studying religion based on five key disciplines.

ods. In fact, one can study religion using the methods of almost any established academic discipline, such as aesthetics, economics, or even physics. But for practical purposes Smart argued that it is best to limit the study of religion, at least in its initial stages, using three main academic traditions: philosophy and logic, history, and the social sciences, particularly anthropology and sociology. Thus anyone who wishes to understand a religious movement needs to approach it both anthropologically/sociologically and historically. Then they need to analyze their findings using logic and the tools of philosophy. Later it may be important to take into account geographic, economic, and other methods to understand the nature of a particular religion.

The approach taken here is to view religion as an area of human life that needs to be studied using various well-established academic disciplines. Thus, to really study a religion, students need to examine its history and beliefs as well as its current cultural context. Such a multidisciplinary approach is both challenging and very exciting, as I hope you will discover in reading this book.

CHAPTER 2

A BIASED CANON

INTRODUCTION

Recognizing bias is the first step toward critical thinking in academic work, and you can do it if you develop confidence in your own judgment. By their very nature biases are ingrained. Therefore, most people do not recognize a bias even when it is staring them in the face. Yet once this is pointed out and you begin looking for biases, they are relatively easy to find. You can discover the truth of this statement the next time you read a book. All you have to do is ask yourself, "What is the author's bias?" Then begin looking for it. You will be surprised how much this simple question reveals. To help you see how biases can be recognized with a little effort, this chapter provides one example of the way racism has clearly affected modern thinking about the nature of religious studies.

The pervasiveness of biases and their ability to distort our understanding are not something new, discovered by postmodern philosophers in the last fifty years. They have been known for centuries. Recognizing bias has always formed the basis of a good education. For example, in 1873, Herbert Spencer (1820–1903) wrote a wonderful book exposing the role of bias in human thinking. The book, *The Study of Sociology*,[1] is a classic that discusses in great detail the numerous ways bias can enter into our thinking. It reminds us that recognizing bias is nothing new. Yet it is something we must learn.

To demonstrate how frequently unrecognized biases appear in textbooks, this chapter will examine the attitude toward Africa and Africans in religious studies textbooks. Even though most of the authors of the books we will examine are self-proclaimed liberals who would be horrified at the

Photo 2.1 Herbert Spencer, whose work on bias is relevant today and exposes the modern tendency to think that serious criticism began only a few years ago.

---

1. This is available for free in electronic form from The Liberty Fund. It may be downloaded from http://oll.libertyfund.org/?option=com_staticxt&staticfile=show.php%3Ftitle=1335. The main website of The Liberty Fund is found at http://oll.libertyfund.org/index.php?option=com_frontpage&Itemid=149.

suggestion that their books are riddled with racism, there can be no doubt that textbooks dealing with African religions suffer from a racist heritage. But until this is pointed out to students, few people consciously recognize the fact, even though many have a subconscious feeling that something is wrong with what they are reading.

To show how deep the problem of bias runs in religious studies textbooks, we will survey a number of different works from the late 1960s to the present. Ninian Smart, in his popular *The Religious Experience of Mankind* (1969), devoted exactly 5 out of 576 pages to a consideration of African religion, while the British writer Trevor Ling, in *A History of Religions East and West* (1979), managed to avoid the discussion of African religions altogether. Robert S. Ellwood, in *Many Peoples, Many Faiths* (1982), and David S. Noss, in *The World's Religions* (1984), make no mention of African religions, nor, more recently, do John L. Esposito, Darrell J. Fasching, and Todd Lewis, in their 550-page *World Religions Today* (2002). In Willard G. Oxtoby's massive two-volume, 1100-page edited work, *World Religions* (2002), only 4 pages are devoted to African religions, with another 4 pages to African religions in the Americas. Yet 6 pages are devoted to Baha'i and 5 to the "New Age." Warren Matthews is slightly better in his *World Religions* (2004), including 22 pages on African religions; yet of these he devotes 10 pages to ancient Egyptian religions, weakening his treatment of contemporary religions, especially those practiced south of the Sahara. In like manner, Christopher Partridge, in his edited work *Introduction to World Religions* (2005), treats African religions in a mere 8 pages, while devoting 14 to the Baha'i and 22 to the Zoroastrian tradition, even though it is so small as to be virtually extinct.

More recently, Theodore M. Ludwig, in *The Sacred Paths: Understanding the Religions of the World* (2006), classifies African religions under the heading "Among Indigenous Peoples." In this section of his book he weaves African religions together with the native religions of Australia, North and South America, Indonesia, the South Pacific, and various other areas where he finds similar patterns of myth and ritual. Not to be outdone, Willard G. Oxtoby and Alan F. Segal, in their *Concise Introduction to World Religions* (2007), classify African religions under "Indigenous Religious Traditions," devoting only 17 of the section's 48 pages to Africa. Although in terms of space this is an improvement, it is hard to justify in terms of the sheer size and diversity of African religious traditions and clearly shows the insensitivity of scholars to this issue.

Books of readings containing "sacred texts" are no better. For example, *Sacred Texts of the World: A Universal Anthology*, edited by Ninian Smart and Richard D. Hecht, devotes a mere 5 out of 408 pages to things African. In Lessa and Vogt's classic anthropological *Reader in Comparative Religion* (1979), only 22 out of 488 pages are devoted to African religions. The one minor exception to this almost total boycott of African religions by Western scholars is the 48 pages Whitfield Foy gives to the subject in his 725-page selection of readings for the British Open University entitled *Man's Religious Quest* (1978). But even there the attention is limited and disproportionate to that devoted to other traditions, such as Zoroastrianism, which receives 60 pages.

If one surveys academic journals in religious studies, one finds a dearth of articles on African religions and few reviews of books about Africa. The uninitiated might attribute

Photo 2.2 At first glance this print seems to present a picture of Arab or Persian Sufi dancers. Take a closer look and you will see that the man in the middle is clutching a crosslike symbol. Actually, it is a mid-nineteenth-century print of Ethiopian Christian dancers. What is often forgotten is that Christian traditions in Africa go back to the time of the conversion of the Ethiopian eunuch in Acts 8:26–39 and are among the oldest in the world, with deep roots in Judaism. What this shows is that the African religious tradition is far more complex than generally thought.

this lack of attention to a lack of scholarship dealing with African religions. But this is not the case. When Hans–Jürgen Becken and Londa Shembe translated some of the works of Isaiah Shembe, the founder of one of the most important new religious movements in Africa, into English, the book received very few reviews even though it was published by an established academic press. This is all the more surprising because at the time of their publication the Shembe texts were the only English translation of the scriptures of a major contemporary African religious movement. Instead of being welcomed as the major breakthrough that they were, they were ignored by journals. Even *Religious Studies Review*, which is devoted to reviewing books on religion, pays virtually no attention to books on African religion and acts as though many of them do not exist.

One could go on providing example after example of the almost total neglect of African religious traditions in standard religious studies texts, but the examples cited make the point. Finally, before looking at the history of the study of African religions it is important to remember that all of the authors mentioned above would probably see themselves as "liberal," or even "very liberal," and none are even remotely racist. Nevertheless, the ethos of religious studies in which they work has blinded them to the importance and complexity of African religious traditions.

AFRICAN RELIGIONS IN THE CONTEXT OF WORLD RELIGIONS

Every author of a textbook has to make hard decisions about what to include and what to leave out. Therefore, to gain some insight into the importance of African religions for the study of religion, it is perhaps worth surveying the state of world religions over the past century. When Louis Henry Jordan published his book *Comparative Religion*[2] in 1905, he provided the following details about the state of religion in the world:

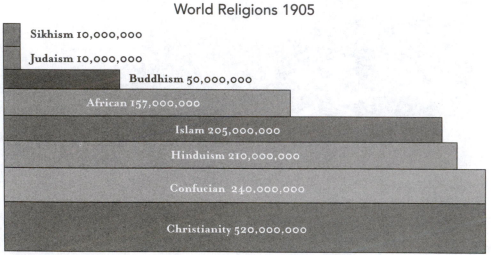

Figure 2.1

More recent figures show that over the twentieth century the relative distribution of world religions changed as follows:

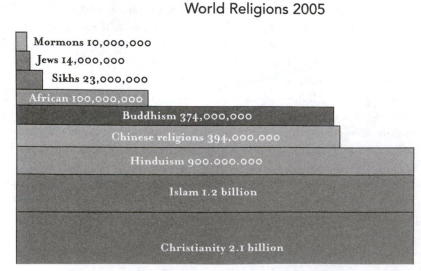

Figure 2.2

From these charts it is clear that African religions form a significant segment of world religions. Further, while the number of people practicing traditional African religions fell over the century, the influence of African traditions on other religions, such as Christianity and African Islam, remains great. Therefore, there is no excuse for ignoring African religions in religious studies textbooks. Yet African religions are ignored, and they are usually treated in a very dismissive way when they are actually included in such texts or mentioned in academic journals.

TEXTBOOK PORTRAYALS OF AFRICAN AND INDIAN RELIGION

To illustrate the unfavorable treatment received by African religions in popular textbooks, those sections dealing with them in Ninian Smart's otherwise excellent *The World's Religions*[3] will be examined in detail.[4] I chose Smart's work because he was politically liberal and certainly *not* a racist. Therefore, his work may be criticized without fear of suggesting his approach to African religions was motivated by racism, which it most certainly was not. As a result, if his approach is judged harshly, it ought to provoke us to ask deeper questions about the study of African religion rather than criticize an individual who wrote a particular book.

To gain some idea of how biased Smart's approach actually was, we will compare what he says about African religions with what he says about the religions of India. Here the aim is simply to draw attention to the relative neglect of African religions, not to suggest that anything said about India is, in the correct context, incorrect or inappropriate. Anyone who wishes to repeat this type of experiment using other religious studies textbooks will find that they all treat African religions in essentially the same way.

First, throughout his book Smart treats the diversity of religion in the Indian subcontinent as an exciting and creative phenomena. But he dismisses African religious diversity, arguing that African religion "has never been a single system" and implying that this makes it inferior to "historical world

Photo 2.3 This Coptic ikon came from Upper Egypt, which most people forget is part of Africa. In style it is similar to many Ethiopian ikons and can be seen as part of an ancient tradition belonging to a geographical area that forms an arc from Ethiopia to Italy. Many African Independent Churches, south of the Sahara, have also developed their own rich ikonic traditions.

---

3. Ninian Smart, *The World's Religions* (Cambridge: Cambridge Univ. Press, 1989).

4. This argument was briefly raised in my "African Religions: Some Recent and Lesser Known Works." *Religion* 20 (1990): 361–72. I also discussed it at greater length in my chapter "African Religions and the Nature of Religious Studies," in *Religious Studies: Issues, Prospects and Proposals* (Atlanta, Ga.: Scholars Press, 1991), 361–79, which was based on a conference paper given at the University of Manitoba in 1988.

religions."[5] Second, he notes that Indians direct their worship toward "a large number of gods" because "God is described ... as taking many forms," with the result that the numerous gods become "manifestations of the One Divine Being." Yet, although similar practices may be observed in Africa, Smart says Africans enjoy a "refracted theism," which he clearly considers an inferior form of religious consciousness.[6]

Third, Smart says Indians possess a mythic system with "a thousand themes." On the other hand, equally rich African mythologies are reduced to "myths of death and disorder," to which "trickster" myths are added, as though these three themes exhausted African mythic consciousness.[7]

Fourth, when discussing sacrifice in the Indian context, Smart tells us it is a "central ritual" which must be interpreted as part of a vast system of interrelated beliefs. But in the African context he dismisses sacrifice: "as elsewhere in the world," it is "a gesture of communication with god."[8] Recognizing that it was not Smart's intention to denigrate African religions, we must nevertheless observe that his use of words is unfortunate, suggesting very clearly that African ritual sacrifices are really not worth serious consideration because they simply duplicate things that happen more interestingly elsewhere.

Fifth, Smart says Indian expressions of anthropomorphism represent a "splendid act of imagination," but he sees African societies as possessing anthropomorphic religions, which in the context of his discussion appear rather limited and simplistic.[9]

Of course some people will object to these compari-

Photo 2.4 Smart sees the many gods of India through the lens of Vedanta philosophy, which reduced them to one essential essence, but when he looks at African religions, he sees many different gods. This is simply inconsistent, because not all Hindus think that all the gods are "the same" god. The above picture, from a Hindu temple, is of a small altar with pictures. While it is permissible to look behind the gods of Hinduism to one God, the same courtesy ought to be extended to African religions.

---

5. Smart, *The World's Religions*, 42, 310.

6. Ibid., 45–47, 300.

7. Ibid., 47, 300–310.

8. Ibid., 54, 302.

9. Ibid., 54, 299–300.

Photo 2.5 When Africans sacrifice, Smart and other writers see it as simply another example of what people do elsewhere. Thus they never bother to investigate what actually goes on or to see African religion as *at least* on the same level as Indian and other religious systems.

sons and attempt to dismiss them as trivial quibbles. Surely, they will argue, "one cannot compare African and Indian religious traditions," because "African religions lack philosophic sophistication, while Indian religions share a rich philosophical tradition." Therefore, they will conclude, critical comments about Smart's text are inappropriate. This argument sounds good initially, but it can be questioned by comparing what Smart, or almost any other religious studies textbook writer, says about other religious traditions which lack philosophical refinement. For example, Smart comments favorably on Polynesian religion, whereas in his section on Africa one finds no appreciation at all. Polynesian myths, he argues, express "vast resources," but African myths simply "leave much to reflect on."[10]

Sixth, in Smart's judgment African religions have a particular problem in terms of their relation to "modern science" and their potential to produce "the philosophical basis for religious pluralism." On the other hand he gives a positive assessment of Australian Aboriginal religion on these issues.[11] Thus, when writing about Australian Aboriginal society, which is a fragmented society far smaller than almost any African society, Smart comments, "No doubt the Aborigines are on the verge of (a new pan-Aboriginal religion) creating an . . .

Photo 2.6 Overall the impression given in most textbooks is that African religions are crude affairs led by unsophisticated people. In reality many African religious leaders are well-educated men and women. For example, before becoming a religious leader, Londa Shembe, right, was a successful lawyer.

10. Ibid., 166, 531.
11. Ibid., 529–31, 494–95.

all-embracing reaffirmation of values, helped too by the interpretation of Aborigine religion created by writers on them, such as Mircea Eliade."[12] Yet, for some reason, he feels that African societies "are on the whole too small to be able to bear the full impact of modern social change."[13]

Seventh, while Smart acknowledges that Christianity had "a long history" in Africa and that "dynamic" Christian movements have developed on the African continent, he gives no hint that such church fathers as St. Augustine of Hippo and Tertullian were African, and in all probability Black. As a result the encounter between Christianity and African religion is seen as essentially a one-way transaction, with Africans adapting Christianity to their needs but not really influencing the outside world.[14]

Yet it can be argued that the impact of Africa on Christianity is as great as the impact of Christianity on Africa. For example, there is considerable evidence that the modern charismatic movement was of African origin and that without an appreciation of African culture one cannot really understand either classical or contemporary Christianity. Taking these considerations into account, it is clear that in religious studies texts, like Smart's, African religions get a very raw deal. To understand this general neglect and disparagement of African religion in the West, we need to look at the treatment of Africa and Africans in European history and European thought generally.

Photo 2.7 St. Maurice as depicted in a statue from Magdeburg Dom (Cathedral). Quite clearly the crusader in this sculpture is an African. Yet he stands in the cathedral alongside Europeans as a great lord who is clearly pious.

AFRICA BEFORE THE ENLIGHTENMENT

Prior to the Enlightenment, Africans were thought to have much in common with Europeans. Indeed, in the eighteenth century one Ghanaian, Anton Wilhelm Amo (1703–1759), actually gained a considerable reputation as a rationalist philosopher and in 1737 was appointed lecturer (*Privatdozent*) at the German University of Halle. He had graduated from Halle in 1727 and obtained his doctorate from the University of Wittenberg in 1734.[15]

Amo is but one of a number of Blacks who were well received and respected in Europe before the Enlightenment. There is also some evidence that Africans were regarded as a religious people with a deep spirituality.[16] All of this changed with the Enlightenment in the eighteenth century.

---

12. Ibid., 495.

13. Ibid., 529.

14. Ibid., 297, 517–20, 523–31.

15. Hans Werner Debrunner, *Presence and Prestige: Africans in Europe; A History of Africans in Europe before 1918* (Basel: Basler Africa Bibliographien, 1979), 107.

16. Debrunner, *Presence and Prestige*, 35–36; Graham W. Irwin, *Africans Abroad: A Documentary History of the Black Diaspora in Asia, Latin America and the Caribbean during the Age of Slavery* (New York: Columbia Univ. Press, 1977), 34–35.

AFRICA AND THE ENLIGHTENMENT

While it is usual to regard the Enlightenment as a period of reform and progress, it was anything but progressive for Blacks. A good case can be made that modern racism originates in the Enlightenment.[17]

The French philosopher François-Marie Arouet, known as Voltaire (1694–1778), set the general tone of Enlightenment attitudes to Africans. Although derogatory remarks may be found throughout his work, his short essay "The Negro"[18] outlined his position. He tells his readers, "The NEGRO race is a species of men as different from ours as the breed of spaniels is from that of greyhounds ... if their understanding is not of a different nature from ours, it is at least greatly inferior. They are not capable of any great application or association of ideas, and seem formed neither of the advantages nor abuses of our philosophy."[19]

In another place Voltaire talks about "uncultivated coasts where Pelsart and his companions, in 1630, found black men

Photo 2.8 Voltaire, the great philosopher of the Enlightenment, who was particularly unenlightened when it came to Africans.

who walked on their hands as upon feet ... and ... a race of negros who had no fore teeth in their upper jaws."[20] More importantly, Voltaire advocated the theory of polygenesis, or the separate creation of different human races: "You may, if you please, reduce all mankind to one single species, because they have the same organs of life, sense and motion; but this species is evidently divided into several others, whether we consider it in a physical or moral light."[21] David Hume (1711–1776) expressed similar views: "I suspect that negroes ...

Photo 2.9 David Hume's statue in his native city of Edinburgh, Scotland. Hume's skeptical works on religion were largely ignored during the period immediately after his death, only to be taken up in the mid-nineteenth and twentieth centuries.

---

17. George L. Mosse, *Toward the Final Solution: A History of European Racism* (New York: Howard Fertig, 1978), 1–7, 19–20.

18. Voltaire, "The Negro," in *The Works of Voltaire: A Contemporary Version*, trans. William F. Fleming (London: E. R. DuMont, 1901), 19:240–42.

19. Ibid., 240.

20. Ibid., 268.

21. Ibid., 270.

be naturally inferior to the whites. There never was a civilized nation of any other complexion than white."[22]

Similarly, while Jean-Jacques Rousseau (1712–1778) is remembered for his attack on slavery, it is forgotten that he also spoke quite freely of "negroes and savages." In fact, when Rousseau's views are examined in detail, his assessment of the "noble savage" mirrors modern racism. In his essay "What Is the Origin of Inequality among Men, and Is It Authorized by Natural Law?"[23] he wrote: "We should beware, therefore, of confounding the savage man with the men we have daily before our eyes. Nature treats all the animals left to her care with a predilection ... By becoming domesticate they lose half these advantages ... there is still a greater difference between savage and civilised man than between wild and tame beasts ..."[24] These comments lead to the view that " ... they [savages] go naked, have no dwellings, and lack all superfluities which we think so necessary ... Their children are slowly and with difficulty taught to walk."[25]

Such racist comments are followed by the observation that, "Solitary, indolent, and perpetually accompanied by danger, the savage cannot but be fond of sleep; his sleep too must be light, like that of the animals ... Such in general is the animal condition, and such, according to travellers, is that of most savage nations ..."[26] And again: "Savage man ... must accordingly begin with purely animal functions ... being destitute of every species of intelligence ... his desires never go beyond his physical wants ... food, a female, and sleep."[27] Moving from "the savage" in particular to people in general, Rousseau says, "Everything seems removed from savage man ... He is so far from having the knowledge which is needful to make him want more, that he can have neither foresight nor curiosity ... He has not understanding enough to wonder at the great miracles; nor is it in his mind that we can expect to find that philosophy man needs."[28] After all of this, Rousseau makes it quite clear that his "savage" is no abstract entity but can be identified with Africans in particular.[29]

The philosopher Immanuel Kant (1724–1804) was more cautious in his essay "On the Different Races of Mankind."[30] Nevertheless, he did appear to think that racial mixture was to be discouraged and laid a highly theoretical basis for segregation. With such biased philosophical judgements behind him, the later German philosopher Georg Wilhelm Friedrich Hegel (1770–1831) had no hesitation in saying, "The peculiarly African character is difficult to comprehend ... In Negro life the characteristic point is the fact

---

22. David Hume, *Essays* (London: Routledge and Sons, 1906), 152.

23. Jean-Jacques Rousseau, "A Discourse on a Subject Proposed by the Academy of Dijon: What Is the Origin of Inequality among Men, and Is It Authorized by Natural Law?" in *The Social Contract and Discourses*, trans. G. D. H. Cole, Everyman's Library 660 (1913; New York: Dutton, 1966), 165.

24. Ibid., 168.

25. Ibid.

26. Ibid., 169.

27. Ibid., 171.

28. Ibid., 172.

29. Ibid.

30. Immanuel Kant, *Immanuel Kants Werke*, Band 2, *Vorkritische Schriften* (Berlin: Bruno Cassirer, 1922).

that consciousness has not yet attained to the realization of any substantial objective existence ... The Negro, as already observed, exhibits the natural man in his completely wild and untamed state. We must lay aside all thought of reverence and morality. Among Negroes moral sentiments are quite weak, or more strictly speaking, non-existent ... At this point we leave Africa to mention it no more. For it is no historical part of the World."[31]

From these examples it is clear that the leading figures of the Enlightenment, and of the subsequent Romantic Movement, held a very low opinion of Africans. This explains not only their failure to study African religion and society but also the continuing neglect of such studies by their disciples and eventually by the founders of religious studies such as Max Müller. But is this the whole story?

EARLY-NINETEENTH-CENTURY EUROPEAN REACTIONS TO INDIA

In light of the reaction of Enlightenment thinkers to Africa and Africans, it might be expected that similar attitudes would have influenced European scholarly views of India. In fact, during the early years of the nineteenth century there was considerable anti-Indian propaganda. Popular accounts of Africa and India, written by traders and missionaries, painted equally bleak pictures of both continents and their peoples.[32] James Mill (1773–1836), Thomas Babington Macaulay

Photo 2.10 Bust of Hegel, for whom Africa had no history. Without doubt Hegel remains one of the most influential of all philosophers. Although his work has been largely ignored by professional philosophers in the English-speaking world, its influence lies behind such movements as Marxism, postmodernism, and even some forms of fascism.

(1800–1859), and a host of other "experts" considered Indian civilization degenerate and described it in terms very similar to contemporary descriptions of African life.[33] Nor did the philosopher Hegel have much more use for India or Indian religions than he had for Africa or its religions: "Absolute Being is presented here in the ecstatic state of a dreaming condition ... The Character of Spirit in a state of Dream, is the generic principle of the Hindoo Nature ... which involves a monstrous bewilderment in regard to all phenomena and relations, we have already recognized as the principle of the Hindoo Spirit. The Hindoo Mythology is therefore only a wild extravagance of Fancy ... Their whole life and ideas are one unbroken superstition, because among them all is revere and consequent enslavement."[34] Here we have an attack on Hindu society and religion harsher than any similar contemporary account of Africa.

31. Georg Wilhelm Friedrich Hegel, *The Philosophy of History* (New York: Willey Book Co., 1944).
32. Kenneth Ingham, *Reformers in India* (New York: Octagon Books, 1973), 1–54.
33. James Mill, *The History of British India*, abridged by William Thomas (Chicago: Univ. of Chicago Press, 1975), 137–89; Raghavan Iyer, ed., *The Glass Curtain between Asia and Europe* (London: Oxford Univ. Press, 1965), 211.
34. Hegel, *Philosophy of History*, 139–41, 155, 157–58, 167.

Yet by the mid-nineteenth century the outlook of many Europeans had changed, and India began to benefit from a growing appreciation of its religious and cultural heritage. Clearly, Kantian philosophy, Hegelian dialectics, and other, similar forms of philosophical idealism affected Western scholarly views of Indian religions,[35] but Hegel's disciples, and thinkers such as Arthur Schopenhauer (1788–1860), who detested Hegel, were enthusiastic about Indian thought.[36]

AFRICA ABANDONED

No parallel appreciation of African values developed during the nineteenth century. In fact, if anything, the descriptions of Africa and Africans written by European writers caused Black Africans to sink lower and lower on the scale of humanity.[37] Once again, it would be easy to explain this devaluation of African life in terms of its "primitive" state as compared to the "richness" of Indian culture, especially Indian philosophy. Such an explanation overlooks the fact that American Indians and similar groups did not suffer the same negative reactions by nineteenth-century writers as Africans did.[38] Therefore it is increasingly difficult not to see an element of racism in the neglect of African religions.[39] The truth is that the more one probes the treatment of Blacks and Black religions by Western scholars, the more disturbing the issue becomes.[40]

THE HISTORY OF AFRICAN RELIGIONS IN EARLIER EUROPEAN TEXTBOOKS

The neglect of African religions by scholars is not a new phenomenon. A quick survey of religious studies texts from an earlier era shows a similar disregard for African traditions long before the growth of modern departments of religious studies.

In 1813 John Belamy devoted fifteen pages of his *History of All Religions*[41] to the religions of India and two pages to African religions, which he describes as "paganism." A few years later, in 1835, Charles A. Goodrich, in *Religious Ceremonies and Customs*, allowed ten pages to "the Hindoos" and three pages to "African Tribes."[42] James Gardner's popular *Faiths of the World* has many references to India and Indian deities, but avoids African

---

35. Ibid., 139–81.

36. Joachim Deppert, ed., *India and the West* (New Delhi: Manohar, 1983), 221–35; Arthur Schopenhauer, *The World as Will and Representation* (New York: Dover, 1969); Carl T. Jackson, *The Oriental Religions and American Thought: Nineteenth-Century Explorations* (Westport: Greenwood Press, 1981), 45–62.

37. Christine Bolt and Seymour Drescher, eds., *Anti-Slavery, Religion and Reform*, (Folkestone, U.K.: W. Dawson, 1980), 109–56; Phillip D. Curtin, *The Image of Africa* (Madison: Univ. of Wisconsin Press, 1964), 377–86.

38. Joseph R. Washington Jr., *Anti-Blackness in English Religion: 1500–1800* (New York: Edwin Mellen, 1984), 24, 349; Bolt and Drescher, *Anti-Slavery*, 234–43.

39. Okot p'Bitek, *African Religions in Western Scholarship* (Nairobi: East African Literature Bureau, 1970).

40. Jordan, *Comparative Religion*; Eric J. Sharpe, *Comparative Religion: A History* (London: Duckworth, 1975); Max Müller, *Anthropological Religion*, Gifford Lectures of 1891 (London: Longmans, Green, 1898), 286–90.

41. John Bellamy, *The History of All Religions* (London: Longman, Hurst, Rees, Orm and Brown, 1813).

42. Charles A. Goodrich, *Religious Ceremonies and Customs, or The Forms of Worship Practiced by Several Nations of the Known World, from the Earliest Records to the Present Time* (Hartford: Hutchinson and Dwler, 1835).

religions altogether.[43] Later still (1883), James Clarke's *Ten Great Religions* shows a typical disrespect for African religions. Unlike modern writers, Clarke does not hesitate to tell his readers, "The negroes of Africa have been charged with all sorts of vices and crimes ... But it must be remembered that the negroes of whom we have usually heard have been for centuries corrupted by the slave-traders ... Travellers who have penetrated the interior ... have met with warm hospitality ... They have, in short, found the rudimentary forms of the kingly and queenly virtues of truth and love, justice and mercy, united in the hearts of these benighted heathens ... Such are the virtues which already appear in primitive man, rudimentary virtues, indeed ..."[44]

No wonder that by the time of the World Congress of Religions, in 1893, African religions had completely disappeared from the vision of progressive scholars. As a result the proceedings of the Congress give no attention whatsoever to African religions. Early-twentieth-century descriptions of African religions are equally prejudiced. Edwin W. Smith, for example, in his tellingly entitled book *The Religion of Lower Races, as Illustrated by the African Bantu*, describes African religion as "elementary" and "a religion of fear."[45]

Clearly, the neglect of African religion and religions has a long history. Modern textbooks, which almost totally neglect African religion, are simply continuing a two-hundred-year tradition deeply rooted in European racism. Consequently, when students read popular textbook accounts of African religion or encounter its almost total neglect, they quickly form the opinion that African religions are unworthy of serious study. Thus existing textbooks confirm old prejudices and lead to the further neglect of Africa by anyone interested in the serious study of religion.

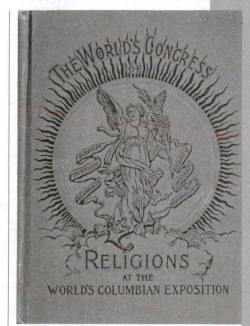

Photo 2.11 The proceedings of the World Congress of Religions, held in Chicago in 1893. It claimed to represent all the religions of the world, but totally ignored African religions.

THE IMPORTANCE OF SACRED TEXTS

Clearly, one reason why an appreciation of African religion did not develop in the nineteenth century is the unavailability of religious texts containing the scriptures of African religions and the reliance of most scholars on written texts containing the scriptures of various religions for their interpretation of religion. Although Indian texts, often directly

43. James Gardner, *The Faiths of the World: A Dictionary of All Religions and Religious Sects* (Edinburgh: A. Fullarton, 1858).
44. James Freeman Clarke, *Ten Great Religions* (Boston: Houghton Mifflin, 1883), 293–94.
45. Edwin W. Smith, *The Religion of Lower Races, as Illustrated by the African Bantu* (New York: Macmillan, 1923), 2–3, 66.

based upon oral traditions, were translated into first Latin and then German and English during the early part of the nineteenth century, no similar translations were made of African traditions. Indeed, often all that Western scholars knew about African religions were sensational accounts of "primitive" practices by traders and missionaries.

That Africa could have its own epics that might rival the Mahabharata, and that apparently irrational behavior, such as witchcraft, might have a logical basis simply did not occur to nineteenth-century scholars.[46] One need not argue that African epics are better or worse than Indian epics. All that needs to be recognized is that in the nineteenth century very few people, in Europe at least, took African oral traditions seriously.[47]

Indian religions, on the other hand, attained a respectability never attained by African faiths.[48] While James Mill could see Indian rituals as essentially expressions of barbaric superstitions, scholars studying Indian beliefs slowly began to recognize an underlying order behind the rituals. Indologists therefore began to attribute meaning to these apparently meaningless acts, thus weakening Mill's arguments.[49] Later intellectual movements like Vedanta and, at a more popular level, Theosophy, which was founded in America in the 1870s by Helena Petrovna Blavatsky (1831–1891), allowed even the crudest ritual acts to be reinterpreted in sophisticated ways.

But this is not all. The very fact of interpretation led to further refinement and produced schools of apologists who saw in Indian religions an alternative to the spiritual bankruptcy of the West.[50] That the Buddhism of C. A. F. Rhys-Davids (1857–1942) is far removed from Buddhism as actually practiced by tradi-

Photo 2.12 An African healer performing a complex ritual in the Transkei. Although religiously and numerically important, African religions have been mostly ignored because the traditions they follow remain largely oral rather than written.

46. E. E. Evans-Pritchard, *Witchcraft, Oracles and Magic among the Azande* (London: Oxford Univ. Press, 1937).

47. Isidore Okpewho, *The Epic in Africa: Toward a Poetics of the Oral Performance* (New York: Columbia Univ. Press, 1979); Elizabeth Gunner, "Forgotten Men: Zulu Bards and Praising at the Time of the Zulu Kings." *Langues Africaines* [African Languages] 2 (1976): 71–89; D. K. Rycroft and A. B. Ngcobo, eds., *The Praises of Dingana: Izibongo zikaDingana* (Pietermaritzburg: Natal Univ. Press, 1988).

48. R. Radhakrishnan, "Hinduism and the West," in *Modern India and the West*, ed. L. S. S. O'Malley (London: Oxford Univ. Press, 1941), 338–53; Bruce F. Campbell, *Ancient Wisdom Revived: A History of the Theosophical Movement* (Berkeley: Univ. of California Press, 1980).

49. M. E. Chamberlain, *Britain and India: The Interaction of Two Peoples* (Newton Abbot, U.K.: David & Charles, 1974). 8.

50. Carl T. Jackson, *Oriental Religions and American Thought*.

tional Buddhists is unimportant.[51] To rephrase the well-known comment by Karl Barth (1886–1968) on the famous German liberal theologian Adolf von Harnack (1851–1930), in the nineteenth century Western orientalists looked deep and long into the well of Indian spirituality and saw their own reflection. One result was the development of what we now know as religious studies, which highly prizes Indian religions while almost totally disregarding African religions.

CONCLUSION

The examples presented in this chapter are so gross that it seems unbelievable that Black Americans are not protesting loud and clear about the prejudice found in religious studies texts. Yet they are not. This is probably because these prejudices are so deep and appear so scholarly that no one really notices them. Instead they lie on the edge of the reader's consciousness.

The significance of this is important because although the evidence is clearly there in the writings of Martin Luther (1483-1546) it is only recently that David D. Daniels and several other scholars have shown that the young Luther was fascinated by Ethiopian Christianity and had an African friend who was a Coptic priest. This "discovery" suggests a strong link between African Christianity and the Protestant Reformation which earlier scholars totally overlooked.[52]

Yet once the way African religions are treated in textbooks is realized, it becomes possible to look out for similar biases elsewhere, and then it quickly becomes clear that textbooks are full of bias and prejudice. We all notice these things at a subliminal level, but few of us really trust our own judgment enough to point out the biased nature of textbooks. Yet this is what we all must learn to do if scholarship in religious studies is to advance. So the task is now handed over to you the reader. What biases can you find in the textbooks you read?

---

51. Edward Conze, *Buddhism: Its Essence and Development* (Oxford: Bruno Cassirer, 1957), 27.

52. See: https://divinity.uchicago.edu/sightings/martin-luther-and-ethiopian-christianity-historical-traces.

PART 2

AFRICAN TRADITIONS

CHAPTER 3

AFRICAN RELIGIOUS TRADITIONS

INTRODUCTION

Although scholars may disagree about the exact nature of various religious traditions, there is general agreement in religious studies textbooks about the existence of what may be called the "Great Traditions," or "World Religions." These are usually listed as Buddhism, Christianity, Confucianism, Hinduism, Islam, and Judaism, all of which have long histories and written texts. Apart from these major traditions there are numerous smaller religious traditions that are sometimes called "traditional" or "primal" religions because they are usually found in non-Western societies that lack written scriptures. Probably the greatest concentration of this type of religion is found in Africa.

Writing about "African religions" is like writing about "European religions" or "Indian religions." There are many very different African religious traditions; therefore, it is impossible to speak about "African religion" without qualification. Here I offer an overview of some common features of many different African religions. These shared beliefs and practices, it should be noted, are often found in other traditional religions throughout the world and are not exclusively African, although they take on a particular form in Africa.[1]

Such religions lack written scriptures and recorded histories and often share a belief in evil power identified with sorcery or witchcraft, specialized healers, psychic events, and the importance of ancestors. Recognizing the similarity between such religions, John Taylor identified them as "primal religions," because in his view they draw on deep-rooted primal, or basic, experiences common to all humans, experiences capable of being formed into coherent ways of seeing the world. Although often very different from each other in

---

*   Shortly before his final illness and death, Fred Welbourn and I planned to rewrite *Atoms and Ancestors.* For a variety of reasons this was never done. This and the following chapter make extensive use of Welbourn's work.

1. For a critique of European scholarship on African religions, see Okot p'Bitek, *African Religions in Western Scholarship* (Nairobi: East African Literature Bureau, n.d.). Although it was written over thirty years ago, little has changed since then in the area of religious studies.

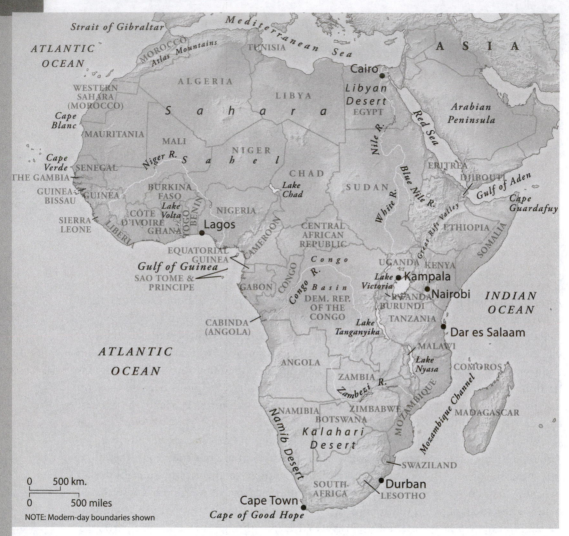

Map 3.1 Map of Africa showing today's political divisions and the cities of Cape Town, Durban, Dar es Salaam, Nairobi, Kampala, Lagos, and Cairo. The borders of today's African states are outlined, and the name of each state is given. Looking at this map, one gets an idea of the vastness of Africa in relation to Europe and the rest of the world.

detail, Taylor argued, African religious traditions share many common features that can be seen as a worldview which may be identified as the "primal vision."[2]

The study of African religions is difficult also because of the relative lack of interest in the topic among religious studies scholars, as was shown in the last chapter. Consequently, at present we simply cannot write an introductory section, like the one on the yogic tradition, outlining the history of African religions because at present the material for such a chapter does not exist. As pointed out earlier, this is a result of the bias against things African in both scholarly discourse and popular culture. Hopefully, it will change in the future.

---

2. John V. Taylor, *The Primal Vision: Christian Presence amid African Religion* (London: SCM Press, 1963).

Photo 3.1 This famous painting, *The Monk by the Sea* (1808–1810) by Caspar David Friedrich (1774–1840), captures the essence of the power of the primal over the human being. The monk standing on the sea shore contemplating the vastness of the ocean and the sky evokes a sense of the finitude of life. The original may be seen in the Old National Gallery, Unter den Linden, Berlin, Germany.

THE PRIMAL CORE

African traditional religions, like most grassroots religious movements, are based on the religious experience of their founders and members. These religions may be called "primal religions," because they are essentially oral traditions that give primacy to the interpretation of experience rather than to a collection of sacred scriptures. Primal religions include most African traditional religions, African Independent Churches, Native American religions, and many new religious movements in Western society.

Primal religions are identifiable with what Robert Redfield calls "little traditions," where charismatic experiences, healings, prophecies, visions, and so on are the principal concern of devotees. In primal religions shamans or similar ritual figures communicate between this world and the next, often with the aim of placating the ancestors.

At the core of all primal religions are primal experiences. These are intense experiences which defy rational explanation. Primal experiences are unexpected vivid encounters so unusual that they can be explained only by reference to a religious mythology. Such experiences take many forms. Above all, they shock those who experience them, bringing about a change in their attitude toward the material world. Primal experiences involve such things as dreams, visions, voices, spiritual healings, a sense of presence or awe, notions of destiny, sightings of the dead, and inexplicable spiritual phenomena.

Primal experiences are important for African religious movements because they affirm the reality of traditional mythologies and the foundation myths of new religious movements like the amaNazaretha. Before a person has a primal experience, he or she may view the traditional mythology, or myths of a particular new religious movement, as unbelievable fairy tales which only uneducated traditionalists believe. Following a primal experience, the "old ways," or teachings, of a new religion become a reality.

As it turns out, primal experiences are remarkably common among humans. In the 1970s David Hay became interested in the phenomenon when some postgraduate students at the University of Nottingham, England, responding to a social survey, admitted that they had had primal experiences that profoundly affected their outlook. The majority of these students said that they had no adequate explanation for their experience and would welcome one. Following this initial survey, Hay and Ann Morisy arranged a statistically valid national survey of the British population. In this more qualified survey they found that 36.4 percent of those included in the random sample reported having had such experiences. Significantly, 45 percent of those who had these experiences had no real contact with churches or organized religions.[3]

In a national survey in the United States, some 30 percent of Americans responded positively to questions about primal experiences. A much higher figure was obtained by Rob-

Religious Traditions and Primal Experiences

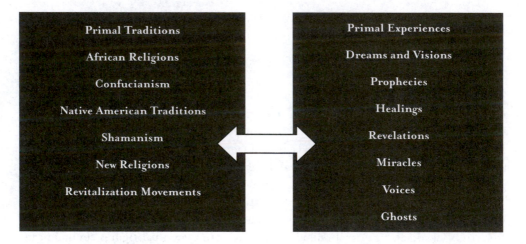

Primal Traditions	Primal Experiences
African Religions	Dreams and Visions
Confucianism	Prophecies
Native American Traditions	Healings
Shamanism	Revelations
New Religions	Miracles
Revitalization Movements	Voices
	Ghosts

Figure 3.1 Primal religions are those that generally lack strong written traditions or rigidly organized priesthoods. Instead they rely on direct experiences of the "supernatural," which, it must be stressed, is always seen as a natural continuation of this life.

3. David Hay, "Reports of Religious Experiences by a Group of Postgraduate Students: A Pilot Study," and "Religious Experiences among a Group of Postgraduate Students: A Qualitative Survey," unpublished papers presented at the Colloquium on Psychology and Religion, Lancaster University, 1975; David Hay and Ann Morisy, "Reports of Ecstatic Paranormal or Religious Experiences in Great Britain and the United States: A Comparison of Trends," *Journal for the Scientific Study of Religion* 1/7 (1978): 255–65.

ert Wuthnow in his survey of the San Francisco Bay area population. There Wuthnow's positive response rate went up to 50 percent.[4] In Canada, Reginald Bibby found that 60 percent of Canadians reported postively when asked about primal experiences. All of this evidence suggests, Bibby observed, a "pool of religiosity" that is largely untapped by established religions.[5]

Similar findings have been reported from other parts of the world. In his studies of hundreds of Zulu in South Africa, for example, S. G. Lee reports that before individuals became diviners, they reported a variety of primal experiences, including numerous visual and auditory hallucinations. Fifteen percent reported a history of possession experiences that involved fatigued states, hallucinations, dreaming, and so on. Seventeen percent reported diseases that they attributed to sorcery. The difference between those who merely consulted diviners and those who actually became diviners was largely a matter of the severity of their condition. Chronic or severe sufferers went through rigorous, six-month-long initiations, and converted from client to diviner.[6]

UNDERSTANDING TRADITIONAL SOCIETIES

To understand traditional religions, particularly African religions, it is necessary to suspend judg-

Photo 3.2 A Zulu becomes a diviner after an intense primal experience followed by a long apprenticeship with an established diviner. The man shown above is in the process of becoming a fully fledged diviner. Each white bead in his braided hair represents a successful healing.

ment as to which view of the universe—the secular, traditional, modern Christian, or any other alternative view—is true. We must enter as fully as possible into the perspective of someone living in a traditional society which sees all phenomena as an expression of mysterious power. But to do so we need to understand not only the thought world of tradi-

4. Robert Wuthnow, *Experimentation in American Religion: The New Mysticisms and Their Implications for the Churches* (Berkeley: Univ. of California Press, 1978), 64–65, 100.

5. Reginald Bibby, "Religionless Christianity: A Profile of Religion in the Canadian 80s," *Social Indicators Research* 13 (1983): 1–16. See also Rodney Stark and William Sims Bainbridge, *The Future of Religion: Secularization, Revival and Cult Formation* (Berkeley: Univ. of California Press, 1985), 325–45; Alister Hardy, *The Spiritual Nature of Man* (Oxford: Clarendon, 1979).

6. S. G. Lee, "Spirit Possession among the Zulu," in *Spirit Mediumship and Society in Africa*, ed. John Beattie and John Middleton (New York: Africana, 1969), 28–55. See also S. G. Lee, "A Study of Crying Hysteria and Dreaming in Zulu Women" (PhD diss., University of London, 1954); and Max Köhler, *The Izangoma Diviners*, trans. and ed. N. J. van Warmelo (Pretoria: Government Printer, 1941).

Photo 3.3 and 3.4 Traditional African life in South Africa's Transkei in the 1970s was hard and in many ways close to the way people lived in biblical times. Consequently, Africans saw in the message of the Bible a reflection of their own personal realities. Note the hard labor of the woman and that the oxen are drawing a sledge, not a wheeled vehicle.

tional people, but also their traditional social order. This exercise will cause us to reflect on our own society and our most dearly held beliefs, and then to agree with Shakespeare's Hamlet that "there are more things in heaven and earth, Horatio, / than are dreamt of in your philosophy."[7]

EXPLAINING PRIMAL EXPERIENCES

In his book *Atoms and Ancestors*,[8] Fred Welbourn pointed out that until recently few Europeans or North Americans had seen bacteria. In fact, he argued, we rarely think about bacteria unless there is an outbreak of disease that we believe they have caused. It is equally significant that even today many people do not realize that bacteria not only cause illness, but are also essential to healthy organic life. The truth is that if we have to think about bacteria at all, whether we want to know how to kill the malign variety that cause dysentery, or to increase their benign activity in a compost heap, we do so because we see them at work. Normally, however, we simply take the existence of bacteria on trust.

Yet for the last hundred years most people in the West, if challenged, would have said that bacteria are a natural and inescapable part of life. They are something which pervades our environment, yet which we normally do not think about and only very rarely see. Only when they begin to cause problems do we consult specialists who can heal illness or tell us why our compost heap is not working properly.

---

7. William Shakespeare, *Hamlet*, 1.5.166–67.
8. Fred B. Welbourn, *Atoms and Ancestors* (London: Edwin Arnold, 1968). This and the next chapter are a revision of Welbourn's work, as agreed with him before he died. Welbourn's *East African Rebels* (London: SCM Press, 1961) is a classic study of African Independent Churches that also throws light on traditional religions.

Similarly, people living in traditional societies, like the Zulu in South Africa, often claim to have seen an Ancestor, or what in the West we call a ghost. Among the Zulu, and many other African groups, Ancestors are not expected to be seen. They work in other ways and are experienced as part of everyday life. Yet they are rarely thought about unless, like bacteria, they begin to cause problems. Among the Ganda, sometimes called the Baganda, of Uganda, custom directs that shrines to the dead should be tended regularly, yet they are usually neglected unless the ghost of the deceased causes trouble. Likewise, people in Zulu homesteads only think about deceased Ancestors when problems arise in daily life.

The benign activity of ghosts—or Ancestors, as both the Ganda and Zulu call them—is taken for granted in most traditional societies. Therefore, Ancestors are hardly mentioned except on very special occasions. When an outbreak of disease occurs or misfortunes continually arise, a specialist is consulted. Like the Western medical specialist or horticultural expert, Africans who know how to communicate with the Ancestors to bring healing or good fortune are highly prized. They are specialists, or people with a calling who have entered their profession after a long training and many years of study. And as with the Western specialist, the proof of the pudding is in the eating. If health and good fortune are restored, then it is clear that the specialist has placated the Ancestors, whose activity is beyond doubt.

Sometimes, however, Ancestors are experienced in a much more frightening way. When interviewed by the author, Estelle Nxele, a Zulu woman in Natal, South Africa, described her encounter with them as follows: "In nineteen sixty-six my spirit came up very strong. At work I used to have a bad, sharp headache. In one minute, it would come up like a balloon. Just like a balloon. I couldn't see. The doctor was frightened to give me an injection, gave me pills for pain. They sent me home and I slept. The next day, I was all right. Then when I was sleeping here, I could hear people talking, but I was sleeping like a dream. I used to see them when I was sleeping. They talked to me, my grandfathers and my granny too. 'This is how you—you're going to help people.' That is what they told me."

Photo 3.5 Estelle Nxele dressed in preparation for a healing ceremony at her home near Durban, South Africa.

As a result of this and many other very frightening experiences, Estelle eventually sought the services of a specialist who could deal with her "African disease." It got its name from the fact that it had defied the efforts of Western doctors to find a cure. Even though she was a baptized Christian, she went to a traditional Zulu diviner. The diviner explained that Estelle had received a call from the Ancestors and that in consequence she must not wear Western shoes or enter a church building. She also had to undergo years of rigorous training before she too became a well-respected diviner who practiced the old ways of healing through communication with the Ancestors. On the other hand, she could remain a Christian provided she did not go into a church building, which the Ancestors found "frightening." Despite this restriction on Estelle's behavior, her children and grandchildren were encouraged to go to church.

THE "SECULAR" AND THE "SACRED"

Behind this type of experience lies a deep division between the way most Western people see the world and the way traditional Africans see the world. Western people tend to think of the "natural" and "supernatural" as two entirely different realms. As a result many people find it extremely difficult to believe that any form of reality exists beyond what is directly observed by our senses. But, as we shall see, what is "reality," how it is best observed, and what counts as "sense experience" are not easy questions to answer. In most traditional African thought, there is nothing more natural than the supernatural. Any attempt to understand the religious experience of traditional Africans must, therefore, begin by suspending our normal "educated," secular, but not particularly Christian, idea that the "natural" and "supernatural" are different.[9]

Traditional Africans, such as the Baganda and Zulu peoples, do not make distinctions between the natural and supernatural. This means they do not recognize a distinction between the secular and the sacred. Yet the idea of the "sacred" or "holy" is deeply ingrained in religious studies.

A good example of the way "the sacred" plays a key role in religious studies can be found in James C. Livingston's popular *Anatomy of the Sacred: An Introduction to Religion*: "most scholars today agree that religion is a system of activities and beliefs directed toward that which is perceived to be sacred ... Here we shall discuss the sacred or the holy as the root of religious experience and practice."[10]

After a short discussion he introduces students to the work of "the Dutch scholar Gerardus van der Leeuw"[11] with the comment that van der Leeuw "points to the preconceptual experience of sacred power as the root of all religion."[12] Livingston then argues that the root of the experience of the sacred is summed up by "Rudolf Otto in his classic and influential study *The Idea of the Holy*,"[13] where it is "a category of interpretation and valuation

---

9. See Harriet Ngubane, *Body and Mind in Zulu Medicine* (London: Academic Press, 1977).

10. James C. Livingston, *Anatomy of the Sacred: An Introduction to Religion* (New York: Macmillan, 1989), 47.

11. Ibid., 48.

12. Ibid., 47–48.

13. Ibid., 50.

Photo 3.6 Sociologist Émile Durkheim made the "sacred-secular" distinction basic to his definition of religion. In doing so he appealed to the religion of Australian Aborigines, even though he had never visited Australia or had direct contact with Aborigines. As a result, he constructed an appealing theory on the basis of secondhand observations and theoretical speculation.

peculiar to the sphere of religion …"[14] Developing his argument, Livingston goes on to cite Mircea Eliade as a scholar whose work generally supports that of Otto. He argues that Eliade improves on Otto's insights by utilizing Émile Durkheim's "fundamental contrast between the sacred and the profane."[15]

The popularization of Durkheim's, Otto's, van der Leeuw's, and Eliade's ideas about the sacred-secular distinction has been accepted without question by most Western scholars. Today this distinction is seen by most writers as the fundamental category of religious thought.[16] Yet, as we have just argued, this "fundamental contrast" is absent from most African religious systems. This means that the study of African religions forces us to rethink popular interpretations of religion. It also means that we must pay attention to empirical evidence rather than theorizing about the way we think religion and religious people ought to behave.

PROBLEMS WITH THE SACRED-SECULAR DISTINCTION

Durkheim developed his theory about the origins of religion from a sharp distinction he claimed to observe between the sacred and the secular in "the most primitive and simple religion which is actually known …"[17] Starting from a theory of "the Holy" which he found in William Robertson Smith's *Lectures on the Religion of the Semites: The Fundamental Institutions*,[18] Durkheim read many works on totemism, particularly among Australian Aborigines, to develop his own wide-ranging theory, which he published in *The Elementary Forms of Religious Life.*

14. Rudolf Otto, *The Idea of the Holy* (Oxford: Oxford Univ. Press, 1923), 5.

15. Livingston, *Anatomy of the Sacred*, 55.

16. E.g., David S. Noss and John B. Noss, *Man's Religions* (New York: Macmillan, 1984), 10; Denise Lardner Carmody and John Tully Carmody, *Ways to the Center: An Introduction to World Religions* (Belmont, Calif.: Wadsworth, 1984), 45.

17. Émile Durkheim, *The Elementary Forms of Religious Life* (London: Allen & Unwin, 1915; repr., 1964).

18. Hans G. Kippenberg, *Discovering Religious History in the Modern Age*, trans. Barbara Harshav (Princeton: Princeton Univ. Press, 2002), 144–45; William Robertson Smith, *Lectures on the Religion of the Semites: The Fundamental Institutions* (1889; repr., London: A & C. Black, 1927).

Similarly, Otto, van der Leeuw and Eliade used a wide range of documentary sources to develop their own contributions to the theory of religion as a manifestation of the sacred. Although Otto alludes to Kant and to the theologian Friedrich Schleiermacher (1768–1834), he never really outlines his own methodology.[19] By contrast, van der Leeuw's approach is essentially similar to that of Eliade, who clearly states in the introduction to his *Shamanism: Archaic Technique of Ecstasy*[20] that he is not interested in "history" as practiced by historians but rather in "the history of religion,"[21] which he defines as "a hierophany realized at a certain 'historical moment'[which] is structurally equivalent to a hierophany a thousand years earlier or later."[22]

The problem with all of these approaches is that they impose a preexisting theory on the empirical data. Durkheim, Otto, van der Leeuw, and Eliade knew what they would find with regard to the sacred before they ever opened a book to prove their theories. And none of them, despite Durkheim's reputation as a sociologist, did fieldwork. Commenting on Durkheim's study, the great British social anthropologist E. E. Evans-Pritchard writes, "Durkheim's theory is more than just neat; it is brilliant and imaginative, almost poetical ... While various logical and philosophical objections could be raised, I would rather base the case for the prosecution on ethnographical evidence. Does this support the rigid dichotomy he makes between the sacred and profane? I doubt it. Surely what he calls 'sacred and profane' are on the same level of experience, and, far from being cut off from one another, they are so closely intermingled as to be inseparable."[23]

What is more, Evans-Pritchard points to Durkheim's selective use of Australian evidence and his clear misunderstanding of how "sacred" objects are treated in practice. Jim Bellis illustrated this issue very well in relation to the "sacred" drums of the Ashanti of West Africa. According to many accounts, the Ashanti regard their drums with awe because the Ancestors speak through them. But Bellis points out that in everyday life the drums are neglected and often treated quite badly until the occasion arises when they are needed. Then, and only then, do they become objects of power. As soon as communication with the Ancestors is broken, however, the drums revert to their former low status. An extreme example of Ashanti disregard for the sacred nature of the drums is found in the following story.[24]

During a battle between the Ashanti and another group of warriors, a group of Ashanti were cut off from the main force. Things looked desperate, so the Ashanti used their drums to appeal for help from the Ancestors. When no help was forthcoming, the Ashanti urinated over the drums to show their contempt for the stubborn refusal of their Ancestors to come to their aid; then the warriors fought their way through enemy lines to rejoin the

19. Mircea Eliade, *Shamanism: Archaic Technique of Ecstasy* (Princeton: Princeton Univ. Press, 1972).

20. Ibid., xvi.

21. Ibid., xvii.

22. E. E. Evans-Pritchard, *Theories of Primitive Religion* (Oxford: Oxford Univ. Press, 1965), 64–65.

23. The preceding passage and following story are based on a lecture given by Bellis during his visit to the University of Calgary in 1988.

24. Note that traditional African cosmologies refer to God as 'him 'or 'it'; they do not see God in feminine terms. See, e.g., Gabriel M. Setiloane, *The Image of God among the Sotho-Tswana* (Rotterdam: Balkema, 1976).

main force. Such coarse treatment of "sacred objects" does not fit any model created by Durkheim, Otto, van der Leeuw, or Eliade.

From these comments it seems safe to conclude that if the reality of African religion contradicts some pet theories current in religious studies departments, it is because those theories are flawed in their very essence. The problem, simply stated, is that Durkheim, Otto, van der Leeuw, and Eliade were armchair theorists. They analyzed written texts. But to study African religions meaningfully we must move beyond the text to the life experience of living people.

THE REALITY OF POWER

It is important, however, to note that when we say traditional Africans do not recognize the distinction between the secular and the sacred, we are not denying that in the thought of many African societies a hierarchy of power exists. The creator God, if there is a belief in him or it, is the source of this power, as he or it is the source of all things. But power is found, in descending order, in lesser spirits, in ancestral ghosts, in chiefs (often the focus of communication with the spirits), and in witches and sorcerers. Finally, it occurs in ordinary men and women, animals, plants, and inanimate things.

Photo 3.7 A traditional Xhosa man and his wife. Notice the hierarchy of power implied by his riding a horse while she walks behind him.

Sometimes this power is personalized. Both the Baganda and the Zulu, for instance, have many stories of pregnant girls, deserted by their lovers, who gave birth to water instead of a child. The water became a river, and in this way the girl's spirit catches unwary travelers and drowns them. In other cases the power takes on animal form. Thus in one Ugandan village there lived a leopard which kept the local people under its care and warned them if other leopards were coming to steal their stock. Villagers could visit the leopard's lair without fear of being molested, and, to prove the point, one student from Makerere University actually took an unwitting Fred Welbourn with him to "see" the leopard. Although Fred got the fright of his life when he realized what he was facing in that dark cave, the leopard ignored its visitor, and Fred lived to tell the tale.

Photo 3.8 On 4 November 1980, the day before the crucial American election that brought Ronald Reagan to power, the New York newspaper *News World* went out on a limb to predict a Reagan victory. Its headline read, "Reagan landslide: Will win by more than 350 electoral votes and carry New York as well." This lead story was dictated to the editor by Sun Myung Moon, who owned the newspaper. He claimed to have had a vision that gave him the election results. In the event, Rev. Moon's forecast was remarkably accurate. Did this show a keen political understanding that professional forecasters lacked, or was it a premonition, as Rev. Moon's followers claimed?

TELEPATHY AND TECHNIQUE

Sometimes "the power" can to be put into things. For example, among the Ganda, an animal's horn, when filled with suitable ingredients and empowered by a spirit, could be used by its owner to do jobs for him at a distance. It could also speak to him secret messages and enable him to communicate with others over vast distances. A similar belief, rationalized in terms of "telepathy," can be found among traditional, white South Africans known as Afrikaners.

When I interviewed the brilliant Afrikaner philosopher, H. G. Stoker, in 1972, he told the following story: "When I was a young student at Potchefstroom University in 1914, I had a friend who was very homesick. Each Sunday afternoon he would go out into the veld and sit under a particular tree from where he communicated with his twin brother in the town of Uitenhage hundreds of miles away. His brother also sat under the same type of tree on the family farm. This was done by telepathy. But the tree had something to do with it, even though I do not understand quite what it was. Somehow it seemed to amplify his thoughts."

As a Christian, Professor Stoker found no difficulty accepting this story. Indeed he knew that it was true. As a skeptical Englishman I was incredulous. But, as Stoker said, with a twinkle in his eye, that was because I had just arrived in Africa. Almost forty years later, I am more inclined to agree with him.

PATTERNS OF POWER

At other times the power is inherent. Among the Buganda a man who killed the animal after which his clan is named was believed to have killed his clan totem, and when he died immediately afterward, his death was regarded as punishment. If a pregnant woman laughed at a lame person, her child would be born lame. If a sheep, a goat, or a dog got onto the roof of a house, the inhabitants would leave it at once, saying it was unlucky to live there. All these things were "taboo" and in many ways reflect similar folk traditions in Europe and America.

Traditional Africans describe this power as an all-pervasive psychic force behaving very much like electricity is believed to behave in our society. People and things which are "positively charged" with power can pass it on by contact to anyone who is "negatively charged." Unless this process is properly controlled, damage will result. A positively charged chief, for instance, might come into contact with a commoner. The chief loses some of his power, but the commoner is injured.

Although not usually recognized by most Westerners who read the Bible, an example of power very similar to that accepted by many Africans and other traditional peoples seems to be reported in the Bible in 2 Samuel 6:6–9: "When they came to the threshing floor of Nacon, Uzzah reached out and took hold of the ark of God, because the oxen stumbled. The LORD's anger burned against Uzzah because of his irreverent act; therefore God struck him down and he died there by the ark of God. Then David was angry because the LORD's wrath had broken out against Uzzah, and to this day that place is called Perez Uzzah. David was afraid of the LORD that day and said, 'How can the ark of the LORD ever come to me?'"

Photo 3.9 The leader of an African Independent church prepares to perform a baptism ceremony in the sea near Durban. The red and white cords around his neck and body are believed to give him the power to ward off evil spirits that seek to prevent baptism.

No wonder so many Africans and other traditional peoples look to the Bible for inspiration and see in it a reflection of their own life and experience. The truth is that at their core the religious practices of the Bible are very similar to the everyday practices found in numerous African traditional religions. To recognize these similarities, however, we have to strip away many of our exclusively Western, particularly Enlightenment, methods of interpretation.

ATOMS, ELECTRICITY, AND UNSEEN POWERS

The electrical metaphor, which was a brilliant insight by Fred Welbourn, can be used to illuminate the relation between the "natural" and "supernatural." The British physicist Sir Arthur Eddington once pointed out that a physicist's description of matter in terms of electrons and protons might easily give the impression that a chair consists largely of wide-open space. Thus when a child is first taught physics, they might be tempted to think that a particular chair which was described as "made of electrons" is unsuitable for sitting. The commonsense account of the same chair, however, is entirely different, and the child sits in the chair without hesitation. In everyday life, therefore, we follow the commonsense account, which normally disregards the electrical basis of matter.

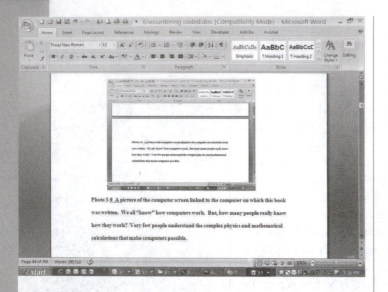

Photo 3.10 A picture of the computer screen linked to the computer on which this book was written. We all "know" how computers work. But how many people really know how they work? Very few people understand the complex physics and mathematical calculations that make computers possible.

Electrical forces, however, become of concern to common sense in Western society when they are not properly controlled, for example, when lightning strikes. Therefore, when electricity is harnessed for human welfare, special care must be taken to produce effects that are both safe and impossible without it. To harness electricity requires the knowledge and skill of specialists. But, even though lightning may be extremely frightening, Western people do not regard it as supernatural. They recognize that electricity is an inescapable part of their natural environment with special powers for good or ill.

This analogy illustrates the way traditional Africans and other traditional peoples understand the power which operates through their Ancestors, ghosts, and the spirits. Such power underlies all life, but "common sense" normally disregards it. When out-of-the-way things happen, or when a person needs special power for a particular purpose, for example, to deal with misfortune or to seek unusual success, he or she becomes aware, as we become aware of electricity, of something which he or she believes to be around him or her and available all the time.

To appreciate what this means in practice, it is necessary to recognize that when ghost stories are told in Western society—and we must remember that there

Photo 3.11 Marley's ghost is probably the best-known ghost in English literature, with the possible exception of the ghost of Hamlet's father. What do these stories tell us about European attitudes to ghosts?

are sane and intelligent Westerners who believe in ghosts—there is usually an atmosphere of horror. In the West ghosts are usually malicious.

But in many traditional societies, ghosts are felt to be an integral part of society, deeply concerned for its welfare, interfering, it is true, if they do not receive the attention which is their due, but expecting to play their part in its smooth running. Most traditional African, and other, ghosts carry over into the next world the characteristics that they acquired in this. Thus, a man caught thieving might ask to be killed rather than have his hand cut off, lest he should enter maimed into the world of ghosts.

Therefore, among the Ganda, it was not surprising that the ghost of a paternal aunt, always in life an oppressive, authoritarian figure, was frequently thought to be the cause of sickness. Among the Zulu the ghosts of fathers and grandfathers, who in life expected respect, also became angry if their memory and wishes were not respected. In a similar vein, special precautions were taken to avoid the ghosts of people with abnormalities and people who had been social misfits. Ghosts, in other words, easily become the source of danger and evil.

THE PRESENCE OF EVIL

To understand this way of thinking in Western terms, consider the popular TV series *Doctor Who*. The BBC began broadcasting the show on children's television in 1963. In North America, *Doctor Who* films became late-night adult viewing. Recently the original scripts of the series were turned into paperback books, and most of the shows are available on DVDs in public libraries. This television series develops the theme of the misuse of electrical and atomic power by evil men, a theme found in many science fiction stories. The show's popularity suggests that in the popular imagination a fear of unseen forces like electricity and atomic power that is not unlike traditional fears about ghosts still survives.

A faulty cord on an electric iron may give a fatal shock. The atom can be used to produce electricity or an atomic bomb. So, too, a man or woman in a traditional society who can control power may be feared as well as admired. If they can use power to improve their own crops or those of others, their help may be sought. Alternatively, such a person may use their power to harm others.

Among the Lugbara of Uganda, a man who consistently has better crops than his neighbors is liable to be accused of witchcraft and punished. In the nineteenth century among the Zulu, enterprising young men who worked in "white" towns such as Pietermaritzburg, South Africa, and saved their earnings to buy plows were also accused of witchcraft, because the plow enabled them to cultivate far more land than their neighbors, and their material success was then interpreted by their neighbors as "witchcraft." As a result many had to flee for their lives and ended up living in mission stations under the protection of missionaries. In Africa it is sometimes dangerous to be excellent.

TRADITIONAL BELIEFS AND MODERN MEDICINE

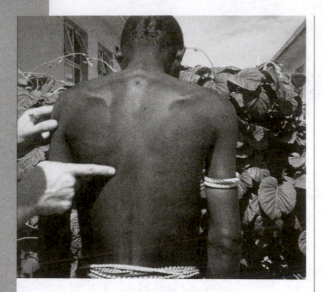

Photo 3.12 An African patient with severe TB is examined by a Dutch doctor at Madlawani Hospital, Transkei, South Africa, in 1974. The scars on the man's skin were made over many months as the man was "treated" by an African healer. In this case the delay in his receiving Western medical attention created a grave risk to the man's health.

The attitudes of African and many other traditional peoples to modern medicine can be summed up by the following story. In the 1970s tuberculosis was a major problem in the Madlawani district of South Africa's Transkei. Although the area had an excellent teaching hospital, funded by the Dutch Reformed Church and staffed by Dutch and Afrikaner doctors, TB remained endemic. The major problem was that most Africans who contracted TB went to see local healers before attending the "white hospital." As a result they came to hospitals months, sometimes years, after contracting the disease, when it was much harder, if not impossible, to treat.

To overcome this problem the doctors, in cooperation with the missionary doctor, Hennie Pretorius, devised a scheme whereby they cooperated with local healers. Instead of condemning African healers as superstitious charlatans, as many whites had done in the past, Pretorius and the doctors at the hospital acknowledged the value of local healers and traditional medicines. They also conceded the psychological value of visits to traditional healers. Therefore, they embarked on a campaign to win over the healers through mutual respect and cooperation. The essence of this campaign was to admit that African healers could help TB victims with psychic problems caused by the anger of ghosts, but that the "white doctors" were able to cure the symptoms. This approach to a deadly disease worked remarkably well, as the healers learned to identify the symptoms of TB and send their patients to the hospital for "further" help.

For this approach to work, the doctors had to set aside their skepticism about ghosts and other psychic forces. Instead they allowed their patients to believe whatever they wanted about the ultimate cause of their illnesses and concentrated on treating their medical causes. For most of the Africans who came for help, ghosts and psychic agents were the primary cause of their sickness. Yet even traditional healers admitted that although ghosts and other forces accounted for sickness, and their rituals freed patients from the power of such evil forces, there was still a need to cure the material expression of such attacks. It was here that Western medicine could be useful. To appreciate the implications of these ideas we must attempt to understand the role of witchcraft and sorcery in traditional societies. It is to this task we now turn.

CHAPTER 4

WITCHCRAFT AND SORCERY

INTRODUCTION

Today it is difficult to talk about "witchcraft" as an evil force without someone objecting that they are a witch and that such accusations amount to open persecution of an ancient, pre-Christian religion. Therefore, it is important to remember that this chapter is about the way traditional peoples see the world, not about modern neopagan religions or European history. For better or worse, almost all traditional societies recognize a category of people who are believed to systematically harm those around them by psychic power. The various names given to these people translate as "witches" and their powers as "witchcraft."

This chapter is not about Wicca, about various new religions that claim their members belong to an ancient pre-Christian faith, or even about the majority of westerners who say they are witches. It is about traditional witchcraft in Africa, which is clearly believed to be evil by members of the societies where it occurs.

TRADITIONAL AFRICAN BELIEFS ABOUT WITCHCRAFT

Belief in traditional witches and witchcraft arises naturally from the structure of traditional African beliefs. In African societies ancestral ghosts are often regarded as the agents of disease. Other psychic forces, such as curses, are also recognized as important facts that govern life. Thus curses are known to be as real as if someone stabs another person with a knife. Most traditional peoples who believe in curses put limits on them. Curses can be used only when someone has done another person real harm. Therefore, they are just. When someone who has done no harm is cursed, the curse is unjust and is believed to rebound onto the curser. If a curse is just, it may cause illness or even the death of the cursed and can be active even after the death of the curser.[1]

Theoretically, curses create balance in society by causing a person who has been justly cursed to seek the curse's removal before the person who cast it dies. After death, there is no hope. Among the Maasai, a nomadic people group of East Africa, an undetected

---

*   As explained earlier in connection with the previous chapter, this one also develops the original ideas of Fred Welbourn.

1.   The classic study of witchcraft in Africa is E. E. Evans-Pritchard, *Witchcraft, Oracles and Magic among the Azande* (London: Oxford Univ. Press, 1937).

Photo 4.1 A traditional healer and her husband in their consulting room. She makes the diagnosis while he runs the business and, when necessary, helps with the rituals. The setting, organization, and even many of the practices are not very different from those of many alternative healers such as chiropractors and herbalists in North America.

murderer or thief may be publicly cursed; similarly, a Zulu cattle thief may be cursed in this way to help a Zulu farmer regain lost cattle. Many stories are told of criminals who suffered such hardship as a result of a curse that they confessed their crimes and took the appropriate punishment.

Another psychic cause of disease is the "evil eye," a power which tends to run in families. Someone with such power has only to look at another person to cause illness and death. Although some traditional peoples believe that the evil eye can be cultivated and used deliberately by a man or woman with the power, many others believe that it occurs naturally and is rather like what Western people describe as a "carrier" of a disease such as TB. Therefore, its possession is regarded as a misfortune rather than a genetic defect. Among the Marakwet of East Africa a person with this affliction will warn the inhabitants of a house they visit so that its members may take the necessary precautions to protect themselves. In such cases the evil effects may sometimes be counteracted by the owner spitting on the victim or by somebody with appropriate psychic powers. Where beliefs of this sort flourish, it is an easy and logical step to believe that other people have similar powers that they are able to use to cause evil to those around them. Such beliefs are the basis of witchcraft.

THE PROBLEM OF WITCHCRAFT

Witches and sorcerers are found almost universally, and it is now usual to distinguish between these two types. Either may be male or female, and in some societies male witches predominate. The Azande of the Southern Sudan believe that a man can transmit witchcraft only to his sons, a woman only to her daughters. Witchcraft is an innate power, which can be used by its owner only, to do harm to others. I may not know that I am a witch until, in a fit of anger, I say, "I wish X were dead," and find that X dies. Making this discovery, I may be horrified and try to get rid of the power.

On the other hand, I may welcome it and begin to associate with other witches. This association may take place only in immaterial form. Witches' bodies may be soundly asleep in their beds, while their witch-souls meet with the rest of the "coven" to perform all sorts of strange activities. Among the Pondo of South Africa, witches are supposed to have animal "familiars" of the opposite sex, with whom they have sexual relations. Among the Nyakyusa of Tanzania, they eat human flesh in an immaterial, or psychic, manner. Consequently, the only evidence for this is when the victim becomes ill and withers away before they finally die.

In Tanzania witches are believed to travel naked, walk upside down, and smear their skins with white ashes; and this belief shows, more clearly than any of the others, that witchcraft beliefs express deep-rooted fear about the disruption of the normal order of the world. Significantly, among the Xhosa of South Africa, young men undergoing initiation rites prior to being accepted as full adults lived apart from their families and other people for around six months. During this time they smear their bodies with white clay and live in isolated areas. It was known that, while in this state, they were dangerous and had the right to attack any women who approached them.[2]

WITCHCRAFT AND SORCERY

Usually anthropologists argue that, in sharp contrast to witchcraft, which is psychic in nature, sorcery involves the use of material objects. Sorcerers, therefore, are specialists who have learned their trade by apprenticeship to another sorcerer or through a direct call from a spirit. What sorcerers produce—their potents, powders, and charms—are available to anyone who can buy them; and, in principle, anybody can learn the trade. There is no question of an innate power. The powers used by sorcerers are usually used for evil purposes, but they can be used for good, just as the powers of healers may also be used for evil. These matters are infinitely complex and vary from society to society.

It is extremely difficult to distinguish the techniques used by sorcerers and healers except by their results and intention. These good and bad powers and the related knowledge are usually called by different names. At the same time, it is recognized that a man who has developed powers for good may be tempted to use them for evil.

Photo 4.2 A child's body that has been mutilated to obtain body parts for use by a witch or sorcerer.

---

2. For more information and a variety of approaches to this topic, see Paul Parin, Fritz Mortgenthaler, and Goldy Parin-Matthey, *Fear Thy Neighbor as Thyself: Psychoanalyis and Society among the Anyi of West Africa* (Chicago: Univ. of Chicago Press, 1980); Leny Lagerwerf, *Witchcraft, Sorcery, and Spirit Possession: Pastoral Responses in Africa* (Harare, Zimbabwe: Mambo Press, 1987); Francis Schimlek, *Medicine Versus Witchcraft* (Mariannhill, Natal, South Africa: Mariannhill Mission Press, 1950). A Christian perspective is attempted by Aylward Shorter in his *Jesus and the Witchdoctor: An Approach to Healing and Wholeness* (New York: Orbis, 1985).

The methods which such people use are often called "magic." If that word means the use of methods and substances which cannot be scientifically demonstrated to produce the intended effect, then it is almost certainly the wrong word to use in this case. The word "magic" comes from the art practiced by the Magi, who were Persian sorcerers; and some sorcerers certainly know poisons which are pharmaceutically effective, although they do not distinguish them from other substances that are supposed to cause death but are pharmaceutically neutral. At the other end of the scale, herbs used to cure disease may be pharmaceutically ineffective but may, on the other hand, contain ingredients which can be isolated and used in scientific medicine. Digitalis was discovered by taking seriously the use of foxglove by traditional healers in England.

TRADITIONAL HEALING

In traditional societies herbs are widely used for curing disease. Knowledge of how to use them may be inherited, or it may be revealed in dreams, and there is ample evidence of one herb being preferred to another because it has proved, in practice, to be more effective. But perhaps more typical examples of sorcery is the use of hair cuttings or nail parings or feces to work harm to the person from whom they came. For this reason, members of Baganda society were extremely careful to bury these objects. More exciting were the charms which could be obtained only from specialists—to make a woman fertile, to preserve a man's life in war, to make a thief invisible. There were also the horns which could be used to bring luck to the owner or to harm an enemy at a distance.

Traditionally, a convicted witch or sorcerer was liable to meet an unpleasant end. Throughout most of sub-Saharan Africa they were burned alive. Under British and other forms of colonial rule in Africa, the practice of witchcraft and bad sorcery was made illegal, and those accused of either were punished. Allowance was made by European administrations for "witchcraft" and "sorcery" allegations that could be linked to poisoning, but without any evidence of poison, these ideas were not tolerated. As a result of European rule, such allegations gradually declined until they were almost nonexistent in places like South Africa during the 1960s. Then, in the late 1970s, they slowly began to rise again, becoming an epidemic in the troubled times leading to the downfall of apartheid.

Some writers suggest that, however much witchcraft and sorcery may have been feared, they nevertheless served a definite social function. For example,

Photo 4.3 A traditional diviner reads the signs to either diagnose illness or foretell future events.

the fear of a curse often served the social function of imposing a degree of respect within a family, and it was wise to fulfill one's obligations to a neighbor, because otherwise they might employ witchcraft or sorcery to get their rights. Similarly, a suspected witch should not be offended, for fear she might retaliate with her mysterious power. Outward relations, at least, were therefore kept smooth. Negatively, a man who was more successful than his neighbors at farming—through good techniques—or with women might be suspected of using sorcery. Such fears and the fear of denunciation and punishment created pressure toward equality. In small, intimate societies, with few technological resources for the material betterment of their members, such sanctions can be interpreted as important factors in preserving social harmony.[3]

THE QUESTION OF BLAME

At the same time, beliefs in psychic forces as the cause of evil offer the opportunity to blame others for one's own misfortune, thereby relieving the frustrations which misfortunes inevitably bring. After disasters, people in Western society inevitably look for scapegoats. Who caused the flooding in New Orleans? Was the city government, the state governor, or President George W. Bush to blame? Questions like these are akin to the questions traditional people ask when seeking a cause for misfortune. Instead of hounding people through the media, they accuse them of witchcraft and sorcery, disregarding more complex reasons, technological failures, and pure accidents.

Similarly, during the first three centuries AD, Christians were commonly accused of being atheists, eating their own children, and practicing incest. Consequently they were punished by Roman state officials, who saw themselves as upholding the social order and protecting the innocent. Later, during the Middle Ages, Christians made similar accusations against the Jews. Many people today regard immigrants as the cause of economic problems and crime, often without any objective evidence to support such claims. Like African witches, such people are seen as a threat because they disrupt the normal order of things.

Modern "witch hunts," of course, do not attribute mysterious, immaterial power to their victims. Our society tends to think in terms of invisible electrical forces, while people in traditional societies think in terms of psychic forces, such as witchcraft and sorcery. Yet both reactions involve types of blame that point

Photo 4.4 A traditional prophetess performing a healing ritual.

---

3. Max Gluckman, *Custom and Conflict in Africa* (Oxford: Blackwell, 1970).

to a human need to put the blame on something outside ourselves, to find other persons, and not merely impersonal causes, who can be held responsible when things go wrong.[4]

THE PSYCHIC CAUSES OF MISFORTUNE

In traditional societies not only sickness but many other misfortunes are attributed to psychic causes. Yet this does not mean, as many early anthropologists argued, that traditional peoples do not, or cannot, recognize the material cause of such events. In many parts of Africa it is widely known that malaria is caused by the bite of a mosquito and that the most effective cure is go to a doctor or get an injection at a hospital. But for the person schooled in traditional thought the question remains: "Why did the mosquito bite me and not the person next to me?" This question quickly becomes "Who sent the mosquito to bite me?" The logical answer for someone living in a traditional society is that it may be a ghost or a witch; and, unless the malevolent force can be appeased, it will send another mosquito to bite again as soon as the sufferer is released from the hospital or otherwise cured. Therefore, the psychic cause must be dealt with before the material medicines can really take effect. This means that the sufferer, or their relatives, must seek out a specialist skilled in curing such misfortune.

Here it is important to understand that African and other traditional peoples recognize what we see as the natural cause of problems. For example, a rock stands precariously at the top of a steep slope. Eventually the supporting soil is eroded by rain and the rock falls with a crash to the bottom. So long as nobody is hurt, no questions are asked. The "natural explanation" is accepted. Curiosity is not aroused by an event which has no personal consequences. There is no urge to look for religious, or for deeper scientific, explanations.[5]

But if the falling rock hurts a man, some personal cause will almost certainly be invoked to explain why natural causes intervened at this particular point in his personal history. Again, it may be a ghost or a witch. It may be the spirit of the rock, which has in some way been offended. Now the impersonal explanations that are usually used by Western peoples, such as "bad luck" or "accident," are felt to be wholly inadequate.

So it is with death in general. African peoples, for instance, recognize the "natural causes" of death: disease, physical accident, war, or simply old age. But in every case—and this is still true even of some who call themselves Christian—no real satisfaction is felt unless an act of sorcery, the ill will of a particular individual, can be invoked to explain why this natural cause produced the death of this person at this time.

A useful illustration of this approach to events is the man who cuts his finger while chopping firewood or who is injured in a mining accident. He will use some effective material means of stopping the bleeding, of healing the wound. It will be known to most adults, and more than likely it has been selected over the centuries as the most effective of several pos-

---

4. For a discussion of modern witch hunts in South Africa, see Adam Ashforth, *Witchcraft, Violence, and Democracy in South Africa* (Chicago: Univ. of Chicago Press, 2005).

5. For a discussion of some of the issues involved in relating traditional African and modern medicine, see M. Vera Bührmann, *Living in Two Worlds: Communication between a White Healer and Her Black Counterparts* (Cape Town, South Africa: Human & Rousseau, 1984).

sible means of cure. If he cuts his finger several days running, the material treatment is still required. But, in addition, it will be supposed that an evil, personal force is making him do this. He will go to a "diviner," a professional who names the spirit or witch responsible and prescribes a ritual by which the evil force can be neutralized. There is another possibility—that the man chopping wood cuts his finger right off or the miner looses a limb. In that case, no cure is possible. But the evil force must still be dealt with, lest the patient cut off yet another finger or looses another limb.

Photo 4.5 Seeking protection from evil. The above photograph shows a Christian prayer group accompanied by a healer who, while a Christian, employs traditional means to ward off evil. While many Western Christians may be shocked by this, the response of the group leader was to point out that most Christians have no objection to vaccination or taking drugs to kill "unseen" germs. Therefore, they argued, there is nothing unbiblical in taking precautions to ward off evil spirits that attack people just like viruses.

It is extremely difficult to know how to define the difference between these two types of treatment and the kinds of causation they imply. Neither "natural and supernatural" nor "scientific and magical" is satisfactory. Moreover, recent tests have shown that the value of some modern pharmaceutical drugs depends on whether or not doctor and patient believe in their efficacy. It is extremely difficult to distinguish this kind of medicine, which involves a psychosomatic element, from traditional sorcery. Equally, there is ample evidence of Africans, and even of some Western people living close to traditional societies, whose sickness has defeated the skill of scientifically trained doctors but has yielded to traditional practitioners who interpreted it in terms of witches and ghosts. The existence of these entities must, in all fairness, be regarded as a hypothesis which, in certain circumstances, works. The question remains open whether, like the aether of the nineteenth-century physicists, it is a hypothesis which can be discarded in favor of a more general concept, or whether, like the alternatives of the wave and particle theories of light, it is applicable in certain contexts but not in others.

PSYCHIC AND PHYSICAL CAUSES

Perhaps the least unsatisfactory terms we can use to describe these things are "physical" and "psychic." They correspond to distinctions recognized in the language of both the Baganda of Uganda and the Zulu of South Africa, although they cannot be easily defined. In Western usage "physical" events can be located accurately in space and time, although that is hardly true of an electron. "Psychic" events cannot be located by physical methods and do

Photo 4.6 In this picture a traditional healer performs a ritual cure on a sick woman as the woman's friend joins in with shouts and gestures of encouragement.

not obey known physical laws. On the one hand are phenomena, such as ghosts and extrasensory perception, that are considered by "psychical research" and which many people regard as superstitious to believe in. On the other hand are such concepts as "consciousness" and "the unconscious," in psychology, that many contemporary people regard as referring to "real" effects in the physical world. From the immediate point of view, this ambiguity in the use of the root term "psych" is an advantage. It can be used to refer to a number of allegedly nonphysical entities without discussing whether or not they "really" exist.

Many traditional medicines have been proved and improved by experience. A diviner—whose primary function is to discover the psychic cause of trouble—is often himself, or less commonly herself, a medicine man. It is just as likely that, having divined the psychic cause, the diviner will send the patient to another specialist for physical treatment; and there are specialists not only in herbal medicine but in bonesetting. Increasingly they may also send people to Western doctors or to a hospital, because they have recognized that Western medicine is the best method of dealing with physical causes, while they themselves deal with the psychic aspects.[6]

One way of understanding the difference between "physical" and "psychic" is to say that every event has both general and unique characteristics. It can be put in a class with other events and seen to be subject to general laws, or it can be seen as unique and unrepeatable. This is true even of a controlled laboratory experiment, because the time factor is always different and the personal factor can never be wholly eliminated.

It is, perhaps, more strikingly true of such events as death from lung cancer or from road accident. It is possible to say, with a high degree of statistical accuracy, how many people of particular ages, sexes, and occupations will die from these causes in a particular year. It is not possible to say which individual will so die; and perhaps the only difference between ascribing it to "luck" or "fate" and holding a witch responsible is that one response is less personal than the other. In both cases there is the recognition that general causes show themselves in unique effects.

By and large, the majority of contemporary people living in Western countries tend to emphasize the importance of general laws and thus attribute their unique effects to impersonal

---

6. For a discussion of the role of African healers in South Africa, see Gerhardus C. Oosthuizen, *The Healer-Prophet in Afro-Christian Churches* (Leiden: Brill, 1992).

causes. The majority of contemporary Africans and people living in traditional societies still tend to be more concerned with the uniqueness of things and to think in terms of personal causes. When Britons, during World War II, thought that they would be hit by a bomb only if it "had my name on it," they were adopting very much the same attitude. "It won't happen to me. I'm different" is a fairly common way of expressing the converse of this attitude.

THE "CALLING" OF A DIVINER

In the early 1960s Fred Welbourn observed a young Muganda (a member of the Buganda people of southern Uganda) who was awarded a university scholarship to study in Britain. On his way to the airport at the start of his journey, he suddenly went blind and his head began to ache terribly. He was taken home and consulted a diviner. He was told that he had been chosen by a spirit to be its medium and that unless he accepted the choice he might go mad. Many Africans—though not always so highly educated—have had similar experiences; and in Buganda their initiation takes some such form as follows.

On the appointed night, the young man and his relatives went to the shrine of a diviner, where a fire was kept burning throughout the rite. They were washed with water from Lake Victoria, and the juice of leaves was smeared on their heads. They were given branches and spears to hold. The diviner's assistants started to beat drums in a peculiar rhythm, shake rattles, and sing special spirit songs. After this had been going on for some time, the initiate started to shake. The drumming and singing grew wilder. The shaking affected him more and more violently until he rose and started to dance wildly.

The drumming and singing became more and more excited. He danced in the fire, apparently

Photo 4.7 As the healing ritual progresses, notice the involvement of the sick woman's companion. African healing is both a personal and a communal affair.

Photo 4.8 A healing dance in the surgery of Estelle Nxele. Her consulting room was in her home, but for rituals and dance she often used her garage, pictured right, as a surgery.

without being burnt, till at last he fell on the floor and started speaking in a strange voice. This was said to be the voice of the spirit which had chosen him. It said it had been neglected by the family and promised that, if all the right ceremonies were carried out, and the initiate set aside as a diviner, it would give the whole family wealth, a successful life, and many children. From now on, the initiate was to be known by a new name. Then it left him and he once again behaved normally.

The next day, a goat and hen were killed and eaten at a feast. Then the whole party returned to the shrine. There was drumming and singing, and the spirit again entered the initiand. But this time there were no violent movements. Since he was a Christian, he was given a Bible to read to ensure that the spirit would have no objection to his going to church; and the spirit once again spoke of the good things it would bring to the family. On the third day the young man was given his equipment as a diviner—a bark cloth to wear, a knife, and cowrie shells. He continued to live in his own home, and, as success brought him wealth, he was able to build a well-constructed brick house for himself and live as an important member of the community.

For his work as a diviner he built a shrine of grass, where a fire burns day and night, whether or not he is in session. There, when he is being consulted, he sits on a goatskin with a bark cloth wrapped round him. Some diviners smoke a long pipe; some chew tobacco; some do neither. Stored in the shrine are parcels of dried plants which are used as medicines to anoint, or to be drunk by, the patient. There are also dry bones and other parts of animals and birds to be used as charms. Of one such diviner it was told that, every Saturday at midday, he would dismiss any patients whom he had not yet seen with the words, "Now I must iron my clothes ready to go to church tomorrow."

Of all ancient practices, that of divination has survived perhaps more actively than any other. It may be defined as the discovery of the psychic aspects of events. It may be used to find out whether or not the psychic forces are favorable to a proposed venture—war, a hunt, a proposed marriage, a business undertaking. But much more commonly it is used to discover why things have gone wrong—why this man is sick, that woman has no children, why X has lost his job or Y has failed in his examinations. As noted, a diviner may also be a

Photo 4.9 The dark side of traditional healing appears when a healer diagnoses the cause of an illness or other affliction as "witchcraft" and initiates a witch hunt. In the above sketch a healer has become a witch finder who sniffs out witches. The look of terror on the face of the man being sniffed tells it all. If convicted of witchcraft, a victim was burned alive.

medicine man. But his primary function, as a diviner, is to unravel psychic causes; and he may well hand a patient over to another specialist for physical treatment.

It is perhaps worth noting that in Europe and North America the common practice is to go first to a physician, who may refer a patient to a psychiatrist. In Buganda, it is the psychic expert who is the general practitioner. But the woman who gazes into a crystal ball at a psychic fair, or for wealthier customers in a downtown office; the astrologer who writes columns in the newspaper; the spiritualist medium who investigates a haunted house—all these are catering to a contemporary desire to get below the surface of physical events. Whether the desire is rational or irrational is entirely another matter.

In Africa the methods used by diviners vary greatly, though most of them depend on the pattern in which certain objects arrange themselves. In Buganda, for instance, nine flat pieces of leather may be thrown onto a cowhide. Cowrie shells or coffee berries might be thrown in the same way. Powdered herbs, or nine twigs, might be thrown onto water in a pot, which is rocked and the arrangement then studied. The arteries in a hen's throat might be cut, and the diviner may count the number of spurts till the blood stops flowing. An even number was a bad sign, an odd number good. A hen might be cut open from throat to tail and the omens judged by examining the arrangement of the fat round the entrails and the marks on them.

Welbourn recorded the following detailed account of such a session that he observed in the region of Ankole in Uganda. The patient arrives. The diviner, who, in Ankole, is quite likely to work in the open air, spreads his hide on the ground and throws the cowrie shells onto it. He examines them to ensure that his spirit is favorable to a divination. "He who divines," runs a proverb, "begins with himself." He tells the patient to spit on the shells. The patient does so and explains that she has a terrible backache and thinks she is going to die. The following dialogue captures the gist of what happened next:

Diviner: She dies that her name may disappear. Her garden let another take. She is dead. These are her mourners. [Throws pumpkin seeds onto cowhide and examines them.] But you don't seem about to die. If you are dying, what is this heap of seeds for? Spit again. [Patient spits on seeds; diviner examines them.] It looks as if you are troubled by a spirit.

Patient: It is the spirits! They broke my back. They want to take me out of this world. I die and go to the grave.

Diviner: It is the spirits! It is the spirits which intend to kill this child. But have you a guardian spirit, O woman? Spit! [Patient spits on seeds.]

Photo 4.10 An African diviner reading the signs in the throwing stones.

Photo 4.11 Estelle Nxele in her consulting room. Note the medicine cabinet where she kept patent herbs and other treatments. On top of the cabinet are a number of pamphlets from the local hospital. A skilled diagnostician, Mrs. Nxele worked in close cooperation with Western-trained doctors, taking various courses the hospital offered and frequently referring patients to the hospital or a medical doctor when she believed they were the ones who were better equipped to heal a particular sickness.

It is Mugasha [one of the Ankole spirits], our Mugasha. It wants a cow. It is Mugasha and it demands a cow. [Throws seeds again and examines them.] It is true! This seed is Mugasha. Go and give it its own. It wants beer. But that other seed seems to be yet another spirit.

Patient: Let me go and buy beer, call the people, men and women. We will sacrifice to Mugasha. I will bring a cow too, so that I am kept from my enemies.

Diviner: She is healed. [Throws and examines seeds.] You are healed. Mugasha, go! It has agreed. Take this seed and say, "Tomorrow I will bring sacrifice" [etc., etc.].

During the whole of this scene the diviner is supposed to be "possessed" by his spirit. It may be that very often this "possession" is feigned. But there are plenty of genuine cases where the diviner goes into a trance and may not remember, when he returns to normal, what happened while he was in the trance. Sometimes, in order to encourage the trance, diviners smoke strong tobacco or take a hypnotic drink. Others can become possessed without any physical help of this sort.

POSSESSION

What is called "possession" may in fact take widely different forms. At one extreme is that described earlier in this chapter, during the first stage of initiation, when the initiand behaves like a teenager at a pop concert or a new convert at a charismatic Christian meeting. At the other extreme is the mild state of a diviner in action, similar to that which is induced by drugs or by sleepwalking.[7]

In contemporary Western society, conditions of this sort are normally described in terms of drugs or of a psychological disturbance — of something inside the individual. In many traditional societies, they are attributed to a psychic force entering the individual from outside and taking over his body for its own purposes. When it enters a diviner, these purposes are good — they are directed toward healing his patients. But in many other cases it enters a person to show its annoyance at being neglected, and almost any unusual behavior — talking wildly, for instance, when a person has a high fever, behaving strangely, as many people do under the influence of strong emotions, or simply a failure in muscular

---

7. A good discussion of the issues related to "possession" is to be found in Heike Behrend and Ute Luig, eds., *Spirit Possession: Modernity & Power in Africa* (Madison: Univ. of Wisconsin Press, 1999).

coordination—may be attributed to "possession." It is then the job of a diviner to discover which spirit is responsible and how it can be prevented from doing further harm.

Whether or not this form of diagnosis is acceptable to scientific thought, it is essential to remember that it is often successful in effecting a cure. One reason may be that a great deal of both sickness and lack of success in life may be due to psychological causes or to being on bad terms with one's relatives or acquaintances. A man who is constantly cutting himself at work is said to be "accident prone" in Western societies, and this may well have been due to some anxiety or worry

Photo 4.12 The principal of Mapamulu Lutheran Theological College, Dr. Hans-Jürgen Becken, a pioneer of Christian interaction with traditional healers and African Independent Churches, stands with two traditional healers.

or quarrel. Western doctors are becoming increasingly aware of this factor in disease, and some of them spend a great deal of time trying to discover the psychological causes of a physical trouble which no medicine seems to cure.

A man may suffer from headaches because he is on bad terms with his wife. In our society this may be very difficult to put right without, at the least, many discussions by both parties with "marriage guidance counselors." In African and other traditional societies, the headaches might be interpreted as due to interference by the wife's ancestral ghosts; and, because both parties believe this explanation, a ceremonial sacrifice might do the trick. On the other hand, it might be said that the wife has been practicing witchcraft against her husband; and that would be equivalent to advising divorce.[8]

CONCLUSION

What these examples show is that despite various cultural differences people are remarkably alike whether they live in

Photo 4.13 The healers begin to search the forest for medicinal plants that they will then use in healing rituals.

---

8. Some of the legal issues raised by witchcraft accusations are discussed in Onesmus K. Mutungi, *The Legal Aspects of Witchcraft in East Africa* (Nairobi: East African Literature Bureau, 1977).

modern, Western societies or in traditional African societies. Therefore, instead of viewing African religious traditions as exotic, "primitive," or strange, we need to see them in comparison with similar traditions in our own society. The practice of charismatic Christianity, for example, including the belief by some charismatics that "normal illness" is caused by evil spirits, bears many resemblances to African traditional beliefs and practices. Therefore, once we recognize that there is a logic to traditional beliefs that is not very different from the logic of everyday life and among religious groups in our own society, we are on the road to appreciating the continuing appeal of African religions and religious practices.

CHAPTER 5

GOD IN ZULU RELIGION

INTRODUCTION

While most scholars ignore African religions, those who pay any attention to them at all tend to argue that in many ways traditional African beliefs are based on the idea of a High God. Since the High God is not very prominent in most African societies, they then argue that either the belief was in decline or that it was so sacred that most Africans never spoke about it. This chapter examines this belief in the context of Zulu society and shows that the available evidence points to a different conclusion.

SLAVERY AND THE INTERPRETATION OF AFRICAN RELIGION

Christianity is unique among religious traditions in the way it quickly came to disapprove of slavery and inspire antislavery movements.[1] As a result, by the time of Thomas Aquinas (1225–1274), slavery was regarded as a sin practiced by Muslims and people living on the edge of civilization. Things changed in the sixteenth century with the development of the transatlantic slave trade, which, as Rodney Stark points out, was conducted despite the opposition of the pope and Protestant theologians.

Thus by the time a powerful antislavery movement developed in the late eighteenth century, European slavers had developed the argument that slavery was justified because the people they enslaved, Africans and other native peoples, lacked souls and were therefore not fully human. Later, as a result of growing secularism and the theory of evolution, this argument was replaced by the claim that such peoples were lower on the evolutionary scale than Europeans. They were not fully human, but were more closely related to monkeys than to men and women. Therefore, slavery and other forms of discrimination and exploitation were fully justified.

Photo 5.1 British Anti-Slavery Society leaflet, 1795, from a medallion designed by Josiah Wedgwood. Led by evangelical Christians, the antislavery movement was at the heart of the nineteenth-century missionary movement. At its core was the biblical teaching that all people were created by God and that humanity shares common ancestors.

---

1. Rodney Stark, *For the Glory of God* (Princeton: Princeton Univ. Press, 2003), 291–365.

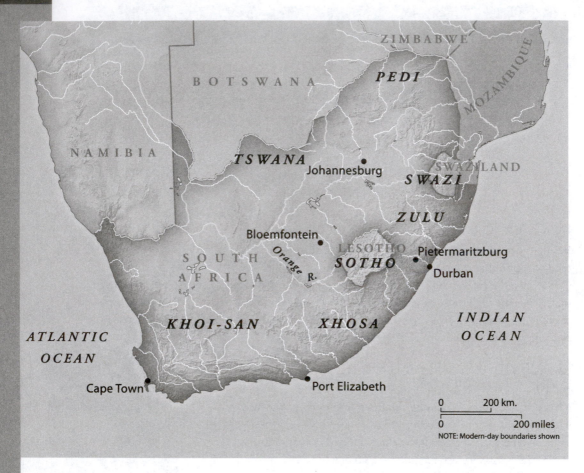

Map 5.1 South Africa and its neighboring countries. The main areas where different African groups traditionally lived are indicated by the name of each African nation. Traditionally the Zulu, who are discussed in this chapter, lived north of the port city of Durban. The Zulu language is, however, similar to that of both the Swazi and Xhosa, and today one can find Zulu as well as members of all the major African groups all over South Africa, where they are often intermarried.

Although most theologians and devoted Christians rejected such arguments as cynical justifications for an evil trade, the arguments had a profound effect on the way European missionaries and Christian travelers viewed African peoples. If they possessed souls or other human attributes, what better way of proving slavers and evolutionists wrong than pointing out that they all worshiped God in their own way and responded to the Christian gospel when it was presented to them. Since you need a soul, or a level of intellectual sophistication, to understand Christian theology, the argument that Africans and others lacked souls or intelligence was easily disproved by showing that they could embrace Christian worship.

Things were not that easy, though. Even as late as the 1880s and 1890s debates took place at the Anthropological Institute in London, where scholars disputed with missionaries, arguing that while Africans appeared to embrace Christianity and education, in fact they were merely imitating Europeans. In this view, which became known as scientific racism, such peoples were too low on the evolutionary scale to think for themselves.[2]

One important effect of these arguments, which determined how various peoples throughout the world were treated by imperial powers, was to make the defenders of indigenous peoples react violently against anyone who suggested that even though traditional peoples may be fully human they nevertheless did not worship God. Therefore, in the study of African religions, it became a given that however different traditional African religions might be from the great religious traditions, they all shared a belief in at least a distant High God.

While the insistence that African religions included knowledge of a High God was clearly well meaning, the truth is that many African and other traditional, or primal, religions appear to lack any awareness of God or, in some cases, even gods. Nevertheless, such peoples had religions of their own and quickly accepted the existence of God once Christian or Muslim beliefs were presented to them. To illustrate this process and the way African religions may not include an awareness of God, the case of traditional Zulu beliefs will now be examined.

ZULU RELIGION

Anyone who reads a modern book on Zulu religion, like Axel-Iver Berglund's fascinating book *Zulu Thought-Patterns and Symbolism*,[3] is presented with compelling evidence for the existence of a coherent Zulu religious system that involves the worship of a heavenly being, the Lord-of-the-Sky. Other works, like Isaac Schapera's edited book *The Bantu-Speaking Tribes of South Africa*, appear to confirm this view. Writing with W. M. Eiselen, Schapera says, "The Zulu have a sky god ... 'The Lord of Heaven.'"[4] Equally adamant is Edwin Smith in *African Ideas of God*, where, speaking about the Zulu, he says, "Unkulunkulu was spoken of as Creator; but the hint seems to be conveyed that

Photo 5.2 The Tugela River, which marks the traditional boundary between Zululand and territories to the south. On the left-hand side of the picture is what was the province of Natal, on the right Zululand. On their way to meet Zulu leaders, all the early white missionaries and traders crossed the Tugela.

2. This type of debate raged during the nineteenth century between missionaries and anthropologists who considered themselves the representatives of modern science. The missionaries, like Henry Callaway (1817–1890), defended belief in a common humanity descended from one original set of ancestors. The anthropologists argued for polygenesis and the separate evolution of numerous human races. See *Anthropological Review* 2 (1864). A detailed attack on the missionary claim is found in *Anthropological Review* 3 (1865).
3. Axel-Ivar Berglund, *Zulu Thought-Patterns and Symbolism* (Bloomington: Indiana Univ. Press, 1989).
4. Isaac Schapera, ed., *The Bantu-Speaking Tribes of South Africa* (Cape Town: Masken Miller, 1937), 262–63.

he made things below, as the slave of the Lord above who created the great things which exist and come from the sky."[5] Smith, too, argues strongly that the Zulus believe in a Lord of Heaven. This Lord, Smith claimed, was far more important than the archetypal ancestor Unkulunkulu, who, he suggests, was spoken of in awe and whose name was actually a veiled reference to the Lord of Heaven. Smith bases this claim on his belief that, like the Jews of Jesus' day, the Zulus thought the name of God too sacred to utter.

Should any doubts remain as to whether Zulu traditional religion believed in a High God, an examination of Eileen Krige's *The Social System of the Zulus* (1936) seems to support this view: "Unkulunkulu (the old, old one) is the Creator of First Cause. If a Zulu is asked about the origin of man and the world, he will say Unkulunkulu made all things ... In addition to Unkulunkulu the Zulus believe in a power which they call Heaven or The Lord of Heaven."[6] Nevertheless, after she read my original paper on this topic, she wrote to say that in her view the Zulu did not have a conception of God prior to the arrival of missionaries.[7]

W. D. Hammond-Tooke also supported arguments for a Zulu High God in *The Bantu-Speaking Peoples of Southern Africa*: "The Zulu also seem to have a personified Sky God, other than Unkulunkulu."[8] Similarly, the Ugandan writer John Mbiti makes great play of the Zulu belief about God in heaven,[9] as does the Nigerian author Bolaji Idowu, who uses evidences about the Zulu belief in a Lord of Heaven to comment upon African ideas of justice.[10]

Quite clearly, the existence of a Zulu belief in a sky deity, the Lord of Heaven, is well established in the literature on both the Zulus in particular and African religions in general. Having examined this evidence in detail, one quickly discovers that a key source for this belief is *The Religious System of the Amazulu*, first published by Henry Callaway (1817–1890) in 1870 with an English translation, notes, and comments on his informants. Thus Krige, Schapera, and Smith all acknowledge Callaway as their source, while Mbiti quotes Smith. Hammond-Tooke and Idowu fail to cite their authorities but cite examples given by Callaway. A careful analysis of Callaway's evidence is therefore essential for understanding Zulu statements about God. When this is done, we surprisingly discover that Callaway's statements differ greatly from later writers' use of them.

THE EVIDENCE OF CALLAWAY

Two main expressions of Callaway's are taken up by later writers in their discussion of Zulu religion, and these are repeated in modern religious studies textbooks to prove that traditional Zulus believed in a High God. These are "Unkulunkulu" and the "Lord of Heaven." Most writers pay the most attention to Unkulunkulu, while Berglund develops the significance of the Lord of Heaven at great length. All of these writers support their arguments by citing the work of Henry Callaway.

---

5. Edwin W. Smith, ed., *African Ideas of God: A Symposium* (London: House Press, 1950), 108.

6. Eileen J. Krige, *The Social System of the Zulus* (Pietermaritzburg: Shuter & Shooter, 1936), 280, 282.

7. Personal correspondence with Eileen Krige.

8. W. D. Hammond-Tooke, *The Bantu-Speaking Peoples of Southern Africa* (London: Routledge & Kegan Paul, 1974), 321.

9. John S. Mbiti, *African Religions and Philosophy* (London: Heinemann, 1969), 49, 52–54.

10. E. Bolaji Idowu, *African Traditional Religion* (London: SCM Press, 1973), 164.

Callaway devotes 104 pages to Unkulunkulu, eleven to Utikxo (a term dismissed by later writers), and eight to the Lord of Heaven. It should be noted that the idea of a Lord of Heaven occurs several times in his discussion of Unkulunkulu. Callaway argues, and later writers seem to agree, that Unkulunkulu can be understood as meaning "the old-old one."[11]

Later Callaway adds this very important note: "Mr. Hully, a missionary for some years connected with the Wesleyans, went up to the Zulu country as interpreter to Mr. Owen, in 1836. He says the word Unkulunkulu was not then in use among the natives; but that Captain Gardiner introduced it to express the Greatest, of the Maker of men. Mr. Hully refused to use it in this sense. He allowed that the word *kulu* meant great, but denied that Unkulunkulu existed in the language to express that which Captain Gardiner wished."

Photo 5.3 Henry Callaway, whose book *The Religious System of the Amazulu* (1870) is one of our main sources for information about Zulu religion as practiced by traditional Zulu in the nineteenth century. A pioneer missionary, he was remarkably sympathetic to African views of religion and African spirituality.

CALLAWAY'S UNDERSTANDING OF UNKULUNKULU

The last statement about the role of Captain Allen Gardiner (1794–1851), the first European missionary to the Zulu, is perhaps the key to some of the obvious confusion in the minds of Callaway's informants when they talked about Unkulunkulu. Again and again there is ambiguity and hesitation in their accounts. Thus one informant could say, "The old men say … they did not know Unkulunkulu."[12] And another said, "The ancients used to say before the arrival of the missionaries that all things were made by Umvelinquangi; but they were not acquainted with his name. But they lived by worshipping snakes."[13] Yet another added, "So finally we hear that Unsondo is, as it were, a man … Unsondo is the same as Unkulunkulu, who we say dies."[14]

Reading these texts, one soon sees that if "Unkulunkulu" had any meaning at all prior to Gardiner's use of the term, it was as a name or way of referring to an early ancestor and carried with it no implications of deity. That the Zulu worshiped or could possibly worship Unkulunkulu was denied repeatedly by Callaway's informants.[15] Callaway also admits that he often had difficulty getting information about Unkulunkulu,[16] and in doing so makes it clear that in collecting his information he and his helpers asked questions of their informants which were designed to elicit a response that assumed the Zulus had a belief in a High God.

11. Henry Callaway, *The Religious System of the Amazulu* (London: Folklore Society, 1870), 54n3. The full text is found on the internet under "African religions" at www.sacred-text.com (accessed 10 May 2010).

12. Ibid., 7–8.

13. Ibid., 10.

14. Ibid., 14–15.

15. Ibid., 16–17, 25, 34.

16. Ibid., 33.

Photo 5.4 The introduction of the plow by missionaries in the late nineteenth century created major disruptions in Zulu and other African societies. Because plows needed oxen and because cattle were part of the male realm, men began to take over one of the traditional roles of women in agriculture. More importantly, the owner of a plow could cultivate as much land as a man with ten wives. Consequently, plows undermined the old social system, where older men dominated society. This in turn changed marriage patterns and led many more progressive young people to convert to Christianity.

Thus, as one reads the texts and attempts to see the question which the informant was asked to answer, one is struck by the desire of informants to give the answers which they believed were sought. For example, Callaway writes, "Two natives, perfect strangers ... overheard what I was saying, and asked, 'Are you talking about the origins of men?' ... I asked what he knew of Unkulunkulu; He replied ..."[17] Here Callaway admits the Africans knew the answers he sought before he talked to them. One informant gave the clue to the origins of Zulu beliefs about Unkulunkulu: "We used to hear it said by our fathers, they too having heard it from others."[18]

The significance of "having heard it from others" becomes clearer when statements by Callaway like the following are taken into account: "This is a very common occurrence. Very old Amazulu, when asked to speak about Unkulunkulu, are apt to speak not of the first Unkulunkulu, but the Unkulunkulu of their tribes."[19] What he means by this is that old Zulu would not speak of a "first being," or creator, but simply of their tribal ancestors. In Callaway's report of the response of one old woman we read, "Truly Unkulunkulu is he who is in heaven. And the whitemen, they are the lords who made all things."[20] Here Unkulunkulu and whitemen are linked together with the idea of creation. This association becomes understandable when it is realized that if Unkulunkulu was thought of as the first ancestor, he would be the one who, according to Zulu mythology, had created the nation by giving it its basic technology. Taking the dominant view that Unkulunkulu was God makes no sense here. But it becomes understandable when Unkulunkulu is seen as the first ancestor, who, according to Zulu mythology, created the nation by giving it its basic technology.

What this means is that many Zulu at the time Callaway was studying them thought of Unkulunkulu as an ancestor who had brought a more advanced technology to the Zulu people by providing the original Zulu with fire and iron weapons. In this sense the whites were similar to Unkulunkulu, because they too brought advances in technology in the form of guns and other products which were changing their way of life.

17. Ibid., 39–40.
18. Ibid., 45.
19. Ibid., 54.
20. Ibid., 55.

Another informant whose conversation Callaway records seems to confirm this interpretation. Callaway wrote: "And when I enquired, saying, 'Do not your teachers tell you that the lord which is in heaven is Unkulunkulu?' he replied with a start, 'Hau! by no means. I have never heard such a word, neither did I ever hear them mention the name. It is your teacher alone with whom I have ever spoken it."[21]

Callaway admits in a footnote that he was "the teacher." The same informant waxed lyrical about the superiority of the whitemen over blacks and said, "Now they [whitemen] tell us all things …"[22] Similarly, Callaway cites a missionary who told him, "Since you were here I have questioned the bearer about Unkulunkulu, as also others. But *unless I first give them the idea*, they know very little or nothing about it …"[23] (italics mine).

From these passages it is clear that Callaway's texts show that the Zulu usage of Unkulunkulu in and prior to his time had the primary meaning "ancestor," to which overtones of a Christian view of God were later added. According to his informants, it was from Europeans, both through direct teaching and in response to the sort of questions they were constantly asking, that the Zulus developed ideas about a High God.

Photo 5.5 The Great Dance at Embellybelli. Dancing figured largely in traditional Zulu life. It created a sense of the sacred in relation to the Zulu nation and their king. From the evidence, it seems that most Zulu and many other African groups had no clear idea of God at the time of their first contact with Europeans. Instead their religion was rather like Confucianism in the ways that it centered on the ancestors and on the everyday concern of living. Nevertheless, in a relatively short time they not only accepted Christian ideas about God, but quickly developed their own interpretations of the Bible, incorporating into their beliefs and practices many African customs like communal dancing.

---

21. Ibid., 62–63.
22. Ibid., 79.
23. Ibid., 86.

Turning to the closely related term "Utikxo," Callaway has no hesitation in saying that it was "a word adopted for God by the early missionaries among the Kxosa (Xhosa) or Frontier Kafirs ... And it is generally supposed that the word does not properly belong to the Kxosa or any other of the alliterative dialects spoken in South Africa; but has been derived from the Hottentots."[24] He then discusses its meaning amongst the Khoi-San peoples and whether it really had the connotations of deity understood by the missionaries in their use of it.

THE LORD OF HEAVEN

Callaway says comparatively little about "the Lord of Heaven," presumably because his informants did not use the term very often, but what he says is informative. It is mentioned by some people in connection with Unkulunkulu and seems to represent the Lord of Heaven as similar to the Christian God. When Callaway first mentions the Lord of Heaven, it is to report an informant who said, "When we were with the Dutch they did not tell us that there is a Lord above; but said that we black people should be burnt and that we have no spirit, but are like a dog, which has no spirit."[25] Later another informant added, "And the King which is above we did not hear of him (first) from whitemen. In summer time, when it thunders, we say, 'The King is playing ...' This is why I say, that the Lord of whom we hear through you, we had already heard of before you came."[26] The same informant went on to distinguish between the heavenly king and Unkulunkulu and insisted that while Unkulunkulu was the creator of men, he died, unlike the heavenly king who reigns above.[27]

Another informant claimed that the heavenly Lord was the creator of the world.[28] An old woman began by denying that Unkulunkulu had gone "above" to become the "creator which is in heaven."[29] A different informant mentioned a Lord in Heaven but was careful to distinguish him from Unkulunkulu.[30] It was said that Unkulunkulu was the creator of human beings and human social institutions but could not be spoken of as a lord.[31] Yet another informant emphatically denied that the Lord of Heaven was the Zulu god. He said, "The ancients said that it was Unkulunkulu who gave origin to men, and to everything else besides, both cattle and animals. They said it was an ancient man who gave origin to these things, of whom it is now said that ancient man is lord; it is said, he is the Lord which is above. We have not heard from you that the Lord which is above made everything. The old men said that Unkulunkulu was an ancestor and nothing more ..."[32]

---

24. Ibid., 105.
25. Ibid., 10.
26. Ibid., 19.
27. Ibid., 21.
28. Ibid., 50.
29. Ibid., 53–55.
30. Ibid., 56.
31. Ibid., 59.
32. Ibid., 63.

The same informant told of how the efforts of a missionary so impressed the people that they ultimately came to accept and use the term *Utikxo* as referring to a being who was above. But the informant adds, "We used to speak of the whole heaven, saying Utikxo dwells in the whole heaven[,] but did not clearly understand what we meant."[33] The final reference to the Lord of Heaven in this section comes in a very confused dialogue where the informant at first denies that he knows Unkulunkulu and then points to heaven and says, "There is Unkulunkulu."[34]

In commenting on this, Callaway says that at first he had not intended to use this piece of evidence but later thought that when the informant denied knowledge of Unkulunkulu he was in fact speaking of the first man, while when he again acknowledged Unkulunkulu he was speaking of the ancestor of his tribe or clan. In this incident, as with the other reports, the reader is left in confusion about both Unkulunkulu and the Lord of Heaven.

When Callaway turns from these remarks about Unkulunkulu to a discussion of the Lord of Heaven, the information he gives throws light on the entire debate. Callaway begins his discussion with an overview of belief in a heavenly lord amongst the nations of the earth. In this, as in many footnotes, he shows both his wide reading and his interest in the comparative religion of his day. He also lays bare his own predisposition to believe in a god who is in heaven.[35] Then he records the comments of his informants, apparently without realizing exactly what they were saying or the implications of their statements for an understanding of the development of religious ideas amongst the Zulu.

His first informant is quite explicit: "It is by no means clear what is really said about the lord of heaven. For when the heaven (lightning) has struck any place, it is said, 'The lord is angry' ... It is not very clear which is the lord that strikes—whether it is the lightning, or whether the lightning is the lord's power.... But there are many who are called lords by

Photo 5.6 With the introduction of European ideas about God into African societies like that of the Zulu, converts were slowly attracted to various Christian missions. Very soon afterwards thousands of indigenous religious groups that were quite independent of the missionaries developed. These are usually known as African Independent Churches, or AICs. In the scene above, two strong men struggle with the baptismal candidate, who under the influence of an evil spirit is resisting submersion in the healing waters of the sea. In this case the Christian ritual of baptism has been adapted as a rite for existing church members intended to ward off evil spirits, defend against witchcraft, and bring about healing.

33. Ibid., 69.
34. Ibid., 83.
35. Ibid., 117.

men...."[36] The same man told Callaway, "It is not permitted that there should be any greater than the chief. The greatness of heaven was said to belong to Upanga, who was a great Zulu chief; for you can see by this that it is merely something done for the purpose of exalting a man when it is said that the heaven too belongs to him. It used to be said if any omen happened to a village, that it was occasioned by the chief ... 'it was done by heaven' ... and the people understood ... it is a mere exaltation of the chief."[37] Another man said, "Among the Amazulu they use the name of heaven; when it thunders they say, 'the heaven of the chief thundered.' They do not mean the owner of the heaven who made it, but a mere man who is chief; he is exalted by saying the heaven is his ... They say this because they see no one else but the chief himself, who if he chooses can command any particular person to die, and he will die at once."[38]

CALLAWAY'S CONCLUSION

Callaway concludes by saying, "It appears, therefore, that in the native mind there is scarcely any notion of Deity, if any at all, wrapt up in their sayings about a heavenly chief. When it ['heavenly chief'] is applied to God it is simply the result of teaching."[39] This is a strange conclusion for a man who began his discussion of the heavenly Lord by affirming that such a belief is found in "almost every country," and who was predisposed to finding the belief amongst the Zulu people.[40] It is significant in light of this that these comments were ignored by later users of Callaway's texts.

THE VIEWS OF WHITE TRADERS

Lest it be thought that too much is being read into the evidence of Callaway, it is worth surveying the very scanty evidence about Zulu religious beliefs from the earliest period of recorded contact between Zulu and European cultures. There are four major sources for information about Zulu beliefs in the years 1836–37. They are the trader Nathaniel Isaacs' (1808–72) *Travels and Adventures in Eastern Africa* (1836), Captain Allen Gardiner's *Narrative of a Journey to the Zoolu Country* (1836), *The Diary of Henry Francis Fynn*, and another missionary work, Owen's *Diary*, edited by Sir George Cory in 1926. The picture of Zulu religion given in all of these documents is of an essentially secular society, where the ancestors and witchcraft were important, but where there was no belief in a High God or Lord of the Sky.

Photo 5.7 Captain Allen Gardiner, who in the early nineteenth century became the first European missionary to the Zulu. A former sea captain who fought in the Napoleonic wars, he converted to evangelical Christianity after one particular naval engagement. Following the end of the wars, he became an Anglican missionary.

---

36. Ibid., 118.
37. Ibid., 120.
38. Ibid., 122.
39. Ibid., 124.
40. Ibid., 117–18.

Nathaniel Isaacs' first mention of religion is in connection with a conversation with the Zulu king Chaka, during which the king asked Isaacs what the sky was made of. When he found Isaacs' answer unsatisfactory, he "introduced the subject of religion." Isaacs comments, "We explained to him that the religion of our nation taught us to believe in a Supreme Being, a First Cause, named God, by whom we swore, in whom we believed and trusted: that he created all things, and was the giver of light and life." Isaacs notes that this caught the king's attention, although he found the story of creation astonishing. He then says, "We told him that we had not brought any doctors [missionaries] with us to instruct the ignorant in the ways of God; this he appeared to regret, and expressed the wish for them to come and teach his people, observing, 'that he had discovered we were a superior race,' and that he would give the missionaries abundance of cattle to teach him to read and write."[41]

After living amongst the Zulu for some time, Isaacs, who was Jewish, made the following observations: "Religions. They have none. The Zoolas have no idea of a Deity, no knowledge of a future state. They cannot comprehend the mystery of creation … and though they could not comprehend the worship of an invisible Creator, they seemed to be somewhat convinced that our motives had more in them than they, poor illiterate beings, could possiblly fathom or divine."[42]

EARLY MISSIONARY REACTIONS

Captain Allen Gardiner, the first Christian missionary to the Zulu, arrived in Zululand after the death of Chaka and met his successor Dingaan. He gives the following account of an interview with Dingaan, whom he considered "very intelligent": "That my views were not in any degree connected with trade he could understand, but what was God, and God's word, and the nature of the instruction I proposed, were subjects which he could not at all comprehend."[43]

Gardiner was, however, convinced that all men have some natural knowledge of God. He was therefore able to assert, "We seem to have arrived here at a period when the *traditional knowledge* of a Supreme Being is rapidly passing into oblivion" (italics mine).[44] As a basis for this statement, he repeats a Zulu legend which he takes as a creation account, and in doing so he assumes that the Zulu originator of life is equivalent to God. This is, of course, highly suspect when, in fact, other Zulu accounts of creation clearly refer to an original ancestor rather than to God in the Christian sense. Even here, however, it is doubtful if Gardiner is relating a story which is uninfluenced by European contact, because on the next page he adds, "The generality of the people are ignorant even of this scanty tradition; but *since their recent intercourse with Europeans* the vague ideal of a Supreme Being has *again* become general" (italics mine).[45] After making this observation, he adds the highly

---

41. Nathaniel Isaacs, *Travels and Adventures in Eastern Africa* (London: Edward Churton, 1836), 1:119–20.

42. Ibid., 2:301–2.

43. Allen Gardiner, *Narrative of a Journey to the Zoolu Country* (London: William Crofts, 1836), 30–33.

44. Ibid., 178.

45. Ibid., 179.

Photo 5.8 The great Zulu king Shaka or Chaka.

significant statement that "at present, the reigning king absorbs all their praises, and he is, in fact, their only idol."[46]

The diary of Gardiner's successor, the Reverend Francis Owen (1802–1854), an Anglican minister, is a mine of information. Owen arrived in Natal in 1837 in response to a call for missionaries by Captain Gardiner. Soon after arriving in Zululand, he made the following comment in his diary: "Dingaan then asked how old I was ... He then called for an old print he had of the Kings of England ... He then asked me if God was amongst these kings ... The Indoonas asked me if I had seen God ..."[47]

From this narrative it is clear that Dingaan and his chiefs, the *Indoonas*, thought of God as an ancestor and, despite the teaching of Gardiner and other whites to the contrary, found it difficult to conceive of God in another culture's terms. When Owen tried to explain his evangelical understanding of the fall to Dingaan, he encountered a host of questions about the death of God. These questions show quite clearly that the concept of an undying Supreme Being was foreign to Zulu thought, because none of Dingaan's chiefs could understand what Owen was talking about.[48]

Commenting directly on the Zulu notion of God, Owen says, "The Zoolas have no word in their own language to express the sublime object of our worship ... the word Unkulunkulu ... being applied by the natives to a certain ancient chief ..."[49] Given this problem, Owen was unsure how to refer to God and seems to have favored the suggestion that the Hebrew "Elohim" be introduced into the Zulu language.

LATER MISSIONARY OBSERVATIONS

Much later, in 1857, the missionary Joseph Shooter asserted that the Zulu had a tradition of a "Being" whom he identifies as Unkulunkulu who was a kind of creator. However, he adds, "This tradition of the Great-Great is not universally known among the people. War, change and the worship of false deities have *gradually darkened their minds, and obscured their*

---

46. Ibid.

47. Francis Owen, *The Diary of the Rev. Francis Owen*, ed. George Edward Cory (Cape Town, South Africa: Van Riebeeck Society, 1926), 39. Henry Francis Fynn, *The Diary of Henry Francis Fynn*, ed. James Stuart and D. McK. Malcolm (Pietermaritzburg, South Africa: Shuter and Shooter, 1950), adds little to our knowledge of Zulu religion, and his diary throws no light on the subject at hand.

48. Owen, *Diary*, 74.

49. Ibid., 90.

remembrance of the true God" (italics mine).[50] Clearly, Shooter wanted the Zulu to have a "traditional" belief in God and was forced to interpret their apparent lack of such a belief in terms of their degeneration as men in rebellion against the truth of God.

Nine years later, in his book *The Past and Future of the Kaffir Races*, William Holden argued that the Zulu were "literally without God"[51] and went on to argue that although amongst some people there appeared to be a belief in a godlike being, it was wrong to interpret this as a belief in God. He was dogmatic in asserting that "they do not recognize a Supreme Being in the sense that we use the term ..."[52] Although a few Zulu had some vague idea of deity, the vast majority, he argued, had no such belief. More importantly, those who did have some indistinct beliefs which seemed like a belief in God really should be seen as worshiping their ancestors.

This point about misunderstanding Zulu belief was developed by J. A. Farrer in *Zululand and the Zulus* (1879). He saw ancestor worship as the basic Zulu religious response and stated that the Zulu understanding of Unkulunkulu was essentially a belief about the ancestors of the people, even though, through the attribution of creation and other actions to Unkulunkulu, it could be said to function in a similar way to beliefs about God.[53] Farrer also discussed the Zulu traditions concerning a "lord of the sky" or heavenly deity, whom he saw as "subordinate" to Unkulunkulu. He then added, "It is possible that missionary teaching has somewhat modified the original conception of the king of heaven ..."[54]

This last statement fits well with the accounts recorded by Callaway indicating an original usage which referred to the Zulu king and not to God. Thus we see that there

Photo 5.9 Initiation rites that mark the transition from childhood to adulthood are an important aspect of most traditional African societies. Among the Xhosa this begins with the circumcision of boys, who then live in an initiation lodge while their wound heals. During the time of preparation they are separated from the rest of society, cover their bodies with white clay, and are taught the history, myths, and ritual practices of their clan. A small boy accompanies the initiates wherever they go, running ahead of them to warn women, who are ritually impure, to keep out of their way. The hut at the side of the picture is a traditional initiation lodge.

50. Joseph Shooter, *The Kafirs of Natal and the Zulu Country* (London: E. Stanford, 1857), 160.

51. William C. Holden, *The Past and Future of the Kaffir Races* (London: privately printed, 1866), 297.

52. Ibid., 298.

53. J. A. Farrer, *Zululand and the Zulus* (London: Kirby, 1879), 128–29.

54. Ibid., 131.

is ample evidence supporting the interpretation given earlier of Callaway's testimony and the assertion that before the coming of Europeans the Zulu had no traditional belief in a supreme deity. What then are we to understand by the evidence that today, modern Zulu have such a belief, which they cast in traditional terms?

SOME SUGGESTIONS ABOUT ZULU RELIGION AND RELIGIOUS CHANGE

It appears that when Europeans first arrived in Zululand, they were welcomed by the Zulu because of their trade goods and their technological superiority, which the Zulus recognized. The great desire of the Zulu kings was to acquire the knowledge which made "whitemen" superior to their people. This superiority was bound up with the possession of firearms and, in the eyes of the Zulus, the ability to read. Therefore, when Captain Gardiner told them such things as, "They were now a great people but I wished them to know these words that they might become greater ...,"[55] the Zulus listened with great interest and care. The promise to make them "greater" must have seemed a hopeful one, because these new strangers sought to teach the Zulus the art of reading, which seems to have been seen as the key to European power.[56]

Photo 5.10 Once the period of training is over for initiates, they are given their final instructions. Then, after various rituals, which begin while it is still dark, their heads are covered, they are given new clothes, and they are led away from the hut, which is set on fire.

It is clear that in inviting missionaries, Dingaan wished to obtain gunpowder and the means of producing firearms. It seems that when the missionaries refused to do this, he thought that by learning to read and by listening to the missionaries his people would acquire the skills of the whites. This understanding is probably best seen as interpreting white technology in terms of a new magic which reading would make available to his people.[57]

The missionaries and traders who visited the Zulu during this early period of contact did so with an overwhelming confidence in the superiority of their civilization, which they were quick to point out to the Zulus and which they attributed to the Christian religion.[58] Their belief in the truths of Christianity could, however, have been severely challenged by the existence of Zulu society. The

55. Gardiner, *Narrative*, 133.

56. Ibid., 33, 133.

57. Owen, *Diary*, 46–47; Gardiner, *Narrative*, 32–33, 132–33.

58. Owen, *Diary*, 39, 40, 47, 53–55, 56, 59, 65–66, 72–73; Isaacs, *Travels and Adventures*, 120.

Zulus were a people who appeared not to have heard the gospel. The question could therefore have arisen as to how a just God could judge people who were totally ignorant of his commands. But this question never seems to have been asked, because a theological interpretation of Zulu life existed which allowed for the Zulus' apparent ignorance of the gospel.

This interpretation depended upon the assumption that the Zulu people must at one time have known the truth of God and that their present state of ignorance was a result of willful rebellion against God's commands. There was, for the missionaries, no real possibility that the Zulus did not know about

Photo 5.11 While leaving the hut on their final journey to manhood, initiates must not look back at the burning hut, which contains their old clothes and childhood toys. Now they are men.

God at some time in their history. If the Zulus they encountered denied such knowledge, this was simply the result of their sinful nature.[59] Gardiner observed, "What an awful condition for an immortal being! Man, when once departed from God, goes out, like Nebuchadnezzar in his banishment.... Breathe, Lord upon these dry bones, and they shall live."[60] For him, and later missionaries, it was obvious that they had "arrived at a time when the traditional knowledge of a Supreme Being ... [was] rapidly passing into oblivion."[61] This interpretation was neatly summed up by Shooter: "False deities have gradually darkened their minds, and obscured their remembrance of the true God."[62]

As a result, the missionaries set about proclaiming the truth of God without making any concessions to Zulu religious beliefs. As can be seen most clearly in the preaching of Owen, they proclaimed their understanding of the gospel, expecting that the Zulus would be able to understand and respond to it.

By contrast, the Zulu worldview at the time seems to have been entirely bounded by their social needs. When Owen asked them "where the rain came from," they told him that the clouds were made by their "doctors."[63] Again and again Zulu questioners asked him if he had "seen God," while other questions indicated that they saw God in ancestral terms. Above all, the impression gained from reading Owen's account of his own mission work is that he must have created confusion in Zulu minds. He told them that they were sinners whom God would punish and send to hell if they did not repent

---

59. Romans 2:1–16.
60. Gardiner, *Narrative*, 179.
61. Ibid., 178.
62. Shooter, *Kafirs*, 160.
63. Owen, *Diary*, 94.

Photo 5.12 Mission stations like the well-equipped Mariannhill Mission in Natal, South Africa, were usually self-contained communities with their own farms, workshops, printing presses, and medical facilities. As such, they often gave birth to similar communal settlements among members of African Independent Churches. Above is a picture of the tower at Mariannhill; Photo 5.13 is the tower of the sacred place of the amaNazarites, Ekuphakameni. Notice the similarity in style, with the exception of the amaNazarite version of a Celtic cross.

and believe in the "blood of Jesus," the Son of God, who had died for them and risen from the dead. Such concepts were, by Owen's account, beyond their comprehension; and their questions, which he sometimes records, reflect their confusion.[64]

Yet from later evidence it is clear that, despite the original confusion created in Zulu minds, certain beliefs were implanted which, in time, came to be regarded as "traditional" Zulu beliefs. One of the most important of these is belief in the existence of a Lord of the Sky. An important clue to understanding how the Zulu people came to accept this belief is to be found in a discussion of swearing in Owen's *Diary*: "I had a long argument with the boys this morning on the subject of swearing ... They asked, 'Are we not to swear when we are at our home? How are we to confirm our words without an oath? Who will believe us?... the king himself swears; he swears by Chaka, and Chaka used to swear by the chief who was before him.'"[65]

Two things need to be noted. First, swearing was the traditional way of making an agreement. Second, one swore by one's ancestor or the king. When Isaacs spoke to the Zulu king, Chaka, about God, he told him that "our nation taught us to believe in a Supreme Being ... by whom we swore ..."[66] Years later Callaway's informants told him that "the white men used to make us swear to the truth of what we said; for they did not understand what a man said when he swore by our chiefs; so the oath was ... I swear by the Lord of heaven ..."[67] From this comment it appears that whites encouraged the usage of the phrase "the Lord of Heaven" in their business dealings with the Zulu without understanding its true significance. In doing so, they gave the phrase a new meaning which detached it from its original context. If this is so, the remark by an earlier informant that "the white-men are the lords who made all things" takes on added significance.

By their power whites challenged the power of traditional chiefs, and as a result they came to be referred to in terms reserved for chiefs. When they further insisted on oaths to seal contracts, Zulus complied by using terminology which forged a link between traditional Zulu understandings of the powers of their chiefs and the metaphysical statements

---

64. Ibid., 30, 37, 39, 74, 102.

65. Ibid., 69.

66. Isaacs, *Travels and Adventures*, vol. 1, 119.

67. Callaway, *Religious System of the Amazulu*, 121.

Photo 5.13 The tower of Ekuphakameni.

Photo 5.13 The tower of Ekuphakameni.

which whites thought essential to the binding of oaths. But in the process of these transactions the phrase "the Lord of Heaven," detached from its original context and meaning, began to take on a life of its own in Zulu thought.

CONCLUSION: THE DYNAMICS OF ZULU CONVERSION

If this interpretation of the origin of the Zulu High God is correct, it fits very well with Wittgenstein's comments on the word "God" in his *Lectures and Conversations on Aesthetics, Psychology, and Religious Belief* (1970): "The word 'God' is amongst the earliest learnt ... The word is used like a word representing a person ... If the question arises as to the existence of a god or God, it plays an entirely different role to that of the existence of any person or object I ever heard of. One said, *had to say* [italics mine], that one *believed* in the existence, and if one did not believe, this was regarded as something bad."[68]

This description of the way people learn to use the word "God" fits exactly the case presented in this chapter. The Zulu had to learn to use a phrase which Europeans would recognize as referring to God if they were to deal with them. Fortunately such a phrase existed in "the Lord of Heaven," making a bridge possible between the two cultures. The result of this interaction was not simply the destruction of a traditional Zulu phrase, but the adaptation of it and the Zulu belief system to extend that system and widen the horizons of Zulu society.[69]

Zulu beliefs and practices were challenged by the arrival of Europeans and their "strange" beliefs, but within several generations an adap-

Photo 5.14 The complex relationships between African traditional religions, mission Christianity, and African Independent Churches (AICs) are often misunderstood, while scholars speculate about them on the basis of hearsay evidence and published books. What is needed most of all is careful fieldwork. In the above picture one of the pioneers of the study of AICs, G. C. "Pippin" Oosthuizen, interviews the leader of an African religious group on the Durban beachfront after a baptismal ceremony.

68. Ludwig Wittgenstein, *Lectures and Conversations on Aesthetics, Psychology and Religious Belief*, ed. Cyril Barrett (Oxford: Blackwell, 1970), 52.

69. Ibid.

tation had taken place which enabled Zulus to deal with the Europeans on their own terms. Zulu society met the challenge of European beliefs through a creative response which drew upon its own traditions to create a new tradition. The "traditional religion" which then came into existence not only enabled the Zulu to deal with Europeans, but also gave pagan and Christian Zulu a common heritage which acknowledges the existence of a Supreme Being.

Thus, while the conversion of sections of the Zulu nation to Christianity originally created a sharp division in Zulu society, the emergence of this "traditional religion" provided all Zulu with a common heritage and identity as well as a basis for the secondary virtues which are necessary in everyday life.[70] The present belief regarding the Lord of the Sky that Berglund emphasizes may therefore be seen in terms of the development of a civil religion of Zululand.

---

70. Monica Wilson, "The Shades, Medicines, Witchcraft and God" (Cambridge: Cambridge Univ. Press, 1971), chapter 2 in *Religion and the Transformation of Society*; David Welsh, *The Roots of Segregation* (Cape Town, South Africa: Oxford Univ. Press, 1971); Alisdair MacIntyre, *Secularisation and Moral Change* (Oxford: Oxford Univ. Press), 1967.

CHAPTER 6

THE CASE OF ISAIAH SHEMBE

INTRODUCTION

This chapter deals with some problems encountered by scholars who attempt to study primal religions. To bring these issues alive, we will examine the major scholarly literature and some traditions surrounding perceptions of the Zulu religious leader Isaiah Shembe, who is arguably the most famous founder of an African Independent Church in the whole of Africa. The movement he founded, known as the amaNazarites, is the main subject of the BBC film *Zulu Zion* (1977), and more books have been written about him and his followers than about any other modern religious movement in Africa.

THE STUDY OF AFRICAN RELIGIONS

As Rodney Stark shows in *For the Glory of God*,[1] antislavery movements began to develop early in the history of Christianity, leading to the virtual abolition of slavery by the high Middle Ages. During the sixteenth century slavery returned with a vengeance as plantation farming was developed in the New World. Even the pope, Catholic scholars, and a growing number of Protestants protested against the practice, forcing slave owners and traders, who shipped millions of captives from Africa to the Americas, to find new justifications for their evil deeds.

One of these justifications was to claim that Africans were not truly human because they lacked a soul.[2] This argument was developed on the basis of supposed observations of African life showing that Africans, unlike the Chinese and Indians, had failed to develop anything like Buddhism or Hinduism and that African society lacked all manifestations of religion.[3] If Africans lacked religion, it was argued, they must not have a soul and were therefore not fully human.[4]

---

1. Rodney Stark, *For the Glory of God: How Monotheism Led to Reformations, Science, Witch-Hunts, and the End of Slavery* (Princeton: Princeton Univ. Press, 2003), 291–365.
2. This argument was being used as late as the 1840s by B. H. Payne in *The Negro: What Is His Ethnological Status?* (Cincinnati, 1840). See David Brion Davis, *The Problem of Slavery in Western Culture* (Ithaca: Cornell Univ. Press, 1970), n.b. 453.
3. Joseph R. Washington, *Anti-Blackness in English Religion, 1500–1800* (New York: Edwin Mellen, 1984), 110. Cf. *Anthropological Review* 3 (1865), clxv.
4. Josiah Priest, *Bible Defense of Slavery, or The Origin, Fortunes, and History of the Negro Race* (Glasgow: W. S. Brown, 1852).

Photo 6.1 An older prayer counselor comforts a younger woman during a baptismal ceremony on the Durban beachfront. While nineteenth-century secular writers argued that Africans lacked spiritual feelings and were therefore not fully human, missionaries were always impressed by the depth of African piety.

Later the argument was modernized. Instead of having no soul, Africans were now said to be lower on the evolutionary tree than Europeans. For example, *The Anthropological Review* reported that at a meeting of the Anthropological Society in London on 17 November 1863, "A comparison was drawn between the anatomical differences existing between the Negro and the ape." Consequently, Africans were said to be nearer to apes than Europeans.[5] A particularly repulsive article, with the title "Anatomico-Anthropological Observations upon the Body of a Negro," appeared in *The Journal of Anthropology* in 1871.[6] Africans, it was supposed from such observations, lacked the intelligence to develop religions of their own. In 1865, *The Anthropological Review* published a long debate about the effectiveness of Christian missions in Africa. The main points made by the critics of missionaries was that Africans lack religious sentiments.

All of the racist arguments against the missionaries were linked by the critics to criticisms of "Exeter Hall," which was the headquarters of the Anti-Slavery Society, the Aborigines Protection Society, and other evangelical Christian organizations seeking to protect native peoples. Further, it was confidently asserted by critics of the missionary movement that "not only has the negro race never civilised itself, but it has never accepted any other civilization …" During these debates various Christian members of the Anthropological Society vigorously objected to this view, arguing that it was plainly untrue.[7]

Thus, the claim that Africans lacked religion justified their exploitation. The first argument, that Africans had no soul, legitimated slavery.[8] The second, that Africans were low on the evolutionary ladder, justified colonialism.[9] Many people, particularly Christian missionaries, argued against both of these assumptions and the exploitation they justified. But for their arguments to be effective it was essential to prove that Africans were just as religious as other humans. Bishops Colenso (1814–1883) and Henry Callaway (1817–1890), in South Africa, played a prominent role in these debates by making a great effort to explain the apparent lack of religion among many African peoples and to

---

5. Numerous articles on this topic are to be found in *The Anthropological Review*. See, e.g., vol. 2 (1864): xv–xxlvi, n.b. xv; vol. 3 (1865): 120ff.
6. *Journal of Anthropology* 3 (January 1871): 245–58.
7. *Anthropological Review* 3 (1865): clxiii–ccxciii, esp. clxvi, clxxi, cxcix.
8. See Priest, *Bible Defense of Slavery*.
9. See *Anthropological Review* 1 (1863): 3–4, 12–14, 16–17; George W. Stocking Jr., *Victorian Anthropology* (New York: Free Press, 1987), 62–69, 248–54, 271–73.

discover a High God behind African mythologies and ways of thought.[10]

As discussed in the last chapter, many missionaries and scholars apparently "discovered" a Christian type of God "hidden" in African culture. Such discoveries served a political purpose but, as was shown, distorted the reality of many African religions just as much as the earlier claim that Africans had "no religion."[11] A similar distortion, for very similar reasons, took place in the twentieth century with regard to the discussion of new religions in Africa. At first such movements were dismissed as a return to heathendom. Today, many scholars embrace them as pure forms of African Christianity. It will be argued in this chapter that both attitudes are wrong and distort the reality of African religion.

Photo 6.2 Early photograph of the great Zulu prophet and teacher Isaiah Shembe, who founded the Nazareth Baptist Church, more commonly known as the amaNazarites.

The academic debate between G. C. Oosthuizen and various critics, particularly Bengt Sundkler and Absolom Vilakazi, illustrates the problems involved with understanding new religions in Africa. Oosthuizen claims that the amaNazaretha of Isaiah Shembe represent a new religion distinct from Christianity. Sundkler and Vilakazi claim that Oosthuizen is wrong and that the amaNazaretha are an authentic form of Zulu Christianity.

CHANGING PERSPECTIVES ON AFRICAN RELIGIOUS MOVEMENTS

Initially, African Independent Churches and other religious movements were called "Ethiopian." Later, in the 1930s, the term "Independent Churches" came into use to refer to such groups, whether or not they were Christian. Although this might seem an improvement, it is important to realize that until the 1980s such movements were widely regarded as deviant social groups motivated more by politics than by religion. At first most observers, including Edgar Brookes (1907–1979), the great South African Liberal writer and defender of Black Africans' political rights, saw them as positively dangerous. More recently attitudes have changed, but an essentially hostile attitude toward such movements remains.[12]

John Buchan's best-selling novel *Prester John* vividly illustrates popular attitudes toward African religious movements early in the twentieth century. Buchan was a very successful mystery writer best known for his book *The Thirty-nine Steps*. He later became the governor general of Canada, Lord Tweedsmuir. His novel was written on the basis of his experiences working for the British governor of South Africa, Lord Milner, during and following the Second Anglo-Boer War (1899–1902). From his writing it is clear

10. Henry Callaway, *Fragment on Comparative Religion* (Natal, South Africa: privately printed, 1874), and *On the Religious Sentiment amongst the Tribes of South Africa* (n.p., 1876); John W. Colenso, "On the Efforts of Missionaries among Savages," *Anthropological Review* 3 (1865): ccxlviii–cclxxxix.

11. Okot p'Bitek, *African Religions in Western Scholarship* (Kampala, Uganda: East African Literature Bureau, 1970).

12. See, for example, Allister Sparks, *The Mind of South Africa* (New York: Knopf, 1990), 293.

that Buchan had access to British intelligence reports on African religions. In the novel Buchan uses highly offensive language that enables the modern reader to grasp the depth of prejudice against African religions in the early part of the twentieth century. So-called Ethiopian movements—and, later, African Independent Churches—were uniformly seen as political movements in disguise.[13] Consequently, they were viewed by colonial administrators as cunning attempts by Blacks to organize politically under the guise of religion. In this sense, Buchan's description of a Black revolt mirrors the reality of white perceptions.[14]

Photo 6.3 John Buchan, Lord Tweedsmuir, was the author of immensely popular books such as *The Thirty-nine Steps* (1915), which Alfred Hitchcock made into a film. Less well known today was his *Prester John* (1910), which presents a very unflattering picture of African Christian converts and African Independent Churches (AICs). Although a novel, his work had a strong negative influence on European attitudes to AICs.

British missionary leaders agreed with colonial administrators in their analysis of Ethiopianism, but added a religious twist. African religious movements, they argued, aimed to convert members of established mission churches to new forms of paganized Christianity. It was claimed that, unlike "true Christian Churches," the new African Independent Churches did not convert the heathen. Instead they led Christians astray through their recognition of witchcraft and acceptance of polygamy.[15] Many Black converts contributed to this negative view, arguing that the growing popularity of African Independent Churches was due to a lack of moral discipline and their toleration of practices like polygamy, moral laxity, and superstitious rituals.

Mission churches were said to oppose witchcraft and polygamy, but African Independent Churches incorporated these beliefs and practices into their theology. Therefore, it was argued that "young converts," who were "weak in faith," were easily attracted to these halfway houses between "true Christianity" and African traditional religions. Such movements, it was said, sanctioned the grossest forms of behavior.[16] Behind the negative reaction of white observers, be they administrators or missionaries, lay the deeply ingrained belief that Black Africans were incapable of developing a genuine interest in religion qua religion.[17]

13. Edgar Brookes, *The Colour Problems of South Africa* (Alice, South Africa: Lovedale, 1934), 34.

14. Public Record Office, United Kingdom, "Ethiopianism," *Africa South, Secret Correspondence Registers, Supplementary*, CO 537 (London, 1904), report no. 513.

15. "The Ethiopian Church," editorial, *Christian Express*, April 1897; "The Negro Spirit," editorial, *Christian Express*, April 1900; Francis Wilson and Dominique Perrot, eds., *Outlook on a Century* (Alice, South Africa: Lovedale, 1973), 153–55, 158–60.

16. John Henderson Soga, *The Ama-Xosa: Life and Customs* (Alice, South Africa: Lovedale, 1931), 134–35, 248, 253.

17. See Fred B. Welbourn, "Reuben Spartas against Paternalism: The African Greek Orthodox Church," in *East African Rebels* (London: SCM Press, 1961), 77–110.

CHANGING PERCEPTIONS OF AFRICAN INDEPENDENT CHURCHES

Bengt Sundkler,[18] and then Katesa Schlosser,[19] challenged such prejudicial views by publishing more informed studies in 1949. Their work was followed by that of Fred Welbourn[20] and later by the works of Harold Turner,[21] G. C. Oosthuizen,[22] and David Barrett.[23] These books slowly turned the tide of academic opinion in favor of taking African religions seriously. Academics gradually came to see that Africans were capable of adapting Christianity to meet their own needs.

Today, scholars recognize that African traditional religions are also capable of modernizing to compete with Christian churches, although this acceptance was a slow process. One of the biggest obstacles to the recognition of revitalized forms of African traditional religions is an overreaction by many scholars to the crude stereotyping of the past. As a result many scholars now accept all African religious movements as indigenous forms of Christianity, even though many are not.

Photo 6.4 Fred Welbourn with the founder of the African Israel Church Nineveh and his sons. A physicist by training and an ordained Anglican clergyman, he began researching African religious movements while lecturing at Makerere University, where he pioneered the study of African Independent Churches.

PAGAN, CHRISTIAN, OR SIMPLY AFRICAN?

G. C. Oosthuizen attempted a new interpretation of African Independent Churches in his controversial book *The Theology of a South African Messiah*.[24] Oosthuizen argued that seeing the movement "in the context of the Zulu religion" produced a very different understanding of groups like the amaNazarites. Correctly understood, within the context of Zulu tradition and popular language, Isaiah Shembe, he said, was seen by his followers as "the manifestation of God."[25] To see Shembe as simply a prophet was wrong. He was far more. Therefore, Schlosser and like-minded scholars were wrong in saying that amaNazarite religion was "an interesting mixture of redemption and legalistic religion."

18. Bengt Sundkler, *Bantu Prophets in South Africa* (Oxford: Institute of Race Relations, 1948).

19. Katesa Schlosser, *Propheten in Afrika* (Braunschweig, Germany: A. Limbach, 1949).

20. Fred B. Welbourn, *East African Rebels* (London: SCM Press, 1961).

21. Harold Turner, *A History of an African Independent Church*, vol. 1, *The Church of the Lord (Aladura)* (Oxford: Clarendon, 1967).

22. G. C. Oosthuizen, *Post-Christianity in Africa* (Stellenbosch, South Africa: T. Wever, 1968).

23. David B. Barrett, *Schism and Renewal in Africa* (Nairobi, Kenya: Oxford Univ. Press, 1968).

24. G. C. Oosthuizen, *The Theology of a South African Messiah: An Analysis of the Hymnal of "the Church of the Nazarites,"* (Leiden: Brill, 1967).

25. Ibid., 4.

Rather, Oosthuizen argued, "every religion is an organic whole ..." and must be seen as such. Consequently, Isaiah Shembe had produced "a Zuluized religion"![26] In making this argument, Oosthuizen believed he was respecting the true intent of Shembe, rather than reinterpreting the movement in Christian terms.

Oosthuizen's work was strongly attacked by Lutheran bishop and missionary scholar Bengt Sundkler, who countered that an African religious movement "should be understood, *not* from the outside, from a Western standpoint, measuring its contents according to the standards and ideas of a European catechism, but rather from its own presuppositions."[27] This is exactly what Oosthuizen was attempting to do, and his essentially Western perspective, according to Sundkler, had "led him astray."[28] Sundkler further claimed that Oosthuizen "constantly misread the most simple and direct statements of faith and trust."[29] Thus he suggested that Oosthuizen really did not understand the Zulu.

This accusation was repeated by Absolom Vilakazi in his book, *Shembe: The Revitalization of African Society*,[30] where he explicitly claimed that Oosthuizen misunderstood both the Zulu language and its numerous idioms.[31] To Vilakazi, the issue was one of cultural insensitivity and Oosthuizen's ethnic background as a white Afrikaner. Oosthuizen, he said, embraced "a particularly insular view" that represented "the views of his own church," which was at heart an "argument for the colonization of the African soul by accepting anything which comes from European Christianity and rejecting all African cultural contributions to the understanding and enrichment of worship in African Christian Churches."[32]

Photo 6.5 Anthropologist Karla Poewe interviewing the Right Reverend Londa Shembe during the annual July celebrations of the amaNazarites at Ekuphakameni. Rev. Shembe, who considered himself the "Third Shembe," and therefore more than merely a prophet, is dressed in traditional amaNazarite ceremonial attire. Professor Poewe holds a tape recorder while also taking notes.

26. Ibid., 10.
27. Bengt Sundkler, *Zulu Zion and Some Swazi Zionists* (London: Oxford Univ. Press, 1976), 190−97.
28. Ibid.
29. Ibid., 191−92.
30. Absolom Vilakazi with Bongani Mthethwa and Mthembeni Mpanza, *Shembe: The Revitalization of African Society* (Braamfontein, South Africa: Skotaville, 1986), 88−111.
31. Ibid., 89.
32. Ibid., 100.

In these ways, by ad hominem attacks on both his linguistic abilities and his ethnic background, both Sundkler and Vilakazi sought to undermine the legitimacy of Oosthuizen's work. Against his position they argued that "Shembe's Church is deliberately and unapologetically Zulu."[33] Further, Sundkler claimed that even if "Shembe's theology was far from being orthodox Christian," it was, nevertheless, Christian.[34]

Given that Vilakazi was a native-speaking Zulu and well-respected anthropologist, it is understandable that many scholars automatically assumed that both Sundkler's and Vilakazi's interpretations of amaNazarite religion must be correct. Not surprisingly, Sundkler cited Vilakazi's work with the comment, "Dr. Vilakazi is a Zulu himself and is therefore in a privileged position to understand the movement."[35] With this comment, the argument appeared to be closed.

A QUESTION OF METHOD

Actually, Sundkler was right when he suggested that "a fundamental methodological factor"[36] created the differences between the interpretation he and other writers gave of the amaNazarites and that of Oosthuizen. Where he went wrong was in his use of ad hominem arguments and locating the issue of methods in Oosthuizen's supposed lack of empathy for the amaNazaretha. Actually, Oosthuizen's *empathy* for Zulu religion led him to recognize that the amaNazaretha could not be interpreted as just another Christian church, thus creating his problems with Sundkler and Vilakazi.

Oosthuizen erred in his initial publication by allowing his work to be governed by prevailing norms of academic scholarship in the area of theology and religious studies. He accepted conventional standards and wrote in a style more appropriate for the discussion of literary texts. This made him appear to deduce the beliefs of the amaNazarites from their published texts without reference to his local knowledge of their rich oral culture. Consequently, he made it easy for his critics to charge him with imposing Western theological thinking and interpretations on the amaNazarites texts.

Anyone who knew Oosthuizen and his approach to scholarship soon realized that in fact he based his conclusions on fieldwork carried out over a long time. For him the anthropological techniques of participant observation, life history, and focused interviews were the key in coming to grips with amaNazarite beliefs and practices. Nevertheless, because of his thorough theological training at places like the University of Marburg in Germany and his background in the classics, Oosthuizen lacked the confidence to publish a book based on anthropological methods.

Consequently, he chose to offer an interpretation of amaNazarite religion which *appeared* to be based on written documents when in actuality he was interpreting the *Hymns of the amaNazaretha* in light of information gleaned from informants. A close examination of his work shows that Oosthuizen interpreted textual documents relative to Isaiah

---

33. Ibid., 155.

34. Sundkler, *Zulu Zion*, 196.

35. Ibid., 328.

36. Ibid., 190.

Photo 6.6 A small amaNazarite worship service in a South African shack area. Here a group of women dance to the rhythm of what they consider heavenly music.

Photo 6.7 The faithful wait to hear a sermon by Bishop Amos Shembe. The congregation is dressed in white, one of the colors of heavenly clothing.

Shembe, and particularly the amaNazarite hymns, in light of his knowledge of the living amaNazarite community.

Unfortunately, because of his background and the time when he was writing, Oosthuizen never discussed his method in his book. Only in conversation did he admit that he had expected his readers to recognize the extent to which he was dependent on his informants. When he wrote, he believed he was simply reporting what all amaNazarites knew to be true at the time of his interviews.

It should come as no surprise, then, that Isaiah Shembe's son, Bishop Amos Shembe, and grandson, the Right Reverend Londa Shembe, who led rival factions of the amaNazarite movement, preferred Oosthuizen's representation of their beliefs to that of his critics, even though they differed with each other on most issues. When Amos Shembe first read Vilakazi's manuscript in 1986, he was furious and immediately applied for a court injunction to prevent its publication. According to him, the book was blasphemous because it completely distorted the life and teachings of Isaiah Shembe.[37] Londa Shembe, similarly, believed that scholars like Sundkler and Vilakazi, whom he greatly respected as scholars, had allowed their own prejudices against Afrikaners to color their judgment on this important issue. "About Prof. a. Vilakazi's book," he wrote, "I leafed through the pages and there was nothing that I could find in it that gave joy to my heart. I was sorry in fact that I had ever looked at it ... My hope is that with the passage of time brave authors will come forward and really get into the meat of the matter: the spiritual identity of the man. Who was he in the realm of the Spirit?"[38] Later he added, "I have it in my mind to write a short work on the work life of Baba inKhulu Isaiah Shembe to counter the poison-pen of Vilakazi's."[39]

37. Amos Shembe, interviewed by Karla Poewe and Irving Hexham, July 1987. Shembe made identical comments in April 1986 when visited by Terry Muck, Paul Robbins, Frederick Hale, and Irving Hexham. He also told these visitors about his lawsuit to prevent the publication of Vilakazi's book.

38. Londa Shembe to Bengt Sundkler, 10 June 1986, from a collection of letters given to Professor Karla Poewe which Londa Shembe thought would clarify his ideas for us.

39. Londa Shembe to Karla Poewe, 22 October 1987.

For them, and other amaNazarite leaders, such Christianizing scholarship, which attempted to make the amaNazarites acceptable to members of the South African Council of Churches, and to international groups like the World Council of Churches, was well meaning but totally unacceptable. Amos Shembe believed Isaiah Shembe created an entirely new form of Christianity quite distinct from existing churches. Londa Shembe, on the other hand, believed his grandfather had founded an entirely new form of African religion. Both strongly supported Oosthuizen by rejecting the interpretations of Vilakazi or Sundkler, noting that Oosthuizen really understood their faith.[40]

Photo 6.8 Rev. Petrus Dhlomo, the original archivist of the amaNazarites, was a former school teacher with a university degree who was commissioned by Bishop Johannes Galilee Shembe to preserve the records of the church.

Summing up the situation, Londa Shembe explained, "In the past Christians used a stick to beat us. They said we were pagans and that our followers ought to join *real* churches. Now they are using a carrot. They say we are just another Christian denomination. In this way they are trying to bring us under their control by using promises of recognition and financial assistance as bribes to lead our people back into their churches." Therefore, Londa Shembe argued that "only Oosthuizen understands us. The others want to re-make us in their own image."[41]

STUDYING LIVING RELIGIONS

This dispute about the nature of a particular African religion can be placed in a wider context. Few New Testament scholars would dare to suggest that there is no development in doctrine between the writing of Q and

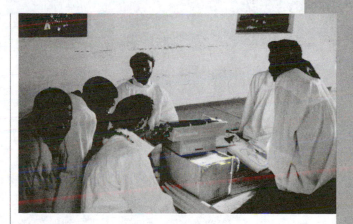

Photo 6.9 Under Dhlomo's direction, a team of amaNazarites painstakingly collected, recorded, and typed out their tradition: the stories about Isaiah Shembe and his successors, as well as their teachings. This collection of documents is unique in the history of AICs.

Mark or that the theology of Matthew, Luke, or John depicts a static situation.[42] Nor would any reputable scholar suggest that there was no development in Christology during the

40. Amos and Londa Shembe, interviews by author, July 1987.
41. Londa Shembe, interview by author, August 1987.
42. N. T. Wright, *The New Testament and the People of God* (Minneapolis: Fortress, 1992), 1:371–443.

first few centuries of the early church.[43] Nevertheless, many scholars expect new religious movements to appear in history with mature and essentially stable theological systems.

In the case of the amaNazaretha we are probably dealing with a shorter period of time than was involved in the writing of the Gospels. Yet many scholars continue to believe that what was taught in the 1930s, 1940s, or 1950s defines amaNazarite theology. This assumption is clearly flawed. Sundkler and Vilakazi appeal to statements made years earlier by Johannes Galilee Shembe about the way his followers viewed Isaiah Shembe. They seem to assume that this view did not change over time.

The fact is that both Sundkler and Vilakazi carried out their primary research, on which they based their criticisms of Oosthuizen, in the 1940s and 1950s. Oosthuizen, on the other hand, worked among the amaNazarites in the mid–1960s. Significantly, although both Sundkler and Vilakazi updated some aspects of their presentation, and added some new material when they published their later books, they appear to have done no significant new research among the amaNazarites following the publication of their original studies. Hence, it is easy to see that the differences between these writers may well be due to the development of doctrine within the amaNazarite movement itself.

Photo 6.10 The prophet Bishop Johannes Galilee Shembe (1904–1975), who succeeded his father, Isaiah Shembe, as leader of the church. He commissioned Rev. Petrus Dhlomo to begin the collection of oral traditions concerning his father and the church in order to create a unique source for both church members and scholars. Later he asked Rev. Hans-Jürgen Becken to translate these texts into English. Before assuming the mantle of his father, Rev. Shembe obtained a university degree from the University College of Fort Hare, South Africa. (Fort Hare was founded in the nineteenth century as a school for Africans by Scottish missionaries. It eventually became a university college and later a full university. Among its graduates were many African leaders, including Nelson Mandela.) Later Shembe worked as a school teacher. After his call to the leadership of the amaNazarties he encouraged education among his followers.

PRIMAL EXPERIENCES AND THE BIRTH OF THE AMANAZARITES

Anyone who has spent time with the amaNazarites knows that primal experiences play a key role in the formation of their beliefs and practices. When Londa Shembe described

---

43. See, e.g., Larry Hurtado, *One God, One Lord: Early Christian Devotion and Ancient Jewish Monotheism* (London: SCM Press, 1988).

Photo 6.11 The Right Reverend Londa Shembe having dinner in a Durban hotel with the author. Before receiving a call to succeed his father, Rev. Johannes Galilee Shembe, he completed a law degree and practiced as a lawyer in Durban. A highly educated man, he was brutally assassinated in 1989.

his call to the office of prophet and leader of the amaNazarite movement, he explained that as a young man and successful university graduate he was originally only interested in making money. For this reason he became a lawyer and developed a highly successful law practice in the city of Durban. After the death of his father, Johannes Galilee Shembe, he experienced three visionary dreams of such intensity that he gave up his law practice to become a spiritual leader. In these dreams his father's and his grandfather's hands reached toward him to pull him into the office of prophet, thus making him "the third Shembe."

His decision to abandon the bar in favor of becoming a religious leader was a difficult one, made even more difficult by the fact that his uncle, Amos Shembe, also claimed to be the rightful successor. The matter was complicated by the fact that his uncle was the older man. In Zulu society respect for the elder relatives and all older people in general is a cardinal virtue. Nevertheless, the power of the dreams was so great that he knew he had no choice but to assume the mantle of prophet. By contesting his uncle's claim to the leadership of the movement, Londa Shembe knew that he risked his life. Indeed, at the close of our last meeting in 1987 he described himself as a "hunted man," who lived in constant danger of assassination. Even so, he claimed that it had been revealed to him that he had nothing to fear because he would die at the age of 84. Two years later, when he was 48, the assassins struck and he was brutally murdered.[44]

Londa Shembe, an intelligent and well-educated man, gave up a promising future to risk death daily as a religious leader because he felt that this was what God, and his ancestors, had called him to do. In reaching this decision, he relied on amaNazarite myths and oral traditions for a framework to interpret his visions. For him, the reality of these visions was beyond doubt. They came to him as messages from his grandfather, Isaiah Shembe, and were vivid encounters with the divine that *compelled* him to lead the amaNazaretha, even at the risk of his life.

The role of myths in the life of Londa Shembe is crucial and helps explain why Oosthuizen and his critics so sharply disagreed about amaNazarite beliefs while remaining true to their own data. The myths of the amaNazaretha, some of which are recorded in various documents collected at the instigation of Bishop Johannes Galilee Shembe, enabled Londa Shembe and other members of the movement to continually interpret and reinterpret their

44. *Weekend Mercury* (Durban, South Africa), 8 April 1989; *Daily News* (Durban, South Africa), 8 April 1989.

primal experiences in terms of the group's own tradition. This very process of interpretation created new myths, which in turn shaped amaNazarite beliefs and practices and continue shaping them today.

It does not work to appeal to written or published texts to establish the correct interpretation of those same texts, as scholars like Sundkler and Vilakazi do. The texts of the amaNazarites may be subject to theological exegesis in the future, but at present they can be understood only within the context of the life of the community, where there is a dynamic interaction between primal experiences and an ever-evolving mythology.

INTERPRETING ISAIAH SHEMBE

Who was Isaiah Shembe? And is the amaNazarite movement an authentic expression of African Christianity? Or is it a syncretic cult merging African beliefs with Christianity to the detriment of both? By their own admission, neither Amos Shembe nor Londa Shembe really knew. In repeated interviews, they both affirmed quite openly that at times even they were uncertain as to the true identity of Isaiah Shembe and their own persona. Even so, both men acknowledged a historic debt to Christianity. Yet they both recognized that a wide spectrum of belief existed among their respective followers.[45]

Photo 6.12 Bishop Amos Shembe (1907–1996), uncle of Londa Shembe and leader of the larger of the two major amaNazarite movements. He was concerned to lead his group in a biblical direction and made no direct claim to be anything other than a bishop of the church. Like his father and other members of the Shembe family, he was a well-educated man with a university degree who also worked as a schoolteacher before assuming the leadership of the more traditional branch of the amaNazarites. In this photograph he is explaining the significance of various ceremonial robes.

Because he saw the future of the amaNazaretha within the Christian community, Amos Shembe encouraged his followers to read the Bible and sought to establish contacts with the South African Council of Churches and other bodies, as well as to educate his people in more generally accepted aspects of Christian theology. It is therefore safe to say that under his leadership the amaNazarites moved from being a new religious movement with distinctly prophetic elements toward being a more traditional Christian church. The prophetic remained, and remains, but the role of the Bible in the church grew under his guidance. He also sought to root the church's history in a broader Christian history and continued the projects of Johannes Galilee Shembe to gather and publish the texts and oral

45. These observations are based on interviews by the author with Amos and Londa Shembe in 1987 and subsequent telephone conversations.

histories of the church as a contribution to both its members and the Christian community generally.

Londa Shembe took a different tack. He did not encourage his followers to read the Bible, but rather told them to look to the life and teachings of his grandfather to find their own identity. At the time of his murder he was studying Hebrew through the University of South Africa in an attempt to probe the Jewish roots of the movement. In this way he hoped to find what he considered to be the true religious source of the amaNazarite movement outside of the Christian fold.

He believed amaNazarite roots were deep and complex and were to be found in a combination of the Hindu tradition, through contacts his grandfather had with Gandhi; in Judaism, through similarities between Old Testament practices and Zulu tradition; and, most surprising of all, in the religion of New Zealand Maoris.

The last claim, that somehow the Maoris influenced the rise of the amaNazarites, will no doubt strike many people as wishful thinking and quite absurd. Yet Londa Shembe insisted that his grandfather had met Maoris and spent a considerable amount of time discussing religion with them when he worked on the docks in the port city of Durban. The possibility that he was right is made clear by New Zealand historian James Belich in his book *Making Peoples: A History of New Zealanders*.[46] Belich points out that not only did Maoris join the crews of whaling ships as early as the 1820s, but they frequently visited the port of Durban, where Londa Shembe said his grandfather met them. Even more significant is the fact that prophetic movements

Photo 6.13 A group of dancers in traditional amaNazarite dress during their July Festival. These dancers were the followers of Bishop Amos Shembe.

Photo 6.14 A group of dancers belonging to the Right Reverend Londa Shembe's group, wearing new dancing attire, which he claimed was revealed to him in a dream.

46. James Belich, *Making Peoples: A History of New Zealanders from Polynesian Settlement to the End of the Nineteenth Century* (Auckland, New Zealand: Penguin, 1996).

appeared among Maoris as early as the 1830s and were a major social movement by the 1880s. Therefore, it is quite possible that Isaiah Shembe met Maori sailors and learned from them about the prophetic movements that played such an important role in their own society, where they revitalized traditional Maori religion by adding biblical insights.

The claim by Londa Shembe that he was the "third Shembe" also requires explanation. What he meant by this was that he had assumed the mantle of his father and grandfather as the spiritual leader of the amaNazaretha. In a letter he wrote, "Europeans call Isaiah Shembe a prophet." Then he explained that this term did not convey the full reality of the person of Shembe.

For him his grandfather was far more than a prophet. Who was Isaiah Shembe? To this question Londa Shembe answered, "I have made it plain to you again and again who I think Shembe was within the bounds of safety which the cultural domination of the West permits me (at the cost of my being called a lunatic)."[47] On another occasion he wrote, "Think about me as being both Londa Shembe and Isaiah Shembe and then you will understand ... Then move on and think again that to you I am Londa Shembe (or Johannes Galilee Shembe for that matter) and then you will see ... I am making an attempt to make you see my God through my eyes."[48]

RELIGIOUS STUDIES AND THE AMANAZARITES

Photo 6.15 A group of young children wearing the traditional dancing attire of the amaNazarites. Children like these represent the future of AICs throughout Africa and demonstrate the deep family roots of these movements.

The majority of religious studies scholars concentrate on religions of the written word. But as soon as we attempt to study African religions, primal religions, or new religions generally, we face a different task. Such religions are primarily based upon dynamic oral traditions that involve the ongoing interpretation of primal experiences. Therefore we must use different tools from those used to study established traditions with long literary histories.

Years ago Fred Welbourn argued, "Scholars of religion cannot simply sit in their studies to reflect on intellec-

47. Londa Shembe, undated letter to author, received February 1988.
48. Londa Shembe, letter to author, 29 February 1988.

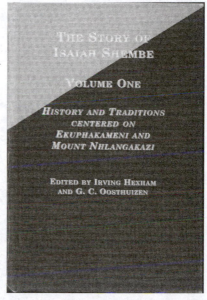

Photo 6.16 A picture of the first volume of the amaNazarite oral histories, which provide future generations with a record of the life and teachings of Isaiah Shembe.

tual truth. They must do that, but they must also go out into the world and get their hands dirty."[49] What this means is that if we are serious about studying the full spectrum of religion, and not just tidy traditions with long-established scriptures, we need to incorporate anthropological methods to allow us to engage in the empirical study of living religions. This, if nothing else, is the lesson we can learn from the debates about the person and work of Isaiah Shembe.

THE STORY OF
ISAIAH SHEMBE

VOLUME ONE

HISTORY AND TRADITIONS
CENTERED ON
EKUPHAKAMENI AND
MOUNT NHLANGAKAZI

EDITED BY IRVING HEXHAM
AND G. C. OOSTHUIZEN

---

49. Fred B. Welbourn, conversations with author, 1970–1974.

PART 3
THE YOGIC TRADITION

CHAPTER 7

THE ORIGINS OF YOGIC RELIGIONS

INTRODUCTION

The Indian subcontinent, or peninsula, can be roughly divided into three geographic regions. In the north the Himalaya Mountains separate India from Central Asia. Below the Himalayas are two vast plains irrigated by the Indus and Ganges rivers and separated by the Vindhya Mountains. Anyone who takes a close look at a relief map begins to see the natural zones of the Indian subcontinent. These three zones subdivide into numerous other geographic and cultural areas which today bear the names of distinct states. Close to the Himalayas are the Independent States of Nepal and Bhutan and the area known as Kashmir. Further south are the states of Bengal and Assam, while toward the southern tip of the subcontinent are places like Goa and Kerala, both of which have large Christian populations.

Many writers argue that the Himalaya Mountains isolated India from the outside world, allowing it to develop its own unique culture. Actually, in the northwest there are good passes through the mountains that over the centuries provided easy access to invaders. Less accessible passes also exist in the north and northeast of the subcontinent. Consequently the real importance of the Himalayas is that they acted as the barrier against the effects of chilling winds from the Arctic while trapping the monsoon winds to the south. The result was to create a highly fertile region capable of supporting a large population, even in ancient times.

Militarily, Afghanistan played a significant role in Indian history. From Afghanistan numerous invaders entered India, with the result that many Indian rulers, from the Mongols to the British, attempted to control Afghanistan. Anyone who was in the Boy Scouts or Girl Guides or has seen Walt Disney movies will know about Rudyard Kipling's famous *Jungle Book* stories and probably his less well-known adventures of *Kim*. In the stories about *Kim*, a young boy acts as a spy in what was known as "the Great Game," which is the term used by the British for their struggle against Russia to control Afghanistan.

One of the problems that plague those writing about the Indian subcontinent is what to call it. India, after all, is the British name for the entire area. Therefore, because it was the most widely used name for the area, it was retained by the Indian government after independence.

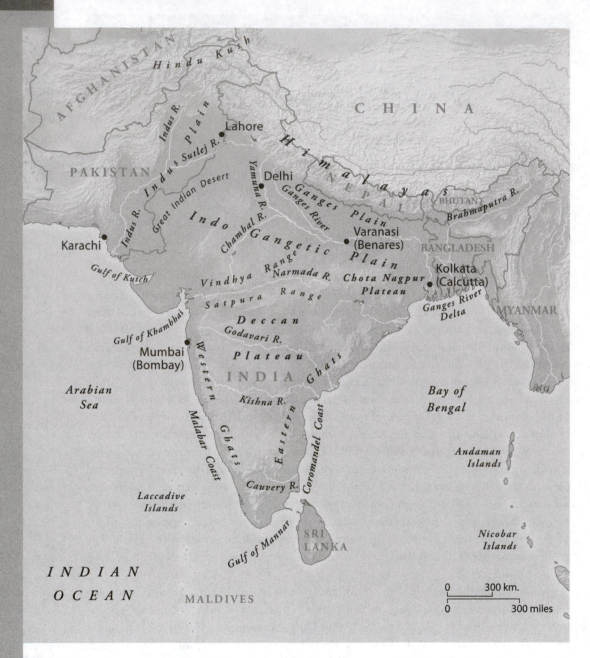

Map 7.1 Topographical map of the Indian subcontinent, showing its main cities and political boundaries as they exist today.

The problem, though, is that because India is a state, it excludes Pakistan and Bangladesh, both of which were part of "British India." For convenience, most people today use "India" or "modern India" to refer to the name of that state and speak of the entire area as "the Indian subcontinent."

IS "HINDUISM" THE RELIGION OF HINDUS?

Another problem concerns the major religion of the people of India. Both Muslim rulers and the British after them called the non-Muslim inhabitants of the subcontinent Hindus. Consequently, the term "Hinduism" began to be used to describe the religion of indigenous peoples. Following independence from British rule, many Indian intellectuals rejected the terms "Hindus" and "Hinduism" as something imposed by the British.

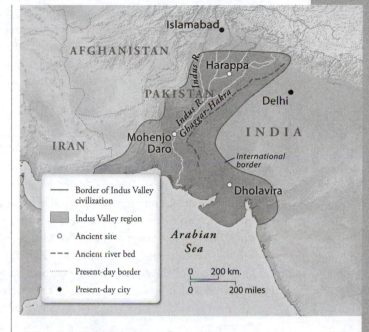

Map 7.2 The area occupied by the Indus Valley civilization, with the key cities identified.

Jawaharlal Nehru (1889–1964), who became prime minister of India, argued in his book *The Discovery of India* that words like "Hindu" and "Hinduism" ought to be discarded in favor of the word "Hindi."[1] This suggestion was quickly rejected by most people in India because Hindi is also one of the languages of India. Since there are fourteen main languages in modern India, with around 2000 dialects, each dialect being so different that they are virtually separate languages, no one wanted to privilege one language over another.

The philosopher Radhakrishnan (1888–1975), who became the vice-president of India, also argued in his book *The Hindu View of Life*[2] that "Hindu" actually referred to a particular territory and not a religion. Therefore, he believed it could easily be used to refer to all peoples of India. This suggestion was also rejected by many, because the term "Hindu" itself is of Persian origin and was used to designate a particular area for hundreds of years. Later, Muslims used it to refer to particular religious practices, not a territory.

Since the early 1970s the term "Hinduism" has gradually fallen into disuse among many scholars in Britain and North America, partly because of the objections of Indian intellectuals, like Nehru, following India's independence, and partly because of the feeling that somehow "Hinduism" connotes a unified religious system which never really existed. Therefore, it was seen as a category created by British imperialists and imposed on native

1. Jawaharlal Nehru, *The Discovery of India* (New Delhi: Oxford Univ. Press, 1959), 75–76.
2. Sarvepalli Radhakrishnan, *The Hindu View of Life* (London: Unwin, 1971; first published 1927), 12.

Indians. Most religious studies textbooks now use terms such as "the Hindu religious tradition" to identify the religions of India. It is important to note, however, that in India itself the terms "Hindu" and "Hinduism" are increasingly used by most Indians to refer to their own religious beliefs and practices. These preliminary considerations lead to a discussion of Indian religious beliefs and practices traditionally associated with Hinduism.

THE HISTORICAL ORIGINS OF HINDUISM

According to the historical framework of the great nineteenth-century scholar Max Müller, which still dominates scholarship today, Indian religious history began around the middle of the second millennium BC, when Indo-European-speaking peoples invaded India from the northwest. These peoples called themselves Aryans and were described by scholars as a warrior community equipped with horses, chariots, armor, and metal weapons. According to this account, the Aryans overran the dark-skinned indigenous peoples, known as Dravidians. Some of these Dravidian peoples were said to have lived in fortified cities that were destroyed by the militarily superior Aryans.[3]

The exploits of the Aryans, Müller argued, were reflected in religious texts, the most important of which was the *Rig Veda*. These were passed down for centuries as part of a carefully preserved oral tradition until around the fifteenth century AD. At that time various Hindu oral traditions were written down in the Mughal Courts on the orders of Muslim rulers who wanted to know what Hindus believed. Later, during the nineteenth century, the British continued the tradition of converting these rich oral traditions into written texts, even though the idea of a written text was totally foreign to the peoples for whom these traditions were sacred.

Photo 7.1 An Indus Valley site before excavation. Note that today the area is semidesert. Yet at its height the Indus Valley civilization supported a large population in a rich agricultural area, suggesting major climate change.

This basic theme of Aryan exploits as the key to Indian history was further elaborated in the 1920s with the discovery of what became known as the Indus Valley civilization. The accidental discovery of this large, clearly prosperous, and previously unknown civilization revolutionized the history of India. These discoveries appeared to provide a context to the hymns of the *Rig Veda*, the earliest scripture of the Hindu tradition, thus confirming Müller's speculations. Passages in the *Rig Veda* that referred to gods such as Indra hurling thunderbolts were now seen as mythological references to the destruction of the Indus Valley civilization.

---

3. An interesting discussion of these ideas and more recent opinions is found in Gavin Flood, *An Introduction to Hinduism* (Cambridge: Cambridge Univ. Press, 1996), 23–50. The issue is also discussed in more detail later in this chapter.

Suddenly, Indian history became surprisingly clear. Prior to the Aryan invasions, a flourishing civilization, founded about 2500 BC by dark-skinned peoples, had existed in the Indus Valley. This civilization was said to have been based on the "twin cities" of Harappa and Mohenjo-daro, the "mound of the dead," which are about four hundred miles apart along the Indus Valley. By ancient standards both cities were large and sophisticated. Harappa had a circumference of almost four miles and at its peak supported a population of around 40,000. It also had advanced sewage and drainage systems and was built on grid patterns that allocated clearly defined living areas to different trades and other classes.

Around 1500 BC, however, the Aryan invaders massacred the inhabitants of these large cities to establish a new order in India based on skin color. At the top of the new system were the light-skinned Aryans, who were priests, warriors, and traders. At the bottom were the dark-skinned Dravidian peoples, who became members of a large servant class.

The new invaders brought with them a series of gods similar in many ways to the gods of the Greeks, to whom the invaders were physically related. The story of these gods and, many believe, of early Aryan history is found in the earliest Hindu scriptures, the Vedas.

Consequently, ancient history was fairly easily explained. The Aryans had originated somewhere in Central Asia, from where a wave of migrations led different tribal groups to invade parts of northern Europe, Greece, Persia, or modern Iran, and eventually India. These invaders originally shared a common language and religion, but over time the languages diverged to create a family of languages known as the Indo-European languages. Religiously, too, the different groups of Aryans gradually drifted apart, merging with local populations and adopting local customs and beliefs.

In India this meant that over a long time, estimated at around a thousand years, the Aryans gradually absorbed the customs, practices, and beliefs of the Dravidians they had conquered. This absorption, historians argued, led to the development of what became the caste system within Indian society, which was clearly based on skin color. Thus lighter-skinned peoples retained key governmental and religious functions, while darker-skinned peoples did menial work.

Indian religion, which scholars originally called Hinduism, was then placed within a general evolutionary framework. First, it was said, the Aryans had little interest in philosophical speculation or any of the basic beliefs that typify modern Hinduism. Rather, they adhered to a warrior creed that centered on sacrifice. At the center of the sacrificial system were the priests, whose sacrifices sometimes involved the death of as many as a thousand horses.

All the time, however, the rather materialistic rewards of sacrifice provided less satisfaction for a people that had transformed itself from nomadic warriors to sedentary agriculturalists. Therefore, a new set of religious interests gradually emerged, clearly incorporating ideas from the pre-Aryan cults of India. At first these were simply magical treaties intended to make the life of the farmer more livable. Later, over several hundred years, a new set of philosophical beliefs emerged that were actually in sharp contrast to the earlier form of sacrificial religion found in the Vedas. Instead of sacrifice, self-knowledge and questions about the essential nature of existence came to the fore. Somewhere around 700 BC these speculations gradually distilled into what became known as the Upanishads. Now a new, world-renouncing religion

Early Evolutionary view of Indian Religious Traditions

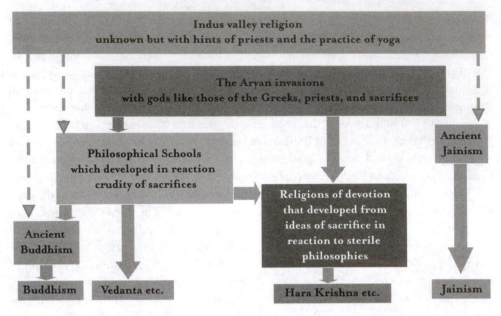

Figure 7.1 The traditional view of the development of Indian religions. In this view the Aryans, northern warrior tribes who resembled the ancient Greeks, conquered preexisting Indian societies and imposed their own religion on them, which was centered on sacrifices to many gods. Centuries later, philosophical Hinduism developed, but this proved too abstract for most people, leading to the development of devotional Hindu traditions several centuries later. Buddhism became a reform movement within Hinduism, while the Jains occupied an uncertain position, either as an ancient survival from earlier Indian religions or as another Hindu reform movement.

came into being that saw all things as part of an original being or essence, known as Brahman. Life became a series of rebirths. Thereafter the aim of religion was to break the bonds of karma and enter into union with either God or the gods, or to be absorbed into the Void.

It took around a thousand years for this religion to permeate Indian society. At the same time, many other Hindu reform movements, such as Jainism and Buddhism, sprang up. All these religions embraced philosophical reflection and the renunciation of life.

Toward the end of this period of Indian history, popular discontent with an abstract and impersonal religious quest spread among the common people. As a result Indian religious history entered a new phase that combined the personal deities of the Vedic tradition with aspects of ideas found in the Upanishads, modified by intense personal devotion to individual gods. These new religions became known as Bhakti, or devotional movements. With the emergence of Bhakti, numerous groups devoted to personalized gods flourished, reaching a height between AD 700 and 1200.

Popular epics such as *Mahabharata* and *Ramayana* predated the emergence of full-blown Bhakti; nevertheless, they were ideally suited for incorporation into this outpouring of popular piety. Over time a number of extremely gifted philosophers, such as Sankara (788–838) and Ramanuja (1017–1130), added depth to what would otherwise have remained shallow folk religions.

Indian religious history changed decisively when Islamic invaders began a series of incursions in the eighth century, leading to the conquest of northern India and the establishment of a sultanate in Delhi in the thirteenth century. Gradually, Muslim control spread over a large part of India, culminating in the establishment of the Mughal Empire in the sixteenth century.

During the long period of Muslim rule in northern India, Hinduism generally went into decline. When European traders arrived in the sixteenth century, Hinduism appeared to be a jumble of superstitions and fanatical practices that sharply contrasted with the orderly religion of the Muslim courts of

Photo 7.2 An Indian holy man walking through the Srinagar Bazaar. Although made in the early twentieth century, the painting suggests that such figures are to be found throughout Indian history going back to the Indus Valley civilization.

northern India. By the time of the establishment of the British East India Company's empire, Hinduism appeared to be a dying religion. As a result, James Mill (1773–1836), the father of famous British philosopher John Stuart Mill (1806–1873) and an agnostic exponent of utilitarian philosophy, wrote at length about the superstitions of the Hindus in his book *The History of British India*.[4] He respected ancient Hinduism and the achievements of Hindus in the past, but he considered the Hindus a largely degenerate people and regarded Muslims as infinitely superior.

Despite the scorn that East India Company officials expressed for Hinduism, they were nevertheless very conscious that religious strife might disrupt their trading activities. Therefore, as far as possible, they attempted to maintain the status quo. This meant the exclusion of missionaries, particularly Christian missionaries, from areas under their control. Only in the 1820s, yielding to public pressure in England, where the

Photo 7.3 This painting by Lord Robert Baden-Powell, the founder of the scouting movement, was made while he served as an officer in India. It captures the essence of "British India" by depicting the entrance to a major Punjab fort with a Sikh lancer, from the fiercely proud Indian army, in the foreground. Although the British ruled India for almost 250 years, they never had more than six thousand British troops at their service. The bulk of the highly efficient Indian army was made up of local troops.

GATEWAY OF THE FORT, PATIALA

---

4. James Mill, *The History of British India* (London: Baldwin, Cradock, and Joy, 1820).

evangelical revival had brought about a major change in religious consciousness, did they allow missions and missionaries to enter areas under their control. Before that, missionaries had to go to parts of India controlled by other European powers.

With the arrival of Christian missionaries and the gradual expansion of East India Company control, leading to the eventual creation of the Indian Empire and the direct British control of the entire subcontinent, the religious situation changed again. Hindus and many Muslims generally welcomed Christian schools and sent their children to them to obtain a better education than was otherwise available. The missionaries welcomed such pupils in the belief that eventually they would convert to Christianity. Many did, but many others did not, with the result that most Indian leaders in the twentieth century were educated at mission schools and colleges, regardless of their religious beliefs and background. All this led to what became known as the Hindu renaissance of the late nineteenth century.

Following Indian independence in 1948, the predominantly Muslim areas of northwest and northeast India separated from the largely Hindu areas that constitute modern India. The new Muslim state that resulted was known as Pakistan. It eventually split into Pakistan and Bangladesh in 1971, when Bengali East Pakistan separated from Pakistan in the West. India, however, remained a unified nation with a large Muslim population of around 50 million people. Today India dominates the entire subcontinent and is a rapidly expanding industrial power. In this new state, since 1948, the Hindu religion has revived and revitalized itself.

THE INDUS VALLEY CIVILIZATION

Until recently, the "timeless civilization" of the Indus Valley, which lasted over a thousand years, was said by scholars to have been ruled by priest kings who reigned from an area of cities that were dubbed "citadels." Then, it was argued, sometime around 1500 BC the cities were destroyed by a cataclysmic event that British archaeologists Sir Mortimer Wheeler (1890–1976) and Stuart Piggott (1910–1996) identified with the supposed Aryan invasions. To support this hypothesis they pointed to skeletal remains found in Harrappa as evidence that the city's inhabitants were massacred.

Various pieces of art engraved on soft stones, known as seals, were used to interpret the religion of the people, to claim that it had an affinity with latter-day Hinduism, and to suggest that over time the "Aryan invaders" had slowly absorbed the religion of their conquered peoples. Therefore, the religion of the *Rig Veda* was interpreted as an expression of Aryan religion that later was reinterpreted to incorporate it into what became Hinduism.

Since Indian independence, the governments of both India and Pakistan have lavishly promoted archaeological research into the prehistory of the subcontinent. Over the past twenty-five years, the findings from this research have gradually

Photo 7.4 Grave of an adult man from Harappa.

changed perceptions of the Indus Valley civilization and seriously challenged the received interpretation, which still holds sway in most religious studies textbooks. Perhaps the best introduction to these discoveries is Gregory L. Possehl's *The Indus Civilization*.[5] In this work numerous myths about the Indus Valley civilization and its religion are discussed. What follows summarizes this work and the scholarship it presents.

The first misunderstanding to be debunked is that the Indus Valley civilization centered on the "twin cities" of Harappa and Mohenjo-daro. We now know that there were at least ten cities in the network of urban centers that belonged to this civilization. In addition there were at least seventy other, smaller settlements.

The second misunderstanding is that the Indus Valley civilization was ruled by priest kings. This was based on the discovery of a small figurine identified as representing such a ruler. Recent archaeological work has thrown doubt on this popular interpretation. The figurine originally identified as a priest king now seems far more ambiguous than originally thought. It may be the bust of a priest or even a king, but more recent finds of numerous human figures in a variety of poses throughout the Indus Valley area show that the figure could equally be simply a seated man.

Photo 7.5 The "Narrative" or "Deity" seal from Mohenjo-daro. A human figure appears to be kneeling before another figure. Although the seal's meaning is not certain, it is usually described as "narrative seal with a deity, human head on a stool, kneeling worshiper, and seven figures."

The third misunderstanding to be corrected concerns the "citadels," which, it is now recognized, were not citadels at all but raised mounds, whose purpose is unclear. What is clear, though, is that they were not used for defense.

Fourth, it is now known that the buildings earlier archaeologists identified as granaries were not, though what they were remains unclear.

Fifth, the towns and cities of the Indus Valley civilization were not all built from baked brick as was previously thought. The only city in the Indus Valley built of baked brick was actually Mohenjo-daro, a fact that demolishes the idea of identical cities built to serve some ritual purpose.

Sixth, archeologists now recognize that not one ethnic group but many inhabited the Indus Valley. Therefore, the idea that its inhabitants were Dravidians who were replaced by invading Aryans is dealt a serious blow.

A final misunderstanding is that the skeletal remains found in Mohenjo-daro were evidence of a massacre by Aryan invaders. Today it is recognized that these deaths were not the result of a massacre, and there is no evidence that the civilization was destroyed by an invading force.

Although no one knows for certain what brought about the decline of the Indus Valley civilization, some sort of ecological disaster seems most likely. This hypothesis is supported by satellite photograph indicating a major geological change around 1700 BC. Whatever happened toward the end of the Indus Valley civilization, it caused one major river to dry up and another to change its course.

5. Gregory L. Possehl, *The Indus Civilization* (Walnut Creek, Calif.: AltaMira, 2002).

Photo 7.6 The so-called Yoga Seal. Notice the way the matchstick figure seems to be sitting in a yoga position reminiscent of later Hindu practices. Compare this with a photograph of a modern Hindu, or Westerner, sitting in the yoga position, and you will immediately recognize the similarity.

All of this points to massive flooding and widespread chaos similar to the floods that engulfed New Orleans in 2005, yet without modern means of rescue or pumps to remove floodwaters. Consequently, most Indus Valley cities, though not all, seem to have been abandoned around this time.

One feature of the Indus Valley civilization that separates it from later Indian religious practice is that no clearly identified places of worship have been discovered. Although there is no firm evidence about the religion practiced by the people of the Indus Valley civilization, it seems likely that it was based on a religion much like later Hinduism.

Other features have come to light that support the idea of continuity between the religious practices of the Indus Valley civilization and later Hinduism. First, it seems likely that many of the large number of the terra-cotta figures discovered in the Indus Valley served a religious function. While there is no overwhelming evidence of a mother goddess cult, these figures, which prominently display sexual organs, suggest fertility.

Second, among the seals discovered in the Indus Valley is one that some archaeologists have claimed represents a forerunner of the Hindu god Shiva. Although the Shiva seal is unique, there are several other seals that are similar, supporting the idea that some sort of religious cult with yoga-like practices existed in the Indus Valley. A number of other seals, and some buffalo figurines, seem to have religious significance. There are also a number

of seals with sexual connotations similar to those found in what is known as Shaktism, which is a highly sensual form of mysticism that occurs in later Hindu traditions. In particular, one seal appears to show a bull

Photo 7.7 The "Great Bath" at Mohenjo-daro. Anyone who has visited a Hindu temple with its own bath cannot avoid noticing the similarity in structure between later Hindu ritual baths and the one at Mohenjo-daro.

about to have intercourse with a woman. There are also indications of a male-female duality similar to that found in later Shaktism, involving objects known as *lingams* and *yonis*, which represent sexual organs and play an important role in later Hinduism.

Equally important to the reconstruction of Indus Valley religion is the fact that everyone agrees water played an unusually prominent role in this civilization. There appears to be little reason to doubt that its inhabitants revered water and participated in water rituals, the most famous being associated with what is known as the Great Bath in Mohenjo-daro. This, of course, is highly significant, because ritual ablutions play an important part in the development of later Hinduism. Apart from water, which is a recurrent theme throughout the area, there seems to be some indication that fire altars existed, although the evidence remains unclear.

Another Hindu feature was discovered in the city of Lothal, Gujarat, 450 miles southeast of Mohenjo-daro. This involved three sets of graves, each containing the remains of a male accompanied by a female. To some this suggests an early indication of the later Hindu practice of *suttee*, involving the death of widows, who are expected to accompany their husbands to the grave. Even more intriguing was the discovery in 1946 of burial urns used in conjunction with cremations at Harrapa. These were

Photo 7.8 Statuette known as the "Priest King," found at Mohenjo-daro. Whether he is a priest or a king is highly debatable.

decorated with peacocks, bulls, and the *pipal* leaf. The significance of this is that in later Buddhism the papal leaf became an important motif. Taken together, all of this evidence suggests a wide diversity of religious belief and practice throughout the Indus Valley area.

Finally, it is important to stress that many small carved stones identified as seals have been discovered throughout the Indus Valley and elsewhere. These "seals" contain pictures of humans, animals, and vegetation, as well as a distinct written script. Yet, despite repeated claims to the contrary, the script itself has not been deciphered. Nevertheless, from the appearance of the script some of its features become clear. For example, it is generally agreed that this was a system of pictographs and not an alphabet. It is also thought that the system employed suffixes and not prefixes. If this is correct, then it seems to indicate that whatever the language was, it did not belong to the Indo-European group. Therefore, it is possibly a form of a pre-Aryan language.

All this means that a great deal of mystery still surrounds the Indus Valley civilization. Yet with advances in computer technology and the application of DNA research it may be possible both to decipher the language and to reach credible conclusions about the ethnic origins of the Indus Valley peoples. How long such research will take is anyone's guess.

THE ARYAN INVASION THESIS RECONSIDERED

Several things need to be considered when assessing the Aryan invasion thesis, which is still taught as fact in many religious studies textbooks. First, fifty years of intensive archaeological research in both the Indus Valley area and the northern part of the subcontinent has failed to uncover any evidence of a violent invasion corresponding to the assumed dates of the Aryan invasion. Equally significant is the fact that no evidence of a mass migration has been clearly demonstrated. Instead, numerous sites show continuous occupation, with intact pottery traditions from the distant past to around 500 BC.

Second, most peoples retain some legendary accounts about ancient migrations and a distant homeland from which their first ancestors came. Such stories are totally absent from traditional Indian folk tales and literature. Instead, it is always assumed that India was the home of Indians. This assumption that Indians were indigenous to India is supported to some extent by archaeological evidence.

From around 5000 BC various pottery traditions and other archaeological finds suggest distinct regional cultures. Then, by 2600 BC there is a gradual merging of cultures in the area that are recognized as part of the Indus Valley civilization. For about a thousand years after 1700 BC there is scant archaeological evidence. Then, gradually, a homogeneous culture seems to emerge that by AD 700 is clearly Hindu. What stands out in Indian archaeology is that, as far as pottery and other archaeological remains are concerned, there is a remarkable continuity from earlier to later periods.

Another key feature of the Aryan invasion theory was the possession of horses by the Aryans and the assumption that the indigenous peoples of India did not possess horses, or at least had not domesticated them. More recently, archaeological evidence for the domestication of horses has been found at various Indus Valley civilization and earlier sites. Cave paintings of mounted riders dating back to before 4000 BC have also been discovered. Archaeology also shows that the skeletal remains found in the Indus Valley cities display the same range of ethnic diversity found in modern India. This suggests that light- and dark-skinned peoples lived alongside one another for at least five thousand years.

Another piece of evidence is the *Rig Veda*'s description of a river system in India that appears similar to the one revealed by satellite imagery as having existed before 2000 BC. Similarly, astronomical references in the *Rig Veda* suggest a well-developed calendar system that was capable of tracking the movement of the planets as they would have been seen in India at least as far back as 3000 BC.

All these considerations imply that the Aryans may well have originated in India. This raises important

Photo 7.9 The Great Bath at Mohenjo-daro, seen in photograph 7.7, is one of the main pieces of evidence used by scholars who link Indus Valley religious practices to those of later Hindu religion. The photo above of the great bath in the Hindu temple at Madura, in South India, seems remarkably similar to the Mohenjo-daro bath, despite an interval of almost four thousand years.

questions about the relationship of the Aryans to the Hittites, Greeks, and other European peoples to whom they are said to be linguistically related. Is it possible, some Indian historians ask, that instead of invading India, the Aryans actually moved out of India into other areas? If so, the whole of prehistory will have to be rewritten.

REACTIONS TO NEW IDEAS ABOUT INDIAN HISTORY

Despite the radical suggestions considered above, most historians reject these views on linguistic and other grounds. They continue to believe that the Aryans originated in the area around the Caspian and Black seas, from where they began to migrate around 2000 BC. As a result they are seen as ancestors of Italian, Greek, German, English, Celtic, and Indian peoples. Modifying the earlier "invasion theory," some scholars suggest that although the Aryans may not have invaded India or entered it as part of a mass migration, they gradually moved into India over several hundred years as part of a migration that may have begun as far back as 3000 BC. This modified view explains the diverse races found in Indus Valley cities and seems to meet many of the objections to the earlier theory. It also fits with the linguistic evidence upon which the Aryan invasion theory was based.

Photo 7.10 An ancient Indian reliquary from around AD 700, said to contain the relics of the Buddha. Note the style of the pot.

To place these issues in context, consider the changes in Europe that have taken place over the last fifty years. Before 1945 Europe was inhabited primarily by light-skinned Caucasian peoples who nominally, at least, were Christians. Although there were a few Africans and Indians living in Europe from at least the Middle Ages, their numbers were very small. Then, from the 1960s onward as a result of migration, large numbers of African, Indian, Turkish, and to an extent Korean and Chinese peoples have settled in Europe.

So great and yet so gradual has this migration been that today it is estimated that many Europeans cities, like London, Berlin, and Paris, already have large non-Caucasian minorities. Further, many people

Photo 7.11 Picture of a potter with his pots, painted around 1900 by Mortimer Menpes.

The Origins of Yogic Traditions in India

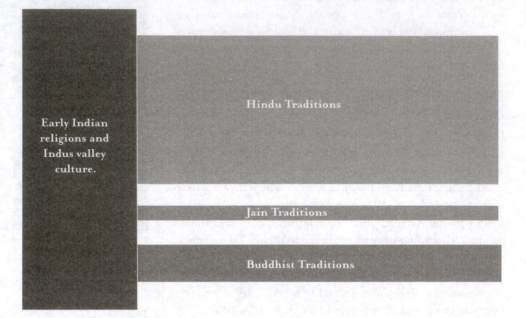

Figure 7.2 An alternative view of the development of Indian religions, based on a changing understanding of Indian history. In this view the Aryan invasion thesis is downplayed and all major Indian traditions have roots that go back to the earliest times.

believe that by AD 2020 the majority of people living in the major cities of Europe will be Muslim.

Imagine an archaeologist in three or four thousand years attempting to explain the rapid change in population and places of worship in European cities during the late twentieth and early twenty-first centuries. Surely, it would be very easy to argue that Europe was devastated by war, followed by the invasion of technologically superior Asian races who were followers of Islam.

This example shows how dangerous it is to speculate about the past. Although an enormous amount of archaeological work has taken place in India over the last fifty years, less than 1 percent of all possible archaeological sites have been excavated. In the future, new archaeological finds could totally revise our view of Indian history, and the Aryan invasion theory might be reinstated as the undisputed truth.

CHAPTER 8

THE RICHNESS OF THE HINDU TRADITION

THE LITERATURE OF THE HINDU TRADITION

The meaning of "Veda" is knowledge. There are four main collections of Vedas which together constitute the Vedic corpus: the *Rig Veda*, the *Sama Veda*, the *Yajur Veda*, and the *Atharva Veda*.[1] Each Veda in turn contains various types of text. The *Samhitas* are collections of hymns, the *Brahmanas* are ritual treaties, the *Aranyakas* are forest writings, and the *Upanishads* are the instructions of a teacher.[2]

Closely associated to the Vedas are the Upanishads, each of which relates to a specific Veda. Thus, the *Taittiriya Upanishad* expounds the meaning of verses in the *Yajur Veda*, while an interpretation of the *Sama Veda* is found in the *Chandogya Upanishad*. Expositions of the *Rig Veda* are found in various Upanishads, such as the *Aitreya Upanishad*.

The most problematic of the Vedas for European scholarship and sophisticated Hindus is the *Atharva Veda*, which consists of magical spells, healing remedies, love potents, curses, and similar incantations. To modern readers, and scholars like Max Müller, this Veda appears to be particularly "primitive" and lacking in spirituality, although it contains much information similar to that found in many so-called New Age texts.

For Hindus the Vedas are sacred texts and the basis of all Indian philosophical thought. But unlike the Bible, they are rarely read or studied by anyone other than ritual specialists and students in Western countries. The sounds associated with the various Vedas and their repetition are more important to Hindus than the study of the Vedas. This is because reciting the Vedas is believed to have cosmic significance. Therefore, although a few Vedic hymns are well known and in common use in major rituals and private devotions, most are unknown to the average Hindu.

---

1. An excellent and free source for Hindu and other sacred texts is J. B. Hare's *Internet Sacred Texts Archive*, which is also available at a modest price on CD. It can be found at www.sacred-texts.com. Some of the translations are dated, but it is free and contains many classic works.
2. The classic discussion of these and other Indian texts is found in J. N. Farquhar, *An Outline of the Religious Literature of India* (Oxford: Oxford Univ. Press, 1920; Delhi: Motilal Banarsidass, 1967). Generally, Farquhar's comments and conclusions hold even today.

Within the Hindu tradition the Brahmins are an exclusive class, or caste, whose duty it is to preserve the purity of the Vedas and repeat them from memory on ritual occasions. Not all Brahmins perform this function, but only Brahmins are considered worthy of such honors. Therefore, the Brahmins as a group are the true custodians of the Hindu religious tradition and its sacred texts. Assuming this role, they preserved the Vedas as an oral tradition for centuries, and many, even today, maintain that only the memorized and sung or spoken Veda is truly a Veda. Because the Vedas were preserved orally for many centuries, dating them is notoriously difficult. According to tradition, the most famous Veda, the *Rig Veda*, was composed around 2000 BC, if not much earlier, while all of the other Vedic hymns are said to have been composed before 900 BC. In the nineteenth century, Western scholars like Max Müller (1823–1900) dated the *Rig Veda* around 1500 BC, while Max Weber (1864–1920) thought 2000 BC was a more accurate date.[3] Modern scholars rarely deviate from these dates. Flood, for example, provides a concise discussion of the issue, suggesting that the "earliest text" of the *Rig Veda* was "composed probably around 1200 BCE."[4] Yet like other authors, he fails to discuss the issue of documentary sources.

The first attempts to preserve the Vedas in writing began in the Muslim courts of India in the sixteenth century. Later in the nineteenth century, various British administrators and scholars began to systematically collect and record Hindu traditions, including sacred texts. Consequently, our earliest extant copies of the Vedas date from the sixteenth century, while the majority of preserved Vedic texts are no older than the nineteenth century. On the other hand, we have many Buddhist and other texts that cite passages from the Vedas dating from the seventh century onward.[5]

Given the amount of space in introductory textbooks devoted to discussions about the date and sources of both Old and New Testament documents, it is surprising that questions about the source, date, origins, and reliability of Vedic manuscripts are ignored by most textbooks. Instead, readers are provided with either the traditional dates or those suggested by scholars like Müller for the composition of Vedas without any consideration of the dates or condition of the earliest surviving manuscripts.

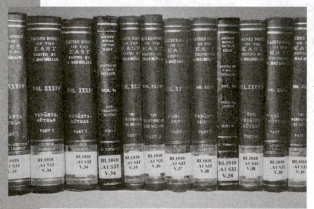

Photo 8.1 Max Müller's fifty-volume *Sacred Books of the East*, published between 1879 and 1894, with an Index volume appearing in 1910, established the study of religions of Indian origin in the universities of Europe and North America. It also made the study of published texts central to what became religious studies.

3. Benjamin Walker, *Hindu World* (London: George Allen, and Unwin, 1968), 2:294.
4. Gavin Flood, *An Introduction to Hinduism* (Cambridge: Cambridge Univ. Press, 1996), 37–78.
5. Walker, *Hindu World*, 370.

As sacred texts, the Vedas are considered by most Hindus to be a revelation and, as such, authoritative. Exactly what is meant by revelation in the Hindu tradition is a matter of dispute. For some philosophical schools, the Vedas are supernatural revelations lacking human involvement. For others, such as the logicians of the Nyaya School, the Vedas are the revelation of God and, as such, infallible. Thus, for members of this school, the Vedas have a status similar to that of the Bible among traditional Christians, who believe God revealed the Bible to humans through the medium of inspired individuals.

Other Hindu thinkers took a different view about the meaning of revelation. The best known of these interpretations is that of Vedanta, the dominant school of Indian philosophy today and by far the best known in the West. For members of this school, the Vedas are eternal texts, revealed to humankind by seers known as *rsis*, who merely transmitted their content without any human intervention, simply reciting the divine revelation. In many ways this Vedantic understanding mirrors the Muslim understanding of revelation, or *wahy*, which claims that Muhammad recited the Qur'an as he received it from God.

Interpretation of the Vedas is at least as varied as that of the Bible. Unlike classical Islam, which has several clearly defined schools of interpretation, the Hindu tradition has been remarkably flexible. Through the centuries numerous modes of interpreting the texts and expounding the meanings of the Vedas emerged. These interpretations originated in the great epic poems of the *Ramayana* and the *Mahabharata*, which are sometimes called the fifth Veda. They are also found in those texts known as the *Puranas* and works of the legendary Bharata, who composed his famous *Natya sastra* sometime around AD 300. Although the earliest fragmentary form of this major text dates from the fifth century AD, its exact date of composition is uncertain.

In addition to clearly Vedic works, numerous oral and written compositions, especially in Southern India, rival the Vedas as sources of Hindu piety.[6] Although many of these are presented as commentaries on the Vedas, others have no connection with the Vedic corpus yet are venerated by local communities as equal to the Vedas themselves. Many of these texts take the form of sutras or collections of scripture. These are often said to have been compiled by a great saint, scholar, or holy man and are frequently presented as aphorisms.

HINDU EPIC LITERATURE

Technically the epics are *smri*, or what is remembered and taught. Practically they are the main medium for conveying Hindu beliefs. Composed around AD 500—some say 500 BC—the stories of these epics are taught to young children, who often know the broad outlines as well as particular verses by heart.

The shortest of the epics is the *Ramayana*, which forms the basis of plays, dances, and numerous artistic expressions from India to Thailand and Indonesia. The story is relatively simple. The young prince Rama is born in the capital of the kingdom of Kosala, where he has three brothers from different mothers in polygamous marriages. Unfortunately,

---

6. Julius Lipner provides an interesting survey of Hindu beliefs and practices in relation to the Indian literary tradition in his *Hindus: Their Religious Beliefs and Practices* (London: Routledge, 1994).

Photo 8.2 This Indus Valley seal is typical of a number of similar seals that contain what is clearly some sort of story, with a man killing an oxen on the right and a yoga figure on the left. Here there seems to be some sort of link between the myths and practices of the Indus Valley culture and later Indian religion.

the handsome and intelligent young prince falls foul of one of these wives who is his mother's rival. As a result, on the day of his father's coronation, he is sent into exile to fulfill a promise his father recklessly made to this envious wife.

Although exiling his favorite son breaks the father's heart, he has no other choice but to break a sacred promise. Undaunted, Rama cheerfully leaves home and lives in the forest, accompanied by his beautiful wife, Sita, and a faithful brother, Laksmana, who refuses to leave him. The shock of forcing his son into exile causes Rama's father to die of grief. Bharata, the heir apparent, returns from a journey to find his father dead and his brothers in exile. Although he begs Rama to return to the kingdom, it is to no avail. Rama remains in the forest, believing he must fulfill his father's last wish.

Then Rama's beautiful wife is kidnapped by the demon king of Sri Lanka. When she refuses to abandon her husband and remains chaste, the evil king imprisons her. In the meantime, devastated by grief, Rama begins to search for his wife with the help of his brother and a band of monkeys led by the divine monkey king Hanuman. With the help of the monkeys, Sita's whereabouts are discovered, and an expedition is launched to rescue her. After an epic battle Rama defeats the evil king and rescues his wife. Now a whole series of travails follow, during which Rama doubts the loyalty and chastity of his wife, but she is eventually vindicated by her spiritual goodness and virtue.

Hindus see in this epic all the virtues of a good wife, loyalty between father and son, and numerous other social and spiritual goods. On the surface, this is a rattling good adventure story. For Hindus, however, there is a deeper spiritual significance, with many lessons to be learned.

In one interpretation, dating from around the thirteenth century, the sufferings of the faithful wife, Sita, saved humans from evil. In other interpretations the trials of Rama and Sita represent the trials of the human soul. Still other interpretations see Rama as the incarnation of the god Vishnu and understand the story in terms of the relationship of Vishnu to humans. However the epic is interpreted, the monkey god Hanuman plays a crucial role and becomes a worthy object of worship.

The other great epic is the *Mahabharata*. This enormously long story tells of the trials of descendants of Bharata and of the Great War between the Kauravas clan and their close relatives, the Pandavas clan. Central to this epic is a story of Krishna and the young prince

Arjuna, which forms the basis of the best-known text in Indian literature, the *Bhagavad Gita*, commonly known as the *Gita*.

The *Bhagavad Gita* is regarded by many, and was regarded by Gandhi, as the most important of all Hindu religious books. Written around AD 300 (though some scholars argue it was written as early as 300 BC), the *Gita* tells the story of the interaction of Prince Arjuna with his charioteer, who, unknown to him, is actually a manifestation of the god Krishna. Arjuna, a member of the Pandavas clan, is stricken by grief at the thought of slaughtering his cousins in the Kauravas clan. Before the battle he becomes so downcast that he begins to discuss his troubles, doubts, and questions with his charioteer.

Most of the *Gita* revolves around this great conversation. In it Krishna guides Arjuna to an understanding of the nature of human life and the relationship of the soul to its destiny. Krishna describes the soul as untouched by human senses, thoughts, and actions.

Just as humans change clothing, so too does the soul move from body to body in the cycle of transmigration. Inhabiting numerous bodies that live and die, the soul moves on through time until eventually it is liberated from the vicious cycle of birth and death to which it is bound to the wheel of *samsara*. In the Hindu tradition,

Photo 8.3 The figure of Krishna, seen in many different poses, plays a central role in both Indian art and the *Bhagavad Gita*.

samsara is usually pictured as the ever turning wheel of time to which all living things are bound by karma; in turn, karma is the belief that all things are embraced by a universal law of cause and effect that stretches through time, binding living beings to the wheel of samsara. Consequently, the soul never dies, though numerous bodies die. The soul is never born and never killed, and experiences nothing of the trauma of this world, which in reality is illusory.

Arjuna therefore must learn not to feel pity, sorrow, or grief. His role is to do his duty. This duty, or dharma, is to fight for righteousness and repudiate cowardice. If he fails in his duty, evil will triumph and his people will be lost. Gradually, as the conversation progresses, Krishna reveals his deity to Arjuna. Thus the young prince is granted a vision of the divine that forms the crowning act of the *Gita*.

Through the *Gita*, Hindu monotheism develops from abstract principles and the theoretical identification of individual gods with the one God into an intensely personal form of devotion. The one cosmic being is now identified with a highly personal God who takes an intimate interest in each individual soul. Yet, unlike the attitude of the God Christians worship, this interest in the individual is an interest in the eternal soul, not a particular person. Consequently, Arjuna learns to detach himself from personal feeling and the cares of this life and to act on an intellectual conviction of what he believes is right for his people, regardless of its effects upon himself as a person or on the people he is forced to kill.

Although most Hindus claim that the Vedas are the source of their religious beliefs and practices, the great epics of the *Ramayana* and *Mahabharata* form the practical basis of most Hindu religious life. From the reading of these epics, the presentation of their stories in films and plays, and more recently their appearance on television, Hindus gain entry to the rich mythology and religious teachings of their tradition.

THE HINDU LAW CODES

Two major works provided Hindu rulers and their followers with instruction in government and legal issues. There are the famed *Laws of Manu*, composed between the end of the second century BC and end of the second century AD, and the *Artha-Shastra* of Kautilya (possibly second century BC), which outlines the duties and techniques of government. To a large extent, these works provided the practical basis for Hindu civilization.

THE *PURANAS*

The *Puranas* represent the popular expression of Hindu piety. There are eighteen major Puranas and eighteen minor ones, all of which claim to expound the Vedas. They glorify gods, provide lineages, and develop a rich mythology that supplements that of the epics. Generally speaking, the Puranas are devoted to the virtues of particular gods. For example, the *Vishnu Purana* is written in praise of the god Vishnu and is a product of

Photo 8.4 This small shrine in a temple complex is capped by a scene from the *Ramayana* where King Rama rescues his faithful wife, Sita, from the demon king of Ceylon (Sri Lanka), Ravana, who has kidnapped her in an attempt to enact a forced marriage. With the aid of the monkey king Hanuman, who boldly leads his army to her rescue, Sita is eventually saved and reunited with her husband.

a particular Vaishnavite religious movement. This important work attempts to develop doctrine in such a way that it embraces the entirety of earlier Brahmanic teachings and practices. Consequently, in this Purana, comprising six books, the five traditional topics of older writings are preserved. The first four and final book develop traditional materials from classic texts, weaving a consistent Vaishnavite interpretation of them together with a rich devotional mythology. Only the fifth book contains what may be considered entirely new devotional materials.

This Purana begins with an account of the creation of the cosmos by the god Vishnu, who is identified with Brahman, the power or force which encompasses the whole universe.[7] Vishnu's existence takes many forms. On the one hand he is pure spirit, *Purusa*; on

---

7. Brahman as the sustaining force behind all things must not be confused with its manifestation in the god Brahma, or with the class of Hindu holy men known as Brahmin, or priests.

the other, primary matter, or *Prakriti*. Most important, he is eternal time, or *Kali*, whose actions separate spirit and matter. Creation therefore becomes the sport—a sacred enjoyment known as *lila*—of Vishnu.

All the elements of creation come together to form one vast cosmic egg that floats on an immense sea of primordial water. The creator god Vishnu enters into the egg, from which evolves the earth, the sky, and the heavens, all populated by gods and other sending beings. First Vishnu is the creator and sustainer, the preserver of the world. This cosmic dance, which is usually associated with the god Shiva, continues until the universe is exhausted. Then, taking the form of Rudra, the god Vishnu becomes god of destruction, and the world is destroyed in a fiery apocalypse, dissolving through rain into one vast ocean. Vishnu now sleeps on the ocean while floating in the coils of a great serpentlike sea monster. While at rest, Vishnu reviews the whole panorama of recurring creations and destruction that make up the saga of the universe.

The term *Kalpa* is used to describe what is sometimes called the day of Brahma, which extends from the creation of the universe to the destruction of the worlds. These recurring cycles of creation and destruction are called the Great *Yugas* or *Maha Yugas*. Each of these cycles lasts for 4,320,000 human years, which is reduced to 12,000 years in the lifetime of the gods, in which one day is equivalent to a human year.

Each of these *Maha Yugas* is divided into shorter periods of 4800, 3600, 2400, and 1800 years respectively, during which time the universe decays. Thus, throughout the whole of history the universe steadily declines, and is ultimately destroyed. The final period before this destruction, the *Kali Yuga*, is

Photo 8.5 This ancient depiction of the Aryan horse sacrifice reminds us of the role of propitiation in Indian religion and the need for humans to participate in a vast cosmic drama that involves the creation, destruction, and renewal of the universe.

one of unrighteousness, oppression, and evil. After the final destruction there is a new creation, and the cycle begins once more. Following this cycle of creation and destruction, the universe is destroyed and a new cycle of creation begins. All of the Puranas teach a similar doctrine of creation and destruction based on a cyclic view of time. The entire vision is underwritten by a monistic worldview based upon the Upanishads. At the same time, this religious vision is theistic and manages to incorporate a personalized god.

THE YOGA SUTRAS

The Yoga Sutras of Patanjali, who lived sometime between the fourth century BC and the sixth century AD, provide a systematic interpretation of the practice of Yoga, making clear the significance of Yoga that develops out of the Upanishads. In this influential work, Yoga is defined as the "mastery or suppression of the mind." The goal of Yoga is said to be the attainment of a pure state of consciousness, without any of the distractions of normal mental processes or daily life. By the suppression of all mental activity, this refined state is eventually reached.[8]

Photo 8.6 Like his contemporary Winston Churchill, Lord Robert Baden-Powell, who founded the Boy Scouts and later the Girl Guides, served in the Indian army, during which time he wrote his own highly amusing book about fighting Afghans around Kandahar and in the Kyber Pass. Among his many excellent watercolors is the above painting of an ancient Hindu temple. The serenity and mystical quality of the scene evokes the spirit of the Upanishads.

THE UPANISHADS

Usually introduced, on chronological grounds, after the Vedas and before the epics and other Hindu literature, the Upanishads are discussed last here, because, regardless of their chronological order, they are actually the interpretive texts that explain the meaning of all other Hindu literature.

In the Upanishads, activist and sacrificial themes of the Vedas, epics, and other literature give way to philosophical speculation. Nowhere do the Upanishads reject Vedic or epic themes; rather, they interpret or reinterpret them. Thus they often explain rituals allegorically and see ritual actions, like sacrifice, in terms of their symbolic meaning.

Structurally, the Upanishads take the form of conversations between the teacher, or guru, and the student, or between a husband and his wife. Less commonly they are seen as discussions between equally informed philosophers. A basic assumption of these conversations is that they are expanding Vedic teachings and giving the Vedas their true interpretation.

The distinguishing feature of the Upanishads, in contrast to the stories of the Vedas and epics or the ritual texts, is the quest for truth and philosophical knowledge. Behind this quest is a longing for what becomes known as enlightenment or freedom from the bonds of Karma and the wheel of samsara. This ultimate knowledge, according to the Upanishads, comes through experience. One of the Upanishads describes the liberating experience in terms of the relationship between the divine within the human, Atman, and the ultimate divine being, Brahman. Frequently, Atman is described as the human soul, while Brahman is described as God. Although this is a common interpretation, the exact nature of Atman is not so clear. Atman may, and often is, the

---

8. A good discussion of the way Yoga developed and was practiced is found in N. E. Sjoman's *The Yoga Tradition of the Mysore Palace* (New Delhi: Abhinav Publications, 1996).

term used for the human soul. On the other hand, Atman may also be used to describe a fragment of the divine which is implanted within humans.

Philosophers within the Hindu tradition have interpreted the terms "Atman" and "Brahman" differently. For example, in the eighth century, Shankara interpreted the phrase *tat tvam asi*, found in the *Chandogya Upanishad* in connection with a discussion of the way salt dissolves in water, as meaning "that art thou," signifying that this is a reflection of life and the relationship of the soul to Brahman and that ultimately Brahman and Atman are identical. On the other hand, the equally famous philosopher Ramanuja rejected this interpretation and argued that while ultimately Brahman and Atman are inseparable, they retain their individuality. Therefore they cannot be identical.

HINDU GODS

Avatar figures, usually manifestations of the god Vishnu or Krishna, enter the world of Hindu mythology to restore order and true knowledge after periods of degradation and decline. This idea of the appearance of God or gods on earth is superficially similar to the Christian idea of the incarnation. The big difference, however, is that while in Christian teaching Christ is both God and man, the avatars of the Hindu tradition are entirely divine.

At the top of the Hindu hierarchy of gods is a trinity of beings—Brahma, Vishnu, and Shiva—all of whom are accompanied by their female consorts. Together these pairs of leading gods represent the vital forces of creation known in Indian thought as *shakti, sakti,* or divine power. Here it is important to note that traditional Indian ways of thinking about the relationship between men and women are very different from those found in the West. Until at least the sexual revolution of the 1960s, the dominant idea of the female in Western thinking was that of a relatively passive being. In India, however, it is the male who is seen as essentially passive, while the female is active. Consequently, in at least one Indian religious movement, Saktism, the gods, who are the focus of popular piety, are depicted as female. In these movements the figures of

Photo 8.7 To most Protestant Christians the deities represented in the above altar from one of North America's Hindu temples must seem both confusing and idolatrous. For Hindus they represent a joyful and uplifting expression of sincere devotion. Look at them very carefully and see if they remind you of anything in the Christian tradition.

Durga, a female warrior who often rides on a tiger to slay demons, and Kali, the goddess of time and destruction and the consort of Shiva, predominated.

An interesting fact about these traditions is that the gods are capable of taking many different forms and, in the case of Durga and Kali, can sometimes be identified with each other. For example, in the *Bhagavad Gita* Krishna appears as the charioteer of Prince Arjuna. Yet in other stories Krishna appears herding cows or as a musician. The ability of the gods to take many forms and identities that are sometimes interchangeable has led many Hindu thinkers to argue that all of these forms and all the different gods are simply expressions of the one divine essence. Therefore they argue Hinduism is a form of monotheism that uses many different stories to express the inexpressible truth about God.

Because the gods play such an important role in Hindu piety, it is important to know something about them and their histories. In the conventional chronology found in most books about Hinduism, the earliest gods are said to be those referred to in the Vedas, particularly the *Rig Veda*. Here we find the worship of nature that befits the interests of a pastoral people. The sun god Surya and the fire god Agni are important here. So too is Vayu, the wine god, and Indra, the king of the gods, who is also the god of thunder and lightning. There is also Varuna, the keeper of the cosmic order.

At the time of the writing of the *Ramayana* and *Mahabharata*, somewhere between 300 BC and AD 300, the stories of gods were interwoven with those of human heroes. In these later works various minor Vedic deities like Vishnu and Krishna take on an increasingly important role. Sometime during the fourth to sixth century AD, the mother goddess, Bharat Mata, or Mother India, was added and the use of images in worship became common.

In the *Rig Veda*, Indra is perhaps the most important of the gods. He is a warrior god with cosmic powers who frequently wars with other gods. Another important god is Agni, god of fire, who, like Mercury in Hermes in Greek mythology, is a messenger between humans and other gods. The stories of Agni, therefore, serve to explain the function of sacrifice. Because Agni is the god of fire and a messenger, offerings that human beings burn become messages to the gods. Similarly, the god Soma is both the moon god and a sacred drink, which many scholars identify with mushrooms and hallucinogenic substances. Consequently, Soma is also identified with ecstatic experiences and spiritual insight.

At times Vedic descriptions of the gods and goddesses, or at least the way they are named and described, blend together. Thus the goddess Sarasvati is the god of rivers, or at least a river god, but has also been described as the god of wisdom and learning. In this way the *Rig Veda* can describe Sarasvati as the source of inspired thoughts, truthfulness, beauty, wise words, and dynamism. Later, in the *Brahmanas*, Sarasvati becomes identified with speech and the goddess Vac, who is the consort of a creator god, Prajapati. As the author of speech, Vac, along with Sarasvati, with whom Vac is identified, becomes the Word, rather like the Logos in Christianity. Therefore, she's described as "the mother of the Vedas."

To complicate things still further, Sarasvati is also identified with Savitri the sun god and Gayatri the singer, who in turn is associated with the ritual formula used during the initiation ceremony of young boys. Thus, Gayatri's name becomes a mantra, or ritual incantation, that is chanted when young boys are given a sacred thread to wear throughout their life, thus marking their transition from childhood to the beginning of manhood and the commencement of their studies.

Throughout the Vedas, the dominant theme is that of sacrificial ritual, or *yajna*, which is performed in close association with fire. Although all major sacrifices were conducted by

Photo 8.8 Here North American Hindus present to the gods small offerings, or sacrifices, of food and drink. In India goats and other animals are still sacrificed, though such practices are rare in the West.

ritual specialists who chanted the hymns and performed sacred actions, other sacrifices belonged to the home. In addition to fire sacrifices, other offerings that involved eating and drinking—particularly the drinking of the juice of the soma plant, which, as has been observed, many believe to be hallucinogenic mushrooms—were important.

Philosophically, these sacrifices are justified in terms of the preservation of the cosmic order, or *rta*, which implies truth, justice, and the balance of creation. In *Purusa Sukta*, understood as a hymn to the Supreme Being, the whole creation is depicted as originating from the primordial sacrifice of the cosmic man.

THE CASTE SYSTEM

Probably the most important feature of the Vedas for social life is the division of society into four classes, or castes. These castes are believed to be rooted in the essential ontology of the universe. This understanding of the ontological structure of society is reinforced by the *Institutes of Vishnu*, where we read in book two: "1. Brahmanas, Kshatriyas, Vaisyas, and Sûdras are the four castes. 2. The first three of these are (called) twice-born." The text then outlines the duties of each caste.

These social divisions, or castes, are known as *varanas*, which can also mean colors. Therefore, the suggestion is that the classes or castes of Hindu society were originally based upon racial differences expressed in terms of color. This understanding is reinforced by the fact that the light-skinned people inevitably belong to higher castes than people with darker skin. Some critics suggest that at its crudest this implies that Hindu social life is based upon a form of religiously enforced apartheid. Most Hindus vigorously reject this suggestion, pointing out that apartheid is a modern notion based on scientific racism and that among the Tamils some high-caste people are very dark. Nevertheless, it is important to remember that Hindu reformers like Mahatma Gandhi fought hard to abolish the social effects of caste in India.

THE HINDU CALENDAR

Hindu piety is closely tied to the Hindu calendar, which, like many religious calendars, is a lunar one. As such, it is divided into twelve lunar months, which vary in length between twenty-nine and thirty-two days. Each month, in turn, is divided into dark and bright divisions. An extra month is added, rather like the leap year, every three years. In this sense, it is roughly similar to the Gregorian calendar used in the West.

HINDU RITUALS AND PIETY

The Hindu tradition is both highly philosophical and deeply devotional. Contrary to common expectations, many Hindu philosophers, such as Sankara and Ramanuja, were also deeply devotional. Hindu piety begins in the home, and each home has a place set aside as a shrine to the gods of the household. Sometimes, an entire room is devoted to this purpose. More commonly, the images of deities occupy an alcove in one particular room, which is very often the kitchen. The offering of food, drink, and devotion to the gods the images represent is known as *puja*. Before offering the worship, worshipers are supposed to ritually cleanse themselves. Pilgrimages, often involving tens of thousands of people, are another aspect of Hindu piety usually linked to the performance of cleansing rituals, such as bathing in the River Ganges.[9]

Ritual cleansing plays an important role in Hindu tradition, where washing and bathing are very important. Before prayer can be offered or sacred words chanted, good Hindus will wash their mouths. Another important aspect of the Hindu tradition is the removal of shoes when entering a temple or even when entering a devout household.

Various forms of ritual purity also affect prayers and other religious rights. Menstruating women, or women who have recently given birth, are ritually impure. So too are people who have touched dead bodies or come into contact with any of a large variety of unclean things, such as blood, urine, or excrement. For a more complex discussion of the idea of ritual purity, readers are referred to Roman Catholic anthropologist Mary Douglas's book *Purity and Danger*.[10]

Photo 8.9 A popular bathing area in the holy city of Benares, viewed from across the Ganges River. This watercolor painting by Mortimer Menpes captures the allure of the city and its river for visitors in the late nineteenth century.

RITES OF PASSAGE: BIRTH, MARRIAGE, AND DEATH

The major rites of passage in the Hindu tradition are, as in most other traditions, birth, marriage, and death. Traditionally,

9. Surinder Mohan Bhardwaj, *Hindu Places of Pilgrimage in India* (Berkeley: Univ. of California Press, 1973); Diana L. Eck, *Banares: City of Light* (Princeton: Princeton Univ. Press, 1983).

10. Mary Douglas, *Purity and Danger: An Analysis of Concepts of Pollution and Taboo* (London: Routledge & Kegan Paul, 1966).

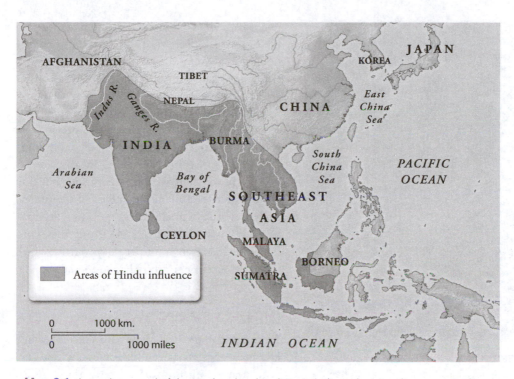

Map 8.1 shows the spread of the Hindu cultural tradition in India and surrounding countries from around AD 300 to 1000.

before birth, prayers are said for the fetus, and the gods are asked to give the woman a male child. After birth, mother and child are regarded as ritually impure for ten days. In this the Hindu tradition has maintained rituals similar to those in medieval Europe. During this time, only midwives and physicians are supposed to have contact with the mother and child. There are elaborate ceremonies, including welcoming the child into the home and whispering the child's name into its right ear. The name given to a child, according to tradition, was always related to the name of a god. But today, Western names are often given to Hindus living in Western countries.

Marriages within the Hindu tradition are elaborate communal affairs. Traditionally, all marriages were arranged. Even today, and among Christian families in India and overseas, many marriages are arranged. Although modern arranged marriages usually allow the couple to meet beforehand to decide whether they will marry or not, the belief persists within the Hindu tradition that love develops during marriage and is not the basis for marriage. In this sense, marriage is an arrangement between families.

When a person is dying, if they are a good Hindu, they ought to be given a sip of water from the Ganges River. Then they are expected, if at all possible, to chant the name of God. Most modern Hindus believe that after death, the soul moves on to another body and another lifetime. Historically, however, a variety of other options, including a belief in annihilation, existed within the Hindu tradition. After death, the names of God ought to be chanted by the mourners, and passages from the *Bhagavad Gita* are read aloud. In India, cremation is most common, although for those who can arrange it, water burial in the Ganges is considered a holy act.

According to Hindu custom, people must remain with the body, chanting and praying and reading from the *Gita* to aid the soul and its journey until cremation takes place. Ideally, cremation ought to occur within twenty-four hours of death. After the funeral, members of the funeral party are ritually unclean and need to take ritual baths to purify themselves. Mourning then continues between ten and thirty days during which time the mourners are still considered ritually unclean.

DIETARY LAWS

Although dietary laws vary with families, many Hindus are vegetarian. Others who are not total vegetarians limit the sort of meats they can eat to poultry and fish. Within the Hindu tradition there are various traditional classifications of food.

Photo 8.10 A water ceremony on the Ganges. These ceremonies take many forms and often include water burials.

Some foods and drinks, such as alcoholic drinks, are believed to provoke anger. Other foods, such as garlic, are believed to create sexual passions. But most vegetables are believed to produce good living and a healthy lifestyle. In traditional families, men eat their meals before the children and women, but for practical purposes, most Hindus in the West, as well as in modern India, eat and drink like everyone else.

HINDU CELEBRATIONS

Because the Hindu tradition is essentially a tradition of the home, there are as many celebrations as there are families. As a result, Hindu celebrations vary from area to area, caste to caste, and family to family. Nevertheless, particularly in Western countries, certain major festivals have become common events within Hindu diaspora communities. Probably the most popular feast is the Diwali, or the Festival of Lights, which is celebrated around the fall with lanterns and fireworks. The winter festival of Shivaratri, in praise of the Lord Shiva, which involves dancing, singing, and feasting, is also very popular. So too is the spring festival of Ramanavami, which celebrates the birth of the god Rama. During this festival, plays from the *Mahabharata* are performed, and stories about Rama are read. The Krishna Janmashtami festival is celebrated in the late summer with feasting. A harvest festival, the Sankranthi, is also often observed. During both Diwali and Sankranthi gifts are exchanged, making it rather like Christmas.

Because of the eclectic nature of the Hindu tradition, most Hindus have no difficulty celebrating Christmas. Indeed, while some agnostics object to things like Christmas greetings, Hindus respect such celebrations and enjoy them.

COMMUNAL WORSHIP

In India, Hindu temples are used on special occasions such as family and communal celebrations. Increasingly, however, both within Hindu reform movements in India and in the Western world, temples resemble churches. As a result, they become centers where people from India can meet and celebrate common traditions.

They also have developed institutions similar to Sunday schools to teach their traditions to children. Worship services are held by priests, who today often give talks rather like sermons in which they remind worshipers what it means to be a Hindu. During such services, offerings of food and drink are made to the images of the deities, which are believed to be indwelt by God or the gods.

THE WESTERN HINDU TRADITION

Although some knowledge about India and its peoples existed among small groups of people in the West from at least the time of the Greek city-states around 300 BC, it was not until the seventeenth century that Roman Catholic mis-

Photo 8.11 This modest building is one of South Africa's Ramakrishna missions. Based on the teachings of Sri Ramakrishna (1802–1886), and decisively shaped by the teachings of Ramakrishna's able disciple Swami Vivekananda (1863–1902), the Ramakrishna movement became a worldwide Hindu revitalization movement. Not only does the building look like a Protestant church, it holds regular worship services and even runs a Sunday school, following the example of Christian missionaries to India. Thus the mission, which seeks to revitalize the Hindu tradition, reaches out to Hindu people living in Western societies.

sionaries based in Goa began to interact with educated Hindus. Other missionaries and traders increased knowledge of Hindu tradition during the eighteenth century.

Charles Wilkins (1749–1836) published an English translation of the *Bhagavad Gita* in 1785, making it the first major translation of a Hindu text into English or any European language. A French translation followed in 1787, and a German one in 1802. It was on the basis of this translation that the philosopher Friedrich Wilhelm Joseph Schelling (1775–1854) developed his early philosophy while popularizing Indian thought in Europe.

Wilkins was encouraged in his work by other British Orientalists such as Sir William Jones (1746–1794), who, like Wilkins, was employed by the British East India Company. Together they created the Asiatic Society of Bengal in 1784 and promoted the publication of Indian literature in India. Later both men returned to Britain, where they pioneered the study of ancient India and its sacred scriptures. The first translation of the Upanishads appeared in 1802, when A.-H. Anquetil-Duperron (1731–1805) published a Latin translation of selected texts taken from a Persian translation. Other translations followed, the most important being that of Max Müller (1823–1900) in 1879. Müller also arranged translations of the Vedas and various other Indian texts, which were published in his series, *The Sacred Books of the East* (1879–1900).

HINDU MIGRATIONS TO THE WEST

Before the nineteenth century very few Hindus visited the West. Throughout that century, however, a growing number visited Europe and North America to study and work. Prominent among these was Raja Ram Mohan Roy (1772–1833), who introduced the term "Hinduism" to the English language. He died and is buried in Bristol, England. Later, at the World Parliament of Religions held in Chicago in 1893, a number of Hindu speakers made a significant impact, including Swami Vivekananda (1863–1902), who stayed on in the West until 1897. During this time he established Vedanta Centers in New York and London and taught hundreds of Westerners, many of whom became converts.

For centuries Hindus had migrated to places like Indonesia and other parts of Asia, as well as the east coast of Africa. During the nineteenth century large scale Indian migrations took place in the form of indentured laborers working in East Africa, South Africa, parts of the Caribbean, Fiji, and even Canada. Although they were discouraged from taking their families with them, their families eventually followed to establish thriving Indian communities in all of these lands.

Small-scale Indian migration to Europe, particularly Britain, began in the 1930s. During the 1950s the number of immigrants began to grow, and large numbers emigrated to Britain as a result of a recruitment drive by the British government to provide low-paid workers for industry in northern England. Many also came from East Africa, where various governments, such as that of Idi Amin (1925–2003), were hostile and sought to expel them. This pattern continued until the late 1970s, when new laws began to tighten immigration rules.

Immigration to America and Canada followed a similar pattern, Canada taking a far larger proportion of Indian immigrants than America. Today Indians can be found across Europe and North America, where there are now thriving Indian communities. The arrival of Indian immigrants has led to the building of Hindu temples and the creation of a network of other religious organizations, the most famous of which is the Hare Krishna movement.

Photo 8.12 A group of Hare Krishnas protest against the "immorality" of San Francisco by chanting the Hare Krishna mantra and dancing on the street.

CHAPTER 9

RETHINKING THE HINDU TRADITION

INTERPRETING HINDUISM

Archaeological discoveries and new thinking about the Aryans have led to a radical revision of the way many educated Hindus understand their own religious tradition. For example, Nirad C. Chaudhuri, in his popular, yet controversial, work *Hinduism: A Religion to Live By*,[1] challenges existing ideas about the origins of the Hindu religious tradition. He points out that although the *Rig Veda* is viewed by Indians as their religion's original revelation, there is no real connection between it and most Hindu cults. He also claims that this is true for the *Gita*, because, while the *Gita* is held in the highest regard by all Hindus, there is no direct link between it and uniquely Hindu beliefs and practices.[2]

Closely related to this point is the fact that no Hindu text can be dated with accuracy before the twelfth century AD.[3] Yet Western scholars, influenced by German Romanticism, were quick to produce a very clear chronology for Hindu texts,[4] based entirely upon linguistic arguments. It was assumed that the Sanskrit of the *Rig Veda* approximates to the date of old Persia, which in turn is dated to the early part of the sixth century BC. On this basis the *Rig Veda* itself is dated somewhere between 800 and 1000 BC. Most orthodox Hindus, in the historical tradition, reject this date as totally untenable, arguing instead that the Vedas are millions of years old. Some European scholars have also suggested that the *Rig Veda* was composed around 4000 BC. This estimate is based upon astronomical data which appears convincing to many.[5]

Whatever the date of the *Rig Veda*, Chaudhuri concludes that clearly the conventional date of between 1500 and 1200 BC is pure speculation, lacking supporting evidence from inscriptions and similar factual sources. The truth is, he argues, we simply lack fixed archaeological points with which to date these documents. Therefore, the entire field is open to speculation.[6]

---

1. Nirad C. Chaudhuri, *Hinduism: A Religion to Live By* (Delhi: Oxford Univ. Press, 1997).
2. Ibid., 29–30.
3. Ibid., 30–31.
4. Ibid., 31.
5. Ibid.
6. Ibid., 29–41.

Photo 9.1 Our earliest external accounts of Indian religions come from Greek writers who visited India either as traders or with the army of Alexander the Great (356–323 BC). The descriptions they left behind are very different from what we would expect, paying far more attention to Buddhism than the Hindu tradition.

The dating of the *Gita* is as difficult as the dating of the *Rig Veda*. The twentieth-century Buddhist scholar Edward Conze (1904–1979) argued that the *Gita* was clearly written as a Hindu apologetic to counter the impact of early Christianity in India. Another scholar, K. N. Upadhaya, argued in his book, *Early Buddhism and the Bhagavadgita*,[7] that it was clear the *Gita* was part of a Hindu apologetic against Buddhism. On the other hand, the great modern Indian historian of Hindu philosophy, S. N. Dasgupta (1887–1952), claimed that the *Gita* lacked any apologetic motif and that he could find no hint of Buddhist teachings in the text. Therefore, he argued, it must have been composed before the spread of Buddhism; otherwise the author would have responded to Buddhist teachings and offered a Hindu apologetic instead of ignoring Buddhism altogether.[8] All these views are well argued and defended. All we can really say is that it seems likely that the *Gita* was composed sometime between 300 BC and AD 300. Nevertheless, even this is not certain, and no one really knows the author or where it was written.

Lacking firm external evidence or extant texts that can be accurately dated, many scholars rely upon a comparative-religion approach to date Hindu literature, speculating about the literature itself on the basis of the supposed dates at which certain ideas became popular. This technique, however, is questionable. As Chaudhuri points out, without knowing anything about the lives of Swami Vivekananda (1863–1902) and Mahatma Gandhi (1869–1948), it is possible to reach some very strange conclusions from an examination of their philosophies. Taken in isolation, their works have similarities that suggest Vivekananda was a student of Mahatma Gandhi, when actually we know that they wrote independently of each other.

This question of dating on the basis of intellectual ideas and supposed borrowing is highlighted in the conversations of the great German writer and critic Johann Wolfgang von Goethe (1749–1832) as recorded by his assistant, Johann Peter Eckermann (1792–1854), in his "Eckermann's Conversations with Goethe" (1836–1848). "I am," Goethe said, "always surprised at the learned, who seemed to suppose that poetizing proceeds not from life to the poem, but from the book to the poem." Later Goethe continued with this idea:

---

7.   K. N. Upadhaya, *Early Buddhism and the Bhagavadgita* (Delhi: Motilal Banarsidass, 1971).

8.   Surendranath N. Dasgupta, *History of Indian Philosophy*; Chaudhuri, *Hinduism*, 32.

Photo 9.2 The older interpretation of "Hinduism," as the Hindu tradition was called, assumed a progression from the ancient sacrificial religion of the Aryans to the philosophy of the Upanishads among the elite. In the same schema, *bhakti*, or the religion of devotion, replaced crude sacrifices among the masses. This photograph of the sacrifice of a goat shows that things are not so simple. Taken in the late nineteenth century, it shows that sacrifice was alive and well long after scholars assumed it had been abandoned. Indeed, it continues today. Thus Hindu religious traditions overlap and do not fall into neat evolutionary categories. It also illustrates that Indian and African religions, at the popular level, are not so different as is sometimes thought.

"The Germans," he said, "cannot cease to be the Philistines. They are now squabbling about some verses, which are printed in both Schiller's works and mine, and fancy it is important to ascertain which really belong to Schiller and which to me; as if anything could be gained by such investigation — as if the existence of such things were not enough." Then he explained, "Sometimes I gave the thought, and Schiller made the verse; sometimes the contrary was the case; sometimes he made one line and I the other."[9] If a great writer like Goethe acknowledges many sources, and even has found it difficult to identify his own sources, how easy is it to identify sources simply on the basis of ideas when no solid textual evidence can be assigned to them?

THE RIDDLE OF SANSKRIT

The fact is, we cannot accurately date Sanskrit literature of the classical period even when we know the names of the authors and some basic information about them. How much less can ancient literature that is not even written in standard Sanskrit be dated? Most classical Hindu texts are indeed written in Sanskrit, and this gives us a clue to their dates, but nothing more. Classical Sanskrit is an artificial language, created as a written language for a literary task. On the other hand, Prakrit was the colloquial language of the people. Although we cannot be sure how and why Sanskrit was created, Chaudhuri suggests it seems reasonable that its use was intended to stem the disintegration of a common language into numerous dialects that were becoming increasingly incomprehensible.

---

9. Johann Wolfgang von Goethe, "Eckermann's Conversations with Goethe," in *The German Classics of the Nineteenth and Twentieth Centuries*, vol. 2, *Goethe*, ed. Kuno Francke (New York: German Publication Society, 1913), 422, 443.

The earliest evidence we have about the development of Sanskrit comes from inscriptions. And the earliest readable inscriptions are those of the great Buddhist king Ashoka, created in the third century BC. The language of these inscriptions is, however, not Sanskrit but Prakrit. Being written in Prakrit, these inscriptions are found over a remarkably wide area of India. Yet none give any hint that Sanskrit was in use at that time. Some scholars argue that the failure of Ashoka to use Sanskrit was due to the fact that he was a Buddhist, who preferred to use the language of the common people. The problem with this argument is that some of his inscriptions also contain an identical message in Greek and Aramaic. Therefore, it seems that Ashoka was concerned to communicate to people regardless of the language they spoke and read. Thus, it is very surprising that Sanskrit is not found on any of these inscriptions. This seems to indicate that the Sanskrit language was not in general use or perhaps was not even known at that time.

Photo 9.3 This late-nineteenth-century painting, showing the Martand Temple of the Sun, located on a plateau near modern Islamabad, illustrates the complexity of Indian religion. Archeology shows that long before the temple was built, which was probably in the eighth century, the area supported a thriving Buddhist community. This was gradually replaced, first by Hindu worship, and later by Islam.

The earliest inscriptions containing classical Sanskrit words appear two centuries after those of Ashoka, during the first century BC. But it is not until AD 150 that complete inscriptions are written in Sanskrit. After that they become increasingly frequent, and by the fifth century AD, Sanskrit was a common language used in India. All this suggests that Sanskrit did not develop until the beginning of the Christian era.[10]

The earliest evidence for the existence of Hindu belief in gods comes from a tablet written in cuneiform script that contains the names of four Hindu gods. It was written as part of a treaty by a Hittite king sometime around 1350 BC. This tablet, however, was not found in India but in Cappadocia. What is even more puzzling is that there are no other examples of the use of names associated with Hindu gods for over a thousand years after the date of the tablet.

The next solid evidence showing that the names of these gods were in use is found in an inscription on the Garuda pillar at Besnagar in modern Madhya Pradesh. This inscription, written in Prakrit, is usually dated toward the end of the second century BC. Surprisingly, none of the relatively numerous Ashokan inscriptions mention Hindu gods, though they do refer to the small priestly class of Brahmins, who were the ritual specialists in ancient India.

---

10. Chaudhuri, *Hinduism*, 38–40.

From the time of the Besnagar inscription to the fourth century AD, scattered inscriptions mentioning the names of Hindu gods are to be found all over India. The most important of these are found in the Nanaghat cave, near modern Mumbai (formerly Bombay), and are generally dated to the first century BC. They mention Indra, the Dharma, and Vedic sacrifices. Other inscriptions refer to the worship of Shiva. After AD 320, inscriptions become both more numerous and more informative, until by the seventh century there is ample evidence of full-blown Hindu worship as it is known today.

THE EMERGENCE OF HINDU ART AND ARCHITECTURE

Art objects add little to our knowledge of Hinduism before the fifth century AD, which is in sharp contrast to the abundance of Buddhist art from earlier periods. When they appear, however, they do so as a fully developed art form similar to anything found in modern Hinduism. The earliest examples of Hindu art are found on coins and seals, some of which date to the third century AD. Only after AD 400 do we find fully developed sculptures of gods and goddesses.

Nor do Hindu temples or similar buildings appear in India before the fourth century, and some scholars argue that even these belong to the seventh century. Actually, the earliest Hindu-style temple was discovered in 1952 at Surkh Kotal, in Afghanistan. It is generally thought to date to the second century AD. The earliest Hindu temples in India are two small buildings. One, built of stone, is found in Deogarh, in the state of Madhya Pradesh. The other, built of brick, is found near Bhitargaon, in the state of Uttar Pradesh. Both date from the fourth century AD. Yet by the fifth century temples are found all over India, and the seventh century witnessed a temple-building boom.[11]

EARLY OBSERVATIONS ON INDIAN RELIGIONS

Written accounts by foreign travelers confirm the general impression of Hinduism gained from archaeological sources. Greek and Roman authors, for instance, incorporated into their works extracts of a Greek account of India from the time of Alexander the Great's expedition there (327 to 325 BC),

Photo 9.4 A third-century-AD sculpture of the nature goddess Yaksi. Note that she is fully clothed and stands in a rather chaste pose, quite unlike the goddesses and female sculptures of the classical period of Hindu art. Although relatively few sculptures exist from this period, and some are similar to later art forms, this type of image is typical for the early period.

11. Ibid., 49–53.

and, in agreement with the archaeological evidence, none of them mention the names of Hindu gods, though there are hints of gods like Shiva and Krishna. They confirm, on the other hand, the existence of a small priestly class known as Brahmins and regarded as great philosophers. Classical accounts also mention the existence of Buddhists and a group of people whom the Greeks described as "naked philosophers." The Greeks also mention wandering teachers, recluses, and hermits and comment on the popularity of religious discussion among Indians.

In the fifth century AD, the Chinese writer Fa-Hien gives a fairly comprehensive account of Indian life. But in his treatment of Indian religions he describes only Buddhism in detail, and gives the impression that Hindu temples were few and far between, though he does mention rivalries between Hindus and Buddhists and offer observations about such Hindu temples as he found. Another Chinese writer, Yuan-Chwang, gave a very different picture of Hinduism two hundred years later. He records numerous temples and talks at length about the various gods that Hindus worshiped. He also says that in one kingdom Buddhists had to worship secretly for fear of persecution by Hindus. Equally important is his description of the Ganges as a sacred river central to Hindu life.

THE EPIC POEMS AND WHAT WE REALLY KNOW

Two other important sources of information about early Hinduism are the great epic poems,

the *Ramayana* and the *Mahabharata*. Although, as with other Indian literature, the date of these poems is uncertain, what they say about Hinduism is highly significant. Both contain the basic framework of Hindu mythology that, together with the *Puranas*, provides a comprehensive account of mythological thinking similar to what exists today. What is interesting about these epics is that actual teachings and comments about religion are missing. Although they provide the imaginative framework for Hindu religious beliefs, they say very little about those beliefs or Hindu practices.[12]

Photo 9.5 This sixth-century-AD sculpture of a Naga king and his voluptuous wife stands in sharp contrast to the earlier sculpture of the goddess Yaksi. It is typical both of the later period and of what follows. It also echoes the changes in culture and religious patterns that took place around this time. The Nagas were a northern people whose women were reputed to be extraordinarily beautiful. They also enter Hindu mythology as enemies of the god Vishnu.

12. Ibid., 53–60.

Taking all these pieces of evidence together, it seems clear that we know very little about Hinduism before the fifth century AD. Yet what appears between the fifth and seventh centuries AD is Hinduism as we know it today. The mythology is virtually unchanged, the gods are clearly recognizable, and the practices are essentially the same. From this it is safe to argue that what we know today as Hinduism, and possibly all we can ever know about the history of Hinduism, dates from around the fifth century AD, when it developed as a coherent and comprehensive religion in its own right. This means that whatever its antecedents, whatever all the sum of its stories, mythologies, and practices, Hinduism as a coherent religion belongs to the same creative era that saw the birth of Christianity, Rabbinic Judaism, and Islam.

THE DEVELOPMENT OF CLASSICAL HINDUISM

During the period from the fifth to seventh centuries AD, a series of cities grew up along the Ganges River, where numerous temples are now to be found. Additionally, both Buddhism and Jainism were thriving. At this time three forms of religious practice are clearly identifiable. First is the practice of yoga in its various forms. While the origins of the various forms of yoga are lost in antiquity, they all shared the common goal of training the mind. Yoga, then and now, is not to be exclusively identified with strenuous bodily exercises that are said to be good for the health. It consists, rather, of a vast range of techniques aimed at stilling the mind to draw the practitioner toward the recognition of true reality.

The second clearly developed practice was that of worship in all its forms, which in Hindu tradition is known as *puja*. At the heart of Hindu worship is the adoration of images of the gods and great teachers. The veneration of teachers was also found in various forms of Buddhism.

The third major expression of religion was the recurring practice of sacrifice. At the top of the sacrificial hierarchy were the Brahmin, who performed temple and other sacrifices at the behest of their patrons. These sacrifices were often closely linked to temple rituals and seasonal festivals. They were also associated with self-mortification and ascetic practices. Although the Brahmins dominated temple practice, all members of society, down to the lowliest household, could perform sacred offerings. These offerings very often involved the death of animals, and on occasion that of humans. Other forms of ritual offerings, more commonly occurring in the home, involved small birds or animals, fruit and vegetables, and things like butter.

While it would be nice to talk about Hindu traditions as clearly defined as those found in Buddhism, Judaism, Christianity, and Islam, such a neat description is not possible. If the foregoing account sounds confusing and contradictory, it is helpful to think of the Hindu tradition as a matrix, or ever-changing mosaic, bound together by certain underlying assumptions and common mythological stories.

At its core Hinduism is the religion of Hindus living in small villages and extended family communities. Consequently, ritual practices such as daily devotions, communal festivals, pilgrimages, beliefs, and allegiances vary from community to community and group to group. As people who share a common literature, developed philosophical

Photo 9.6 The intensely personal and essentially familial aspects of the Hindu tradition continue today. Here a family brings their new pickup to be blessed by the priest. The father proceeds around the car holding a sacred flame, while the priest chats to the daughter and a relative looks on. Fruit offerings for gods can be seen on the ground.

traditions, great festivals, and pilgrimages, all Hindus have many things in common. Therefore, it is possible to speak about Hinduism. Yet it remains true that at least until the Hindu Middle Ages it is difficult to distinguish clearly defined religious movements resembling sects or what might be called denominations.

Consequently, it makes little sense to attempt to force the Hindu tradition into a mold that concentrates on specific institutions. Of course, institutions such as great monasteries existed within the Hindu tradition. And today there are distinct Hindu movements such as the Ramakrishna movement and the Hare Krishna movement. Yet such movements within Hinduism do not define the Hindu tradition in the way that the eleventh-century breach between Eastern Orthodoxy and Roman Catholicism define medieval Christianity. Nor is there anything in Hinduism similar to the Reformation. In fact, although there are monasteries, they are not part of organized movements similar to the great monastic movements of Catholicism. However, it is possible to identify religious movements associated with figures like Sankara (788–838) and Ramanuja (1017–1130), both of whom were also great Hindu philosophers.

Finally, it is important to recognize that some scholars argue that "Hinduism" as such emerged in the late eighteenth and early nineteenth centuries as a result of British rule in India. The argument here is that prior to the eighteenth century India was a continent inhabited by numerous ethnic groups lacking a unified religion or religious system. Today such groups are called "tribals" in India.

With the coming of the British, Western education arrived in India, and the children of collaborating elites were sent to the best British schools. In these schools they were taught the history of India as construed by British scholars such as Sir William Jones (1746–1794). This history presented a view of the Indian past as one in which Indians were unified by religion and the Sanskrit language—implying a process of sanskritization that drew very different peoples into a common history and religion.

HINDU PHILOSOPHY

Hindus have a rich mythology about gods like Shiva, Kali, Vishnu, and a host of others, which is recorded in their sacred books such as the *Mahabharata*. Strangely enough, Hindus have not developed a theology, possibly because they do not have conflicting, or potentially conflicting, doctrines like the Christian Trinity. On the other hand, the Hindu tradition has produced numerous intellectually challenging philosophical systems and endless religious speculation. The earliest Hindu scriptures, the Vedas, possess only a rudimentary philosophy. They are more concerned with practice and issues like sacrifice. Within the Hindu tradition, philosophy emerges with the Upanishads.

Hindus recognize six orthodox schools of philosophy. These are the Nyaya, Vaiseshika, Sankhya, Yoga, Purva Mimamsa and Uttara Mimamsa schools. Each of these schools has its own collection of writings, or Sutras. That said, the systemization of these schools and their ideas is generally recognized to have taken place long after the Sutras were compiled.

Both the Nyaya and Vaiseshika schools, which eventually merged to form the Nyaya-Vaiseshika school, trace their origin to a sage called Gautama, whose *Nyaya Sutras* are the foundational documents of the school. Most scholars agree that the school itself is older than these sutras. Exactly when Gautama lived is uncertain. The earliest commentary on the Sutras is by Vatsyayama, who is believed to have lived around the fourth century AD. The main commentary, however, was written by Gangesa, a Bengali philosopher who lived in the twelfth or thirteenth century AD. His work is taken to be the definitive interpretation of the system.

This system teaches that all true knowledge arises from the processes of sense perception, inference, comparison, and trustworthy testimony. Untruth gives rise to evil actions, which lead in turn to successive rebirths. All human suffering originates in false knowledge, and liberation depends upon true knowledge.

The importance of this system is not that it is a living reality today, but rather that it forms the foundation for Indian logic and many other philosophical arguments. In a sense it is the equivalent of Aristotle's philosophy and logic in the Indian context.

The *Vaiseshika Sutra* is ascribed to Kanada, whose date is unknown. The earliest commentary on it is by Bhasha of Prasastapada in the fifth century AD. The definitive interpretations, however, are the *Kiranavali* of Udayana and the *Kandali* of Sridhara. Both of these writers lived in the tenth century AD.

Because of the similarity between Nyaya and Vaiseshika teachings, these two schools are often seen as a unified system known as the Nyaya-Vaiseshika. The two share a common view of knowledge and its importance in salvation. The Sutras themselves make no mention of God or of any

Photo 9.7 Scene from the Hindu classic the *Bhagavad Gita*. In this picture Prince Arjuna rides to battle with his charioteer, whose blue skin identifies him as the god Krishna. Before hostilities commence, they carry on a long dialogue about the nature of duty and meaning of life and death.

form of universal soul. These ideas are, however, found in the commentators. Some commentators even attribute to God the work of creation and see him as a first cause. The commentators insist that the existence of God can be proved by deduction, without the aid of revelation.

The goal of life, according to the system, is release from the bonds of karma. The system teaches the existence of individual souls and preaches salvation from the bondage of this life through the acquisition of correct knowledge; to attain this, the initiate needs a good teacher, or guru, to help them reflect on what they have learned. This leads to meditation upon the nature of self, which brings about an experience of truth.

The oldest Indian philosophical system, which is rooted in the Upanishads, is that of Sankhya. As a system, it is traced to the teacher Kapila, to whom the *Sankhya Sutra* was traditionally attributed. Yet the sutra is probably not more than six centuries old. The earliest systematic work on Sankhya is that of Isvarakrishna's *Sankhya-karika*, written around the fifth century AD. Although containing only seventy stanzas, this work clearly outlines the basic teachings of the system.

The Sankhya system is based upon a cosmic dualism that divides the universe into matter and the self, or soul. Each individual self is infinite and eternal. Yet they are in some strange way bound up with matter. This bondage is linked to karma, necessitating liberation. The self, however, cannot liberate itself except through the destruction of ignorance and the gaining of enlightenment. Sankhya makes no mention of God or a universal soul. Therefore, in a certain sense, it is atheistic, because it explains human life without reference to a first cause or a creator. Because living beings consist of three elements, the soul, a subtle body, and the gross body, transmigration (the process by which a soul migrates from one body as it dies to a new one as a child is born) is a complex matter. At death, the gross body is lost and the subtle body transmigrates, but the soul, which is above experience, is not transmigrated because it is eternal.[13]

Further, because all life is essentially suffering, the Sankhya system teaches that the liberation of the soul from bondage to matter is the goal of every reasonable human being. Nevertheless, while preaching liberation, this system provides no methods by which liberation can be attained. Probably the greatest influence of the Sankhya system was on the development of Buddhism, with which it shares many similarities.

The Yoga system, as a philosophy, is a discipline that leads to salvation. Thus, the practice of yoga, or meditation exercises, has to be distinguished from the philosophical system itself. The appeal of the system is found in the practical ways it guides practitioners toward attaining liberation.

Although Yoga is mentioned in the Upanishads, the system itself is attributed to Patanjali, a fifth-century teacher who wrote the *Yoga Sutras*. The earliest commentary on these texts was written by Vyasa in the sixth century. Unlike the other systems mentioned, Yoga is intensely practical. Its concern is not with the nature of the universe or with the soul, but with the liberation of the soul from bondage. Thus, Yoga accepts an essentially pessimis-

---

13. Western writers often call transmigration *reincarnation*. For a philosophical discussion of the issue, see Paul Edwards, *Reincarnation: A Critical Examination* (Amherst: Prometheus Books, 2002).

Photos 9.8 and 9.9 A devout Hindu prepares an offering of milk before the sacred lingam and yoni, which represents the union of creative forces in the universe. Such offerings are both sacrifices and forms of devotion that may be described as a type of yoga.

tic view of life, teaching that release from the cycle of births and deaths is the only hope for humans. To attain release, one must become detached from the world. When, through the practice of yoga, this happens, liberation may be attained.

Traditionally, Yoga involved long hours of training and rigorous discipline. In return, the Yogi, or practitioner, was believed to gain tremendous power. They were said to be able to make themselves invisible, to levitate, to travel through space at the speed of light, and to perform miracles. Some observers claim that it is fairly common practice among Yogis to expel their intestines and wash them. Others say that they can stop their hearts from beating for more than a minute, or be buried alive for several hours before they are dug up again, in perfect health. Whether such claims are true or not is difficult to judge.

The Purva Mimamsa system originated with the *Mimamsa Sutra*, which is attributed to Jaimini, who lived in the third century AD. It consists of over 2500 stanzas and is the largest of the philosophical sutras. A complex text, it is described by many as unintelligible. Therefore, the system depends upon commentators to develop its meaning. The earliest surviving commentary is that of Sabarasvam in the fifth century.

The aim of this system is to demonstrate the revelatory nature of the Vedas by reasoning, and to show that their most important sections are the *Brahmanas*, which deal with ceremonial issues and ritual. Originally, the system lacked reference to God, but later the concept of God was introduced. Overall, this system is very similar to that of the Nyaya-Vaiseshika school, except that the emphasis is placed on religious practice.

Uttara Mimamsa is a coherent system of teaching based upon the Upanishads. This is the dominant school in the Hindu philosophical tradition. The earliest work of the system is known as the *Vedanta Sutras* of Badarayana, written in the fourth century AD. There are numerous commentaries on these sutra and dozens of philosophical works that claim the name Vedanta. The most important of these, however, is the Advaita school of Vedanta.

This school stands in sharp opposition to the atheistic Sankhya system, claiming that all is God and that there is nothing but God. Paradoxically, however, it also claims that God

Photo 9.10 The great Hindu reformer Ram Mohan Roy (1772–1833) cofounded the Brahma Sabha in 1828, out of which the influential organization the Brahmo Samaj developed. He appears to be the first person to have used the word "Hinduism" to describe the Hindu tradition. As a young man he learned English from the Baptist missionary William Carey (1761–1834). After an eventful career, he died of meningitis in Bristol, England, on 27 September 1833, and is buried in Bristol's Arnos Vale Cemetery. The above statue proudly stands outside Bristol Cathedral. Although he never converted to Christianity, he accepted monotheism and was an ardent campaigner for social reform in India.

cannot be said to exist, because everything that exists is conditioned by space and time and therefore subject to causality, but God is beyond all these things. God is Brahma, and Brahma alone is real. Essential to this school is the famous saying "You are that." This identifies the individual with the whole of creation.

In the teaching of this school, the phenomenological world, or world of appearances, is unreal, and life is meaningless. All our ideas of duty, virtue, or morality are nothing in reality, but appear to exist only because we are bound to existence. Consequently, while duty, morality, and so on ought to be observed, the essential thing is to recognize that they are nothing in themselves. As a result, the purpose of life is not liberation, but realization. Through knowledge derived by training, one comes to realize the true nature of reality. And this resolves all other issues.

The great philosophers of this tradition are Sankara (AD 788–838) and Ramanuja (AD 1017–1130), who lived three hundred years apart and developed Vedanta in very different ways. For Sankara, nondualism was the key to understanding. He held that while Brahman and individual soul exist separately, essentially they are the same. Besides Brahman, all is unreal, an illusion from which we must escape. Liberation comes from lifting the veil of ignorance and realizing our basic identity with Brahman.

Sankara's great rival, Ramanuja, proposed a diametrically opposite interpretation. He claimed that the physical world, sense of self, and Brahman are all real. Therefore, ultimate reality is expressed through the world of sense impressions. Consequently, he posited a threefold reality that distinguished between the self, matter, and God, which he saw as having real, separate, but interrelated and interwoven existences.

No survey of Indian philosophy would be complete without mentioning the materialists, about whom we know only from the writings of their enemies, because their own works were systematically destroyed. These philosophers rejected the Vedas and the existence of the soul. Like the Epicureans in ancient Greece, they claimed that heaven and hell were to be found on earth and that life ends with death. The best known of the materialists was Charvakas, who held the Vedas in contempt, claiming that they were composed by unscrupulous fools.

Nevertheless, although Charvakas held asceticism in contempt, he hated animal sacrifice, and was actually a vegetarian. He called upon the rich to abandon the practice of pilgrimage, supporting Brahmins, and building temples. He rejected dharma and moksha, which is translated as "liberation" or release from the wheel of dharma. In the Hindu tradition, it became identified with personal salvation. Because these ideas challenged the very basis of Hindu society, they were suppressed by the Brahmins and eventually forgotten.

HINDU REFORM MOVEMENTS

Kenneth Ingham's book *Reformers in India*[14] painted a dire picture of Indian society in the late seventeenth century. Things began to improve in the early nineteenth century as Hindus responded to the challenge of Christian missions and Western education. One of the first and most influential early Hindu reformers was Ram Mohan Roy (1772–1833), who founded the Brahmo Samaj, or Divine Society, in 1828. An admirer of Christianity and the teachings of Jesus, he sought to remove from Hindu life what he saw as ethically questionable practices,

such as *suttee*, *sati*, or the suicide of widows, which was often involuntary, as well as sacrifices and most aspects of the caste system. He published a translation of the five main Upanishads in 1816 and *The Precepts of Jesus* in 1820 with the aim of bringing Hindus back to what he saw as their religious roots. Essentially, as a result of his contact with Unitarian

Photo 9.11 Suttee (sati), or the ritual sacrifice of a widow, was supposed to be a voluntary act of pious devotion. From contemporary accounts in the eighteenth and nineteenth centuries AD, it appears that in many cases devoted wives and pious widows willingly threw themselves on the flames of their late husbands' funeral pyres, although this verdict needs to be qualified by the fact that most accounts also state that they were high on drugs before doing so. Nevertheless, the necessity of abolishing of this practice, which was seen as "barbaric," served as a justification for British rule, and all the great Hindu reformers of the nineteenth century fought to abolish it as well. The above print, from 1723, makes it clear that in many cases the wife's death was far from voluntary.

14. Kenneth Ingham, *Reformers in India, 1793–1833* (Cambridge: Cambridge Univ. Press, 1956; repr., New York: Octagon, 1973).

missionaries, he taught a monistic system involving belief in the one true God, rejected the worship of idols, and called for social reform. His message was carried on by Devendranath Tagore (1817–1905) and Keshab Chandra Sen (1838–1884).

The next great Hindu reformer was Dayananda Sarasvati (1824–1883), who founded the Arya Samaj, or Aryan Society, in 1875. He too attacked image worship, demanded far-reaching social reforms, and adopted a Unitarian-type theology. His most radical reform was to open the movement to women and people from all castes, encouraging all to read the Hindu scriptures. Interestingly, the Arya Samaj influenced a far greater proportion of Indians living in places like South Africa and Fiji than of those in India itself. The movement encouraged egalitarianism and political involvement, which led it to become one of the sources of modern Indian nationalism.

More than anyone else, Ramakrishna (1836–1886) and his disciple Vivekananda (1863–1902) provided modern Hindus with a contemporary creed to live by in the modern world. The reformers did this by adapting the philosophy of Sankara to Western thinking. Fortunately for them, the philosophy of Hegel (1770–1831) held pride of place in the various Christian colleges and universities of India at that time. As a result, it was easy to move from Hegel's idealism to the idealism of Sankara. Indeed the whole Hindu tradition seemed to lead up to the work of philosophers in the Hegelian tradition, thus giving Indian thinkers a primacy over the West and legitimating Indian metaphysics.

Under Vivekananda these teachings developed into the view that behind the illusory nature of our world lies its true reality. Although we cannot know the higher nature of the divine, we can know its manifestations through its incarnation in Shiva, Kali, Vishnu, and a host of other deities. Thus all worship is the worship of the one God, even though worshipers express this in numerous ways. Further, he argued, we all participate in the divine and are in sense divine ourselves. Recognizing this, we must love all our fellow humans and develop a universal ethic of love that leads to social involvement. Thus Vivekananda set the tone for most of modern Hindu thought by adapting Hindu ideas to the West and arguing that they were better suited for a scientific age than Christianity.

It is out of this rich tradition of thought that the Hindu reformers of the twentieth century emerged. One of the greatest of these was the philosopher Sarvepalli Radhakrishnan (1888–1975), who also engaged in politics and eventually became India's president from 1962 to 1967. His book *The Hindu View of Life*[15] is a classic statement of modern

Photo 9.12 A modern Hindu temple in a large western city in North America.

15. Sarvepalli Radhakrishnan, *The Hindu View of Life* (London: Unwin, 1971; first published 1927).

Photo 9.13 The stunningly beautiful Hare Krishna temple outside of Durban, South Africa.

Hindu beliefs. The other great twentieth-century Hindu was, of course, Gandhi, whose ideas are discussed in the next chapter.

Finally, no survey of the Hindu tradition is complete without reference to the vast outpouring of missionary zeal of the late twentieth century, led by men like Abhay Charanaravinda Bhaktivedanta Swami Prabhupada (1896–1977). A pharmacist for many years, he retired from both business and family life in 1959, when he took a vow of renunciation. For the next seven years he deepened his study of the Hindu scriptures before embarking in 1965 for America, where he founded the Hare Krishna movement in 1966, thus launching the most successful Hindu mission to the West.

The growth of Hindu mission movements like that of Hare Krishna and the growing acceptance of Indian philosophical ideas among ordinary people in the West coincided with the mass migration of skilled Indians to Europe and North America. Thus in the last decades of the twentieth century the Hindu tradition became truly a world tradition and was no longer restricted to India and nearby lands.

CHAPTER 10

GANDHI THE GREAT CONTRARIAN

INTRODUCTION

Mohandas (Mahatma) Gandhi (1869–1948) in a very real sense is the father of modern India. Gandhi was born into a devout Hindu family in the seacoast town of Porbandar, in what is today the Indian state of Gujarat. At the time of his birth it was a royal state ruled by a prince supported by the British. Here his father, Karamchand Gandhi (1822–1885), was the prime minister.

Both his parents were devout Hindus, and they raised their children in a rich, but relatively liberal, Hindu tradition. His mother's piety, which deeply impressed her son, was of the Vaishnavista variety, which centered on the worship of the supreme god Vishnu through his avatars (manifestations in human form) Rama and Krishna and was rooted in the great Hindu epic of the *Mahabharata*. The young Gandhi also found himself surrounded by people of other faiths, including Jains, whose piety and commitment to nonviolence and vegetarianism impressed him.

At the age of thirteen Gandhi was married to a fourteen-year-old bride in an arranged child marriage, following local customs. A year later they had their first child, who died shortly afterwards. Four other children followed in later years. It seems the marriage was successful in traditional terms, although his wife, Kasturbai Makhanji, remained uneducated and possibly illiterate throughout her life, which seems to have caused him some concern later on.

Gandhi's family wanted him to become a barrister, which in the British system is the top legal position before becoming a judge, but in his school years they discovered to their horror that he was an indifferent student. Nevertheless, in September 1888 he sailed for London, England, where he studied law at University College. Until this time he appears to have had little personal interest in religion, although in London he came into contact with both the Vegetarian Society, which he joined, and the Theosophical Society, whose lectures he sometimes attended and whose members became some of his closest British friends. Encouraged by Theosophist friends, he began reading the *Bhagavad Gita*, while at the same time carefully examining the Christian scriptures.

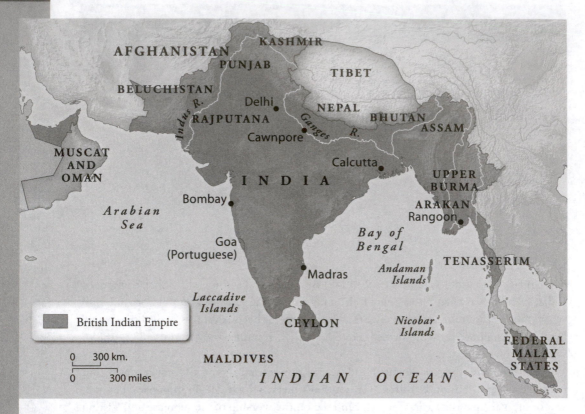

Map 10.1 The British Indian Empire at its height in the late nineteenth century. British expansion in India began in the seventeenth century as a result of the activities of the private British East India Company. Gradually most of India came under the company's control. Then in 1857 Muslim troops in the East India Company's army rebelled. Once the rebellion was suppressed, the British government took over the rule of India from the company. Whatever its shortcomings, the British Indian Empire gave India a unifying language, English, a superb railway system, and a good administration that was largely run by Indians. It also brought to an end Muslim rule over most of the country and created the conditions that led to the Hindu revivals of the early and late nineteenth century. The British directors of the East India Company, like James Mill, were freethinking agnostics who appreciated religions other than Christianity and discouraged missionary activity, which they saw as detrimental to trade.

After completing his studies, he was called to the bar in 1891 and returned to India to practice law in what was then Bombay, modern Mumbai, but failed to make a success of his new venture. Therefore, after teaching for a short time while continuing to work as a lawyer on the side, he accepted a post in South Africa with an Indian company that traded there. As a result he moved to Durban in 1893 on a one-year contract. In South Africa Gandhi thrived and soon established his own law firm working in Johannesburg and Durban.

According to tradition, while on his way to Pretoria by train, Gandhi, who was by now a well-spoken and immaculately dressed Indian gentleman, was thrown out of his first-class compartment by an uncouth railway porter in Pietermaritzburg, the capital of

Natal Province, in May 1893. As a result he spent a very cold night shivering in an unheated waiting room. Out of this traumatic experience Gandhi developed his abiding passion for social justice and developed his philosophy of nonviolence. After this incident he remained in South Africa, developing his religious philosophy and experimenting with social protest against injustice and with various types of communal living.

In 1913 he met the Anglican clergyman and social activist Charles Freer Andrews (1871–1940), who was visiting South Africa from India. Andrews was impressed by Gandhi's philosophy and what he saw as his deeply Christian vision. Therefore, he cooperated with Gandhi on various projects and eventually persuaded Gandhi to return to India, which he did in 1915.

Back in India, Gandhi developed the views on nonviolence that he would use to great effect against British rulers to bring about the eventual independence of India in 1948. A few months later he was murdered by a Hindu fanatic who thought he was too liberal and therefore not a true Hindu. Gandhi left behind him hundreds of books and articles and a rich political tradition of nonviolence as a means to achieve social reform.

The remainder of this chapter deals with some little-known aspects of the life and teachings of Mohandas Gandhi, who, it will be argued, was a great contrarian, deeply rooted in both Indian and Western traditions of thought. Anyone who examines his work looking for passages that deal with topics like education soon runs across some very curious remarks that illustrate his contrarian spirit. For example, his writing about the Anglo-Indian poet Rudyard Kipling (1865–1936) and his famous—or infamous—poem "The White Man's Burden" shows that, against all expectations, Gandhi appreciated Kipling's work.

Indeed, whenever the reader thinks they have understood Gandhi, a few pages further he says something quite unexpected. Unlike so many people today, Gandhi did not toe a party line, allow an overarching ideology to shape his ideas, nor did he become what Sir Karl Popper called "addicted to theory."[1] Rather, he reacted to living situations in terms of his own understanding of the good and the true, and his ideas developed over time; yet there is a consistency to them

Photo 10.1 The young Gandhi as a successful South African lawyer during a visit to England in 1906. At this time he was widely respected and was at the height of his secular career.

Photo 10.2 The English poet Rudyard Kipling, whom most literary critics and many others scorn today as an unreflective imperialist. In fact, Gandhi admired his work. The sketch is by the Marchioness of Granby.

---

1. Karl Popper, *The Myth of Framework*, ed. M. A. Notturno (London: Routledge, 1994), 53.

based on his commitment to the search for truth. Therefore, in the spirit of contrarianism, this chapter offers some provocative comments on our own times by attempting to identify those themes in Kipling's poem that probably appealed to Gandhi in terms of his own outlook.

GANDHI AND "THE WHITE MAN'S BURDEN"

To illustrate what is meant by describing Gandhi as a contrarian, let us begin by quoting the first three stanzas of Rudyard Kipling's once-popular poem "The White Man's Burden," published in 1899 as a comment on the occupation of the Philippines by the U.S.

Take up the White Man's burden—
　　Send forth the best ye breed—
Go bind your sons to exile
　　To serve your captives' need;
To wait, in heavy harness,
　　On fluttered folk and wild—
Your new-caught sullen peoples,
　　Half devil and half child.

Take up the White Man's burden—
　　In patience to abide,
To veil the threat of terror
　　And check the show of pride;
By open speech and simple,
　　An hundred times made plain,
To seek another's profit,
　　And work another's gain.

Take up the White Man's burden—
　　The savage wars of peace—
Fill full the mouth of Famine,
　　And bid the sickness cease;
And when your goal is nearest
　　The end for others sought,
Watch Sloth and heathen Folly
　　Bring all your hope to nought.[2]

Whenever students read these lines today, they gasp in astonishment, shock, and unbelief. To most students these verses are the ultimate heresy. They see them as an expression of colonial prejudices that prove the evils of imperialism. For them such sentiments have no place in a multicultural world. No doubt many of you will share these feelings of revulsion toward Kipling's imperial sentiments. Therefore, it comes as a complete surprise to learn

---

2. Rudyard Kipling, "The White Man's Burden," in *Rudyard Kipling's Verse* (London: Hodder and Stoughton, 1949), 323–24.

that Gandhi defended the poem, arguing that it had "been very much misunderstood" and that Kipling was not a racist.[3]

This comment is quite remarkable. The first question it forces upon us is, why was Gandhi not appalled by this seemingly jingoistic poem? The answer seems to be that because Gandhi did not see Kipling as a racist, he was able to look beyond the first line and ponder the author's intent. It seems probable that, instead of understanding "White Man" as a racial category, Gandhi interpreted the phrase "White Man's burden" to mean "civilization's burden." Despite all his Romanticism and love of villages, Gandhi was a great lover of civilization and acutely aware of the dangers of tyranny and chaos facing civilized life.

Thus, if we substitute "civilization" for "White Man," we get a very different reading of the poem:

Photo 10.3 Gandhi outside his law office in Johannesburg with members of his staff in 1905. On the left is his colleague, Mr. Polak; on the right, his European secretary, Miss Schlesin. Note the multiracial and multicultural nature of his team.

> Take up civilization's
> burden —
> Send forth the best ye
> breed —
> Go bind your sons to exile
> To serve your captives'
> need.[4]

Of course we may object to the term "captive," but if we contextualize the expression in terms of America's invasion and conquest of the Philippines, it is actually quite appropriate. Seen in this light, the poem takes on a completely different tone.

GANDHI AND THE EVIL EMPIRE

Using words echoed by the Ayatollah Khomeini, with reference to the United States of America, Gandhi argued that the British Empire represented "Satanism," adding, "and they who love God can afford to have no love for Satan." As an empire, he said, it "certainly has been guilty of misdeeds" and "terrible atrocities," while the British government in India was best compared "to a robber."[5]

Nevertheless, this empire, which Gandhi spent a large part of his life criticizing, was not beyond redemption. Its failure was the failure to be what it was destined to be, not

3. Mahatma Gandhi, *Collected Works of Mahatma Gandhi* (New Delhi: Ministry of Information and Broadcasting, 1988), 8:320.
4. "The White Man's Burden," lines 1–4.
5. Ghandi, *Collected Works*, 20:362.

that it was an empire. Gandhi outlined this position on the British Empire during a trial of Indian protesters in Johannesburg in 1908, when he argued, "The Transvaal Indians have to shoulder a burden on behalf of the whole of India." This burden was that of opposing the views of white settlers, who sought to create a racist state that was in Gandhi's view "a change [for the worse] in British policy."

Such people, Gandhi said, "represent a rather unworthy aspect of British policy and, if they gain currency, they will herald the decline of the Empire. Therefore, the Indians' resistance tends to the good of the British Empire, too." Gandhi claimed that it was racist white colonists, not Gandhi himself, or other Indian protesters, who were the real "enemies of the British Empire." The Indians, Gandhi argued, were actually the true "friends of the Empire."[6]

From these and many similar comments scattered throughout his *Collected Works*, it is clear that Gandhi was not opposed to the idea of empire as such. Nor was he hostile to the British Empire as an empire. What he rejected was the illusion of empire—that is, when one group of people was allowed to lord it over all others because the empire was *their* empire. For him, the idea of empire was not necessarily a bad thing, provided it was an inclusive empire that gave citizenship and equal rights to all.

Gandhi's open-minded reaction to both Kipling's poem and the British Empire allowed him to reach quite unexpected conclusions based on what he saw as truth. The key issue for Gandhi was always the question of truth. What we find in his writings is a commitment to the idea of truth, not the claim that he possessed the truth. Rather, as the title of his famous book *My Experiment with Truth* (1927) proclaimed, Gandhi was on a lifelong pilgrimage as a seeker of truth. For this reason he was able to appreciate what he saw as good and true in both Kipling's poem and the British Empire, while strongly rejecting racism and popular ideas that justified European arrogance.

Gandhi opposed only empires that oppressed their subject peoples and failed to fulfill their promise of peace, security, and the betterment of their peoples. Over time Gandhi's attitude toward the British Empire

Photo 10.4 Victoria Station (now called Chhatrapati Shivaji Terminus) in Bombay, modern Mumbai, which for many Europeans and Indians alike represented all that was best in the British Empire. This is the world into which Gandhi was born and reflects those values of progress—in the best sense of the word—that he wished to preserve.

6. Ghandi, *Collected Works*, 9:219.

changed, becoming increasingly critical. What did not change was his willingness to judge every situation on its own merits.

Gandhi could take this approach because he was committed to the importance of civilization.[7] While highly critical of "Western civilization," "British civilization," and "modern civilization,"[8] he was equally critical of "Indian civilization."[9] Nevertheless, for him civilization was a basic necessity and a right that all people deserved to enjoy. Gandhi's severe, sometimes shrill, denunciations of both Western and modern civilization, as Anthony Parel points out, are "likely to mislead," because his attitude, even toward modern civilization, was "not wholly negative."

For Gandhi, criticism implied "the desire to improve the object criticized." Hence there were many aspects of modern civilization, such as "civil liberty, equality, rights," and "the liberation of women," that he welcomed.[10] Looking at the world around him and the history of humankind, Gandhi was all too aware that society can easily collapse into chaos and barbarism.[11] Avoiding this danger was a constant struggle and one of the factors that motivated his pacifism.[12]

Gandhi defined civilization quite explicitly, as "that mode of conduct which points out to man the path of duty."[13] As such, true civilization represented "good conduct" or "a good way of life."[14] Americans and Canadians pride themselves that their lands are blessed with natural resources and good government, making them great places to live. Yet it seems unlikely

Photo 10.5 Gandhi and Muhammad Ali Jinnah (1876–1948), the secular leader of India's large Muslim minority in Bombay, April 28, 1938. Throughout his life Gandhi strove to bring peoples of different creeds and belief systems together to create a good society. Later, in 1948, Jinnah went on to help create the separate state of Pakistan leading to the partition of the Indian sub-continent. He is usually regarded as the "father" of Pakistan.

that Gandhi would see things in this way. He would ask, as he did so often, do we do our duty to our own people and others throughout the world? Do we promote good conduct

7. Ghandi, *Collected Works*, 10:258–62, 279–81. Cf. Mahatma Gandhi, *Hind Swaraj and Other Writings*, ed. Anthony J. Parel (Cambridge, Cambridge Univ. Press, 1997), 66–71.

8. Gandhi, *Hind Swaraj*, 34–38.

9. Ibid., 70–71.

10. Ibid., xvii; Gandhi, *Collected Works*, 95:208.

11. Gandhi, *Hind Swaraj*, xviii; Gandhi, *Collected Works*, 79:40–41.

12. Gandhi, *Collected Works*, 42:362.

13. Gandhi, *Hind Swaraj*, 67.

14. Ibid., 67n124.

and a good way of life, or are we allowing our material wealth to blind us to social reality by promoting illusions about the purpose of life itself?

THE CALL TO SERVICE

Although Gandhi and Kipling both died less than a hundred years ago, a huge cultural gap separates them from our own time. Reading the poem today in any meaningful way is almost impossible, because the ideas are expressed in ways that seem totally alien to us.

Consider again the lines:

> Send forth the best ye breed—
> Go bind your sons to exile
> To serve your captives' need.[15]

Today these lines sound hypocritical and absurd, and appear totally meaningless. Yet to Gandhi and numerous others, the idea that individuals would sacrifice themselves for the good of other people in an empire was an acceptable notion. Gandhi admired British society for sending some of its elite from schools like Eton overseas to govern their empire with a degree of fairness and justice.[16]

Of course, Gandhi clashed with many colonial administrators and frequently pointed out unfairness and injustice. Nevertheless, overall, he had great respect for imperial administrators both as individuals and as a class. Surprisingly, he believed that many servants of the empire actually attempted to be fair and just.[17] My question is, can we say the same of the neoimperialism we see at work in the world today?

Most Christians in Europe and North Americans support their governments when they

Photo 10.6 Despite his great admiration for the English and all that was good in the British Empire, Gandhi was well aware of the injustices of history. He also recognized the power of propaganda contained in prints like the one shown here, entitled *The Massacre at Cawpur, June 26, 1857.* What it depicts is the killing of British civilians and some army officers by Indian troops during what Indians call the First War of Independence and the British refer to as the Indian Mutiny. Although this event took place long before Gandhi was born, the memory of the rebellion by Indian troops and local rulers remained strong in the minds of both the British and Indians. In Gandhi's philosophy it was memories like this that needed to be transformed and used to demonstrate the evils of violence.

15. "The White Man's Burden," lines 2–4.
16. Gandhi, *Collected Works,* 6:457.
17. Ibid., 4:73, 475–76.

go to war. Yet how many worry about the children who are being born with genetic defects caused by radiation from the depleted uranium that makes the casing on many modern bombs? Or how many think about the numerous people who lose limbs because of bombs that explode years after conflicts have ceased? This selective way Christians see the world was one of the things that turned Gandhi away from embracing Christianity as a young man.

Here it is important to emphasize that in supporting "peace-keeping missions," in bombing places like Serbia, or in calling for troops to be sent to places like Darfur, we are actually engaging in what Kipling more honestly called "the savage wars of peace" (line 18). We are engaging in a form of imperialism and imposing our will on people who reject our values, even though our leaders deny that this is what they are doing.

The truth is, despite all the so-called moral relativism of our society and our desire to respect other cultures, we do not, nor should we, accept evils like genocide as morally acceptable or something we can stand by and watch. Nevertheless, it is time to be more honest about our values and recognize that both Kipling and Gandhi have a lot to teach us about truth.

Politicians go to great lengths to stress that imperialism is dead and that as soon as freedom, democracy, and peace are "restored" in some trouble spot, the task is complete. This is a slash-and-burn, empire-on-the-cheap neoimperialism that imposes Western control without taking responsibility for what follows. Since, like the poor, imperialism seems to be an abiding fact of human life, my question is, which type of imperialism do we prefer: one that simply exploits through the imposition of acceptable local rulers, or one that accepts responsibility for intervening in a country and attempts to actively improve the lot of the people whose lives it controls?

CHARITY BEGINS AT HOME

Today we pride ourselves on combating famines and aiding the poor throughout the world. It seems unlikely, therefore, that anyone will take offense at the line "Fill full the mouth of Famine." A more likely reaction to these verses is to ask why Kipling felt it necessary to utter them, and to see in them something so trite that they really say nothing. Once again the distance between our time and that of Gandhi and Kipling clouds our understanding. What we must not forget is that when Kipling wrote these words, the principle they expressed was by no means a generally accepted norm.

Anyone who reads issues of the *Anthropological Review* or *Journal of the Anthropological Institute* from the last decades of the nineteenth century soon discovers that there was an intense debate, often between missionaries and anthropologists, about the wisdom of feeding the hungry. On the one side were humanitarians who sought to aid the poor. On the other were social Darwinists who used the idea of the survival of the fittest to justify accepting the arguments of Thomas Malthus (1766–1834) that famines are a natural way of reducing the population and ought not to be prevented.

Here it is important to note that Gandhi, like Kipling, was well aware of the devastating effects of famines, which, in 1902, he said, "as a rule, recur in India every four years."[18] Forty-five years later, toward the end of his life, he was still scheming ways to "be rid of

18. Ibid., 2:17.

Photo 10.7 This picture of young children with their teachers is from a Christian mission school taken in the late nineteenth century. Surprisingly, Gandhi and most other Hindu reformers were supportive of Christian schools which, along with hospitals, they saw as a practical expression of Christ's teachings. As a result most, if not all, of the first generation modern political leaders of India, Africa, and many other parts of the world were educated by Christians. Today this rich heritage of education and service is in decline among Christians which is something Gandhi would have lamented because he always worked closely with his many Christian friends.

famines" and alleviate grinding poverty.[19] Today Kipling's words and Gandhi's concerns still challenge us to take seriously the alleviation of hunger throughout the world. Yet how often do I ever think about the abject poverty found in Canada and even my own province of Alberta? Sadly, our sense of social responsibility does not even reach beyond our own backyard.

Anyone who doubts this has only to drive into a run-down, downtown area in almost any North American city. For example, at the corner of Center Street and Eleventh Avenue southwest in the Canadian city of Calgary, one can always see long lines of ill-clad and undernourished people gathered in the vicinity of the Mustard Seed, a Christian aid agency, where they are given food and shelter. Most of these people are not the victims of a natural disaster such as famine. Most are the victims of a man-made disaster brought about by the closing down of long-term mental wards throughout Canada. Turning them out onto the street was justified in terms of pseudoacademic theories about the need to integrate the mentally ill into the community. All that the last ten years has achieved is the creation of a growing underclass of homeless people unable to care for themselves.

Another good example of institutionalized poverty in places like Canada is found in the system of Native reserves, homelands, nations, or whatever you want to call them. With few exceptions, most Native Canadians live in substandard housing, sometimes even without basic facilities like running water and electricity. Anyone who has visited a Native

19. Ibid., 98:89.

area is bound to be shocked.[20] Yet how many Canadians are aware of the extent of poverty among Native Canadians? And how many Americans or Europeans are aware of similar problems in their own countries?

MEDICAL MISSIONS

No doubt everyone also agrees with Kipling's line "bid the sickness cease" (line 20). North Americans are proud that their governments are helping fight AIDS and other epidemics in the world. The question I have is, how seriously do we really take our duty to aid the poor and sick of this world?

Around fifteen years ago Western governments began deliberately cutting back on places in medical school for both doctors and nurses. Now, according to a recent BBC documentary, British hospitals are recruiting nurses from Malawi, one of the world's poorest countries. The harsh fact is that it makes economic sense for Britain to allow Malawi to bear the cost of training nurses and doctors before they are hired to work in Britain at salaries they could never imagine in their home country. What this does, of course, is undermine the medical system of a country where good medical treatment is already almost impossible to come by.

Today many Canadian provinces and American states are facing an acute shortage of doctors and nurses and, like Britain, are recruiting them from countries that cannot really afford to lose any medical personnel at all. All one has to do is count the number of South African doctors and nurses who have flocked to North America since 1990. It seems that almost every rural town in Canada has a South African doctor. Yet South Africa cannot afford to lose such people. Not only has our sense of social responsibility lost its universal appeal; it has become exploitative.

The harsh truth is that Western medical systems are as good as they are today because the citizens of Western

Photo 10.8 The grave of the great English writer John Bunyan, whom Gandhi greatly admired as a true visionary with a strong religious and social vision. Bunyan's *Pilgrim's Progress*, though neglected by today's readers, was considered by Gandhi to be one of the greatest literary achievements of all history. Anyone wondering about this ought to read Christopher Hill's biography of Bunyan, *A Tinker and a Poor Man* (1988),[21] to understand why Gandhi was attracted to Bunyan.

---

20. "Building Success on Native Reserves," *National Post*, 8 September 2004, A10. Although many will disagree with the argument presented in this article, at least it acknowledges the issue.

21. Christopher Hill, *A Tinker and a Poor Man: John Bunyan and His Church, 1628–1688* (New York: Knopf, 1989).

countries have allowed all levels of their governments to engage in the rape of the health systems of the so-called Third World. Why do we never hear protests against this policy which allows poor nations to pour their resources into medical training that in the longer run only benefits far richer countries?

THE DEMOCRATIC IMPULSE

Another place where Gandhi and Kipling shared a common outlook is found in the following lines, again from "The White Man's Burden":

> No tawdry rule of kings,
>   But toil of serf and sweeper—
> The tale of common things.[22]

With this sentiment Gandhi was in wholehearted agreement. Explaining his pacifism, he once said, "For me 'man is a man for a' that,"[23] citing the Scottish brogue, or dialect, of Robbie Burns' famous poem "Is There for Honest Poverty."[24] Writing about the institution of monarchy, Gandhi observed, "In all civilized communities kings have been reduced to the status of figure-heads." He also argued that "industrious farmers are a far greater and truer treasure for any country than kings and nobles."[25]

Nevertheless, he did not see monarchy as the greatest problem facing ordinary people. Rather, Gandhi warned that in place of kings, "officials have become indispensable and all-important." As a result, "they begin to consider self-interest more important than duty, and sufficient attention is not paid to the welfare of the people." This, he argued, tended to be the case because many officials became "autocratic, short-sighted and haughty."[26] Yet this ought not to be the case, because we need to remember that "high-salaried officers are not our kings, but our servants." This, he reminded his readers, was because "they are paid by us."[27]

Reading Gandhi's works, one notices that he spends far more time criticizing local administrators and various types of officials than he does the British or Indian government. True democracy, he believed, begins at the grassroots level, and unless sufficient attention is paid to reforming local governments, any change of government at the national level is a waste of time.

Do we recognize the need to criticize our own local officials? Rather than simply bemoaning corruption in the federal government, surely a vigorous debate ought to be raging about all aspects of civil society in the West. Frankly, one does not see this debate today. For example, beginning around 1990, the nature of university education began to be transformed. Essentially, the older view that society ought to offer a very good education to all qualified citizens was replaced by a promotion of elite institutions and programs

22. "The White Man's Burden," lines 26–29.

23. Gandhi, *Collected Works*, 48:331.

24. Robert Burns, *Poems and Songs of Robert Burns*, ed. James Barke (London: Fontana, 1987), 642–43.

25. Gandhi, *Collected Works*, 11:186.

26. Ibid., 4:171–72.

27. Ibid., 7:341.

within institutions and a downgrading of the overall level of higher education by starving it of funds.

At the same time a shift has occurred from the humanities and social sciences toward business, medicine, engineering, high tech, and similar faculties. This shift was accompanied by a desire to prepare people for specific careers rather than provide them with a good general education. The biggest problem with this approach is that it mirrors the failed educational systems of Eastern Europe under Communism, where people were unable to respond to changing job markets and economic realities.

Nowhere in North America is this major shift in social and educational

Photo 10.9 The Russian Christian author Count Lev (aka Leo) Nikolayevich Tolstoy (1828–1910), who wrote the novels *War and Peace* and *Anna Karenina*, was another great inspiration to Gandhi, both as a writer and as a man who attempted to live by the gospel. Here Tolstoy, dressed in peasant clothing, is at work on his farm in 1908.

policy a matter of urgent debate. Newspapers essentially avoid serious discussion of these issues, as do radio and television stations. Whether these changes are good or bad, whether they are necessary or reflect the vainglory of administrators seeking to further their own careers, I do not know. What is clear is that as a nation we are not debating these or a host of similar issues.

PLAIN SPEECH

No doubt Gandhi also liked the lines

> By open speech and simple,
> An hundred times made plain.[28]

Anyone who reads Gandhi's works quickly discovers that he loved plain speech. As a master of the English language, he always sought to make his meaning clear to everyone who could read. In this he follows in the tradition of John Bunyan, whom he admired. Gandhi's commitment to plain speech stands in sharp contrast to much of what passes for erudition today. Anyone who takes a course in the social sciences or humanities at a modern university soon discovers that many professors pride themselves in the use of obscure language and technical terms that appear to enhance their prestige as "deep thinkers."

Such pretensions are absurd. My first encounter with one popular academic fad came when I was a graduate student working in South African archives. Living in the small university town of Potchefstroom, I ate my midday meal with a group of Afrikaner graduate students, most of whom were studying philosophy. Over the year we became friends and had many heated arguments about the injustices of apartheid. After arriving in South Africa

---

28. "The White Man's Burden," lines 13–14.

I had joined both the South African Institute of Race Relations (SAIRR) and the Christian Institute, the two leading antiapartheid organizations within South Africa.

Consequently, I came to our debates well armed with facts and figures from the SAIRR annual *Survey of Race Relations in South Africa*. Eventually, my lunch companions became frustrated with my arguments and responded by telling me that they had to admit they had never realized the power of English empiricism until they met me. Clearly, my empirical approach to "facts" blinded me to the recognition that "all facts are interpreted facts." Therefore, they suggested that I study hermeneutics and the work of scholars like Martin Heidegger (1889–1976) and Hans-Georg Gadamer (1900–2002). They were sure that if I did this I would see the logic of apartheid and abandon my "simplistic empiricism."

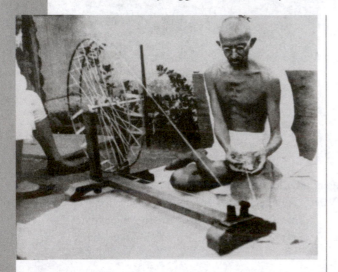

Photo 10.10 Gandhi at his famous spinning wheel, which he used to emphasize the need for India to develop its own industries for the benefit of its peoples. In this and his various communal experiments he was inspired by Tolstoy.

The lesson I took from this experience was that if the work of these men, which the Potchefstroom philosophers understood very well, since many of them had studied with them,[29] legitimated apartheid, then I wanted nothing to do with it. Years later Heidegger was exposed as a strong supporter of National Socialism. Although for a while his supporters denied this, they eventually settled for the argument that his political views did not affect his philosophy.[30]

There is no doubt where Gandhi would have stood on this issue. Like Kipling, he recognized that mystification through the use of high-sounding language is a common tool of tyrants, who blind people to reality through a web of words. As Walter Kaufmann observed, "one has often to ask oneself as a matter of honesty: What does this mean in plain language? And the

29. Martin Heidegger acknowledges the work of Hendrik Gerhardhus Stoker (1899–1993), the Dean of Potchefstroom philosophers in *Sein und Zeit* (Tübingen: Max Niemeyer Verlag, 1979; first published 1927), 272n1. It should also be noted that despite his support for apartheid and his essentially racist views, Stoker was a cultured and charming man who on the personal level treated Blacks well and respected them as individuals. This paradox illustrates the complexity of racism and the relationship between beliefs and actions.

30. Hugo Ott, *Martin Heidegger: A Political Life*, trans. Allan Blunden (London: Fontana, 1994); Tom Rockmore, in *Heidegger and French Philosophy: Humanism, Antihumanism and Being* (London: Routledge, 1995), shows how Heidegger actively rehabilitated himself through his contacts with former students in France following World War II, and how he distorted his own earlier arguments to make himself appear respectable. The most recent blow to Heidegger's reputation is Emmanuel Faye's *Heidegger: The Introduction of Nazism into Philosophy* (New Haven: Yale Univ. Press, 2009).

answer is often devastating."[31] Insisting on the use of plain speech in both public and academic discourse, in politics and philosophy, is not simplistic but a democratic imperative.

THE FINAL JUDGMENT

Today few people spend much time thinking about the way our religious beliefs are viewed by others. Gandhi was different. Like the apostle Paul, he believed that a person's religious faith ought to bear fruit in their lives. Therefore, when Kipling told Americans, "By all ye leave or do, / The silent, sullen peoples / Shall weigh your Gods and you," Gandhi would have understood.

Undoubtedly, the most unexpected political development over the past twenty to fifty years has been the decline of traditional political discourse and the rise of so-called Christian politics in the United States of America. The ability of a small group of self-identified Christian fundamentalists to gain so much power within the Republican Party in the United States is truly amazing. Again and again sociologists and political scientists have declared the "Christian Right" dead and confidently promoted the illusion that this is a passing phenomenon that will soon fizzle out.[32] Yet the Christian Right continues to grow and gain increasing power.

Many people react to the growth of the American Christian Right by seeking the total separation of religion and politics. Gandhi would have found such a reaction laughable. He had no illusions about the close relationship between religion and politics. Religion, in his view, was a necessary element in all moral, social, and political decisions. Therefore, he did not believe that religion and politics could ever be completely separated. Nevertheless, his understanding of how religion affects politics was radically different from that of the spokespeople of the Christian Right in America.

To a surprisingly large extent Gandhi's political views were based on Christian teachings[33] and the example of great Christian leaders.[34] Thus, Gandhi found inspiration in the life and work of Oliver Cromwell,[35] John Wesley,[36] and most of all John Bunyan,[37] who, he noted, spent twelve long years in prison before he "won freedom for his people."[38] For Gandhi, *The Pilgrim's Progress* was "the most beautiful book in the English language."[39] Bunyan's example and writings, he said, were one of the main sources of England's greatness and as such ought to inspire others.[40]

---

31. Walter Kaufmann, *Critique of Religion and Philosophy* (London: Faber and Faber, 1958), 42–43.

32. A good example of this is found in the work of British sociologist Steve Bruce, who confidently proclaimed the demise of the Christian Right in his book *The Rise and Fall of the New Christian Right: Conservative Protestant Politics in America, 1978–1988* (Oxford: Oxford Univ. Press, 1988); cf. Clyde Wilcox, *Onward Christian Soldiers? The Religious Right in American Politics* (Boulder, Colo.: Westview, 1996).

33. Gandhi, *Collected Works*, 63:327–28; 7:429.

34. Ibid., 4:399–400.

35. Ibid., 4:461; 7:87.

36. Ibid., 1:91, 310; 4:474.

37. Ibid., 5:383–84.

38. Ibid., 9:306.

39. Ibid., 5:399; 26:227.

40. Ibid., 26:319–20.

Photo 10.11 Gandhi with the Theosophical leader Annie Besant in Madras, September 1921. During his stay in London (1888–1891), the young Gandhi was befriended by, and grew close to, many Theosophists. Later, as this picture shows, he developed a working relationship with members of the Theosophical Society in India. Besant, an evangelical Christian and British social activist turned agnostic, had converted to Theosophy in 1889. She immigrated to India, where she became one of the founders of the Indian National Congress, which led India to independence from the British Empire in 1948.

Instead of simply criticizing religious people who engaged in politics as fools or fanatics, Gandhi tried sincerely to understand their viewpoint and judge them in their own terms. He read the great works of philosophy and theology alongside the main scriptures of major world religions. Then he offered criticisms in terms of his opponents' understanding of their own belief by citing their sources to prove his point. Surely Gandhi's example remains valuable today; instead of dismissing people who engage in religious rhetoric, we ought to engage them in real political debates, not ridiculing them, but demanding that they take the teaching of their own traditions seriously.[41]

This is what Beyers Naudé did in South Africa when in 1961 he founded the magazine *Pro Veritate* and in 1962 founded the Christian Institute of Southern Africa to criticize and oppose the nationalist government and its policy of apartheid. Instead of simply accepting the common view that apartheid grew out of the outdated sixteenth-century Calvinism of most Afrikaners, Naudé and his coworkers set out to show that the teachings of John Calvin and Calvinism did not support apartheid. So successful was he in this venture that the Christian Institute was banned in 1977 as a subversive organization and *Pro Veritate* was forced to cease publication.[42] The example of Naudé and that of Gandhi before him point forward to how we today ought to deal with increasingly politicized religious groups.

CONCLUSION

Throughout this chapter I have argued that Gandhi's appreciation and defense of Kipling's much-maligned poem "The White Man's Burden" provides us with insights into Gandhi's

---

41. Ibid., 4:242–47; 6:522; 98:109.

42. Colleen Ryan, *Beyers Naudé: Pilgrimage of Faith* (Grand Rapids: Eerdmans, 1990).

attitude to political and social issues that ought to cause us to reflect afresh on the issues of our own times. Finally, it needs to be noted that Gandhi did not always agree with Kipling. Indeed he totally rejected Kipling's lines, "East is East and West is West / And never the twain shall meet."[43]

Against this view Gandhi argued, "Wherever I went in London, in England or in Europe, I was surrounded with the greatest amount of affection and I felt that there was no truth in Kipling's saying that the East and West would never meet ... On the contrary, I have been convinced more than ever that human nature is much the same, no matter in what clime it flourishes."[44] This comment challenges us all to take up civilization's burden and seek the welfare of all people.

43. Kipling, "The Ballad of East and West," *Verse*, 234.
44. Gandhi, *Collected Works*, 54:321.

CHAPTER 11

BUDDHISM

INTRODUCTION

Of all the world's religions, Buddhism is arguably the most misunderstood in Western society. This is the direct result of the work of nineteenth century European writers who embraced Buddhism as an alternative to Christianity. Most of these people were agnostics, although some were nominally Christian or Unitarian. The most successful promoter of Buddhism in the nineteenth century was Sir Edwin Arnold (1832–1904) whose poem *The Light of Asia* (1879) became an instant best seller in Britain and America before being translated into numerous other languages.

Arnold, an editor with the influential British newspaper *The Daily Telegraph*, began his career as a political liberal before becoming increasingly conservative through his whole-hearted support for imperialism and the extension of the British Empire. A well-respected poet in his own right, Arnold remained a liberal Christian, strongly influenced by his second wife, Fanny Maria Adelaide Channing, the daughter of the transcendentalist Unitarian minister William Henry Channing (1810–1884) and great niece of the famous American Unitarian preacher William Ellery Channing (1780–1842).

The Light of Asia, Arnold's most famous work, purports to be a retelling of the life of the Buddha based on original texts. Actually, though it draws upon several early English translations of Buddhist scriptures, it was explicitly written as a testimony to the power of religious liberalism. Arnold drew most heavily on Samuel Beal's *Abhinishkramana Sutra* (1875), supplementing that with Robert Spence Hardy's (1803–1868) *A Manual of Buddhism* (1854) and Max Müller's (1823–1900) *Dhammapada* (1870).

Proud of his literary skills, Arnold unashamedly adapted Buddhism and Buddhist texts to what he saw as the interests of his readers. Therefore, he had no hesitation in removing what he considered tedious passages, expanding on interesting ideas or stories, adding dramatic scenes, and removing what he considered unscientific, such as miracle stories. Only those

Photo 11.1 Sir Edwin Arnold, the author of *The Light of Asia* (1879).

elements of the original which could be readily interpreted within a modern mechanistic worldview entered his fascinating yet deeply flawed text.

Nevertheless, the book was a stunning success, leading to tours of Eastern lands and instant acclaim by respected members of indigenous Buddhist groups. Local politicians, who appreciated the recognition he gave to their traditions in terms of increasing Western interest in Eastern religions, accorded him great respect. In these ways Arnold was a forerunner of modern multicultural thinking and a pioneer in East-West dialogue. But in terms of accurately conveying Buddhist thought to the West, he actually set things on a very distorted path.

It is little wonder that almost a hundred years after the publication of his work, the great twentieth-century Buddhist scholar and practicing Buddhist Edward Conze (1904–1979) could lament that people inspired by Arnold had purged "Buddhism of the doctrine of 'not-self' and of monasticism," arguing instead that "some gospel of 'The Man' is the original gospel of Buddhism." Then Conze pointed out that "H. J. Jennings, in cold blood, removes all references to reincarnation from the Scriptures, and thereby claims to have restored their original meaning. Dr. P. Dahlke, again, ignores all the magic and mythology with which traditional Buddhism is replete …"[1] Such writers, and there are many, simply followed in Arnold's footsteps, taking what they found acceptable and ignoring anything that challenged their essentially agnostic outlook.

Anyone wanting to understand Buddhism has to go beyond such clearly ethnocentric concerns by transcending their own time and place and attempting to understand through empathy and the suspension of prejudice. Like Conze, whose book *Buddhism: Its Essence and Development* is a classic, we must do our best to see Buddhism as it is seen by Buddhists and not as we would like the religion to be.

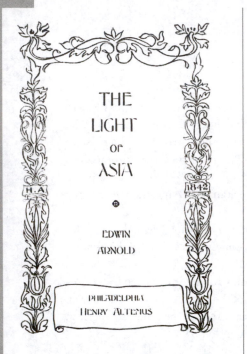

Photo 11.2 This book more than any other popularized Buddhism in the West. In many ways, it misled readers who had no other information about Buddhism, because it presented a highly selective version of Buddhism closer to rationalism than the living religion.

THE BUDDHIST STORY

Buddhism traces its origins back to a teacher known as the Buddha. According to tradition this was a man named Siddhartha Gautauma who lived sometime in the fifth and sixth centuries BC, probably between 563 and 483. Thus, he was 80 when he died. Tradition says that he was a prince in the northern Indian kingdom of Shakyas, which most modern scholars believe lay in the borderland of modern Nepal and India. His father is said to have been a ruler of the Shakya clan, which probably means he was a local chief

---

1. Edward Conze, *Buddhism: Its Essence and Development* (1951; Oxford: Bruno Cassirer, 1957), 27.

of some sort. Nevertheless, in most traditional stories he is a great king who was immensely rich.

The caste into which the Buddha was born was the *kshatriya* or warrior caste, and the town, according to tradition, was Kapilavastu, about 150 miles north of Benares, on the Nepalese border.

As might be expected, the birth of the Buddha is surrounded by numerous stories and legends, some very old, others more recent. A relatively late one, from around the seventh century AD, claims his mother was a virgin and his birth a virgin birth very similar to that attributed to Jesus Christ by Christian tradition. This story is thought by many scholars to be part of a Buddhist apologetic developed in reaction to Christianity.

More popular, and significantly older, is the story of the Buddha's mother's dream, in which, as she lay on a bed, a white elephant appeared, circled her several times, and then miraculously entered her womb through her side. Startled by the dream, she called upon various wise men, soothsayers, and prophetic figures for an interpretation. White elephants are very rare in India, and within the Hindu tradition are regarded as sacred; therefore, the diviners agreed, the dream pointed to some great event. It must mean the child about to be born would become either a great warrior, who would establish a vast kingdom, or a great religious leader, whose wisdom would impress the entire world.

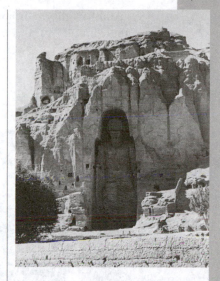

Photo 11.3 A photograph of one of the two massive Bamiyan Buddhas created in 554 and 557 by Afghan Buddhists. They were destroyed by the Taliban in 2001 because they considered them pagan idols.

Another legend tells how, ten lunar months after the Buddha's mother conceived, she visited her parents, who lived in a small town near her palace. As she passed through Lumbini, a beautiful deer park the king kept for recreation and hunting deer, the beautiful queen went into labor and gave birth to a wonderful son. These events are held by tradition to have occurred at a place called Rummindei, in modern Nepal. Centuries later this spot became a center of Buddhist pilgrimage, and, following his conversion, the great Indian king Ashoka (born between 304 and 270 BC, probably died 237 BC) erected a monument on the spot where the Buddha was said to have been born.

Photo 11.4 The giant Buddha statue on the Likr temple in Ladalk, India.

Another story tells how a great Hindu sage called Asita recognized the significance of the child. By various means of divination, he predicted that the boy would become a great teacher. Other Hindu priests who attended the queen after her son's birth are said to have made similar prophecies. All agreed that if the child remained with his father, he would be a great king, but that if he wandered away from home and mingled with religious teachers, he would become a great sage.

Photo 11.5 The column of King Ashoka the Great in Nepal, erected around 250 BC, which, according to tradition, marks the location of Lumbini, where the Buddha was born. Although today this is a World Heritage Site, the photograph above, taken in the late nineteenth century, reminds us that after the decline of Buddhist civilization in India, Buddhism was neglected for many centuries.

Horrified by these predictions, his father determined to entertain his son and ensure that he was attached to this world. He occupied the boy constantly and lavished gifts upon him, so that all he experienced was enjoyable. The legends tell how he was entertained by over forty thousand beautiful dancing girls, had numerous palaces, and was continually surrounded by friends.

Yet Siddhartha's life was not easy. His mother died seven days after his birth, and he was raised by his aunt. Buddhist texts tell many stories of wonderful and miraculous happenings that accompanied his childhood, rather like those told of the child Jesus by the apocryphal Gospels. For example, one story tells how one day Siddhartha's nurse briefly wandered away and returned to find the child practicing yoga and sitting in the lotus position, legs crossed.

All of these traditions agree that around age sixteen Siddhartha was married to the beautiful Yasodhara, his cousin and the daughter of a local chief or king. Whatever her rank, she was subsequently called a queen. Siddhartha's bride bore him at least one son, significantly named Rahula, indicating that he was given or held by Rahula, a demon thought to have devoured the moon. Although there were probably other children, none are mentioned in traditional accounts of Siddhartha's life. All we are told is that during this period he lived in great luxury, verging on decadence, and that, rather like Sleeping Beauty in Western fairy tales, he was systematically shielded from everyday life and anything that might lead him to leave home or associate with the wrong kind of religious person. His father went to great lengths to protect his son from unwelcome influences and train him to fulfill his role as a ruler.

Then, about age thirty, a series of experiences dramatically changed Siddhartha's life. Depending on which tradition one uses—and there are several early ones—four encounters shook the young prince's complacency and dramatically changed his way of life. As the story goes, one day he was out riding, when he encountered, in quick succession, a young child full of energy and joy, an old, decrepit man in great pain, a very sick younger man, clearly near death, and finally a funeral procession carrying a decaying corpse. Seeing the passage from life to death in a very short time made the young prince question his existence, ask about the purpose of life, and vow to find life's true meaning.

After brooding over the significance of these encounters, Siddhartha made the momentous decision to leave his home, abandon his family, and search for spiritual truth. To Western readers, this act of abandonment sounds callous and self-centered. It must be remembered, however, that Hindu tradition expected men over the age of sixty to renounce family and friends, and that by that age they had children who were considered adults and able to take over the family responsibilities of their fathers.

Photo 11.6 This ancient statue of the Buddha from Lahore, created in the second or third century AD for use in a monastery, reminds the onlooker of the transience of life and the imminence of death.

This act of wrenching himself free from his family and normal social commitments is known as Siddhartha's "Great Renunciation." It began a period of wandering that the tradition tells us lasted around six years, during which Siddhartha is said to have visited numerous sages and holy men who practiced various forms of meditation and arduous spiritual exercises. Yet none provided him with the knowledge or satisfaction he sought. Siddhartha tried solitude, studied philosophy, and became an ascetic, eating only six grains of rice a day. He also experimented with drinking alcohol to excess. But none of these things brought him closer to his goal.

Then one day, at the end of his tether, as he sat under a fig tree, he struggled with Mara, a supernatural being of godlike proportions who was thought to lead humans astray by blinding them to the illusory nature of this world. In the struggle, he faced severe temptations. First, he received news that his father's kingdom had been conquered and his relatives were prisoners of an evil king. But this vision did not affect his resolve. Whatever happened to his family was not his concern; his goal was to discover the truth of existence. In a second vision, or temptation, three voluptuous women tried to seduce him. Again Siddhartha was unmoved. He had renounced the joys of sex. Finally, a host of demons savagely attacked him, firing arrows, throwing spears, and launching stones at him from a slingshot. None of these missiles harmed him, because he was so detached from the world that, as soon as they entered the emanating fields of concentration surrounding him, they turned to rose petals and gently fluttered to the ground. Recognizing that all of these temptations were illusory, Siddhartha placed his fingers on the ground, and an enormous roar, like a thousand lions, echoed throughout the night.

Then Mara attacked him with the final temptation. He appealed to reason, arguing that nobody would ever understand the truths the Buddha had discovered. Surely all of his efforts to attain enlightenment were a waste of time and no one would take any notice of his teachings. Given the perversity of mankind, why not simply wash one's hands of the cares of the

Photo 11.7 A modern representation of the Buddha on the altar of the Buddhist Center in Möhra, Thüringen, Germany. Ironically, this small town is the ancestral home of the Luther family and was visited several times by the Protestant Reformer Martin Luther (1483–1546), whose uncle lived there. Luthers still live in the neighborhood today. Möhra is a short distance from Eisenach, where Luther translated the Bible into German.

world and enjoy oneself? To this the Buddha replied that someone was bound to recognize his truth, making everything worthwhile. At that, the tempting visions ceased and Mara fled, never to return, leaving the young prince alone under the night sky. Following these events and his victory over Mara, the bodhi tree under which he sat came to full bloom, and red blossoms fell to the ground surrounding him.

During that long and terrifying night, Siddhartha gained ever deeper levels of consciousness, seeing visions of his past lives and gaining an understanding of the essence of all things. Now he had resolved all his questions, found answers to the puzzle of existence, and gained true understanding. Life, he recognized, means suffering. All life is full of suffering. Suffering is the essence of all things in this earthly existence. Now he knew that the only solution to the anguish of life comes not from a severe asceticism, nor profligate Tantric hedonism, which involves the use of magic and sexual rituals, but only from embracing what he came to call the middle way.

Traditional Buddhists believe that, following the enlightenment of the Buddha, the heavens shook, stars deviated from their course, and the whole cosmos was deeply affected. Blossoms became fruits, fruits ripened on trees, and the sky shone with unseen glory. A pivotal event in human history had taken place.

Following his enlightenment, the Buddha spent five or six weeks meditating on the truths he had discovered, considering how best to communicate them to others and wondering whether his truth was the truth for him alone. Eventually, he decided to share his newly discovered truth and, to that end, began making disciples. Humans, he came to believe, are like lotus plants. Some lotuses float on water, others float beneath its surface, and others fluctuate between the two; some people are capable of seeing the truth and obtaining it for themselves, others will never see the truth and never be enlightened, and still others fluctuate between the truth and error and need someone who can save them from themselves. Therefore, he concluded, most humans need someone to show them the way, even though they themselves must walk the path.

Since all the Buddha's Hindu teachers were dead when he attained enlightenment, he could not share his joy with them. But many of his former companions, with whom he had sought spiritual truth by visiting numerous masters, were alive and still seeking truth. Therefore, he decided to seek them out and proclaim his good news to them. Eventually, the Buddha encountered a group of his former companions on the road to Benares, also known as Varanasi, a city in the northern Indian state of Uttar Pradesh. When he first met them, they wanted nothing to do with him, because, in their eyes, he had abandoned the ascetic practices of their masters. A heated argument broke out, his friends rejecting everything he said. Finally, in frustration, the Buddha cried out, "Surely, my friends and fellow monks, you have to admit that I've never spoken with such authority before." Startled by this, his companions admitted that he spoke the truth and that he had indeed changed. So impressed were they by his sincerity that they became his first disciples. Together with these men the Buddha founded the Sangha, or monastic order of Buddhism.

For the rest of his life the Buddha preached the truth as he discovered it. He then traveled throughout India and the northern states that border India. In time his father, stepmother, and even his wife and son were converted by his teachings. Many of these converts came from the higher castes, such as those of the priests and warriors, although a significant number came from the lower castes. As numbers grew, the Buddha began to send out what in Christian terms would be called evangelists, traveling preachers, who traversed India. All of the Buddha's early followers were men, and it seems he had no intention of

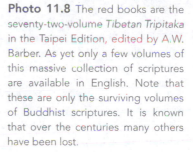

Photo 11.8 The red books are the seventy-two-volume *Tibetan Tripitaka* in the Taipei Edition, edited by A.W. Barber. As yet only a few volumes of this massive collection of scriptures are available in English. Note that these are only the surviving volumes of Buddhist scriptures. It is known that over the centuries many others have been lost.

including women in his movement. Then, one day, his cousin and chief disciple, Ananda, came to him and pleaded for the inclusion of women in the movement. Ananda's arguments were so convincing that the Buddha founded an order of nuns.

The tradition also hints at early conflicts within the movement. It is said that even within the Buddha's lifetime, his cousin, Devadatta, challenged the Buddha's leadership and attempted to found his own religious movement. It is also said that this evil cousin attempted to kill the Buddha, but that his numerous plots came to nothing. Some later apocryphal Buddhist writings called the *Sutras*, which are collections of scripture that often appear as aphorisms, also say that in a later incarnation Devadatta was born in Arabia, where he founded Islam.

The Buddha lived forty years after his enlightenment, to the age of eighty. Buddhists believe the last words of the Buddha were, "All things are conditional and transient; try to attain your salvation with diligence." A week after his death, the Buddha was cremated at the place called Kushinagra, near the modern town of Gorakheura in the Indian state of Uttar Pradesh. Relics were removed from the ashes and distributed among eight groups of

Photo 11.9 This ancient Buddhist stupa, or repository for relics, of the Buddha and his close disciples, once stood at the center of a large monastic complex near the city of Benares, also known as Varanasi, a city in the northern Indian state of Uttar Pradesh. Stupas, or at least their ruins, are the most common form of early Indian architecture, testifying to the fact that Buddhism was once widespread across the Indian subcontinent.

followers, who spread them throughout India, where they became the focus of local cults.

THE HISTORY OF BUDDHISM

Buddhist tradition tells us that after the Buddha died, around 483 BC, his disciples and all the monks held a great council, where over five hundred monks formulated an authoritative canon and established the rules of the order of monks. Around a century later, according to tradition, another great council was held, and this one led to a schism in the order.

After this the Buddhist movement divided into two groups: the Hinayana and the Mahayana, also known as the lesser and the greater vehicles. The Hinayana was known as the lesser vehicle because Hinayanists argued that only monks can possibly attain enlightenment. Followers in the Mahayana, however, countered that pious members of the laity had a place within the Buddhist movement and could attain enlightenment by their own efforts. Eventually the Hinayana tradition developed into what today is known as Theravadin Buddhism, which spread from India to Sri Lanka and throughout Southeast Asia. Mahayanan Buddhism, on the other hand, spread from India into Tibet, Korea, and China. From Korea it then spread into Japan.

Buddhism experienced its greatest and most rapid period of growth during the third century BC, beginning sometime after 261 BC with the conversion of the great Indian king Ashoka (273–232), who placed the resources of his great empire, which extended over a large part of the Indian subcontinent, at the service of Buddhism. He built temples, schools, and holy places while generally supporting the Sangha, or order of monks. Ashoka did everything in his power to promote Buddhism, sending missionaries from his kingdom throughout India. Four or five centuries later, Buddhist missionaries moved eastward into China and westward toward Europe; a thousand years later, north into Tibet.

Buddhism began to penetrate China in the first century of the Christian era, in a pincer movement of missions organized by both Theravadin and Mahayanan groups from the north and southeast, respectively. With the great success of these missions, the regions that are today Pakistan and Afghanistan became thriving centers of Buddhism, from which the religion spread along what is known as the silk route into Central Asia and from there into China.

Buddhist Tradition

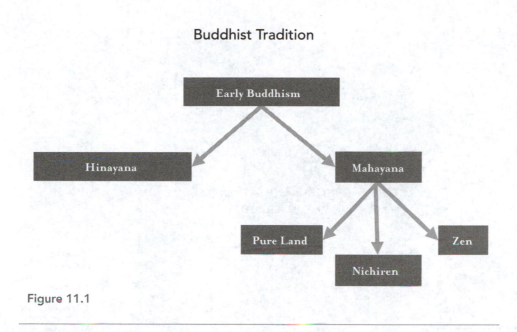

Figure 11.1

When Buddhism first entered China, the Han dynasty was firmly in control of a vast area stretching from Turkistan to Korea and from Vietnam to the Gobi Desert. Officially the Han dynasty was committed to Confucianism as a way of life that emphasized filial piety, the maintenance of social rights, and an explicit moral code with clearly defined social rules.

According to tradition, around AD 65 Emperor Ming (reigned AD 58–76) had a vision of the Buddha that led him to permit the building of the Whitehorse Temple. Within a hundred years, Buddhist worship and practices were common at the imperial court. In AD 399 the Buddhist monk Fa-Hsien made a historic journey to India, where he gathered source materials about the life and teachings of the Buddha. This journey encouraged a series of pilgrimages to India by Chinese Buddhists seeking to discover more about the founder of their religion. In addition to India, Fa-Hsien visited all the major Buddhist pilgrimage sites throughout the subcontinent and even went to Sri Lanka. He returned to China in 414, laden with priceless Buddhist manuscripts.

Around the same time an Indian Buddhist monk, Kumarajiva, was kidnapped by Chinese pirates and sold into slavery in the provincial capital of Ch'ang-an. There he eventually gathered around him three hundred Chinese scholars and supervised the translation of numerous Mahayanan sutras into Chinese. By the end of the late fourth century AD, most of northern China was converted to Buddhism. Things changed in 446, when one of the northern Chinese rulers apostatized and initiated a period of savage persecution. Eventually he was overthrown, and Buddhism was restored as a religion of the people by his successors.

Another period of vicious persecution occurred from 574 to 577 during the reign of the Emperor Wu, who drove over a million monks and nuns from their temples, forcing them to become laypeople. Much like Henry the VIII and his supporters in Reformation

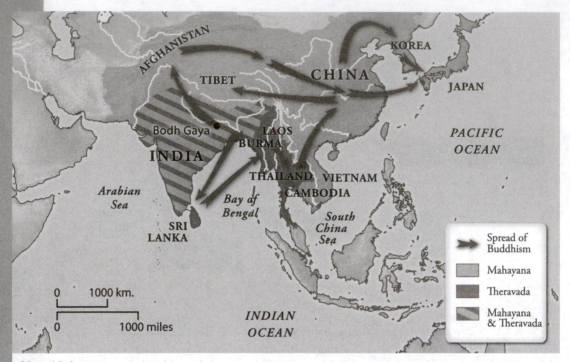

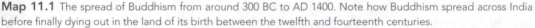

Map 11.1 The spread of Buddhism from around 300 BC to AD 1400. Note how Buddhism spread across India before finally dying out in the land of its birth between the twelfth and fourteenth centuries.

England, the imperial family, local aristocrats, and opportunist individuals benefited from these persecutions by seizing temple lands and enriching themselves on the accumulated treasures of Buddhist communities.

This period of persecution came to an end when the Emperor Wen founded a new dynasty in 581. Identifying himself as a disciple of the Buddha, he ushered in a golden age of Buddhist art and scholarship. Like the Indian emperor Ashoka, he supported missionary efforts and sought to spread Buddhism far beyond the borders of his realm. In particular he sought to convert Koreans and Japanese people to Buddhism. For the next 250 years Buddhism spread throughout the regions bordering on China without encountering serious opposition. In 845 a third wave of bitter persecution swept through China. From that time forth, Chinese Buddhism grew or declined depending on the inclination of the ruling regime.

Buddhism fared much better in Korea following its introduction in 372, when it became the major religion of the country. Then, after the establishment of the fiercely pro–neo-Confucian Choson, or Yi, Dynasty, the religion was savagely suppressed before being marginalized in Korean society without further state support. Nevertheless, it remained a strong undercurrent in the religiosity of the common people and preserved some of the most important collections of Buddhist scriptures.

Buddhist civilization reached the height of its power in Korea between the twelfth and fourteenth centuries, when it attracted the best of the aristocracy and ruling elite. So great

Photo 11.10 As Buddhism spread throughout Asia, Mahayana missionaries developed the doctrine of "skill in means," which allowed them to adapt their teachings to local cultures. In this west coast North American Buddhist temple, the main shrine is flanked by small photographs of numerous ancestors of members of the local Chinese Buddhist community. Thus the Chinese reverence for the aged and for ancestors is blended with Buddhist worship.

was the influence of Buddhism during this period that even the death penalty was abolished in 1036. Although the change of dynasty in 1392 led to the establishment of a strict neo-Confucian regime that excluded Buddhism from the circles of power and persecuted it in varying degrees, it continued to be supported among the common people.

Buddhism was introduced to Japan from Korea in 552 with support of members of the Japanese nobility. Although periods of persecution and neglect followed, Japanese Buddhists in general fared much better than their Korean neighbors, leading to the development of a number of important schools of Buddhist thought and practice. The best known of the schools is, of course, Zen. In Japan, Buddhism's fortunes declined from the fifteenth century onwards and went into sharp decline during the Tokugawa period (1603–1867), when neo-Confucianism became the dominant philosophy and militant Shinto led to sporadic persecutions of Buddhists. By the late nineteenth century it appeared that Buddhism would die out in Japan, but a revival occurred that continued throughout the twentieth century until the present.

In India, Buddhism succeeded remarkably at first, and for a time Buddhist culture flourished throughout most of the subcontinent, particularly in the north. All this came to an end around 900, when large areas of northern India were overrun by Muslim invaders. Suddenly, Chinese and Tibetan Buddhism were cut off from the source of Buddhist scholarship and piety, as Muslims massacred thousands of priests, destroyed ancient Buddhist temples, and annihilated centers of Buddhist learning. From the Buddhist viewpoint, these massacres were nothing less than a holocaust.

A similar fate almost simultaneously befell the area we know today as Afghanistan, as well as numerous smaller kingdoms along the silk route. Between 700 and 900, one after another of the Buddhist kingdoms of Central Asia fell to the fury of invading Arabs, who quickly established Islamic states throughout the region. Thus, within a couple of centuries, the heartland of Buddhism became a wilderness, where Islam alone flourished. Only in small pockets—in isolated mountain valleys and remote regions—could an emasculated form of Buddhism survive, cut off from the roots of its tradition until the twentieth century.

WESTERN BUDDHISM

The most recent development in a long history of Buddhism is its spread into the West. Although it seems clear that the Vikings encountered Buddhism—they brought statues of the Buddha back to Scandinavia from places they had visited—in reality, Buddhism did not penetrate Western societies until the late nineteenth century. Although a knowledge of Buddhism circulated among Western intellectuals from at least the beginning of the sixteenth century, not much was really known about this great religious tradition. One reason for this is probably that, during the great ages of Buddhist expansion outside of India, the route to the West was blocked by Muslim kingdoms.

In the nineteenth century everything changed. Western technology increasingly made the world smaller. Fast sailing ships were replaced by far more reliable steamships, making it possible for colonial administrators and even what we would now call tourists to visit India, Japan, and other parts of Asia. The most important role in spreading Buddhism to West, however, was played by British colonial officials, a small number of whom converted to what they believed was Buddhism. Actually, as noted earlier, what they understood as Buddhism was often a sanitized version of the religion closer in form to deism or agnosticism than to Buddhism proper.

Nevertheless, such people played an important role in bringing Buddhism to the attention of Western scholars. Germans in particular embraced Buddhism under the influence of Hegel's idealism, the brooding philosophy of Schopenhauer, and the

Photo 11.11 Berlin's Buddha House, Das Buddhistische Haus in Berlin, located in the quiet suburb of Frohnau, is one of the oldest Buddhist communities in Europe. Established in 1924 by a homeopathic physician, Dr. Paul Dahlke (1865–1928), it has played a key role in the spread of Buddhism in the German-speaking world and beyond.

linguistic interests of the brothers Grimm. These latter linguistic interests developed into a quest to discover the roots of Western culture in a common Aryan past shared by Europe and India. As a result, in the first half of the twentieth century, Buddhism gradually began to take root in Western societies. At the same time, our scholarly understanding of the Buddhist tradition increased enormously through the work of scholars like Edward Conze and others.

As observed earlier, the writings of Sir Edwin Arnold, particularly his *The Light of Asia* (1879), played a key role in the development of Western Buddhism. More significant for the serious study of Buddhism was the founding of the Pali Text Society by Dr. Thomas William Rhys Davids, who lectured at Manchester University in 1881. The society aimed at promoting the translation and publication of Sri Lankan Buddhist texts.

Another key figure in the formation of British Buddhism was Alan Bennett, who was born in 1872 to a middle-class family. After reading *The Light of Asia* as a teenager, he became fascinated by Buddhism and read anything he could get his hands on. Then in 1898 he moved to Sri Lanka, where he proclaimed himself a Buddhist. He studied under a well-known teacher and in 1901 began lecturing on Buddhism. He entered the Sangha by joining the Burmese order, because they were more open to receive Europeans than were the Sri Lankans. At his ordination he was given the new name Ananda Maitriya, and announced his intent to found an international Buddhist society. The first meeting of this group took place on 15 March 1903.

Photo 11.12 A Buddha statue at Berlin's Buddha House.

Back in England a small group of people who read *The Light of Asia* had begun to meet fairly regularly in London. When they heard about Bennett's ordination, they began to correspond with him, and also opened a bookshop at 14 Bury Street, close to the British

Photo 11.13 The Buddha House library.

Museum. In the front room of the shop they sold books, and in a small room at the back they held regular lectures. It was out of these meetings that the Buddhist Society was founded in 1907, with Dr. Rhys Davids playing a leading role.

In these ventures they gained strong support from Professor Hermann Oldenberg in Germany, various Theosophists, and writers like Sir Charles Elliott.

The excitement generated by these events led the society to invite Ananda Maitriya, who had changed the spelling of his last name to Metteyya, in keeping with the Pali. Consequently, the first Buddhist mission to Britain can be dated from his arrival in London on 23 April 1908. It lasted until the 2 October, when Metteyya was forced to return to Burma as a result of severe asthma attacks brought on by the cold and damp British climate. Buddhism has grown slowly but steadily in Britain ever since, and today it is a well-established part of British life. According to the 2001 National Census, there are now 152,000 Buddhists in Britain, comprising 0.3% of the population. Although this is a very small number, it is actually quite impressive considering that a hundred years ago there were fewer than one hundred Buddhists in Britain. And, unlike Muslims and followers of other immigrant religions, most British Buddhists are actually converts.

In America, Buddhism was popularized through the activities of the Theosophical Society, founded in 1875. Here again, Sir Edwin Arnold's *The Light of Asia* played a key role in promoting an interest in Buddhism. Equally important in terms of preparing the way for the spread of Buddhism in America is the popular, although highly misleading, notion that the New England Transcendentalists were somehow influenced by Buddhism. That Transcendentalism is in many ways similar to Buddhism and was no doubt influenced by a growing awareness of Eastern religious ideas cannot be disputed. Yet it is equally true that there is no direct link between Buddhism and Transcendentalism.

Perhaps more important than any other factor in popularizing Buddhism and Eastern religions generally in America was the World Parliament of Religions held in Chicago in 1893. At these meetings, two highly articulate Buddhists, Anagarika Dharmapala and Soyen Shaku, made a strong impression on many people. In particular they effectively converted Paul Carus to Buddhism. Following these meetings, he began to seriously study Buddhism, and he eventually wrote numerous books and articles on the topic. More importantly, he was instrumental in bringing the young Japanese scholar D. T. Suzuki to the U.S.

Photo 11.14 Although many North American Buddhist temples occupy ordinary houses, a growing number, like the one above, are purposely built by local Buddhist communities.

Photos 11.15 and 11.16 Many professing Buddhists maintain personal shrines in their homes. These are often fairly inconspicuous while at the same time they serve as the household's center for personal and family devotions.

Although Carus's understanding of Buddhism was probably as poor as that of Sir Edwin Arnold, like Arnold he made a profound impact on his contemporaries, and he did more than anyone else to popularize Buddhism in America during the early twentieth century. Another outcome of the World Parliament of Religions was the establishment in 1899 of a Buddhist mission to California, which eventually led to the creation of the Buddhist Churches of America. The Parliament also encouraged a considerable number of itinerant Buddhist scholars and teachers, mainly from Japan, to visit the U.S.

The aftermath of the Second World War was a further impetus to Buddhism in the U.S. Many American servicemen stationed in Japan married Japanese wives. Others simply developed interest in Buddhism. During the same period, D. T. Suzuki gave a series of lectures at Columbia University between 1950 and 1958 that stimulated American interest in Zen. During the 1950s interest in Buddhism increased in the U.S. as a result of the so-called beat movement. Writers like Jack Kerouac (1922–1969), Allen Ginsberg (1926–1997), and Gary Snyder (1930–) did much to popularize Buddhism. So too did Alan Watts (1915–1973), who converted to Buddhism in Britain before emigrating to America, where he became something of a guru.

The Buddhist Churches of America in San Francisco was founded in 1898 and claims to be the oldest Buddhist institution in the United States. It belongs to the Japanese Jodo Shinshu, or Pure Land, community and is essentially an ethnic Japanese church. In recent years it has attracted an increasing number of Caucasians. Large-scale immigration to America from various Southeast Asian countries from the 1960s onward has led to the growth of a relatively large Buddhist community in America with roots in non-Western cultures that are historically Buddhist. Today it is estimated that there are between three and four million Buddhists in America. By way of contrast, there were 253,735 Buddhists in Canada according the 2001 Census.

CHAPTER 12

THE DEVELOPMENT OF BUDDHIST BELIEF AND PRACTICE

INTRODUCTION

The history of Buddhist expansion is paralleled by the history of Buddhist dogma. Buddhist history may be conveniently divided into periods of five hundred years. This division is actually the one preferred by Buddhist scholars since at least the first century AD. Essential to this way of thinking is the view that the world, indeed the entire universe, is in decline. Consequently, the beginning of the Buddhist era marked a relative high point from which everything gradually degenerates.

Buddhism has remained stable through most of its history, yet in many periods, particularly the early history of Buddhism in India, the historical facts are scarce and highly debatable. Despite the self-confident assertions of many writers, we really know very little about early Buddhism. Nor do we know what the Buddha actually taught. All we know is what later generations said he taught.

Unlike the search for the historical Jesus in Christianity, there is no search for the historical Buddha. Such a search is virtually meaningless because of a lack of historical data over several hundred years. What we do know is that throughout its long history of approximately 2500 years, certain features seem to have accompanied the religion and growth of Buddhist communities: first, a monastic organization upon which everything else is based; second, a series of mediatory practices accompanying Buddhist monastic orders and lay piety; and third, an ultimate goal, for all Buddhists, of the death of individuality, in what may be described as "the extinction of self." Thus, despite the arguments of historicist scholars who claim that Buddhism as such does not exist, and that we should talk about "Buddhisms" rather than "Buddhism," there does seem to be a remarkably unified Buddhist ethos. In other words, Buddhism appears, like many other religious traditions, to have an organic structure.

BUDDHIST COMMUNITIES AND SECTS

During the first period of Buddhist expansion and development, the religion spread through-out the Indian subcontinent. Questions about psychology and the nature of the person—or in reality, the nonexistence of a person—dominated Buddhist thought. Therefore, the fol-lowers of the Buddha attempted to master their thoughts to gain control over the inner work-ings of their minds. Using techniques of philosophical and psychological analysis, Buddhist monks saw self-control of the psychological process we call thinking as a goal that would enable them to escape the bonds of existence. Because of the totally absorbing nature of these exercises, few people could aspire to complete mastery of their thoughts and thereby attain the desired goal. As a result, what Buddhists call enlightenment, similar to what Christians call salvation, was reserved for an elite group of monks known as arhats.

This period of development concentrated on the rules of the Sangha, or monastic discipline, and is asso-ciated with the Council of the Rajagrha, which some scholars describe as "legendary." It was here that the Buddhist scriptures are said to have been collected for the first time. The period ends with the Council of Vaisali, which formulated the disciplinary practices for the monastic order.

It is the Sangha, or community of monks, that dominates the first period. Even to speak of a commu-nity is misleading, because many communities, each with slightly different practices and beliefs, existed. Throughout this period laypeople remained on the sidelines. Although the monks and nuns depended upon the laity for their livelihood, the latter were accorded no place in the Buddhist scheme of things except, perhaps, to be reborn in a future life, perhaps in such favorable circumstances that they would be able to enter the Sangha.

Although numerous branches, or sects, of Bud-dhism existed during this period, they may generally be grouped under the heading Hinayana, or lesser vehicle, to which the Theravadin school, which was distin-guished by its strict interpretation of which texts were to be admitted into the canon of Buddhist scriptures and its emphasis on the monastic order, belonged. The term "lesser vehicle" comes from the fact that this branch of Buddhism restricted access to membership, or at least to salvation, to members of the monastic orders.

Photo 12.1 A Chinese Buddhist monastery in the nineteenth century. It was in China that the Mahayana tradition flourished and devel-oped into numerous schools.

During the second period, Buddhism began to spread throughout Asia, whose cultures were modified by contact with northern Indian thought and practice. At this time questions of ontology predominated. What exactly is the nature of the world? What sort of being is the Buddha? These and similar questions led to the creation of a vast literature that significantly shaped the development of Buddhism. By questioning the nature of reality, Buddhism was able to develop into a more comprehensive religion that offered a form of salvation to laymen and laywomen who by their efforts supported the order of monks, the Sangha. Now the focus of Buddhism moved from the *arhat*, a being who earned his or her own individual salvation, to the *bodhisattva*, who temporarily renounced his personal salvation in a bid to bring enlightenment to all sentient beings.

The reason Buddhists used terms like "lesser vehicle" and "greater vehicle" is both important and easy to understand. The dharma, which in Buddhism is understood primarily as the truth or essence discovered by the Buddha, is described in Buddhist scriptures as a raft that carries the practitioner of Buddhist meditation over the river, or ocean, of this world to the realm, or nonrealm, that is represented by the term "nirvana." For Buddhists, this is described as enlightenment and is the equivalent of salvation for Christians. Exactly what enlightenment or nirvana are like is impossible to describe, according to the Budda, and is best understood in terms of the question, Where does the flame of a candle go when it is extinguished?

Photo 12.2 The centerpiece of this shrine and the dragon on the left clearly convey the Chinese origins of this particular Buddhist group in a large North American city.

The second period of Buddhist expansion began around the beginning of the Christian era, when what became known as the Mahayana, which is best translated "the great vehicle," formed. The movement takes its name from its deliberate attempts to include the laity within the sphere of Buddhist activity and salvation. This movement within Buddhism appears to have developed simultaneously in northwest and southern India, where large non-Buddhist populations existed and Buddhists came face-to-face with foreign influences. It was these "foreign influences" that enabled Buddhism to adapt, so that through the appropriation of new ways, it could spread beyond the borders of India.

Before the development of the Mahayana, many obstacles impeded the spread of Buddhism outside India. For example, monks were supposed to wear simple cotton robes and refrain from eating meat or wearing clothing created from animal skins. Practically, this meant that it was impossible for Buddhist teachers to spread the dharma northward over the Himalayas into Central Asia. The altitudes, intense cold, reliance upon animal products, and the need for protective clothing made from animal skins made such an undertaking impossible.

Therefore, Buddhism could only spread southward into low-lying warm areas. With the development of the Mahayana, new doctrines arose that allowed for the adaptation of Buddhism to hostile climatic conditions. These doctrines were associated with "skill in means" and the idea that it was the duty of Buddhists to spread the dharma by whatever means possible.

As a result of these developments, Buddhism, in its Mahayana form, was able to spread from India to Central Asia and into Korea, China, and Japan. At the same time ideas about bodhisattvas and skill in means led to similar modifications in Theravadin practices; and although these were far less than those found in the Mahayana tradition, they nevertheless enabled Theravada missionaries to spread to Burma, Thailand, and other countries. Thus Buddhism saw a remarkable period of expansion.

It was during the second period that the terms "lesser vehicle" and "greater vehicle" began to make sense. According to this distinction, to a large extent based on Mahayanan usage, Theravada Buddhism was the lesser vehicle because, according to it, salvation was open only to members of Buddhist monastic orders. On the other hand, the Mahayana tradition, which flowered during the second period of Buddhist history, became known as the greater vehicle, because it created a role for laypeople and included them in its scheme of enlightenment or salvation.

The third period of Buddhist development saw the rise of cosmic speculation, developing directly from the bodhisattva ideal that arose during the second period. The ideal in this period was the *siddha*, a man who had gained control over himself to the extent that he was in complete harmony with the cosmos, unaffected by external constraints. Thus, as a free agent, he was able to control and manipulate cosmic and magical forces. This ideal led to the development of what became known as the Tantra.

Early developments of Tantric or magical practices often associated with sexual rituals go back to the fourth century and rapidly developed throughout the fifth and sixth centuries. From the Buddhist point of view, the development of a magical Buddhism was different from popular folk magic. Ordinary people, in Buddhist thinking, use magic to cast spells, attack enemies, or bring good fortune. But Buddhists use magic to free themselves from the bonds of this world and so gain enlightenment. Within Tantric Buddhism the historical person of the Buddha fades into insignificance as new cosmic Buddhas, located in some far distant realm, both in space and time, take precedence.

The development of the Tantra, with its emphasis upon the miraculous aspect of Buddhism, and magical powers, aided Buddhism as it spread northward into Tibet, where Tantric teachings easily blended with the existing folk religion of the Tibetan people. Traditionally, the conversion of Tibet is said to have begun around 632, but it really began to make an impact only in the eighth century. The first Tibetan monastery is usually dated from 787, while the patronage of Tibetan kings began in the ninth century.

The fourth period of Buddhist history began around 1000 and rapidly became a story of death and decline in India, while Buddhism continued to spread outside the Indian subcontinent. In northern India Buddhism died around 1200, and in the south around 1400, for various reasons.

First, Buddhists appear to have lost the support of ruling elites. Without funding and other support from influential landowners and royal patronage, the now large monastic communities were unable to survive on their own. Unlike Christian monasteries in Europe, Buddhist monasteries had not developed agricultural and other enterprises as a source of income. Rather, in keeping with the traditions, they relied on begging and the support of wealthy patrons. As this support waned, the monastic orders faced extinction.

Second, a Hindu renaissance appears to have taken place as a result of Hindus' incorporating Buddhist philosophy, practices, and even deities into their own religious pantheon. At the same time, revised Hindu philosophies attracted the intelligentsia away from Buddhism to Hinduism, while highly emotional devotional movements attracted the masses.

Third, and perhaps most important, the Muslim invasions, beginning in northern India, destroyed Buddhist centers of learning and civilization. Muslims found it far easier to tolerate what they saw as "Hindu idolatry" than the "idolatry of Buddhists." The reasons

Photo 12.3 Today it is not uncommon to see Buddha statues for sale in furniture, art, and other more specialized shops like the one pictured above. Buddhism has become part of Western society.

for this are not entirely clear, but perhaps it was because Hindus had clearly identifiable gods, while Buddhists had none and therefore seemed to worship a man. Another possible reason is that Buddhism possessed a centralized organization including monastries and universities, which could be easily destroyed, while the Hindu tradition was located in the family. Whatever the reasons, Buddhist monasteries were destroyed and the monks slaughtered on a scale that made the Viking invasions of Britain seem like a summer school picnic.

Because of multiple persecutions, many monks and scholars, bringing with them books, images, and sacred relics, fled to Nepal, where a Buddhist community had already been established. Thus Nepal became an important center of Buddhist scholarship and art in the later Middle Ages. Later, Nepalese Buddhism went into a long decline. Eventually, in the middle of the eighteenth century, the Nepalese state became predominantly Hindu because of the invasion of western Indian peoples.

Buddhism fared better in Tibet, where there was a revival around the year 1000. Contact was established with Buddhists in India, before the Muslim occupation, and with Buddhists in other parts of the world. For the next four hundred years Buddhism flourished in Tibet, with the creation of many monasteries and distinct traditions. In the fourteenth century Tibetan Buddhism became fairly centralized, and Buddhist literature was codified. Buddhist texts were

Photo 12.4 Perhaps more than any other form of Buddhism, various Tibetan schools have taken root in all Western societies. On the wall of the house in the above picture is a large photograph of the current Dalai Lama, who is largely responsible for the spread of Tibetan Buddhism to the West.

collected and preserved with great diligence, making Tibet one of the major centers of the Buddhist world. At the same time Tibetan Buddhism took root among the ordinary people, creating a strong support base rooted in all sectors of society. From Tibet, Buddhist missionaries spread into Mongolia, where they had remarkable success and many Mongolians became devout Buddhists.

A similar fate to that which overtook northern Indian Buddhism awaited southeast Asian Buddhism. Sometime after 1200, Buddhism in Sri Lanka began a long and slow decline. During this period Buddhism spread into Burma, where both Mahayana and Theravadin Buddhism flourished until at least the fifteenth century. From then on Theravadin Buddhism dominated the area and the Mahayana was suppressed. From these countries Buddhism entered Thailand and parts of Indochina. Here Buddhist culture flourished for many centuries. When Buddhist missionaries entered Indonesia, they encountered large Indian communities, and many converted to Buddhism, so that it flourished there too, until it was suppressed in the fourteenth and fifteenth centuries by Muslim rulers.

By the sixteenth century, when Portuguese traders and missionaries arrived in Sri Lanka, many of the common people converted to Catholicism. During the following centuries, first Portuguese and then British rule led to the slow decline of Buddhism in that country, until a nationalist revival in the mid-twentieth century that saw Buddhism as the true religion of the area.

Over the centuries numerous Buddhist schools of thought developed in China, Korea, and Japan. In particular the Ch'an school developed in China; after it was taken to Japan, it eventually evolved into Japanese Zen. The more radical branches of the Ch'an school rejected the sutras, the historical Buddha, and everything not based upon immediate experience. In addition to Zen, various Buddhist groups worshiping Amida Buddha, who is represented as a being of infinite light and a powerful savior figure, sprang up throughout these regions. These developed into what became known as the "Pure Land" school, which emphasizes a Buddhism of faith that is expressed through the repetition of a mantra declaring faith in Amida as a personal savior.

BUDDHIST SCRIPTURES

Unlike other religious traditions, Buddhism has a vast number of scriptures. Traditionally these are divided into two groups, known as the Dharma, or Sutras, and the Vinaya. The Dharma consisted of doctrinal texts, while the Vinaya contained the rules of monastic discipline. Later, a third division was added, the Abhidharma, which aimed at systematizing the contents of the Sutras.

A sutra is a text that was traditionally believed to have been spoken by the Buddha himself. All sutras begin with the words, "Thus have I heard that the Lord …" Here the speaker is assumed to be Ananda, the Buddha's cousin and favorite disciple. In actuality, many sutras were composed hundreds of years after the death of the Buddha.

One of the major divisions between the Hinayana — later Theravada — tradition and that

Photo 12.5 A huge crowd gathers in front of Berlin's famed Brandenburg Gate to welcome the Dalai Lama on one of his numerous visits to Germany and express their support for a "free Tibet." Whatever else the Dalai Lama may be, he is a superb publicist who knows how to use spiritual values in a political cause.

of the Mahayana revolved around the issue of which scriptures were to be accepted as authentic. The Hinayana position was that only those scriptures recited at the first council following the Buddha's death were to be accepted. The Mahayana, on the other hand, believing that the Buddha was simply an incarnation of the Buddha principle and that there are other Buddhas, accepted numerous scriptures as equally authentic.

Some Mahayana teachers even asserted that many of the sutras composed long after the death of the Buddha were actually spoken by him but stored in the netherworld because they were too difficult for the people of his time to understand. Only when the time was ripe, said these teachers, were these sutras brought into our world to the medium of committed Buddhists.

The dates of the scriptures are particularly difficult to ascertain, and only a few can be dated in terms of when they were discovered and where. Generally, modern scholars take the death of the Buddha to be around 483 BC or 150 years later. But traditional Indians give a variety of dates from 852 BC to 252 BC. All this becomes understandable when it is realized that Buddhism is ahistorical. What matters is the teaching itself, not how we got it.

Clearly, for many centuries Buddhist teachings were part of an oral tradition transmitted from teacher to pupil or pupils. Later they were written down. The earliest written works we possess date from around the second century AD, although there are inscriptions from the time of Ashoka. This means that the earlier scriptures were written between two hundred and three hundred years after the death of the Buddha and possibly longer. Equally important, the earliest extant copies come from around the third century AD, about seven hundred years after the probable date of the Buddha's death.

Photo 12.6 The Girnar Rock, which bears one of the surviving inscriptions by the Buddhist king Ashoka (273–232), which were carved around 240 BC and are the oldest surviving inscriptions in India after the decline of the Indus Valley civilization. While historicity is essentially unimportant for Buddhist philosophy, the inscriptions of King Ashoka which are to be found in India, Nepal, and Pakistan testify to the size of Ashoka's kingdom and the wide distribution of Buddhism some 250 years after the Buddha's death.

One of the earliest collections of Buddhist scriptures, one that the Theravadin tradition considers complete, is the Pali Canon, composed in Sri Lanka in the Pali language. Also known as the Tripitaka, it consists of works grouped together under three headings to form three distinct sections called *pitakas*, "baskets." The three baskets are those of discipline pertaining to monastic life, sermons that report the teachings of the Buddha, and metaphysical texts dealing with philosophical issues. The other major collection of this sort is the Chinese Tripitaka, which is generally broader in its scope than its Pali counterpart. The oldest catalogue of this Chinese collection can be dated to 518, when it was said to contain 2113 works. Of these, only 276 still exist.

Another major collection of Buddhist texts is the Tibetan *Kanjur* and *Tanjur*. The Kanjur contains between 100 and 108 distinct volumes, the Tanjur between 209 and 225. There are also many other scriptures, ultimately based on translations from Sanskrit texts. These include a collection of stories about the birth of the Buddha known as the *Jataka*. Altogether there are thousands of Buddhist manuscripts, many still are not translated into English. Many of these were found during the twentieth century in remote areas of central Asia, carefully buried to protect them from invaders and preserved for hundreds of years by the dry climate.

WHAT BUDDHISTS BELIEVE

For the outside observer, particularly one from a Christian background, two beliefs of Buddhism present an immediate problem: its belief about God and its belief about the nature of the person. Many years ago, a friend of mine was interrogated by South African security police shortly after she interviewed an African religious leader. When she learned that the African "prophet" whom she had interviewed the previous day had been taken into custody, she exclaimed in horror, "Oh! My God!" to which the South African police officer wryly replied, "God has nothing to do with it." In a way the officer's answer was profoundly Buddhist, for although Buddhists do not deny the existence of God or, for that matter, the existence of gods, they do argue—and, as far as we can tell, the Buddha taught—that God or the gods have nothing to say about our ultimate fate. Only the Buddha has shown the way beyond this realm of existence.

The nonimportance of God in relation to the ultimate fate of humans is closely linked to the Buddhist view of the nature of the human being. Most of us are used to thinking of ourselves as individual persons, possessing something we all call "the self." For the Buddhist, whether this self is a living soul or simply a being who has some sort of individualized existence does not really matter, because God does not exist, and the soul or any form of self or personal identity is an illusion.

One could also say that for most Buddhists there is no such thing as "the person," although in the first period of Buddhist history an important school of Indian Buddhism was known as the Personalists. Yet the Personalists, while believing it possible to talk about a person, simultaneously denied the existence of a self. On the basis of Buddhist philosophy, they argued that, on the one hand, over and above the sense impressions that create our awareness of the world there is also something that can meaningfully be called "a person," but on the other hand, this person is not to be thought of as in any way permanent, nor anything beyond a momentary surge of consciousness. The person was real, while the self was not. Although influential at one time, the school was vanquished and eventually disappeared.

Photo 12.7 A group of North American academics receive a short lecture on Buddhism at one of North America's thriving Buddhist centers.

For the vast majority of Buddhists there is neither a self nor a person. All that exists in terms of the human being are a series of sense impressions that can be analyzed with great precision. The sense impressions are made up of the *skandhas*, or groupings, and are part of an impersonal dharma.

In the Buddhist scheme of things there are three jewels, or treasures, to which each individual must cling if they are to attain enlightenment. The first jewel is a Buddha himself. Contrary to some popular Western interpretations, and even some more ancient developments of Buddhism, such as certain branches of Zen, the Buddha is absolutely essential to Buddhist teachings, because it is a Buddha who guarantees their truth, and all Buddhas are represented in the Buddha who is both a human and cosmic being.

Equally confusing for many Westerners is the fact that, like the term "Christ," the term "Buddha" is not a personal name but a title. Actually it means "the enlightened one." The meaning of "enlightenment" in this case is a state of total freedom from any spiritual or material forces that hinder one's appreciation of the truth of reality itself, the dharma, and the teachings of the Buddha. Yet within Buddhism too, the Buddha is far more than simply a historical human being; he is identified with the essence of what is called "Buddha nature," or "the Tathagata," also referred to as "the dharma body of the Buddha." In other words, there is a supermundane, or perhaps we should say supernatural, aspect to the Buddha. Originally, or at least within early Buddhism as we know it, people spoke about seven Buddhas, of which the historical Buddha was the last. Each was said to have appeared on earth during a period of great need with the expressed intent of preaching the dharma to all sentient beings and thus restoring balance to the universe.

This view of the Buddha, as a manifestation of the principal Buddhahood which eventually developed from seven Buddhas to twenty-four Buddhas, and in some traditions many more, gave way to the idea of the Buddha body. But it came to be believed that even when he was on earth, there was over and above the physical appearance of the Buddha's body an ethereal, all-supernatural body only visible to highly spiritual people. This spiritual body of the Buddha is said to have been sixteen feet high and to have contained thirty-two marks of a superman, including wheels engraved on his feet, webbed fingers, and what Christians would call a halo around his head. Thus the Buddha was seen not just as a man, nor as a god, but rather as an extraordinary being who brings enlightenment to other sentient beings. The full development of this doctrine of the Buddha, his various manifestations, and his supernatural body took centuries. It appears it was only at the end of the first millennium of Buddhism that all these beliefs were firmly in place.

Photo 12.8 A small personal shrine in one of North America's western Buddhist centers.

Alongside doctrines about the Buddha there developed new understandings of the dharma, the impersonal spiritual reality upon which everything is based. The dharma, the second jewel to which Buddhists must cling, was said to protect, transmit, and maintain the truth of Buddhism. So important was the dharma within the community that in Asia, Buddhists were not known as Buddhists but rather as followers of the dharma. Grasping the true extent of the dharma is like trying to drink all the water as it flows from a tap or down a mountain stream.

"Dharma" has various meanings in Buddhism. First, it refers to that which represents, or comprises, the whole of reality. The dharma is the only true reality, in contrast to the world of illusion in which we all live. Second, the word refers to the teachings of the Buddha: his doctrines; the sutras, the writings expressing those doctrines; and the truth of his message—in other words, the sum total of Buddhist teaching. Third, "dharma" can refer to actions by human beings and in that sense is like the biblical concept of righteousness, or the ancient Roman concepts of virtue and gravitas.

Within Buddhist writings there are frequent references not simply to the dharma, but also to dharmas. This plural usage signifies the basic elements of consciousness or whatever ties experienced reality together. The dharmas are like atoms to the physicist. As a result, within Buddhism there are many lists of dharmas. For example, the five skandhas that make up the basic elements of human personality are dharmas. These are corporality, feelings, perceptions, volition, and consciousness. Identifying the dharmas and understanding the workings of consciousness are essential to Buddhist meditation. It is only in this way that the Buddhist comes to see the nonreality of everything which we consider reality.

The last of three jewels is the Sangha, or Buddhist community, which preserves the teachings of the Buddha, the lifestyle of his followers, and practices of meditation, which are only possible within a supportive community. Although many so-called Western Buddhists play down the importance of the Sangha, it is nevertheless absolutely vital for authentic Buddhism.

Buddhism is both a highly philosophical and an ultimately experiential religious system of spiritual practices. Central to these practices and beliefs are the four Noble Truths. The first Noble Truth is the truth of *dukkha*, or impermanence, often rendered "suffering," though in fact they are separate entities, impermanence being the cause of suffering. The truth of dukkha is that nothing in life is lasting; everything is in a constant state of flux. Therefore, even if you are happy today, you may be sacked tomorrow. If you are young today, you will be old tomorrow. Everything changes: the flowers bloom, and then they wither away. This is the essence of life. There is no permanence, no lasting satisfaction, only eternal change and impermanence. Hence, all life is described as suffering.

Photo 12.9 The colorful entrance to a North American Buddhist temple.

The second Noble Truth is the cause of impermanance and suffering, which, according to Buddhist thought, is our craving or thirst for existence. In other words, our consciousness emerges from constant activities that are bound to the totality of all things, which are in constant motion. This consciousness, which results from individual events, creates the illusion that an individual person, or self, actually exists, when in reality all that exists is a constant motion of impermanent sense impressions.

The third Noble Truth is that the cause of this impermanence or suffering can be eliminated. There is a way that leads to the annihilation of consciousness and the cessation of all activity. This is the way that the Buddha has shown to his followers.

The fourth Noble Truth is that way and is known as the Noble Eightfold Path. This path consists of eight levels, or steps, that lead the individual consciousness to enlightenment. The full path has three basic elements: trusting in the teachings of the Buddha, living an ethical and pure life, and meditating in the correct way and thus bringing the mind totally under control. The first two steps on the path deal with the essence of trust. They are right belief and right attitude. Without knowing what is true and without having a receptive attitude, one can never enter into the path.

The next three steps deal with the way we live. They are right speech, right actions, and right livelihood. The Buddhist must constantly be aware of what they say, because their words reflect their thoughts. Since thoughts lead to action, and actions reflect thoughts, how a Buddhist behaves is essential to correct living. Finally, how a person makes their living will obviously affect their speech and actions. For example, if a person works in a slaughterhouse killing animals, their thoughts and actions lead them away from the truth of Buddhism. Therefore this cannot be done.

The final three steps concern the control of the mind, what we call meditation, or yoga. These are right effort, right awareness, and right meditation. To act rightly, one must always struggle to do what is good in terms of the Buddhist teaching about right and wrong. Right awareness, or contemplation, means that one must learn to control the mind so that emotions and all the concerns of life do not affect one's inner being. Thus neither joy and sorrow, nor heat and cold, nor wealth and poverty, nor any other transitory state should affect the inner thoughts of the true Buddhist. Finally, there is right meditation, which may be described as a form of advanced contemplation, or perhaps we should say the right practice of Buddhist yoga. Only when all the other stages of the eightfold pattern have been followed can one bring the mind totally under the control of the will. Only when all is still can one attain enlightenment, the ultimate goal of Buddhism.

Photo 12.10 A nineteenth-century painting of a Chinese Buddhist pagoda. Although the term "pagoda" refers to a layered building in the Buddhist tradition of China, a pagoda was the equivalent of an Indian stupa, which housed a relic of the Buddha or one of his close disciples. Relics of holy men—and they were men—help the believer attain merit, thus lightening the burden of their quest for enlightenment.

BUDDHIST ENLIGHTENMENT

But what is enlightenment? Buddhists call it nirvana and then have great difficulty explaining what it is. Perhaps the best explanations come from the Buddhist sutras, thought to have been given by the Buddha himself. According to these traditions, to the question "What is nirvana?" the Buddha answered that it can be best understood as a blowing out of a candle. "Where," he asked, "does the flame go when it is blown out?" On another occasion the Buddha is said to have described his teachings, the dharma, as a raft that ferries people over a river so wide that the passenger never knows what the other side looks like until reaching it. Entering nirvana is like crossing this river. Nirvana is the unknown, the unconditioned enlightenment.

Edward Conze (1904–1979) begins his introduction to Buddhism with the statement that "the Buddhist point of view will appeal only to those people who are completely disillusioned with the world as it is, and with themselves, who are extremely sensitive to pain, suffering, and any kind of turmoil, who have an extreme desire for happiness, and a considerable capacity for renunciation ... The Buddhist seeks for a total happiness beyond this world."[1]

To most Westerners, Conze's view of the human condition seems extremely pessimistic, but practitioners of Buddhism would disagree. Buddhism portrays a very different form of salvation than do the Abramic religions. The latter place primary value on human personality and emphasize the salvation of the individual, while yogic religions speak of salvation *away from* individuality. As Ninian Smart has written, yogic thinking, upon which Buddhism is based, holds that men and other living beings are continually being reborn. With death, the individual is reborn in a different form. This everlasting recurrence of births and deaths can only be stopped by transcending it, by attaining a liberation in a transcendental sphere where the self is freed from mental and bodily encumbrances. Typically, this is achieved by the practice of austerity and yoga: self-denial and self-discipline are means of destroying that which leads to rebirth and karma.

Buddhist ideas of rebirth are logically related to a belief in karma and need to be sharply differentiated from many Hindu views. Buddhists deny the existence of the soul, arguing that the continuation of sense impressions at the point of death deludes those who suffer near-death experiences into thinking that they have an essence or soul. Buddhists postulate reincarnation rather than transmigration of the soul. They define rebirth through transmigration as the continuation of sense impressions, not the movement of the soul from one body to another.

From the Buddhist standpoint all humans are trapped in the "wheel of existence," known as *samsara*. This is the name given to a vast network of births and deaths through endless lifetimes involving incarnations in many worlds, heavens, and hells. For Buddhists samsara holds together everything and every being in an infinite repetition of birth and death driven by the bonds of karma.

Ordinarily, people do not experience the bonds of karma, nor are they aware of the wheel of existence. Instead they experience what they take to be their individual lives as a fleeting moment of consciousness to which they ascribe ultimate significance. But this awareness of one's individuality and belief in the significance of one's present life is an illusion brought about by the effects of karma. Karma blinds us to the reality of samsara and thus to the possibility of escaping our karmic bonds and attaining liberation. Karma creates the illusion of individuality and of a permanent creation, when in reality everything is in a state of constant flux. The illusory nature of our experience of reality is brought about by *maya*, which magically conjures up an unreal world. Therefore maya is understood as illusion, or the essence of all illusions, which can manifest itself as a god. Once we see through the illusion, however, we realize that we need to be liberated from samsara and the bonds of karma.

Thus in Buddhism, dharma means a teaching about what is right or the truth about reality, and liberation, or freedom from the bonds of karma and release from samsara, is

---

1. Edward Conze, *Buddhism: Its Essence and Development* (1951; Oxford: Bruno Cassirer, 1957), 22.

called nirvana. Buddhists teach that we cannot really say what nirvana is, because it is not conditioned by our universe of cause and effect and is consequently beyond our comprehension. We can do no more than affirm our belief in it. All we can really know is that nirvana is freedom from the wheel of samsara and the bonds of karma. It is the cessation of our present mode of existence. Buddhist teaching also maintains that while we cannot explain what nirvana is, we can know what enables people to attain it.

BUDDHIST VIEWS OF THE STATE

Initially, Buddhism represented a radical call to renunciation and the leaving behind of everything we would consider normal life. In the hierarchy of Buddhist thinking, monks were at the top, followed by nuns, whose status was always somewhat ambiguous. Below them were the laity, who were to be taught the dharma in return for food and other gifts. The relationship between the laypeople and members of the Sangha was theorized through a doctrine known as merit. By their actions, meditations, prayers, and general lifestyle the monks and nuns generated merit which mitigated the effects of karma. By supporting the monks and nuns, laypeople earned a share in this merit. Hence there was a symbiosis between society and the Sangha.

Early in the development of Buddhism, various kings adopted the religion. The most famous of these was the great King Ashoka, whose grandfather had led resistance against Greek rule in northern India. Eventually, Ashoka's empire stretched over most of the areas we now consider India. According to tradition, Ashoka converted to Buddhism following a major battle in which he was sickened by the slaughter. Under his patronage Indian Buddhism entered the golden age. He built temples, erected pillars, and arranged for the moral instruction of his subjects. His understanding of the duties of a Buddhist king involved the bringing of justice, the avoidance of harsh penalties, and the protection of his people. This of course meant that he maintained an army to protect the state, the equivalent of what we would today call police. Most important of all, he became a vegetarian and encouraged his subjects to practice vegetarianism.

As kings converted to Buddhism, there slowly developed an understanding of what it meant to be a Buddhist king. This appears to have incorporated existing Indian views of the king as a pivotal figure in society. He was called "the wheel turner," a term that referred to both his secular, material role and his spiritual role. His secular role was signified by the turning wheels of a chariot, and his spiritual role was signified by the dharma,

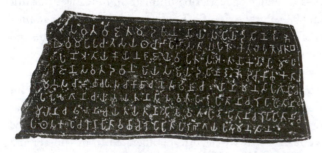

Photo 12.11 The inscription of Ashoka from the Girnar Rock. Importantly for the study of ancient India, this is written in Prakrit and not Sanskrit, raising the question as to when Sanskrit developed as a living language.

pictured as the wheel of existence. The king held together both society and the super-natural realm.

From early times the Buddhist king was seen as having a duty to promote the dharma. This meant he must care for the welfare of his subjects, ensuring that they had sufficient food, shelter, and protection. As Buddhism spread to other parts of Asia, this conception of kingship was adapted by existing cultures. In every case, support of the Sangha, or community of monks, was seen as one of the central responsibilities of the king.

As in the case of Ashoka, there is no evidence that the majority of Buddhist rulers were essentially pacifist. Many ostensibly Buddhist states fought wars. After the collapse of the Central Kingdom of Burma in the thirteenth century, for example, the area divided into numerous small warring kingdoms, all claiming to be Buddhist. Similarly, in Tibet many of the monasteries maintained large standing armies that continually warred with one another, and in Japan the samurai tradition was strongly influenced by various schools of Buddhism. Generally, however, Buddhist kings were restrained by their religion from conducting aggressive wars. In theory, at least, nonviolence remained a Buddhist ideal, violence was regarded as a last resort, and only defensive war was really permissible.

BUDDHIST PIETY

Buddhist piety centers on practices of meditation that were originally designed for monks. These practices aim at bringing the mind under control so that the meditator recognizes the true nature of reality and is able to escape from it. In many respects, Buddhist meditation is a form of yoga. Therefore, talk about meditation is somewhat misleading. What in English we call meditation covers three different ideas within Buddhism. First, there is the idea of mindfulness, which is the first stage in meditation. Traditionally, this is seen as a quieting of the mind, a calming down of thought. Mindfulness, in turn, leads to wisdom and ultimately trance.

Second, there is the idea of concentration, which draws upon the Buddhist belief that our mind has two levels. The first level is that of ordinary consciousness. It is the surface level of the mind. Beneath this is a deeper level that is calm. Few people are aware of or can reach this deeper level. Therefore most people live in a state of constant turmoil.

Finally, there is the idea of wisdom, which in Buddhism is the highest of all values. For the Buddhist the idea of wisdom is quite specific. The great Buddhist scholar Buddhaghosa (fourth to fifth century AD), of Ceylon (modern Sri Lanka), defines it as "whatever penetrates

Photo 12.12 Kemp's view of the inside of a nineteenth-century Buddhist monastery in China.

into the Dharmas destroying all the illusions of darkness which distort our understanding the Dharma." It may be said, therefore, that wisdom concerns the meaning of life, our daily conduct, and the essence of reality.

THE BUDDHIST CALENDAR

Because Buddhism has taken root in various cultures and societies, there is no one Buddhist calendar like the Christian year. Instead we have various Buddhist calendars adapted to different countries and traditions. In attempting to understand Buddhist festivals it is important to recognize that, as in Jewish and other traditions, Buddhists work with the lunar calendar. The Buddhist year begins with the full moon that marks the day on which the Buddha is said to have been born.

Most Buddhists celebrated two major festivals. In the Theravadin tradition these are known as Wesakh and Kathina. Wesakh celebrates the birth, death, and enlightenment of the Buddha on the first full moon of the second lunar month. During this festival people wear white gowns, raise flags, light lanterns, and attach money to branches known as money trees. Kathina is a time to celebrate the poor, give gifts, and endow monks with new robes. Other festivals, such as a celebration of the Chinese New Year, are often incorporated into Buddhist celebrations.

Photo 12.13 A Buddhist priest delivers a homily.

DAILY DEVOTIONS

Most Buddhists maintain a small shrine in their homes to aid them in meditation. In such a shrine there will be at least one statue of the Buddha and very often candles or a low light. There may also be other decorations depicting the Buddha or Buddhist scriptures. Most Buddhists use a rosary, that is, a string of beads, usually 118 in number, to aid them in their meditations.

COMMUNAL MEDITATION

Buddhists wear ordinary clothes while attending communal celebrations which Christians tend to describe as worship. Of course, since God and the gods are essentially unimportant for Buddhism, it is somewhat misleading to speak about Buddhist worship. Perhaps a more accurate term is communal meditation or the veneration of the Buddha. When entering a Buddhist temple, which in North America and Europe is sometimes called a Buddhist church, participants remove shoes and often sit cross-legged on the floor.

THE BUDDHIST TRADITION AND MODERN SCHOLARSHIP

Buddhism is unique among world religions in that it is the least affected by modern historical scholarship. This is because it is the teachings of the Buddha, not events in his life or any other historical data, that is important. Therefore, even if all Buddhist scriptures were found to be very recent inventions without any connection to the historical Buddha, this discovery would not affect Buddhism. Nor would Buddhism be affected by the discovery that the Buddha was a totally fictitious being and that the historical Buddha never really existed. None of this matters to Buddhism.

Therefore, everything modern scholarship contributes to the study Buddhism is essentially positive. The greatest contribution of modern scholarship has been in the rediscovery of lost texts, such as the truly fascinating Buddhist play *Joy for the World* (1987),[2] written by the Buddhist scholar Candragomin (fifth century AD?) and recently translated in English by Professor Michael Hahn of the University of Marburg. Hahn's publishing company Indica-Tibetica has produced many rare texts. So too has the American publishing company Dharma Publishing. These are just two examples of the way modern scholarship has enriched Buddhism by recovering numerous long-lost manuscripts.

Photo 12.14 To survive today, Buddhist groups emphasize meditation and adapt to modern society by creating their own schools, like the one in this picture, for children of community members.

---

2. Candragomin, *Joy for the World*, trans. with notes by Michael Hahn (San Fransisco: Dharma, 1987).

CHAPTER 13

THE MORAL QUEST OF EDWARD CONZE

INTRODUCTION

By general agreement, Edward Conze, whose full name was Eberhard Julius Dietrich Conze (1904–1979), was one of the greatest Buddhist scholars of the twentieth century and a truly remarkable man. He helped shape the reception of Buddhism in the English-speaking world during the twentieth century. His many books and continued influence in the field testify to his scholarship and devotion to the Buddhist cause. Recognizing Conze's great importance as a scholar and the value of his works, it is worth attempting to understand the background out of which his work developed.

This chapter is based on his privately published *The Memoirs of a Modern Gnostic*,[1] which is now quite rare, plus my own memory of Conze as an unforgettable teacher who took time to talk with his students. Conze begins his *Memoirs* by telling his readers that the book was written at the request of friends and that he intended to "merely record honestly what has happened to me."[2] It was, he said, "a thoroughly honest book" that "tells you what I think and not what I ought to think."[3] The book is certainly honest, so much so that the third volume was withheld from publication until after his death for fear of libel suits. Unfortunately, it will probably never appear because his wife is said to have destroyed the manuscript.

CONZE'S MEMOIRS

What is surprising about the *Memoirs* is that although Conze spends a lot of time discussing his interaction with various individuals, very little of his narrative concerns the development of Buddhist ideas or philosophy. Instead the overriding theme is a passionate concern with the moral questions raised by war. Again and again Conze reiterates his commitment to pacifism and his horror at the brutality of modern warfare. Against this background he is highly critical of people, particularly professing Christians, who ought to know better, yet who enthusiastically support war when it becomes a reality.

---

1. Edward Conze, *The Memoirs of a Modern Gnostic* (Sherborne, U.K.: Samizdat, 1979).
2. Ibid., iv.
3. Ibid., v.

Photo 13.1 This rare photograph of Professor Conze was taken by Herbert Elbrecht, who kindly allowed its reproduction in this book.

Therefore, anyone wishing to understand his scholarship needs to place it in the context of his moral concerns. To view his scholarship apart from his life is to miss an important dimension of modern Buddhism. In this chapter the life of Edward Conze will first be explored in terms of what James Richardson identifies as a "conversion career"[4] and then as the life of a mature Buddhist apologist. In this way we hope new light will be thrown on the development of Western Buddhism, its interaction with Christianity, and the important role played by Fascism and Marxism in shaping many twentieth-century Western Buddhists.

CHILDHOOD INFLUENCES

Although in most respects a very typical German, Conze was British born by one of those chance events that make history interesting. While his father was working as the German vice-consul to Britain, in 1904, his mother gave birth. Consequently, he was entitled to British citizenship by right of birth. Shortly afterward his parents returned to Germany, and Conze grew up in a very respectable, wealthy, upper-class family. His paternal grandfather was a factory owner and "devout Christian" who, in his quest for industrial consolidation, married his two sons to the two daughters of another manufacturer, attempting to merge the two businesses. The business venture was a success, but both marriages, which were arranged with a total disregard for the true feelings of the people involved, or their religious commitments, were disasters.

From his paternal grandfather, whom he describes as a highly educated man, Conze claimed he "absorbed" an "abiding love of the Greek Classics."[5] From what Conze says about him, anyone familiar with Peter Gay's classic work *The Enlightenment: An Interpretation; The Rise of Modern Paganism*,[6] will immediately realize that Conze's grandfather's views were probably closer to those of Enlightenment thinkers and liberal Christians than to those of German Pietists. This is because, as Gay argues, there is a close link between the reading of Greek and Roman classical authors and modern skepticism.

By contrast, Conze says that his maternal grandfather "thought little of Christianity and never went to church."[7] Conze also notes that "other ancestors had shown great interest in psychic matters and in mystical religion."[8] Consequently, throughout his life Conze

---

4. James T. Richardson, ed., *Conversion Careers: In and out of the New Religions* (Beverly Hills: Sage, 1978).

5. Conze, *Memoirs*, 1.2.

6. Peter Gay, *The Enlightenment: An Interpretation; The Rise of Modern Paganism* (New York: Knopf, 1966).

7. Conze, *Memoirs*, 1.2.

8. Ibid.

was fascinated by the supernatural and occult powers, though when he first encountered astrology from a professor at the University of Bonn, he rejected it as unscientific. Later, as will be explained, he changed his mind.

Commenting on his family background, he observes that a "latent conflict or perhaps tension between capitalist activities and Christian profession was never far from the surface."[9] This led him to comment that "in some ways the message of the gospel did not go any too well with the way in which we amassed our wealth."[10] Nevertheless the young Conze grew up in the heyday of the German Empire. Like many wealthy Germans, he was sent to a private school modeled after the English public school. There, he claims, he was given a concern for social justice derived from the Hebrew prophets.

Photo 13.2 Trafalgar Square, at the heart of London, with the National Gallery in the background. The German Embassy, where Conze's father worked, is in nearby Belgrave Square. Born in England because his father was a German diplomat, Conze automatically gained the right to British citizenship, a fact that saved his life after the Nazis came to power.

At his first boarding school he acquired a love for England and for what he describes as "a simple life in the country as against the wastefulness of big cities." This distaste for big cities, which, he observes, was part of the ethos of the time, led him to join the *Wandervoegel*, a Boy Scout–type group that wandered barefoot in the woods. More significantly, and something Conze does not say, the Wandervoegel in many ways was the cradle of National Socialism, because it was here that what is known as the *völkisch* ideology, which popularized occult and nationalist ideas, was popularized among young people based on a sharp contrast between the "deadening effects of modern civilisation" and the "lifegiving nature of German culture."

Apart from these three influences—family, school, and Wandervoegel—which Conze considered valuable, he also imbibed two other far less desirable notions: a rabid anti-Semitism and a "noisy, ultra-patriotically Pan Germanic militarism."[11] Both of these influences he ultimately rejected, although the insidious effects of anti-Semitism were particularly difficult to root out.

Conze describes himself as possessing "a deep-seated and instinctive aversion to killing,"[12] which he attributed to the influence of his mother's family. This aversion gave him

---

9. Ibid., 1.2.
10. Ibid., 1.3.
11. Ibid., 1.5–6.
12. Ibid., 1.6.

Photo 13.3 The Berlin Dom, or cathedral, which houses the tombs of the German emperors. In his autobiography Conze describes how as a child he grew up to admire the achievements of the Hohenzollern dynasty, with its apparent Christian piety and moral uprightness.

a natural predisposition toward Buddhism, which he first encountered when he was thirteen years old through a book in his father's library. The book was a German translation of Lafcadio Hearn's (1850–1904) *Gleanings in Buddha-fields*.[13] He wryly remarks he discovered Buddhism through "a German translation of an English translation of a Japanese translation of a Chinese translation of a Sanskrit original."[14] If nothing else, this remark shows the power of translation and casts doubt on the craze for purity. In some religions, like Islam, it may be impossible to translate sacred texts, and therefore learning the original language is absolutely necessary for reading a book like the Qur'an. But, as with the Christian scriptures, translation has been crucial to the transmission of Buddhism.

UNIVERSITY YEARS

After completing high school, which in Germany was known as the *Abitur*, Conze went to university. He began at Tübingen, where on his father's insistence he studied law, which thoroughly bored him. From there, following the usual German pattern, he moved to the University of Heidelberg to study philology, which his father reluctantly permitted, having forbidden the study of philosophy, which he saw as useless. Here Conze discovered his great linguistic talents and once more came under the influence of Buddhism, particularly Zen. From Heidelberg he moved to the University of Kiel, where he hoped to write his PhD dissertation on either Schopenhauer or Spinoza. His doctoral adviser, Professor Heinrich Scholz (1884–1956), forbade this and insisted that he write on the Jesuit scholar Franciscus Suárez.

Despite Conze's misgivings, this proved a very profitable project, bringing him into contact with ideas about the perennial philosophy. The idea of a "perennial philosophy" is associated with a group of early twentieth-century thinkers who adopted the name "Traditionalists."[15] This group centered on the French writer René Guénon (1886–1951),

---

13. Lafcadio Hearn, *Gleanings in Buddha-fields: Studies of Hand and Soul in the Far East* (Boston: Houghton Mifflin, 1897).

14. Conze, *Memoirs*, 1.7.

15. Mark J. Sedgwick, *Against the Modern World: Traditionalism and the Secret Intellectual History of the Twentieth Century* (Oxford: Oxford Univ. Press, 2004).

whose book *The Crisis of the Modern World*[16] caused something of a sensation when it was first published in 1927 and resulted in the development of a small but devoted following. The term itself appears to go back to the fifteenth-century Roman Catholic writer Marsilio Ficino (1433–1499), who created a form of Christian Platonism. As a result of Guénon's work, the idea was revived in a new form that embraced all religious traditions through the belief that they share common esoteric features. Among the advocates of this view were writers like Ananda Kentish Coomaraswamy (1877–1947), the distinguished art historian; the self-appointed Sufi master Frithjof Schuon (1907–1998); and the historian of religions Mircea Eliade (1907–1986).

From Kiel Conze moved on to the University of Cologne, which at the time had one of the best philosophy faculties in Germany. There he came under the influence of Max Scheler (1874–1928), "to whom," he said, "I owe more than I can say in a few words. Many of my brightest ideas … go back to him."[17] Eventually, in 1928, upon acceptance of his dissertation, "The Concept of Metaphysics in Franciscus Suárez," he was awarded his doctorate by the University of Cologne. Then he moved to the University of Bonn, where Johannes Maria Verweyen (1883–1945) introduced him to Theosophy and astrology, which he initially rejected. It was here that he also began to learn Sanskrit from Walter Ruben before moving on to Hamburg, where he hoped to obtain his second doctorate, the German "habilitation," which is necessary for anyone embarking on an academic career, under Ernst Cassirer (1874–1945). To his dismay, Cassirer was dismissed by the Nazis when they came to power, and Conze's habilitation was never completed, although he did write a large book called *The Principle of Contradiction*. Shortly after this, early in 1933, he was forced to flee to England to escape the wrath of the Nazis.

The entire Conze family, like many elite Germans, were solidly anti-Nazi. Conze tells how, in protest against their actions against the Jews, his mother deliberately held conversations with Jewish acquaintances in the middle of the street. To further irritate the Nazis,

Photo 13.4 Käthe Kollwitz (1867-1945) moving war memorial, in Magdeburg Dom, to the fallen in World War I. What horrified her, and many like her, including Conze, was that supposedly Christian nations could sanction such butchery. The horrors of the First World War and its patently false propaganda profoundly affected Conze, creating a reaction similar to that of the hero of Erich Maria Remarque's novel *All Quiet on the Western Front* (1928). His disillusionment after the war propelled him toward the Communist Party, which he saw as the only bulwark against fascism.

---

16. René Guénon, *The Crisis of the Modern World*, trans. Arthur Osborne (London: Luzac, 1942).
17. Conze, *Memoirs*, 1.9.

she conspicuously converted to Roman Catholicism, which the Nazis despised. Around the same time, his father was dismissed from his position as a judge, and his legal career suffered throughout the Nazi period.

Against the background of the growing power of National Socialism, Conze joined the German Communist Party in 1928 and thereafter dedicated himself to organizing opposition to Nazism. Although the Nazis tolerated his party activities for a long time, they tightened the noose after they came to power in 1933.[18] This was brought home to him by a visit from several SS officers, who, being Theosophists, knew of his interest in Buddhism. They warned him that while they tolerated his activities as "Comrade Ackermann," his Communist Party pseudonym, the Gestapo would not, and the Gestapo was about to take over control of the police on July 1. He was advised to get out of Germany. Conze, admittedly terrified, took their advice, since the "Nazis had introduced a new element into political strife by the widespread use of torture." And he feared being slowly beaten to death in a dark Gestapo cell, which had happened to some of his comrades.[19]

CONZE'S MARXISM

Conze first encountered Marxism during his school years, when an able boy from a lower-class family, whose father was a "mere school teacher," befriended him. In itself this was a rare event in a society rigidly divided along class lines. Nevertheless, from him Conze learned the basic principles of Marxism. On several occasions he was also taken to the boy's home, which he described as "working class," even though in reality it was middle-class. The bareness of the home, with its lack of comforts or reading materials, shocked the young Conze, adding an experiential reality to Marxist theories.

Subsequently, he became a full-fledged Marxist who never deviated from Stalin's views until he fled to England and left the party in June 1933.[20] As he explained, what attracted him to Marxism was its philosophy of history and that it seemed to offer the only credible resistance to National Socialism. In becoming a Communist, Conze was not alone. As he observes, many upper-class Germans, as well as the cream of English society, flocked to Marxism as a credible alternative to Fascism during the 1920s and 1930s. It was, as he said, "the fashionable thing to do."[21] Nevertheless, certain Marxist analytic techniques served him well throughout his life and, by his own admission, "never left" him.[22]

Toward the end of his time in Germany he began to develop doubts about the theoretical basis of Marxism, which he eventually came to view as "a *surrogate for religion*."[23] More importantly, contact with the economist Joseph Schumpeter (1883–1950) led him to recognize "a serious weakness in the Marxist explanation of surplus value."[24] Marxist economics, he realized, simply did not work.

---

18. Ibid., 2.8.
19. Ibid., 2.12.
20. Ibid., 2.9.
21. Ibid., 2.19.
22. Ibid., 2.17.
23. Ibid., 2.18.
24. Ibid., 2.20.

Contact with real workers while organizing Communist resistance in Bonn also made him realize that the workers were not interested in some Communist paradise; all they wanted was simple improvements in their standard of living. To his shock, he discovered that what they really wanted was to be middle-class, take good holidays, live in decent houses, and eat good food. They were not impressed by Soviet achievements, but only by things that made their lives better.[25] By the early 1930s he had begun to be disillusioned with Marxism, although as a committed anti-Nazi he continued his membership in the Communist Party and worked tirelessly to oppose the emerging tyranny of National Socialism. In his own words, he remained "a faithful servant of Stalin" until he left the party after fleeing to England.

The success of Hitler in forming a coalition government on 30 January 1933 was followed by the burning of the Reichstag on 27 February. Whether the Nazis set fire to the German Parliament themselves or whether some deranged individual committed the act, it gave Hitler the excuse he needed, and the Nazis, who controlled the police in the coalition government, seized power. This led to the Enabling Act, or Law for Removing the Distress of the People and the Reich, which was passed by a large majority on 23 March 1933. After that there was little anyone could do.

Photo 13.5 A street in central Hamburg. It was here in the 1920s that Conze was both a university student and a Communist Party organizer helping working class members oppose the Nazis.

FLIGHT TO ENGLAND

Taking his Jewish Communist girlfriend, who he married after they arrived in London so that she would be allowed to stay in Britain, he fled to England as a British citizen. Soon after they arrived, his wife converted to Catholicism and they separated. After this, by his own account, Conze spent several months on a lonely retreat in the woods, where he discovered the full powers of meditation for the first time, and almost killed himself through rigorous ascetic practices.

He eventually returned to society to become a sectional lecturer for various universities and the Worker's Education Society. Along the way he met his future wife Muriel, who, because his Catholic wife refused a divorce, changed her name to Conze and moved in with him. Thus began the pattern of life that he followed until he died. After the end of World War II, Conze held several temporary university positions in Britain and America. Yet, though he published prolifically, he never gained tenure, which is more a comment on

25. Ibid., 2.15–24.

the fickle nature of academic appointments than on either Conze's teaching skills, which were outstanding, or his extensive scholarly work.

CONZE'S CONVERSION TO BUDDHISM

In England Conze came to see himself as bogged down in a hopeless mire. What rescued him was his rediscovery of Buddhism. Here D. T. Suzuki played a key role. Conze dated his Buddhist conversion to 1938, when he published a refutation of Major John Morris's review of Steinilber-Oberlin's *The Buddhist Sects of Japan*.[26] From 1938 or 1939—even Conze was not sure—he devoted all his energies to the study of the Mahayana as a believing Buddhist.

While recommitting himself to Buddhism, Conze discovered astrology and developed a love for it which remained with him for the rest of his life. After the breakup of his first marriage, he despaired of ever finding a suitable partner. Then he came across a booklet on astrology that changed his life. To his surprise, it described to a tee all his failed relationships and drew attention to the fact that all women who had attracted him up to that point were Capricorns. This made him curious, and he began to study astrology seriously, learning to read and cast horoscopes. Later, when he settled in Godshill, in the English countryside, he discovered that many people regarded astrology as a natural part of life. This discovery, he claimed, set him free from the domination of technology and the tyranny of science.

He also claimed to have developed various psychic faculties as a result of years of meditation.[27] For example, he claimed to be able to communicate telepathically and to be able to see people at a distance. He also claimed that he had a premonition of the first air raid on London.[28] Consequently, he despised what he called "verbalised religion," which he described as "a whistling in the dark, [which] has little to do with the spiritual life."[29]

Despite these developments, he continued to be profoundly attracted to Christianity, noting that many Western Buddhists eventually become Christians. This was,

Photo 13.6 The open-air Topography of Terror exhibit in central Berlin is built on the site of a Nazi interrogation center. It documents in vivid detail the horrors of the Nazi regime. In his autobiography Conze comments on the fact that the Nazis introduced terror as a political tool into German life. After they came to power, he took the hint, assumed British citizenship, and with his Jewish wife fled to England.

26. Ibid., 1.16.
27. Ibid., 1.79.
28. Ibid., 1.46–47.
29. Ibid., 1.37.

he opines, because most Western Buddhists "are at heart disappointed Christians."[30] Then he admits that he too was tempted to become a Catholic, but a priest, later defrocked for homosexual activities, rejected him in the mid-1930s.[31]

DISILLUSIONMENT AND CONZE'S MORAL QUEST

The key to Conze's spiritual development appears to lie in the disillusionment he felt as a child with his parents' generation, the society in which he lived, and the actions of supposedly Christian leaders. By his own admission, as a young boy, he admired the kaiser and the society over which he ruled. Like other Germans of his generation, Conze thought that the moral issues surrounding the outbreak of World War I were clear. The Austrian heir to the throne, the Archduke Franz Ferdinand (1863–1914) and his wife Sophia (1868–1914) were on a state visit to Sarajevo, the capital of Bosnia-Herzegovina, which was an Austro-Hungarian province. At 10:15 a.m. on 28 June 1914, a group of terrorists mounted an assassination attempt that initially went wrong when a hand grenade missed its target, killing innocent bystanders. Afterwards the royal couple insisted on visiting the hospital to comfort the injured. On their way the driver of the royal car took a wrong turn, realized his mistake, and slowed to correct it. At that point another of the assassins, Gavrilo Princip (1894–1918), who had gone for a coffee in a local café, saw his opportunity and gunned them down. The archduke and his wife died within minutes.

Although the two main assassins were caught, others escaped to nearby Serbia, where they were given sanctuary. Naturally, the Austrian government demanded that they be handed over for trial. The Serbs refused, and Austria mobilized its army. To appreciate the situation, it is necessary to imagine what would happen if the American vice president was assassinated while visiting San Antonio or some other town close to the Mexican border. Suppose the assassins escaped to Mexico and the Mexican government not only refused to hand them over, but clearly regarded them as national heroes.

This was the situation in Sarajevo in August 1914. When the Austrians threatened Serbia, the Russians responded by beginning to mobilize their army. At that point the Germans appealed for peace. But when the Russians refused to stop the mobilization, the Germans followed suit and mobilized their own army. France then scrambled to

Photo 13.7 This Topography of Terror exhibit in Berlin shows less fortunate opponents of the Nazis who suffered for their opposition through torture and death. To his credit, Conze admitted that, after the horrific death of a Communist colleague through torture, he was terrified and decided to leave for England.

30. Ibid., 2.81.
31. Ibid., 2.34–35.

mobilize its army in support of the Russians, triggering the events that began World War I. From the German viewpoint, as expressed in a famous declaration drawn up by German academics, including men like the great liberal Protestant theologian Adolf von Harnack (1851–1930), the German government was entirely in its right to mobilize its army and go to war in support of its Austrian ally. Austria was the wronged party, Serbia had broken international law, and Germany was merely defending itself as an ally against hostile threats.

As a young man Conze accepted these arguments without question. Then doubts gradually began to accumulate. In particular, he came to see the Protestant clergy as "the slavish lackeys of the bourgeoisie, and other militarists." The German upper classes, to which he belonged, treated pastors as their slaves as long as they preached obedience to the government and warned against godless political movements. They were, in his view, "sycophants," who preached the gospel of a Germanic god leading his people into battle. In his words, "I will never forget nor forgive these blasphemies which have shaped my attitude to Christianity for this life at least."[32]

The event that shaped Conze's attitude to war more than any other was his discovery of his father's war diaries when he was seventeen years old. These detailed diaries told the story of his father's experiences as a German officer serving on the eastern front against the Russians. What horrified Conze was a series of "pictures of naked dark-haired girls lying in fields where they had they had been raped, with their legs wide apart and a bayonet rammed in their belly."[33]

Even more horrifying in gross barbarism were another set of pictures, a few pages further on, of Russian girls raped by Germans. In this case, and Conze said that the photographs haunted him all his life, not only were the

Photo 13.8 Behind this wall and beyond a double row of trees lies the former concentration camp of Sachsenhausen, in the small town of Oranienburg just outside Berlin. As Conze noted, Nazi terror was carefully targeted and concealed. Long before the mass arrests and deportations of Jews, the Nazis rounded up the leaders of opposition groups and transported them to camps like this one. The very secrecy of the arrests added to the psychological terror induced by the regime. The brutality of the Nazis and their ability to squash all opposition was something Conze never forgot. Among those held at Sachsenhausen was Martin Niemöller (1892–1984), one of the leaders of the Confessing Church, who was detained "at Hitler's pleasure."

32. Ibid., 2.32.
33. Ibid., 2.46.

women raped and murdered, but they had been subjected to torture and mutilation. As the commanding officer in the area, his father had mounted an investigation, arrested the culprits, court martialed them, and had them executed. He was an honorable German horrified by the barbarity of his own troops. Since Conze's father was eventually transferred to the Military Court of Justice, there were many similar accounts throughout his diaries.

What horrified Conze even more was that these brutalities were magnified thousands of times during the Second World War. Conze had no illusions about the Holocaust and the evil that brought it about. What shocked him was the self-righteousness of the Allies, particularly the English, because he believed that World War II could have been avoided if only the English and other powers had supported the opponents of Nazism. He also believed that many of the worst atrocities against the Jews were modeled on British actions as a colonial power. After all, it was, as he pointed out, the British who invented the concentration camp during the Second Anglo-Boer War. All the Nazis did was develop the original model.[34]

RUSSIAN ATROCITIES AND ALLIED BOMBING

Although the published volumes of *Memoirs* do not mention it, presumably because he reserved the material for the unpublished third volume, Conze was painfully aware of Russian atrocities toward the end of World War II, when, encouraged by Stalin and his generals, Russian troops went on a rampage of rape and murder. What Conze could not understand was that the English and their American allies suddenly turned a blind eye to this, never even hinting at such things in their history books. It was not simply that the Russians took revenge on the Germans. That would have been bad enough, but the Russians murdered and raped anyone who came their way, be they Czech, Pole, Jew, or German.

Later, after the end of the war, even the wives of German Communist Party officials, who had taken refuge in Moscow during the 1930s and who returned to the Russian Zone of Germany as its new rulers, were not immune from such treatment from Russian troops. The Russian army, until 1948, at least, was above the law and had the right to shoot anyone who refused to cooperate with them. In fact, only recently have books like Christopher Duffy's *Red Storm on the Reich: The Soviet March on Germany, 1945,*[35] Alfred de Zayas's *A Terrible Revenge: The Ethnic Cleansing of the East European Germans, 1944–1950*[36] and Norman M. Naimark's *The Russians in Germany: A History of the Soviet Zone of Occupation, 1945–1949*[37] begun to explore this issue. Despite the Cold War, Conze found the silence of the West hard to understand, but suspected that it was rooted in a reluctance to open Pandora's box by examining the conduct of war.

---

34. Ibid., 2.1.
35. Christopher Duffy, *Red Storm on The Reich: The Soviet March on Germany, 1945* (London: Routledge, 1991).
36. Alfred-Maurice De Zayas, *A Terrible Revenge: The Ethnic Cleansing of the East European Germans, 1944–1950,* trans. John A. Koehler (New York: St. Martin's, 1994).
37. Norman M. Naimark, *The Russians in Germany: A History of the Soviet Zone of Occupation, 1945–1949* (Cambridge, Mass.: Harvard Univ. Press, 1995).

When he first went to England in 1933, Conze described Winston Churchill, who at that time was in the political wilderness, as the only British politician who really understood what was going on in Germany. Therefore, he virtually idolized Churchill. Later, he came to regard Churchill as one of the greatest killers in history.[38] What upset Conze was British bombing of civilian areas in German cities. Mass air raids and the creation of firestorms in cities like Hamburg were particularly galling to him, because the areas that were attacked were the very ones that had resisted the Nazis to the end. Instead of bombing the industrial areas, the docks, or those suburbs that had supported the Nazis, the British chose to destroy those very areas were anti–Nazi sentiment was the strongest. Thus, Conze spoke of "villainous scientists" who "experimented with their firestorms" and "killed up to 30,000 people in one go, by a mixture of explosive phosphorus bombs."[39]

The horror which Conze so vividly described is well documented in Martin Middlebrook's *Battle of Hamburg*,[40] which deals with the devastating British air raid that destroyed the working class areas and civilian population of Hamburg on the night of Saturday, 24 July 1943. Yet it was only with the appearance of Jörg Friedrich's *The Fire*[41] that the full extent of the horror and the deliberate, cold-blooded planning that preceded it became fully public. As Conze pointed out, "The official history of the politics of the Thirties is bathed in moral indignation."[42] Yet the fact that his anti-Nazi comrades in Hamburg were roasted alive seemed to concern no one.

The Allies' callous disregard of the treatment of German civilians, who were automatically identified as "the enemy," troubled Conze deeply. With the exception of the Labour politician Ernest Bevan, the British public, in Conze's view, looked to "the archbishop of Can-

Photo 13.9 After arriving in England, Conze lived in woods like these for almost a year. His wife had converted to Catholicism while he rediscovered Buddhism, which he had encountered as a teenager. After arriving in England he gave up on politics, and literally took to the woods, where he lived in a small shack without any of the amenities of modern life. During this time he engaged in fasting and various ascetic practices of Tantric origins. At the end of this experiment, he emerged a convinced Buddhist, and he devoted the rest of his life to the study of Buddhism.

38. Conze, *Memoirs*, 2.74.

39. Ibid., 1.113.

40. Martin Middlebrook, *The Battle of Hamburg: Allied Bomber Forces against a German City in 1943* (London: A. Lane, 1980).

41. Jörg Friedrich, *The Fire: The Bombing of Germany, 1940–1945*, trans. Allison Brown (New York: Columbia Univ. Press, 2006).

42. Conze, *Memoirs*, 2.13, cf. 61.

terbury," who, "while there is peace he is all for it, but as soon as he sees the chance of a War he is prepared, 'with a heavy heart' to find a godly reason for it."[43] Given this attitude among publically recognized Christian leaders, it did not surprise Conze that Bishop William Temple (1881–1944) became the archbishop of Canterbury in 1942. Temple, despite his extensive writings on ethics and supposed sympathy for ordinary people, fully supported all aspects of the war effort.

On the other hand, Bishop George Bell (1883–1958), who was in line for the archbishopric, was sidelined because he spoke out in protest against the bombing of civilian targets. Thus Bell was relegated to insignificance while Temple was lionized by the British ruling class.

A CONSISTENT PACIFIST

True to his pacifist convictions, Conze later expressed equal contempt for the South Vietnamese Buddhist monks who scattered holy water on American tanks. Buddhists who supported war were just as bad as the German pastors who urged men to die in vain. Even Zen, he argued, had been corrupted by human folly and bloodlust. Modern religion, he believed, had lost its true root in spirituality. After his negative experiences with Christians, Conze never visited a Buddhist land, because he "feared that actual existing Buddhists would probably turn me against Buddhism, just as the actually existing Christians have turned me against Christianity."[44]

In many ways, Conze seems to have regretted his rejection of Christianity and longed to see Christians take up these causes for themselves. Once, when I was his student, he encouraged me to write my PhD thesis on the morality of area bombing and attacks on civilian targets. When I said that I intended to study the origins of the ideology of apartheid, he admitted that this was a good subject. Nevertheless, he protested that if Christians and other spiritual people did

Photo 13.10 Apart from becoming a committed Buddhist and one of the leading Buddhist scholars of his generation, Conze became convinced of the truth of perennial philosophy, the belief that behind all religious traditions is an essential spiritual core. This belief system is associated with what is often called "Traditionalism." His approval of perennial philosophy led him to be fascinated by places like Glastonbury Tor, seen above. The dark, mysterious hill, with its church tower but no church, and with the brooding clouds above, evoked a sense of awe and mystery that Conze saw as moving people indoctrinated with materialism toward the spiritual realm.

43. Ibid., 1.23.
44. Ibid., 1.31.

not take up issues like the morality of war and such things as mass expulsions, rape, and area bombing, they would eventually be discovered by atheists and used to destroy Christianity and all true religion on the basis that religion turns a blind eye to human suffering.

His "prophecy" appears to have come true almost thirty years later when the British philosopher A. C. Grayling, a prominent member of what has been labelled the "new atheism," associated with Richard Dawkins and Christopher Hitchens, published his book, *Among the Dead Cities*.[45] Although Grayling does not make the same link as Conze did to Christian morality, there is no doubt that he has laid the foundation for such an argument. Anyone who doubts this should visit websites like those of the Freedom from Religion Foundation[46] to see how Christianity is being increasingly assailed for its supposed lack of morality and support of war and for the inconsistency of professing Christians.

ENCOUNTERING CONZE

My first encounter with Conze was as a student at the Lancaster University in 1968, when I took his Buddhism course. The first class, which was a small seminar of about ten students, was the most unusual I have ever experienced. Professor Conze came in with a notepad, which he gave the nearest student. He then asked us all to write down our names and dates of birth. Once these were returned to him, he announced that the class was over and that after he had cast all of our horoscopes he would decide whether anyone had to leave the class or not. Then he explained that he never permitted a student whose horoscope conflicted with his to remain in one of his classes.

When we returned for the second class, Conze said he was pleased to announce that we were all acceptable to him and that the course could now proceed. After this he gave his reasons for casting our horoscopes. First, he explained that he had experienced some very uncongenial students in the past and therefore was determined not to attempt to teach someone who did not want to learn or whose horoscope conflicted with his own. Second, he said, we needed to realize that Buddhism was a full-blooded religion in which the supernatural plays a significant role. It was impossible to teach students about Buddhism if they refused to at least recognize that, for a true Buddhist, things like horoscopes and psychic events are a living reality. Finally, he argued, by telling us he planned to cast our horoscopes he would prompt anyone indoctrinated into a rationalistic ideology of science to think he was crazy and leave the class immediately. That was how it should be, he said, because he had no time to argue about the pastime of modern science with people who were closed to spiritual realities.

From then the class progressed remarkably well, even though he often made caustic remarks about contemporary Christianity and churches. Conze did not like established churches and modern Christians, or trendy clergy, whom he thought hypocritical. To him most of the Christianity preached in churches was nonsense, because it stripped the message of Jesus of its supernatural elements. He maintained that by adapting their faith

---

45. A. C. Grayling, *Among the Dead Cities: Was the Allied Bombing of Civilians in WWII a Necessity or a Crime?* (London: Bloomsbury, 2006).

46. This is found online at http://ffrf.org/ (accessed 27 November 2008).

Photo 13.11 Today the ruins of St. Nicholas Church in Hamburg stand as a memorial to the folly and deadly destruction of war. The fire bombing of Hamburg on 24 July 1943 shocked Conze to the core, because the British had not targeted the docks or other military targets, but rather working class neighborhoods which before the war had been centers of staunch opposition to the Nazis. Many of Conze's former colleagues who had fought pitched street battles against the Nazis were killed in this raid, confirming to Conze the totally futility and essential evil of war.

to modern science, most so-called Christians had made themselves people who were not Christians at all but agnostics in disguise. He did not like agnostics, or atheists, because he had noticed "that the German free thinkers" harbored "a most incredible spite of all the things spiritual."[47] In fact, they were not agnostics or atheists at all. They were believers in a new secular religion.

Consequently, while he castigated Christianity, by which he meant the modern expressions of Christianity represented by theologians like Rudolf Bultmann (1884–1976), Paul Tillich (1886–1965), and John Robinson (1919–1983), he respected believing Christians and had a great deal of time for students who belonged to groups like the evangelical InterVarsity Christian Fellowship. But for Christians like Robinson he had nothing but contempt, describing his ideas about the "Death of God" as "so incredibly silly as to be unanswerable."[48]

For him the great men were "first Aristotle, then Marx, and then the Buddha,"[49] closely followed by Jesus and various Christian writers like as Thomas à Kempis,[50] Thomas Aquinas,[51] and Tolstoy, whose *The Gospel in Brief*[52] he loved just as Gandhi had. Most of all, however, he claimed that the Jewish-Christian philosopher Max Scheler (1874–1928) was a man of true genius who deeply influenced his work and from whom all his best thoughts came.[53] Another Christian who strongly influenced him was F. A. Voigt (1892–1957), who worked as a journalist on the *Guardian* newspaper. In his book, *Unto Caesari*, Voigt argued that "Communism and Nazism are secularised religions which try to establish the

47. Conze, *Memoirs*, 2.31.
48. Ibid., 2.67.
49. Ibid., 2.71.
50. Ibid., 2.1.
51. Ibid., 1.50, 145.
52. Ibid., 1.40.
53. Ibid., 1.9.

kingdom of Heaven on Earth."[54] This Conze thought was an insightful and true judgment. Thus, while he saw most mainline churches as empty vessels where faith had been replaced by ill-informed social activism, he respected believing Christians who took their faith seriously.

CONZE'S MORAL CRITICISMS OF WESTERN BUDDHISM

Conze's attack on the churches was surpassed by his virulent attacks on modern Buddhists like the prominent British lawyer Christmas Humphries (1901–1983), who also fully supported the British war effort before serving as a prosecutor at the Japanese War Crimes Tribunal. After his return to Britain, Humphries was appointed a senior crown prosecutor. In 1950 he secured the conviction of Timothy Evans (1924–1950) for the murder of his infant daughter, and Evans was subsequently hanged. Three years later it was discovered that the real murderer was the serial killer John Christie (1898–1953). In 1975 Humphries also passed a suspended sentence on a man convicted of two brutal rapes. Such actions by someone who paraded his Buddhism for all to see angered Conze. Therefore, he was scathing in his criticism of what he saw as Humphries' hypocrisy.

To Conze, men like Humphries were disguised agnostics who misused Buddhism to promote a ritualistic form of agnosticism with all the trappings of religion but none of its content. Similarly, he had no time for scholars who wished to remove magical and other texts from the Buddhist canon. Holding such views, he saw himself as a crusader for true Buddhism unsullied by secularizing modernity. If he were alive today, he would likely be called a "Buddhist fundamentalist."

Many other Western Buddhist leaders were equally problematic to Conze, because he knew many of them had embraced Fascism, or National Socialism, in the 1920s and 1930s. As he once told his class, "When the Americans decided they needed expertise in Asian studies, they hired a large number of European professors. Half of us were ex-Communists, the other half were former Fascists or National Socialists. Yet neither

Photo 13.12 Lancaster University, the site of Britain's first religious studies department, in winter. While he taught there in the late 1960s, Conze and his wife, Muriel, lived in one of the apartments seen on top of the main building. Towards the top left can be seen the round multifaith center, which was one of the first of its kind in England.

54. Ibid., 1.27.

side dare denounce the other for fear of raking up their own pasts. So an armed truce existed between us."

Among the people he particularly disliked because of his political views was Mircea Eliade, of whom he wrote, "Eliade's book on *Shamanism* (1951; 1964 in English) is probably the best we have on the subject. The more one re-reads it, the more unconvincing it becomes ... he spoke on these matters without authority, like the Scribes and Pharisees."[55] Although he never said so publicly, he was convinced that Eliade was a Fascist to the root of his being and that his books on religion were simply a subtle means of promoting Fascist ideas in America. No doubt if Conze had lived long enough, he would have enthusiastically supported Adriana Berger's claim that not only was Eliade a lifelong Fascist,[56] but he worked as a Nazi spy during World War II. These are claims that Conze's friend Ninian Smart (1927–2001) was inclined to accept.

Bryan S. Rennie has persuasively argued that Berger was wrong and implies that she falsified her evidence, because "she has referred to Foreign Offices Files which, although listed in the index, are no longer extant and which cannot provide any real evidence."[57] The fact that these files, which were so important to Berger's argument, have gone missing is very troubling, yet it does not prove that Berger did not read them. Letters from Eliade to the Nazi ideologue and professor of religious studies Jakob Wilhelm Hauer (1881–1962) have also gone missing from the German Federal Archives in Koblenz suggests that someone has gone to a lot of effort to cleanse the record by removing potentially explosive archival material that might implicate Eliade.

Similarly, in his *The Politics of Myth* (1999), Robert Ellwood argues that Eliade was not pro-Nazi because

Photo 13.13 A statue of the Protestant Reformer Martin Luther towers over the ruins of Dresden's once beautiful Church of Mary (Frauenkirche), which was destroyed by the firestorm created by the Allied air raid on 13 February 1943. Conze would have found this picture, taken in 1991, symbolic, because he believed the Reformation had gutted Christianity of its spiritual core. He blamed Luther for the dour pietism of his own family and the "ungodly" mixing of religion and business which made the pursuit of profit the true faith of many modern people despite their privatized Christianity.

---

55. Ibid., 1.60.

56. Adriana Berger, "Mircea Eliade: Romanian Fascism and the History of Religions in the United States," in *Tainted Greatness: Antisemitism and Cultural Heroes,* ed. Nancy A. Harrowitz (Philadelphia: Temple Univ. Press, 1994); "Mircea Eliade's Vision for a New Humanism," *Society* 30, no. 5 (July/August 1993): 84–87; "Fascism and Religion in Romania," *The Annals of Scholarship,* 1989, 6:4:455–465.

57. Bryan S. Rennie, "The Diplomatic Career of Mircea Eliade: A Response to Adriana Berger," *Religion* 22 (1992): 387.

"he prided himself on his friendship with a Jewish novelist ... and relatively moderate stance on 'the Jewish question.'"[58] There are two major flaws in this argument. First, why would anyone "pride himself" on his friendship with a Jew if he was not anti-Semitic? Second, one is not "relatively moderate" on things like "the Jewish question." These are issues that should never be considered in the first place. "Moderate on the Jewish question" is a contradiction in terms, like "opposed to the segregation of blacks." Such language is unacceptable.

Further, to argue that Eliade, Jung, or anyone else "had Jewish friends" or was critical of aspects of Fascism and National Socialism, as Ellwood and other well-meaning writers do, means very little indeed. All it does is show how very little they understand about National Socialism and the extent to which Hollywood images and American propaganda have clouded their vision. Magda Goebbels, the wife of Propaganda Minister Joseph Goebbels, had a Jewish stepfather whom she loved. Goebbels himself, like many National Socialists, had Jewish friends and girlfriends before the Nazis came to power in 1933. What National Socialist ideology condemned was not individual Jews but what they identified as the "spirit of Judaism," which they saw individual Jews furthering whether they liked it or not. Thus the ideology depersonalized Jews to allow Nazis to acknowledge friendships with Jews even as they sent them to concentration camps for what they saw as the greater good.

This Conze recognized all too well, which is why former Nazis who promoted Buddhism angered him. A case in point was his troubled relationship with Herbert V. Guenther (1917–2006), whose writings he dismissed as "turgid ululations."[59] Writing of his encounter with Guenther, Conze described his meetings as "eye opening."[60] Guenther, or Günther, completed his doctorate at the University of Munich in 1939 under the direction of Walter Wüst (1901–1991), who in 1937 became president of the research unit of the German *Forschungsgemeinschaft Deutsches Ahnenerbe*, or SS Ancestral Research Unit, established by Reichsführer-SS Heinrich Himmler (1900–1945). Whether or not Guenther was in the SS is unclear; what is certain, from archival records, is that his studies were at least partially financed by the SS. No wonder Conze did not like him and saw in his work echoes of National Socialist thinking.

Apart from his ideological enemies, Conze despised what he called "sectarian Buddhism," because it attracted "rich women" who accepted the doctrine of reincarnation because it enabled them to claim that in a past life they were an Egyptian princess. Such a misuse of reincarnation, he claimed, was embraced by the rich because it freed them "from any sense of social guilt" by convincing them "that they deserve their money and privileges as a reward for merit gained in the past." These beliefs, he caustically remarked, convince the rich "that their precious selves will not be lost when they die." Yet, as he pointed out in his classic work, *Buddhism: Its Essence and Development*, this notion of self goes against the most basic principles of Buddhism.[61]

58. Robert Ellwood, *The Politics of Myth: A Study of C. G. Jung, Mircea Eliade, and Joseph Campbell* (New York: State University of New York Press, 1999), 84.

59. Conze, *Memoirs*, 2.60.

60. Ibid., 2.120.

61. Edward Conze, *Buddhism: Its Essence and Development*, 18–21.

EDWARD CONZE: CONTINUING QUESTIONS

Despite his outspoken opinions on the supernatural nature of religion, his scholarship was so good by the standards of his age that it was hard to reject his work. Therefore, although he never held a permanent academic position, his work laid the foundation for the development of Buddhist studies in the West. As he said himself, "It was after all Hitler who blew my life off course."[62] There is little doubt that, without Nazism, Conze would have held one of the top chairs in Indology or Buddhist studies in Germany. As it was, he became a vagabond, a wandering scholar, and a thoroughly interesting man.

Finally, toward the end of his *Memoirs*, he describes his profound sense of disappointment with life, saying, "My entire life can now be seen as one long process of disenchantment ... As a boy I looked upon the Kaiser and Hindenburg as knights in shining armour ... For many years I was proud of being a German, but after 1933 I have often been ashamed of Germany, and have played down my own Germanness ... After worshipping the English ruling classes from afar I have now come to look upon them as a bunch of decadent ninnies. Likewise closer acquaintance with Buddhists has not increased my respect for them

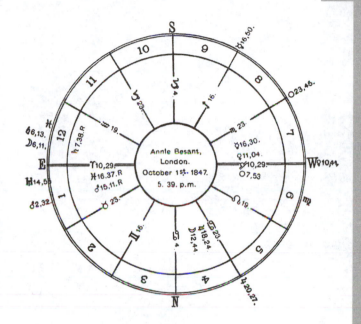

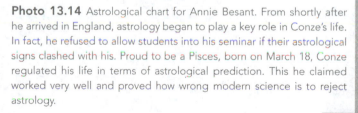

Photo 13.14 Astrological chart for Annie Besant. From shortly after he arrived in England, astrology began to play a key role in Conze's life. In fact, he refused to allow students into his seminar if their astrological signs clashed with his. Proud to be a Pisces, born on March 18, Conze regulated his life in terms of astrological prediction. This he claimed worked very well and proved how wrong modern science is to reject astrology.

... How many of the holy lamas of my expectations have turned out to be gun toting whisky-swilling philanderers!"[63] Reading this movingly honest testimony, one cannot help wondering at the curious remark Conze made at the beginning of his *Memoirs*, describing them as a "kind of end of term report to the Almighty, or an account of this incarnation for Yama, Judge of the Dead."[64]

62. Conze, *Memoirs*, 1.10.
63. Ibid., 1.86.
64. Ibid., 1.iv.

Although it is possible that in saying this he was teasing Christian readers, the remark is typical of his ongoing interaction with Christianity and curious fascination with the Christian faith. Perhaps if he had lived a few more years, or met the right people along his life's path, he might have ended up like Paul Williams, writing an account of his conversion to Christianity.[65] Who knows? All this shows is that human lives are complicated and cannot be separated from the trials and tribulations of the times, while most modern scholarship about religion is intimately tied up with the experiences of the writer.

---

65. Paul Williams, *The Unexpected Way: On Converting from Buddhism to Catholicism* (Edinburgh: T&T Clark, 2002).

CHAPTER 14

OTHER YOGIC-TYPE TRADITIONS

INTRODUCTION

Apart from the major Buddhist and Hindu yogic traditions, a number of other religious traditions fall within the general rubric of yogic religions. Some are extremely small; others, such as the Jains and Parsees, although small, are worthy of mention. The Sikhs are one of the largest small religions originating in the sphere of the yogic tradition. Although they are found worldwide, they do not quite fall into the category of world religion because of the highly exclusive and essentially ethnic nature of the Sikh movement. Finally, there are the once great Confucian and Taoist traditions, which were virtually exterminated during the twentieth century. Although they continue to have an ethical and social influence, they no longer exist as viable religious traditions on a world scale. They are included here because although they are not strictly yogic religions, they traditionally shared many social and other features with the yogic religions and generally fall within the sphere of yogic influence.[1]

Photo 14.1 Tiger Gate in the Jain city of Palitana in the late nineteenth century. Today most courses on Indian religion emphasize the Hindu tradition, treating the Jains almost as a "dead" religion, like those of ancient Egypt. Actually, there are still somewhere between 10 and 12 million Jains in India and many small Jain communities scattered around the world.

1. I am grateful to Dr. Chang-han Kim for reading this section and making suggestions for its improvement. As a Korean brought up in a Confucian society, he appreciated the issues involved from both an academic and a personal perspective.

THE JAINS

Jainism is one of the ancient Indian religions to emerge, centuries after the collapse of the Indus Valley civilization, out of the general social and religious matrix that created the complex Hindu tradition. The traditional founder of the Jain tradition was an Indian sage, Nataputta Vardhamana (599–527 BC), who is known as Mahavira, a title similar to "Christ" in Christianity. The meaning is "great hero." According to tradition, he was born in the Bihar province of India and, like many other great teachers of the yogic tradition, became an ascetic before attaining the equivalent of enlightenment.

The earliest surviving records of his life come from almost a thousand years after his death; therefore it is difficult to obtain reliable information about him. Traditionally he was supposed to be the son of a king who had experienced rebirth several times before his last appearance on earth. It is said that during these existences he was both a king and a priest. Like the Buddha, he became disillusioned with the life of comfort and turned to religion for solace. Then he again became disillusioned with ascetic practices, because he saw them as a sham, preferring more extreme forms of asceticism.

Again like the Buddha, Vardhamana appears to have challenged certain aspects of the caste system and to have proclaimed a faith that was open to all, although in practice it was limited in its appeal because of its rigorous nature. He appears to have taught that there is only matter and spirit, both of which are eternal, and that a creator god does not exist. The exact nature of his teachings is uncertain, however, because the Jain scriptures, known as the *Puvaras*, do not appear for over three hundred years after his death.

Apart from denying the existence of a creator god, Vardhamana taught that formless time continues forever. Within it there are two basic entities: the *jiva*, all conscious mental functions which form the principle of life itself, and *ajiva*, or the lifeless characteristics of matter. Each of these is divided into various subgroups for the type of logical analysis of existence that later became popular within Buddhism. Within this framework karma becomes a glue-like substance that binds consciousness and matter, and both to eternity.

In this rather dismal situation, the only escape is by a liberation from rebirth that comes about as a result of right knowledge and practice in terms of austere asceticism. This releases a few souls from the bonds of rebirth to a realm of bliss that is envisioned at the top of the universe. To attain this, Mahavira followers are required to take five binding vows:

Photo 14.2 This late-nineteenth-century photograph shows the interior of the ancient Jain temple at Mount Abu-Dilwara in India. Note how similar it is to Buddhist temples.

1. To abstain from killing of any kind.
2. To abstain from all desires arising from greed, laughter, fear, or anger and to reject all lies.
3. To not steal or take anything that is not freely given.
4. To renounce all forms of sexual activity and contact with women.
5. To reject and renounce attachment to anything that causes either pleasure or pain and to avoid contact with anyone who displays such attachment.

Taking these vows seriously means the renunciation of family and all social obligations. Ultimately they lead dedicated Jains to the final sacrifice of death through their chosen path of starvation, which in turn is believed to lead to liberation for the true ascetic.

THE PARSEES

Although the Parsees originated in Iran as part of the Zoroastrian tradition, the Parsee community began their migration to India after Muslim invaders destroyed the Sassanid Empire in AD 651. Then, as a result of persecution and Islamization in the ninth century, most other Parsees fled to India. Today they are one of the smallest religious communities worldwide, yet remarkably wealthy.

Photo 14.3 is a modern Jain temple in a midwestern North American city.

The Parsees trace their origins to the prophet Zoroaster, who lived centuries before the Christian era. The dates given for the birth of Zoroaster range from 1500 to 500 BC, which makes it difficult to make reliable statements about him or to know any historical information about his life. There are numerous legends about him: he is said to have been trained as a priest, to have married several times, and to have fathered numerous sons and daughters. Then, like

Photo 14.4 shows the inside of the Jain temple. Note the simplicity of the decoration and compare it to the lavish color and decorations found in the Buddhist or Hindu tradition. In some respects the Jains are the Protestants of India.

many other sages, he left home on a quest for truth, and on his quest he experienced visions and revelations.

According to tradition, Zoroaster's first vision came when he was attending a spring festival. An angel appeared to him and led him into the presence of God, known as Ahura Mazda, the all-knowing one. It was he who gave Zoroaster his mission to proclaim the true religion to the world. Therefore, it is thought, around age thirty he began his life's work. It appears that at first he was seen as a failure, because his preaching brought him into conflict with existing priesthoods, and after ten to fifteen years he had converted only one person, his cousin. Eventually, however, the king and court of a small state in northern Iran were converted, and Zoroastrianism became the state religion for over a thousand years.

Zoroaster's message appears to have been relatively simple. Taking a stand against polytheism and pantheistic forms of religion, he proclaimed one creator God, who was the principle for good in the universe. He preached against sacrifices and existing priesthoods, which he believed led to drunkenness and the use of drugs. For Zoroaster, Ahura Mazda was the source of all life, the beginning and the end, and the master of mankind.

Zoroaster's teachings seem to have divided humanity into two camps. On the one hand there were the enlightened followers of truth, who seek justice. These people desire to serve God. On the other hand there are many people who choose evil and destroy peace on earth. This view is a highly dualistic one. There is some argument among scholars as to whether Zoroaster's dualism extended throughout the whole of creation or applied only to life on Earth.

Photo 14.5 The Zoroastrians and Parsees of India were forbidden to either bury or cremate their dead. Therefore, they exposed them to the elements to allow birds and other predators to devour them. The above photograph is of an ancient "Tower of Silence," where the dead were laid to rest.

Unfortunately, our knowledge of the history of Zoroastrianism is limited by the fact that when Alexander the Great (356–323 BC) conquered Persia, he sacked the capital of the Persian empire, destroying the royal archives and the authoritative copies of the Zoroastrian scriptures. As a result, only incomplete copies of these texts survived. Later, after the Islamic conquests of Iran, many remaining fragmentary copies of these scriptures were destroyed. Today four groups of writings, known as the *Avesta*, are all that remain of the once extensive scriptures of Zoroastrianism.

For Parsees, modern Zoroastrians, the central symbol and practice of their religion is the fire ceremony. In both their homes and their temples, sacred fire is kept perpetually burning, and believers must visit the temple to participate in a ceremony at least once every four months. During these ceremonies, prayers are said while worshipers go to great lengths to preserve the ritual purity of the fire, even wearing facemasks to prevent any saliva from accidentally entering the flames.

Today, there are perhaps 100,000 Parsees in the world. Their members do not seek to make converts to a large extent. Marriage is supposed to take place within the community, limiting both its growth and its vitality. Like many religious traditions of the past, the Parsee religion appears to be a dying tradition overwhelmed by history.

CONFUCIAN AND TAOIST TRADITIONS

It seems almost perverse to treat the once great Confucian and Taoist traditions as relatively minor. Yet the truth of the matter is, as a result of the great upheavals of the twentieth century, they have been reduced to a remnant. Although Confucian and Taoist ideas clearly influenced Chinese social life and culture in the past, today they appear to have lost most of their historic power as functioning religions, because they were both linked to a specific form of society that no longer exists.

China's long history begins around 3000 BC; the first archaeological evidence of a distinctly Chinese culture appears around 1500 BC. Although tradition talks about an early Chinese kingdom that belonged to the Hsia dynasty, no solid archaeological evidence informs us about its nature or even its existence. This was followed by the Sang dynasty, which lasted from around 1500 to 1125 BC, and it is with the end of this dynasty that the historical record begins.

The first great Chinese dynasty, however, was the Chou dynasty, which lasted from 1125 to 225/21 BC. The rulers of this dynasty developed ideas about virtuous ruling and the state as guardian of the people. Early in this dynsasty, written records appear. The dynasty appears to have gone into gradual decline from the middle of the eighth century BC, when local warlords arose to protect China from Asian invasions. As a result, a series of civil wars led to the breakup of the state between 481 and 21 BC. After that, China was once more unified and had a strong emperor. Out of this period of political confusion, the Chinese sought to discover a basis for social stability. Among the possible alternatives was the adoption of either a Confucian or a Taoist system.

Throughout this time, and indeed down to the present, various forms of Chinese folk religion flourished. Traditionally there appears to have been belief in a high God who was the supreme ruler of the universe. The messengers of this God were minor deities identified with the wind, clouds, the sun and moon, and the four points of the compass. There were also local deities associated with mountains and rivers. Most important of all, however, was the veneration, or perhaps worship, of the ancestors.

Sometime around 1000 BC the Chinese developed ideas about what they call Yin and Yang, which were seen as two fundamental forces lying behind everything in the universe. On the one hand, Yang was seen as the masculine, active and good force; on the other hand, Yin was seen as a feminine and passive force with the potential for evil. Both forces were believed to indwell everyone and everything. Therefore it was important to take active steps to establish harmony between them.

Another characteristic of Chinese folk religions is the use of divination. In these religions, as in other primal religious traditions, understanding coded messages on the basis of

Photo 14.6 The holy mountain of Tai Shan, one of the five holy mountains of Taoism in China. The stairway leads to the Taoist temple at the summit. According to tradition, anyone who climbs these stairs will live to be one hundred years old.

the examination of entrails, bones, throwing of a die, or interpretation of dreams became important. Where the Chinese tradition differed from most others of this sort was the codification of divination in what became a classic Chinese text, the *I-Ching*.

Because the welfare of the people was seen as both the duty of the ruler and the expectation of his subjects, a series of emperor rites developed that saw the emperor as a mediator between ordinary humans in the spiritual world. But in this system, due reverence for the imperial ancestors became very important.

Over time Chinese literature produced five classical works that governed the religious and social order. The original texts were destroyed during the civil unrest that ended the Chou dynasty. Later, during the early Han dynasty, sometime after AD 206, the texts were said to have been rediscovered, although there is some dispute concerning to what extent the later texts were faithful to the earlier ones. The five classical scriptural texts that emerged were as follows:

1. The *Shu Ching*, the *Book of History*.
2. The *Shih Ching*, the *Book of Poetry*.
3. The *I-Ching*, the *Book of Changes*, which guided divination.
4. The *Chun Chiu*, or *Annals of the Seasons*.
5. The *Li Chi*, or the *Record of Rites, Rituals and Ceremonies*.

In addition to these, four other key texts, explaining the system, came into general use. These were as follows:

1. The *Analects of Confucius*.
2. The *Analects of Mencius*.
3. The *Book of Higher Education*.
4. The *Doctrine of the Mean*.

CONFUCIUS

Sometime during the Chou dynasty, a philosophical teacher whose work had religious overtones began to articulate what became known as Confucianism. According to traditional accounts, Confucius was born around 550 BC in the state of Lu, which today would be in the northern province of Shantung. His father was a valiant soldier; his mother came from a distinguished family. Both parents, however, died when Confucius was young. It is said that later he went into service with the local ruler, where he was given the task of organizing various rituals. As a result, he began the serious study of traditional worship and gained a reputation for his knowledge of the history of Chinese sacraments. He is said to have married, had children, and failed in his attempt to pass the examinations that would have allowed him to become a civil servant of the central government. Consequently, he gave up thoughts of a government career and became a teacher. Late in his life he was able to pass the exams and become a government magistrate, before rising rapidly in the service of the state.

In later life, it is said, Confucius gathered around him a group of disciples and spent at least ten years traveling around China, spreading wisdom and teaching about the correct mode of government. According to tradition, local rulers recognized wisdom and welcomed him wherever he went. Later still, he devoted himself to the study of the five classical scriptures, while his disciples were appointed to important offices in the state. He is said to have died at the age of seventy-two, after effectively reforming the Chinese system of government and establishing schools that would guarantee the continuation of his ideas.

Although we have little reliable information about Confucius, we are on better ground when we come to his great disciple, Meng Tzu, or Mencius (*ca.* 371–*ca.* 289 BC), who wrote a classic text outlining the Confucian system. In this work he sought to provide stable government to China by teaching the importance of government by a form of consent, based upon the virtue of the ruler. He argued that sincerity and righteousness, rather than brute force, are the marks of good government. Like the French philosopher Jean-Jacques Rousseau (1712–1778), Meng Tzu based his system on his belief in the innate goodness of mankind. Therefore, in his view, the task of government was really to allow humans to become what in the depths of their being they really were before they were corrupted by society.

Photo 14.7 The tomb of Confucius as it was in the late nineteenth century. Whether or not Confucius initiated a new religion or simply offered a philosophy of life and means for ordering society is a matter of intense debate among scholars and has profound implications for how one views Chinese ancestor rites. Are such rites simply an expression of social solidarity or an act of religious worship?

Opposed to this view was the work of another group of Confucian scholars associated with Hsun Tzu, who rejected the idea of the innate goodness of humans. They argued instead that conflicts arise out of human desires common to all people, desires similar in many ways to the effects of what Christians call original sin.

Nevertheless, all Confucian writers, regardless of their view of human nature, recognized the potential for social chaos and destruction, which they believed could be averted by teaching the correct modes of conduct. Good conduct, they argued, was based upon a series of relationships rooted in the family, especially the relationship between father and son. This system is sometimes known as filial piety and includes within it respect for age and veneration of one's ancestors.

TAOISM

Sometime during the sixth century BC, a new religious or philosophical system with both popular and elite mystical elements emerged to challenge Confucian ideas. This became known as Taoism. Its traditional founder was Lao Tzu, about whom little is known. In fact, his name simply means "the Old Master." The name first appears in the *Chuang Tzu*, which seems to have been written in the third or fourth century BC. In this work Lao Tzu is described as a wise government official who opposed the Confucian system.

By the second century BC, various other works belonging to this tradition had emerged. In one early source it is claimed that Lao Tzu was actually one of the teachers of Confucius. Although most of these works are clearly legendary and intended as polemics against Confucianism, they seem to have some sort of historical context in an era that saw the growth of local warlords and great families of landowners. Eventually, however, Confucianism gradually triumphed by offering practical solutions to the confusion of the times and the need for stable government.

During the Chin dynasty (221-206 BC), from which China gets its name, the Great Wall of China was started and the Chinese system of writing standardized. At this time the ideas of a group of teachers known as Legalists, who sought to impose a totalitarian form of government, came to the fore. This led to conflict with Confucian officials and teachers, resulting in what became the great persecution of 213 BC, during which a concerted attempt was made to exterminate Confucianism by burning books and executing the Confucian teachers.

After the collapse of the short-lived Chin dynasty in 206 BC, the Han dynasty (206 BC−AD 220) seized power, leading to a revival of Confucianism, which at this time came into conflict with Taoism. As the Han dynasty itself disintegrated with the growth of local warlords, the Confucian system was increasingly ignored. The Sui dynasty, from AD 589 to 618, and the Tang dynasty, from AD 618 to 907, saw the ebb and flow of Confucian fortunes and the spread of Buddhism throughout China, which put the Confucian tradition on the defensive.

Photo 14.8 A traditional ancestral shrine in a Chinese temple. Ancestors are venerated in Taoism and all other major Chinese religious and philosophical traditions.

Things changed dramatically with the establishment of the Sung dynasty in 960, when the Confucian system, or what scholars more accurately call neo-Confucianism, emerged to become the dominant force in Chinese intellectual history. This new form of Confucianism incorporated elements from both the Buddhist and the Taoist traditions and provided the basis for the Chinese administrative system until the Communist Revolution in the 1940s, despite major changes early in the twentieth century. During this time neo-Confucianism spread to Korea and Japan.

The Confucian era, during which Confucian teachings played an officially recognized social and religious role in society, came to an end with the revolution in government that occurred in 1905. This revolution abolished the traditional state exams for entry into the civil service, which were based on the study of Confucian classics. A few years later, with the revolution of 1911, led by Sun Yat-sen (1866–1925), who is known as "the father of modern China," the anti-Confucian revolution in government was completed. After that, the new Republic of China, established in 1912, sought to create a modern state, following Western principles of government.

The final death knell of both the Confucian and Taoist traditions came with victory of Chinese Communism and Mao Tse-tung in 1949. As well, the final remnants of the Confucian system and Taoist practices were brutally suppressed and removed from social life in mainline China. At the same time, the flight of anti-Communist refugees to Taiwan, who created a new modern Chinese society, had equally disastrous results for the traditional religious and social systems associated with Confucianism and Taoism. The upheavals created by the Communist victory on the Chinese mainland totally disrupted traditional practices and local customs, to the extent that, while the refugees in Taiwan brought with them Confucian and Taoist customs, they were too fragmented to continue as a coherent religious tradition. Hence neither survives as an intact tradition today.

The influence of both of these traditions can still be seen in fragmentary forms in contemporary Chinese social and religious practices. The veneration of ancestors remains an important aspect of Chinese thought and practice. Filial piety lingers on as a basis for Chinese social thinking, although increasingly eroded by modern views of the family. Perhaps most important of all, various folk practices associated with healing, divination, and healthy exercises, connected with martial arts and forms of meditation, flourish at the popular level. Yet all of these are fragmentary, lacking the coherence of the traditional religious, philosophical, and social systems associated with the long history of China.

Today there is a large Confucian university in Korea, but it is now a secularized institution that has lost most of its religious roots. In this it is similar to universities like Harvard, Princeton, and Yale in the United States, and McMaster in Canada, which were originally founded as Christian institutions but long ago lost all real connection with Christianity as a basis for their teaching and research.

In Japan, similarly, although Confucian ideas and practices still provide the bedrock for many social and religious customs, a great synthesis is taking place, and in the rest of Asia as well. Many ideas, often of Christian origin, are fundamentally changing these societies. The Confucian ethic has merged well with the reforms introduced into Japan and other areas by

Photo 14.9 Confucian temple in China.

General MacArthur after the end of World War II to produce new industrial societies. Where this will lead in the future is anyone's guess. Arguably there could be a revival of a new form of the Confucian tradition, but at this stage it looks unlikely, if for no other reason than the relatively low status of women in Confucian society. Aspects of this tradition, such as respect for the government, filial piety, and the belief in the welfare of the citizen as a duty of rulers, will no doubt continue as the broad basis of Asian societies.

THE SIKH TRADITION

Shortly after 9/11, several men wearing turbans were beaten up or refused entry to airplanes by people who thought they were Muslims. The irony of the situation is that they were Sikhs, members of an Indian religious community that has fought for its independence from Muslim rule for over four hundred years. The Sikhs are an Indian-based ethnic religious community with a rich tradition that is essentially uninterested in making converts. During the past half century, an increasing number of Sikhs migrated to Europe and North America. Therefore, it is important to know something about this community.

SIKH HISTORY

Sikhism originated in the late fifteenth century in what is today the Indian state of Punjab, a traditional Hindu area that at that time was under threat of Muslim conquest. Arab armies entered India early in the eighth century and in 712 conquered the area known as Sind. Although initially the conquerors repressed the conquered and destroyed both Buddhist and Hindu temples, the sheer number of non-Muslims enabled local peoples to follow their own Hindu traditions and in some cases flourish for several hundred years. Then in 1022 Turkish Muslims gained control of Punjab, founding a major Muslim empire based upon the city of Lahore. Eventually, as the empire spread to other parts of India, its capital was moved to Delhi.

During this time many Hindu temples were completely destroyed, and mosques were usually erected on the site where a temple had once stood. Thus the seeds were sown for present-day conflicts between Hindus and Muslims in areas of India where Hindus want to destroy mosques to rebuild temples on what were traditionally important Hindu holy sites. At the same time many lower-class Hindus converted to Islam, thus freeing themselves from the constraints of the caste system.

By the thirteenth century most of northern India was under Muslim control. At this time parts of the Muslim heartland, including the sultanate of Baghdad, were conquered

by Mongols, who promptly converted to Islam. In the early fourteenth century, the Mongol ruler
Tamerlane, or Timur the Lame,
invaded India and overthrew the
sultanate in Delhi without establishing a new empire of his own,
plunging the area into chaos which
lasted until the invasion of the
Muslim ruler Babar in the early
fifteenth century. A devout Muslim, Babar attempted to Islamize
northern India by removing the
traditional rights of non-Muslims
and attempting forced conversions.

It was at this time that a young
Indian named Kabir (1438–1518),
whose mother, a Hindu widow,
gave him up for adoption by a
Muslim family, joined a Hindu

Photo 14.10 The Golden Temple of the Sikhs in Amritsar, the Sikhs' most important shrine.

religious order in the tradition of the great Hindu teacher Ramanuja (1017–1137). Kabir began preaching throughout India. His message was one of the need for devotion and for the reconciliation of Muslims and Hindus. He wrote hundreds of hymns, three hundred of which were later accepted by the Sikhs as sacred texts.

Guru Nanak (1469–1539), the founder of what became Sikhism, was a much younger contemporary of Kabir. He was born to Hindu parents in the Punjab village of Talwandui, around forty miles, or a good day's walk, from Lahore. According to tradition, Nanak's father was an educated man who served as a village administrator in what today we would call the local civil service. His mother is described as an exceptionally pious woman who devoted herself to her children. As a young man, Nanak studied the Hindu scriptures and, under the influence of Kabir, read the Qur'an.

Traditional sources, the earliest of which were written around seventy years after Nanak's death, claim that, in accordance with Hindu custom, it was arranged that he be married as a teenager, but the marriage, though it produced at least two sons, was deeply unhappy. At some point, possibly in his midthirties, when his family would be regarded as fully grown, Nanak left his home to become a wandering mendicant. He is said to have wandered through India in the company of a friend who was a gifted musician. He is said to have visited many holy places and conversed with the disciples of various gurus and religious leaders. He may even have made a pilgrimage with his friend to Mecca.

Tradition says that one day, while meditating in the tradition of the Upanishads in a forest setting near Sultanpur, in what is today the eastern part of the Uttar Pradesh state of India, he received a revelation from God which instructed him to proclaim the oneness of God, who was to be praised. After this he began preaching that there is neither Hindu nor Muslim in the sight of God, only true worshipers. He appears to have spent several decades traveling in India and preaching his message, which took hold on Hindu groups in his native Punjab. To emphasize the reconciliation of the Hindu tradition and Islam, he developed a new form of dress for himself and his followers, consisting of traditional Hindu clothing on the lower part of his body but identifiable Muslim clothing on the top.

Photo 14.11 A modern Sikh temple in western North America.

The hymns Nanak composed during this time, along with around three hundred hymns composed by Kabir, were to become the basis of secret scriptures known as the Adi Granth. Eventually Nanak returned to Punjab, where he spent his last years instructing what was to become the Sikh community. Setting itself apart from Hindu and Muslim traditions, the Sikh community met regularly to eat a common meal centered on a communal kitchen where all caste distinctions were obliterated. This meal continues to remain the central communal rite of Sikhism. At the same time Nanak's followers retained various Hindu beliefs, such as that in the wheel of existence, or samsara; karma; and transmigration.

Following Nanak's death, his disciple Agnad, whom he had designated his successor, assumed the leadership of the Sikh community. Agnad is mainly remembered for developing the distinctive Punjabi script and beginning the compilation of Sikh scriptures. A succession of nonhereditary "gurus," as Sikh leaders are called, followed, along with a time of relative peace and prosperity. The fourth guru, Ram Das Sodhi (1534–1581), is remembered for beginning work on the great Sikh temple in Amritsar. This was completed under the leadership of his son, the fifth guru, Arjun Das (1563–1606), who also oversaw the final rendition of the Sikh holy book, the *Granth Sahib*.

During Nanak's time as guru, things went relatively well until the Sikhs were drawn into revolt against the Muslim emperor Jahangir (1569–1627) by Nanak's own son. The revolt was unsuccessful, and the fifth Sikh leader, Guru Arjun Das, was executed. The situation became worse after Jahangir's death, when a new emperor, Shah Jahan (1618–1707), best known for building the Taj Mahal, embarked upon a new campaign of Islamization. Shah Jahan not only attacked and destroyed Hindu temples; he also turned on the Sikhs, who at that time were led by Arjun's able son Har Gobind (1595–1645). Har Gobind began to organize resistance against the Muslims by retreating from the plains of Punjab into the more easily defensible mountainous regions of the Himalayas. He and his followers also fortified the town of Amritsar, where the main Sikh temple was located. It was at this time that the Sikhs emerged as a formidable military force.

Things became critical during the reign of the Mughal emperor Aurangzeb (1618–1707), who ruled northern India for forty-nine years, from 1658 until his death. Determined to complete the Islamization of his realm, Aurangzeb launched furious attacks upon the Sikhs, who resisted with great bravery. By this time the leadership devolved to the last of the Sikh gurus, Gobind Singh (1666–1708), who yet again transformed the Sikh community by strengthening its social and political structures. Now both men and women were given military training, and a highly committed military elite, the *Khalsa*, or brotherhood, was formed. Most importantly, Gobind Singh revealed that the succession of Sikh gurus was to end. Instead Sikhs were to be ruled by their holy book.

Although the succession of religious leadership came to an end, a series of gifted military leaders virtually assumed control of the Sikh community. The first of these was Banda Singh (1670–1716), who led the Sikhs in a series of brilliant military campaigns before eventually being defeated, captured, and executed in Delhi. The next significant military leader, Ranjit Singh (1780–1839), gained control of a large area of the Punjab, establishing a secure Sikh rule. The Sikh kingdom was racked by unrest and civil war following his death, by which time the British had become a major force in India. Between 1845 and 1849 the British waged a successful war of conquest against the Sikhs, for whom they devel-

Photo 14.12 Under the richly embroidered covering is a copy of the Sikh scriptures, the Adi Granth. Note the ceremonial shields and sword in front of the altar. These symbolize the Sikh struggle for survival against overwhelming odds brought against them by the Muslim rulers of India.

oped great respect. After their defeat as an independent kingdom, the Sikhs were quickly incorporated into the British Raj (as Britain's Indian Empire was known),[2] where many would have important administrative positions and play leading roles in the Indian army.

In the 1920s and 1930s, Sikhs played a leading role in the movement for Indian independence, which came to fruition in 1948. At that time the Sikhs felt deeply betrayed, because, exhausted and on the verge of bankruptcy as a result of World War II, the British hurriedly left India without providing the Sikhs with their own independent homeland. The results were tragic. Because of the violence that led to the partition of India between

---

2. It is important to realize that the Indian Empire was always distinct from the British Empire, even though the term British Empire included India. After the British government took over the empire created by the British East India Company in 1858, India was the responsibility of the India Office in London. Other British possessions and colonies, like Canada and South Africa, were the responsibility of the Colonial Office, also in London.

the secular state of India and the Muslim state of Pakistan, traditional Sikh lands were divided between the two warring parties. Most areas of the Punjab went to India, although a smaller territory, which included a number of sacred Sikh sites, was included in Pakistan. The partition of the Indian subcontinent and what Sikhs see as the unjust division of the Punjab have been a continual thorn in the flesh of the Indian body politic and Sikh society ever since.

SIKH BELIEFS

As indicated, the Sikh religion is based upon both the tradition of the gurus and, more importantly, the interpretation of the Sikh holy book, *Granth Sahib,* a highly devotional text consisting mainly of hymns. It is divided into three main sections: the Japji, which embodies the teachings of Guru Nanak; the Ragas, or joyful music, which is divided into four major sections; and twenty-six books interpreting and elaborating upon these hymns. This sacred book is a focal point of each Sikh temple, and all true Sikhs are expected to set a room aside in their homes to house a copy of the *Granth Sahib*, allowing them to perform daily readings and rituals.

Sikhs believe that there is only one God, Sat Nam, the Truthful Name, who, as the uncreated, immortal creator of the universe, takes a personal interest in his people. Although in practice Sikhism is essentially an ethnic religion followed by people from the Punjab, Sikh teachers insist that they are not a special chosen people. They insist that, although the Sikhs have a special role to play in God's plan for salvation, God has chosen all mankind to serve him.

The idea of transmigration, that is, of the soul moving from one body to the next after death, is an essential Sikh belief. Humans are locked into the wheel of samsara until their souls obtain release to union with God.

Photo 14.13 Friends greet the bride and groom at the end of the formal ceremonies of a Sikh wedding. As with most religious traditions, the Sikhs place great value on the integrity of the family.

SIKH SECTS

Although the Sikh community is relatively homogeneous, several sectarian groups exist among them. The most important of these are traditionalist groups that seek to restore the full independence of the Punjab as a Sikh state. There are also smaller groups, like 3HO, or the happy, healthy, holy organization, which seeks to spread the Sikh message to the rest of the world and make converts among other ethnic groups. They are generally regarded as something of a cult by mainline Sikhs and members of the societies where they seek to make converts.

THE SIKH CALENDAR

Generally, Sikhs follow a Hindu lunar calendar, marked by various festivals. The most important of these festivals is Vaisakhi, a three-day celebration that commemorates the formation of the Khalsa, which created a military and religious elite. During the festival, new members of the Khalsa and the initiated in the community join together in parades and feasting.

Like Hindus, Sikhs celebrate Diwali, or the Festival of Lights, which takes place at different times during the fall according to the lunar calendar. Sikhs also use the occasion to remember the sixth guru's release from captivity when, according to tradition, he was pardoned by the emperor but refused to leave prison until fifty-two Hindus who were imprisoned with him were also released. Reluctant to allow this, the emperor compromised by saying that the guru could take as many Hindus with him as could hold a part of his cloak. By a miracle the cloak had fifty-two tassels. Thus everyone could take hold of a tassel and leave the prison.

SIKH CEREMONIES AND PIETY

Sikhs meet together weekly in a center known as a *gurdwara*, or the gate to the guru. There they worship God by reading scripture, hearing sermons, and singing hymns. Before entering, Sikhs must remove their shoes and cover their heads. Inside, men and women sit in separate areas. At the end of the service, the Sikh community meets together for a communal meal.

All Sikhs celebrate these ceremonies, but there is also within the Sikhs an order called the Khalsa, or "brotherhood," which includes both men and women who are obliged to bear five signs: (1) Never cutting their hair. This is the sign of faith. (2) A comb that holds together the top knot of their hair and is used to comb the hair at least twice a day. This symbolizes order within the community. (3) A steel wristband, known as the *kara*. This symbolizes the unity of the Sikh community. (4) A sword, which today is represented by a symbolic dagger. (5) An undergarment known as a *kaccha*, to facilitate rapid and unhindered movement in time of danger.

DIETARY LAWS AND OTHER RELIGIOUS OBSERVANCE

Sikhs are expected to eat a healthy, moderate diet, fast regularly, and generally abstain from alchohol, and they are forbidden from eating food prepared according to either Jewish or Muslim religious law. Otherwise they are free from dietary constraints.

Within Sikh communities women play an important role, although traditionally their chief task was the raising of children. Unlike in Islam, or certain branches of the Hindu tradition, women are at no point considered unclean, either during their menstrual cycle or after childbirth.

As with all religious traditions, the birth of a child is an important event, and babies are taken to the gurdwara to be dedicated in a ceremony of prayer and thanksgiving. Today

Photo 14.14 As with most weddings, a celebratory meal follows the formal ceremonies. Here a vegetarian feast is served to the guests.

all Sikh males are given the surname Singh, which means lion. This name reflects the military origins of the Sikh community. Girls, on the other hand, take the surname Kaur, which means something like little princess. At the end of the ceremonies the babies are given sweetened water to drink.

Marriage is also an important festivity and rite of passage within the Sikh community. Even today many Sikh marriages are arranged, because Sikh women are expected to marry Sikh men. The wedding ceremony is relatively simple, and marriages are fairly egalitarian.

At the time of death, the family is supposed to gather around the dying person to chant prayers and recite scripture. If a dying person is a member of the Khalsa, they are buried with the five symbols of membership. Because death is seen as the gateway to a new and better life, grief is muted. Since Guru Nanak was unconcerned about what happened to his body after death, Sikhs may be buried or cremated without causing any religious problems.

PART 4
THE ABRAMIC TRADITION

CHAPTER 15

EARLY JUDAISM

INTRODUCTION

Probably the best introduction to Judaism for Christians would be an adaptation of a sentence from Walter Martin's *The Kingdom of the Cults*: "On encountering a cultist then, always remember that you are dealing with a person who is familiar with Christian terminology, and who has carefully redefined it to fit the system of thought he or she now embraces."[1] Replace the word "cultist" with "Christian" and "Christian" with "Jew," and you will begin to understand how most Jewish people view Christians and Christianity.

For Christians, Christianity is the fulfilment of the teachings of the Hebrew Bible and the natural completion of Judaism. For Jews, Christianity is a systematic distortion of Jewsih religion that creates something almost totally unrecognizable. For this reason many Jews are genuinely offended when Christian churches organize what they call a "Seder meal" as part of their Easter celebrations. To Jews the Christian appropriation of the Seder is an affront that strikes at the root of their being, even though many recognize that Christians who do such things do them with the best intentions, that is, to recognize the importance of the Hebrew heritage to Christianity.

As Professor Eliezer Segal puts it, "Ask a Christian how important Judaism is to their faith and they have to admit that their religion depends on Jewish texts and interpretations for its ultimate meaning. Ask a Jew how important Christianity is to them and their religion and they will tell you that it is not important at all. Judaism can exist without Christianity but Christianity is totally dependent on Judaism for its basic frame of reference." Therefore, when attempting to explain Judaism to a Christian, or someone from an essentially Christian background, it is particularly important to carefully distinguish Christian interpretations of Judaism and the religion of Israel from the way Jews themselves see these things.[2]

To make this distinction, we must attempt to see Judaism as a religion in its own right. We need to see it as totally separate from the Christian tradition, and not interpret

---

1. Walter Martin, *The Kingdom of the Cults* (Minneapolis: Bethany Fellowship, 1976), 20.
2. A good overview of the Jewish perspective on Jewish beliefs and history is provided in Michael Fishbane, *Judaism* (San Francisco: Harper, 1987). For a more complex account see Dan Cohn-Sherbok, *Judaism: History, Belief and Practice* (London: Routledge, 2003).

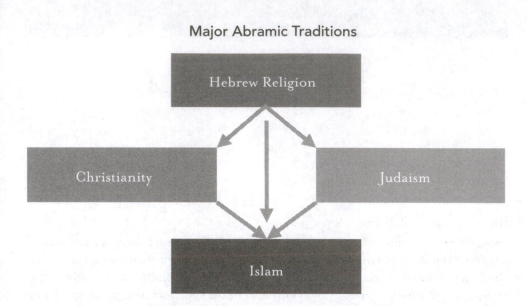

Major Abramic Traditions

Figure 15.1

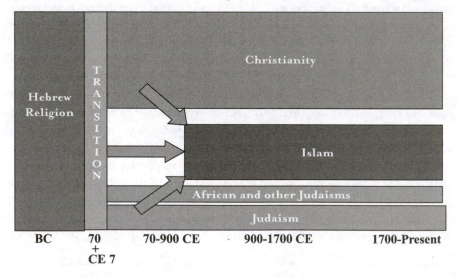

Abramic Religious Tradition

Figure 15.2 Timeline of the Abramic traditions. Note how the ancient religion of Israel is not the same as Judaism, which developed after the destruction of the Jerusalem temple in AD 70.

it through a Christian lens. Only then can we begin to understand the appeal of Judaism to Jewish people.

Finally, it needs be noted that talking about Judaism is problematic, because many Jews dispute the term almost as much as they dispute what it means to be Jewish. The problem here is that Jews belong to an identifiable ethnic group which is neither a religion nor a race. Hence, it is possible to have nonreligious Jews who practice Jewish rituals as a means of affirming their identity. Historically Jews originated with the family of Abraham, but over time they incorporated people from many different families—what we now call nations and races—making any definition of Jewishness exceptionally difficult. Nevertheless, most Jews are proud to be Jewish, and most other people accept their self-identification. According to Michael Fishbane, "Judaism is thus the religious expression of the Jewish people from antiquity to the present day as it has tried to form and live a life of holiness before God."[3] With this definition in mind, we will attempt to explore the rich world of the Jewish religion.

THE JEWISH STORY

Like all religious traditions, Judaism depends upon a rich body of narrative in both written and oral forms as the basis of its beliefs and practices. What makes Judaism different from other ancient religions is that its narratives are firmly rooted in the claim to historicity. That is, Jewish holy books and scholars claim that at their core the stories about their origins are based upon historical events, not fictitious legends or sagas. It is these events that give Jewish narratives a dynamic structure which over the centuries and millennia shaped the life and thought of individuals and an entire people.

When Christians approach Judaism, they tend to think about it in Christian terms. Therefore, they begin at the beginning of the Bible with the story of the creation, Adam and Eve, and the garden of Eden. Then they assume that Jews read these stories in the same way they do. This approach leads to many misunderstandings. To understand how Jews view creation, one must look not to the Bible alone but to that vast collection of interpretation known as the Talmud, where the creation is described in the following way:

> In the beginning, two thousand years before the heaven and the earth, seven things were

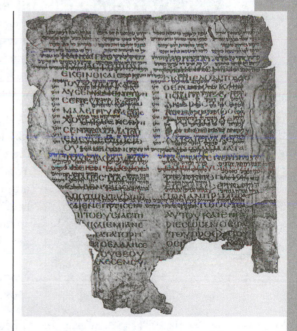

Photo 15.1 One of the earliest surviving manuscripts of the Jewish scriptures. This is a fragment from the book of Kings from the fifth or sixth century AD.

---

3. Fishbane, *Judaism*, 12.

created: the Torah written with black fire on white fire, and lying in the lap of God; the Divine Throne, erected in the heaven which later was over the heads of the Hayyot; Paradise on the right side of God, Hell on the left side; the Celestial Sanctuary directly in front of God, having a jewel on its altar graven with the Name of the Messiah, and a Voice that cries aloud, "Return, ye children of men."

When God resolved upon the creation of the world, He took counsel with the Torah. Her advice was this: "O Lord, a king without an army and without courtiers and attendants hardly deserves the name of king, for none is nigh to express the homage due to him." The answer pleased God exceedingly. Thus did He teach all earthly kings, by His Divine example, to undertake naught without first consulting advisers.

The advice of the Torah was given with some reservations. She was skeptical about the value of an earthly world, on account of the sinfulness of men, who would be sure to disregard her precepts. But God dispelled her doubts. He told her, that repentance had been created long before, and sinners would have the opportunity of mending their ways. Besides, the Temple service would be invested with atoning power, and Paradise and hell were intended to do duty as reward and punishment. Finally, the Messiah was appointed to bring salvation, which would put an end to all sinfulness.[4]

From this long passage it can be seen that the Jewish view of creation places the original act long before the story found in the book of Genesis, and that the Torah is personified as a female figure who in communication with God planned everything from the beginning. This emphasis upon the Torah is central to an understanding of Judaism and is a source of misunderstanding for Christians who see things differently.

Christians usually see the story of Abraham as the central narrative in Jewish history, with stories about Moses and other biblical figures following naturally from it. Jews read the biblical narratives somewhat differently than Christians. Although the story of Abraham is very important and can be described as

Photo 15.2 In a very real sense, Judaism begins with the story of God's call to Abram. This African tapestry depicts the key story of Abraham's sacrifice of his son and God's intervention at the last moment to save Isaac by substituting a ram caught in a thicket.

---

4.   www.sacred-texts.com\jud\loj\loj103.htm; from Louis Ginzberg, *The Legends of the Jews* (Philadelphia: Jewish Publication Society, 1909), 1:3.

the founding story of Jewish origins, it is not the centrally important founding story that defines Judaism. Nor is the story of the exodus, which many Christians take to be the central narrative of Jewish life. What is important for Jews and Judaism is the revelation of the Torah (which according to Jewish tradition began with the giving of the Law) to Moses described in Exodus 19. The divine revelation which took place at Sinai plays a role in Judaism similar to the role of the crucifixion in Christianity.

According to Jewish tradition, God revealed the Torah to Moses, and through him to the Jewish people. With this partly written and partly oral revelation—the oral part being preserved in traditions of the Jews—went the obligation to enter into what is known as the covenant. The idea of a covenant is first mentioned in the story of Noah in Genesis 9:8–17. Later it is developed in the story of Abraham found in Genesis 12–25.[5]

The idea of covenant is based upon the ancient Near Eastern practice of conquerors and kings, who entered into binding relationships, or covenants, with subject peoples. Enacting a covenant meant that the king, or conqueror, gave the conquered a choice of entering into a relationship which was quite unlike a modern contract. It was not something that could be negotiated. Rather, it was imposed by the more powerful party upon the weaker party. This implied that the conquered accepted certain obligations and responsibilities in return for the protection of the conqueror. At the core of a covenant was the idea of obedience. In return for obedience the conquered entered into a protected relationship which brought with it peace and other blessings.[6]

Thus, in creating a covenant between himself and his people, God makes his demand that his people fulfill their obligations to him in return for his blessings. With the covenant goes a series of blessings and curses such as those found in Deuteronomy 27–28. The covenant calls upon the Jewish people to respond to God in terms of their duty to him and binds them together as brothers and sisters.

In this scheme of things, the Torah is God's instrument for the creation of a covenantal people and is the true heritage of his people (Deuteronomy 33:1–4). Although Christians often talk about Judaism and the five books of Moses as "the Law," it is far more than law to Jewish believers. It is a guide to life. Consequently the word "Torah" is seen by Jewish people in two ways. In the narrow sense, it means the scrolls of the five books of Moses that are preserved in all synagogues. More generally, it signifies the teachings of these books understood within the context of the other Jewish scriptures and Jewish tradition.

Seen in this way, the Torah is a dynamic source of life and legislation that speaks to each generation anew. Therefore, Jews have a duty to preserve the Torah and interpret it. Traditionally the rabbis, or Jewish teachers, considered every single letter, every word, and every sentence to be of the greatest importance. As a result, many learned men

---

5. The relationship between the Hebrew Bible and Jewish history often becomes a heated academic debate. For a provocative approach, see K. A. Kitchen, *On the Reliability of the Old Testament* (Grand Rapids: Eerdmans, 2003); *Ancient Orient and Old Testament* (Downers Grove, Ill.: InterVarsity Press, 1975). A more standard approach is found in John Bright, *A History of Israel* (London: SCM Press, 1976); Peter Craigie, *The Old Testament: Its Background, Growth, and Content* (Nashville: Abingdon, 1986).

6. For a discussion of this complex issue, see Bruce Waltke, with Charles Yu, *An Old Testament Theology* (Grand Rapids: Zondervan, 2007), 287–90.

Photo 15.3 Wall painting of an Egyptian pharaoh from around the time of Moses.

within the Jewish community have spent their lives interpreting the Torah and discussing interpretations of interpretations. Early interpretations were codified in the first few centuries of the Christian era to create what became known as the Babylonian Talmud, which forms one of the great sources of Jewish self-understanding. To appreciate these things further, we now turn to the Jewish scriptures and Jewish history as understood by the Jewish tradition.

JEWISH SCRIPTURES

Over the centuries early Jewish writers produced the collection of religious texts we know as the Hebrew Bible. The Hebrew Bible has three parts. The first is the Pentateuch, or five books of Moses, which traditionally were attributed to Moses. The second part is known as the Prophets. This includes books which Christians call "historical." Further, there are two parts to the prophetic books of the Hebrew Bible. The first section includes the books of Joshua, Judges, Samuel, and Kings. The second section consists of the books of Isaiah, Jeremiah, Ezekiel, and the twelve remaining minor prophets. Finally, there is a third section known as "the Scriptures." In this section we find the books of Psalms, Proverbs, Job, Song of Solomon, Ruth, Lamentations, Ecclesiastes, Esther, Daniel, Ezra, Nehemiah, and Chronicles.

The Hebrew Bible is supplemented, however, by a number of books known as the Apocrypha. These books include Tobit, Judith, Maccabees 1–4, Ezra, Ecclesiasticus, and the Wisdom of Solomon. They were not included in the Hebrew Bible itself because the rabbis considered them repetitious or believed that their teachings were not entirely consistent with Judaism. Others were excluded because they were regarded as too "modern." Since some of these books were translated as part of the Septuagint, the Greek translation of the Hebrew Bible made by Jewish scholars around 260 BC, they acquired a certain degree of authority among Greek-speaking Jews.

It is worth noting here that the earliest fragmentary evidence for manuscript sources we have for the Hebrew Bible date back to the second century BC. These come from both the Dead Sea Scrolls and a vast collection of documents known as the Cairo *Genizah*. There are also amulets bearing inscriptions from the Torah and other forms of inscription dating back to about the seventh century BC. Nevertheless, the first complete set of manuscripts dates from the tenth century AD. This is known as the Masoretic text, which is the received, or authoritative, text of the Hebrew Bible. Other earlier manuscripts confirm the reliability of these texts through quotations scattered throughout thousands of documents. There are also earlier Greek and Latin manuscripts, both of which are in relative agreement with the later text.

THE JEWISH UNDERSTANDING OF HISTORY

Against the background of the revelation of the Torah, the stories of creation, Adam and Eve, Noah, and Abraham form a pattern of events related to the birth of Israel as the people of God. These stories have two main themes. First, they deal with the establishment of an "everlasting covenant" by God with Abraham and his legitimate descendents. This covenant involves the obligation of living a blameless life before God, the sign and seal of which is the practice of circumcision (Genesis 17:1–14).

Following the establishment of the covenant, the blessings pass on to Abraham's son Isaac and his grandson Jacob. Jealousy within the family of Jacob leads his older sons to conspire against Joseph, their father's favorite. When Joseph angers his brothers, they sell him to slave traders, who eventually take him to Egypt and resell him to an Egyptian nobleman, Potiphar. In Egypt Joseph prospers, rising to the top executive position and becoming the de facto ruler of the country under the pharaoh. Drought and famine then force Jacob and his remaining sons to seek refuge in Egypt. After testing them, Joseph identifies himself to them, forgives their earlier evil deed, and welcomes them to settle in the country, where they prosper (Genesis 32–50).

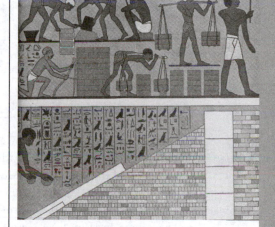

Photo 15.4 Hebrew slaves making bricks as depicted in an ancient Egyptian mural.

Although nineteenth-century biblical critics raised doubts about the historical reliability of this and other early biblical accounts, it is nevertheless full of remarkably accurate minor details. For example, according to the biblical story, set in the early or mid-second millennium BC, Joseph was sold as a slave for twenty shekels. We now know that twenty shekels was the average price for a slave in the eighteenth century BC. Similarly, in the same story, the title given to Joseph's master, Potiphar, is a term that at the time meant "an official." Over the next few centuries the meaning of this term changed to "eunuch."[7] These incidental comments are either an amazing coincidence or confirmation of the story's authenticity. These small pieces of evidence are not something a forger could have invented centuries later, and thus point to an origin around the date when the story is set.

The biblical story continues in the book of Exodus with the ominous words, "Then a new king, who did not know about Joseph, came to power in Egypt." (Exodus 1:8). Thus, the children of Israel come to be seen as potential subversives and a threat to Egyptian unity. As a result, a period of intense persecution follows, leading to a decree ordering the murder of all male Israelite children (Exodus 1:9–22). Against this background a child is born whose mother seeks to protect him by hiding him in the foliage along the banks of the Nile. There he is discovered by "Pharaoh's daughter," who adopts him as her own son

7.   K. A. Kitchen, *The Bible in Its World* (Downers Grove, Ill.: InterVarsity Press, 1977), 74.

Photo 15.5 Egyptian depiction of the Pharaoh Ramases defeating the Hittites around 1273 BC. Some scholars suggest that he was Pharaoh at the time of Moses and the Exodus.

and raises him as an Egyptian prince named Moses. After reaching manhood the child sees an Egyptian foreman brutally beating a Hebrew slave. Moses is outraged and strikes the Egyptian and kills him. At first Moses attempts to hide his crime, but word of it spreads, and he flees Egypt, fearing the wrath of Pharaoh.

Moses takes refuge in the land of Midian, where he marries the daughter of a local priest and becomes a herdsman. Years later, when a new king is appointed in Egypt, "the Israelites groaned," and "God heard their groaning and he remembered his covenant with Abraham, with Isaac and with Jacob" (Exodus 2:23–24). God now appears to Moses in a "burning bush" and calls him to serve God by freeing the Israelites from bondage (Exodus 3).

Following this, and Moses' initial reluctance to accept his new role, a struggle of wills takes place between Moses and Pharaoh. Assisted by his brother Aaron, who is the better speaker, Moses commands Pharaoh in the name of God, "Let my people go" (Exodus 5:1). Pharaoh refuses and intensifies the suffering of the people. Despite numerous miracles performed by Moses and a certain amount of wavering, Pharaoh remains obstinate and refuses to free his Hebrew slaves (Exodus 7). All of this leads to a series of plagues which God inflicts on the Egyptians, to no avail (Exodus 8–10). Finally, in a great act of punishment, all the firstborn in the land of Egypt are slain (Exodus 11). Only the Israelites escape this fate, by obeying God's commands, reinstituting the practice of circumcision, originally given to Abraham as a sign of the covenant (Genesis 17), and participating in what becomes the feast of Passover (Exodus 12). Now the Israelites are allowed to despoil the Egyptians by taking their clothing and gold and silver jewelry as they depart from Egypt.

After the shock of these events, Pharaoh recovers his nerve and pursues the fleeing Israelites, determined to punish them and recover what the Egyptians now see as stolen wealth. God decisively intervenes in the history of his people, allowing the Israelites to safely cross the Red Sea by miraculously dividing the waters. When the Egyptians attempt to follow, they are engulfed in a tidal wave which kills Pharaoh (Exodus 14). Following these events, the Israelites wander in the wilderness until they reach Mount Sinai, where God renews his covenant by revealing the Torah to Moses (Exodus 19).

The revelation of the Torah and the exodus from Egypt, therefore, are the central events of Jewish history, and the story of them is the formative narrative of both Jewish experience and Jewish ritual. The narratives relating these events and their interpretations define Judaism.

JEWISH HISTORY AFTER MOSES

According to the Bible, it took another forty years of wandering in the wilderness before the Israelites entered the Promised Land of

Photo 15.6 Lucas Cranach the Elder's (1472–1553) crossing of the Red Sea. Painted in 1530, it tells biblical story, found in Exodus 14:21–31, of destruction of the Egyptian army as it pursued Moses and the children of Israel during their flight to freedom from Egyptian bondage. The original painting can be seen in Munich's excellent art gallery known as the Alte Pinakothek.

Canaan, which they then conquered. Moses does not live to see this happen but dies in the wilderness. The Promised Land is gradually conquered under Joshua and his successors, during which time Israel is led by charismatic leaders known as judges and prophets. Around 1000 BC, under Saul, a monarchy is established. Following Saul's death, David becomes king after a short civil war, and Jerusalem becomes the capital of the kingdom. Although he is remembered as Israel's greatest king, David is prevented from building the temple of the Lord because of his failings. That task falls to his son Solomon, who extends Israelite rule from Damascus to Egypt.[8]

A savage civil war follows Solomon's death, with the northern half of the kingdom, consisting of ten tribes, making Jeroboam king of Israel. To the south, the kingdom of Judah is established by the remaining two tribes under their king, Solomon's son Rehoboam. From now on the kingdoms have separate but equally confusing histories. To the north there are frequent changes of dynasty in the state of Israel. To the south the kingdom of Judah remains loyal to the house of David. In each case, character and piety, or lack of piety, determine the welfare of the nation. The southern kingdom, with Jerusalem as its capital, retains a greater sense of its calling and duty to God, while the people of the northern kingdom more fervently follow after other gods.

Beginning around the eighth century BC and lasting until the end of the fifth century, a series of itinerant preachers known as prophets dominate Jewish history. Their works are recorded in the various prophetic books of the Bible and represent a profound yearning of

---

8. Paul Johnson, in *A History of the Jews* (New York: Harper and Row, 1988), provides a good overview of Jewish history, particularly after the end of the biblical period.

Photo 15.7 Nineteenth-century picture of the valley of Jericho, where the Israelites first invaded the Promised Land.

the human spirit for God and justice.

In 722 BC the northern kingdom of Israel was conquered by the Assyrians, and its people lost to history. To the south the kingdom of Judah submitted to Assyrian rule, which permitted its continued existence as a tributary state. From this time on, the children of Israel become the children of Judah, the Jewish people as we know them today.

One of the greatest events in the history of Judah was the reforms initiated by King Hezekiah during his long reign (715–687 BC). The coming of a plague which destroyed a besieging Assyrian army is seen as confirmation of God's miraculous preservation of the people. Pagan shrines were destroyed, and all evidence of the worship of other gods was removed from the land. Despite the success of Hezekiah's reign, his son, Manasseh, restored pagan worship during his fifty-five-year reign. Following Manasseh's death, his son Josiah once more restored the worship of the one true God, and a religious revival took place. At

this time, in 622 BC, repairs carried out in the temple uncovered an early copy of the book of Deuteronomy that had been lost. This version of Deuteronomy was used to initiate further reforms. While many modern scholars doubt the authenticity of this story and believe that the priest or someone else "planted" the manuscript to promote the reform agenda, there can be no doubt that the traditional story of the discovery of a lost manuscript of Deuteronomy changed history.

Throughout this history, one sees the continued conflict between reformers,

Photo 15.8 An early depiction of King Solomon from the Bible of Karl the Bald (823–877). It was painted around 880 AD. The scene is from 1 Samuel.

who seek to establish the worship of the one true God, and others who allow lapses into polytheistic paganism. Then, between 598 and 586 BC, the Babylonians conquered Judah, destroyed the city of Jerusalem and its temple, and enslaved its people.

For seventy years the Jewish people were in exile, or Babylonian captivity, as it is sometimes called. During this time a sense of hopelessness set in while Jewish leaders struggled with the question of why God allowed his people to be treated in this way. They determined that this was a just punishment for their failure to keep the covenant. God had not failed them; they had failed God. From now on the central mark of the Jew became his or her obedience to God.

At the end of seventy years, following the conquest of Babylon by Cyrus in 538 BC, the Jews were permitted to return to Judah and rebuild Jerusalem with the exile ending around 516 with the dedication of the Temple. They did so, and two great leaders, Nehemiah and Ezra, established the covenant of obedience. A second temple was built, and a priestly cult established, that dominated the religion of the people.

JEW AND GREEK

Judaism underwent further changes following the conquest of the entire Near East by Alexander of Macedonia (356–323 BC), better known as Alexander the Great, whose attitude toward the Jews was one of tolerance. After his death, Judea became a province ruled by Alexander's general Ptolemy, who proclaimed himself ruler of Egypt. So great was the influence of Greek rulers on the Jews, who prospered in cities like Alexandria, that many abandoned the Hebrew and Aramaic languages. Consequently, around 260 BC seventy Jewish scholars in Alexandria began to translate the Hebrew Bible into Greek in a translation known as the Septuagint.

Shortly thereafter, the land of Judea was annexed by the kingdom of Syria and its Seleucid rulers, who were Greek in origin. One of their kings, Antiochus IV, also known as Antiochus Ephiphanes, determined to unify his empire under one religion. Therefore, encouraged by some modernizing Jews, he sought to suppress traditional Jewish religious worship and transform the Jerusalem temple into a Greek temple. In 166 BC, a rebellion broke out under the leadership of the priestly Maccabee family. The outcome of the rebellion was the independence of Judah, which Jews today remember by celebrating the festival of Hanukkah.

During this period of political independence, Jewish groups such as the Pharisees, who stressed obedience and religious observances; the Sadducees, a Hellenized priestly group that later cooperated with the Romans; and the scribes and teachers, encountered

Photo 15.9 Nehemiah inspects the walls of Jerusalem (Nehemiah 2:11–18) by Jacques-Joseph Tissot (1836–1902). It was painted in the late nineteenth century. The original is in the Jewish Museum in New York.

in the New Testament, became established. Squabbles among political parties eventually led to civil war, in which the Roman general Pompey was called upon to act as an arbitrator in 63 BC. As a result, Judea became a puppet state of Rome, with Roman advisers guiding the policies of a nominally Jewish king. The most important of these kings was Herod the Great (37–4 BC).

During this time, there emerged in Palestine various apocalyptic movements that called for the expulsion of the Romans and the establishment of the kingdom of God. These calls became more intense after the death of Herod, when the Romans dropped all pretence of independence and assumed direct control of the country. Under the rule of Pontius Pilate, who ruled from AD 25 to 36, Jewish rebellions grew in Palestine, while other Jewish revolts broke out throughout Roman-ruled provinces, including Egypt. But it was Pontius Pilate's successor, Florus, appointed in AD 64, who provoked the deadliest rebellion in Palestine.

THE DESTRUCTION OF JUDEA

As with many historical disputes, the events leading up to the Roman-Jewish war were complex. When Romans instituted a census in Judah early in the first century AD, a resistance movement known as the Zealots quickly developed. For the rest of the century they would cause the Romans continuous trouble. The Sadducees, however, collaborated with the Romans. They also controlled the priesthood and temple in Jerusalem. One of the key complaints of the Zealots and their sympathizers was against the medallions on the standards of the Roman legions, which bore the image of the Roman emperor. They saw these as idolatrous symbols of a pagan god.

Around the same time, the Hellenized Jews in the Egyptian city of Alexandria came into conflict with the Roman authorities and the local Greek community. At issue was the request by members of the Jewish community to be granted full citizenship. Riots broke out and synagogues were ransacked by the pagan Greeks, who erected statues of the emperor in them. In AD 40, members of both the Greek and Jewish communities appealed to Emperor Caligula for a judgment. Apparently, when he heard their case, Caligula thought the Jews were completely mad because they failed to acknowledge him as a god. At the same time, Greeks living on the Palestinian coast built a temple in honor of Caligula, to the outrage of local Jews. Caligula ordered the local Roman governor to set up an altar in his honor in Jerusalem itself. Before this could be done, Caligula was assassinated and Claudius became the new emperor.

One of Claudius's first challenges was to bring to an end the conflict between Jews and Greeks in Egypt. At first he tried to reconcile them, urging the Greeks to be more tolerant and the Jews to stop disparaging pagan gods. He also ended direct Roman rule over Judea, allowing it to become a client kingdom under the rule of Agrippa I. When Agrippa died in 44, the area exploded with apocalyptic movements, riots, revolts, massacres, and what we would today call ethnic cleansing, caused by tensions between Galileans, Greeks, Samaritans, and Jews. The countryside rapidly became dangerous, with robbers and "freedom fighters" terrorizing travelers.

As tensions mounted, Florus, the Roman governor—known as the procurator—was faced with an increasingly unstable situation. Ethnic riots between Greeks and Jews in the coastal city of Caesarea Maritima were the last straw. Exasperated with the Jews, Florus allowed his troops to run riot in Jerusalem itself and executed a number of Jewish leaders. In retaliation, Jewish rebels began to murder pro-Roman Jews and wealthy citizens who favored the Romans. They also began a series of attacks on outlying Roman garrisons, which they slaughtered. Faced with a

Photos 15.10 and 15.11 The Roman emperor Claudius (left), who attempted to reconcile Jews and Gentiles, and General Vespasian (right), who dealt harshly with the Jewish revolt against Rome. Vespasian later became emperor.

growing rebellion, the Roman governor of Syria invaded Judea; but when he attempted to capture the Jerusalem temple, his troops were driven back and he retreated to the coast.

A new general, Vespasian, was now appointed by Emperor Nero in 67. At that time Zealots seized control of Jerusalem, massacring its Jewish Roman sympathizers. In March of 67, Vespasian began his march into Judea. Fighting continued to 68, when Nero died. There followed a brief lull in Vespasian's campaign as he was appointed emperor of the eastern provinces. He then appointed his son Titus as commander of the Jewish campaign. Jerusalem was besieged, and five months later it fell to the Romans. Titus laid it waste, and the Jewish population was severely punished, with many of them either being enslaved or sent to the arena to face certain death.

Following these events, the Romans carried out cleanup operations. The last Jewish fortress, Masada, fell in April of 74.

Photo 15.12 Mount Masada, where a Jewish fortress held the Romans at bay until it was eventually overrun after a long siege. This siege has become one of the national myths of modern Israel and was the subject of an American television series.

According to popular legend, its inhabitants boldly resisted Roman attacks before committing suicide on the eve of the final Roman assault. Many historians now doubt this claim and believe that the inhabitants were captured and enslaved. Nevertheless, the Masada story has become one of the foundation myths of modern Israel. Historians estimate that around 1 million Jews died during this rebellion and its brutal suppression by the Roman legions. At this point traditional Judaism, and what may be identified very broadly as biblical Judaism, came to an end.

LATER JEWISH REVOLTS

The destruction of the Jerusalem temple in 70 sent shock waves throughout Jewish communities in the Roman world and beyond. In a relatively short time, the Romans had depopulated Palestine, razed Jerusalem to the ground, and destroyed the temple, and with it a whole system of sacrifices, religious pilgrimage, and supporting priesthood. The result was one of the most significant religious transformations in history.

Photo 15.13 Jewish captives depicted in the Arch of Titus.

Despite these traumatic events—perhaps because of them—Jewish rebellions continued for several centuries throughout the Roman world. When the Romans attempted to invade Persia under the emperor Trajan (53–117), the Jews of Babylon revolted. Other revolts and riots took place in Alexandria, throughout Egypt, and in Cyprus between 114 and 117. The most significant in shaping long-term attitudes toward the Jews in the Roman world, particularly in Greek speaking areas, was the Jewish revolt in Cyprus.[9] Here the fighting centered on the city of Salamis. After capturing it, the Jewish rebels sacked it and slaughtered all the Greeks they could find.[10] Figures for the number of Greeks killed during this revolt range from around 200,000 to 500,000. Given the scale of the slaughter, rumors quickly spread throughout the Roman world about Jewish atrocities. Even allowing for blatant anti-Semitism, these stories seem to indicate exceptionally cruel deeds on the part of the Jewish insurgents before they were finally defeated by Roman troops. The net result was that Jews became associated

---

9. Alexander Fuks, "Aspects of the Jewish Revolt in AD 115–117," *Journal of Roman Studies* 51 (1961): 98–104.
10. Ibid., 99.

with the worst kind of terrorism and seen as people capable of the grossest cruelties against their enemies. In modern terms, the Romans viewed the Jews like Americans view Islamic terrorists.

Another serious revolt occurred in Palestine in 132 under the leadership of Simon Bar Kochba. It was provoked by Emperor Hadrian's colonization program. As a result of this revolt, Judea was depopulated and Judaism was outlawed by the emperor. After his death in 138, this decision was reversed. These defeats led the surviving Jews of Judea to reconcile themselves to the Romans, and Jewish scholarship began to flourish.

The significance of these revolts is that the latent anti-Semitism of the late Roman world appeared to be confirmed by the actions of the Jews themselves. This anti-Semitism, particularly among Greeks who had suffered the most, became established among educated people, only to poison the preaching of later Greek Christian leaders.

THE NEW JUDAISM

Into the breach created by Roman savagery and Jewish apocalyptic movements, a new generation of Jewish scholars stepped to make the study of the Torah the central feature of Jewish worship. In filling this gap the Jewish community was aided by people who today would be called "collaborators." Certainly, they knew how to communicate with the Romans and convince their political masters that the encouragement of Jewish scholarship was in their best interests. It is arguable that in this way Judaism was saved from extinction. Naturally enough, one of the overriding concerns of these scholars was to play down apocalyptic teachings and discourage any movement that held out the lure of messianic promises. Consequently, a number of academies, or schools of learning, were established, laying the foundation for a new form of Judaism.

This change produced an increased emphasis on textual interpretation and the need to generate rules for exegeting the sacred texts. Out of this renewal of scholarly activity came a collection of laws and practical rules known as the *Midrash*. This highly influential text, compiled around 200, contained six parts: seeds, feasts, women, damages, holy matters, and purities. These parts were subdivided using a complex system of organization. As the titles suggest, each part dealt with a different area of life: "seeds" with agricultural affairs, "women" with family matters, and so on.

The Midrash was only the beginning. From the second century AD Jewish authors produced a host of scholarly works. Many of these were eventually compiled into what became known as the Talmud. In the mid-fourth century AD the Jerusalem Talmud, as it was

Photo 15.14 The ruins of the Bir'im Synagogue as they were seen in the late nineteenth century.

known, came into being. A century later saw the production of the Babylonian Talmud. These two works laid the foundation for what was to become known as Rabbinic Judaism. Both of the Talmuds developed the implications of the Midrash. Sometimes contradictions were harmonized; at other times the legal position was discussed from a myriad of different perspectives. An enormous amount of legendary, theological, and exegetical material, often suitable for teachers, also entered the collections. These texts preserve discussions in an almost shorthand form, giving the essence of arguments and creating endless problems of interpretation that have occupied Jewish scholars ever since.

The aim of all this activity was to provide the people of Israel with a comprehensive guide for life. Although the Ten Commandments are clear enough, the implications are not always clear. What, for example, is meant by the commandment in Exodus 20:8–11, which reads, "Remember the Sabbath day by keeping it holy. Six days you shall labor and do all your work, but the seventh day is a Sabbath to the LORD your God. On it you shall not do any work, neither you, nor your son or daughter, nor your manservant or maidservant, nor your animals, nor the alien within your gates. For in six days the LORD made the heavens and the earth, the sea, and all that is in them, but he rested on the seventh day. Therefore the LORD blessed the Sabbath day and made it holy"?

This, of course, was one of the issues that troubled Jesus and his disciples in Matthew 12:9–14, where we read, "Going on from that place, he went into their synagogue, and a man with a shriveled hand was there. Looking for a reason to accuse Jesus, they asked him,

'Is it lawful to heal on the Sabbath?'" Jesus, according to the New Testament, provided his opponents with a good answer. He countered their question with a question about whether the owner of a sheep or goat could rescue it or not when it fell into danger or was hurt on the Sabbath. This type of argument occurs again and again in the Talmud, except the context given is an academic debate rather than a living situation.

The discussions of the rabbis on these matters were filled with passion and great profundity. The ability to argue and interpret texts was of crucial importance. Yet, despite apparently endless discussion, most of the conclusions were left open, to allow the student to reach a decision for themselves. In many ways this is like the process of case law in the English

Photo 15.15 The Ark of the Law, which is found in all synagogues on a wall that faces Jerusalem. Inside it are kept the scrolls of the Torah.

legal system, which was adapted to the American situation and forms the basis of American law. The difference, of course, is that the Talmud is religious law based upon Scripture.

Just like lawyers today, Jewish men had to go through rigorous training which required them to remember not only cases but also the arguments about those cases and the best ways of presenting their own views. Rabbis went through similar, but more rigorous, training. Thus Judaism developed an extensive educational system based upon local congregations in cooperation with specialized rabbinic academies that created an ethos enabling Jewish people to thrive in the modern world.

By the third century a measure of prosperity had returned to Jewish communities in Palestine. Other communities flourished throughout the Roman world and further east. In 313, after a series of savage persecutions by his predecessors, Emperor Constantine officially confirmed the toleration of Christianity, and the conversion of the peoples of the Roman Empire to Christianity gained momentum. Initially, these events did not have a very great impact on Judaism. But slowly anti-Jewish sentiment grew, and by the middle of the fourth century imperial laws were passed prohibiting Jews from converting Christians, particularly through marriage. In the fifth century, laws were passed to prevent Jews from holding government posts. In the view of Christian theologians at this time, it was the duty of Christians whenever possible to convert Jews. In eastern parts of the empire, where memories of the Jewish revolts lingered, anti-Semitism was strong and was often encouraged by the exaggerations of fiery preachers.

Further east, Jewish communities flourished in modern Iraq, then known as Babylonia. Jews had originally been deported there by Nebuchadnezzar in the sixth century

Jewish Religious Traditions

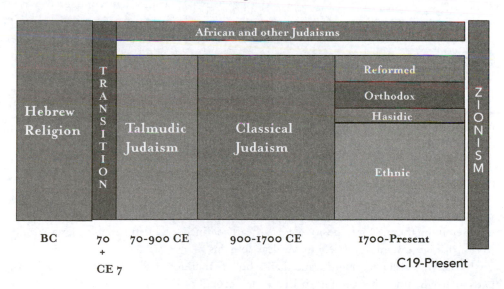

Figure 15.3 The later development of Judaism.

BC. Although many had returned to Palestine as soon as the opportunity presented itself, others remained to make Babylon a center of Jewish scholarship. The conversion of the Roman Empire to Christianity actually helped the Jews of Babylonia, because the local rulers, fearing Roman conquest, favored the Jews while persecuting Christians, whom they suspected of supporting Rome. Thus, by the fifth or sixth century, Judaism was flourishing in Babylonia and border areas beyond the boundaries of the Eastern Roman Empire. At the same time, its status in the Roman Empire itself, particularly in the Greek-speaking Eastern Empire and areas that once belonged to the Roman Empire in the West, was somewhat less stable. Nevertheless, Judaism had staged a remarkable recovery from the dark days of the first century and the Roman destruction of Jerusalem.

The unity of the Mediterranean world under Roman rule was shattered in the seventh century by the rise and rapid conquests of Islam. At first it appears that Muhammad welcomed the Jews, whom he hoped to convert to his new religion. Their rejection of him as the true prophet then led him to denounce them.

As a consequence, at least one Jewish tribe living in Arabia was exterminated, and two others were expelled or enslaved. By 644, Muslim armies had conquered Syria, Palestine, Egypt, Iraq, and Persia and were on the verge of entering India. They then swept across North Africa and entered Spain, where they

Photo 15.16 The above nineteenth-century view of Jerusalem is probably fairly similar to how the city looked in the seventh century following the conquest of Jerusalem by the Arabs. The mosque of the Dome of the Rock, which dominates the landscape, was built on the site of the Jewish temple and is intended to signify the triumph of Islam over both Christianity and Judaism.

conquered two-thirds of the territory. The treatment of Jews varied from area to area, depending upon the local ruler. Later on, what was known as the Pact of Omar, drawn up in 800, came to define Jewish-Muslim relations.

Under this treaty—or perhaps one should say declaration—numerous restrictions were placed on Jewish communities. They were not allowed to make converts or build new synagogues. They were prohibited from carrying weapons and from riding horses. Worst of all, they had to wear clothing that clearly identified them as Jews. Numerous taxes were imposed upon them. On the positive side, a clearly defined legal status enabled Jewish trade to flourish, as Jews moved freely in Muslim domains.

Initially, Jewish communities and their scholarly traditions flourished in Muslim lands, particularly Spain. Changes within Islam itself brought to an end these times of relative prosperity for Spanish Jews when in 1086 the Spanish rulers invited North African Muslims to help them lead an attack on the Spanish Christian communities remaining in the north of the peninsula. Preparations for a new holy war led to the persecution of Christians under Muslim rule, and this soon led to the persecution of Jews as well. After a short period of persecution things calmed down, and the Jews of Spain enjoyed two centuries of unprecedented prosperity, accompanied by a golden age of Jewish scholarship and learning.

This prosperity came to an abrupt end in the middle of the twelfth century, when a Moroccan Berber dynasty took control of Muslim Spain. A new wave of persecution ensued. Jews were given the choice of converting to Islam or leaving Muslim-ruled Spain. In practice, this often meant the choice of converting to Islam or being killed. Many Jews, including the great Jewish philosopher Moses Maimonides (1135–1204), moved to securer areas of the Islamic world like Egypt and the Middle East, where less fanatical rulers held power. Others migrated to Christian parts of Spain and to other areas in Europe. It was in northern Europe that the Jewish community was to face its greatest challenges, produce much of its best scholarship, and create many vibrant communities.

CHAPTER 16

RABBINIC AND OTHER JUDAISMS

INTRODUCTION

Jewish communities were established in northern Europe during the days of the Roman Empire, particularly along the banks of the Danube and Rhine rivers. Consequently, cities like Mainz and Worms in the German-speaking lands and Troyes and Sens in France became important Jewish centers, producing distinguished scholars. As tensions rose between what was then known as Christendom and Islam, leading to the Crusades of the eleventh century, the situation of Jews became precarious and tragedy often followed in their wake.

JEWISH COMMUNITIES AND SECTS

Around the seventh century AD, European Judaism developed into two major groups, the Sephardic Jews of Spain and the Ashkenazy Jews of northern Europe. Within these communities, philosophy, mysticism, and occasional fundamentalist movements like the Karaites, which were founded in Babylon and flourished between the eighth and eleventh centuries, could also be found. The important thing to remember, however, is that Judaism defined itself not as a creed, as Christians and, to a lesser extent, Muslims generally did, but as a way of life. At the core of traditional, or rabbinic, Judaism was what Michael Fishbane calls "the matrix of traditional Jewish life,"[1] which was kept alive by liturgical practices, communal involvement, and the daily life of Jewish families.

Living in what were often hostile and potentially dangerous environments, Jews in both the Christian and Muslim worlds looked inward to their own people for solace and protection. These were traumatic times that created memories of "tears and martyrdom."[2] In Muslim lands Jews and Christians alike shared the status of *dhimmitedu*, or second-class citizens, protected by the law, but not as well protected as true Muslims, to whom they were subservient. In Christian lands Jews were protected by secular rulers and church authorities against the whims of an unstable and ill-educated populace. In both geographic areas, the situation of Jews was at best precarious.

---

1. Michael Fishbane, *Judaism: Revelation and Traditions* (San Francisco: HarperSanFrancisco, 1987), 49.
2. Ibid., 51.

Photo 16.1 A traditional Jewish betrothal contract from the Jewish year 5555, or AD 1794. Such contracts bound Jews together in a Europe-wide community that often had strong ties beyond Europe into the Islamic world, making the Jews a truly international, or global, community.

Most important of all, Jewish isolation from the surrounding society brought about the acceptance of "love and care for fellow Jews" as a central value of Judaism, based on the belief that "all Jews are responsible for one another."[3] Perhaps more than anything else, this principle held Jews together over the centuries.

SEPHARDIC AND ASHKENAZY JUDAISM

The origin of the term "Sephardic" is unknown. Some argue that it came from the Hebrew name for Spain. Others suggest it had a much older meaning which goes back to either Persia or the Greek city of Sardis. Whatever its origin, Sephardic Judaism came to be identified with Jews living in the Iberian Peninsula until they were expelled from Spain by Ferdinand and Isabella in 1492. At that time the majority of Sephardic Jews took refuge in Muslim lands, moving to Constantinople, North Africa, or Egypt. Others settled in Portugal or immigrated to northern Europe, particularly the Netherlands, where Amsterdam became a Jewish center.[4]

Ashkenazy Judaism, on the other hand, originated in northern Europe, particularly German-speaking lands in the tenth century, although it was not until the eleventh century that the term came into common use.

It is believed that at that time Ashkenazy Jews costituted about 3 percent of the total Jewish population. Later they spread to the Netherlands, Poland, Russia, and eastern Europe. In Europe they distinguished themselves by their relatively high levels of literacy and aptitude for education. Initially, many were moneylenders, but later, as the times allowed, they took up other professions, such as medicine and law.[5]

The main difference between Ashkenazy and Sephardic Judaism lies in the liturgy and in cultural practices within families. Liturgically, the order of prayers, the number of prayers, the type of script used to write Torah scrolls, the way Torah scrolls are kept and handled, the use of lights, and various other details of the liturgy differed between the two communities. Another significant difference is that Sephardic Jews refuse to eat fish and milk in the same meal, while Ashkenazy Jews reject this food law. As for cultural practices, the Sephardic Jews reflect aspects of Arabic culture, while Ashkenazy Jews were strongly influenced by German culture. Today approximately 17 percent of Jews throughout the

---

3. Ibid.
4. Leo Trepp. *Judaism: Development and Life* (Belmont, Calif.: Wadsworth, 1982), 60–66.
5. Ibid., 66–75.

Photo 16.2 Eighteenth-century Sephardic Jews attending a funeral. These were Jews of Spanish origin, who developed differently from the more Germanic Ashkenazy Jews. After their expulsion from Spain in the fifteenth century, many Sephardic Jews who fled to other European lands and found refuge in the Netherlands.

world are non-Ashkenazy, the majority of whom are Sephardic. In the state of Israel, however, the number of Sephardic Jews is around 50 percent, which makes the Jews of Israel significantly different from many other Jewish communities throughout the world.[6]

MEDIEVAL TRAUMAS

In 1095 the First Crusade was proclaimed by Pope Urban II to defend Christian pilgrims visiting the Holy Land and to relieve the Byzantine Empire from attacks by Muslim invaders. In the wake of his declaration, as Rodney Stark points out in his book *One True God*, from which the argument of the following discussion is drawn,[7] the Duke of Lower Lorraine, Godfrey of Bouillon, recruited an army at Verdun. In doing so, Godfrey boldly declared that as he marched east he would avenge the death of Christ by killing Jews. When the chief rabbi of Mainz heard about this, he wrote to the Holy Roman emperor, Henry IV, demanding protection. The emperor responded by commanding all his subjects to guarantee the safety of Jews. When Godfrey reached Mainz, the local Jews paid a ransom to ensure their safety. Godfrey marched on, leaving Emich of Leisingen in charge of the area with a small garrison. On 3 May 1096, Emich marched to the cathedral city of Speyer, where the archbishop provided protection for those Jews who came to him. Unfortunately, a small group was captured and brutally murdered by Emich, who then marched his men to Worms, where they attacked the Jews, killing as many as they could. Once again the local bishop gave protection to the Jews, but Emich's forces attacked the bishop's palace and massacred about five hundred refugees.

Emich then doubled back to Mainz and attacked the bishop's palace again. The bishop narrowly escaped with his life, but about a thousand Jews were massacred. Emich then continued his march to Cologne and massacred Jews hiding in nearby villages. News of these massacres inspired another local warlord, Volkmar, to massacre the Jews of Prague, whereupon another would-be crusader, Gottschalk, launched an attack upon the Jews of Regensburg. In the meantime Emich's forces rampaged through the Mosel Valley, killing as many Jews as they could find—about five thousand, by some estimates.

---

6. Information on Jewish demographics can be found on the Central Bureau of Statistics website for the state of Israel: http://www1.cbs.gov.il/reader/cw_usr_view_Folder?ID=141 (accessed 25 March 2009).

7. Rodney Stark, *One True God* (Princeton: Princeton Univ. Press, 2001), 124–56.

Photo 16.3 The above pictures depict accusations against a Jew, who is then arrested and burned at the stake. Although relatively rare, such barbaric treatment was meted out to Jews, heretics, and other outsiders by enraged mobs and is a dark chapter in European history.

Once he realized what was happening, the emperor had rallied his forces, and Volkmar's troops were hunted down and executed in Hungary. A similar fate awaited Gottschalk, whose forces were destroyed by a Hungarian army that went on to confront and annihilate Emich's force. As Steven Runciman points out, most Christians viewed the destruction of these murderers as just punishment. Nevertheless, these events set a pattern. When, eventually, knights of the First Crusade captured Jerusalem, it was Godfrey of Bouillon's troops who were responsible for the massacre of Jews, although there is some evidence that other commanders protected Jews and many escaped the carnage.

The problem, as Stark points out, is that the work of these renegades set a pattern that was repeated during the Second and subsequent Crusades. During the Third Crusade this bloodlust spread to England, and the people of York massacred its Jewish community. Even though King Richard immediately reacted by hanging the ringleaders of this gruesome act, other Jewish communities were attacked and plundered as soon as he left the country. The final wave of bloodletting appears to have occurred in the mid-fourteenth century in the wake of the bubonic plague, better known as the Black Death. What is significant here is that, in this outburst of communal insanity, the Jews were blamed in some areas, Muslims in others, and different ethnic groups, including the English, in other areas, leading to the lynching of anyone who was unfortunate enough to belong to the wrong ethnicity.

Against this background of the persecution of Jews by renegades claiming to be Christians, it is important to note that bishops and popes, as well as preachers like Bernard of Clairvaux (1090–1153) and many kings and princes, did all they could to protect Jews.[8]

---

8. Ibid., 140–42.

At the same time, we really know very little about the fate of Jews in Muslim countries, where, as in Europe, they often thrived between periods of intense persecution. Only recently have historians begun to probe this; and the picture of a golden age in Spain, or anywhere else, has become increasingly questioned. For example, the life of the great Jewish philosopher Maimonides (1135–1205) was anything but tranquil. He had to flee again and again from persecution, or for fear of persecution, by Muslim authorities.[9]

Nevertheless, the Christian reconquest of Spain brought little relief to the Jews living there. During the fourteenth century, Jewish communities were massacred in both Aragon and Castile by local mobs. Consequently, thousands of Spanish Jews converted to Christianity. These people, known as *conversos*, flourished under the new dispensation, many moving into government as minor officials, and very often as tax collectors. During the fifteenth century anti-Jewish feeling, which originated in a general dislike of tax collectors, grew, and rumors spread that the Jews were not true converts. They were given the name "Marrano," or pig, and were said to practice Judaism in secret.

Urged on by popular unrest and wild rumors about the alleged murder of a Christian boy by Jewish witches, King Ferdinand and Queen Isabella initiated the Spanish Inquisition in 1480. This disgraceful episode of history led to the execution of around 30,000 people and the eventual expulsion of the Jews from Spain on 31 March 1492. Only those Jews who now converted and submitted to baptism would be allowed to live in Spain. When the Marranos and other Jews fled Spain, some went to Portugal, others into northern Europe, and the majority to North Africa and Turkey.

Not surprisingly, messianic movements erupted among this dispersed and threatened population. Many Spanish Jews went to Constantinople and were welcomed by the Sultan of Turkey, who was astonished at what he saw as the stupidity of the Spanish rulers in expelling an educated and productive segment of their population. From all accounts, these refugees were very confused, many not knowing whether they were Jewish or Christian, and as a result a significant

Photo 16.4 As far as we know, Jews first settled in England after the Norman Conquest, when they served Norman kings. After the coronation of Richard I, known to history as Richard the Lionheart, a series of anti-Jewish riots broke out all over England, leading to the deaths of scores of Jews. The worst occurred in March 1190 in the city of York, where around 150 Jews took refuge in the local fortification known as Clifford's Tower. Here they were brutally massacred by a raging mob. Later King Richard punished the perpetrators, though too late to help the victims. The fact that the ringleaders in these attacks were local nobles who owed large sums to Jewish moneylenders supports the notion that greed and not religion lay behind the attacks.

9. Ibid., 81–82, 128–33; Rodney Stark, *For the Glory of God* (Princeton: Princeton Univ. Press, 2003), 48–49.

number converted to Islam. For the next few centuries, Jews generally flourished in the Ottoman, or Turkish, Empire.[10]

NORTHERN EUROPEAN JEWS

From the early Middle Ages, Jews migrated through Germany and areas of the Byzantine Empire into Russia and Poland. In 1264, Prince Boleslav V (1226–1279), Duke of Krakow, granted the Jews a charter guaranteeing their legal rights and protection. A century later, during the rule of King Casimir III (1310–1370), a series of decrees extended rights to Jews throughout Poland. Then, in 1388, the Grand Duke of Lithuania welcomed the Jews to his lands. These developments, though good for Jewish immigrants, providing them with considerable protection under the law, had a dark side which appears to have affected the fate of the Jews in modern times. As earlier in Spain, the Jews, an educated people, provided reliable and able recruits for government service. As a result many became tax collectors, estate managers, and agents of the government, and they were feared by the common people, who saw them as oppressors. To make matters worse, as in Spain, they were required to wear their own distinctive clothing. Therefore, no one could fail to know that the hated tax collector or government bailiff was a Jew. Undoubtedly these developments laid a foundation for later anti-Semitism. By the early fifteenth century there were around 15,000 Jews in Poland. A century later that number had grown to around 150,000 as Poland became a center of Jewish life and scholarship.

Jewish prosperity in Polish areas came to a dramatic end in the seventeenth century, when Ukrainian Cossacks revolted against their Polish masters and massacred Jews and Polish landowners alike. In what became a major peasant revolt, Polish gentry and their Jewish administrators were slaughtered in gruesome ways.

Eventually the rule of the Cossacks led to the separation of Poland and the Ukraine as well as intervention by the Russian and Swedish armies. The involvement of foreign troops gave birth to a Polish partisan movement that resisted both the Russians and the Swedes. In the pro-

Photo 16.5 This woodcut shows Sabbatai Zevi (1626–1676) in a Turkish prison. He declared himself the Messiah in 1648 and was eventually imprisoned in Constantinople, where, in the castle of Abydos, he converted to Islam on 16 September 1666. Later he vacillated between Judaism and Islam. His followers, known as Sabbateans, drew inspiration from Jewish mysticism, especially the kabbalah, and are believed to have influenced the development of the Hassidic movement in Poland and elsewhere.

10. Dan Cohn-Sherbok, *Judaism: History, Belief and Practice* (London: Routledge, 2003), 210–19.

cess these groups identified the Jews with Russian and Swedish ambitions and turned on them too. Caught up in bloody warfare and attacked from all sides, thousands of Jews perished.[11]

THE IMPACT OF THE PROTESTANT REFORMATION

During these upheavals Jews in Lithuania remained relatively safe, while Vilnius, its capital, became the northern center of traditional Talmudic belief and practice. Here "the last great theologian of classical rabbinism," Rabbi Elijah ben Solomon (1720–1797), lived and died as a staunch critic of modernity who held fast to medieval Jewish traditions.

To the south, in German-speaking lands, the Reformation and Counter-Reformation created uncertainty and numerous problems for Jews. In 1553 Pope Paul IV (1476–1559) ordered the burning of the Talmud, and two years later he promoted the segregation of Jews into ghettos. On the Protestant side, Martin Luther (1483–1546) initially took a highly favorable stance toward the Jews. Then, toward the end of his life, as a result of Sabbatarian messianic movements that threatened revolution in Bohemia, and on the advice of a Jewish convert to Christianity, he turned against the Jews. Worst of all, in 1543 he published his notorious tract *Against the Jews and Their Lies*.[12] Despite this, as Uwe Siemon-Netto shows in his book *The Fabricated Luther*, it is unjust to blame Luther for the later anti-Semitism of the Nazis.[13] Luther's work on the Jews was largely forgotten after his death and only rediscovered after Nazi anti-Semitism was well established. Therefore, it is not a source, as some have alleged, for the twentieth-century Holocaust.

The Thirty Years' War of the seventeenth century, which brought devastation to anyone unfortunate enough to be living in the path of an invading army or roving group of mercenaries, brought prosperity to European Jews. This was a time when the Jewish traders flourished in northern Europe by providing both funds and supplies to various warring governments, which rewarded them with special privileges. Because Jewish moneylenders and merchants "made themselves indispensable to all sides," many Jews "were treated better, rather than worse, than the population as a whole." After the war, Jews continued to enjoy the privileges they had earned during this time of terrible devastation. As a result, resentment grew among their neighbors, who resented the Jew's role as middlemen with special trading privileges. To a large extent this resentment laid the foundation for later anti-Semitism.[14]

In England, the Jews were expelled in 1290 by Edward I (1239–1307), and only welcomed back in 1656 by Oliver Cromwell (1599–1658) and the Puritans. In the Calvinist Netherlands Jews had been welcome since the sixteenth century. Nevertheless, in central Europe, Jews were forced to wear distinctive clothing and live in their own areas until the late eighteenth century. In German-speaking countries, despite the efforts of men like

11. Trepp, *Judaism*, 78–84; Paul Johnson, *A History of the Jews* (New York: Harper and Row, 1988), 231, 251–52.

12. First published in Wittenberg in 1543. The only complete English translation is Martin Luther, *Luther's Works*, vol. 47, *The Christian in Society IV*, ed. Franklin Sherman, trans. Martin H. Bertramis (Philadelphia: Fortress, 1971), 123–306.

13. Uwe Siemon-Netto, *The Fabricated Luther* (Saint Louis: Concordia, 2007).

14. Johnson, *History of the Jews*, 254–58; Cohn-Sherbok, *Judaism*, 225–32.

Photo 16.6 The great English Puritan and political leader of the parliamentary forces in England's Civil War, Oliver Cromwell (1599–1658), the Lord Protector, who granted Jews the right to live in England in 1656.

Philipp Jakob Spener (1635–1705), the father of German Pietism, who sought to improve their lot, the status of Jews changed very little until the nineteenth century.[15]

MODERN TIMES

The history of modern Judaism begins in the mid- to late eighteenth century, when, as a result of various social and intellectual trends, Jews began to be slowly integrated into the life of continental European countries. Agitation by the Prussian official Christian Wilhelm von Dohm (1751–1820), a friend of the distinguished Jewish philosopher Moses Mendelssohn (1729–1786), began to have an effect. His two-volume work *Concerning the Amelioration of the Civil Status of the Jews* (1781) was enormously influential in helping change public attitudes toward Jews. A wave of emancipation swept continental Europe in the late eighteenth and early nineteenth centuries. For this reason many Jewish scholars argue that it is accurate to see the Jewish Middle Ages as lasting until the late eighteenth century, by which time some 2 million Jews lived in Europe.[16]

In 1781 the reforming Holy Roman emperor, Joseph II (1741–1790), abolished distinctive clothing for Jews and restrictions on travel. A year later he issued an Edict of Tolerance that allowed Jews to live where they liked in Vienna and fully participate in commercial and industrial activities. Similar, though less sweeping, reforms were enacted in many other German-speaking states, greatly improving the lot of Jews. In France the position of Jews in the south improved as

Photo 16.7 Menasseh ben Israel (1604–1657) was one of the most successful diplomats for Judaism in the early modern world. Through his efforts Oliver Cromwell sanctioned the return of Jews to England and their eventual recognition as citizens.

15. Ibid., 213, 276–77; Philipp Jakob Spener, *Pia Desideria*, trans. Theodore G. Tappert (Minneapolis: Fortress, 1989), 68–69.

16. For further reading related to this and the following sections, see Johnson, *History of the Jews*; Howard Morley Sachar, *The Course of Modern Jewish History* (New York: Dell, 1977); David Rudavsky, *Modern Jewish Religious Movements* (New York: Behrman House, 1979).

well as in cities like Paris, although in other areas they remained as they always have been, a second-class and despised group.

The French Revolution of 1789 brought sweeping changes, as the National Assembly declared all human beings free and equal. Two years later Jews were granted full citizenship, although during the Terror from 1793 to 1794, many Jews died as a result of their association with aristocrats or simply because they were denounced. With the seizure of power by Napoleon Bonaparte in 1799, the situation of Jews greatly improved. Five years later, when he issued his Civic Code, Jews were given the full rights of citizenship. This was extended to Jews living in all the areas of Europe conquered by the French. Napoleon went further in 1806 by convening an Assembly of Jewish Notables to harmonize French-Jewish relations. This was followed in 1807 by a Grand Sanhedrin, a gathering at which rabbis and laymen pledged allegiance to the French state and brought Jewish laws under the umbrella of French civic law. Finally, in 1808, Jewish affairs were regulated by two edicts which set up an organization to oversee the running of synagogues and regulate trade.[17]

Following the defeat of Napoleon at the Battle of Waterloo in 1815, the victorious Allies, at the Congress of Vienna, attempted to raise the status of Jews in the newly created states of continental Europe. Unfortunately, in many places the instructions issued by the congress were ignored and restrictions were reimposed on the Jews. Throughout Europe, nationalism spread as a new ideology, fanned by the impact of the French Revolution and subsequent Napoleonic invasions. Almost without exception these nationalist movements quickly developed anti-Jewish sentiments, which were reinforced by the works of numerous academics. There were anti-Jewish riots in 1819 throughout Europe. By 1830 a more lenient and positive attitude prevailed, but the failure of the reforming Frankfurt Parliament in 1848 led to a worsening of the situation for Jews, who were identified by the authorities with political radicals. Consequently, although the lot of Jews gradually improved in German-speaking countries, it was not until 1869 that the Northern German Federation proclaimed Jewish emancipation. Two years later the Jews were emancipated in all German-speaking areas.[18]

DEVELOPMENTS IN EASTERN EUROPE

The situation of Jews in eastern Europe was far worse because they faced more legal restrictions and open hostility than Jews in the West experienced. In Russia, for instance, Catherine the Great (1729–1796) tolerated Jews, but numerous restrictions remained upon their freedom of movement. Alexander I (1777–1825), after first attempting to expel Jews from many areas, changed his policy to one of integration that encouraged the conversion of Jews to Christianity; his successor, Nicolas I (1796–1855), however, increased pressures on Jews by conscripting young men into the army, where conversion was encouraged. At this time many Jews were deported from their villages and expelled from cities like Kiev. These policies of ethnic cleansing were revised in 1835, when a new set of laws came into effect governing what was known as the Pale of Settlement, an area on the western borders

---

17. Johnson, *History of the Jews*, 305–10.
18. Cohn-Sherbok, *Judaism*, 241–43.

of Russia where Jews were allowed to live. Under the leadership of the Jewish reformer Max Lilienthal (1815–1882), an attempt was made at the Russification of Jews through the introduction of a new school system established in 1844. Then, once again, in 1850 the government reversed its policies, insisting that traditional Jews dress like everyone else. Slowly Jewish emancipation got underway, and Jews entered Russian society by the late nineteenth century.[19]

EMANCIPATION AND REFORM

The emancipation of northern European Jews had its intellectual roots in the Dutch Republic and in the work of authors like Baruch Spinoza (1632–1677), who argued that the essence of religion was an ethical system. Although he was excommunicated by the Jews of Amsterdam, Spinoza's work inspired Jews and non-Jews alike. In Germany, the great Jewish philosopher Moses Mendelssohn (1729–1786) developed Spinoza's ideas and became one of the leading figures of the German Enlightenment and a friend of many German intellectuals in Berlin, the capital city of Prussia.

Among Mendelssohn's colleagues was a German writer and philosopher, Gotthold Ephraim Lessing (1729–1781), whose play *Nathan the Wise* (1779) did much to promote favorable attitudes toward the Jews. Among other things, Mendelssohn sought to modernize Jewish life so that Jews would be fully accepted as citizens in the states where they lived. The poet Goethe (1749–1832) was also widely regarded as a "friend of the Jews," and Jews in return promoted his work, which many genuinely loved.

Photo 16.8 Baruch Spinoza (1632–1677), the first great secularized Jewish philosopher. His work made a major impact on European thought and promoted the idea of religious tolerance.

The belief that Jews ought to modernize, and particularly that eastern European Jews who were immigrating to the west ought to abandon their traditional dress and mannerisms, grew rapidly during this period. In the 1820s a new Jewish journal, *The First Fruits of the Times*, was published in Vienna, arguing for the reform of Judaism. In the German state of Westphalia a Jewish financier, Israel Jacobson (1768–1828), began his own reform program by establishing schools for Jewish children that employed ordinary German teachers for everything except religion. The first of these schools was founded in Seesen, Brunswick, in 1801.

Jacobson also persuaded the local Jews to begin the reform of worship by including hymns, sermonlike addresses, and prayers in the vernacular. Further, the worshipers were allowed to go with their heads uncovered and in most respects behaved like congregants in a typical Protestant Christian church. In 1810, Jacobson financed the first Reform Jewish synagogue, or temple, in Kassel; he later built one in Berlin and another in Hamburg in

19. Cecil Roth, *History of the Jews* (New York: Shocken, 1963), 327–46.

Photo 16.9 The simple but dignified grave of the great Jewish philosopher and Enlightenment thinker Moses Mendelssohn (1729–1786) in Berlin.

1818, as well as supporting other Reform temples in different parts of Germany. Thus the city of Frankfurt-am-Main became the center of the Reform movement in Judaism.

From Frankfurt-am-Main the ideas of Reform Judaism spread to other parts of Europe, and by 1824 they had appeared in North America when a small group of Jews in South Carolina introduced reforms based on Jacobson's practices in Hamburg. These ideas caught on, and an indigenous Reform movement took root in New York and Baltimore. The first conference of American Reform Rabbis took place in Philadelphia in 1869. Four years later the Union of American Hebrew Congregations, the main Reform group in America, was founded. Two years later this group established the Hebrew Union College as a center of Reform scholarship and a place to train its leaders.

Back in Germany other reforming movements quickly developed among German Jews. The most important of these was what became known as Conservative Judaism. This movement gained momentum in 1845 when Zacharias Frankel became the principal of the Jewish theological seminary in Breslau. Criticizing Orthodox and Reform Judaism alike, he helped develop a new form of modernizing Judaism.

In America, people attracted by his ideas founded the Jewish theological seminary in 1887 in New York. Its most influential leader was Solomon Schechter (1847–1915), a Cambridge-educated scholar who sought a compromise between modern scholarship and traditional practices. For him, rituals, traditional customs, and accepted observances were all important in maintaining a Jewish religious and ethnic identity while at the same time integrating socially with the surrounding culture. Many regard Schechter as "the architect of American Conservative Judaism."

In reaction, other scholars like Samson Raphael Hirsch (1808–1888) sought to develop a new, invigorated form of Orthodox Judaism that maintained traditional Jewish beliefs and practices while making practical accommodations to the

Photo 16.10 A print of Moses Mendelssohn himself.

modern world. For him the purpose of life was to serve God in obedience, setting aside questions about personal fulfillment and romanticized spirituality.[20]

JEWISH CONVERSIONS TO CHRISTIANITY

As all these developments were taking place within European and North American Jewish communities, an increasing number of Jews converted to Christianity. These converts included two of Moses Mendelssohn's daughters and most of his grandchildren, one of whom was the famous composer Felix Mendelssohn-Bartholdy (1809–1847), whose oratorio *Paulus* (1836) movingly portrays both the conversion of Paul and his own. Other converts included David Mendel (1789–1850), better known as the church historian Neander, who became something of a legend because of the respect in which his students held him at the University of Berlin. The jurist Friedrich Julius Stahl (1802–1861), who later influenced the Dutch Christian leaders Guillaume Groen van Prinsterer (1801–1876) and Abraham Kuyper (1837–1920), was another of these highly influential Jewish converts.[21]

Photo 16.11 A picture of Moses Mendelssohn's grandson, the great German Jewish-Christian composer Felix Mendelssohn-Bartholdy (1809–1847), whose moving oratorio *Paulus* was inspired by his conversion to Christianity.

The most famous convert of all was Karl Marx (1818–1883), the communist theorist whose works became the basis of Soviet Marxism. Marx's family converted to Christianity when he was a child. Although most of these converts retained a deep respect and love for Judaism, Marx turned against his Jewish heritage with a vengeance when he published *On the Jewish Question* in 1844.[22] In this tract he set the tone for later thinking about Judaism by accusing Jews of being interested only in money and exploitation of workers. While Marx turned against Judaism, others, like the theologian Friedrich Schleiermacher (1768–1834), regretted the conversion of so many Jews to Christianity and attempted to discourage it.

In the Netherlands, on the other hand, the conversion of a number of Jewish intellectuals like Isaac da Costa (1798–1860) and Abraham Capadose (1795–1874) led to a revival of Calvinism and what became known as the Anti-Revolutionary Movement, associated with Abraham Kuyper.

Another prominent Jewish convert of this period was Alfred Edersheim (1825–1889). Born in Vienna, he moved to Hungary, where he was converted by a Scottish engineer. He went to Scotland, studied at the universities of Edinburgh and Berlin, and became a Presbyterian minister and missionary to his fellow Jews. His most famous book is *The*

20. Johnson, *History of the Jews*, 311–421.
21. Surprisingly little has been written on this topic. One of the few recent books on this topic is Deborah Sadie Hertz, *How Jews Became Germans: The History of Conversion and Assimilation in Berlin* (New Haven: Yale Univ. Press, 2007).
22. Karl Marx, *On the Jewish Question*, trans. Helen Lederer (Cincinnati: Hebrew Union College, Jewish Institute of Religion, 1958).

Life and Times of Jesus the Messiah (1883), which, remarkably, is still in print and use today. These conversions, and the success of many converts, created a crisis for European and North American Jews, and many denied that the conversions were genuine. Although many Jews probably did "convert" for social reasons and opportunities for advancement, others, like Neander and Edersheim, were deeply moved by Christian teachings and were therefore genuine converts. Nevertheless, a far greater crisis was looming on the horizon.

THE RISE OF ANTI-SEMITISM

From the 1850s onward a new threat against the Jews and other peoples emerged with the development of what became known as "scientific racism." This enormously successful idea was propagated by the French nobleman Joseph Arthur Comte de Gobineau (1816–1882) in his book *An Essay on the Inequality of the Human Races* (1853–1855). A few years later its basic ideas appeared to be confirmed by the publication of Charles Darwin's *The Origin of the Species* in 1858. As a result, the Jews were now scorned, not because of their religion, but because they were an "Asiatic race" incapable of assimilation into the population of Europe.[23]

Photo 16.12 During the Middle Ages Jews were forced to wear distinctive forms of dress. This practice was reintroduced by the Nazis, who insisted on Jews wearing a yellow star on their normal clothing. Where the Nazis differed from earlier forms of anti-Judaism was in the supposedly "scientific" basis of their judgments. Now religious differences, which could be changed by conversion, were replaced by unchangeable racial differences. Ironically, in 1933 there were only around 650,000 Jews in Germany, yet there were over 1 million Jewish Christians who, even though they often had no connection to Judaism, were considered by the Nazis to be Jews. These people suffered enormously and are often overlooked in standard accounts of the Holocaust.

23. A vast literature exists on the topic of anti-Semitism. For more on the argument presented in this and following sections, see George L. Mosse, *Toward the Final Solution: A History of European Racism* (Madison: Univ. of Wisconsin Press, 1985); Peter G. J. Pulzer, *The Rise of Political Anti-Semitism in Germany and Austria* (New York: Wiley, 1964), esp. 62–63; Paul Lawrence Rose, *German Question/Jewish Question: Revolutionary Antisemitism from Kant to Wagner* (Princeton: Princeton Univ. Press, 1990).

By the end of the nineteenth century, many Jews in Europe and North America were increasingly integrated into the life of the societies in which they lived, and yet they were increasingly seen as strangers. In fact, their very success fueled the new anti-Semitism. The term "anti-Semitism" was coined by the journalist Wilhelm Marr (1819–1904), who was expelled from the Swiss city of Zürich in 1843 for alleged Communist activities. From there he moved to Lausanne, where he became involved with various secret societies that promoted anarchism, atheism, and various other radical causes. Leaving Switzerland, he became a delegate to the Frankfurt Parliament of 1848, where he advocated German unification. After various failed business ventures, including one in Costa Rica, he moved to Hamburg, where he married Johanna Bertha Callenbach, the daughter of wealthy Jewish businessman, in 1854. They were divorced in 1873 and a year later he married another Jewish woman, Helene Sophia Emma Maria Behrend, who tragically died shortly afterward. A year later he married yet another Jewish woman, Jenny Therese Kornick; but in 1877 they too were divorced. Finally, in 1877 he married the daughter of a German dockworker.

Marr's speeches contained anti-Semitic elements from at least 1848, despite his close association with Jews and his numerous Jewish wives. In 1879 he published an anti-Semitic tirade, *The Way to Victory of Germanicism over Judaism*, in which he coined the term "anti-Semitism" and argued that the liberal policy of emancipation had allowed Jews to gain control over German finance and industry. Since the Jews could not be assimilated, he believed this would lead to the destruction of the German people. Therefore, in 1879 he helped found the Anti-Semitic League. Around the same time similar anti-Semitic movements were developing in Austria, particularly Vienna, where conflict between a socialistically inclined city council and local Jewish businessmen centered on the issue of increasing the number of city parks, an action to which the businessmen were opposed. Thus, in both Germany and Austria, anti-Semitic political parties that were closely associated with working class movements came into being.[24]

In France, where emancipation appeared to be working, the Jewish community was shattered by what became known as the Dreyfus affair, in which a French army officer, Alfred Dreyfus, was accused of spying for the Germans and imprisoned under appalling conditions in 1894 on Devil's Island. Eventually Dreyfus was acquitted when it was shown that the evidence against him was forged. Nevertheless, the shock waves created by his trial and unjust treatment caused many Jews to rethink their attitude toward assimilation.[25]

To make matters worse, anti-Semitism became the official policy of the Russian government following the assassination of Alexander II (b. 1818) in 1881. The assassination led to a massive pogrom against the Jewish population of the Ukraine, while over twenty thousand Jews were expelled from Moscow and numerous restrictions placed upon them. Sporadic pogroms continued into the twentieth century.[26]

Apart from appeals to "scientific racism," the prevailing anti-Semitic sentiment of the times was given a sinister twist by the publication of the so-called *Protocols of the Elders of*

---

24. Rose, *German Question/Jewish Question*, 279–95.

25. Pulzer, *Rise of Political Anti-Semitism*, 62–63; Johnson, *History of the Jews*, 379–80; 384–91.

26. Cohn-Sherbok, *Judaism*, 273–75.

Zion (1903), which described in lurid detail a secret Jewish plot to take over the world. This publication, said to be a document obtained from Jews by a member of the Czarist secret police, was quickly discredited as a forgery. Despite this, it had an enormous circulation, influencing writers in Nazi Germany and even people like Henry Ford (1863–1947) in America.[27]

Arguably even more insidious was the the publication of Houston Stewart Chamberlain's *The Foundations of the Nineteenth Century* (1911),[28] which became an instant best seller in both the English- and German-speaking worlds despite its great size and turgid prose. Unlike *Protocols*, *Foundations* was not conspiratorial but rather presented a seemingly ordered and academic theory of history that blended with the findings of scientific racism. Therefore, although many rejected its implications, it had considerable influence.[29]

THE ZIONIST REACTION

Taken together, these events caused many Jews to despair of finding peace in Europe, with the result that many sought to emigrate with the majority going to North America. A small minority, however, traveled to Palestine, which was part of the Turkish Empire, in the hope of establishing a "Jewish Homeland."[30]

The idea of a Jewish homeland was promoted by Leon Pinsker (1821–1891), a Jewish doctor living in Russia who published a German pamphlet titled *The Auto-Emancipation: A Call to Comrades Bound Together by their Common Linguistic Heritage by a Russian Jew* (1882). In this work, he identified the roots of anti-Semitism in the social and historical conditions under which Jews lived in Europe, not in religious prejudice as many thought. "To Europeans the Jew is a cadaver," he wrote, "to natives a foreigner, to farmers a vagrant, to the property owners a beggar, to the poor a rich exploiter, and to the patriot a man without a country. All share a common hatred." Juxtaposing

Photo 16.13 Captain Dreyfus, who was unjustly accused of being a German spy and sent to Devil's Island by a French military court. His only crime was being Jewish.

---

27. Norman Cohn, *Warrant for Genocide: The Myth of the Jewish World Conspiracy and the Protocols of the Elders of Zion* (Harmondsworth, U.K.: Penguin, 1970).

28. Houston Steward Chamberlain, *The Foundations of the Nineteenth Century*, 2 vols. (London: John Lane, 1911).

29. Geoffrey G. Field, *Evangelist of Race: The Germanic Vision of Houston Stewart Chamberlain* (New York: Columbia Univ. Press, 1981).

30. Zionism is a complex and particularly complicated issue. For Jewish accounts of the rise of Zionism, see Arthur Hertzberg, ed., *The Zionist Idea: A Historical Analysis and Reader* (New York: Doubleday, 1959); Nahum N. Glatzer, *Franz Rosenzweig: His Life and Thought* (New York: Schocken, 1961); Steven J. Zipperstein, *Elusive Prophet: Ahad Ha'am and the Origins of Zionism* (Berkeley: Univ. of California Press, 1993); Melvin I. Urofsky, *American Zionism from Herzl to the Holocaust* (Lincoln: Univ. of Nebraska Press, 1995).

Photo 16.14 An early Jewish agricultural settlement in Palestine at the turn of the twentieth century. At that time the area was ruled by the Turks.

anti-Semitism with what he called Judeophobia, Pinsker argued that only a Jewish homeland where Jews could toil on the land and build their own country would fully emancipate Jews.

Eventually, with the aid of prominent European Jews like Baron Edmond James de Rothschild (1845–1934), Pinsker was able to establish what became the Zionist movement. In this project he was aided by various Russian authorities who helped establish the "Society for the Support of Jewish Farmers and Artisans in Syria and Israel." At the same time empathetic Christians, including the German kaiser, encouraged and supported Jewish migration to Palestine in the belief that they were helping fulfill biblical prophecies.[31]

The biggest obstacle to the settlement of Jews in Palestine was that the territory was part of the Turkish Empire and was already populated by Arabs. Therefore, for a while, a number of Zionist leaders, like Theodor Herzl (1860–1904), toyed with the idea of a Jewish settlement in some other part of the world. Herzl also suggested that Jewish financiers and industrialists might be willing to pay the Turkish authorities to compensate Arabs living in Palestine, provided they emigrated to other parts of the Turkish Empire. Unfortunately, none of these schemes that would have allowed an orderly occupation of Palestine without dispossessing the residents came to fruition, because of the outbreak of World War I, in which the Turks were allied with the Germans.[32]

THE HORRORS OF THE TWENTIETH CENTURY

After the outbreak of hostilities in 1914, plans for a Jewish homeland seemed a distant dream. Then, after becoming bogged down on the western front, the British, largely for propaganda reasons, issued the Balfour Declaration of 2 November 1917 in an effort to gain Jewish support for their cause. On the surface it appeared to support Zionist plans for a Jewish nation homeland. Of course, the British were careful to state that nothing

---

31. So-called Christian Zionism played an important role in the development of Jewish Zionism. See Stephen Sizer, *Christian Zionism: Road-map to Armageddon?* (Downers Grove, Ill.: InterVarsity Press, 2004); Donald M. Lewis, *The Origins of Christian Zionism: Lord Shaftesbury and Evangelical Support for a Jewish Homeland* (Cambridge: Cambridge Univ. Press, 2009).

32. Probably the best overall history of Zionism is Walter Laqueur, *A History of Zionism: From the French Revolution to the Establishment of the State of Israel* (New York: MJF Books, 1972).

should be done which would jeopardize the rights of the existing occupants.

Therefore, in reality, the Balfour Declaration said very little and promised even less, as was recognized by many Zionist leaders. Yet it had the desired psychological effect, and many Jews, particularly those living in eastern Europe, who were previously sympathetic toward the Germans changed sides, helping to add to the chaos in the east. Not to be outdone, the Germans smuggled Lenin and a small group of supporters into Russia. The Bolshevik Revolution followed, bringing with it the Treaty of Brest-Litovsk of 3 March 1918, which gave respite to the German armies in the East but failed to prevent their ultimate defeat in the West.[33]

In the meantime, in Germany from 1916 onward, the German kaiser and democratic institutions were sidelined. A military council controlled by General Erich Ludendorff effectively ruled the country. With the collapse of the German army's final offensive in the spring of 1918, Ludendorff handed over power to the civil authorities, who were faced with accepting unfavorable peace terms. This led to the Treaty of Versailles, which was signed on 28 June 1918.[34]

In this situation Ludendorff, by withdrawing from the peace negotiations, allowed opponents of democracy to blame what was definitely a bad treaty on the civilian politicians who were forced to accept it. These events laid the foundation for the claim that the army was stabbed in the back and that Germany had not lost the war but was betrayed by its own people, mainly moderate politicians and Jews. As Lord Keynes predicted, the scene was now set for another war.[35]

Photo 16.15 The grave of General Erich Ludendorff described by his son-in-law as "self-consciously pagan." It was designed to show his rejection of "Jewish-Christian imperialism."

Following the war, the situation in Germany was grim. As a result of the British naval blockade, starvation began around 1916 and continued to at least 1922. The official estimate of the number of Germans who died of starvation between 1916 and 1918 was 763,000; how many more died before the blockade was lifted in the summer of 1919 is unknown, as is the number who died of starvation in the next few years.[36] What is certain

---

33. For a discussion of this, see Vejas G. Liulevicius, *War Land on the Eastern Front: Culture, National Identity and German Occupation in World War I* (Cambridge: Cambridge Univ. Press, 2000).

34. A good introduction to this topic is Niall Ferguson, *The Pity of War* (New York: Basic Books, 1999).

35. John Maynard Keynes, *The Economic Consequences of the Peace* (New York: Harcourt, Brace and Howe, 1920).

36. For a discussion of this little-known episode in World War I, see C. Paul Vincent, *The Politics of Hunger: The Allied Blockade of Germany, 1915–1919* (Athens: Ohio Univ. Press, 1985), 145.

is that the experience of starvation on such a scale radicalized many young Germans, who later became fanatical supporters of Hitler.

The much-vaunted Weimar Republic was a political disaster, in which rival street gangs, like the reactionary Freikorps and pro-Communist Red Guards, fought for mastery. On 26 August 1921, the Catholic Center Party leader, Matthias Erzberger (1875–1921), was assassinated; his able colleague, Jewish politician Walther Rathenau, was assassinated on 24 June 1922.[37]

Now the government was incapable of preventing the violence because of restrictions on the size of the German army imposed by the Treaty of Versailles, which left the army and the police outgunned by militants. At the same time, inflation destroyed the wealth of the German middle class. Things were slowly improving in the late 1920s when the Great Depression of 1929 led to mass unemployment, with one out of three men lacking work. In this situation a number of prominent German Jews, such as Hugo Preuss (1860–1925) and Walther Rathenau (1867–1922), played an important role at the national level, while men like the Berlin city councillor, jurist, and historian Erich Eyck worked at the local level. All strove to restore stability and order to the economy, with the aim of preserving the best in German culture.[38]

Capitalizing on the economic chaos and loss of the war, Nazi Party propagandists blamed "the Jews" for the government's failure. Yet, despite Nazi propaganda, most members of the various Weimar governments were Catholics, not Jews.

Eventually, in the face of economic crisis and social turmoil, a coalition government, in which the National Socialists had the largest number of parliamentary seats but

Photo 16.16 The grim entrance to Sachsenhausen concentration camp outside Berlin. Here the Nazis imprisoned their political opponents. Long before they embarked on the Holocaust, a regime of terror cowed their critics, thus diverting attention from their ultimate goal of destroying the Jews. In this camp Pastor Martin Niemöller was held in solitary confinement from 1938 on at Hitler's pleasure. Like all the concentration camps in Germany, Sachsenhausen was a transit and detention camp, not a death camp, even though many people died there. Death camps proper were established in Poland and other areas beyond Germany's borders.

---

37. Traditionally historians and other writers, following Erich Eyck's *A History of the Weimar Republic* (Cambridge, Mass.: Harvard Univ. Press, 1962), have praised the achievements of the Weimar Republic and overlooked its failures. More recently Weimar's weaknesses have gained attention. Cf. Michael Burleigh, *The Third Reich: A New History* (London: Pan Books, 2000), 27–145; Richard J. Evans, *The Coming of the Third Reich* (New York, Penguin Press, 2004), 78–153.

38. Through conversations with Erich Eyck's son, the historian Frank Eyck, I acquired a better understanding of this period.

remained a minority in terms of the popular vote, came to power, with Adolf Hitler as chancellor. The burning of the Reichstag, or German parliament, in Berlin on 27 February 1933 gave Hitler the chance he needed to stage what was in effect a coup, made possible by the fact that National Socialists were in charge of the ministries controlling police and army. From then on, pressure mounted on the German Jewish community. Nevertheless, many Jews remained in Germany, believing that the Nazis were a passing phenomenon. By the time it became clear they were not, it was too late to leave, because many countries had closed their doors to Jewish immigration, while the Nazis made it impossible for people to leave.[39]

National Socialist policy and theories about the Jews were inconsistent. Some National Socialist professors—and, sadly, the universities were the first institutions in Germany to fall to the National Socialists—defined race in terms of biology; others saw race more in cultural terms. Even the chief Nazi ideologue, Alfred Rosenberg (1893–1946), is unclear about this issue in his seminal work, *Myth of the Twentieth Century* (1930).[40] Initially, it seems, most Nazis simply wanted to remove Jews from German life. Therefore, they were quite happy to see their emigration and saw the ultimate solution in the Jews moving either to eastern Europe, where many Germans believed the Jews came from, or to Palestine. After the outbreak of World War II, the situation became more desperate and radical ideas came to dominate Nazi thinking.[41]

On the eastern front many occupied peoples initially welcomed the German army, which was seen as a liberating force freeing them from Communist rule. This situation changed rapidly as SS and special police units moved into occupied areas. These groups began rounding up Jews, Socialists, Communists, and anyone suspected of sympathizing with them. The Jews, along with the Socialists and Communists, were either sent to concentration camps or herded into ghettos.[42]

Soon mass killings began, on the pretext of executing partisans and their sympathizers. Special police units known as *Einsatzguppen*, supervised by Reinhardt Heydrich (1904–1942), began by executing Jews, shooting them and burying them in mass graves. It soon became clear, however, that this policy was not working very well. Members of killing squads, nauseated by their own actions, turned to alcohol for relief to such an extent that, by early in the morning, most members of such squads were drunk. Clearly, another

39. See William D. Rubinstein, *The Myth of Rescue: Why the Democracies Could Not Have Saved More Jews from the Nazis* (London: Routledge, 1997).

40. Alfred Rosenberg, *Des Mythus des 20. Jahrhunderts* (Munich: Hoheneichen Verlag, 1930). Although it is often said that this book is unavailable in English, it was translated by James B. Whisker and published by the Noontide Press, Torrance, California, in 1982. It is also widely available in electronic format on the internet. The main value of this book is that it demonstrates beyond all doubt the fanatical irrationality of Nazi beliefs and their similarity to many esoteric beliefs today. For a discussion of Nazi ideology, see Karla Poewe, *New Religions and the Nazis* (London: Routledge, 2006); Irving Hexham, "Inventing 'Paganists': A Close Reading of Richard Steigmann-Gall's *The Holy Reich*," *Journal of Contemporary History* 42, no. 1 (2007): 59–78.

41. Christopher R. Browning, *The Origins of the Final Solution: The Evolution of Nazi Jewish Policy, September 1939–March 1942* (London: Arrow, 2004).

42. Burleigh, *The Third Reich*, 499–500.

solution was needed before the killing groups were totally demoralized and the will of the army undermined. This solution was the death camp, initiated after over a million Jews had been killed by the death squads.[43]

Nazi death camps should not be confused with concentration camps, which the Nazis established in Germany after seizing power in 1933. Concentration camps were initially used to punish the political enemies of National Socialism, regardless of race. Later, during the conquests of eastern Europe, more concentrations camps were created for industrial and armaments production based on slave labor. Although the people in them were treated appallingly, with the result that they were often worked to death, these camps were not death camps as such.

The construction of the real death camps began in 1942, when Adolf Eichmann (1906–1962) began the gassing of Jews in Poland. Eventually camps associated with Auschwitz became the main centers for Jewish extermination. In all, around 6 million Jews perished during what later became known as the Holocaust, totally decimating the Jewish population of Europe, which was estimated at around 9 million before the outbreak of war.[44]

THE BIRTH OF THE NATION OF ISRAEL

The impact of the Holocaust directly led to the foundation of the state of Israel in 1948.

Traumatized Jews fleeing Europe after the war sought refuge in Palestine, but neither the British authorities, who held a League of Nations Mandate over the terri-

Photo 16.17 Budapest's moving and strangely beautiful Holocaust memorial, which stands as a living testimony to a once great community destroyed by the Nazis.

43. The best account of the impact of such killings is Christopher R. Browning's *Ordinary Men: Reserve Police Battalion 101 and the Final Solution in Poland* (New York: HarperCollins, 1993).

44. A lot of confusion exists about the Holocaust. For example, it is popularly believed that 6 million German Jews died in gas chambers as a result of Nazi persecution. This belief allows Holocaust deniers to point out that at most there were around 500,000 Jews in Germany. Actually, the figure of 6 million Jews is for European Jews seized from all over the continent by the Nazis and their allies. Further, many of these deaths were caused by firing squad and other means, not by gas chambers. For a good discussion of these issues, see Leni Yahil, *The Holocaust: The Fate of European Jewry, 1932–1945*, trans. Ina Friedman and Haya Galai (Oxford: Oxford Univ. Press, 1987); Martin Gilbert, *The Holocaust: The Jewish Tragedy* (London: Fontana-Collins, 1986); Yehuda Bauer, *Rethinking the Holocaust* (New Haven: Yale Univ. Press, 2001).

tory, nor local Arabs, the majority of whom were Christians, welcomed massive Jewish immigration. At first the British cracked down on Jewish activists and tried to prevent further immigration. Eventually, on 14 February 1946, the British handed over the problem to the newly founded United Nations, which on 29 November 1947 endorsed a plan for the partition of Palestine between Arabs and Jews. This led to Arab attacks on Jewish settlements and Jewish countermeasures, in which over a thousand Jews and many Arabs were killed. On 14 May 1948, David Ben-Gurion (1886–1973) read a declaration of independence, and a Jewish government was formed. War broke out between the Jewish settlers, local Arabs, and surrounding Arab countries. Eventually, with no clear victory, an armistice was signed on 12 January 1949. By that time around a million Arabs had been displaced from their lands. Thus the armistice sowed the seeds of the conflicts which continue to this day.[45]

Probably the most important event in Jewish history after founding the state of Israel in 1948 was the Six-Day War of 1967, when Israel defeated the combined armies of Egypt, Syria, and Jordan. This war led to major and long-lasting outcomes. On the one hand it galvanized religious Jews, particularly the Orthodox, into supporting the state of Israel, which until then was regarded by many Jews with suspicion. On the other hand it led Arab states to convene a conference to consider why God had apparently deserted them. The outcome was the recommitment of Arab nations, particularly Saudi Arabia, to use their growing oil wealth to further the cause of Islam.

Today we continue to live in the aftermath of these momentous events. The significance of all of this is brought home by the observation of Jacob Neusner that following the Six-Day War, Orthodox Jews, and Jews generally, abandoned the tradition, which had served them well almost two thousand years, of avoiding apoplectic movements and messianic dreams. These ideas, the rabbis taught, invariably lead to disaster and social chaos. Therefore, they instituted study of the Torah at the heart of Judaism and left the restoration of the Jews to the Holy Land in the hands of God. In 1967 this caution evaporated. Instead of seeing dreams for the restoration of Palestine to the people of Israel and the dreams of the Zionist leaders as aberrant, the rabbis embraced what they had previously viewed as political folly.[46]

Where this will end and what it means for the world and the Jewish people is anyone's guess. All we can say with certainty is that it has unleashed a new era of messianic hopes, for the end of the world as we know it and the establishment of a new religious order, among Jews, Christians, and Muslims, each with their own agenda and vision of the future.

---

45. For a discussion of this heated topic, see Chaim Herzog, *The Arab-Israeli Wars: War and Peace in the Middle East* (New York: Methuen, 1982); and Ahron Bregman, *Israel's Wars: A History Since 1947* (London: Routledge, 2002).

46. Jacob Neusner, *The Way of Torah: An Introduction to Judaism*, 3rd ed. (North Scituate, Mass.: Duxbury, 1979), 19. This book is now in its 6th edition.

CHAPTER 17

JEWISH FAITH AND PRACTICE

JEWISH PHILOSOPHY

From at least the time of the Hellenized Jewish scholar Philo (20 BC–AD 50), who lived in the Greek city of Alexandria, Jews have taken a close interest in philosophy. Probably the most famous of all Jewish philosophers was Moses Maimonides (1135–1204), who was one of the great medieval exponents of Aristotle. Written in Spain, his *Guide for the Perplexed* took the form of a three-volume letter to one of his students. It is one of the great classics of medieval thought.

As a good Aristotelian, Maimonides argued that God was incorporeal, that is, purely spirit, and that his existence could be known by following Aristotelian logic. Maimonides advocated the doctrine of the resurrection, but was skeptical about the meaning of things like prophecy. Above all, however, he sought to preserve Torah and defend it against all criticism. In 1230 a bitter dispute broke out between his followers and other Jews opposing his teachings, but eventually his thought provided the basis for one of the dominant traditions in Judaism.

Apart from providing an Aristotelian interpretation of Jewish faith and practice, Maimonides also sought to provide Jews with a creed, which he wrote in poetic form. As translated, it contains the following thirteen points:

1. Belief in the existence of the Creator, be He Blessed, who is perfect in every manner of existence and is the Primary Cause of all that exists.
2. The belief in God's absolute and unparalleled unity.
3. The belief in God's noncorporeality, nor that He will be affected by any physical occurrences, such as movement, or rest, or dwelling.
4. The belief in God's eternity.
5. The imperative to worship Him exclusively and no foreign false gods.
6. The belief that God communicates with man through prophecy.
7. The belief that the prophecy of Moses our teacher has priority.
8. The belief in the divine origin of the Torah.
9. The belief in the immutability of the Torah.
10. The belief in divine omniscience and providence.
11. The belief in divine reward and retribution.
12. The belief in the arrival of the Messiah and the messianic era.

13. The belief in the resurrection of the dead.[1]

After his death, Maimonides' Creed came under attack from other Jewish scholars who argued that Judaism ought not embrace a creed. These critics claimed that by creating a creed, Maimonides was making far too many concessions to Christians and Muslims and that Judaism was a way of life rather than an abstract expression of belief. Despite the rejection of his creed by many Jews both then and now, it is a remarkable fact that, as Leo Trepp points out, Jewish resistance fighters, who became twentieth-century martyrs in the Warsaw Ghetto, went to their deaths singing Maimonides' affirmation of faith.[2]

Photo 17.1 A page from a medieval manuscript of Maimonides' writings.

Apart from Maimonides, medieval and modern Judaism has produced many articulate philosophers. By far the most famous of these within the Jewish tradition was Moses Mendelssohn (1729–1786). His importance within Judaism can be summed up in the saying "From Moses, to Moses, there is none like Moses." The meaning of this is that Moses of the Bible, Moses Maimonides, and Moses Mendelssohn form a continuous Jewish intellectual and practical tradition.

Like his predecessors, Moses Mendelssohn's aim was to equip Jews to compete intellectually with their contemporaries. Just as Maimonides adapted Aristotle to the Jewish cause, so too Moses Mendelssohn took the best in modern Western scholarship of his time, particularly German scholarship, and used it to defend Judaism. In doing so he created what the philosopher Immanuel Kant (1724–1804) might well have called an Enlightening Judaism. This tradition continues to the present and was represented in the twentieth century by such figures as Martin Buber (1878–1965).[3]

JEWISH MYSTICISM

Although Jewish mystical movements clearly existed around the time of Christ, particularly in cities like Alexandria, where Neoplatonism flourished, it is not until the European Middle Ages that we can form a clear idea about Jewish mystical movements. Despite

1. Rabbi Shmuel Boteach, *The Wolf Shall Lie with the Lamb* (Montvale, N.J.: Jason Aronson, 1993). Found on J. B. Hare's *Sacred Text Archive* CD, version 5, available from *Internet Sacred Text Archive*, P.O. Box 7429, Santa Cruz, CA 95061–7429, USA, or sales@sacred-texts.com. Also found on the internet under Judaism on the website http://www.sacred-text.com.
2. Leo Trepp, *Judaism: Development and Life* (Belmont, Calif.: Wadsworth, 1982), 62–64.
3. Ibid., 94–95; Dan Cohn-Sherbok, *Judaism: History, Belief and Practice* (London: Routledge, 2003), 253–54.

continuous speculation in popular books about the Essenes and other early Jewish groups, scholars are divided on the question of what we know; and the truth seems to be that we actually know very little about them.

The situation changes with the development of medieval mysticism, which grew out of earlier speculation among the rabbis that was based upon the study of biblical texts. In particular, the books of Genesis and Ezekiel provided a rich repository of symbols and imagery for mystical thinkers. Ezekiel's chariot was believed to give insight into the divine nature of God by enabling mystics to enter the spiritual realm through practices that brought on ecstasy, visions, and out-of-the-body experiences. These early movements flourished between the seventh and eleventh centuries and were based on rigid ascetic practices involving fasting, ritual purity, and magical chants.

Alongside speculation about God, numerous mystical ideas about the nature of creation were developed. Most of these ideas originated with the second-century text titled *Sefer Yetsirah*, or *Book of Creation*, which taught that God created the universe following thirty-two mystical pathways that were cosmically bound to the twenty-two letters of the Hebrew alphabet and ten emanations from God himself. The alphabet was further divided into various classes of letters, and links were made to the symbolic nature of the basic elements, fire, water, and air, as well as the various parts of the human body. Added to these notions was speculation about divine emanation which originated philosophically in the teachings of Plato and contributed to what medievals called the "Great Chain of Being." These emanations, linked to the idea of plenitude, or the fullness of creation, were known as the *sefirot*.

As the Middle Ages progressed, more complex systems of mystical thought developed, incorporating ideas found in Talmud together with early mystical texts like the *Book of Creation*. The rabbis who promoted these views saw themselves as members of a secret tradition that was embedded within the chain of being. In this view, life as well as the creation itself was involved in a cosmic struggle for salvation and freedom from evil. Thus the goal of the mystics was to redeem the cosmos as well as themselves. The final act of this great drama would take place with the establishment of the messianic kingdom.

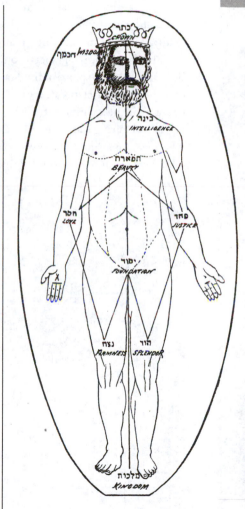

Photo 17.2 Medieval Jewish mystical diagram illustrating the *sefirot*, or divine attributes.

The three main centers of Jewish mysticism in the Middle Ages were Germany, southern France, and Spain. By the ninth century, mystical schools were established in the Rhineland, where they flourished until at least the thirteenth century. Among the German mystics were Isaac ben Kalonymus He-Hasid (d. 1126) of Speyer and his grandson, Judah ben Samuel He-Hasid (1150–1217) of Regensburg. Judah is best remembered for his mystical treatise the *Book of the Pious*. His student, Eliezer of Worms (1176–1238), wrote the popular treatise *The Secret of Secrets*.

These German mystics were captivated by the nature of God and believed it was beyond human reasoning. Therefore, anthropomorphisms and scriptural accounts of God needed to be interpreted as representations of divine truths hidden to ordinary men. The mystics followed a quest whose goal was the vision of God's glory. In this task they believed pious living and ethical behavior, humility, and altruism would lead to spiritual enlightenment based upon a profound sense of God's glory that permeates the universe. The highest honor of all was martyrdom, which many actually suffered.

The theological and social community which these mystical scholars created developed the concept of the pious individual, or *Hasid*, as a role model. Such people were recognized by other Jews, not because of their scholarship or rabbinic skills in argumentation, but because of the quality of their lives. They were seen as people who would overcome the world by bearing the taunts and jibes of hostile nonbelievers. They were also seen as people who developed magical powers based upon their knowledge of the secret names of God, who gave them supernatural abilities.

Both their magical and their mystical powers were usually associated with numerology, or the manipulation of numbers. Hence they interpreted prayers, hymns, readings, and other sacred acts in terms of their numerical values based upon the Hebrew alphabet. They thought that, by finding links between letters and words of equal or varying values and making the correct calculations, they could interpret and control the powers of the universe.

As German-based Jewish mysticism grew, another group of Jewish mystics also flourished in southern France. In the

Photo 17.3 Christian and Jewish scholars disputing the meaning of Scripture during the Middle Ages. Despite periodic outbreaks of persecution by the rabble, Jewish and Christian scholars and religious leaders had remarkably good relationships during most of the medieval period.

twelfth century these people produced the first kabbalistic text, known as the *Bahir*, which interpreted the *Book of Creation* as showing that words constituted the essence of the divine. Among the members of this community, Isaac the Blind (1160–1235) was an outstanding example of someone who incorporated Neoplatonic ideas into his mystical experiences. Later mystics, developing his ideas, replaced the concept of the divine thought with a concept of the divine will, as different mystical schools grew from a common tradition.

Since many of these ideas originated in the third center of medieval Jewish life, Muslim Spain, scholars have seen in them the influence of Islam and movements like Sufism. One of the most important of these kabbalists was Isaac the Blind's pupil, Azriel ben Menaham (1160–1238), who lived in the Spanish town of Girona, close to Barcelona. He played a particularly important role in the history of Judaism by reconciling kabbalistic mysticism with rabbinic traditions. As a result of his work, kabbalah became acceptable in rabbinic circles, which until that time had regarded it with skepticism. In particular, he argued that the divine will, not word or intellect, was the first emanation of the divine being. The significance of this is that an act, rather than thought, became the first manifestation of God.

The nineteenth-century Danish Christian thinker Søren Kierkegaard (1813–1855) developed ideas about God that are somewhat similar. He stressed that the God of Abraham is not the God of the philosophers and that existence precedes essence. Significantly, while Kierkegaard sought to separate his thought from that of philosophers, Jewish kabbalists generally upheld Neoplatonic and Aristotelian philosophies. In a similar way, Abraham ben Samuel Abulafi (1240–1271) combined mystical teachings with an admiration for the philosophy of Maimonides.[4]

Photo 17.4 The medieval Sarajevo manuscript depicting Rabbi Gamaliel instructing his students.

As these mystical schools grew, the idea developed that God himself is beyond human comprehension. Therefore, the mystics developed the concept of the Divine Infinite to express the absolute perfection of God. These ideas found expression in the mystical work *The Zohar*, which appeared in Spain in the thirteenth century. Promoted as a revelation given to Rabbi Simeon ben Yohai and his disciples in the second century, it became immensely popular and was eventually accepted as

---

4. Cohn-Sherbok, *Judaism*, 194–208; Trepp, *Judaism*, 60–89.

a major text by the disastrous millenarian group known as the Sabbatatean movement, led by Sabbatai Zevi (1626–1676). Many Jewish communities were demoralized after their leader, Zevi, converted to Islam. As a result, the very core of Jewish mysticism appeared threatened. At the same time, the Polish Jewish community was demoralized as a result of massacres and continued harassment. In this situation the Hasidic movement arose with a message of personal piety and salvation.[5]

The founder of Hasidism was Israel ben Eliezer (1700–1760), who acquired the name Baal Shem Tov. Hasidic traditions say that he was born in Poland and as a young man traveled to the Carpathian Mountains, where he acquired spiritual wisdom. In the 1730s he began a tour of various Jewish communities, where, it was said, he performed miracles, and where he certainly recruited disciples. After his death, the movement spread throughout Poland, the Ukraine, and Lithuania. Over the years it encountered growing opposition from the rabbinate, which, in Vilnius, excommunicated its members, who were seen as antinomians, showing a lack of respect for the observance of rabbinic customs and the Torah. So bitter was this dispute that the rabbis of Vilnius appealed to the Russian government, which ruled Lithuania at that time, to intervene. Consequently, various Hasidic leaders were arrested and imprisoned. Eventually, however, the persistence of the movement led to its recognition by both Jewish and secular authorities in eastern Europe.

Photo 17.5 For most Jews, as for many Christians, penance has traditionally been an important religious act. In the above print, Jewish followers of the false messiah Sabbatai Zevi (1626–1676) do penance after learning about his conversion to Islam.

Kabbalistic mystical teachings were often accompanied by severe ascetic practices, which the Hasidic movement opposed. Instead they emphasized the need to cling to God in prayer and developed their ideas on the basis of the omnipresence of God, whose divine light permeates creation. Each human, they taught, contained a divine spark that needed to be released to achieve inner bliss. The activities of daily life were also seen as a medium for communication with the divine, turning them into religious acts.

Hasidism made two major innovations within the Jewish tradition. First, it was intensely democratic in the sense that it allowed ordinary people to achieve religious ecstasy. To this end it embraced joyful worship, singing, and dancing as liturgical acts in anticipation of the messianic kingdom. Second, it introduced into the Jewish tradition a new form of leadership, the *rebbe*, a charismatic figure very different from the traditional rabbi. Within Hasidism the rebbe was a superior spiritual being who gained his authority from spiritual experiences.

Within a Hasidic community the rebbe assumed authoritarian powers because the community believed he could work miracles and communicate with the divine in ways that went far beyond the abilities of ordinary mortals. As a result, much of the literature produced by Hasidism concerns the lives of various leaders who, on the basis of their charismatic authority and miraculous powers, were able to develop new customs, doctrines, and practices. The movement also developed the practice of pilgrimage to the graves of famous rebbes, and in doing so gave the movement a dynamic sense of community.

To a large extent the Hasidic movement was looked down upon by educated Jews during the period of emancipation from the mid-eighteenth to the late nineteenth centuries. Putting it bluntly, Polish and other east European Jews who formed the core of a Hasidism were seen as an embarrassment by the sophisticated Ashkenazy Jews of German-speaking lands. There, the reading of Goethe and participation in modern society left no room for magic. Not until the twentieth century, largely as a result of the writings of Martin Buber, did Hasidism come into its own as a religious movement compatible with the modern world.[6]

KEY IDEAS OF JUDAISM

Although many writers, particularly biblical critics, like to find parallels between the religion of the ancient Jews and the religions of the surrounding peoples of the ancient Near East, the differences are far more important. The relationship between God and man found in the Hebrew Bible and that relationship as portrayed in the traditions of other Near Eastern peoples are quite separate. Although many try to blunt the edges of these differences, the God of the Old Testament is quite distinct from the gods of Egypt, Mesopotamia, ancient India, Greece, or even northern Europe. An infinite gulf exists between the God of Israel and his creation. Israel's God did not fashion preexistent material, nor did he fight with rival gods, demigods, evil spirits, or other spiritual beings in the struggle to bring the universe

Photo 17.6 For orthodox Jews, ritual observances are an important feature of religious life. In this nineteenth-century photograph, a young Jewish man wears the *tallit*, or prayer shawl, over his head. On its corners are four knotted tassels to remind the wearer of the laws of the Torah. On his head and bound by leather straps to his body and arm is a tefillin, containing the words of Scripture. The idea behind this complex prayer ritual is that the Scriptures must bind the heart through the obedience of the mind.

6. Ibid., 233–37, 333.

into being. He created it, by his word, out of nothing. Thus God is the supreme creator and sovereign to whom all things owe their existence.

We cannot see God, and we cannot turn him into an object, for this is the root of all idolatry. It is God who speaks and humans who receive his revelation. The relationship between humans and God is the essence of biblical religion. What this means is that we are not dealing with a metaphysical religion which speculates about the nature of God. Rather, as Martin Buber put it, we are dealing with an "I and thou" relationship.[7]

This revolutionary idea of God, which is concerned with ethical and personal relationships rather than metaphysical and ontological issues, has an equally revolutionary impact on our understanding of humanity. According to the Bible, all people are descended from a common ancestor, which means all humans share a common heritage and are in a certain sense equal.

The significance of this can be seen by comparing the Hebrew Bible with the ancient document known as the Code of Hammurabi, compiled by Hammurabi, the king of Babylon, sometime around 1700 BC. This law code was discovered during excavations at Susa in southern Iran in the winter of 1901–1902 by French archaeologists. It appears that it was taken there as booty in the twelfth century BC. From there it was taken to the Louvre in Paris. Although it is not the earliest known law code, it is the most comprehensive and by far the best preserved other than those of the Bible.

In a prologue to the code itself, various practical matters are dealt with, such as the appointment of judges, the role of witnesses, accusations, and various matters dealing with the social system. The central portion of the code provides a systematic account of the law as applied at that time. When this code was first discovered, numerous comparisons were made with the law of Moses. As might be expected, the two are similar in many ways. Nevertheless, there are significant differences.

The Code of Hammurabi is based on two key concepts. First there is the notion that criminal justice consists of precise retribution based upon retaliation. Second, it is fundamental to this body of statutes that the law is a respecter of persons. This means that different standards need to be applied according to the social status of individuals. Consequently, in this leg-

Photo 17.7 The Code of Hammurabi, discovered at Tell Arnamia. Such stones were very important in ancient Israel and in many ways provide a basis for the later development of Jewish law.

---

7. Martin Buber, *I and Thou*, trans. Ronald Gregor Smith (Edinburgh: T and T Clark, 1931). Originally published as *Ich und Du* (Berlin: Schocken Verlag, 1922).

islation human beings are treated as objects, not as individuals. This is where the law of Moses deviates significantly from the Code of Hammurabi.

According to Hammurabi's Code, there are three classes, or castes, of people: aristocrats, commoners, and slaves. Each is governed by unique laws, and each merits a different form of punishment for any given crime. Further, each group is subdivided. For example, the sons and daughters of the nobility get treated differently from established members of the same class.

For example, if a man breaks the arm of his slave, or causes him to lose an eye, there is no penalty. Should he do the same thing to the slave of another man who is of his own social rank, he must compensate the other man in the amount of half the value of the slave. If the slave runs away from his or her master and takes refuge in another person's house, or is helped by another person to escape from the city, then the entire household of the person who aided the slave must be put to death.

Hammurabi's Code also regards a man's children as property and not individuals. Hence, if for some reason a man strikes the daughter of another man and she dies, the daughter of the man who caused injury must also be put to death. The fact that the perpetrator's daughter had nothing to do with the death of the other person is totally disregarded. What is important is that a person is punished in terms of loss of property equivalent to the loss they cause. In this case the daughter is seen as property. Similarly, if a builder builds a house and part of it collapses, causing the death of the son of the owner, then a son of the builder must be put to death. Once again, the son is regarded as property and not a person.

The law of Moses takes a very different approach. Exodus 21 provides an example of a totally different approach. A man who harms a slave, even if only damaging his tooth, must let the slave go free. The principle at work here is that the slave is a human being who has rights, regardless of his social status. Similarly, Deuteronomy 23:15−16 state quite clearly that if a slave escapes from his master and seeks refuge with another person, that person must protect him and give him refuge. Nowhere in the Mosaic law is there anything like the requirement that a man's children be punished for his deeds. Rather, each person is responsible for their own actions.

A superficial reading of Exodus 21:23−25 might lead one to think that the law of Moses is essentially similar to that of Hammurabi, because here it is stated quite clearly, "But if there is serious injury, you are to take life for life, eye for eye, tooth for tooth, hand for hand, foot for foot, burn for burn, wound for wound, bruise for bruise." The reason why this is different from the Code of Hammurabi is that in context, it is clearly not meant to be taken literally. Rather, it lays down a principle to be used as the basis for compensation. Each of these injuries is given a value to avoid applying the punishment literally. In other words, payment in terms of cattle, service, or money replaces brute vengeance on the principle of retaliation. Thus the passage is intended to be used, not to enact revenge, but as the basis for arriving at just compensation.

Another great principle of Jewish thinking is that no human being is equal to God. Thus, no human ought to be worshiped. This prohibition of idolatry, particularly the worship of either living or recently dead persons, is very significant. In China, India, the ancient Near East,

Photo 17.8 Family law always played an important role in Judaism. In the above print, Jewish lawyers argue the pros and cons of a divorce case at a time when divorce was virtually impossible among Christians.

and throughout the Mediterranean world and in northern Europe great men were frequently given divine or semi-divine status. Thus the dividing line between men and God was blurred. No such development took place in ancient Israel, even though according to the Bible the common people often lapsed into idolatry.

Deeply ingrained in the Jewish psyche is the belief that no human is more divine than any other. What interested the Jews was not Moses or any of the prophets, but rather their message. Thus God in his sovereign majesty dominated Jewish thought. The Jews did develop a concept of themselves as belonging to the eternal Israel and as therefore set apart from other peoples. Yet this is very different from the deification of a person.

Finally, it needs to be noted that many people, including a large number of modern Jews, believe that Judaism does not proclaim an afterlife. According to these people it is a purely this-worldly religion. Yet, as Eliezer Segal points out, this belief represents a complete misunderstanding of the Jewish tradition and Jewish sacred literature. From at least the second century BC the Jewish people and their leaders firmly embraced belief in an afterlife and God's judgment.[8]

JEWISH PIETY: THE JEWISH CALENDAR

According to Jewish teaching, the creation took place 3760 years before the birth of Christ, or, as most Jews would say, before the Common Era. Therefore, to know which Jewish year it is, all you have to do is add this figure to whatever date you have at a given time. For example, the year 2000 in the Jewish calendar was the year 5760, while the year 2008 is the Jewish year 5768.

Since the Jewish calendar uses a combination of the lunar and solar calendars, Jewish months vary in length between 29 and 30 days. To harmonize the calendar with the rotation of Earth around the sun, the Jewish calendar works on a 19-year rotation, with 12 years of 12 months and 7 years of 13 months. These monthly leap years are the 11th, 14th, 17th, and 19th

---

8. Several books give a good overview of Judaism. Jacob Neusner's *The Way of Torah: An Introduction to Judaism*, 6th ed. (Belmont, Calif.: Wadsworth, 1997) is a standard text, as is Michael A. Fishbane's *Judaism* (San Francisco: HarperSanFrancisco, 1987). An excellent recent work is Eliezer Segal, *Introducing Judaism* (London: Routledge, 2009).

years. Consequently, there is no relationship between the Jewish months and the secular Western ones. The Jewish months and their secular equivalents are as follows:

Tishrei	September–October
Cheshvan	October–November
Kislev	November–December
Tevet	December–January
Shevat	January–February
Adar	February–March
Nisan	March–April
Tyar	April–May
Sivan	May–June
Tammuz	June–July
Av	July–August
Elul	August–September

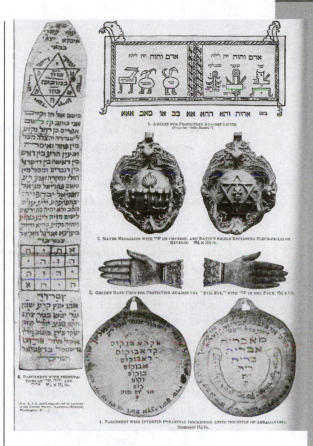

Although Jewish holidays are regular within the Jewish calendar, they vary quite considerably in terms of the secular Western calendar. Similarly, because the Jewish day begins at sunset, it is reckoned quite differently than the normal secular way of counting a day.[9]

Photo 17.9 Despite an insistence on ritual purity and devotion to the one God, magical practices, often related to specific days, crept into popular Judaism. Among these was the common use of amulets to ward off evil. The pictures above show a collection of such magical devices.

JEWISH HOLY DAYS

As with all the major world religions, Jews have their own cycle of religious festivals and holidays. These begin with Rosh Hashanah, on the first day of the month of Tishrei. It commemorates the creation of the world and the opening of the book of life by God. This is a communal holiday, celebrated in the synagogue, unlike most other Jewish holidays,

---

9. A good discussion of Jewish piety and the issues discussed in this and the following sections is found in Stephen J. Einstein and Lydia Kukoff, *Every Person's Guide to Judaism* (New York: UAHC Press, 1989). Similarly, Eliezer Segal's various popular writings on Judaism are an excellent introduction to popular Judaism and religious practices. They include *Why Didn't I Learn This in Hebrew School? Excursions through the Jewish Past and Present* (Northvale, N.J.: Jason Aronson, 1999); *Holidays, History, and Halakhah* (Northvale, N.J.: Jason Aronson, 2000); *Ask Now of the Days That Are Past* (Calgary: Univ. of Calgary Press, 2005).

which are essentially family based. It also marks the Jewish New Year and a ten-day cycle known as the days of awe, when practicing Jews engage in self-examination and reflection.

This ten-day cycle is followed by Yom Kippur, or the Day of Atonement, when Jews come to terms with themselves and make peace with any they have wronged. They are expected to fast and pray, asking God for forgiveness. This is the holiest and most solemn day in the Jewish year.

By contrast, Hanukkah, which has become a sort of Jewish Christmas in North America, is a time of joy and blessing. It is symbolized by the eight-branch menorah, or candlestick, which holds nine candles, four on each side and one in the center. This is a celebration of light in remembrance of a miracle that Jews believe occurred at the time of the Jewish revolt against Syrian domination. According to legend, the Maccabees relit the sacred lamp in the temple which had been extinguished in an attempt to suppress Judaism. When they did so, they had only enough oil for one day; yet miraculously the lamp burned for eight days, giving them time to purify the new oil required to resupply the lamp. Hanukkah is a time of relaxation, fun, and games, during which Christmas-type gifts are exchanged.

Far more solemn is Pesach, or the Feast of the Passover, held in the month of Nisan to commemorate the liberation of the children of Israel from Egyptian bondage. During the eight days of this feast, observant Jews eat unleavened bread called the *matzot*. They also take part in a special meal known as the seder, in which they retell the story of their ancestors' escape from Egypt and eat symbolic foods to remind themselves of the various aspects of the exodus story.

Another joyful, or at least lighthearted, feast is that of Purim, on the fourteenth day of Adar. Purim celebrates the story of the Jewish heroine Esther, who married the king of Persia in the fifth century BC. Neither the king nor his courtiers knew that Esther was Jewish. Therefore, when one of the kings advisers, Haman, plotted to murder the Jews, Esther was able to save her people, and it was Haman who was executed. For many modern Jews, this feast is like Halloween, with a lot of fun.

On the sixth day of Sivan, Jews celebrate Shavuot, a type of harvest festival that celebrates the reception of the Ten Commandments by Moses. This feast centers on a family meal and the reading of the Torah.

Photo 17.10 Medieval Jews prepare the *matzot*, or unleavened bread, in preparation for the feast of the Passover.

Photo 17.11 The entrance to Erfurt's "Small Synagogue" and its commemorative plaque.

Photo 17.12 Although rebuilt in the nineteenth century, a synagogue has stood on this spot since 1137.

JEWISH PRAYER

Prayer is an important aspect of Judaism and takes place at both the individual and the communal level. In many respects Jewish prayer is similar to Christian prayer, having intensely personal aspects but also a liturgical dimension during synagogue services. In some ways a synagogue service resembles an Anglican or even a Roman Catholic service, and there are probably ancient links between the ways these liturgies were compiled. Many synagogues hold daily prayer, although certain types of prayer require at least ten men. Women, at least in traditional synagogues, are kept quite separate from the men.

THE SYNAGOGUE

Following the destruction of the temple in AD 70, Jewish worship quickly came to center on the synagogue, which also served and continues to serve as a sort of Sunday school and, sometimes, a community center. Synagogues have three essential elements: the ark, which is the cabinet where the scrolls of the Torah are stored; the lectern, from which worship is led and sermons are preached; and, in front of the ark, a lamp which burns continually to remind Jews of the ancient menorah that once stood before the ark of the covenant in the temple in Jerusalem. As in many ancient European churches,

Photo 17.13 The entrance to the ancient ritual bath.

there are also tablets on which are engraved the Ten Commandments. No images or other artwork of an anthropomorphic nature are allowed in the synagogue.

JEWISH DRESS CODES

For practicing Jews, the one shared article of dress is what is known in Hebrew as a *kapah* and in Yiddish as a *yarmulke*, a small skullcap worn by men during worship as a sign of respect to God. It is also often worn in the outside world as a means of witnessing to the wearer's Jewish identity. During communal prayers in Orthodox and most other synagogues, Jewish men wrap themselves in a prayer shawl called a *tallit*, which has fringes in accordance with instructions found in the book of Numbers. These fringes are threads with knots in them totaling 613, to symbolize the number of laws identified by rabbinic Judaism as obligatory for all practicing Jews. During certain prayers Jewish men, and occasionally women, strap a small leather box containing four passages from the Torah onto one arm, and another box to their heads, centering it on the forehead. These are known as tefillin or *phylacteries*. This practice is based upon Deuteronomy 6:8.

Photo 17.14 This nineteenth-century photograph shows a Middle Eastern Jewish family celebrating the Feast of Tabernacles, during which time they move into temporary outdoor accommodations to remind themselves of the travail and triumphs of their ancestors.

DIETARY LAWS

As in Islam and some forms of Hinduism, as well as many monastic communities found in all religions, dietary laws play an important role within Judaism. Food which Jews may eat is known as kosher food and must be prepared according to strict rules. Today many Jews do not "keep kosher" or only do so within the confines of their homes or on special occasions. Being kosher involves preparing not only food and the vessels it is prepared in—pots and pans—but also the plates and utensils used to eat it. New pots and plates are needed when different types of food are eaten, and to confuse these utensils makes them ritually unclean.

Generally speaking, fruits, vegetables, nuts, gourds, grains, seeds, and fungi may be eaten without restriction, except on special occasions. The eating of insects is forbidden; therefore, all plant foods, such as salads, have to be washed carefully to ensure that no insects are mixed up with them. Fish, as the Levitical laws outline, may be eaten provided they have both scales and fins. As a result, eels, shellfish, octopuses, turtles, frogs, and similar creatures cannot be eaten. The only permissible meats are those that come from animals that chew the cud and have split hooves. This means that while Jews can eat beef, they are not allowed to eat horse meat, and pork is strictly forbidden. Even so, certain portions of cows, such as sinew and blood, are forbidden. All meat must also be completely drained of any blood, and animals must be slaughtered according to strict, ritually prescribed standards. Dairy products are allowed, provided they are kept separate from meat. Birds raised for eating, such as chickens, are permitted, but wildfowl are banned. Eggs are allowed, provided they come from species that are themselves edible according to Jewish law.

Photo 17.15 The small prairie synagogue now housed in Calgary's Heritage Park, seen during Stampede week—hence the cowboy hats of the visitors.

What this means is that in practice, Jews who strictly abide by kosher rules cannot eat in most restaurants, are limited in what they can buy from supermarkets, and cannot freely eat food at the homes of non-Jewish, or even Jewish, friends who do not keep kosher. Therefore, these rules, as anthropologist Mary Douglas points out in her classic book *Purity and Danger*, set Jews apart from other peoples. This, Douglas argues, is based upon the ancient Hebrew understanding of holiness and God's command in Leviticus 11:45: "I am the LORD who brought you up out of Egypt to be your God; therefore be holy, because I am holy." Holiness, according to Douglas, was a very physical thing in

Photo 17.16 The inside of this rare pioneer synagogue, where Jews far from centers of Jewish culture once celebrated the Sabbath in what was then the Canadian wilderness.

ancient Israel and, understood in this way, the Levitical laws, upon which the practice of kosher is based, make sense.

THE CENTRALITY OF THE SABBATH

Beyond doubt, observance of the Sabbath is by far the most important of all observances of Jewish holy days and rituals. Remembering the Sabbath is what makes Israel Israel. The Sabbath begins at sundown every Friday and ends with sundown the following day. In recognition of the commencement of the Sabbath, the senior Jewish woman in the home lights ritual candles. The senior man then recites the ritual prayer over the bread and wine at the beginning of the evening meal, which joyfully celebrates the coming of the Sabbath.

Many Jews, particularly the Orthodox, attend synagogue before such activities take place. Others, particularly members of Conservative and Reform congregations, attend a late evening service. For all three groups, and various other minor, or sectarian, Jewish groups, Sabbath worship also takes place the following day, that is, on Saturday. Orthodox Jews refrain from all forms of work on the Sabbath and, if very strict, do not even turn on a light or drive a car. Some other groups are more lenient in their interpretation of Sabbath laws; some smaller sectarian groups are even stricter than the Orthodox. The Sabbath concludes with a short ceremony just before sundown on Saturday, when a lit candle is extinguished in a glass of wine and a box of spices is passed around for family members to taste and smell, symbolizing the passing away of the sweetness of the Sabbath.

THE JEWISH FAMILY

According to Orthodoxy, the only true Jew is someone born of a Jewish mother. Some groups argue that because of this, it is impossible to convert to Judaism. Most, however, make some allowance for conversion. Within the Jewish household the circumcision of boys is one of the most important events of all. For Jews circumcision symbolizes the relationship between God and his people. Therefore, it is a religious requirement that cannot be forgone, although in the nineteenth century some modernizing Jewish groups, especially in Germany, attempted to abolish circumcision as "a barbaric act." Today, however, circumcision has regained its traditional place; and all major Jewish groups as well as sectarian ones practice it. In many synagogues there is also a ceremony for the naming of girls.

The next milestone in a Jewish man's life is the bar mitzvah, which literally means "son of the covenant," when, around the age of twelve or thirteen, a boy ritually comes of age. Traditionally there was no similar ceremony for female children, but since the nineteenth century in Germany, increasingly today, there has also been the bat mitzvah, or "daughter of the cov-

Photo 17.17 A traditional bar mitzvah ceremony, in which a young man comes of age by assuming the responsibilities of adulthood and his relationship to God.

enant," for young women. These ceremonies are like super birthday parties and resemble either confirmation or adult baptism as practiced in Christian churches.

The next major milestone is marriage, which traditionally took place at a relatively young age. One interesting aspect of Jewish weddings is that the bridegroom is expected to see the bride before the marriage ceremony, which in most other Western cultural traditions is forbidden. The explanation of this practice is that in Genesis 29, Jacob was tricked into marrying Leah rather than Rachel, whom he loved. After prayers and various other rituals, the rabbi officiating the ceremony gives the couple a glass of wine, which they share. Then the rabbi announces that they are man and wife. At that point the bridegroom throws the glass to the ground and stamps on it. Although various reasons are given for this act, the most likely is that it is a reminder that life is fragile and that even at the happiest moment suffering may be around the corner. Another explanation is that it is done in remembrance of the destruction of the temple and the hardships suffered by the Jewish people. Whatever the reason, this is one of the unique features of the Jewish wedding.

Finally, there are traditions for the time of death. Jews are not permitted to leave a person while they are dying. Once they are dead, however, several rituals take place, including the opening of a window, which some say is to allow the soul to escape the body, while prayers and psalms are recited. For practicing Jews cremation is prohibited, as are autopsies, although on the latter point there is a certain degree of flexibility. By Jewish law a person ought to be buried in a plain casket and placed in the ground, not in some form of crypt or mausoleum. The funeral should take place as soon as possible after death is confirmed, but not on the Sabbath or a major Jewish holiday. At a traditional funeral, mourners tore their garments and cried out aloud to express their grief. Today it is more common for people to wear black as a sign of respect. Another common practice is the placing of a handful of soil from the land of Israel in the casket. Otherwise, most Jewish funerals are little different from any other funeral.

For practicing Jews the family is the most important social institution of all and is closely intertwined in their thinking with the Sabbath. Both of these institutions remind Jews of eternal Israel and their relationship to God. Therefore, the ritual practices associated with the family and the Sabbath are at the heart of Judaism. As Jacob Neusner points out in his book *A Rabbi Talks with Jesus*,[10] the attitude of Jesus toward both institutions is totally shocking. The statement of Jesus in Mark 3:35, "Whoever does God's will is my brother and sister and mother," is the antithesis of Jewish thinking. As Neusner observes, "Jesus calls into question the primacy of the family in the priority of my responsibilities, the centrality of the family in the social order."[11] Jesus, he argues, is asking him to "abandon my home and family" for his sake, yet this runs completely counter to the sacred duties conferred upon a practicing Jew by the Torah.[12] For Neusner the issue is simply the Torah or Christ,[13] because the teachings of Christ strike at the very heart of eternal Israel.[14]

10. Jacob Neusner, *A Rabbi Talks with Jesus* (Montréal: McGill-Queen's Univ. Press, 2001).
11. Ibid., 58.
12. Ibid., 60.
13. Ibid., 64.
14. Ibid., 54.

The teachings of Jesus strike also, in Neusner's view, at the other pillar of eternal Israel, the Sabbath, because "the celebration of the Sabbath defines what makes Israel Israel. The entire way of life of the community centers on that day."[15] Clearly, in Neusner's view, Jesus appeared "not to fulfill but to abolish the Sabbath,"[16] and by implication the Jewish people as they had existed until his time. For this reason he cannot accept Jesus' teachings or Christianity.

Few writers have highlighted the differences between Judaism and Christianity more clearly than Neusner. In doing so, he also shows Christians, who might otherwise construct a Judaism in the image of their own religion, that Judaism is not simply an earlier, or incomplete, form of Christianity. Rather, it is a dynamic religion in its own right which must be respected on its own terms and not reinterpreted through a Christian lens. Neusner eloquently sums up Judaism as follows: "Long ago, far away, God had called the people, a holy, enduring people, into being. God had bound the people to God in the covenant, giving the Torah as terms of that agreement, engraving even into flesh the very sign of the covenant."[17] This then is the dynamic heart of Judaism.

---

15. Ibid., 78.
16. Ibid., 84.
17. Ibid., 157.

CHAPTER 18

MARTIN BUBER'S ZIONIST SPIRITUALITY

INTRODUCTION

In seeking a Jewish religious leader as a representative figure to give readers from a Christian background some insight into the appeal of modern Judaism and the way in which Jewish scholars have negotiated the challenges of the Enlightenment, one is faced with a host of possible subjects. Therefore, in choosing Martin Buber (1878–1965) rather than any other figure, I do not imply that other Jewish figures are not interesting or significant. I chose him, rather, because it is arguable that, more than any other modern Jewish thinker, he has profoundly influenced Christian theology. That said, he has also had an enormous effect on Jewish thinking and practice through his philosophical works and studies of Hasidism.

BUBER'S EARLY LIFE

Martin Buber was born in Vienna, Austria. But when he was three years old, after the mysterious disappearance of his mother, he went to live with his grandparents in Lemberg, the capital of the Austrian province of Galicia. Today part of the Ukraine and known as Lviv, the city was around 170 miles east of Krakow and 60 miles from the Russian border. In 1878 it had a population of just over 95,000, a quarter of whom were Jewish. During the next quarter century the population of the city grew rapidly, as did the number of its Jewish inhabitants. Jews had lived in Lemberg from the fourteenth century. During the eighteenth century it became one of the leading centers of Hasidism.

When Buber moved there, his grandfather, Solomon Buber, was a well-respected Hebrew scholar and a leading figure in the movement for Jewish emancipation and enlightenment. Therefore, Martin received an excellent modern education under the direction of his grandmother, who employed private tutors until he was ten years old. From them he gained a thorough grounding in Hebrew and various other modern languages, including German and Polish. He also gained an excellent knowledge of Jewish history, as well as the traditions and customs of the Jewish people. After his basic education, at the age of ten he was sent to the local gymnasium, or high school, which he would remember with fondness.

Photo 18.1 While he stayed with his grandfather in Galicia, religious festivals like the one shown captivated the young Buber's imagination, shaping his thinking in a religious direction.

Throughout this period he grew to love the Hebrew Bible. But, like his friend Franz Rosenzweig (1886–1929), with whom he later translated the Hebrew Bible into German, he also developed a love for Martin Luther's German translation of the Bible. Later, after making his own German translation of the Hebrew Bible, he came to regard Luther's Bible as particularly German in the sense that in his view it failed to capture and convey the communal nature of Judaism.

It was while visiting his father, a farmer and owner of a large estate, that the young Buber first encountered Hasidic Judaism through a local group in the village of Sadagora. These people initiated him into Hasidic beliefs and practices. Paradoxically, the representatives of Hasidism and the Jewish enlightenment, like his grandfather, were locked in a bitter struggle with each other. Each considered the other a threat to the survival of Judaism. Typically, Buber embraced both traditions, attempting to reconcile them throughout his life.

Following the German tradition, Buber studied at the universities of Vienna, Berlin, Leipzig, and Zurich, gaining a thorough grounding in philosophy and German culture, which for a while distanced him from his Jewish background. Then he read the works of Theodor Herzl (1860–1904) and was captivated by the Zionist vision, though he disagreed profoundly with Herzl's interpretation of it. From then on, Judaism, and its survival, became the dominant theme in Buber's life. As early as 1899, at the University of Leipzig, he founded a Zionist group and participated in the Third International Zionist Congress, held in the Swiss city of Zurich.

Independently wealthy, Buber was able to combine his studies with occasional journalism and work for Jewish organizations. In this capacity he published numerous successful books, mainly on Jewish Hasidism, leading up to his best-selling *I and Thou*

(1923). In 1930 his literary activities led to his appointment to a special professorship at what was then the University of Frankfurt-am-Main. He lost this position after Hitler came to power in 1933, when he became active in providing advanced education for Jews deprived of a university education by the Nazis. He immigrated to the British Mandate Territory of Palestine in 1938, where he received a professorship at the Hebrew University, which he had helped found in 1925. There he taught anthropology and sociology while living in Jerusalem. His beloved wife died in 1958, and Buber seven years later in 1965. In his later life Buber was awarded numerous literary prizes and was a frequent lecturer outside Israel.

BUBER'S ZIONISM

From the outset Buber saw Zionism as a dynamic way of life and not simply a political creed. For him the appeal lay in its ability to revitalize the Jewish people and revive eternal Israel through a combination of modern philosophical reasoning, mystical experience, and messianic expectations. From the time he embraced Zionism until his death, he never doubted that this was the only solution for the survival of Judaism.

For Buber, Zionism was not some narrow and exclusive preserve of Jews. It was an ideal capable of embracing the world. In keeping with his open outlook on life, to the horror of both his family and that of his fiancée, he married Paula Winkler (d. 1958), a young novelist who wrote under the pen name George Mundt, or Munkl. Although she came from a devoted Roman Catholic family, she was a devoted Zionist whom Buber met at university in Zurich. After their marriage she embraced Judaism, going through a complete conversion, including a ritual bath, even though this led to a complete break with her family.

Buber's Zionism is perhaps the key to his thought and released him from what he found the challenging, yet ultimately oppressive, philosophy of Friedrich Nietzsche (1844–1900). Buber's answer to the question of existence was that the individual forms part of a vast chain that embraces the yet unborn, the living, and the dead, stretching back to Abraham and on into the future. Within each Jew, he said, lives the Jewish people as a real historical and ultimately genetic heritage. It is this heritage that liberates the

Photo 18.2 The Second World Jewish Congress, held in Basel, Switzerland, in 1898.

Jew from human alienation. It overcomes his loneliness, isolation, and the sense of being a stranger in a strange land. In the Jew reside those key biblical personages, or offices, of prophet, priest, and king, ensuring that as long as the world exists, an Israel remains.

THE LURE OF GERMAN CULTURE

As a German Jew, Buber lived in a peculiar tension that arose from his Jewish heritage and the attraction of German culture, which, like many German Jewish intellectuals, he loved. German culture was an ever-present temptation. For him the poetry of men like Goethe (1749–1832) and Friedrich von Schiller (1759–1805) was divine. Yet it was German poetry, not Jewish poetry. The art and architecture which surrounded him was German art and German architecture, even if Jews had contributed to it. Therefore, the Jew in Germany was both at home and a stranger in German culture. As Goethe's most famous character, Faust, laments: "Two souls alas! are lodged within my breast, / Which struggled there for undivided reign."[1]

For Buber and many of his like-minded contemporaries, this tension brought about the realization that the Jew was either a German or a Jew but could not be both. Either they knew themselves to be a Jew and, in recognizing their true identity, accepted the Jewish past as a basis for their own personality, or they abandoned Judaism and fully embraced German culture. There was no halfway house. Either a Jew was concerned with the plight of their people worldwide as an existential reality, or they abandoned Judaism. Only by faith in the future of the Jewish people could they be truly called a Jew. This was because in the future of their own people they found their own future and themselves. Therefore, all dedicated Jews must lose themselves in their people and raise their people as a whole from the degradation that so many experienced daily.

But before this could happen, every Jew, particularly every German Jew who felt enticed by German culture, had to fight and win a battle with themselves. They had to return to the core of their being by rediscovering the deep roots of Jewish consciousness. Buber addressed this issue in his seminal essay *Judaism and Humanity* (1911), in which he asked the question, is it possible to identify those aspects of the Jewish people that are unique and eternal? He answered with a resounding "Yes."

For Buber the heart of the problem he sought to address was a philosophical dualism that at the popular level expressed itself in an unceasing struggle between opposite poles of existence. Good and evil, heaven and hell, right and wrong, truth and error, are all ideas that challenge individuals with what the Danish philosopher Søren Kierkegaard (1813–1855) so aptly described as the choice of either/or.[2] Yet for Buber, Kierkegaard's analysis was flawed. In Judaism, even though the Jews of his day felt the tensions created by dualistic thinking even more strongly than Kierkegaard himself, the solution was found in a unity beyond all diversity.

---

1. Johann Wolfgang von Goethe, *Faust*, trans. Anna Swanwick, in *The German Classics of the Nineteenth and Twentieth Centuries*, vol. 1, *Goethe*, ed. Kuno Francke (New York: German Publication Society, 1913), 272.
2. Søren Kierkegaard, *Either/Or*, vol. 1, trans. David F. Swenson, Lillian Marvin Swenson, vol. 2, trans. Walter Lowrie, with revisions and foreword by Howard A. Johnson (Garden City, N.Y.: Doubleday, 1959).

BEING A JEW IN THE WORLD

Later, in his address "The Jew in the World" (1934), Buber articulated his more mature views on Zionism. Although his views developed over the years, in essence they remained fairly consistent. For him, Jews were "hurled into the abyss of the world" by the Roman destruction of Jerusalem.[3] After that, they came to represent "the insecure man," because "every union with other civilizations [was] informed with a secret divisive force," and therefore every social situation into which they moved, however good, also contained what Buber called "an invisible terminating clause." He then pointed out that to host peoples, among whom the Jews lived for so many centuries, the very act of Jewish self-preservation as a people created a separation that turned the Jew into "a 'sinister' homeless specter." This reality, he said, was epitomized by the "myth of the homeless Jew."[4]

To make matters worse, Buber agreed that it was difficult to classify Jews because they were neither a nation nor a creed. They were not a nation because they lacked the experience of a nation occupying land with a common history. They were not a creed because Judaism is a lived experience. They were, very definitely, a people that "experiences history and revelation as one phenomenon, history as revelation and revelation as history." Consequently, "the unity of nationality and faith" is a thing that "constitutes the uniqueness of Israel" and as such is the "destiny" of the Jews. In light of this understanding, he was able to say that "the prophets knew and predicted that in spite of all their veering and compromising Israel must perish if it intends to exist only as a political structure. It can persist—and this is the paradox in their warning and the paradox of the reality of Jewish history—if it insists *on its vocation and uniqueness.*" This, for Buber, was the essence of the covenant.[5]

Photo 18.3 The Mozart monument in Vienna. When Buber lived in Vienna, it was the cultural center of a rich, multicultural empire in which German cultural achievements, like the music of Beethoven (1770–1827) and Mozart (1756–1791), created a pride among all German-speaking peoples. Buber loved this culture but also sensed an alienation from it. Therefore, he longed to see a similar pride in Jewish culture among his own people. Yet at the time many Jews saw Jewish traditions as culturally deprived and were leaving Judaism in droves. This self-imposed cultural exodus troubled Buber, who sought to arrest it through his writings and work for the Zionist cause.

---

3. Martin Buber, "The Jews in the World," in Arthur Hertzberg, ed., *The Zionist Idea: A Historical Analysis and Reader* (New York: Doubleday, 1959), 453.

4. Ibid., 454.

5. Ibid., 455.

The uniqueness of Israel, for him, was that its creation represented "the *first real attempt at 'community'* to enter world history." Israel therefore had a mission to help other nations create their own communities and live in harmony with each other. For him it was here that all attempts at Jewish emancipation failed, because they failed to recognize the importance of the living community of Israel to the Jewish people. Acceptance by non-Jews of Judaism as a religion alongside Christianity, Islam, Buddhism, Hinduism, and any other religion appeared as tolerance and a sign of progress. But to Buber such acceptance turned Judaism into just another denomination or, as he put it, "confession." And this destroyed the essence of eternal Israel as a community.[6]

Judaism, he argued, strives for unity. This unity is found in the person, the people, and ultimately all people, because it is rooted in the unity between God and his world. The Jewish concept of God, therefore, came into being through the search for salvation beyond all Jews. As Deuteronomy 6:4 says, "Hear, O Israel: the LORD our God, the LORD is one." This ultimate monism was for Buber the glory of Judaism.

Everything, Buber argued, is meaningless unless it finds meaning in God and the unity that God brings to all things. Thus Jews are messengers of the one God bringing his eternal reign to earth. Yet this great task of witness could only be fulfilled when the creative Jewish soul found peace in its native land of Palestine. Only the restoration of the Jews to their holy land would bring about a rebirth of the Jewish people. For this reason, long before the coming of the Nazis, Buber believed that Jews must pack their bags and migrate to Palestine.

Unlike many Jews and Christians of more recent times, Buber did not believe that it was the destiny of Jews simply to occupy the land. Rather, he had a vision of peace and prosperity. For him Jews could grow and prosper only if they ensured that the people around them shared in their joy and prosperity. The other residents of Palestine must therefore be welcome to share the blessings God gave to his people. Only then could the real meaning of God's sovereignty be seen, as the Jewish people witnessed to the world the deeds of God. Israel was not called to be God's chosen people for nothing. Nor was their destiny to lord it over other peoples. Rather, their calling was to serve others. The return to Palestine, therefore, could never be for the purpose of exploiting their Arab neighbors.

Photo 18.4 The flight from Jewish culture by Jews living in German-speaking countries originated with the Jewish enlightenment that grew out of the work of Moses Mendelssohn. Not only did most of Mendelssohn's grandchildren become Christians, but others, like the hostess and Berlin socialite Henriette Hertz, seen above, led a wave of cultural and religious conversions.

---

6. Ibid., 456.

Capitalism and imperialism must be forsaken as the Jews discovered themselves through service to others.

BUBER AND THE BIBLE

For Buber the Hebrew Bible was a record of Israel's experience with God. As such, it was absolutely central to his faith. Yet Buber was not a Bible believer like some fundamentalist Christians. In his view, Scripture expressed the longings of men and women for God, but not necessarily a correct understanding of God. In his autobiography he tells how he was "horrified" to read "that section of the book of Samuel in which it is told how Samuel delivered to King Saul a message that his dynastic rule would be taken from him because he had spared the life of the conquered Prince of the Amalekites."[7]

Statement in the Bible like this one, Buber believed, could not possibly express the will of God and led enlightened Jews to reject the religion of their fathers. To illustrate his point, he tells of a conversation with an old Jewish man with whom he discussed this passage after telling him that "I had never been able to believe that this is a message of God. I do not believe it." Buber relates how the man appeared to become angry and repeatedly asked whether or not he believed it. Then, he writes, after they had discussed the passage at length and Buber had reaffirmed that he did not believe it, the man confessed that he too did not believe this passage. Thus Buber hoped that, by rejecting a literal view of the Bible in favor of rational ethics and a living religious experience, he might preserve the essence of Judaism.

For Buber the message was simple. There was "nothing astonishing in the fact that an observant Jew of this nature, when he has to choose between God and the Bible, chooses God: the God in whom he believes, Him in whom he can believe."[8] This passage illustrates Buber's understanding of dialogue. As a Jew he feels himself in constant dialogue with God, testing all traditions against his understanding of the calling of the people of Israel. In this situation, revelation is not the Bible, but the experience of Israel—or rather of the people known as Jews—throughout the whole of history.

PHILOSOPHICAL ISSUES

Deeply immersed in German intellectual life, Buber had a thorough grasp of modern philosophy. Although he was influenced by Kant and Nietzsche, the writer who seems to have influenced his thought about religion most profoundly was Ludwig Feuerbach (1804–1872), whose books, particularly *The Essence of Christianity* (1840)[9] and *Principles of the Philosophy of the Future* (1843),[10] he found exceptionally challenging. What appealed to Buber about Feuerbach was that, "unlike Kant," he "wishes to make the whole person, not human cognition, the beginning of philosophizing."[11]

---

7. Martin Buber, *Meetings: Autobiographical Fragments* (London: Routledge, 2002; first published 1967), 62.
8. Ibid., 63.
9. Ludwig Feuerbach, *The Essence of Christianity*, trans. George Eliot (New York: Harper, 1957).
10. Ludwig Feuerbach, *Principles of the Philosophy of the Future*, trans. H. Manfred Vogel (Indianapolis: Hackett, 1986).
11. Martin Buber, *Between Man and Man*, trans. Ronald Gregor Smith (London: Routledge and Kegan Paul, 1947), 146.

Photo 18.5 One of the key figures to influence Buber and his generation was the philosopher Immanuel Kant (1724–1804). Although few of Buber's generation believed Kant had provided philosophical answers, it was agreed that he raised the key questions. These questions of meaning Buber sought to answer in *I and Thou* as well as his other works.

The importance of Feuerbach to Buber's thinking can be seen in the latter's comment, "By man, whom he considers is the highest subject of philosophy, Feuerbach does not mean man as an individual, but man with man—a connection of *I* and *Thou*."[12] This phrase, "I and Thou," became the title of Buber's most famous book. Perhaps because of this he could say, "I myself in my youth was given a decisive impetus by Feuerbach."[13]

Before discussing the philosophy and significance of Buber's *I and Thou*, it is important to say a little more about Feuerbach. Writing in conscious opposition to the idealistic philosophy of G. W. F. Hegel (1770–1831) and the psychologizing theology of F. D. Schleiermacher's (1768–1834) apologetic, which substituted Christology for a defense of traditional arguments for belief in God and Christianity, Feuerbach sought a consistent materialism. As Karl Barth (1886–1968) argued, Feuerbach was the scourge of nineteenth-century theology, particularly all forms of liberal Protestantism.[14] Feuerbach also, as Buber points out, provided the materialist foundation for the work of men like Karl Marx and Friedrich Nietzsche.[15]

What is significant is that for Christian theologians, particularly Protestant theologians, Feuerbach represents the high-water mark of nineteenth-century anti-Christian apologetics. Not only were Marx and Nietzsche influenced by him, but so were a host of other nineteenth-century writers, from his English translator, George Eliot (1819–1880), to writers like Samuel Butler (1835–1902), and even people like Christopher Hitchens (b. 1949) and representatives of the so-called new atheism.[16] Yet, rather than running from Feuerbach or denouncing him as an atheist, Buber makes him his own.

Buber explains his understanding of God through the story of his encounter with the Reverend Hechler, a pro-Zionist Christian pastor with a firm belief in biblical prophecy. Hechler's discourses on the book of Daniel, the return of the Jews to Palestine, and the significance of biblical prophecy caused Buber to reflect on the nature of God after Hechler pointedly asked him, "Do you believe in God?"

---

12. Ibid., 147.

13. Ibid., 148.

14. Karl Barth, *From Rousseau to Ritschl* (London: SCM Press, 1959), 355–61.

15. Buber, *Between Man and Man*, 146–48.

16. See, e.g., Christopher Hitchens, *God Is Not Great: The Case against Religion* (London: Atlantic, 2007).

This question struck Buber to the core of his being. After reflecting on it, he says, he came up with the following answer: "If to believe in God means to be able to talk about him in the third person, then I do not believe in God. If to believe in him means to be able to talk to him, then I believe in God." Then he adds, "The God who gives Daniel such foreknowledge of this hour of human history, this hour before the 'world war,' that its fixed place in the march of the ages can be foredetermined, it's not my God and not God. The God whom Daniel praises in his suffering is my God and the God of all."[17] These comments, and his reaction to Feuerbach, lay the foundation for understanding his book *I and Thou*.

I AND THOU

Buber begins his classic work with the comment, "To Man the world is twofold, in accordance with his twofold attitude."[18] This twofold distinction is expressed by the primary word "I-Thou" and the primary word "I-It." This is a difficult passage in an equally difficult book. In the book Buber explains, "Primary words do not signify things, but they intimate relations."[19] Therefore, "I-Thou" is an expression of the whole being, or of the person, while "I-It" is fragmentary and incomplete, representing "a thing" and signifying a fractured world. Thus, according to Buber, when we say "It" or "I-It," we are speaking about things, but when we say "Thou," "the speaker has no thing, he has indeed nothing. But takes his stand in relation."[20] Thus Buber rooted his philosophy in Feuerbach's insight into the primary importance of relations.

For this reason, Buber argues, "The primary word *I-Thou* establishes a world of relation."[21] Such relations are mutually affected by "I" and "Thou." When we approach people, we do not experience the person to whom we say "Thou." As soon as we experience "the person," we lose "the Thou." Such relations form our personalities: "A person makes his appearance by entering into relation with other people."[22] By contrast, "I-It" introduces a separation into man's life.

Photo 18.6 Ludwig Feuerbach (1804–1872), who exercised so great an influence on Buber, is not well known today, but his translator and English interpreter George Eliot is. Her novels spread Feuerbach's philosophy in the English-speaking world. Remarkably, like Buber, she came to a Zionist position in her novel *Daniel Deronda* (1876). Eliot translated *The Essence of Christianity* in 1854. Earlier, in 1846, she had translated David Friedrich Strauss's (1808–1874) equally explosive *The Life of Jesus Critically Examined*.

17. Buber, *Meetings*, 52–53.
18. Martin Buber, *I and Thou* (Edinburgh: T&T Clark, 1958), 3.
19. Ibid.
20. Ibid., 4.
21. Ibid., 6.
22. Ibid., 62.

There is no longer a mutual relation. Now my "I" precedes my "It." This means that I experience "the It" and know "It," but no longer share a relationship. This is the "melancholy of our fate."[23] Every Thou is doomed to become an It, except for the eternal Thou. "I-It" is the word of separation, where relation is replaced by the experience of things.

Thus humans need to invoke, or believe in, "It" to form the world of things. But when they enter into relationships, they enter the world of "Thou." Yet, according to Buber, even relationships, or relations, may become things, and this can lead us to despise things, but we must not. Without things we cannot live. The important point is not to reject things, but not to live by them alone. We must remember that "he who lives with *It* alone is not a man."[24]

Things are not evil in themselves, but they belong to the realm of causality in our world. This realm is essential to science, but anyone who lives with "It"-type encounters finds that the "It" becomes a burden by threatening the very nature of their personal being. Left in the realm of causality, we never meet reality, but only the face of "the menace of the abyss." The person who knows relation is very different; "causality does not weigh on" them, and their "freedom is assured."[25] In this way Buber argues that someone who lacks freedom has become an "It" because "he treats himself too as an *It*."[26] As a result, such a person is not fully human.

For Buber, reality is to be found only in what he calls "the real twofold entity *I and Thou*."[27] Therefore, "he who takes his stand in relation shares in reality." This means that all reality is shared reality. Reality is a relationship which excludes appropriation. The more direct the contact, the more real the relationship and the closer the Thou.[28] Each meeting in relation is a glimpse of the eternal Thou. "The extended lines of relation, meet in the eternal *Thou*. Every particular *Thou* is a glimpse through to the eternal *Thou*; by means of every particular *Thou* the primary word addresses the eternal *Thou*."[29] Thus, while all true meeting is characterized by exclusiveness, "in the relation with God unconditional exclusiveness and unconditional inclusiveness are one." God meets us in daily life through our encounters with other people when they are experienced as "Thou." After outlining what can only be called a very human view of religion, Buber adds, "Of course God is holy other; but he also is holy same, the holy present." Only when "you hallow this life do you meet the living God."[30] That is, you experience a revelation of God through your encounters with other people when you know them as a "Thou" and not an "It."

THE PROBLEM OF REVELATION

As E. L. Fakenheim suggests, the work of Martin Buber falls into the category of a Jewish response to the problem of revelation. Without doubt, in the Jewish context, it is an excel-

---

23. Ibid., 23.
24. Ibid., 34.
25. Ibid., 52.
26. Ibid., 68.
27. Ibid., 59.
28. Ibid., 63.
29. Ibid., 75.
30. Ibid., 79.

lent response that taps the roots of the Jewish tradition. The question is, can this approach be applied to other traditions, particularly the Christian tradition? Many theologians have argued that it can and that Buber's work is equally valid for Christian and Jew alike. Others suggest that attempts by Christians to appropriate Buber's work are futile and doomed to failure because they fail to recognize the importance of what Neusner calls "eternal Israel."[31]

Both Christian and Jewish views of revelation demand a minimum factual content as the basis for belief. Buber's factual content rests—or perhaps one should say is rooted—in his consciousness of belonging to a long tradition of physical descent that goes back to Abraham. Thus, Buber's revelation is a revelation of a people, not a revealed scripture, even though it is scripture, the Torah, that binds the people together.

By contrast, for Protestant theologians, Christian revelation rests on the authority of the revelation itself and not upon a particular people bound together by genetic inheritance. Even the Roman Catholic Church, which in its view of the church as the people of God comes closer to the Jewish conception of a historical community, roots the church in the community of the faithful, and in the transmission of the faith through liturgical practices and correct doctrines, not in physical descent.

Martin Buber avoided rationalists' criticism of his work by carefully refusing to add content to his abstract concept of revelation. He writes, "The eternal primal phenomenon, present here and now," is called "revelation," and "it is the phenomena that a man does not pass, from the moment of the supreme meeting, the same being as he entered into it." This, Buber stresses, is not an experience, but rather a revelation "in which something happens to the man."[32] In this situation what a human

Photo 18.7 Friedrich Nietzsche. Through embracing a dynamic form of personalism based on the relationship between I and Thou, Buber believed that he escaped the nihilism he saw in Nietzsche's philosophy.

"receives is not a specific 'content,' but a Presence, a Presence as a Power."[33] This includes three undivided things: "First, there is the whole fullness of real mutual action, of being raised and bound in a relation." This relation is "heavy with meaning ... Secondly, there is the inexpressible confirmation of meaning. Meaning is assured. Nothing can any longer be meaningless ... Thirdly, this meaning is not that 'of another life,' but back to this life of ours."[34]

---

31. Jacob Neusner, *A Rabbi Talks with Jesus* (Montréal: McGill–Queen's Univ. Press, 2001), 45.

32. Buber, *I and Thou*, 109.

33. Ibid., 110.

34. Ibid.

This enables Buber to say, "I know of no revelation and believe in none whose primal phenomena is not precisely this. I do not believe in a self naming of God, a self definition of God before men. The word of revelation is '*I am, that I am.*' That which reveals is that which reveals. That which is *is*, and nothing more."[35]

Theologians who try to make Buber's scheme carry more weight than it will bear are trying to make Buber say things that he has no intention of saying to support a position that in fact he repudiates. In his terms, talk about *kerygma*, or good news from God mediated through Jesus Christ, involves a preoccupation with an experience. This experience of, or with, Jesus can never be pure revelation for Buber. Rather, such experiences belong to the world of the It, because the very language that is used to express the experience involves a thing, that is, "an experience," and not a relation. In Buber's understanding the It has replaced the relation of faith, and God has been reduced to a cult object.

In his book *Christianity and Paradox* (1958), Ronald W. Hepburn attacked theologians who attempted to use Buber's work to bolster Christian theology. Hepburn asks, "Are there no checking procedures relevant to the encounter of a person with a person?"[36] He then goes on to say that there are and there must be such procedures. Therefore, in his view, anyone who wants to talk about an encounter with God in the same breath as they talk about an encounter with another person as though they are talking about the same thing is sadly mistaken. Actually, Hepburn's arguments do not apply to Buber himself but rather mirror his view. Buber makes it very clear that he is only talking about a "relation." When Buber calls God "a person," he does this in the context of the effect which relation has upon a person's life. "As a person God gives personal life, he makes us as persons capable of meeting him and with one another."[37]

"God," for Buber, is not "a Person." He is the "ground and meaning of our existence."[38] Buber argues that humans live in a world of It which is "set in the context of space and time by the relation of It. But, the world of Thou is not set in the context of either of these. Its context is the Centre where the extended lines of relations meet—in the eternal Thou."[39] This "Centre" gives man meaning in his life. As Buber sees it, "Meeting that God does not come to man in order

Photo 18.8 Martin Buber.

---

35. Ibid., 111–12.

36. Ronald W. Hepburn, *Christianity and Paradox* (London: Watts, 1958), 30.

37. Buber, *I and Thou*, 136.

38. Ibid., 135.

39. Ibid., 100.

that he may concern himself with God, but in order that he may confirm that there is meaning in the world."[40]

BUBER'S MESSAGE

Buber does not seek to prove his case. He proclaims his message. He is not trying to "prove that God exists." Rather, "the existence of mutuality between God and man cannot be proved, just as God's existence cannot be proved."[41] Therefore, for Buber, it is a basic presupposition that if humans are to live in the world, they must live in the world with meaning. Buber's comment, "Men have addressed the eternal Thou with many names,"[42] is significant. What he means is that humans have found meaning in many different ways, and in finding meaning have found themselves as humans. This view is perfectly consistent with Buber's view of the significance of Israel and what it means to be Jewish. For him meaning is found in community, and his community is the community of the Jewish people both in space and in time. It is up to others to find and develop their own communities and in doing so find their God.

---

40. Ibid., 115.
41. Ibid., 137.
42. Ibid., 76.

CHAPTER 19

CHRISTIANITY

INTRODUCTION

Every year thousands of students enroll in religious studies courses at colleges and universities throughout the English-speaking world. Usually, they have a choice of taking a broad introductory course on "world religions" or taking a course on such things as "Eastern and Western religions." Whatever their options, the courses usually follow a common pattern. Those sections that deal with Buddhism, the Hindu tradition, Judaism, or Islam take a holistic approach to religious traditions, one that attempts to provide the students with an empathetic understanding of the religion concerned as it is understood by believers.

The courses, or sections of courses, that deal with Christianity frequently take a very different approach. Instead of presenting Christianity as it is found in numerous Christian communities, they tend to concentrate on textual studies and critical issues about the reliability of the Bible. Thus Christianity is often presented in an essentially negative manner, while other religions are presented relatively positively.

Here an attempt is made to present Christianity in the same way that other religions are presented in introductory textbooks, that is, as a holistic religious tradition in which the experience of believers is given precedence; and in the tradition of intellectual history, Christianity is viewed historically, not from a theological perspective.

CHRISTIANITY IS CHRIST

Not very long ago Western writers spoke about Islam as "Muhammadanism," which many Muslims found insulting because it named their religion after their prophet.

Photo 19.1 At the heart of the Christian message is the person of Jesus the Christ, who Christians believe is the Word of God. This medieval Madonna from the Convent of the Sacred Heart in Munich captures this message. The child Jesus points with his right finger to God's Word, the Bible, indicating the reality of his existence.

What upset Muslims was that this usage seemed to remove God as the central object of their worship. Similarly, can you imagine someone referring to Judaism as "Abrahamism" or "Mosesism"? Surely, if someone did this in an introductory textbook, Jews would be outraged. Yet Christians have no difficulty using the name of Christ, who they see as the founder of their religion, as part of the name for that religion. This is one of the peculiarities of Christianity. In fact, in Acts 11:26 we read, "The disciples were called Christians first at Antioch."

The truth of the matter is that in a very real sense "Christianity is Christ." At the heart of the Christian message is not a book, a teaching, a way of life, a particular people, but a person. This person is Jesus of Nazareth, Jesus the Christ; and Christianity is built around him. Therefore, before we can talk about Christianity, we need to talk about Jesus.

JESUS OF NAZARETH

After launching a virulent attack on Christianity, the famous American polemicist Thomas Paine (1737–1809) wrote, "Nothing that is here said can apply, even with the most distinct disrespect, to the real character of Jesus Christ. He was a virtuous and an amiable man, the morality that he preached in practice was of the most benevolent kind; and though similar systems of morality had been preached ... by good men in all ages, it has not been exceeded by any."[1] What is remarkable about this statement is that in essence it has been repeated by numerous other non-Christians throughout the ages. Although, like Paine, such men and women may have hated Christianity and the church, they retained great respect for Jesus. Among religious leaders, only the Buddha, and perhaps Confucius, come anywhere near to Jesus in this respect; and in reality they trail a long way behind him in popular consciousness.

Photo 19.2 Thomas Paine (1737–1809), one of Christianity's most effective critics. His work *The Age of Reason* (Part One, 1794; Part Two, 1796) had a profound effect on many people throughout the nineteenth century. In it Paine presents in embryo all the arguments against traditional Christian teachings about the nature of the Bible that were later developed by nineteenth-century biblical critics in Germany.

Why is it that Jesus is held in such respect when other leaders, including Abraham, Moses, and Muhammad, are not venerated in this way by any other than their followers? Of course, non-Muslims may respect Muhammad as a great general and religious teacher; but few ever make comments about him like those that

1. Thomas Paine, *The Age of Reason*, introduced by Philip S. Foner (1794; Secaucus, N.J.: Citadel, 1974), 53.

non-Christians make about Jesus. The centrality of Jesus to both the Christian message and world history should therefore make us ponder.

WHERE DO WE LEARN ABOUT JESUS?

Our sources of information about Jesus come primarily from the New Testament, which provides a complex portrayal of this important religious leader. Traditionally, Christians have held that Matthew's gospel was the first gospel and was written for Jews, that Mark's gospel was a condensed account of the life of Jesus written for Romans, and that Luke's gospel was written primarily with Greeks in mind. Then they explained that John's gospel was written last, to bring out in a more detailed way the spiritual significance of the stories told in the other three gospels.

In addition to ordering the Gospels in this way, Christians traditionally claimed that they were directly based on the testimony of eyewitnesses. Matthew's gospel was written either by Matthew, who was a disciple of Jesus, or by a scribe at his dictation. Mark's gospel, it was believed, was written by John Mark, the companion to Luke and Paul in the Acts of the Apostles. John Mark was believed to have witnessed some of the events of Jesus' life and to have known others, presumably including his parents, who knew what Jesus had said and done. The gospel of Luke, on the other hand, was said to have been written by someone

Traditional View of Gospels

Matthew

The first gospel to be written. It was intended for Jews. The author was Jesus' disciple Matthew. This is still the official Roman Catholic view and is defended by Joseph Ratzinger.

Luke

The second gospel to be written. It was intended for Greeks. The author was Paul's companion Luke.

Mark

The third gospel to be written. It was intended for Romans and abbreviates both Matthew and Luke. The author was John Mark, who is mentioned in the Acts of the Apostles.

John

The last gospel to be written. It expresses the inner meaning of Jesus' teachings and was written by his disciple John.

Figure 19.1

either of Greek origin or a Jew educated as a Greek who collected eyewitness reports, as the author of the gospel claims in Luke 1:1–4. Finally, the gospel of John was supposed to have been written by the apostle John in his old age to fill in the gaps in the other gospels.

Apart from this traditional scheme, which relies upon a belief that the writers were eyewitnesses or knew eyewitnesses, it was also generally assumed, although seldom explicitly stated except by members of the Eastern Orthodox community, that Jesus spoke and taught in Greek. This being the case, it was easy for writers like John Calvin and a host of other Christian theologians to produce harmonies of the gospels, which were taken to include the actual words of Jesus as he spoke them.

This traditional scheme was challenged in the eighteenth century by various deistic writers, of whom Thomas Paine is probably the best example. These writers denied that gospels were eyewitness accounts, and some, like Paine, suggested that they were written hundreds of years after the event. Then, in the late eighteenth century, the German scholar Johann Gottfried von Herder (1744–1803) suggested that in reality Jesus must have spoken Aramaic. His argument was simple: when Jesus suffered on the cross, he cried out in Aramaic. This, Herder suggested, was actually the language Jesus normally spoke; therefore,

A Modern View of Gospels
The Synoptic Problem

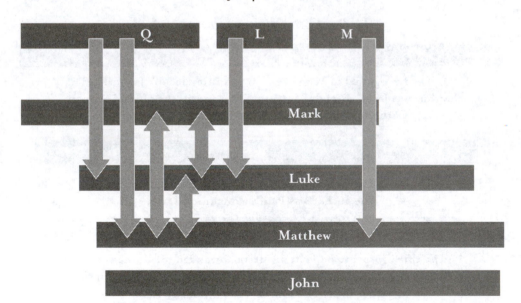

Figure 19.2 A modern view of the relationship between the Gospels. In this view, the existence of a yet-to-be-discovered text, known as Q, which stands for *Quelle*, German for "source," provides the basic framework for the Gospels, whose exact authorship is highly disputed and increasingly seen as the work of entire communities or locally established churches that preserved different fragmented traditions in an oral form. Like Q, sources "L" and "M" stand for lost manuscripts containing the gospel fragments that are unique to the gospels of Luke and Matthew.

out of a deep respect for him the authors of the Gospels, who normally wrote in Greek, preserved his original words in this agonizing instant.

Herder's suggestion was widely accepted, and now it has become the received wisdom that Jesus taught in Aramaic, necessitating the translation of his words into Greek by the gospel writers. The assumption that the words of Jesus in the Gospels are translations from Aramaic into Greek creates a serious problem. First, if the gospel writers are not recording the actual words of Jesus as he spoke them, why do the different authors translate what he said using identical words? Anyone who ever translated from one language to another knows that there are numerous ways of translating a passage. Therefore, translations invariably differ. If the material in the first three gospels, known as the Synoptic Gospels because they present a common picture of Jesus, shows little variation, this implies that the authors must have relied upon a common source or sources that translated Jesus' original Aramaic sayings into Greek, thus explaining why so many passages that cite Jesus' words are identical in the gospels. On the other hand, if Jesus spoke Greek, as earlier commentators assumed, and as the Greek Orthodox Church still maintains, these passages are easily explained as exact quotations from Jesus.

Eventually, as the new "science" of biblical criticism developed throughout the nineteenth century, scholars claimed to have identified various sources in the text of the New Testament. Rejecting the traditional view derived from the arguments of the church fathers that Matthew's is the earliest gospel, it was argued that Mark's gospel must be the earliest. Two main reasons were given for this. First, Mark's gospel lacks an ending. Therefore, it was argued that, contrary to the traditional view that the manuscript was damaged and the ending lost, it must have been written near to the time that the events took place. As a result, the author was unable to bring the story to the type of conclusion found in the other gospels. It was also argued that because Mark fails to mention the story of the virgin birth, the Christology, or view of the person of Jesus, held by the gospel writer was undeveloped and therefore an early account of Jesus' life unpolluted by later theological reflections.

Similarly, the critics argued that John's gospel must be the last to have been written because it contains a highly developed theology of the preexistent Christ, the Logos, found in John 1. This was said to indicate a late date and that the gospel had to be seen in connection with a Christian community that speculated about theological issues. Whether this community knew about the existence of the other gospels was also a matter of debate.

Photo 19.3 Johann Gottfried von Herder (1744–1803), the moving figure in early German Romanticism, and a key player in modern thinking about the origins of the Gospels. Intensely interested in local cultures, Herder questioned the age-old assumption that Jesus spoke Greek, suggesting instead that his language was Aramaic and that the gospel writers therefore translated Jesus' words into Greek.

Such arguments, including the one that 80 percent of Mark's gospel can be found in Matthew's gospel,[2] where, it is claimed, it is repeated word for word, led to the development of ideas about a common source. The most famous of these is the so-called "Q" document, which is said to lie behind the Synoptic Gospels. The only problem with this hypothesis is that in the last two hundred years not one single fragmentary document supporting the existence of such a source has been found. Thus, while biblical scholars may take Q for granted, any historian who looks at the evidence is bound to be skeptical.

Although, as with any other historical document, there are disputes about the origins of the New Testament, the fact remains that it is the best attested of all ancient manuscripts. The earliest surviving portion of a New Testament text is the famous John Rylands fragment, which contains a passage from the gospel of John. This is dated to AD 125. From the next few centuries, hundreds of manuscripts containing at least segments of the New Testament exist, while by the fourth and fifth century there are literally thousands of such manuscripts. Therefore, compared to other ancient manuscripts, those of the New Testament are not only remarkably well preserved but far earlier, and closer to the events.[3]

WHO WAS JESUS?

Many students, particularly those from Christian backgrounds, are often shocked to discover that we do not know the exact date of Jesus' birth. Actually, in historical terms this is not a great problem. The dates of Jesus' life are known fairly accurately, give or take ten years. By comparison, we can only guess at the date of the birth of the Buddha within a range of about three hundred years. About the dates of birth and death of many other religious leaders and founders there are similar disputes involving hundreds of years. Even in the case of Muhammad, scholars argue about exactly when he was born, although the date of his death is fairly certain.

With Jesus the problem concerns various events mentioned in the New Testament that need to be related to what is known about Roman history. For example, the author of the book of Matthew says that Jesus was born in Bethlehem, in Judea, during the reign of Herod the King. Since Herod died in 4 BC, Jesus must have been born before that time. The biblical account also talks about a star which guided the wise men; consequently, some scholars have attempted to harmonize this with known astronomical events. Again these seem to indicate a date around 5 BC. On the other hand, the gospel of Luke says that Jesus was born when Quirinius was governor of Syria. This poses a difficulty, because Quirinius is known to have ruled Syria from AD 6–9, although there is some evidence that perhaps he was there earlier, sometime around 5 BC, which would fit the biblical account.

Similar problems relate to the year of Jesus' death. To the historically naïve, such problems may appear major difficulties in accepting the New Testament account as histori-

---

2. Raymond E. Brown, *An Introduction to the New Testament* (New York: ABRL, Doubleday, 1997), 171. My thanks go to Katrine Brix for her comments on this and other sections dealing with early Christianity.

3. F. F. Bruce, *The New Testament Documents: Are They Reliable?* (1943; London: InterVarsity Press, 1970).

Photo 19.4 An early Christian painting of the death of Jesus from the sixth-century Syriac gospel book *The Rabbula Gospels*, now housed in Florence.

cally reliable. But anyone who has done historical research using archival materials soon discovers the difficulty of exact dating and the problems involved in confirming a date, even when you know something happened at a particular time. Anyone who doubts this has only to look at the biographies of any major historical figure, like Adolf Hitler, to discover that biographers even of people who lived quite recently often provide contradictory information about when certain events happened.

The biggest problem with dating the life of Jesus comes from the fact that in the sixth century the Christian monk Dionysius Exiguus (b. 525) used the existing Roman calendar to devise a system for identifying years since the birth of Jesus, for which he used the term AD, meaning *Anno Domini* or "in the year of our Lord." The system gradually gained acceptance throughout Western Christianity, although it was not accepted in Portugal until the sixteenth century. The term BC, or "Before Christ," was added centuries later by the English monk Bede (673–735). In the process of these calendar reforms, the date of Jesus' birth became confused. This, however, is not a great problem, because the New Testament does not use this dating system and therefore does not say exactly, in terms of our calendar, when Jesus was born.

On the basis of what the New Testament teaches about Jesus, Christians believe that he was the incarnation of God. Yet they do not believe that he was a demigod like the Greek gods, many of whom were born through the union of gods with humans to produce a creature that is half god and half human. Rather, Christians argue that the New Testament teaches that Jesus is fully God and fully human. This belief, which is central to traditional Christian teaching, involves the further belief that Jesus was conceived in a supernatural manner and born of the virgin Mary. Although many people throughout history have found this belief hard to accept, from the early gnostics to today's Jehovah's Witnesses, it seems to be the only one that really fits the full spectrum of New Testament teachings about Jesus and his relationship to God.

Belief in the incarnation implies that Joseph was not Jesus' physical father, although, knowing the nature of Jesus' conception, Joseph assumed the legal responsibility for

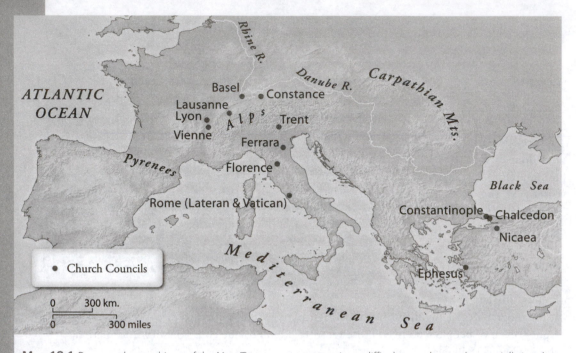

Map 19.1 Because the teachings of the New Testament are sometimes difficult to understand, especially in relation to the person of Jesus, leading theologians and Christian leaders met at regular intervals in the early centuries of the Christian era to try to express New Testament teachings in a systematic and noncontradictory manner. These meetings are known as the "church councils," the most important of which were the councils of Nicaea and Chalcedon in 325 and 451. Although many sensationalist authors, like Dan Brown, try to make a great mystery out of these meetings, we have good historical records about what took place and can be certain that there were not hidden agendas or unrevealed mysteries. All the evidence points to sincere Christians discussing and attempting to reach agreement about what the New Testament teaches.

him as his father. It also seems from the New Testament that Jesus had several brothers and sisters, although the Roman Catholic Church denies this and claims that the people referred to as "brothers and sisters" were actually cousins. The Gospel of Luke says that before Jesus' birth, Mary and Joseph traveled to Bethlehem to participate in a Roman census. They then fled as refugees to Egypt because King Herod had heard that a child born in Bethlehem would become the king of Judea and had ordered the killing of all male children in the area to eliminate possible rivals to his heirs. Mary and Joseph remained in Egypt until after the death of Herod, when they returned to the town of Nazareth. There Jesus spent his youth, learned Joseph's trade as a carpenter, and lived until he began his ministry around the age of thirty. Beyond this, the New Testament tells us very little about the early life of Jesus.

Here it is worth noting that the New Testament, like the Hebrew Bible, is written in what might be described as a minimalist style. Unlike other ancient texts, such as the poems of Homer, the Bible tells a straightforward story without elaboration. What is meant by this is carefully described by Eric Auerbach in his study *Mimesis: The Representation of*

Reality in Western Literature.[4] This now classic work begins with his essay "Odysseus' Scar,"[5] where he describes an incident in book 19 of the *Odyssey* and compares it with the story of Abraham and the sacrifice of Isaac.

Auerbach writes of Homer, "What he narrates is for the time being the only present, and fills both the stage and the reader's mind completely." It is Homer's style to leave "nothing which it mentions half in darkness and an unexternalized ... nothing must remain hidden and unexpressed."[6] This he contrasts with the biblical style, arguing that it tells the reader only things the reader needs to know. There are no frills, but only the bare bones of the story directed toward a religious goal. Despite the richness of the Homeric style, Auerbach concludes that there is far more psychological depth to the biblical narrative because it leaves the reader with a feeling of suspense. By contrast with Homer, which he describes as highly detailed but flat, the biblical style is multilayered and realistic.[7]

Above all, biblical writing is pregnant with meaning and a quest for truth. Auerbach writes, "The Bible's claim to truth ... is tyrannical" and "excludes all other truth claims."[8] "It would," he writes, "be difficult, then, to imagine styles more contrasting than those of these two equally ancient and equally epic texts. On the one hand, externalisation, uniformly illuminated phenomena, at a definite time and in a definite place, connected together without lacunae in a perpetual foreground. On the other hand, the externalisation of only so much of the phenomena as is necessary for the purpose of the narrative, all else left in obscurity ..."[9]

What Auerbach says of the Hebrew Bible is equally true of the New Testament. Unlike Homer, the New Testament never gives us a description of Jesus; we do not know how tall he was or the color of his hair or of his eyes, nor do we know any physical details about him. What the reader is presented with is a dynamic portrait of a living individual who commands authority among all around him. The bulk of the New Testament concerns the last few years of Jesus' life, teaching, ministry, and

Photo 19.5 Rembrandt van Rijn's (1606–1669) painting of the Greek bard Homer (1663). Over the past two centuries the study of Greek literature has profoundly shaped theories about the authorship of biblical texts.

---

4. Eric Auerbach, *Mimesis: The Representation of Reality in Western Literature*, trans. Willard Trask (New York: Doubleday Anchor, 1953), 1–20.
5. Ibid.
6. Ibid., 3–4.
7. Ibid., 5–8.
8. Ibid., 12.
9. Ibid., 9.

death. It begins with his baptism by John the Baptist when he was around the age of thirty. Jesus then begins preaching the coming of the kingdom and the demand for repentance. In the process he recruits twelve disciples, who remain with him as his close companions until the time of his death. The preaching ministry of Jesus is depicted in a variety of situations, where he enters into conflicts with religious leaders and teachers concerning the correct interpretation of the Torah and God's intentions for mankind. Alongside these incidents are a series of healings described as miracles. Sick people come to Jesus, and he invariably heals them, to the astonishment of all around.

Both Christians and academics disagree as to whether or not Jesus intended to found the Christian church from the beginning of his ministry. Joseph Ratzinger, the current pope, argues in his book *Jesus of Nazareth* that this was Jesus' intention. Indeed, Roman Catholic theology teaches that Jesus went further than simply founding a church; rather, he appointed one of his disciples, Peter, to be the head of the church. Other Christians dispute the claim that the Roman Catholic Church was directly founded by Jesus in this way. Some even suggest that Jesus did not intend to form a church at all but that it simply grew up after his death. This latter position is the one taken by most modern scholars, who see the Gospels as products of various communities of believers, who projected their own origins as a church backward into the teaching of Jesus, when they claim he never mentioned the church at all. Therefore verses such as Matthew 16:18 and 18:17 are seen to be the result of an editing process that met the needs of a local Christian community or a group of Christian communities.

Photo 19.6 Pietro Perugino's (1445–1523) fresco of Jesus giving Peter the key to heaven. In the background stands a church, while Peter is symbolized as the rock upon which the church is built, following the Roman Catholic Church's interpretation of Matthew 16:18.

Eventually, however, Jesus' teaching was seen as a threat by the religious authorities of his day, who controlled the temple in Jerusalem. He was arrested, brought before a religious court, and then taken to the secular authorities in the person of the Roman governor of Judea, Pontius Pilate. According to the New Testament, Pontius Pilate was unable to find any fault in Jesus; nevertheless, fearing a riot, he gave in to Jesus' accusers and executed him for treason, or fomenting rebellion against Rome. After this Jesus was buried in a secure grave, and the story appeared to have ended. The religious authorities, however were worried that Jesus 'disciples would steal his body and claim a miracle. Therefore, according to the New Testament, a Roman guard was placed at the tomb. Despite this, on the third day, Jesus was miraculously resurrected from the dead. The guards fled and his disciples were terrified when Jesus appeared among them.

The interpretation given to these events in the New Testament is that Jesus' death was prophesied in the Hebrew Bible and was an act of reconciliation between God and humanity. Through his death the sacrifices of the Hebrew Bible were abolished, and a new covenant, as predicted in Jeremiah 31:31, was established between God and mankind that includes all people, not simply the Jews. This interpretation is developed in the earliest writings of the New Testament, known as the Letters, or Epistles, of Paul and other apostles, such as Peter, James, Jude, and John.

The impact of these events on Jesus' disciples and the spread of Christianity to the rest of the world are described in the Acts of the Apostles, which immediately follows the gospel of John in modern New Testaments. Finally, at the end of the New Testament, following the epistles of John, is the book of Revelation, a highly figurative work which is so poetic and elusive in its meaning that even the great biblical commentator John Calvin (1509–1564) refused to attempt to interpret it. To appreciate the way the New Testament interprets the life and death of Jesus, it is necessary to understand the framework within which it interprets and claims to explain the significance of the Hebrew Bible, which for Christians became the Old Testament.

FROM "HEBREW BIBLE" TO "OLD TESTAMENT"

For Christians the only way to understand their religion is to begin at the beginning with the story of God's creation, the transgression of Adam and Eve, known as "the fall," and the subsequent revelation of God's will to the Jewish people, found in what Christians have traditionally called the "Old Testament." Whatever the reader may think of these stories, particularly the story of creation and the way this story is interpreted by Christians, there is no doubt that it sets the tone for the whole drama of Christian experience. Without an understanding of the Jewish scriptures, these stories that grip the mind and imagination of Christians make no sense.

According to Christians, God created the universe out of nothing. Unlike some other religious traditions, Christianity does not teach that the world was created out of preexisting matter, energy, or anything else. Rather, the story of creation begins with God and God alone. This God, who is spoken about in masculine language, created all that is by an act of his sovereign will. In Latin this belief is known as creation *ex nihilo*, "out of nothing."

Photo 19.7 Giovanni Battista Cima da Conegliano's (1459–1517) *The Presentation of the Baby Jesus at the Temple* draws attention to the continuity between the Old Testament and the New. What is striking about this picture is that the baby Jesus is nowhere in sight, although, if you look carefully, you can see Mary in the group at the bottom of the stairs. What the picture does is draw attention to the fact that Christians have always maintained that first his family and then Jesus fulfilled the law of the Hebrew Bible and thus completed the mission of Judaism. On the other hand, numerous heretical movements have sought to cut Christianity off from its Jewish roots.

Once the universe was created, God proceeded to form the earth and populate it with all that we see of plants, animals, and everything that lives. Finally, God created humans, whom he placed in "a garden" known as "Eden." Here our original ancestors were told that they would inherit the earth, which God pronounced good. The one condition was that they obey the command of God their creator.

The specific command given to the first humans, who are spoken of as Adam and Eve, was simple. They could eat from every tree in the garden except one, identified as the tree of the "knowledge of good and evil." At first our original ancestors obeyed their creator. But then, something happened to cause them to disobey. In chapter 3 of the book of Genesis we are told that Adam and Eve were tempted by a serpent who convinced them that they ought to eat of the forbidden tree.

Once they did so, a change came over the entire creation, and for the first time they became self-conscious. In biblical language, they realized their nakedness. Consequently, they could no longer face God or commune with him as they had done in the past. Not only that, but each human, Adam and Eve, blamed the other for what they had done, and they both blamed the serpent.

Although this story may sound quaint, the moral behind it is far from trivial. Essentially, the whole issue of the fall revolves around the question of whether humans trust and obey their creator or whether they go their own way. The key passage in this story is Genesis 3:1, where we are told that "the serpent" asked the question, "Did God really say ..." In other words, the word of God was thrown into question and doubted.

The Bible says that, as a result of this act of disobedience, Adam and Eve were expelled from the garden of Eden, or paradise. Once again an important point is made. Because of an original act of disobedience, which involved the failure to trust God and obey his word, communication between humans and their creator broke down. As Genesis continues, the effects of this sin are seen in a breakdown of human relations, human pitted against human, as deceit and murder enters their world. These stories are intended to say something very significant about the situation in which humans find themselves living throughout human history.

After relating how human communication breaks down and life on earth becomes hellish, Genesis tells the story of Noah and the flood. This is important because it is the first mention of God's entering into a covenant to save, or redeem, humans from the mess into which they had fallen. The story of the flood is followed by the story of the Tower of Babel, which stresses that although different races speak different languages and have very different customs, they are indeed part of one human race created by God.

The story becomes more specific with the account of Abraham and his descendants, beginning in Genesis 11:27. Although in many ways Jews and Muslims share these stories with Christians, the interpretation each religion gives them is significantly different. For example, while Christians see in the account of the creation and the flood evidence of God as a loving father of mankind, such an idea as calling God our father is blasphemous to Muslims. Similarly, while Jews see Abraham as their physical father, Christians see him as their spiritual father. What is important for Jews is descent

Photo 19.8 Adam and Eve's expulsion from paradise, as portrayed by the Italian painter Tommaso di Giovanni di Simone Cassai Masaccio (1401–1428).

from Abraham. What is important for Christians is acting in the way Abraham acted in terms of exercising trust in God.

The next important step in the unfolding drama is what Christians call redemption. This begins with the story of the exodus and the Jewish liberation from Egyptian captivity. Here again the basic story is shared with Jews and Muslims. The difference is that Christians have traditionally seen the story as conveying a spiritual message that goes far beyond the actual events. For them the story of the exodus is a type, or analogy, of redemption. Living in Egypt is a vivid image of life in this world, while the salvation of the children of Israel becomes an image of salvation in Christ. It is not, therefore, the possession of the land which is important to Christians, but rather acting in faith, as Moses and those who were faithful to his message acted in faith.

Like Jews, Christians see the development of God's covenants, first with Noah, then with Abraham, and later with Moses and the people of Israel, as a hermeneutical tool with which to understand the history of redemption. In the Christian view, the covenants prepared the people of Israel as God's chosen people who would be a witness to him in the world. At the same time, through the covenants, other nations would learn about God's nature and his interest in humankind. Most importantly, the covenants laid the foundation for the coming of the Messiah who Christians believe is Jesus Christ. Here it should be

Photo 19.9 *God's Covenant with Noah*, by Anton Koch (1768–1839). Painted in 1803, this work captures the covenantal structure of the Bible.

pointed out that the name "Christ" is actually a title for the Messiah and not the surname of Jesus which, in practice, it has become over the centuries.

Where Christians depart from the Jewish interpretation of the covenants is in their insistence on the spiritual core of the covenants and on the importance of faith in establishing their validity. These teachings, found in the New Testament, are based upon the Christian belief held by most Christians, but rejected by dispensationalists, that all the covenants are part of God's one covenant with mankind. Therefore, his covenant with the Jews is simply a preparation for the revelation of an even greater covenant that fulfills the covenant with Israel. As a result, Christians speak about a "new and everlasting covenant" (Mark 14:24; 1 Corinthians 11:25; 2 Corinthians 3), which is "a better covenant" (Hebrews 7:22). In this sense, although Christians have always accepted the Hebrew Bible, they gave it a radically new interpretation based upon their reading of Jeremiah 31:31–34.

This interpretation can be seen in the way Christians look at the other books in the Hebrew Bible—the histories, prophetic writing, and poetry—which are all interpreted by Christians in a similar way. For them, those books point forward to Christ and provide examples of faith to be followed. They also act as a warning of what happens when people lose faith and wander from obedience to their God. This method of interpretation, which takes the history seriously but gives it a spiritual importance in terms of faith, is derived from the New Testament. Unlike Jews, who read the Hebrew Bible in terms of itself, Christians have traditionally read the Hebrew Bible through the lens of the New Testament, and particularly the work of Christ.

Consequently, figures like Joshua, Elijah, David, Isaiah, and numerous others who appear in the Hebrew Bible are seen as, in some respects, prefiguring the life and work of Jesus. Similarly, the sacrifices initiated by Moses and eventually centralized at the temple in Jerusalem become figures, or illustrations, of the meaning of the sacrifice of Christ. Likewise, verses which in themselves appear to be talking about events in a given historical situation are reinterpreted as evidence of prophetic foresight that points forward to the life and death of Jesus.

The best examples of such usage are found in Isaiah 7:10–17 and 9:2–7, which are interpreted as prophecies of the birth of Jesus. Chapter 53 is seen as a prophecy of his death. Since the Enlightenment and rise of modern biblical criticism, the predictive elements of these verses, and others like them, have been cast into doubt. For example, it is often said that Matthew's use of Isaiah 7:14 as evidence of the virgin birth (Matthew 1:22–23) actually shows that Matthew, or whoever wrote his gospel, misunderstood the text of the Hebrew Bible, because, the critics claim, the Hebrew word used by the author of Isaiah for "virgin" actually means "young woman." Yet the author of Matthew's gospel translates it as virgin.

What could possibly be a better example of the confusion of the author of the gospel? Surely, some might say, this shows how unreliable the New Testament actually is. All this sounds very convincing until it is realized that the author of Matthew's gospel was actually using the Greek translation of the Hebrew Bible, where the Greek word for "virgin" is used to describe the young woman in Isaiah 7. Further, it is important to recognize that this was

Photo 19.10 The annunciation, or announcement of the coming of the Messiah, Jesus the Christ, from a book of hours (a devotional genre) commissioned by the French duchess Anne de Bretagne (1477–1514).

no scribal error. For whatever reason, the translators of the Greek version of the Hebrew Bible, known as the Septuagint, deliberately chose this word to express what they believed Isaiah meant when they translated the Hebrew some 250 years before the birth of Jesus. From this it is clear that at least one group of Jews prior to the time of Jesus believed in something like the virgin birth in connection with their expected Messiah. Therefore, the use made of this verse by the author of Matthew was in line with at least one tradition of Jewish interpretation.

What is important here is that the early Christians saw themselves in a particular tradition of biblical interpretation that gained its fullest expression in the teachings of Jesus. For them, the New Testament interpreted the Old; the Old Testament did not interpret the New, even though it was very important for understanding the meaning of the New Testament.

Historically, Christians paid little attention to the events in Jewish history from the closing of the Old Testament canon, with the writing of the book of Malachi, to the coming of Jesus. Although the stories recorded in the various apocryphal books were seen as useful for filling in historical details, they were not seen as revelation in the same way as the Old and New Testaments. Therefore, Christians view the Old Testament as laying an indispensable foundation for their faith.

THE RESURRECTION

For all Christians the most important events in the New Testament are the death and resurrection of Jesus and the events leading up to them. His death is seen as both a fulfillment of Old Testament prophecy and an act of propitiation for the sins of humankind. Then, it is believed, as proof of the truth of Jesus' teaching and that God accepted his act of atonement, Jesus was raised from the dead.

According to the gospel accounts, the disciples were initially terrified by the risen Jesus, and many refused to believe that he had actually risen. Eventually, they became convinced, and, according to the Acts of the Apostles (Acts 2), the Holy Spirit came upon them on the Jewish feast of Shavuot, or the harvest, which became known as the day of Pentecost. From then on they boldly proclaimed the resurrected Christ whenever and to whomever they could. In particular, those disciples who actually saw the risen Christ became known as apostles.

As a result of these preaching activities, the temple authorities began to persecute the early church. One of the earliest martyrs was a bold Christian preacher named Stephen, who was stoned to death by his opponents for blasphemy (Acts 6–7). According to the Acts of the Apostles, one of the people who incited the crowd against Stephen was a young rabbi called Saul (Acts 8:1).

Later the story develops by explaining that this same Saul, who hated the emerging Christian church, was sent to Damascus to warn Jewish congregations there against the claims being made by Christian preachers. On his way, Saul was transformed. The writer of Acts, who is generally thought to be the author of the gospel of Luke, writes, "As he neared Damascus on his journey, suddenly a light from heaven flashed around him. He fell to the ground and heard a voice say to him, 'Saul, Saul, why do you persecute me?'" (Acts 9:3–4).

The story then goes on to describe how this bright light temporarily blinded Saul, how he was guided by God to the home of a Christian, how he was baptized, and how he became a Christian. He then studied the Christian message and the Jewish scriptures for around three years, after which he became the leading evangelist of the Christian church. St. Paul, as he is known to Christians, was also counted as an apostle, because it is said that he encountered and saw the living Christ.

For Paul the central message brought to earth by Jesus is that God forgives sins on the basis of faith in the saving death of Jesus Christ. This, Paul argues, God confirmed through the resurrection. In 1 Corinthians 15:1–22, Paul describes the significance of these events: "Now, brothers, I want to remind you of the gospel I preached to you, which you received and on which you have taken your stand. By this gospel you are saved, if you hold firmly to the word I preached to you

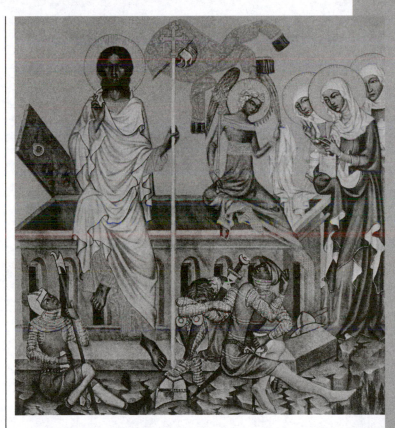

Photo 19.11 *The Resurrection of Christ* (ca. 1350), by the Master of Hohenfurth. This picture captures the essence of the Christian message: "Christ is Risen."

... Christ died for our sins according to the Scriptures, ... he was buried, ... he was raised on the third day according to the Scriptures ... If Christ has not been raised, our preaching is useless and so is your faith. More than that, we are then found to be false witnesses about God ... If only for this life we have hope in Christ, we are to be pitied more than all men. But Christ has indeed been raised from the dead, the firstfruits of those who have fallen asleep ... For as in Adam all die, so in Christ all will be made alive."

With this powerful argument in mind, we now turn to what happened to the Christian church after the end of the apostolic age—that is, from the beginning of church history to our own time.

CHAPTER 20

CHRISTIAN HISTORY

INTRODUCTION

The history of the Christian church can be divided into several distinct periods. The first concerns the ministry of Jesus and the apostolic age. The second is the period of the early church until about the fifth century and the destruction of the Western Roman Empire. During this time churches were established throughout the Roman Empire and beyond. To appreciate the extent of Christian expansion, one must realize that most maps of the Roman Empire at the height of its power are highly misleading, because they usually give the impression that the civilized world was restricted to the Roman Empire, India, and China, all of which had little or no contact with each other.

GLOBAL CHRISTIANITY

While it is true that contact between these great civilizations may have been minimal, there is no doubt that contact did take place. Further, beyond the borders of the Roman Empire were other civilizations that belonged to neither India nor China. Most importantly, there was a thriving Persian empire which occupied parts of the Middle East, including Iraq. In addition, there were friendly states in Africa that traded with Rome. In fact, in many ways, Roman Africa stretched as far south as Ethiopia and included the present-day Sudan, which was a source of gold and other minerals to the Romans. And the first kingdom on the borders of the Roman Empire to become Christian was the kingdom of Armenia, where the king and his people were baptized in 301.

Therefore, when thinking about the expansion of the Christian church, we must recognize that it very quickly established itself beyond the borders of the empire in both friendly areas of Africa and hostile regions of the Persian Empire. For example, the Christian kingdom of Nubia, in the modern Sudan, survived until around 1350, yet no one remembers this today, nor do we study the long history of Armenian Christianity. There also seems to be growing evidence that Christian missionaries reached India and China by the second century. Therefore, Christian history really needs to be rethought and taught in terms of world Christianity.

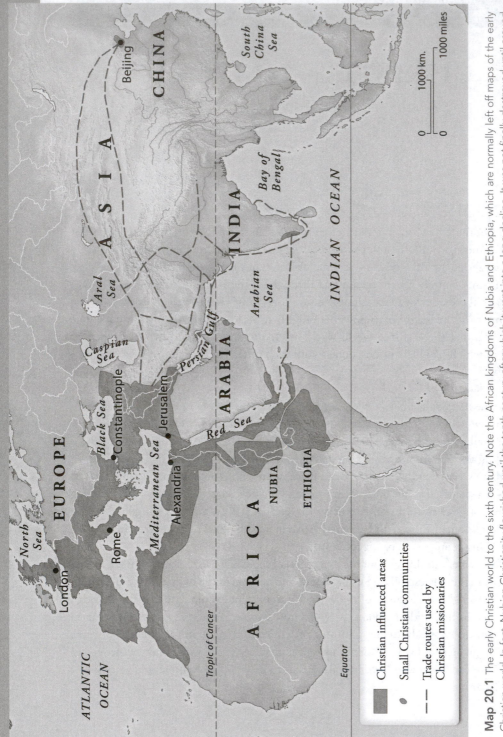

Map 20.1 The early Christian world to the sixth century. Note the African kingdoms of Nubia and Ethiopia, which are normally left off maps of the early Christian world. In fact, Nubian Christianity flourished until the tenth century after which it went into a long decline. It was not finally destroyed until around 1350; scholars argue about the exact date. Similarly, Ethiopian Christianity has survived until the present. Also by the sixth century, Christianity had spread along trade routes to both China and India. Although we know little about these early Christian communities, we know they existed. This global expansion of Christianity ended in the seventh century with the rise of Islam. At that time the traditional trade routes along which Christian missionaries traveled to both China and India fell, along with the African kingdoms of Ethiopia and Nubia, under Muslim control, and contact with European Christianity virtually ceased.

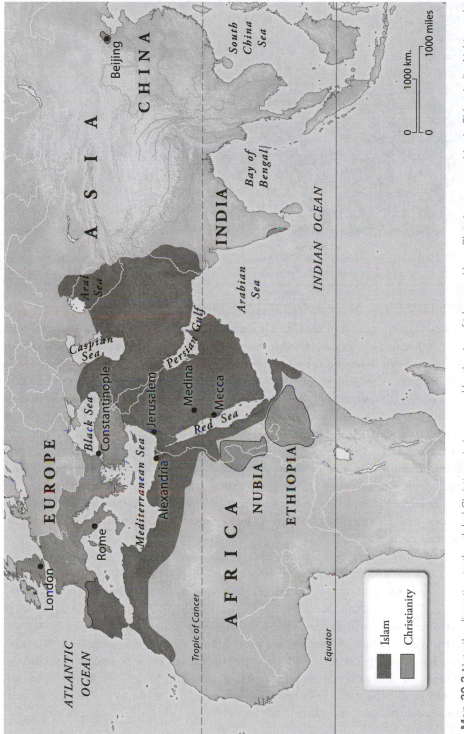

Map 20.2 Note the disruption to the global Christian mission caused by the rise of Islam, and how Christian communities in China, India, Nubia, and Ethiopia are now isolated from European Christianity.

Photo 20.1 The above scene is from Piero Della Francesca's (ca. 1415–1492) fresco *The Triumph of Constantine*, painted between 1452 and 1456. This battle ended the era of Christian persecution.

CHRISTIANITY IN THE ROMAN EMPIRE

Nevertheless, for practical purposes, this account of Christian history will concentrate on Europe, particularly western Europe, because it was in these areas that those forms of Christianity which dominate the world today came to fruition. After years of both mild and severe persecution, Emperor Constantine issued what is known as the Edict of Milan in 313. Although Constantine (288–337) had a Christian mother, he was not baptized until near death, and at no time did he make Christianity the religion of the Roman Empire, as is so often claimed. All he did was issue an edict of tolerance and stop the official persecution of Christians.

After the death of Constantine, the persecution of Christians resumed until the time of Emperor Theodosius (347–395), who did make Christianity the official religion of the Roman Empire. Yet, contrary to some reports, he did not attempt to obliterate Roman paganism as practiced by pagan families. All he did was make Christianity the state religion for state functions.

During this early period of church history, Christians struggled in two main realms. The first was the doctrinal. Unlike all other major world religions, Christianity places its primary emphasis upon right belief and secondly upon right practice. Orthodoxy, therefore, is far more important than liturgical forms. For early Christians the great challenge was deciding what to make of Jesus and his relationship to the God of Abraham. According to the Torah, which the earliest disciples of Jesus, all of whom were Jews, accepted, there is only one God. Yet during his life, as recorded in the New Testament, Jesus did and said things that God alone can do and say. For example, in Matthew 9:2, a paralytic was brought to Jesus, who said, "Take heart, my son; your sins are forgiven." Such statements are problematic because, according to Jewish teachings, only God can forgive sins.

Throughout the New Testament there can be found other examples of Jesus taking upon himself the attributes of God. In the prologue to the gospel of John we read, "In the beginning was the Word, and the Word was with God, and the Word was God. He was with God in the beginning. Through him all things were made; without him nothing was made that has been made. In him was life, and that life was the light of men. The light shines in the darkness, but the darkness has not understood it" (John 1:1–5). A few verses later the meaning of this text is explained, when the author of John's gospel writes, "The Word became flesh and made his dwelling among us. We have seen his glory, the glory of the One and Only, who came from the Father, full of grace and truth ... For the law was given through Moses; grace and truth came through Jesus Christ. No one has ever seen God, but God the One and Only, who is at the Father's side, has made him known" (John 1:14–18).

To someone brought up to be a Jew, such statements and explanations were extremely problematic. How could Jesus be a man and yet God? How could Jesus be God when there is only one God— God the Father? What did all this mean? During the first few centuries of the Christian era, well-educated thinkers struggled with the meaning of Jesus in terms of the clear teachings of the Bible. In the end these issues were resolved by a series of church councils, the most important of which was probably the Council of Nicaea in 325. There and at the other councils, as well as in the works of numerous Christian authors, the doctrine of the person of Jesus Christ and his relationship to God was carefully worked out in what became known as the doctrine of the incarnation, which teaches that God became man. That is, Jesus was fully human (unlike Krishna, who as a god took human form), yet at the same time he was fully God. Closely related to this was the doctrine of the Trinity, which states that while there is only one God, he exists in three persons—Father, Son (Jesus), and Holy Spirit.

Photo 20.2 Jesus in glory. This mosaic stands over the Communion table in the Peace Church of the palace of Sanssouci, in Potsdam, Germany. On the wall above the mosaic is a biblical quotation from Colossians 2:9: "For in Christ all the fullness of the Deity lives in bodily form." Of Italian origin, the mosaic was brought to Germany in the nineteenth century to save it from destruction.

On the practical side, Christians in the early centuries struggled with both slavery and the Roman games. Although the New Testament does not condemn slavery, and Jesus never mentions it, implicit in the message of Jesus is the dignity of each human being. Therefore, by around the sixth century slavery was in decline and in many areas banned outright as a result of Christian agitation. Similarly, the Roman games held throughout the empire in thousands of stadiums were opposed by Christians, because literally

Photo 20.3 Bethlehem in the late nineteenth century, looking very much as it probably did in the first century, at the time of Jesus' birth. The Christmas story has reminded Christians through the ages that their Savior was born as a refugee in a town where there was "no room in the inn." This powerful image has given Christianity a strong social conscience and concern throughout the centuries.

thousands of people died horrible deaths in them every year. As a result of Christian opposition, they were banned in 404, although they probably lingered on in some areas until the mid-fifth century.

The next great challenge faced by the church was the eruption of barbarian invasions from the fifth century onward. Although these invasions initially led to the destruction of many churches and the persecution of Christians, before long the barbarians adopted the religion of the conquered. During this period Christians were taunted by their pagan compatriots with the charge that Christianity had only brought destruction to Rome. This charge was answered by St. Augustine of Hippo (354−430) in his classic work *The City of God* (412−413).[1] In this complex treatise Augustine argued for a view of providence that recognized God as the God of history.

THE BYZANTINE EMPIRE

At that point Christian history divides between the history of the Byzantine Empire in the East and the barbarian kingdoms in the West. In the East the capital of the Roman Empire was established by Emperor Constantine in the city that became known as Constantinople, from which the Eastern, or Byzantine, Empire was ruled. This empire, little known among Western Christians, continued as a Christian civilization until the city of

---

1. A good modern translation of this Latin work into English is Augustine, *The City of God against the Pagans*, ed. and trans. R. W. Dyson (Cambridge: Cambridge Univ. Press, 1998).

PLAN OF CONSTANTINOPLE IN 1481

Photo 20.4 Constantinople in 1481, twenty-eight years after its conquest by the Turks. Already the great Church of St. Sophia, the second largest building in the picture, has been converted into a mosque with two minarets, one on either side.

Constantinople was captured by the Turks in the name of Islam in 1453. Since then it has been a Muslim city which until the twentieth century had a large Christian population. From Byzantium, Christian missionaries penetrated into Russia and the Ukraine as well as other areas of eastern Europe.

CHRISTIANITY IN THE WEST

Compared to the steady development of a Christian civilization in the East, until it was challenged by Muslim invaders in the seventh century, the history of Christianity in the West is best seen as two steps forward and one step backward. Until around the tenth century, western Europe was unstable, continually threatened by external, pagan, invaders. The devastating effects of such invasions are well documented by the seventh-century historian known as the Venerable Bede (673–735), a monk who lived in Jarrow, part of the kingdom of Northumbria in northern England. His great work, *The Ecclesiastical History of English People* (731),[2] is not only the first history of England but a fascinating account of the trials and tribulations of Christians living on the northern frontier.

---

2. Bede, the Venerable, *Ecclesiastical History of the English People*, trans. Leo Sherley-Price, rev. by R. E. Latham, new introduction and notes by D. H. Farmer (Harmondsworth: Penguin, 1990).

Christianity reached Northumbria around the second century, when the island was still part of the Roman Empire. As in other parts of Europe under Roman rule, Christianity was brought by missionaries, traders, and soldiers drafted into the Roman army. Over the next few centuries Christianity took hold, and churches were established and flourished in many areas. Then came the withdrawal of the Roman legions and the barbarian invasions, as pagan Anglo-Saxon tribes moved into Britain, destroying the existing Christian society. In the fifth century the process of reconversion began when missionaries were sent to England by the pope in Rome, and it was remarkably successful. This is a story Bede records.

Following Bede's death, Viking invasions destroyed the new Anglo-Saxon Christian culture he described so well. Consequently, large areas of Britain reverted to paganism. The process of converting the invaders and reconverting British people who had lapsed into paganism was begun again by surviving Christian communities with the help of missionaries from Europe. This time the people living in Britain became and remained Christians until modern times. A similar process is documented all over western Europe in Richard's Fletcher's excellent book *The Conversion of Europe*.[3] Noting that the motives for conversion were always complex, Fletcher observes that the historian must take into account the motives of both the preachers and those who received their message. Pagans did not simply convert because they were forced to convert. They converted because they saw something in Christianity which attracted them.

The task of the historian, in Fletcher's view, is to attempt to understand what message was communicated to these pagans and why they responded to it. He further observes that the criteria for conversion were not simple. Rather, most Christian missionaries required that a person meet rigorous standards before being baptized. One of the more puzzling, and for modern writers difficult, issues is what to do with the numerous accounts of miracles that appear in our earliest archival documents.

RESVREXI ET ADHVC TECVM SVM. PS. CXXXVIII.

IHESVM QVERITIS NASSARENVM SVRREXIT NON E HIC. M. VL.

Photo 20.5 People who are troubled by miracle stories in early Christian histories overlook the fact that the great miracle of the resurrection stands at the heart of Christianity. The above painting by Fra Giovanni da Fiesole (ca. 1387–1455), nicknamed "Angelico" because of the angelic nature of his work, shows the women discovering the empty tomb of Jesus and being told of his resurrection by an angel.

---

3.   Richard Fletcher, *The Conversion of Europe* (London: Fontana, 1998). The American title is *Barbarian Conversion* (Cambridge, Mass.: Harvard Univ. Press, 1998).

Fletcher observes that again and again people were converted because they "accepted without question that the miraculous could weave like a shuttle in and out of everyday reality." He then adds, "we need to remember this, and to resist the temptation to dismiss it out of hand as infantile credulity: patronising the past never helped anyone to understand it."[4]

This was a world very unlike our own, a world where not only was the miraculous taken for granted, but martyrs, pilgrimage, and exemplary Christian living played key roles in the conversion of pagan peoples. The conversion process, Fletcher notes, "was a very slow business," where missionaries were engaged "in an urgent and competitive enterprise" with the living paganism that often opposed their activities with violent brutality.[5] For their part, Christian missionaries and evangelists worked "miracles, wonders, [and] exorcisms" and indulged in "temple-torching and shrine-smashing." While we may find such activities embarrassing, for centuries they were accepted as quite normal. Therefore, Fletcher advises, "It is usually fruitless to indulge in speculation about what might have been the 'real' basis of miracle stories."[6] Wisely, he concludes that while such stories may embarrass us, we must remain faithful to our sources, because "this is what our sources tell us; we have to make of it what we can."[7]

THE MEDIEVAL ACHIEVEMENT

Throughout this early period the great monastic orders played a key role. For this reason *The Rule of St. Benedict*,[8] which was followed by members of the Cistercian monastic order and became the basis for Western monasticism, is one of the most important documents in the Christian history of the West. As a missionary order, the Cistercians were unrivaled. All over Europe, particularly in border areas at the interface between Christianity and paganism, Cistercian

Photo 20.6 The ruins of the once great Cistercian Abbey of Rievaulx, in a remote part of Yorkshire, England.

4. Ibid., 11.
5. Ibid., 64.
6. Ibid., 45.
7. Ibid., 65.
8. Benedict, *The Rule of St. Benedict*, in Owen Chadwick, ed. and trans., *Western Asceticism* (London: SCM Press, 1958), 291–337. For a discussion and explanation of the *Rule*, see Hubert van Zeller, OSB, *The Holy Rule* (New York: Sheed and Ward, 1958).

Photo 20.7 Part of an exhibit in the abbey's Interpretive Centre that documents the many activities and commercial enterprises of the monks. This particular exhibit emphasizes the development of sheep farming and the manufacture of wool.

monasteries revolutionized agriculture and developed mining, manufacturing, and trade, while at the same time spreading the gospel.

It is easy for Protestants to dismiss these ventures as a distorted form of asceticism. To do so is to misunderstand the times. In an age of chaos, the monasteries were islands of stability that preserved education and civilization, even though the ascetic practices that many of the greatest monastic leaders observed appear to many to undervalue the importance of faith.

Until at least the eleventh century, the majority of parish ministers were married clergy, many of whose children inherited the churches where their fathers preached. Because of the obvious potential for abuse, reforming bishops of Rome, known as popes, such as Pope Gregory VII (1020 or 1025–1085), also known as Hildebrand, outlawed the practice, although it continued in many areas for centuries. In England clerical celibacy was promoted by St. Dunstan (born sometime before 925), archbishop of Canterbury from 960 to 988. But it was not until William the Bastard, also known as the Conqueror, the Duke of Normandy, invaded England and imposed Norman rule and policies of cultural genocide on the native English that the practice of celibacy became widespread. For example, the great medieval spiritual teacher, Aelred of Rievaulx (ca. 1110–1167), who was called "the St. Bernard of the North," came from a long family of clerics who inherited the ancient priory of Hexham, which in the time of Bede was one of the most important churches in northern Europe. Aelred's classic work *Spiritual Friendship*, written shortly after he became abbot of Rievaulx in 1147, is still read today and is a testament to a depth and wealth of monastic spirituality from which all Christians can benefit.

Starting around 940, a little-known and quite remarkable popular movement known as the Pax Dei, or "the peace of God," spread throughout Europe. This great movement gathered momentum in the eleventh century and remained active well into the thirteenth. Arguing that to kill a fellow Christian was to kill Christ, the movement sought to bring an end to the intermittent warfare that plagued medieval Europe. Despite its ultimate failure, the movement succeeded in bringing about various peace treaties, such as the Treaty of Cologne in 1083. It also went a long way to regulating warfare, protecting civilians, and promoting peace as an ideal among both rulers and ordinary people.

During the Middle Ages the Roman Catholic Church flourished in western Europe, while the Eastern Orthodox churches were missionizing Russia and the Slavic realms. All the evidence suggests that communities like Rievaulx flourished for several hundred years before they went into a slow decline. Certainly, by the sixteenth century, many were struggling to survive. Although recent historical work has cast doubt on the more dramatic denunciations of the medieval church by

Photo 20.8 The restored Abbey Church of Iona, which today houses the ecumenical Iona Community. St. Columba founded the monastary of Iona in 563. It rapidly became known as a place of piety, learning, and evangelism from which missionaries were sent to Europe. The community was destroyed by the Vikings in 794.

Protestant Reformers, and although popular piety may have flourished among the laity, there seems little doubt that many of the monastic orders were in serious trouble by the sixteenth century.

Yet at the height of their power, the monastic orders created the basis for modern Europe. They built great monastic complexes in the countryside and provided the churches and cathedrals of cities with many of their best preachers. They created a communications network that crisscrossed Europe at a time when secular powers could barely control their own realms. Through their excellent system of hospitals and medical training, they provided hospitality to pilgrims and other travelers, and medical aid to the sick and injured. They supported the universities, often providing them with their greatest scholars, and they sent out evangelists and preachers throughout the known world.

THE REFORMATION

However, by the sixteenth century, many monasteries were failing to attract new

Photo 20.9 Martyrs Bay, Iona, where in 806 the eighty-six monks who remained after the Viking destruction were slaughtered.

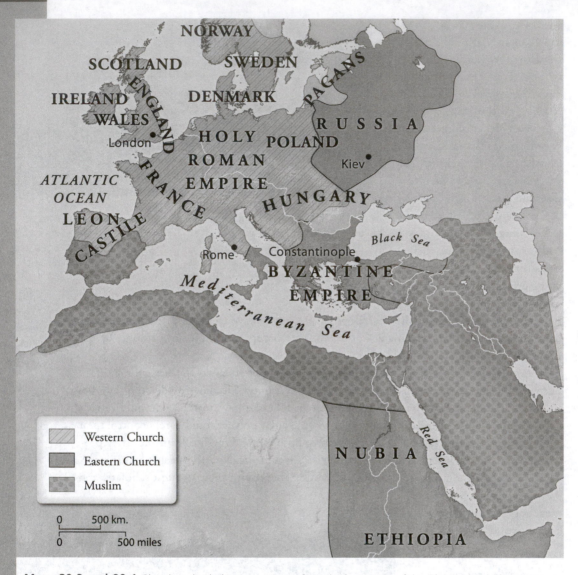

Maps 20.3 and 20.4 Churches divided in various ways from the beginning of the Christian era. The most important division was that between what became the Orthodox and Catholic traditions on the one hand and the smaller Coptic, Syriac, and Nestorian traditions on the other. Nevertheless, Christians retained a remarkable sense of unity, reinforced by numerous church councils and well-organized administrative arrangements. By the eleventh century European Christian churches had separated into two major divisions along linguistic lines. In the East the Orthodox tradition developed, using Greek and later other languages like Ukrainian and Russian for worship. In the West the Roman Catholic Church based its worship on the use of Latin. Another major division following tenth- and eleventh-century reforms in the Roman Catholic Church was that the clergy were forbidden to marry, while in

the East clergy could marry. By the eleventh century these divisions, which stretched back to the beginning of the Christian era, became formalized. Map 20.3 above shows the situation around the year 1000. The next major division among Christian churches came in the sixteenth century when the Western Roman Catholic Church rejected the reforms proposed by Martin Luther (1483–1546). Subsequently, between 1525 and 1648, the Western church divided into numerous smaller groupings, including Anglicans in England; Calvinists in Scotland, the Netherlands, Hungary, and various other parts of Europe; Lutherans in Germany and Scandinavia; and the Roman Catholic Church largely in southern areas and Poland, as Map 20.4 shows.

recruits, and the standard of discipline and spirituality in many houses had fallen to a low ebb. At this point a German monk and pious Augustinian, Martin Luther (1483–1546), set off a chain reaction that was to change Europe and the world. This reaction, which arose out of his search for peace with God and an authentic spiritual life, tore apart the unity of medieval Christendom, creating two great blocks. The countries of the north, except Poland and parts of Ireland, became Protestant. In the south, Italy, France, Spain, and Austria remained loyally Catholic.

Luther's transformation began when he was appointed professor of theology and lecturer of interpretation of Scripture at the University of Wittenberg in 1512. In studying the Bible, he slowly came to the conviction that Christians find peace with God through their faith in Jesus Christ. He termed this doctrine "justification by faith alone," based on the arguments of Paul found in chapters 3 and 4 of the book of Romans and in the book of Galatians.

The Reformation is usually said to have begun on 31 October 1517, when Luther nailed ninety-five theses onto the door of the palace church in Wittenberg. This act, which was a normal way in which medieval scholars entered into academic debates, launched the Reformation. In his theses, Luther questioned the basis of salvation as taught by the Catholic Church, in particular the practice of selling indulgences, which were said to free people from their sins. He insisted that, based on Scripture, only faith in Christ leads to the forgiveness of sin.

At first, all Luther wanted to do was reform the church and remove practices like indulgences, which he believed were contrary to the clear teaching of Scripture. But the conflict with church authorities soon escalated. Instead of responding to Luther's detailed criticism of their practices, Catholic authorities hardened their stance, eventually condemning Luther as a heretic.

Luther's study of Scripture led him to abandon more and more traditional Catholic doctrines. He abandoned belief in purgatory, a realm somewhere between heaven and earth where the dead were said to go until ready for heaven. He also realized that Catholic teachings about celibacy lacked a biblical foundation; therefore, he encouraged his followers to marry even though they were priests. Eventually, in 1525, he too was married, to a former nun, Katherina von Bora (1499–1552), entering into what was by all accounts a very happy marriage.

Photo 20.10 Martin Luther (1483–1546), disguised as Junker Georg, the Knight George, as sketched by Lucas Cranach the Elder (1472–1553). After his trial at the Diet of Worms, Luther's friends staged a kidnapping and took him to the safety of the fortress of Wartburg, near Eisenach. There he translated the New Testament into German.

Luther's guiding principle was to remove from the Catholic Church anything contrary to Scripture. Things about which he believed the Scriptures said nothing, such as the appointment of bishops, were for him simply useful traditions that could be accepted or rejected depending upon their pragmatic value. Other Protestant Reformers, the most important of whom was John Calvin (1509–1564), went far beyond Luther. For Calvin and his followers, Scripture was the foundation upon which the church must be built. Therefore, if something was not clearly mandated in Scripture, it had to be removed from the practice of the church. Consequently, Calvinist

Photo 20.11 The Wartburg castle overlooking Eisenach in Thüringen, where Luther lived from 4 May 1521 to 1 March 1522, during which time he translated the New Testament into German.

churches rejected forms of church government that involved bishops in favor of a presbyterian system, which was regulated by the clergy and congregations.

Other groups went even further than Calvin. The most important of these were the Baptists, who emerged in England and on the continent in the mid-sixteenth century. They took literally the command of the resurrected Jesus in Matthew 28:19–20, which says, "Therefore go and make disciples of all nations, baptizing them in the name of the Father and of the Son and of the Holy Spirit, and teaching them to obey everything I have commanded you. And surely I am with you always, to the very end of the age." The Baptists argued that these verses, and others like them, clearly showed that only adults, or at least people capable of making reasonable judgments, ought to be baptized.

"How," they asked, "could a child a few days old receive baptism when it was incapable of believing anything?" Therefore, in their view, only people capable of making a decision for Christ and capable of exercising a public faith could possibly be baptized.

Calvin countered this argument, as did Luther before him, by arguing that baptism was a sign of membership in the Christian church and a part of God's new covenant. For Calvin, Romans 4:9–12 was a key passage in

PROMPTE ET SINCERE·

Photo 20.12 Portrait of John Calvin (1509–1564) from 1562.

this heated argument. He asked how was it possible for Paul, in Romans 4:11, to say that circumcision, which according to Mosaic law was to be given to children eight days old, was a sign of faith? Therefore, Calvin reasoned, if circumcision was given to Abraham as a sign of faith for the old covenant, then baptism was given to the folds of Jesus as a sign of faith in the new covenant. In both cases, he claimed, this faith was covenantal and included the children of believers.

The rise of the Baptist movement, and of the Anabaptists in continental Europe, who developed into the Mennonites, Hutterites, and various other small groups, split the Protestant movement. Similarly, in England, as a result of Henry VIII's divorce, a compromise church had been created which was Catholic in form and ritual but Protestant in doctrine. This was known as Anglicanism, and it was challenged by the rise of the Puritan movement. The Puritans were followers of Calvin whose slogan was that the church ought to be reformed "root and branch." For them, the Anglican compromise was unacceptable, because many things, like the appointment of bishops, were in their view against Scripture. Nevertheless, unlike the continental Anabaptists, the Puritans strongly endorsed infant baptism, attempting to preserve a strong theology of the covenant.

THE COUNTER-REFORMATION

In the immediate aftermath of the Reformation, the Roman Catholic Church looked inward to create a remarkable renewal movement known as the Counter-Reformation. Spearheading this movement was the Society of Jesus, better known as the Jesuits, founded in 1540 by the Spaniard Ignatius Loyola (1491–1556). Their motto was, "for the greater glory of God." Contrary to popular belief, the Jesuits were not founded in opposition to the Reformation. Rather, they were founded to spread the word of God. What distinguished the Jesuits from other Catholic orders was that far greater authority was vested in their vicar general, making them a highly centralized and efficient organization.

Inspired by the Jesuits, more traditional Catholic orders, such as the Franciscans and Dominicans, received a new lease on life. Like the Jesuits, they established schools, universities, and numerous charitable institutions. In terms of popular piety, these movements sought to triumph over Protestantism by creating a rich artistic and musical culture.

While the composers Dietrich Buxtehude (1637–1707) and Johann Sebastian Bach (1685–1750) represented the height of Protestant musical achievement, composers like Joseph Haydn (1732–1809), Ludwig van Beethoven (1770–1827), Wolfgang Ama-

Photo 20.13 Ignatius Loyola (1491–1556), the founder of the Jesuit Order.

deus Mozart (1751–1791), and Franz List (1811–1886) provided Catholics with rich liturgical resources. Similarly, in art, the work of Protestant painters like Rembrandt van Rijn (1606–1669) and Jan Vermeer (1632–1675) was more than equaled by Catholic painters who created the baroque style, which quickly spread to Protestant lands. Thus Catholicism responded to the challenge of Protestantism.

THE THIRTY YEARS' WAR AND THE CREATION OF RATIONALISM

As rulers in Europe chose between Catholic and Protestant forms of Christianity, their political allegiances changed, leading to one of the most devastating wars in European history—the Thirty Years' War. Although ostensibly about religion, this war was as much about dynastic succession and who should rule where. Starting in 1618, the war raged throughout the German-speaking lands of northern Europe until the Peace of Westphalia in 1648. During this time many areas were totally devastated, losing as much as two-thirds of their population. Yet the war was not simply a war between Catholics and Protestants. Catholic France and Cardinal Richelieu (1585–1642) funded German Protestants because they were fighting Austria, the perceived enemy of France.

The importance of this war is its effect on the German psyche and that of Europe generally. In its wake a wave of revulsion swept across Europe. "How," people asked, "could people professing to believe in Christ kill one another simply because of differences in doctrine?" Questions like these gave rise to a growing skepticism, leading directly to the Enlightenment and the rejection of Christianity by many European intellectuals. Anyone wishing to grasp the effect of the Thirty Years' War on subsequent generations would do well to read the play *The Thirty Years' War* by German writer Friedrich Schiller (1759–1805), as well as his histories.

THE BIRTH OF PIETISM

Apart from giving birth to what became a violently anti-Christian nationalist movement opposed to all dogma, the Thirty Years' War played a significant role in the development of what became known as Pietism. The origins of German Pietism can be traced to the English Puritans and to writers such as Johann Arndt (1555–1621), whose *True Christianity* (1610) had a profound influence on many people. Pietism proper took shape as a result of the energetic preacher Philipp Jakob Spener (1635–1705), who edited Arndt's works. Spener's influence grew after he became a senior minister at St. Paul's Church in Frankfurt. There he encouraged pious Bible study based upon the traditional Lutheran belief in the priesthood of all believers. For him the daily practice of Christianity meant unselfish works, love for others, and praying for unbelievers instead of arguing with them or calling them "heretics." Spener also sought to engage unbelievers in constructive discussions in a spirit of love.

Spener's enthusiasm caught on among theological students and clergy, although it appears to have had little effect on his Frankfurt congregation. Perhaps the person who had the greatest influence in promoting his vision, although they never got along personally, was August Hermann Francke (1663–1727), a young lecturer at the University of Leipzig who met concerted resistance from his fellow professors because of his pious Christian influence on students. From Leipzig, Francke moved to the town of Halle, where he became professor of theology at the newly founded university, created largely as a result of Spener's influence on the court in Berlin. There he also founded his famous Francke Foundations, known in German as the *Franckesche Stiftungen*. The foundations engaged in numerous philanthrothopic and educational ventures, including the creation of what became the first modern orphanage. This later encouraged the modern Protestant missionary movement. Francke promoted the teaching of academic subjects from primary school through university in the vernacular, which for his compatriots was German. The university where he worked was also highly innovative in accepting women into its medical school and at least one black African, who eventually became a professor, into its philosophical faculty.

Initially the movement known as Pietism flourished in German-speaking lands, particularly Prussia, where it practically became the state religion. It also had an enormous influence outside Germany, especially through its English offshoot, Methodism. This was stimulated by the influence of Count Zinzendorf (1700–1760) on John Wesley (1703–1791). In Germany, however, Pietist fortunes changed when the old Prussian king Frederick William I (1620–1688), known as the Great Elector, died and his son, Frederick II (1712–1786), known to history as Frederick the Great, assumed the throne. Unlike his father, Frederick II despised Pietism and did all he could to eradicate it from

Photo 20.14 Outside the original Methodist Chapel in London, England, stands this bronze statue of the father of Methodism, John Wesley (1703–1791), who was profoundly affected by German Pietism. Wesley's work helped revolutionize English-speaking societies in the eighteenth and nineteenth centuries.

his realm. Practically, this meant appointing university professors like Christian Wolff (1679–1754), who developed the rationalistic elements in the thought of G. W. Leibniz (1646–1716). From the 1740s, an intellectual battle raged in Germany between Pietist scholars and the followers of rationalistic Wolff. The Pietists eventually lost this battle, because the power of the state was behind their opponents, who made all new university appointments and influenced church appointments.

THE DECLINE OF PIETISM

Yet strangely enough, both sides shared a common appreciation for what might best be termed "inwardness," an appreciation shaped by Leibniz's views about the dynamic nature of the universe. Within Pietism this quest for inner reality encouraged the growth of what became known as the radical Pietist movement, which drew heavily upon the writings of spiritualistically inclined mystics such as Jakob Böhme (1575–1624) and various medieval writers. On the rationalist side, the teachings of Wolff influenced a peculiar form of German intellectual development which retained a disdain for orthodox Christianity. At the same time, affinities to deism were blended with an aesthetically motivated spiritual quest. This new religious expression found its major exponent in the greatest of all German writers, Johann Wolfgang Goethe (1749–1832); philosophers like Immanuel Kant (1724–1804); and theologians in the tradition of Friedrich Schleiermacher (1768–1834).

Although both Kant and Schleiermacher attended "Pietist" schools, questions remain as to what sort of Pietism was affirmed there. From the late 1740s, Pietist strongholds like the University of Halle came under rationalist control, while the Pietist movement itself attracted many less orthodox spiritualist types. The claim that centralized government developed in response to a Pietist desire for authority is highly misleading and requires further investigation.

Photo   20.15   Friedrich   Schleiermacher (1768–1834), one of the founding professors at the University of Berlin, whose bust still stands in the office of the dean of theology.

What is certain is that under pressure from Enlightenment rulers like Frederick the Great, the Pietist movement lost influence and generally became inward looking. These developments allowed the growth of a radical spiritualized rationalism that, as Nicholas Boyle points out, led Goethe and many other leading German intellectuals and statesmen to embrace a new paganism.[9] All this happened while Pietism's stepchild, Methodism, was transforming the English-speaking world in a Christian direction and agitating for social reforms, such as the abolition of slavery.

At the same time the late eighteenth century saw the popularization of Christian missions among both Protestants and Roman Catholics. Throughout the nineteenth century the missionary movement gathered momentum, with remarkable results worldwide. In places like South Africa, missionaries like John Philip (1775–1851) and John William Colenso (1814–1883) opposed colonial oppression of Blacks and fought for a just society. In India and China other missionaries both preached the gospel and sought social reforms that eventually transformed these societies. Meanwhile, on the continent of Europe, anti-Christian sentiment was taking root in northern European Protestant universities.

9. Nicholas Boyle, *Goethe: The Poet and the Age*, vol. 1, *The Poetry of Desire* (Oxford: Clarendon, 1997), 352–55, 641–66.

THE AGE OF REVOLUTIONS

Initially this anti–Christian spirit found expression in two great revolutions that changed world history. The first, the American Revolution of 1775 was led by deists like Benjamin Franklin (1706–1790) and the great revolutionary publicist and critic of Christianity, Thomas Paine (1737–1809). The forces of Methodism, however, were gaining momentum in America, where many people had been touched by what was known as the Great Awakening, which preceded the revolution. Consequently, the new American state developed in an increasingly Christian direction, reflecting the beliefs of ordinary Americans.

The second great upheaval, the French Revolution of 1789, followed the American Revolution but took a totally different direction. Beginning as a fairly conservative reform movement, it rapidly became increasingly radical. Ironically, many modern historians believe that the roots of the financial troubles of the French monarchy that initiated the revolution lay in its support for the American Revolution and the financial burden this imposed upon France. As the revolution proceeded, the king's intransigence and hesitation created a spiral of action and reaction, until the radicals gained control. This led to the execution of Louis XVI and what became known as the Reign of Terror, in which even revolutionary leaders were sent to the guillotine. During this time of chaos, the Christian calendar was abolished in France and a festival of the Supreme Being was initiated in Paris. The church, particularly the Catholic Church, was viciously persecuted, and thousands of Christians fled France or died in the Terror.

Photo 20.16 *Oath of the Horatii* (1784), the masterpiece of Jacques-Louis David (1748–1825), captures the grim self-righteousness of the French Revolution, in which death for an abstract cause was placed above all other values.

The chaos was brought to an end in 1797, when the commander of French armies in Italy, Napoleon Bonaparte (1769–1821), defeated an Austrian army and was given command of French forces in preparation for a planned invasion of England. At this point he staged what was effectively a coup and embarked on a series of military campaigns that made him the master of Europe. Then, in 1804, Napoleon was declared emperor of France. For the next eleven years, a series of wars known as the Napoleonic Wars ravaged Europe, until in 1815 Napoleon's forces were finally defeated, and the Treaty of Vienna imposed a new order in Europe that effectively lasted until 1914.

FROM FOLKLORE TO BIBLICAL CRITICISM

During this period English deism, which had been effectively refuted in Britain, took root on the Continent, particularly in Germany at universities like Göttingen. Stimulated by Napoleon's invasion of Egypt and his visit to the pyramids, widespread curiosity developed about the ancient world, leading to a growth of interest in archaeology, which at that time was a very crude science. Running parallel to this was the growth of folklore studies, initiated by a rather obscure Scottish clergyman, James MacPherson (1736–1796), whose *Odes of Ossian* (1761–1765) purported to be the remains of an almost forgotten folk memory of pre-Christian religion in Scotland. This work, which subsequently proved to be a forgery, caught the imagination of Europeans to such an extent that even Napoleon carried a copy of the *Odes* in his saddlebags while on campaign.

In Germany, MacPherson's work encouraged a pair of scholarly brothers from Kassel, Jacob Grimm (1785–1863) and Wilhelm Grimm (1786–1859), to develop what became known as "the science of folklore." Able linguists, they began work on a major etymological dictionary of the German language. More importantly, they are remembered as the authors of *Grimm's Fairy Tales* (1812), which were part of a much larger project for preserving what they presented as authentic German folk traditions that included sagas and legends of the German peoples. In his provocative book *One Fairy Story Too Many* (1983),[10] John Ellis has challenged the claim made by the brothers that they collected authentic folktales. Although their articulation of the method they claimed to have used was sound, Ellis argues, they did not follow it themselves. Rather, he claims, the evidence suggests the stories were of French origin and were told to the brothers by Jacob's fiancée, Dorothea Wild.

Photo 20.17 The brothers Jacob and Wilhelm Grimm, whose *Fairy Tales* captivated generations, are representatives of a far more important cultural movement that began to search for the pre-Christian roots of European culture.

Whatever the truth about the origin of these stories, the fact is they fitted into a cultural context where the manufacture of ancient, pre-Christian ethnic traditions was a booming industry. Similar inventions of tradition occurred all over Europe. More significantly, the "recovery," or "rediscovery," of "lost traditions" was closely related to the growth of nationalist movements that mushroomed following the Napoleonic conquests and to attempts to impose French

---

10. John M. Ellis, *One Fairy Story Too Many: The Brothers Grimm and Their Tales* (Chicago: Univ. of Chicago Press, 1983).

culture on subject peoples. With the exception of the Netherlands, where the Christian Antirevolutionary Movement became the main focus of Dutch national feeling, these incipient nationalist movements were deeply pagan. Frank Eyck, the author of the classic work on the German Frankfurt Parliament of 1848, which was the first attempt to create a unified Germany, observed that many of the delegates to the parliament were deeply involved in neopagan cultural movements. This was a fact, he regretted to say, he had not included in his book.[11]

Although such developments may seem remote from the history of Christianity, they were very important, because to a large extent it was people involved in the German nationalist movement, and influenced by the folklore movement, who helped develop what became known as the higher criticism of the Bible. Rabbi Solomon Schechter (1847–1915), perhaps the dominant figure in the establishment of American Judaism, in his *Seminary Addresses and Other Papers*,[12] argued that the origin of the new "Higher anti-Semitism" was "partly, though not entirely ... contemporaneous with the genesis of the so-called Higher Criticism of the Bible." Few theologians writing the history of biblical criticism have followed his lead, yet in recent years a few have recognized that the history of biblical criticism needs serious reevaluation because of its clearly anti-Semitic roots.[13] As Schechter warned, the work of scholars like Julius Wellhausen (1844–1918) is "full of venom against Judaism,"[14] while that of Adolf von Harnack (1851–1930) displays "not so much his hatred as his ignorance of Judaism."[15]

Encouraged by politicians like the German chancellor Otto von Bismarck (1815–1898), the higher criticism of the Bible, particularly arguments like that for the priority of the gospel of Mark over the priority of the gospel of Matthew, gained acceptance for the simple reason that academic appointments in Germany were made by state officials and not universities. The appointment of critics suited Bismark, because he saw things like Markan priority as a way of undermining the Roman Catholic Church by devaluing the gospel of Matthew. Therefore, biblical critics became his allies in his *Kulturkampf*, or cultural war, against Catholicism. Backed by the prestige of German intellectual accomplishments, these ideas swept into the English-speaking world, gaining ascendancy in leading universities in America, while in Britain they met with considerable resistance from the entrenched Anglican hierarchy.

THEOLOGICAL LIBERALISM AND ITS CRITICS

By 1900 the dominance of liberal theology in America led to the development of the fundamentalist movement, which sought to restore the primacy of traditional Christian doctrines in seminaries and within the church. Although initially fundamentalism was represented by a series of highly academic papers circulated under the title *The Fundamentals:*

11. Personal conversations.

12. Solomon Schechter, *Seminary Addresses and Other Papers* (New York: Jewish Publication Society of America, 1915).

13. Alan T. Davies, *Infected Christianity: A Study of Modern Racism* (Kingston, Ont.: McGill-Queen's Univ. Press, 1988); Shawn Kelley, *Racializing Jesus: Race, Ideology and the Formation of Modern Biblical Scholarship* (New York: Routledge, 2002).

14. Schechter, *Seminary Addresses*, 36.

15. Ibid., 36–37.

A Testimony Compliments of Two Christian Laymen,[16] the movement quickly disintegrated following World War I.

As a result, numerous fundamentalist movements emerged, each questioning the scriptural basis of the other. By the 1950s American conservative Christianity appeared to be in disarray. Then, largely as a result of the success of the Billy Graham campaigns, fundamentalism saw a significant revival as what some called "the new evangelicalism." The new evangelicals were cynically labelled "fundamentalists with a PhD" by their critics. Despite this and attempts by scholars like James Barr,[17] a former fundamentalist himself, to label all evangelicals as unthinking fundamentalists, the movement took root and flourished, creating the religious situation in which we find ourselves today.

Photo 20.18 The grave of the greatest of all liberal theologians, Adolf von Harnack (1851–1930).

During the twentieth century, liberal theologians dominated universities. In English-speaking countries they helped produce such things as liberation theology and black theology. More ominously, in the German-speaking world, many German liberal theologians, as Karla Poewe[18] points out, supported National Socialism and found their way into the German Christian movement. Those in this movement attempted to accommodate themselves to the world of science and modernity. The result was an enthusiastic embrace of National Socialism. Thus Schechter's musings about the relationship between anti-Semitism and biblical criticism became a horrific reality. According to such prominent liberal theologians as Gerhard Kittel (1888–1948), Jesus was of Aryan stock and not a Jew at all. Such nonsense was propagated by the best and brightest of German scholars. Only a small group of despised conservatives such as Karl Barth (1886–1968) and Dietrich Bonhoeffer (1906–1945) stood against it, and some, such as Bonhoeffer, paid for their opposition with their lives.

On the Catholic side, bishops like Clemens August von Galen of Cologne (1878–1946) stood firmly against the denigration of the Jews and the atrocities done to them by the Nazis. Out of this maelstrom, the Roman Catholic Church produced two of the great popes of history, the Polish Pope John Paul II (1920–2005) and his successor, a German theologian and former university professor, Joseph Ratzinger (b. 1927), Pope Benedict XVI. Shaped by the temptation of modernity as represented by National Socialism, both men took a firm

---

16. Two Christian Laymen, eds., *The Fundamentals: A Testimony Compliments of Two Christian Laymen*, 12 vols. (Chicago: Testimony Publishing Company, n.d.), various authors for different articles.

17. James Barr, *Fundamentalism* (London, SCM Press, 1967).

18. Karla Poewe, *New Religions and the Nazis* (Oxford: Routledge, 2006).

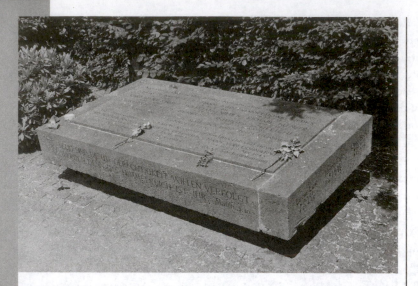

Photo 20.19 A Berlin memorial to Dietrich Bonhoeffer (1906–1945) and other leaders of the German Resistance. Bonhoeffer was executed days before American troops liberated Flossenbürg concentration camp. On the orders of Hitler, his body was cremated and the ashes scattered in a river to prevent his grave becoming a site of pilgrimage to future generations.

stand against the cultural relativism of accommodation to the times. Ratzinger's book *Truth and Tolerance* (2003)[19] is a model of Christian scholarship that displays a wide vision, approvingly citing various North American evangelical Christian authors, while his *Jesus of Nazareth* (2007)[20] is a passionate defense of orthodox Christology.

THE CHALLENGE OF THE NEW ATHEISM

So the twentieth century ended with Christianity facing some of the greatest challenges of its entire history. Prompted by the American invasion of Iraq and the policies of President George W. Bush (b. 1946), a new, self-proclaimed atheism arose, led by such people as Christopher Hitchens (b. 1949), the British scientist Richard Dawkins (b. 1941), and groups like the Freedom From Religion Foundation. How Christians respond to this challenge will be the story of our time, as will be their response to the growing number of non-Christians from other religious traditions living among them in the formerly Christian countries of western Europe and North America.

19. Benedict XVI, *Truth and Tolerance: Christian Belief and World Religions*, trans. Henry Taylor (San Francisco: Ignatius, 2004; first published in German in 2003).

20. Joseph Ratzinger, *Jesus of Nazareth: From the Baptism in the Jordan to the Transfiguration*, (New York: Doubleday, 2007).

CHAPTER 21

CHRISTIAN FAITH AND PRACTICE

INTRODUCTION

Unlike the other major world religions, Christianity has paid at least as much attention to correct belief as to right practice. Although beliefs are important in both Judaism and Islam, it is orthopraxis, or the way people live, that is decisive for determining who is a Jew or a Muslim. Similarly, in Buddhism and the Hindu tradition, practice has traditionally been far more important than doctrines. In Christianity, things are different to the extent that some criticize Christianity as being an intellectual construct rather than a living practice. Indeed, some even argue that it was the church in the early centuries of the Christian era that distorted the "simple" message of Jesus by adding layers of intellectual understanding.

Actually, a Christian emphasis on belief, or what goes on inside a person, goes back to the teachings of Jesus himself. In Matthew 5:21–22 Jesus says, "You have heard that it was said to the people long ago, 'Do not murder, and anyone who murders will be subject to judgment.' But I tell you that anyone who is angry with his brother will be subject to judgment." Then, a few verses later, he says, "You have heard that it was said, 'Do not commit adultery.' But I tell you that anyone who looks at a woman lustfully has already committed adultery with her in his heart" (Matthew 5:27–28). In both of these statements, and many others like them, Jesus makes intent, not action, the fundamental issue in judging whether something is right or wrong.

Following Jesus' example, the early disciples preached a message that demanded a decision. They proclaimed Jesus as Lord, and they expected anyone who joined their community to acknowledge this proclamation. Evidence of this highly intellectual stance is to be found in the fragmentary sermons recorded in the Acts of the Apostles. Peter, for example, in his Pentecost sermon (Acts 2:14–36), gives a systematic interpretation of biblical history, and the hearers are called to make a decision on the basis of it.

Later in the New Testament we find a series of letters, known as the Epistles, from Christian leaders to the followers of Jesus. Some of these writings are in fact earlier than the Gospels or Acts. In numerous places they record creed-like statements, expressing the essence of the Christian faith in terms of acknowledgment of explicit beliefs. For example,

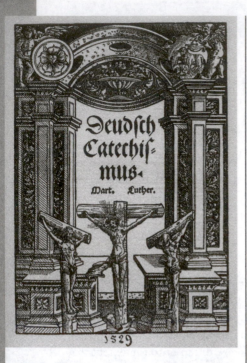

Photo 21.1 Throughout Christian history new converts and candidates for either baptism or confirmation were required to give their assent to a set of basic beliefs. Above is the title page of Martin Luther's catechism, in which he outlines the basic beliefs of what became known as Lutheranism.

in Colossians 1:1–20, the author, traditionally said to be Paul, makes a long statement of faith that resembles what later became known as a creed. In it he clearly states those things that all Christians are expected to believe. Similarly, in the letters of John, toward the end of the New Testament, the author takes great pains to distinguish between true and false belief. In fact, throughout the New Testament, from the teachings of Jesus to those of Paul and the other writers of the Epistles, knowledge and acceptance of the truth is the key issue.

Of course, this is never separated from practice. Again and again Jesus teaches his disciples how they should live. Again and again Paul rebukes Christians for not living in accordance with their beliefs and the high moral standards demanded by the church. Faith and works go together in the New Testament scheme of things, because works grow out of faith. What is important here is that in Christian thinking right conduct must be guided by and based upon a sincerity of heart and committed relationship to God.

CREATION, FALL, AND REDEMPTION

As explained in chapter 19, the doctrines of creation, fall, and redemption form the core of Christian belief. For the purposes of this discussion, we can say that they form a major Christian theological unit, defining the relationship between God and humans. If the actions of Adam and Eve broke the trust between man and God, God restored it through the life and death of Jesus. In the process, human beings learned who they are—finite creatures who nevertheless have a freedom of choice. And they learned who God is—a being both infinite and divine.

Mistrust entered the relationship between humanity and God with the fall. God became suspect. To redeem humans from suspicion and regression, God redeemed mankind with an act of infinite love. He gave them Jesus, leaving humans free to choose their attitude and relationship to him. Reflection on the fact that we chose to crucify him might have left humans wallowing in guilt, but by resurrecting him, God not only redeemed humans but also showed them that he alone is infinite. God redeemed humans by redeeming himself at the same time. He defined humans as distinct and different from himself, subject to his divinity yet free in their humanity.

The Christian notion of redemption, as interpreted here in this admittedly limited way, fits well with Western attitudes toward science and knowledge. It grants humans knowledge and choice within the confines of God's universe but dictates that since we are not granted ultimate or God-like knowledge, our pursuit of knowledge can never be complete. It does not allow humans to rest in the comfort of having attained union with the One, as the believers of Eastern religions do, but it thereby prevents humans from stagnating. Its emphasis is not on *being* (except in the sense of being at peace) but rather on *becoming*. It entails that exploration and the pursuit of knowledge is never-ending for humanity, that we will always be able to experience growth, development, and, above all, hope.

Nor does the Christian sense of development necessarily have anything to do with evolution, especially not with the myth of evolution. Our development as sentient beings may be regressive or progressive, good or bad. This central Christian theme assures us

Photo 21.2 The story of the creation and fall is told in pictorial form in the late medieval Grabower Altar (1375–1383).

humans that we were given the opportunity to choose whether to build or destroy. It leaves us with the hope of finding ever-new frontiers to conquer, without the delusion that all "conquest" will be ipso facto "higher" and "better." The paths we travel are a matter of our choosing. These Christian doctrines leave humans with a feeling of exhilaration, for they indicate that we have the opportunity to direct all that God has given to us. And we can do so without having to hallucinate spirit helpers. Choice is conscious, not fortuitous, not subject to the occult, not even subject to a belief in the evil powers of humanity. It allows humans to act in the world from the healthy perspective of trust.

THE IMPORTANCE OF FAITH

All Christians believe that the way humans reenter a living relationship with God is through faith. Faith is an act of trust based upon knowledge of God and his deeds. It is not a blind leap into the unknown but a confident step into enlightenment about the nature and love of God. Faith is the opposite of doubt and magical power. Faith is to redemption what magic and doubt are to the fall. Faith frees humans of anxiety because it entails our accepting our identity as creatures made in God's image.

Of course, some Christian groups introduce ideas about the sacraments and good works as necessary supplements to faith. Nevertheless, the inspiration for the distinctively

Christian understanding of faith is found in the story of Abraham, who left the security of Ur of the Chaldees to become a wanderer and nomad in response to God's call (see Genesis 12–24 and Hebrews 11:8–19). Theistic faith is an expression of trust. It leads to a new way of life based on a living relationship with God.

The longest exposition of the meaning of faith in the Bible is found in the book of Romans. It starts with Paul's observation that people have renounced truth and "served created things rather than the Creator" (Romans 1:25). The essence of Paul's argument is that human beings, having lost the ability to trust God, made gods out of created things. In so doing, they lost the ability to trust each other, with disastrous results. But faith restores not only our relationship with God but also our relationship with our neighbors.

Photo 21.3 Dieric Bouts' (ca. 1415–1475) painting of the meeting of Abraham and Melchizedek as recorded in Genesis 14:18 reminds the viewer that according to the New Testament, particularly the book of Hebrews, Abraham is the great example of what faith means in Christianity.

Unfortunately, it is difficult to have faith. Many people choose to be satisfied with the sort of apparent reconciliation to God and neighbors that is achieved by observing rigid codes, ritual actions, and prescribed ways of living. They look to laws rather than faith for instruction concerning how all people must live. These laws appear to restore human relationships and create communion with God, but in fact they produce a new kind of servitude. Paul describes this servitude as "being slaves" to the law (Galatians 4:3) and discusses it at length in the book of Galatians.

Such legalism leads to magical practices and the observance of "a festival or a new moon or a sabbath," which are justified by appeals to what Paul calls "hollow and deceptive philosophy, which depends on human tradition" (Colossians 2:8, 16). The "law" also includes such things as observing genealogies, continuing ancient rituals such as circumcision, and keeping dietary rules. Paul and other New Testament writers condemn reliance on ritual observances as a means to salvation, denouncing such practices as a form of bondage (see Acts 10; 15:1–29; Galatians 2–4; 1 Timothy 1:4).

In Galatians 3:1 Paul describes people who have submitted to legalism as "bewitched." Usually people regard this phrase as a figure of speech. When read in conjunction with Galatians 5:20, however, in which "witchcraft" is classified with idolatry and other sins as a "[work] of the flesh," a different interpretation suggests itself. In Paul's view, legalism is akin to bewitchment and is therefore nothing other than the power of sorcery.

In the Christian tradition, faith is presumed to free people to enter meaningful, nonexploitative relationships, whereas legalism is presumed to create dependence, addiction, and exploitation. The essence of legalism is the replacement of trust in God with manipulation through rituals. Legalism is therefore the continual reenactment of the fall.[1]

THE RETURN OF CHRIST

Ideas about the "return of Christ" give many contemporary Christians their distinctive emphasis. These ideas arise out of the interpretation of the eschatological passages of the Bible, such as those in the books of Daniel and Revelation, as well as key passages in the Gospels such as Matthew 24. Attempting to understand the "true" meaning of prophetic passages in the Bible, new religious movements ignore established methods of exegesis and often use novel interpretive tools. For example, Charles Taze Russell (1852–1916), the founder of the Jehovah's Witnesses, found in the Great Pyramid of Egypt "sacred measurements" that he believed unlocked the meaning of the Bible.

Photo 21.4 *The Last Judgment*, by Stefan Lochner. The painting dates from 1435 and reminds us that eschatology, or the study of last things, has always played an important role in Christian theology.

The key to this type of esoteric interpretation is the magical manipulation of numbers. In essence it involves ways of thinking that display an obsession with coincidence and the creation of sacred patterns. Recently, some new Christian groups have tried to introduce similar numerological ideas into Christian circles, and ads have appeared in magazines like *Charisma* promoting such things.

TYPES OF ESCHATOLOGY

There are three basic theological understandings of biblical eschatology: postmillennialism, premillennialism, and amillennialism. For our purposes, it will only be necessary to look at the first two. The postmillennialist position and its variations is the more historical position, being held by the majority of Christians throughout history. It holds that the gospel must be preached to every nation, after which there will be a thousand years of peace before Christ returns to judge people and nations. The Puritans held a particularly optimistic version of this view, maintaining that the millennium would be a period of continuous progress and human advancement.

Until recently, the premillennialist position has had few supporters. It achieved widespread popularity only in the nineteenth century through the writings of the founder of the Plymouth Brethren, John Nelson Darby (1800–1882). Today it represents the dominant

---

1. D. Martyn Lloyd-Jones, *Spiritual Depression: Its Causes and Its Cure* (Grand Rapids: Eerdmans, 1984).

Postmillenialism

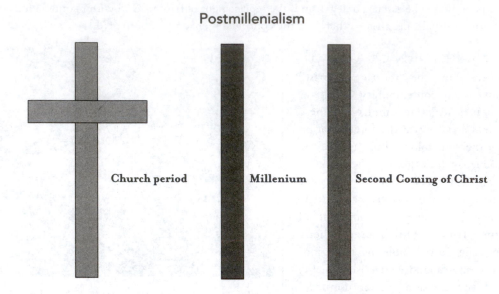

Figure 21.1 In the classic postmillennial view, the "church period" is a time in which the Christian gospel is preached throughout the world, bringing with it peace and prosperity. As a result of the preaching of the gospel, the millennium, or thousand years of peace ruled by God, is established. After the thousand years, Christ returns and a new heaven and earth is created. One of the implications of this view is that Christians need to work for the long term and build for the future. This vision inspired the great cathedrals of Europe and various other ventures.

mode of interpretation in North America. One of the best-known presentations of this position is Hal Lindsey's book *The Late Great Planet Earth* (1967).[2]

Essentially, premillennialists believe that society will disintegrate into chaos before the second coming of Christ. Instead of a thousand years of peace, there will be universal unrest and widespread persecution of Christians. In recent years this view has been directly linked with the expectation of atomic war, because the New Testament speaks of the world being destroyed by fire (2 Peter 3:10).

Dispensationalism is a variation of premillennialism that was popularized by the *Scofield Reference Bible* (1909) and is taught at such places as the influential Dallas Theological Seminary. Dispensationalism adopts the basic premillennial scheme but divides history into seven time periods, or dispensations, during which God is said to have dealt with humanity on the basis of different expectations.

Early dispensationalists, in writings like the *Scofield Reference Bible*,[3] even suggested that God offered different ways of obtaining salvation in each dispensation. Today, most dispensationalists reject this aspect of the movement's early teaching, arguing instead that behind the apparent differences was a constant reliance on faith.

---

2. Hal Lindsey, *The Late Great Planet Earth* (Grand Rapids: Zondervan, 1970).
3. C. I. Scofield, *The Scofield Reference Bible* (New York: Oxford Univ. Press, 1909).

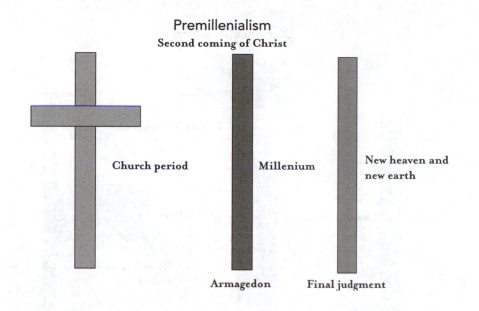

Figure 21.2 This diagram shows the classic premillennial position, which has a long history as a minority view in the church and is often associated with radical social movements. Following the "church period," during which the gospel is preached throughout the world, the state of Israel is established as proof of the veracity of God's word. Then there is a rebellion against God, and the battle of Armageddon takes place. Christ now establishes his thousand-year reign, known as the millennium, which is followed by the last judgment and the creation of a new heaven and earth. The main implication of this view is that Christ may return at any time, because human society is in decline. Therefore, the main task of Christians is to preach the gospel so that as many people as possible are "saved" before the end comes.

An important issue on which postmillennialists and premillennialists disagree is the biblical teaching about Israel. Premillennialists contend that biblical references to Israel are references to the Jewish people. They maintain that the return of the Jewish people to Palestine and the establishment of the state of Israel in 1948 was a fulfillment of biblical prophecy. Consequently, they are strongly pro-Israel. More importantly, they expect a battle between Israel on the one hand and the Arab nations and/or Russia on the other to signal the end of the world.

Postmillennialists reject this type of interpretation, maintaining that the Jews who returned to Palestine cannot be identified with the biblical nation of Israel, which was destroyed in the sixth century BC. The Jews who subsequently returned to Palestine are not really the people of Israel, they argue. They are descendants of the tribe of Judah.

Postmillennialists also argue that the references to the nation of Israel in New Testament prophecies are in fact references to the church of Christ. The references to Old Testament terms for Israel in 1 Peter 2:9 are meant to be applied to Christians. When Paul ponders the fate of Israel in Romans 9–11, he is referring to the church, the new Israel, into which God has "grafted" Gentiles (see especially Romans 11:13–24).

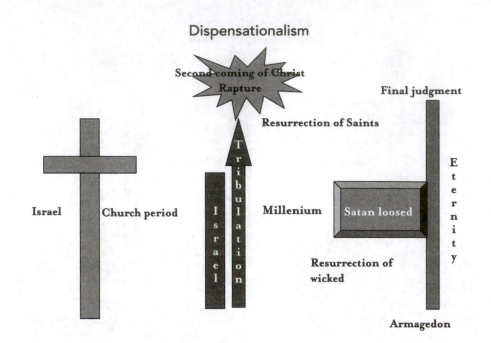

Figure 21.3 Although there are many variants of dispensationalism, the above diagram sums up the main points of the popular viewpoint. In this view, at the end of the present era, known as the "church period," the Jewish people are restored to their own land and eventually convert to Christianity. Then comes a great rebellion, followed by a period of tribulation when Christians are persecuted. At the height of their agony, Christ returns and takes his own people to be with him in heaven. On earth Christ's rule is then established and the millennium follows. After this there is a final rebellion led by Satan, who is defeated at the battle of Armageddon. Finally, God establishes his kingdom. Dispensationalism takes over premillennialism's emphasis on the imminent return of Christ and the need to save souls rather than create a Christian civilization.

Finally, there is the so-called amillennial position, which argues that Scripture is unclear on the exact time of Christ's return or the events leading up to it. Therefore, instead of speculating about the future, Christians should work in the present while always remembering that while Christ could return at any time, his return may be delayed for thousands of years.

ESCHATOLOGY AND CHARISMATIC GIFTS

Christian eschatology has also given rise to significant prophetic and charismatic movements. Christians who call themselves "charismatics" believe that *glossolalia*, or "speaking in tongues"; healing the sick; prophecy; and other "gifts of the Spirit" are signs of "the last days." Verses from Acts 2, John 14–16, and many other passages of Scripture are used to justify such expectations.

In the 1960s, books such as David Wilkerson's *The Cross and the Switchblade* and John L. Sherrill's *They Speak with Other Tongues* popularized the notion that God's Spirit is at

Amillenialism

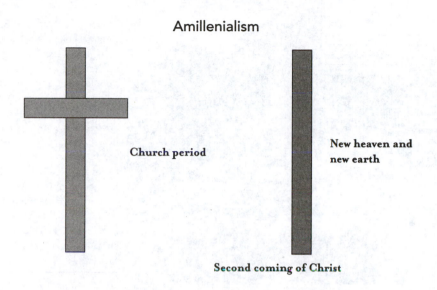

Church period

New heaven and new earth

Second coming of Christ

Figure 21.4 The amillennial position is skeptical about our ability to interpret the eschatological passages of Scripture with any accuracy. Therefore, it emphasizes living in the expectation of Christ's immediate return while building for the future as though his return may be delayed for centuries.

work today in preparation for the end.[4] Charismatics contend that spiritual "leading" is manifested in miraculous acts, visions, prophecies, and other supernatural phenomena. To be a true Christian, one must rely directly upon the leading of God's Spirit. Such teachings have the effect of undermining the established authorities and rational procedures of traditional churches. Spontaneous charismatic leadership, devoid of specific qualifications, is made respectable by appeals to the Bible and becomes the source of authority and direction in small groups, prayer cells, and independent churches. Some of these fellowships have developed further into new religious movements like the Children of God.

THE SEARCH FOR COMMUNITY

Eschatological and charismatic beliefs have led to the formation of many community-oriented Christian groups. A concern with community is another of the hallmarks of the Abramic tradition. In Judaism and Islam, community is clearly identified with ethnic, national, or religious groups, as Christianity was until the Reformation. Luther's Reformation emphasis on the importance of faith led many Christians to return to a concept of community found in the New Testament, which stresses the idea of the fellowship of true believers sharing a common faith in an essentially hostile and unbelieving world.

The Puritans of the sixteenth century and the Pietists of the seventeenth century are examples of Christian groups that sought to establish new communities of faith. Other out-

4. David Wilkerson, *The Cross and the Switchblade*, with John Sherrill and Elizabeth Sherrill (New York: B. Geis, 1963); John L. Sherrill, *They Speak with Other Tongues* (New York: McGraw-Hill, 1964).

Photo 21.5 Although today's charismatic Christians often act and think as though they are the first people after the founding of the early church to display charismatic gifts, the above print shows a medieval pilgrimage to a local shrine where healings were believed to take place. Notice the people in the foreground of the picture rolling on the ground and generally behaving in ways one often sees at charismatic revival meetings.

standing examples of the quest for community include the monastic movements in Roman Catholic, Anglican, Lutheran, and Orthodox traditions and also such groups as the Mennonites, Hutterites, and Doukhobors. Today an emphasis on community has reappeared with new vigor in charismatic circles.

Christian interest in community takes many forms. In the traditional Protestant denominations it has surfaced in revitalization movements that seek to recreate a sense of fellowship among church members. These movements tend to be rational, well controlled, and essentially moderate in beliefs and practices. Within some traditional churches, such as the Roman Catholic and Anglican, charismatic gifts are tolerated and at times even encouraged. They are placed within a framework of tradition and history, however, that tends to encourage respect for rational authority and common sense, thus preventing enthusiasm and cultic practices. The leaders of these mainstream movements tend to be well educated and to have considerable theological and biblical knowledge. By contrast, charismatic groups that emphasize community outside of established denominations tend to arise spontaneously as the result of the conversion experiences of their members. These groups acquire self-appointed leaders who are often poorly educated and theologically unsophisticated. It is out of such groups that many new religions, or cults, develop.

PROPHETIC LEADERSHIP TODAY

The question of authentic leadership and religious authority is clearly important in judging religions. Religions of the yogic tradition revere gurus, who gain complete authority over their disciples. Christian groups have no gurus. Instead, some charismatic groups have the institution of the prophet. A prophet differs from a guru in that the prophet simply declares the word of God.

Prophets are not held to be gods or to share in the essence of God or even to lead the way to God. They simply serve to remind people of God's word. Traditionally, prophets take existing revelation and apply it to particular situations, reminding people of their failures and calling them to restore their relationship with God. Historically, prophets never develop new doctrines or techniques for attaining salvation. They simply apply existing knowledge and allow their words to be tested against the Scriptures.

Throughout the Bible the testing of prophecy is an important theme. Prophets are called to conform to God's revelation, and the conclusions they draw from particular passages must be fulfilled if their words are to be regarded as authentic. Unlike the guru's teaching, which is tested only by experience, the prophet's teaching is tested by experience, Scripture, and history.

CHRISTIAN PIETY AND THE CHRISTIAN CALENDAR

Historically, different peoples and cultures have used different calendar systems. Those in western Europe were dominated by the old Roman republican calendar, which began with the legendary founding of Rome in 753 BC. Later, as part of his administrative reforms, the Roman dictator Julius Caesar (100–44 BC) initiated a major reform of the calendar with the aim of making the months coincide with the seasons. He assigned this task to Sosigenes of Alexandria (first century BC), whose reforms came into effect on 1 January 45 BC, a year before Caesar's death. Practically, however, it was not until AD 8 that the calendar was fine-tuned to allow it to work smoothly. It was this calendar, based on a solar year of 365 ¼ days, that was adopted by Christians in the early church and remained effective in the West until the sixteenth century, when it was known as the Julian, or old, calendar.

Photo 21.6 Statue of Thomas Müntzer (1489–1525) outside the city walls of Mühlhausen, Germany. At the time of the Reformation, premillennialism was discredited as a result of the violence associated with prophetic preachers like Müntzer. To many of his followers Müntzer was both a preacher and a living prophet, just like the prophets of the Bible. Believing that they were living in the last days and that God had restored "the gift of prophecy" to humankind, they were willing to follow him to their deaths, and in doing so left a trail of destruction in their wake. Müntzer's fiery preaching and "prophetic gifts" ignited the Peasants' War of 1525.

The problem with the Julian calendar was that Sosigenes had miscalculated the length of a year by 11 minutes and 14 seconds. This may not seem very much; practically, however, it meant that the length of the year grew by approximately one day every hundred years. Therefore, by the 1500s the seasons were beginning to be out of line with the dates. As a result, Pope Gregory XIII (1502–1585) initiated a calendar reform using the latest astronomical knowledge available to scholars. This is known as the Gregorian, or new,

Photo 21.7 A page from the *Book of Kells*, which contains the four gospels and various other introductory and explanatory materials. In liturgical churches like the Greek Orthodox, Roman Catholic, Anglican, and Lutheran, Scripture is read weekly according to a fixed pattern, so that the congregation hears the entire contents of the Bible over a period of years, usually with the New Testament being read twice or three times in the same period that the Old Testament is read through once.

calendar. He also decided to adjust the calendar according to the new data by taking the year 325, when Emperor Constantine convened the first Council of Nicaea, as the baseline for the new calendar.

This reform, which created a far more accurate calendar, needing fewer adjustments known as leap years, meant removing ten days from the calendar. As a result, there were actually riots in the towns of Europe, where people believed ten days had been stolen from their lives. However, the adjustment worked well and was adopted throughout western and eventually eastern Europe for secular affairs. The churches of western Europe on the whole accepted the new calendar and organized their festivities around it. But in the East, the Greek, Russian, and other Orthodox Churches clung to the old calendar. As a result, there is now a fourteen-day difference between the celebration of any given Christian holiday, like Christmas, in the Western churches and the celebration of the same holiday in the Eastern churches.

CHRISTIAN HOLY DAYS

Traditionally, from the earliest times, Christian liturgies have adhered to what is known as "the Christian year." From the fifth century, this began with a season of Advent, the period leading up to the celebration of the birth of Christ. Advent begins four weeks before Christmas. It is a time of reflection, and in many Christian cultures the beginning of Advent is a time to give gifts to one another and to children. During Advent, Christians meditate on the coming of Christ and his significance to the world (Luke 1; Acts 2:14–36). Usually in churches and private homes, four candles are placed in a special candleholder, of which one is lit on the first Sunday of Advent, two on the second, and so on until Christmas.

The second great celebration of the Christian year is Christmas itself, which is held in the Western, or Gregorian, calendar on 25 December. For those churches following the old, or Julian, calendar, it is now held fourteen days later. Christmas is a time when Christians commemorate the birth of Jesus, remembering his humble origins and the fact that as a baby he was a refugee in Egypt. It is a time for giving gifts and celebrating the incarnation of God in his world (Matthew 1–2; Luke 2). This event has inspired some of the greatest Christian music, including Georg Friedrich Händel's (1685–1759) *Messiah* (1741), Johann Sebastian Bach's (1685–1750) *Christmas Oratorio* (1734), and some great hymns of writers like Charles Wesley (1707–1788).

For many Protestant Christians in North America, the next great event in the Christian year is Easter. But in the traditional Christian year, several other things come first. On 6 January there is the Feast of the Epiphany, commemorating the coming of the wise men, or kings, from the East to worship Jesus. Then sometime in February or March there is Ash Wednesday, a time of repentance marking the beginning of Lent. Usually, in popular custom, the day before Ash Wednesday was the feast day, when people traditionally ate pancakes and finished off all the goodies in their larders. During Lent they were supposed to fast; therefore, all rich food had to be eaten before Lent began.

For Christians, Lent is a period of prayer and fasting during which they give up particular pleasures, such as rich foods and drinks like wine. Unlike Muslims, who, in the month of Ramadan, fast during the hours of daylight but can feast during hours of darkness, Christian fasts make no exceptions and therefore are rarely

Photo 21.8 Christmas is the major religious festival for Christians, shared by people around the world of all faiths. Bernardo Daddi's (ca. 1290–ca. 1349) nativity scene from 1340 captures this timeless message of God's intervention in our world.

total fasts but limited to restrictions on what are seen as luxuries. The meaning given to Lent by Christians is that it reminds them of the temptations of Jesus when he spent forty days in the wilderness before beginning his ministry.

Easter is the greatest of all Christian feasts. Because the date of Easter is fixed, following Jewish custom, in terms of the solar calendar, it takes place on the first Sunday after the full moon of the vernal equinox. This means that Easter can fall on any day between 22 March and 25 April. Because the Eastern Orthodox Churches use both a different calendar and a different method of calculating the date of Easter, it can fall anywhere between one week and five weeks after the Western Easter. On occasion, as in 2010, the dates coincide.

Photo 21.9 While most people have no difficulty responding to the birth of Jesus, few other than Christians understand the significance of his death as an atoning sacrifice for human sin. The painting above, by Mathias Grünewald (ca. 1470–1528), captures the full horror of what Christians know as the passion.

For all Christians the Easter celebration begins with Palm Sunday, which commemorates Jesus' triumphant ride into Jerusalem on a donkey, symbolizing humility. During this ride, according to the Gospels, Jesus was enthusiastically greeted by the people of Jerusalem, who threw their cloaks and palm leaves and branches before him, thus treating him like royalty (see Matthew 21:1–11). In many liturgical churches, Christians are given a small cross woven from palm leaves or a branch of palm leaves. However, the joy of Palm Sunday gives way to a sober tone on Maundy Thursday, which is commemorated as the day on which Jesus celebrated his Last Supper with his closest disciples (Matthew 26:17–35; Luke 22:7–30).

The following day, known as "Good Friday," is both the saddest and, in some senses, the most joyful day of the Christian year, because on the one hand, Christians remember the humiliation, degradation, and torture of Jesus, who died a cruel death upon a Roman cross, but on the other hand, they know that in some ways they can never fully fathom that Jesus died for their sins, making peace with God possible. Although some Christians claim to fully understand the meaning of Christ's death, it is probably wise, as J. I. Packer points out,[5] to view this event in the words of Charles Wesley's great hymn, "And Can It Be?" where in the second verse he writes:

'Tis mystery all: th'Immortal dies!
Who can explore his strange design?
In vain the firstborn seraph tries
to sound the depths of love divine.
'Tis mercy all! Let earth adore;
let angel minds inquire no more.
'Tis mercy all! Let earth adore;
let angel minds inquire no more.[6]

---

5. See Packer's introduction to John Owen's *The Death of Death* (London: Banner of Truth Trust, 1958).

6. Charles Wesley, "And Can It Be?" (1738), in *The Book of Praise* (Don Mills, Ont.: Presbyterian Church of Canada, 1972), 173.

Following the commemoration of Jesus' crucifixion and death comes the greatest of all Christian celebrations—the resurrection, which is celebrated on Easter Sunday. This is the holiest and most joyful day of the Christian year, when Christians remember that Jesus not only died, but had his sacrifice accepted by God, who brought him back to life, thus guaranteeing both the resurrection and the forgiveness of sins of all believers (1 Corinthians 15). Traditionally, in cultures throughout Europe, Christians have celebrated Easter by decorating hard-boiled eggs, which are said to commemorate the rolling away of the stone from the tomb of Jesus, thus reminding everyone that "He is risen" (Matthew 28; Luke 24). In many liturgical traditions the celebration of Easter Sunday begins with the minister's cry "He is risen," to which the faithful reply, "He is risen indeed."

The Christian year, however, does not end with the resurrection. Rather, it is followed by the feast of the Ascension, which takes place on Thursday of the sixth week after Easter. This feast reminds Christians that, after showing himself to literally hundreds of people, the resurrected Jesus returned to his Father in heaven, whence he will come at the end of time to judge all people.

Finally, a week later comes the feast of Pentecost, on the seventh Sunday after Easter. This celebration commemorates the fact, as recorded in Acts 1–2, that after the death of Jesus the disciples were demoralized until he appeared among them and his resurrection was confirmed. Even then, however, they continued to lack courage in the face of opposition by the authorities. But then, on the Jewish feast day of Pentecost, the Spirit of God fell upon them and they were given courage and power to proclaim the Christian message throughout the world.

Although there are many other minor celebrations within the Christian calendar, these are the main ones shared by all of the historic churches. Each is tied to specific events in Jesus' life and intended as a time of prayer and contemplation.

CHRISTIAN PRAYER

While on earth, Jesus taught his disciples to pray according to the formula he laid down in what was recorded in the New Testament as the Sermon on the Mount. He instructed his disciples to avoid hypocrisy and displays of piety by praying in private, and indeed in secret, to God their father. This emphasis on the fatherhood of God, which in the Greek of the New Testament is expressed in a highly personal form similar to today's

Photo 21.10 Jean Francois Millet's (1814–1875) *Evening Prayer* (1857) captures the simple piety of French peasants in the nineteenth century.

expression "Daddy," distinguishes Christian prayer from other forms of prayer by its highly personal content.

For Muslims, to speak of God as father is blasphemy. For Jews, God is indeed the father of the Jewish people, but although some Jews have a personal relationship with him, the mainline tradition sees God in somewhat patriarchal and distant terms. Christians, however, hold a highly personal view of God which some people find flippant and disrespectful. Nevertheless, this is the way Jesus taught his disciples to pray.

The basis of Christian prayer is the idea of a direct relationship with God in which the individual can cast all his or her cares upon God and can worship and glorify him. Developments of Christian views of prayer are found in the liturgies of various traditional churches, where set prayers either replace or are used alongside extemporaneous prayer. Although some people, often religious reformers, object to set prayers as "dead rituals," they are in fact based upon the Lord's Prayer in Matthew 6:9–13. And as the great Christian writer C. S. Lewis and others have observed, in an amazing way such prayers free the mind to concentrate on God.

CHRISTIAN WORSHIP

The earliest Christians were Jews who, as far as they were permitted, continued to worship in Jewish synagogues and even at the temple in Jerusalem (Acts 3:1; 9:20). At the same time, they appear to have worshiped regularly in private homes (Acts 10:9, 27). During the early centuries of the Christian church, when it faced fierce persecution, Christian worship continued in homes and remote places. Eventually, after Constantine's edict of toleration (313), Christian congregations obtained their own buildings, which became known as churches. Very often, as in the case of the basilica in Trier, Germany, these were public buildings that rich patrons converted into churches. Then, as time passed, distinct churches were built throughout the empire, providing a pattern that has continued until this day.

Today Christian worship varies considerably from denomination to denomination. At one extreme there are "house churches" that meet in private homes. At the other extreme

Photo 21.11 The Romanesque Basilica of St. Anne de Beaupré, on the shores of the St. Lawrence River outside of Québec City, is the site of the oldest North American Roman Catholic shrine north of Mexico. The original church was founded in 1658 and quickly became a center of pilgrimage. Today it serves the triple function of a pilgrimage church, a local congregation, and a tourist attraction.

there are large liturgical denominations, like the Anglicans, Lutherans, Roman Catholics, and Orthodox, which build large cathedrals. Finally, in recent times the phenomenon of the megachurch has emerged in America, in which multipurpose buildings that accommodate up to ten thousand people are used for worship services.

CHRISTIAN DRESS CODES

Some extremist sects, offshoots from Christianity, prescribe particular forms of dress. Some older, less extreme, ethnic groups like the Hutterites also retain types of dress that originated in earlier centuries. Yet the vast majority of Christian groups have no particular dress codes except that people ought to dress modestly.

DIETARY LAWS

The New Testament repeatedly repudiates dietary laws for Christians (Acts 10:1–43; Galatians 3:1–29; Colossians 2:16–23). Therefore, apart from a few small sectarian groups, such as various African Initiated Churches, few Christian denominations maintain dietary laws. One possible exception to this statement is the general prohibition of alcoholic beverages among North American Christians of an evangelical or fundamentalist persuasion.

SUNDAY OR SABBATH

Although the earliest Christians were Jewish, the early church significantly changed its pattern of worship by celebrating on the first day of the week instead of the Sabbath. The theological reason given for this was that worship on what we now call Sunday reminds humans of the resurrection of Christ. Only a few sectarian groups, the best known of which are Seventh-day Adventists, retain the Jewish Sabbath as their day of worship.

THE CHRISTIAN FAMILY

As with the Jews, and most other religions, the family is very important for Christians. Yet, as Jacob Neusner observes (see chapter on Judaism), Christ set himself against the Jewish understanding of the family by claiming that loyalty to him came before loyalty to father or mother. Therefore, in all forms of orthodox Christianity, believers have been aware that, while the family is important, it can easily become an object of idolatry, and that devotion to Christ comes before all.

CHRISTIAN CEREMONIES OR SACRAMENTS

Christianity has its own set of ceremonies to mark the passage of an individual's life. In Christian theology these are known as the sacraments. Theologically a sacrament is a religious rite in which God is believed to be uniquely active. Augustine of Hippo, the great theologian of the Western church, described a sacrament as "a visible sign of an invisible reality." In the Anglican *Book of Common Prayer*, this thought is explained in terms of "an outward and visible sign of an inward and invisible grace."

All Christians, except a few sectarian or small groups, such as the Salvation Army, practice two major sacraments. These are baptism, by which a person is formally admitted to the social

Photo 21.12 A group of Africans pray before a baptismal ceremony on the beach in Durban, South Africa.

institution of the Christian church, and the Lord's Supper, or Mass, which commemorates the death of Jesus and looks forward to his coming again. Both of these sacraments are directly grounded in scriptural teachings (Luke 22:19–20; Matthew 28:18–20). Where Christians disagree is on the meaning and means of celebrating these sacraments.

Christians divide on the issue of baptism between those who claim that only people capable of making a decision to serve Christ are fit subjects to receive the sacrament, which is a testimony to their faith, and those who baptize babies. Technically, the baptism of infants is called paedobaptism, and the restriction of baptism to people capable of confessing their own personal faith is called antipaedobaptism.

The paedobaptist position includes the Anglicans, Lutherans, Orthodox Christians, Presbyterians, Roman Catholics, and a variety of other older, or mainline, denominations that believe baptism is a communal act that includes entire families. In defense of this position, they argue that in the New Testament the church seems to have included babies and children (Acts 16:27–34). Further, they argue that under the old covenant, revealed in the Old Testament, the sign of membership of the people of God was circumcision, which was performed when a child was eight days old (Genesis 17:1–27). They then point out that in Romans 4, particularly in verses 11 and 12, circumcision is described as a sign of faith. Therefore, they ask how an eight-day-old child could have faith unless signs of faith have a communal significance.

The Orthodox, Roman Catholics, and many Anglicans and Lutherans go even further, asking their critics to explain the meaning of 1 Peter 3:21. Literally, the Greek of this passage reads "now saves baptism." This is translated in the King James Ver-

Photo 21.13 A group of participants gather for a photograph with their bishop after the service of confirmation.

sion of the Bible as "baptism doth also now save us." The Roman Catholic *New Jerusalem Bible* says, "It is the baptism ... which now saves you." Even the New International Version speaks about "baptism that now saves you." According to paedobaptists, this difficult passage, when seen in context, implies that there is a quality to baptism that goes far beyond a mere confession of faith.

Consequently, such churches usually practice infant baptism by sprinkling water on the head of the infant during a church ceremony. Then, years later, when a child comes of age, they perform a ceremony in the congregation known as "confirmation." This allows the young adult to confess their personal faith and accept the obligations of membership of the Christian community that were assumed at their baptism. In this way, confirmation is similar to the Jewish bar mitzvah.

Members of antipaedobaptist traditions, usually known as Baptists, which are the dominant form of Christianity in North America, claim that only someone capable of making a profession of faith can be baptized. They base this interpretation of the sacrament on verses like Matthew 28:19, where Jesus said, "Therefore go and make disciples of all nations, baptizing them ..." They then ask, "How can a baby be regarded as a disciple?" Further, they point out that Peter, in the earliest recorded Christian sermon (Acts 2:38), tells his hearers, "Repent and be baptized." Again they ask, "How can a baby 'repent'?"

Therefore, members of Baptist traditions argue that someone must profess faith in Christ of their own accord before they are baptized, which usually takes place by immersion. Consequently, churches in the Baptist tradition usually hold a service of blessing, or naming, before the congregation, when a baby is "brought to the Lord," or dedicated. Then, later, when the child is capable of deciding to follow Christ and does so decide, they are baptized, usually by total immersion, in what is known as "believer's baptism." Normally, for children brought up in Christian families, this takes place when the child becomes a teenager.

Photo 21.14 The homily, or sermon, during a Communion service in St. Martin's Cathedral, in Bratislava, Slovakia. After sixty years of Communist repression, the Christian community in the city is largely made up of elderly people. Yet it was here that the Hungarian kings were crowned for almost six hundred years. Later the Austro-Hungarian emperors and empresses, including Maria Theresa, whose rule shaped an age, were crowned here.

Christians also divide over the nature of the Lord's Supper. Once again the issue concerns the correct interpretation of the words of Jesus. At the Last Supper as recorded in Matthew 26:26–28 (and related passages), we are told, "Jesus took bread, gave thanks and broke it, and gave it to his disciples, saying, 'Take and eat; this is my body.' Then he took the cup, gave thanks and offered it to them, saying, 'Drink from it, all of you. This is my blood of the covenant, which is poured out for many for the forgiveness of sins.'"

Since Jesus' death and resurrection, the Christian church has commemorated his death by regularly holding Communion services, known to the Orthodox, Roman Catholics, and many Lutherans and Anglicans as "the Mass." During these services the words of Jesus are repeated to the congregation, and either the officiating minister or the priest, with or without the congregation, participates in the ceremony by eating and drinking bread and wine.

For the Orthodox and Roman Catholics, as well as many Anglicans and Lutherans, this is a profound event that in a certain manner, which we do not fully understand, reenacts the sacrifice of Christ. These churches take literally the statements of Christ, "Take and eat; this is my body" (Matthew 26:26), and, "this is my blood" (Matthew 26:28). Such statements, which in one form or another are found in all accounts of the Last Supper, are taken literally by these historic churches. Therefore, they claim that through the ritual of consecration, the bread and the wine of Communion are actually transformed into the body and blood of Christ.

On the other hand, most Protestant churches claim that such literalism misunderstands Scripture and that Jesus meant something different by these words. Most Lutherans, for example, argue that while Christ is present in the sacrament, the elements remain bread and wine, although they become the body and blood of Christ upon their reception by the believer. Many Anglicans tone this down a little without being explicit about what they mean. Other Protestant groups, influenced by Reformers like John Calvin (1509–1564), argue that Christ is spiritually, but not physically, present in the sacraments. Finally, following sixteenth-century Reformers like Ulrich Zwingli (1484–1531), some say that the sacraments are merely symbols of remembrance that cause us to reflect on Christ's death and resurrection in expectation of his ultimate return.

In addition to these two main sacraments, the Orthodox and Roman Catholic traditions recognize five other sacraments: (1) the rite of confirmation, which includes the laying on of hands and anointing with oil; (2) the sacrament of penance, which used to be called confession, where a person confesses their sins to a priest to obtain absolution; (3) anointing the sick with oil; (4) marriage, which is part of a service that includes a Mass; and (5) the ordination of deacons, priests, bishops, and other ranks of people set aside for the service of God. Within such churches it is believed that, through the laying on of hands by properly ordained members of the clergy, these ceremonies convey a special unction or grace upon the recipient.

The important thing about all of these traditions is that they provide Christians with a framework within which to live and work. Taken together with the Christian year and the Christian community worldwide, they create a highly diverse and colorful religious tradition.

CHAPTER 22

CHRISTIAN POLITICS ACCORDING TO ABRAHAM KUYPER

INTRODUCTION

Anyone wishing to understand modern Christianity in North America needs to begin by recognizing that since the 1980s evangelical Christians have undergone a remarkable political transformation. Until about 1970 the majority of evangelicals were convinced that religion and politics did not mix and should not be mixed. Today, however, many believe that Christianity and politics cannot be separated, although the failures of the Bush administration appear to be leading some to step back from involvement in politics.

According to American sociologist Andrew Greeley,[1] a small majority of the newly politicized evangelicals and fundamentalist Christians are supporters of the New Christian Right. A large minority are political moderates, while a small minority, identified with journals such as *Sojourners*, are on the radical left. What is surprising about this development is that some leaders on both left and right trace their political thought to the work of the Dutch theologian and statesman Abraham Kuyper (1837–1920). Therefore, it is helpful to take a look at his life and his political thought, in order to understand something of the roots of contemporary evangelical political movements.

The earliest systematic expression of Kuyper's thought in English is found in his 1898 Stone Lectures, regarded by Kuyper as an authoritative statement of his views. The Stone Lectures were delivered at Princeton Theological Seminary and are published under the title *Lectures on Calvinism*.[2] In addition to discussing politics, Kuyper also includes his views on religion, art, education, and science. Informed by Kuyper's arguments, readers should be able to understand contemporary issues in religion and politics in North America far better than if they had never studied him.

---

1. Andrew M. Greeley and Michael Hout, *The Truth about Conservative Christians: What They Think and What They Believe* (Chicago: Univ. of Chicago Press, 2006).
2. Abraham Kuyper, *Lectures on Calvinism* (Amsterdam: Höveker and Wormser, 1898).

ABRAHAM KUYPER

Abraham Kuyper was born on 29 October 1837. His father was a Dutch Reformed Church minister who preached a liberal, or modernist, form of evangelicalism. As a student, Kuyper attended the Middelburg Gymnasium and Leyden University, where he gained the highest academic honors. After receiving his doctorate in theology in 1863, he was ordained as a minister in the Dutch Reformed Church. His first parish was in the small northern fishing village of Beesd.

Photo 22.1 Abraham Kuyper, from a commemorative picture issued in 1920.

In Beesd, Kuyper encountered what he regarded as backward, ignorant parishioners steeped in traditional Calvinist doctrines. In attempting to educate these folk and to enlighten them to the truths of the modern world, Kuyper was himself converted from the advanced theological liberalism of his university training to a living faith in Jesus Christ as Lord. As a result of this deeply emotional experience, he reevaluated his theology and returned to Calvinist orthodoxy.

In 1867 he moved from Beesd to Utrecht, and in 1870 to Amsterdam. During these years he developed a comprehensive world-and-life view to express his living faith and Calvinist convictions. In 1869 he met Guillaume Groen van Prinsterer (1801–1876), a fellow Calvinist, who had founded a small Calvinist grouping in the Dutch parliament based upon what van Prinsterer called "anti-revolutionary principles." Kuyper supported van Prinsterer's ideals and helped found the first modern Dutch political party, the Anti-Revolutionary Party. After two years as editor of *De Standaard*, a daily newspaper, Kuyper entered parliament to represent the new party. In 1880 he founded the Free University of Amsterdam. Because of disagreements with the hierarchy of the Dutch Reformed Church, Kuyper led a secession movement in 1886 to found his own independent Reformed Church. The following year his political activities saw fruit in constitutional reforms and the extension of the right to vote to many people, including members of his party. These changes led to an electoral victory that brought the Anti-Revolutionaries to power in 1888 with a small majority.

Several years later, in 1891, Kuyper began a series of attacks upon capitalism in which he pleaded for a form of Christian socialism. As a result, the right wing of his party broke away to form the Christian Historical Party in 1893–1894. It was not until 1900 that Kuyper's Anti-Revolutionary Party gained undisputed power in parliament, and in 1901 Kuyper became prime minister, a post he held until 1905, when he was defeated at the polls after bitter labor disputes and revolutionary ferment by socialist opponents. He retired from active politics in 1913 and died seven years later in 1920.

KUYPER'S CALVINIST FRAMEWORK

Declaring conservatism dead and liberalism dying, Kuyper sought to re-create a Christian perspective on politics and society that would form the basis for Christian social action. This he envisaged as an integral part of a Christian world-and-life view based upon the Scriptures and on their interpretation within the Augustinian-Calvinist tradition. Although he wrote profusely in Dutch on theology, art, politics, education, and a host of other topics, only a few of his writings are available in English translations. The most comprehensive statement of his position in English is to be found in the previously mentioned Stone Lectures. The remainder of this chapter will consist of an exposition and critique of Kuyper's views as set out in these lectures.

For Kuyper, citing the American historian George Bancroft (1800–1891), Calvinism "has a theory of ontology, of ethics, of social happiness, and of human liberty, all derived from God."[3] He notes that, unlike Lutherans, Calvinists did not include the name of Calvin in the church denominations *they* founded, but preferred to call themselves Christian Reformed. Hence he says Calvinists have been known by many names in different countries, and adds, "It may be said, that the entire field which in the end was covered by the Reformation, so far as it was not Lutheran and not Socinian, was dominated in principle by Calvinism. Even the Baptists applied for shelter at the tents of the Calvinists."[4] Thus the difference between the center and the circumference could vary greatly and produce many different types of Calvinist organizations and expressions, but essentially, all "such general systems of life" revolve around three fundamental relationships: "(1) our relation *to God*; (2) our relation *to man*; (3) our relation to *the world*."[5]

Photo 22.2 Guillaume Groen van Prinsterer (1801–1876), who initially inspired Kuyper's political thought.

As examples of what he means, Kuyper argues that paganism is a life system that worships God in the creature. This worship results in a distortion of man's other relationships by allowing some people to become demigods, thus creating caste systems in society. At the same time, too high an estimate is placed on the idea of nature, which leads to a deification of the world. Kuyper offers similar interpretations of Islam, Romanism, and Modernism, all of which he contrasts with Calvinism. It is in Calvinism alone, he argues, that one can find the right balance between these vital relationships.

According to Kuyper's understanding of Calvinism, God enters into immediate fellowship with his creature, Man. This, Kuyper declares, is the true meaning of the doctrine of predestination. So, according to this doctrine, our entire human life is placed immediately

---

3. Ibid., 9.

4. Ibid., 11.

5. Ibid., 16. Italics here and in subsequent quotations are original unless otherwise specified.

Photo 22.3 Willem Bilderdijk (1756–1831), through whom Guillaume Groen van Prinsterer and a host of young men were converted to orthodox Calvinism in the early part of the nineteenth century. He laid the foundation for Kuyper's work, although his own political philosophy was reactionary in relation to that which Kuyper developed.

before God, ensuring, as a result, the equality of all human beings before God and with each other.[6] The world itself is to be honored not because it is divine, but because it is a divine creation—the handiwork of God. Practically, this means for the Christian that "the curse should no longer rest upon the world itself, but upon that which is sinful in it, and instead of monastic flight from the world the duty is now emphasized of serving God in the world, in every position of life … Thus the puritanical sobriety went hand in hand with the recognition of the entire life of the world."[7]

KUYPER'S "CHRISTIAN" POLITICS

The third lecture in the series is entitled "Calvinism and Politics." Here we find a brief but dense outline of Kuyper's political theory, distilled from his great work *Ons Programme* (Our Program [1878]). He argues that the determinative principle for Calvinist political theory is "the Sovereignty of the Triune God over the whole Cosmos."[8] From this statement of principle he deduces three realms of sovereignty: the state, the society, and the church. He then refers to these realms or areas of relationship as integral wholes, which he calls "spheres." In this way, he speaks about his political principle as the application of the principle of "sphere sovereignty" to politics.[9]

KUYPER'S VIEW OF THE STATE

The first application of this notion is to the state. Kuyper does not define what he means by "the state," but assumes that his hearers are in agreement with him as to how the state is to be understood. What he seems to mean by the state is civil government as recognized both by the citizens of a country and by foreign powers.

Mankind, Kuyper argues, is organically related by blood, so that one humanity exists throughout all time. But because of sin and the fall, man's original unity has been fractured, and political life has become a necessity. Had there been no fall, there would have been no need for the establishment of the structures of the state. Instead, all people would be gov-

---

6. Ibid., 18.
7. Ibid., 21.
8. Ibid., 99.
9. Ibid., 116.

erned through family relationships. Thus politics and the state are unnatural developments in human history, the state being a mechanical structure imposed upon the natural organic relationships that bind people together. "God has instituted magistrates, by reason of sin."[10] Therefore, from the viewpoint of God's original creation, the state ought not to exist, but in the light of the fall it must exist to restrain evil and make life in a fallen world tolerable.

Kuyper rejects all theories that imply a social contract as the basis of society, because these are based upon the notion of "the people" as the primary element in the state. He asserts, "No man has the right to rule over another man, otherwise such a right necessarily, and immediately becomes, the *right of the strongest*."[11] Like Calvin, Kuyper does not believe that any one form of government is in itself right for all times and places. Rather, the form that government takes is bound up with changes in historical and social circumstances. This position he traces back to Augustine.

In Kuyper's view, all life systems are to be seen in terms of their deep roots in the past and the ways in which they combine various elements from preceding systems of government. Christians are to seek godly government without demanding a set form.

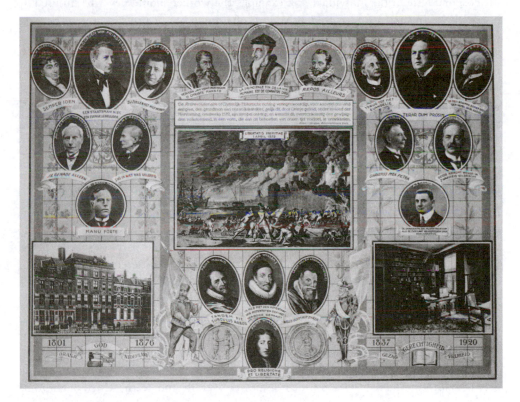

Photo 22.4 The 1920 commemorative picture that puts the Dutch Christian Anti-Revolutionary Party, which Kuyper founded, in its historical and intellectual tradition.

---

10. Ibid., 102.
11. Ibid., 103.

In saying this, Kuyper rejects the idea of a theocracy, which he argues was restricted to ancient Israel. He summarizes Calvinist political thought in three theses:

> 1. God only—and never any creature—is possessed of sovereign rights, in the destiny of the nations, because God alone created them, maintains them by His Almighty power, and rules them, by His ordinances. 2. Sin has, in the realm of politics, broken down the direct government of God, and therefore the exercise of authority, for the purpose of government, has subsequently been invested in men, as a mechanical remedy. And 3. In whatever form this authority may reveal itself, man never possesses power over his fellow-man in any other way than by an authority which descends upon him from the majesty of God.[12]

THE STATE'S DUTIES

The state itself has three duties to perform: (1) It must draw a boundary between the different spheres to avoid social conflict. Thus, there is a boundary between the domestic and the corporate life of the individual. For example, the worker should never be misused by his employer in such a way as to deprive him of a home life or private interest, because such a development would mean that the corporate sphere has illegitimately invaded the domestic sphere. (2) It must defend individuals and weak elements within each sphere. In saying this Kuyper appears to envisage a subdivision of each social sphere into further spheres. Within the domestic sphere, for example, there is a separate sphere of education, which must not be confused with the sphere of marriage, or vice versa. (3) It must coerce all the separate spheres of society to support the state and uphold its legitimate functions. Thus, each sphere has an obligation to render whatever dues necessary for the maintenance of the overall unity of society as protected by the state.[13]

SOCIETY IN KUYPER'S SCHEME

Building on this foundation, Kuyper discusses the sphere of society. This sphere, he maintains, includes the family, business, science, the arts, and so on. It stands in antithesis to the state. Society, he declares, is not one whole, but a number of diverse parts, or social spheres. There is *"sovereignty in the individual social spheres,...* [and] these different developments of social life have *nothing above themselves but God*, and ... the State cannot intrude here."[14]

The family is the basis of all human social relations, and as such is based upon the primal blood relationship. Thus society functions organically and may be compared at this level to a plant. In society, "the chief aim of all human effort remains what it was by virtue of our creation and before the fall—namely, *domination over nature*."[15]

In this view, government, in contrast to society, is a mechanical device, which is set over peoples. Its essential characteristic is its power over life and death, which ought to be

---

12. Ibid., 108.
13. Ibid., 124–25.
14. Ibid., 116.
15. Ibid., 117.

exercised in the administration of justice. This has a twofold application: (1) to maintain internal justice, and (2) to care for the people as a unit at home and abroad. But because government is mechanically imposed upon the organic spheres of society, friction occurs between different social areas and the government: "The government is always inclined, with its *mechanical* authority, to invade social life, to subject it and mechanically to arrange it."[16] At the same time, the various social spheres will endeavor to throw off all restraints of government. Thus society will be continually faced with the twin dangers of statism and anarchy. But Calvinism, Kuyper maintains, avoids these extremes by insisting on the sovereignty of God and the rightfulness of a plurality of social spheres "*under the law*," which is maintained by the government.[17]

Within the social sphere Kuyper finds numerous other spheres. He divides these into four main groups: (1) the sphere of social relationships, or of personality, where individuals meet and interact with each other; (2) the corporate sphere, which includes all groupings of people in a corporate sense, such as the university, trade unions, employers, organizations, companies, and so on; (3) the domestic sphere, which encompasses family issues,

Photo 22.5 The great British Christian prime minister William Ewart Gladstone (1809–1898), whose work Kuyper admired.

marriage, "domestic peace," education, and personal property; and, finally, (4) the communal sphere, which includes all groupings of people in communal relationships, such as those on streets, villages, towns, cities, and so on. Each of these spheres, Kuyper argues, has its own pattern of development and its own specific laws, over which God reigns and which the state has no power to alter.

KUYPER'S VIEW OF RELIGION AND POLITICS

Kuyper's final sphere is the sphere of the church. While admitting that a divided church presents many problems, he believes that implicit in Calvin's teaching about liberty of conscience is the ideal of a free church in a free society. On the top of his newspaper *De Standaard* was the motto "a free Church for a free State." While acknowledging that unity between churches has an aesthetic appeal, he argues that the government must suspend judgment in this area and allow divisions to exist amongst Christians, because "*the government lacks the data*

---

16. Ibid., 120.
17. Ibid., 121.

of judgment," and would "[infringe] the *sovereignty of the Church*."[18] He concludes from this that while extreme forms of puritanical church order are to be avoided, allowances must be made for historical and cultural differences between denominations. In saying this, Kuyper was prepared, as was Calvin, to accept Roman Catholics as allies against atheism.

Photo 22.6 Kuyper's study, where he worked unceasingly, producing a steady stream of newspaper articles on political issues, devotional readings, and theological tracts. His output runs to hundreds of publications that form a three-volume bibliography.

KUYPER AND THE INDIVIDUAL

Kuyper concludes with a short section on the "*sovereignty of the individual person*," in which he argues that "conscience is never subject to man but always and ever to God Almighty."[19] This leads him to declare that "the *liberty of speech*, and the *liberty of worship*"[20] are essential in a just society. Yet, like John Stuart Mill, Kuyper seeks to limit such liberty to the "mature man," and doubts that "undeveloped peoples" experience such liberty.[21] In this, as in all his arguments, Kuyper's overall aim is to enable "every man to serve God, *according to his own conviction and the dictates of his own heart*."[22]

For Kuyper, it was not the desire to ensure one's own personal salvation that inspired Christians, but rather their love for God and their desire to bring all areas of life under his lordship. Through his emphasis on creation-fall-redemption, Kuyper brought a more comprehensive understanding of Calvinist theology and motivations to his work than either Max Weber (1864–1920) or Ernst Troeltsch (1865–1923) in their reporting on Calvinism as outside observers. It is also important to realize that Calvinism is not static, and that in developing Calvinist themes Kuyper was simply carrying on the task of reformation begun by Luther and formulated by Calvin.

CRITICISMS OF KUYPER

Before moving on to the main criticism of Kuyper's work, which concerns his model of society, a number of ambiguities in his writings should be noted. Kuyper refers to spheres

---

18. Ibid., 136.
19. Ibid., 129.
20. Ibid., 141.
21. Ibid., 140.
22. Ibid., 142.

within society, but what does he mean? If these spheres are to be understood as observable entities, why do not all people recognize them? If, on the other hand, they are meant as socially constructed "social facts" in a Durkheimian sense, how do we come to recognize them? In talking about spheres, Kuyper refers to them as "relationships," which indicates that his ideas are somewhat similar to Durkheim's.

Equally important is his observation that some societies are "less developed" than others. This seems to indicate that in certain societies a particular sphere may be "missing"—a point taken up by Herman Dooyeweerd (1894–1977) in his development of Kuyper's thought.

His reference to the sphere of the state as "above" the sphere of society is puzzling. What is the relationship between the state and society? In a similar way, he seems to say that the family takes its form from the state, while insisting at the same time that the state is distinct from society. Here his views seem very unclear.

At times Kuyper almost falls into the class of theologians who say that the state is a result of sin. Yet a careful reading of his work shows that his view is not that simple. He definitely speaks about the state in its present form as being a result of sin. In this sense he sees the state's primary task as the maintenance of law and order. But he also seems to allow for the development of statelike functions in a nonfallen world. What these functions would be he never develops, but the fact that he allows for them is important.

Kuyper bases his analysis of man and society upon what he calls the "three fundamental relations."[23] These begin with man's relationship to God—although Kuyper's analysis does not force one to accept his view of God. By "relation *to God*" he means something like Paul Tillich's understanding of "ultimate concern." How people view their relationship to God, or whatever is the central issue of their lives, affects all of their lives. In this he is also very close to Weber's understanding of religion. The second relationship is that of man to man, and the third, of man to the world. In all of these relationships Kuyper sees the God–man relationship as determinative. How people view their relationship to God (or whatever they see as

Photo 22.7 Much of European history from the coronation of Charles the Great, or Charlemagne, in 800 to today involves an ongoing struggle between church and state. In the above picture of the coronation of Charles V of France, one sees bishops crowning the future king and, in doing so, implicitly claiming authority over him. This view of church and state Kuyper explicitly rejected, substituting his own pluralistic view of sphere sovereignty.

23. Ibid., 16.

ultimate) will affect all other important relationships. In God or an idol people find the starting point that integrates the whole of their existence and provides unity to their lives.

THE ENDURING RELEVANCE OF KUYPER FOR CHRISTIANS

The problem one faces in attempting to evaluate Kuyper's work is the fragmentary nature of his thought and the abundance of his writings. Kuyper uses analogy and imagery to great effect and tends to bewitch the intellect rather than clarify issues. With these skills he was a great politician and leader, because he could offer his followers a vision to follow. But for the distant observer who tries to analyze what he is saying, his work presents many problems. Great ideas are offered, but again and again the question is raised, "What do they mean?" How can these visions be translated and transformed from nineteenth-century Dutch society to twenty-first-century North American society? Kuyper's work is perhaps itself more of a vision and model than a blueprint to be followed. Yet concepts such as the distinction between the organic nature of society and the mechanistic nature of the state are both helpful and informative.

What Kuyper does is to blend two dominant models of society in one political theory. In doing this he brings together the mechanistic image of the state, which is usually associated with radical political thought, with the organic image of society favored by conservative thinkers. As a result, he produces a political theory that is neither radical nor conservative, but which has the potential to be a truly Christian third way, incorporating true understandings of man's state found in both radical and conservative theories.

Kuyper thus provides Christians with a uniquely Christian vision of the state and society. Unlike other Christian thinkers, he does not adopt a conservative or radical stance, but creates his own view, based on Scripture,

Photo 22.8 Founded in 1879 by Abraham Kuyper, the Anti-Revolutionary Party, or ARP, was a formidable force in Dutch politics until its merger in 1974 with three other Christian parties, including its one-time rival the Catholic Party, to form the Christian Democratic Appeal coalition. Today the ARP faction is still an influential voice within Dutch politics. The picture to the left shows an ARP poster from the 1971 election, the last major independent initiative of the ARP.

that allows for both continuity and change in society, but which maintains, above all, the biblical emphasis on justice. Since his day, many Christians have lapsed into either radical or conservative political thinking without adequate models upon which to build their own distinctly Christian theories. By stressing the importance of relationships and seeing the reality of conflict between social forms and the state, Kuyper offers Christians the basis of a position that can be developed into a dynamic and viable Christian alternative to present secular challenges.

CHAPTER 23

THE CHALLENGE OF ISLAM

INTRODUCTION

This chapter attempts to understand Islam as it is presented by Muslim scholars who are best-selling authors in the Muslim world and whose works are popular in English translation among committed Muslims living in the English-speaking world. It will be supplemented by academic studies written by Western-educated scholars, the majority of whom are non-Muslim. Hence the understanding of Islam presented here is significantly different on certain issues from that found in most other religious studies textbooks.

Most religious studies textbooks are written by Western scholars who present their own image of Islam based on other Western-educated scholars' interpretations of primary texts. The problem with this approach is that most Muslims, even those living in Western societies, do not read Western academic studies as devotional texts for inspiration in their daily lives. Like Christians, they turn to trusted Muslim authors, whose works are usually ignored by Western-educated scholars or dismissed as fundamentalist, radical, or extremist.

According to the prominent and immensely popular Egyptian Muslim writer Sayyid Qutb (1906–1966), scholarly interpretations such as those found in popular religious studies textbooks are "the wily attacks of orientalists" who treacherously seek to destroy Islam by reinterpreting its core concepts in terms of secularizing Western ideas.[1] Of course, Qutb is usually dismissed as a "sincere extremist" by Western interpreters of Islam. Nevertheless, his works are immensely popular throughout the Muslim world and among Muslims living in Western countries. Therefore, anyone wanting to understand contemporary Islam needs to take him and writers who share his essentially traditional viewpoint seriously.

For example, when James Dickie, better known as the British Muslim leader Jakub Zaki, taught Islamic studies at the Lancaster University in the late 1960s, he emphasized that after the revelation of the Qur'an, the second great miracle of Islam was the Conquests of the first century of the Muslim era. This emphasis on the military genius of Muhammad and his Companions goes against the tendency of many contemporary Western writers to downplay Islam's military achievements and deny the importance of concepts like *jihad* as core Muslim values. Yet Dickie, who went on to become one of the main organizers of the Festival of Islam held in London in 1976, did not hesitate to directly confront images

---

1. Sayyid Qutb, *Milestones* (Beirut: Holy Koran Publishing House, 1980), 12.

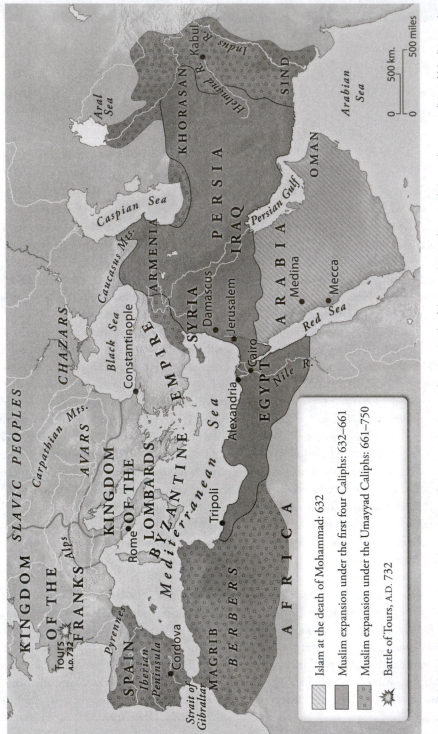

Map 23.1 This map shows the rapid expansion of Islam in the century after the death of the prophet Muhammad. According to traditional Muslim teaching, these conquests were the second great miracle of Islam.

of Islam presented in Western literature in Islamic terms as understood by the majority of committed Muslims today.

On the one hand, Dickie rejected the notion that Islam is just like Christianity with a few minor differences about the nature of God, and that at its core it values a secularized form of pacifism. On the other hand, he rejected attempts by hostile critics to dismiss Islam as a religion that promotes war. Instead he argued that war has its legitimate place in Islamic theology. Anyone wanting to understand Muslims needs to recognize this and not distort the Muslim tradition. Islam is not a milk-and-water religion, like that of the Quakers, but neither does it promote war for its own sake. Rather, Islam seeks to bring about the rule of God on earth through the activities of his people, and these activities include military as well as cultural, intellectual, and every other legitimate activity of human life.

THE ORIGINS OF ISLAM

According to Muslim tradition, Islam came into existence with the creation of humanity by the creator God, known to Muslims as Allah. Following the creation, God revealed his will to mankind through the first man, Adam, and a long line of prophets that included Abraham and Jesus. The last and final prophet was Muhammad, to whom God revealed his will for mankind in the holy Qur'an, and who now serves as a model and inspiration for all men. What follows is an account of the origins of Islam according to Muslim tradition. For most Western scholars this is problematic, because most of the traditional

Photo 23.1 The holy city of Mecca as seen in the nineteenth century, before modern developments changed the landscape.

account lacks external verification, making it a matter of faith rather evidence-based history. Muslims, on the other hand, claim that that tradition is accurate and needs no external verification.

According to tradition, Muhammad was a successful, middle-aged businessman when he first received God's call in 610. He was the son of Abd Allah, born in Mecca as Muhammad ibn Abdullah, in 570. Muhammad's father died before his birth, and his mother, Amina, died when he was six years old. After the death of his parents, his uncle Abu Talib became his guardian. By birth Muhammad belonged to the Banu Hashim clan of the powerful Quraysh tribe, which dominated Meccan society.

The oasis town of Mecca, situated at a crossroads between Eastern countries adjoining the Indian Ocean and the Mediterranean world, was controlled by a group of powerful tribes led by the Quraysh. It was a thriving trading center that depended on agricultural imports, particularly from the area around the town of Yathrib, known later as Medina. This town, about a 250-mile journey north of Mecca, was controlled by a powerful group who became known as the Ansar tribe, or "helpers of Muhammad."

At the center of Mecca was a cube-shaped shrine, the Kaaba, that contained 360 idols belonging to various Arabian tribes. Every year this shrine became the center of a pilgrimage and the location of an important trade fair. The shrine was controlled by the Umayyad clan of the Quraysh tribe, who gained considerable revenue and power from their role as guardians of the Kaaba. Before the birth of Muhammad, according to Muslim tradition, the Arabs of the Arabian peninsula worshiped numerous gods and goddesses; on the other hand, the tradition seems to indicate that they also acknowledged the existence of a High God, Allah, who was the creator of the world. He was accompanied by three goddesses, who were considered his daughters. The Arabs of this time were a fatalistic people who dismissed ideas about an afterlife, rejected teachings related to a divine judgment, and based their justice on a system of vengeance and blood feuds between powerful clans and tribes.

According to Muslim teaching, the Qur'an is not an inspired book like the Bible. Rather, it is the very word of God. Therefore, the Qur'an is pure revelation, unsullied by human intervention.

When Muhammad was a young man, the tradition says, he entered the caravan trade, where he became the business manager for a wealthy widow, Khadija, whom he eventually married. At the time of his marriage he was twenty-five years old and she was forty. The marriage was fruitful, and the couple had seven children, three of whom died early in life. Throughout her life Muhammad remained faithful to Khadija, and, contrary to local customs, did not take a second wife.

Tradition tells us that from his childhood Muhammad was a spiritual person who frequently took time off from his daily tasks to meditate and pray. It also tells us that, although he was a successful businessman, he was illiterate. Therefore, the revelation of the Qur'an is all the more amazing.

On one occasion, when he was forty years old, during the lunar month of Ramadan, he was meditating in a cave near Mecca when the angel Gabriel appeared to him. This event is known as the "night of power and excellence" in Islam. The accounts of what happened next vary. According to the majority, or Sunni, tradition, Muhammad feared that the angel was a messenger of Satan and had to be compelled to follow the angel's instructions. According to the minority, or Shia, tradition, Muhammad recognized Gabriel and willingly followed his instructions. In any event, the command came for Muhammad to begin reciting what became the first revealed Sura, or chapter, of the Qur'an, which literally means "the recitation." In the Pickthall rendition,[2] the first Sura reads as follows:

1 Read: In the name of thy Lord who createth,

2 Createth man from a clot.

3 Read: And thy Lord is the Most Bounteous,

4 Who teacheth by the pen,

5 Teacheth man that which he knew not.

6 Nay, but verily man is rebellious

7 That he thinketh himself independent!

8 Lo! unto thy Lord is the return.

9 Hast thou seen him who dissuadeth

10 A slave when he prayeth?

11 Hast thou seen if he (relieth) on the guidance (of Allah)

12 Or enjoineth piety?

13 Hast thou seen if he denieth (Allah's guidance) and is froward?

14 Is he then unaware that Allah seeth?

15 Nay, but if he cease not, We will seize him by the forelock—

16 The lying, sinful forelock—

17 Then let him call upon his henchmen!

18 We will call the guards of hell.

19 Nay! Obey not thou him. But prostrate thyself, and draw near (unto Allah).

After this dramatic beginning Muhammad returned home, unsure how to respond. Encouraged by his wife and family members, he began preaching in Mecca, condemning paganism, idolatry, and corruption, while other revelations followed his first dramatic encounter with Gabriel. The core of Muhammad's message was the demand that humans

---

2. Muslims believe that the Qur'an is the Word of God, which exists in heaven on golden plates. Muhammad "read" these in some miraculous way, even though he was illiterate, according to most accounts. The language of the Qur'an is Qur'anic Arabic, which, because it is literally the Word of God, cannot be translated into any other language. Consequently, all so-called translations are really renditions and not translations at all. Further, all Muslims must recite memorized Qur'anic verses in their original language.

abandon idolatry and return to the worship of the one true God. For the Meccans this meant renouncing their traditional gods and idols that they worshiped in a shrine known as the Kaaba.

Stung by Muhammad's accusations, call for repentance, and submission to God's will, as well as his practical calls for justice and aid to the poor, the leading families in Mecca began an increasingly harsh series of persecutions, led by the leaders of the the Umayyad clan, who were guardians of the shrine. Eventually, after almost seven years, Muhammad and his followers fled Mecca to live in caves in the mountains. They returned only after Muhammad received guarantees of their safety. The hardships of this time led to the death of Khadija, whom Muhammad greatly loved.

Persecution resumed, and some of Muhammad's followers fled to Ethiopia or other parts of Arabia, where, according to Muslim tradition, they were protected by Christians. Then, to everyone's surprise, the people of Yathrib (later Medina), which lies about two hundred miles north of Mecca, called upon Muhammad to mediate in a blood feud that was tearing their community apart. After accepting this invitation, Muhammad became their ruler. Between the months of July and September, Muhammad led more than two hundred of his supporters from Mecca to Yathrib, which was to be renamed Medina, where he brought about a revolution in morals and government. This migration became known as the *hijra* and is remembered in the *Hajj*, a pilgrimage held annually during Dhu-al-Hijja, the last month of the Islamic year.

Consequently, every Muslim is expected to complete this journey at least once in their lifetime. Today this is the largest pilgrimage in the world.

During this time various other rituals, known later as the five pillars of Islam, were formalized. These are *Shahada*, or the profession of faith; *Salat*, or prayers, which are offered five times a day at fixed hours; *Sawm*, or fasting during daylight hours in the month of Ramadan; *Zakat*, or the giving of alms to the poor, which is similar to what Christians call a tithe; and *Hajj*, the pilgrimage to Mecca mentioned above.

According to the Sunni traditions, Muhammad consulted with his followers before even-

Photo 23.3 A medieval Muslim pilgrim book. Such texts, which also existed in Christianity, were intended to lead the pilgrim both practically and spiritually to their destination. As such, they were rather like a spiritual travel guide.

tually deciding on the advice of one of them to institute the call to prayer using a human voice. The Shia reject this tradition, claiming instead that the angel Gabriel instructed Muhammad about the correct way in which the faithful were to be called to prayer.

As the governor of Medina, Muhammad established laws that regulated the conduct of life and the duties of citizens. He also recognized the rights of Jews to remain a separate community, provided they allied themselves with Muslims. Once his rule was established in Medina, Muhammad once more turned his attention to Mecca, where the people remained adamantly opposed to his preaching.

Since Mecca was the commercial capital of the Arabian Peninsula, control of the city was essential if the Arabs as a whole were to convert to Islam. Therefore, Muhammad initiated a guerrilla war against his enemies' caravans, which succeeded to such an extent that he cut off their trade routes and source of wealth. Things came to a head in 624 at the Battle of Badr, near Medina, when Muhammad's followers decisively defeated a much larger army sent out by the citizens of Mecca to subdue what they saw as a robber chief. This battle was the first decisive victory for Muhammad and was seen as a sign of God's blessing on his divine mission. Two years later the Meccan army defeated Muhammad's forces at the Battle of Uhud, and Muhammad was wounded. The following year Medina was besieged by the Meccan armies; but at the Battle of the Ditch, named after a trench that Muhammad had built to foil the Mecca cavalry, the Meccans withdrew their forces.

Following these wars, Muhammad turned to diplomacy with great effect. A truce was arranged in 628, and Muslims were permitted to visit Mecca on pilgrimage. But in 630 Muhammad accused the leading Meccan clan, the Quraysh, of breaking the treaty and invaded Mecca, backed by an army of ten thousand troops. The Meccans surrendered and Muhammad showed them great leniency. Consequently, many converted to Islam and accepted Muhammad as their leader.

With Mecca securely under his control, Muhammad extended his authority over the whole of Arabia, and many Arabs converted to Islam. Finally, at the age of sixty-two, he

Photo 23.4 The plain interior of this Western mosque is typical of all mosques. Nowhere are there any pictures that represent Muhammad, his Companions or his family, let alone other human beings. Islam takes the commandment not to create a graven image very seriously indeed. To what extent this reflects the Ten Commandments of Exodus 20 is not entirely clear, although Islam clearly shares the spirit of Exodus 20:4. Consequently, there are no pictures of Muhammad except those made by heretical groups or enemies of orthodox Islam.

was able to lead the annual pilgrimage from Medina to Mecca, where he preached what was to be his last sermon. Three months later, in June 632, he died after a severe illness.

Apart from his example as a successful military and civic leader, Muhammad's personal conduct is of great interest to Muslims and serves to guide their daily life. This is why Muslim writers pay close attention to Muhammad's every word, his actions, and his personal conduct. They also learn from the example of his wives and Companions.

The issue of Muhammad's wives is one that Christians have often used as a point of criticism when debating with Muslims and is generally misunderstood. As long as Muhammad's wife Khadija lived, he was faithful to her. After her death, Muhammad, who by this time was known as "the Prophet," married the nine-year-old daughter of his friend and follower Abu Bakr, whom he first saw in a dream. Her name was Aisha, and she is described in the literature as a highly intelligent beauty who was a poet and artist of great piety.

Her age at the time of the marriage has often prompted severe criticism from Western observers, but it has to be remembered that Juliet in Shakespeare's play is only thirteen, and her mother regarded herself as "old" even though she was only in her mid-twenties. Therefore, when seen in the context of the times, there was nothing unusual in such a marriage. Anyone seeking to understand Islam needs to understand that marriage customs of different societies differ greatly over history. What is shocking to modern Western peoples would not have shocked Shakespeare very much and did not shock Muhammad's contemporaries. Further, this was to a large extent a dynastic marriage that cemented a bond between two families. Therefore, it should not be seen in terms of modern ideas about romantic love or feminism, which thinks in individualistic terms.

Later Muhammad took other wives. The exact number is in dispute, but it is usually agreed to be between eight and eleven. To understand his marriages it is important to realize that a number of these women were widows of his followers who died in battles for Islam. These widows included Hafsa, the daughter of Umar Ibn El Khattab; Zenab, whom the Prophet married to provide her with a home; and Um Salama, another widow. He also married Zenab Bint Jahsh, a divorcee whose original marriage was arranged by the Prophet, who felt pity for her after her divorce. Um Habiba was another divorcee, who had emigrated with her husband as a Muslim refugee to Ethiopia during the Meccan persecutions. She divorced her first husband when he embraced Christianity. When the Prophet heard of her fate and her determination to remain a Muslim, he wrote to the Ethiopian king proposing marriage to her. Then there were Safiyya and Rehanna, two Jewish widows who converted to Islam after their husbands were killed when their tribes were defeated and wiped out by the Prophet's forces. Juweria was another widow who was taken prisoner by Muhammad's army. The Prophet felt pity and married her as well.

Finally, Maria needs mention. She was one of four sisters who were among the earliest converts to Islam. She was widowed and was the last wife whom the Prophet married. She was fifty-one at the time. Muhammad was in Maria's house when he was struck by his final illness. At that time he requested to be moved to Aisha's house which is where he died. Maria was given to the Prophet by the king of Egypt. She was a Coptic Christian by birth. She bore a male child, Abraham, to the Prophet, and this incited the jealousy of his other wives. The child died at eighteen months.

To devout Muslims, these marriages are a sign of Muhammad's compassion and care for others. The people he married were often in need and through marriage gained both respect and security. Thus Muslim scholars reason that Muhammad sets an example for all men on how to treat women with respect and dignity.

Our knowledge of Muhammad and his ways comes not from the Qur'an, which is a book of revelation, but from a body of literature known as the *Hadith*. His wife Aisha is said

Photo 23.5 The above scene from a Syrian manuscript shows a meeting of Muslim scholars from the early thirteenth century.

to have played a key role in compiling various sayings attributed to Muhammad after his death. This collection is believed to be the basis of the *Hadith* for Sunni Muslims. Since the Hadith is vast, other Muslim groups often use different collections and which Hadith are emphasized by any one group may vary.

Another important group in Muslim traditions are those men known as "the Companions" of the Prophet. Superficially, these men appear to play a role in Muslim tradition similar to that of the disciples of the Buddha in Buddhism and of Jesus in Christianity. In reality their role is far, far greater than that of any group of disciples in other religions, because they are the people who recorded both the Qur'an when Muhammad recited it and the traditions, or *Hadith*, that tell us about the life, sayings, and conduct of the Prophet. Four members of this elite fellowship later became leaders, or caliphs—literally, successors of Muhammad—of the early Muslim community, known as the *umma*. The story of the Companions of the Prophet begins the history of Islam, which we must now consider.

MUSLIM HISTORY

When studying Islam, it is important to realize that most introductory textbooks in religious studies and most other works on Islam written in English largely repeat the majority, Sunni version of Muslim history. On the one hand, it is acceptable to present this version, because it does represent the view of most Muslims. On the other hand, it has become highly problematic, because it has led people in the West to accept without question a version of Islamic history that is believed to be false by the second largest community of Muslims worldwide. The problem is compounded by the fact that, since there are very few works available in English that present the Shia viewpoint, that viewpoint is difficult to learn about unless one reads Arabic or some other language used by Shia writers. One of the few history books written in English from a Shia viewpoint is Sayed A. A. Razwy's *A Restatement of the History of Islam and Muslims, 570–661*,[3] which presents a radically different interpretation of early Muslim history from that which is usually presented.

Caution in judging one account of Islam superior to another is warranted first of all, then, because one of the major accounts has simply not been heard. It is warranted also because all versions of the Muslim tradition were written down long after the events they recall; the first time Islam enters what we know as history is with the Arab conquests after the death of Muhammad.

Photo 23.6 The emphasis on a written tradition in addition to the sacred Qur'an encourages a high degree of literacy among Muslims, although they tend to restrict their reading to religious texts.

In the following account the majority, or Sunni, view is taken as the basis for our understanding of Muslim history, but we also note Shia views about some key events.

The Companions of Muhammad include Abu Bakr, who became the first caliph in 632 and married four wives. In Sunni tradition he is the best known of the Companions of the Prophet and was the first man to swear allegiance to him. Shia Muslims reject this tradition and claim that Muhammad's nephew, adopted son, and son-in-law, Ali, was the first male to convert to Islam, following the example of Muhammad's wife Khadija. Sunni Muslims, however, make Ali the fourth person to convert to Islam, thus lowering his importance in the ranks of the faithful. Regardless of who was the first male convert, it is agreed that Abu Bakr was a faithful follower of Muhammad who was regarded as a learned interpreter of the Qur'an. He waged successful wars against rebels and various people claiming to be prophets in their own right. Under his guidance Muslim armies invaded Syria, and under his guidance what was to become the official version of the Qur'an was compiled and arranged in its present order. In 634 Abu Bakr fell ill after taking a cold bath. Realizing that his end was near, he nominated Umar to became the next caliph.

Before his conversion to Islam, Umar was a sworn enemy of Islam. But in the sixth year of Muhammad's mission, when Umar was twenty-seven years old, he was converted. Under his rule Muslim armies conquered Iraq, Iran, Syria, Palestine, and Egypt. He was assassinated by a slave who stabbed him several times with a poisoned knife. Uthman became caliph after the death of Umar. He was assassinated in 656 by a group of Muslims discontent with his appointment of his brother as ruler of Egypt.

---

3. Sayed Ali Asgher Razwy, *A Restatement of the History of Islam and Muslims, 570–661* (Stanmore, Middlesex, U.K.: Islamic Centre, The World Federation of KSI Muslim Communities, 1997).

Ali was the adopted son of the Prophet. The Prophet took him into his home when he was five years old, and later Ali became Muhammad's son-in-law by marrying his daughter Fatima, who bore him Hassan, Husayn, and Mohsin, as well as two daughters, Zenab and Um Kulthoom. Ali married eight other wives. He was elected caliph after the murder of Uthman and reigned from 656 to 661. Known for his piety and simple way of life, he was a good ruler. Ali was a poet and the first person to write an Arabic grammar.

Photo 23.7 The shrine of Ali in Najaf, Iraq. This is the holiest site of Shia Islam.

His caliphate was marred by internal unrest and two major revolts against his rule. The first revolt was led by Aisha, the youngest wife of Muhammad and daughter of Abu Bakr. He defeated her forces in the Battle of the Camel, which got its name from the fact that the fighting raged around a camel on which Aisha was seated. This was the first war against Muslims led by Muslims.

Later Mauwiyah, the Muslim governor of the new province of Syria, rebelled against Ali's rule. He was the nephew of Uthman and suspected that Ali was implicated in his uncle's assassination. Ali met Mauwiyah's army at Siffin, in modern Syria, in 657, and Mauwiyah's greatly outnumbered troops seemed certain to be defeated. Therefore, Mauwiyah's men attached Qur'ans to the tips of their spears and called for arbitration. Ali accepted the challenge and made peace with Mauwiyah.

This act of leniency, when victory was in sight, angered and alienated a group of Muslims known as the Kharijites—whose name means "separatists"—who saw Ali's willingness to compromise as an act of weakness and religious betrayal. Four years later, a Kharijite assassin attacked Ali on his way to a mosque. He died from his wounds three days later. Following Ali's death, Mauwiyah proclaimed himself caliph and moved the capital of the Muslim empire from Mecca to Damascus.

With the death of Ali, the era of founding traditions and the recording of revelations comes to a close and we enter the realm of normal history. The first phase of Muslim history coincides with the establishment of the caliphate, which is usually subdivided into three periods. From 632 to 661 is the period known as that of the "Right Guided Caliphs," which ended with the death of Ali. Then there is the Umayyad Empire from 661 to 750, which saw a rapid expansion of Muslim rule in both the West and the East.

In a relatively short time, Muslim rule was established over the whole of North Africa, much of Spain, Persia, large areas of Afghanistan, and most of what is now Pakistan. The rapid advance of Muslim armies during this formative period of Islam came to be seen by Muslims as a miracle that proved the truth of Muhammad's claim to be the true Prophet of God. To outsiders, these conquests seemed to indicate that Islam was "spread by the sword." Actually, during this period Muslims sought to establish their rule over various subject peoples without making much of an attempt to convert them. Throughout most of the conquered areas, conversion to Islam came much later. Perhaps the greatest impact of Islam on Christianity during this period was that it cut off European Christians from other Christian communities in Africa and Asia, which eventually made Europe the main center of Christian civilization.

The Umayyad Empire was followed by the Abbasid Empire from 750 to 1258, which ended with the destruction of the caliphate by the Mongols. It was during this period that Islam enjoyed a golden era and fought against the Crusades, attempts by Christian forces to repossess Jerusalem and the pilgrimage sites of the Holy Land.

After the fall of the Abbasid Empire in 1258, various sultanates sprang up and numerous rival Muslim rulers vied for power. In Egypt the Mamluks established a new dynasty that conquered Syria and expelled the remaining crusaders from Acre and the Palastinian mainland in 1291. Turkish power also grew during this period, leading to the eventual conquest of the city of Byzantium by the Turks in 1453 and the expansion of Muslim power into eastern Europe.

This period of fragmentation ended in the sixteenth century with the consolidation of three new empires: the Safavid Empire in Iran, which collapsed in 1736; the Mogul Empire in India, which was eventually annexed by the British in 1857; and the Turkish, or Ottoman Empire, in the West, which slowly disintegrated until World War I led to its destruction and to the creation of a new secular state in Turkey and various kingdoms, such as Egypt, Saudi Arabia, and Iraq, in former Ottoman provinces.

MUSLIM COMMUNITIES AND SECTS

From the very beginning, divisions emerged within the Muslim community. Mainstream Muslims, that is, the largest Islamic community, comprising around 85 percent of all Muslims, are known as Sunni. The name is derived from *Sunna*, which literally means "the trodden path," "way," or "practice" of the Prophet. They claim to base their religion on the example of Muhammad and to belong to the community he created because they follow the example he set. Today Sunni Islam is to be found throughout the Muslim world and is the dominant expression of Islam in countries like Egypt, Indonesia, Turkey, and Pakistan.

SUNNI ISLAM

Sunni Muslims believe that the Prophet Muhammad was guided by God in all his actions and words and was therefore able to see into the hearts of men and women and judge them according to their true nature. When, after resisting Muhammad's call for twenty

The Islamic Tradition

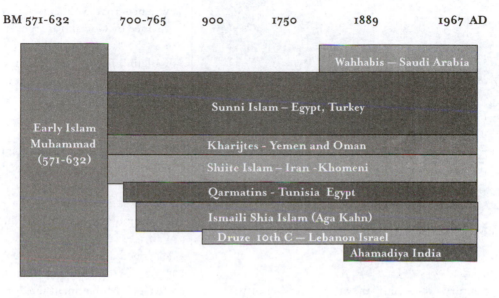

BM 571-632	700-765	900	1750	1889	1967 AD

Wahhabis — Saudi Arabia

Early Islam Muhammad (571-632)

Sunni Islam — Egypt, Turkey

Kharijtes - Yemen and Oman

Shiite Islam — Iran -Khomeni

Qarmatins - Tunisia Egypt

Ismaili Shia Islam (Aga Kahn)

Druze 10th C — Lebanon Israel

Ahamadiya India

Figure 23.1

years and persecuting his followers, the Meccan nobility, particularly members of the powerful Umayyad clan of the Quraysh tribe, professed conversion, Muhammad, knowing their confession was sincere, generously forgave their past actions, embraced them as true believers, and appointed many of their most important leaders to key positions in the Muslim community, making them generals in his armies and governors of conquered territories.

The significance of Muslim belief in the Prophet's divine guidance is seen even more remarkably in the election of Abu Bakr, a member of the Quraysh tribe, as the first caliph, or successor to Muhammad. Once appointed caliph, Abu Bakr appointed kinsmen from the Meccan Umayyad clan of his tribe to key positions in his administration and army. Thus he made Yazid commander of the Syrian invasion and Yazid's younger brother, Mauwiyah, a staff officer during the invasion. In time Mauwiyah became governor of Syria, an opponent of Ali, and eventually the caliph of all Sunni Muslims.

To Sunni Muslims the military victory of Abu Bakr's generals and of his Umayyad successors proves the wisdom and insight of the Prophet in accepting the full integration of the Quraysh tribe, particularly the Umayyad clan, into the Muslim community. Within a hundred years Muslim armies under Umayyad leadership had conquered the whole of North Africa to the south, conquered large parts of Spain and made incursions into France in the west, and in the east had subdued Syria and parts of modern Turkey, conquered Iran, and begun the invasion of India. These remarkable military victories are seen by Sunni

Photo 23.8 Egypt's Al-Azhar University, one of the main seats of learning for Sunni Islam.

Muslims as the seal of God's approval on the caliphate. Thus the conquests are regarded as evidence that Sunni Islam is ordained by God and are spoken of as the "second great miracle of Islam." For all Muslims the first miracle of Islam is the revelation of the Qur'an.

THE WAHHABI

Over time, various schisms and internal groupings developed within the Sunni community. The most important of these reform movements today is the Wahhabi movement, which developed as a revivalist movement during the eighteenth century. Today, it is the official version of Islam in Saudi Arabia. Muhammad ibn Abd al-Wahhab (1703–1792), who founded the movement, was a devout Muslim, well trained in traditional law and Qur'anic exegesis, with a good knowledge of the mystical Sufi tradition, which he rejected. At the core of Wahhabi Islam is a call to return to the pure teachings of the Qur'an and the example of the Prophet.

Ibn Abd al-Wahhab allied himself with a local tribal chief, Muhammad ibn Saud (d. 1765), to inaugurate a formidable reform movement based on military success and desire to suppress all unbelievers. The alliance unified the tribes of Arabia and began attacks on what they saw as remnants of paganism that were corrupting Islam. Thus revered shrines and sacred tombs were destroyed wherever they attracted pilgrims. In Mecca and Medina the tombs of Muhammad and his Companions were wrecked. In Karbala the tomb of Husayn, the grandson of Muhammad, who is venerated by the Shia, was desecrated and destroyed, creating undying enmity between Shia and Wahhabi Muslims that continues today.

After its initial enthusiasm for conquest and military action, the Wahhabi movement turned to missionary zeal and the propagation of its message by more peaceful means. This zeal dissipated over the years but was revived by the defeat of Muslim forces by Israel in 1967. Such an affront to Islam led to serious reflection by Saudi Arabian Muslims on the cause of Islam. That reflection initiated a commitment to a renewed missionary movement and the dedication of a significant proportion of the country's budget to Islamic causes. As a result, schools and missions were established throughout the Islamic world to spread Islam as interpreted by Wahhabi scholars.

THE SHIA COMMUNITY

The second largest Muslim community, the Shia, take a very different view of things. They are the followers of Ali, who remained loyal to Muhammad and his children, particularly those born to Muhammad's daughter Fatima. In 680 a civil war broke out between Mauwiyah's successor, his son Yazid, and the followers of Ali's son Husayn. The army of Husayn was quickly defeated, and a massacre followed during which direct descendents of the Prophet were killed. This event is remembered by the Shia as the "martyrdom" of Husayn, the grandson of the Prophet Muhammad, whom they regard as the rightful heir to the prophetic tradition and true ruler of the Muslim community.

Shia piety and theories of government revolve around the deaths of Ali and Husayn and the fate of the Prophet's family. According to tradition, Abu Bakr seized control of the Muslim community illegitimately, using the pretext of an election to foil the rightful claim of Ali to the caliphate. This situation came about, according to the Shia, because the pagans of Mecca, led by the Ummayad clan, realized that they could no longer resist the preaching of Islam. At that point, the Shia claim, these pagans outwardly converted while secretly planning to restore their old power and wealth within the new Muslim community by seizing control of its leadership. Thus, under Abu Bakr and his successor, Umar, the Ummayad worked for the appointment of their own people to key posts in the com-

Photo 23.9 The Al Askari Mosque in Samarra, Iraq, before it was bombed in 2006. This is the shrine of the tenth and eleventh Shia imams, Ali an-Naqi and Hasan al-Askari.

munity, thus undermining the legitimate authority of Ali and the Prophet's family, who belonged to the Hashim clan.

Worse still, the Shia allege, it was Abu Bakr who organized the compilation of the Qur'an, and he and his successors oversaw the collection of the Hadith, or traditions, about the Prophet. This was done in such a way, say the Shia, as to make the Hadith favorable to the Sunni viewpoint. Thus, while Shia Muslims usually accept the work of Abu Bakr in compiling the Qur'an, they have grave reservations about the collection of the Hadith and claim that many sayings and deeds of the Prophet were fabricated to promote Ummayad claims to leadership, thus legitimating the authority of the caliphate while undermining or ignoring the role of Ali and the Prophet's family.

Therefore, instead of accepting the caliphate, the Shia developed the idea of imamship. The caliph was a political and social leader whose right to govern Muslims depended on his military skill. For the Shia the imam developed as a religious leader who assumed the religious and political leadership of the community by virtue of his piety and scholarship. The Shia also insist that a true imam is a descendant of the Prophet through the line of Ali, the first imam. As such, an imam is the final authority in all things and is believed to be guided by God in his decisions. In the course of Shia history, disputes developed about who was the legitimate imam, with the result that the community split into several subgroups.

THE QARMATINS

The most important breakaway from the main body of Shia are the various Ismaili groups that grew out of a series of schisms in the eighth century. Persecuted by the Sunni Umayyad regimes, the Shia developed a doctrine of concealment that allowed their followers to conceal their true beliefs for self-protection during times of persecution. This policy of secrecy allowed an Ismaili group, the Qarmatins, to attack Syria, Palastine, and Iraq during the tenth century and establish their rule in Bahrain. Other Ismaili groups spread their teachings to North Africa and India. After failing to conquer Syria in the tenth century, one such group established itself in Tunisia in 909 and in 969 conquered Egypt to establish the Fatimid dynasty as an absolute monarchy ruled by an infallible imam. This dynasty expanded its power across large parts of North Africa and as far east as India during the following two centuries, and for a short while captured Baghdad. It built the al-Azhar mosque in Cairo and founded the al-Azhar University there. The dynasty came to an end in 1171 with a Sunni revolt led by Saladin, who conquered Egypt.

THE ISMAILIS

A breakaway branch of the Fatimids was the Nizari sect, founded in 1094 by Hasan al-Sabah. He ruled from Mt. Alamut in Persia and developed the art of assassinating both Sunni leaders and Christian crusaders, only to be defeated by the Mongol invasion of 1258, which broke the sect's power and drove them underground.

From this unpromising beginning, present day Ismailis developed as one of the most advanced branches of Islam in terms of their accommodation with the Western world. A descendent of Hasan al-Sabah married the daughter of the Shah of Iran, thus receiving the title Aga Kahn. After an unsuccessful attempt to take control of Persia in 1840, the Aga Khan fled to the protection of British India, where he established himself in Bombay. Regarded by his followers as the living Imam of Islam, who is directly descended from Muhammad through Ali, he is able to reinterpret Muslim teachings for the modern world.

THE DRUZE

A far smaller branch of Ismaili Islam developed into what today are known as the Druze. They were formed when two Fatimid missionaries were sent by Caliph al-Hakim (996–1021) to make converts in southern Lebanon. In the process they developed a theology that saw al-Hakim as an incarnation of divinity with supernatural powers. When al-Hakim disappeared

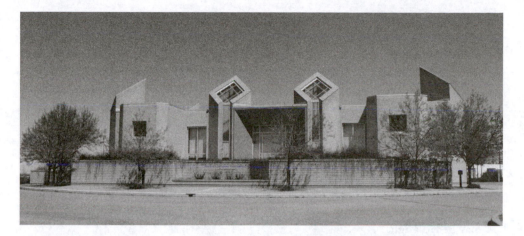

Photo 23.10 This architecturally modern mosque reflects the ethos of today's Ismaili community, which embraces the modern world with a refreshing vitality. Unlike most other Muslim groups, the Ismailis have no problem adopting modern dress, adapting to local cultures, and accepting the equality of women.

suddenly in 1021, his followers argued that he had done so to test his followers and would return at some future date to judge the world. Thus the Druze developed as a new religion quite separate from all other branches of both orthodox Shia and Sunni Islam.

Today small communities of Druze exist in Lebanon and parts of Israel, where they are often recruited into the police force. They maintain their own scriptures in addition to the Qur'an, which is called *The Book of Wisdom* and consists of a series of letters between al-Hakim and his missionary followers. In the Druze religion, the ideas of other Muslim communities about Sharia law are replaced by Druze law, an elite religious leadership, and special places of prayer. The Druze also developed a theory of the transmigration of souls that is unique in Islam. Because they are regarded as outright heretics subject to justifiable persecution by both the Sunni and Shia communities, the Druze have remained a secretive movement that carefully guards its beliefs and practices from outsiders.

THE KHARIJITES

The third major schism in early Islam occurred during the rule of Uthman, with the creation of the Kharijite movement, a radical charismatic group that created a form of Muslim community similar to Christian fundamentalism, supported by a puritanical morality. The group quickly became revolutionary after Ali refused to destroy the army of Mauwiyah when the two met at Siffin. To the Kharijites, all true Muslims were required to wage war against Mauwiyah, who, by challenging Ali's authority, became an apostate. Therefore, Ali's refusal to give battle, and thus leave the judgment to God, was also an act of apostasy, and the Kharijites turned against him too.

The Kharijites were true believers who took the Qur'an and the Sunna, or example, of the Prophet literally, following the teachings found in Sura 7:157–158, which reads as follows:

157 Those who follow the messenger, the Prophet who can neither read nor write, whom they will find described in the Torah and the Gospel (which are) with them. He will enjoin on them that which is right and forbid them that which is wrong. He will make lawful for them all good things and prohibit for them only the foul; and he will relieve them of their burden and the fetters that they used to wear. Then those who believe in him, and honor him, and help him, and follow the light which is sent down with him: they are the successful.

158 Say (O Muhammad): O mankind! Lo! I am the messenger of Allah to you all—(the messenger of) Him unto Whom belongeth the Sovereignty of the heavens and the earth. There is no God save Him. He quickeneth and He giveth death. So believe in Allah and His messenger, the Prophet who can neither read nor write, who believeth in Allah and in His Words, and follow him that haply ye may be led aright.

Here the key passage says, "He will enjoin on them that which is right and forbid them that which is wrong." This verse the Kharijites interpreted to mean that Muslims are duty bound to impose their understanding of law and social conduct on everyone, believers and nonbelievers alike. To do otherwise, they argued, was to compromise the purity of the faith.

After their disillusionment with Ali, the Kharijites withdrew to create their own, egalitarian Muslim community based on charismatic leadership. Then they launched a guerrilla war against all whom they considered "unbelievers," including Ali and his followers. Ali led an expedition against them in 658 and decisively defeated them at the Battle of Nahrawan, but their revolt continued and Ali was assassinated. Then the Kharijites turned their wrath on the new caliph, beginning a revolt that lasted hundreds of years. Over time the zeal of the Kharijites ameliorated, and a moderate branch of the movement, known as the Ibadiyya, or followers of Abd Allah ibn Ibad, emerged. It exercised great influence over the development of Islamic states in Tripoli, Zanzibar, Yemen, and Oman. Today small Ibadiyya communities exist in North and East Africa, and Ibadiyya is the official religion in the Sultanate of Oman.

SUFISM

Probably the best-known group of religious revivalists within Islam are the various Sufi movements that function in both Sunni and Shiite Islam. Essentially, Sufis are mystics who seek to supplement the strict obedience demanded by the Qur'an and orthodox Muslims with a loving devotion to God. The essence of this movement is the personal quest for spiritual experiences based on a living relationship with God. In many ways these Sufi experiences are similar to the "born again" experience of Christians and the sense of God's presence found in the *bhakti* movements of the Hindu tradition.

Prayer, fasting, and meditation on scripture, in this case the Qur'an, are typical of such movements. Sufi groups share four basic ideas. First, they believe that truth is discovered by direct personal experiences, not by rational thinking or intellectual investigation. Second, Sufi masters are the object of veneration during their lifetime and become saints upon their deaths. Therefore, to be buried near a Sufi master enables the deceased to share in the spiritual care of that master. Third, the Sufi follows a tradition similar to that of Christian monastic orders, but without celibacy, which is forbidden in the Qur'an. These orders are normally male, although some female orders exist. Finally, Sufism promotes a form of monism, where God is everything.

Probably the most famous Sufi in the West is the philosopher al-Ghazali (1058–1111), whose work is highly valued by both Sunni and Sufi writers. Although essentially orthodox himself, al-Ghazali provided the basis for numerous heterodox and heretical groups.

Photo 23.11 Today Sufism is viewed as a mystical tradition with little or no connection to orthodox Islam. This popular view overlooks the fact that in its origin Sufism was the ecstatic devotion of military orders devoted to the spread of Islamic rule. In the seventeenth century print shown above, a group of Sufi dervishes perform a ritual dance. The dervishes were particularly feared by European armies in their long wars against Muslim invaders.

Sufis use various techniques to induce hypnotic states that lead to chanting and frenzied dancing. As missionaries, Sufis, particularly Sufi orders, were very successful, partly because Sufism is able to incorporate local practices, thus giving primal religious experiences and traditions a place within Islam.

CHAPTER 24

MUSLIM BELIEFS AND PRACTICES

THERE IS NO GOD EXCEPT ALLAH

Islam is essentially a simple and straightforward system of belief and practice. At its core is the declaration that there is only one God and that Muhammad is his messenger. Implicit in this declaration is the belief that all other claims to deity, such as those made by Christians about Jesus, are false. This basic creed of Islam is found in the Qur'an itself, where, according to the rendition into English of Muhammad Marmaduke Pickthall, we read in Sura 57:

1 All that is in the heavens and the earth glorifieth Allah; and He is the Mighty, the Wise.

2 His is the Sovereignty of the heavens and the earth; He quickeneth and He giveth death; and He is Able to do all things.

3 He is the First and the Last, and the Outward and the Inward; and He is Knower of all things.

4 He it is Who created the heavens and the earth in six Days; then He mounted the Throne. He knoweth all that entereth the earth and all that emergeth therefrom and all that cometh down from the sky and all that ascendeth therein; and He is with you wheresoever ye may be. And Allah is Seer of what ye do.

5 His is the Sovereignty of the heavens and the earth, and unto Allah (all) things are brought back.

6 He causeth the night to pass into the day, and He causeth the day to pass into the night, and He is knower of all that is in the breasts.

7 Believe in Allah and His messenger, and spend of that whereof He hath made you trustees; and such of you as believe and spend (aright), theirs will be a great reward.

Every true Muslim recites, "There is only one God and Muhammad is his prophet," on numerous occasions every day. This statement is also the basis of conversion to Islam. In addition, Muslims accept the obligations of obeying God's law as revealed in his holy revelation, the Qur'an, and through the life and example of Muhammad, found in the

Hadith, which records the traditions of what Muhammad said and did as an example for all Muslims.

The implication of the Muslim declaration of faith is that all true Muslims will strive to obey God according to the example of Muhammad and the teachings of the Qur'an. This means that Muslims are committed to a radical reorganization of human society based on the principle of radical religious and moral reform. The ultimate goal of Muslims is the creation of the rule of God on earth through the activities of God's people, the Muslim community.

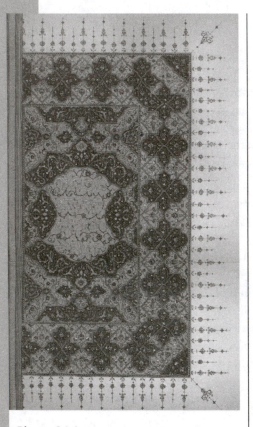

Photo 24.1 For Muslims this page from an ancient Qur'an has a quality of sacredness lacking in the Bible. While the Bible is a historical text, no one doubts that it was written by human beings. Therefore, Muslims see it as inspired in some way, but for them it is not revelation. Only the Qur'an is revelation, and therefore it is totally unique according to Islamic philosophy.

THE MIRACLE OF THE QUR'AN

According to Islamic belief, Adam was the first Muslim. From him a long line of prophets can be traced, through Abraham, to Jesus, and on to Muhammad. Muhammad is the last and greatest prophet of all. Through Muhammad the Qur'an, which literally means "recitation," was revealed to mankind. Usually expositions of Islamic belief begin by discussing the teaching of Muhammad about God. Although this is a good place to start, it is probably better to begin by discussing how one should read the Qur'an and how Muslims view it, because Islamic teaching about God is based on God's revelation in the Qur'an.

Most Christians approach the Qur'an the way they approach reading the Bible. As a result, Christians fail to see the differences between the Qur'an and their own scriptures. According to Christian teachings, all scripture of the Old and New Testaments is inspired by God and is God's revelation to mankind. Therefore, Christians speak of the Bible as the Word of God. Superficially Muslims use the same language when speaking about the Qur'an. Therefore, Christians often assume that Muslims regard the Qur'an in essentially the same way as Christians regard the Bible. They also often think that because the Qur'an mentions the scriptures of the Old and New Testaments, it does so in more or less the same way as Christians think about these books. Nothing could be further from the truth.

The identification of the Islamic doctrine of *wahy*, or revelation, with Christian views about the inspiration of the Bible is a major source of misunderstanding of Islam in the West. To understand why, one must consider two terms usually used to express the idea of revelation as found in Christian thinking: *wahy* and *ilham*. *Ilham* means approximately what "inspiration" of the Bible has meant in the Christian tradition as taught by traditional Roman Catholics and Protestants like the Princeton theologian B. B. Warfield. Literally, *ilham* means "to cause to swallow or gulp down" and is found only once in The Qur'an, in Sura 91:8, which reads: "And inspired it (with conscience of) what is wrong for it and (what is) right for it."

Here, in verse 8, the term for "inspired" is *ilham*, which clearly means that God is working inside the person. As Muslim theology developed historically, this usage was maintained and developed. *Ilham* is said to occur when God reveals himself to an individual by putting his knowledge into their mind. Thus saints are believed to be special recipients of *ilham* or inspiration, and the knowledge a person gains by *ilham* is inspired knowledge, quite distinct from human reason, and is the free gift of God.

This type of idea compares well with traditional Christian views about the inspiration of the Bible. Second Timothy 3:16 reads, "All Scripture is God-breathed . . . ," and 2 Peter 1:21 reads, "For prophecy never had its origin in the will of man, but men spoke from God as they were carried along by the Holy Spirit."

For this reason, B. B. Warfield summed up his understanding of biblical inspiration by saying, "The Biblical books are called inspired as the Divinely determined products of inspired men; the Biblical writers are called inspired as breathed into by the Holy Spirit, so that the product of their activity transcends human powers and becomes Divinely authoritative. Inspiration is, therefore, usually defined as a supernatural influence exerted on the sacred writers by the Spirit of God."[1]

Clearly this interpretation of inspiration is very close to the Muslim concept of *ilham*. The problem is that Muslims do not claim that the Qur'an is inspired in the sense of being the product of *ilham*. For Muslims the Qur'an is the product of *wahy*, not *ilham*. That is,

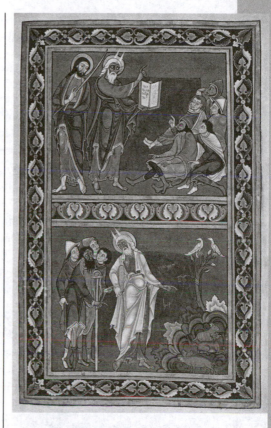

Photo 24.2 This miniature from a twelfth-century illustrated manuscript by Master Hugo shows Moses preaching to the Jews. Islam has no difficulty accepting Moses, Isaiah, and Jesus, as well as a host of other prophets as men inspired by God. Yet it distinguishes sharply between the inspiration of a prophet who speaks for God and the revelation of the Qur'an, recited by Muhammad. The prophets speak inspired words, yet they are their words. But when Muhammad recited the Qur'an, he spoke the literal word of God. The works of the prophets are inspired; the words of the Qur'an are divine.

---

1. B. B. Warfield, *Inspiration and Revelation of the Bible* (Nutley, N.J.: Presbyterian and Reformed, 1951), 131.

it is a revealed, not an inspired, book. *Wahy* literally means "to hasten" and is used as a religious term to denote revelations given to prophets. The Old Testament prophets are said to receive *wahy*, not to speak by *ilham*. This can be seen in Sura 23:27, presented here in its context:

> 23 And We verily sent Noah unto his folk, and he said: O my people! Serve Allah. Ye have no other God save Him. Will ye not ward off (evil)?
>
> 24 But the chieftains of his folk, who disbelieved, said: This is only a mortal like you who would make himself superior to you. Had Allah willed, He surely could have sent down angels. We heard not of this in the case of our fathers of old.
>
> 25 He is only a man in whom is a madness, so watch him for a while.
>
> 26 He said: My Lord! Help me because they deny me.
>
> 27 Then We inspired in him, saying: Make the ship under Our eyes and Our inspiration. Then, when Our command cometh and the oven gusheth water, introduce therein of every (kind) two spouses, and thy household save him thereof against whom the Word hath already gone forth. And plead not with Me on behalf of those who have done wrong. Lo! they will be drowned.

Later, as was already observed, when Muhammad himself received revelation, he was commanded: "1 Read: In the name of thy Lord Who createth" (sura 96).

In this passage *wahy* is clearly described as a reading of a preexistent message, not as the inspiring of a person to compose the message. Muslims do believe that Muhammad spoke under the influence of *ilham*, but his inspired sayings form the basis of the Hadith rather than appearing in the Qur'an. For this reason Hadith may be understood as "revelation" but not "Revelation." That is, it contains words inspired by God, but it is not God's word. Therefore, Muslims argue that, like the Bible, the Hadith may be corrupted, necessitating its critical study to distinguish genuine from spurious traditions.

In the truest sense, only the Qur'an is *wahy* to a Muslim's certain knowledge. Other scriptures may contain *wahy*, but they are not *wahy*, because their transmission has been corrupted. The Qur'an, on the

Photo 24.3 This tenth-century miniature of John the Evangelist dictating his gospel sums up the difference between Christian and Muslim views of scripture. John dictated God's message in his own words; therefore, although they are inspired words, they are not revelation in the sense that Muslims use *wahy*. The Qur'an, on the other hand, is the word of God. It is revelation, and the only reliable revelation available to humans.

other hand, is the pure revelation of God. It is the word of God that exists in heaven, while all earthly editions are simply copies of the eternal heavenly archetype. Being God's word, the Qur'an is one of his Ninety-Nine attributes and coeternal with him. Sura 7:180 says: "Allah's are the fairest names. Invoke Him by them. And leave the company of those who blaspheme His names. They will be requited what they do." This doctrine is supported by Sura 85:21–22, where we read, " Nay, but it is a glorious Qur'an. On a guarded tablet."

Other passages are taken as further evidence of the heavenly nature of the Qur'an, such as Sura 3:44, which describes the Qur'an as "the tidings of things hidden. We reveal it unto thee (Muhammad)." And Sura 18:105 declares, "Those are they who disbelieve in the revelations of their Lord and in the meeting with Him. Therefore their works are vain, and on the Day of Resurrection We assign no weight to them."

The traditions surrounding Muhammad's reception of the Qur'an emphasize that it is "a recitation." Particulars of this tradition are found in the Hadith, which are the traditions about Muhammad's life recorded by his immediate followers. In these Muhammad is reported to have said, "Sometimes it comes as the ringing of a bell … Sometimes it is an angel who speaks to me as a man, and I retain what he says."[2] It is said that when Muhammad recited these revelations to his followers, sweat appeared on his head, even on cold days. On other occasions he covered his face or turned a livid color. Both Muhammad's account of his revelations and the accounts given by his followers emphasize the pain such an event caused him as he recited the Qur'an.

The Qur'an itself clearly teaches that it was revealed by an angel. Sura 2: 97 reads, "Say (O Muhammad, to mankind): Who is an enemy to Gabriel! For he it is who hath revealed (this Scripture) to thy heart by Allah's leave, confirming that which was (revealed) before it, and a guidance and glad tidings to believers." Thus the idea that the Qur'an is the only sure source of *wahy* is confirmed to Muslims by the fact that it was given to Muhammad in its entirety and not the result of the inspiration of his mind.

From this discussion it is clear that the tools of biblical criticism hold no threat to the believing Muslim. The concept of *wahy* precludes a search for the "original message" or "true words" of Muhammad. Rather, the Qur'an is the word of God, pure and simple. Not surprisingly, Muslim scholars have welcomed the rise of biblical criticism and made effective use of its findings. Instead of shaking Muslim belief in the idea of revelation, biblical criticism actually confirms it by making the Qur'an the only reliable scripture, because it is, in their view, the only scripture that is pure revelation. In fact, biblical criticism, Muslims argue, confirms Sura 5:13, which says, "And because of their breaking their covenant, We have cursed them and made hard their hearts. They change words from their context and forget a part of that whereof they were admonished. Thou wilt not cease to discover treachery from all save a few of them. But bear with them and pardon them. Lo! Allah loveth the kindly."

Given this view, it is little wonder that as early as the 1840s, Muslim scholars in India were citing European biblical critics to defend Islam and attack Christian preaching. By the 1850s these attacks had become a tidal wave, sweeping through India and other Muslim

---

2. H. A. R. Gibb and J. H. Kramers, eds., *The Shorter Encyclopedia of Islam* (Leiden: Brill, 1974), 623.

Photo 24.4 This photograph is of one of the earliest surviving fragments of the Decalogue. To Christians and Jews this is an important piece of evidence that helps confirm the truth claims of their religion. To Muslims it simply shows how unreliable Christian and Jewish scriptures really are because the Qur'an exists as a complete text for the simple reason that the early caliphs ordered the destruction of all variant readings and fragments to create a unified whole. Consequently, for Muslims issues like text criticism are not a problem.

countries. In India the works of critics such as J. D. Michaelis (1717–1791), J. G. Eichhorn (1752–1827), and D. F. Strauss (1808–1874) were standard works used by Muslim apologists to prove the unreliability of the Bible. They also used the works of various rationalist writers like "Toland, Chubb, Spinoza, Reimarus, Voltaire and Rousseau."[3] The works of Thomas Paine (1737–1809) were also known and liked. According to local missionaries, "a wretched merchant of Boston" had sent "a whole cargo of copies of Paine's *Age of Reason*" to Calcutta to counter the work of Christian evangelists.[4]

THE DOCTRINE OF ABROGATION

Another factor one must take into account when attempting to understand Muslim views and interpretation of the Qur'an is the doctrine of abrogation. Here it is important to be very careful. Some Muslims totally reject the idea of abrogation and suggest that it is the invention of Muslim scholars who went astray or of the enemies of Islam. Thus, in his article "The Lie of Abrogation: The Biggest Lie against the Qur'an,"[5] published on the internet, A. Muhammad blames the doctrine on a group of tenth-century scholars including Mohammad Khalifa. Similarly, in chapter seven of his book *The Sublime Qur'an and Orientalism*,[6] Muhammad blames the popularization of the doctrine on "Orientalists." Others accept that Islam allows for abrogation but argue that it only takes place on rare occasions. The majority of Muslims, however, appear to accept that abrogation is a normal part of Qur'anic interpretation, and some even say that in the Qur'an itself hundreds of verses are abrogated. The abrogated verses are usually the early, or Meccan, Suras, which are abrogated by the later, Medinan Suras. For a non-Muslim this can be a very confusing doctrine. Therefore, when talking to a Muslim or attempting to understand the views of a particular group, it is important to know how they

3. Avril Ann Powell, *Muslims and Missionaries in Pre-Mutiny India* (London: Curzon, 1993), 232–33.

4. Ibid., 232.

5. Found on the internet at http://www.submission.org/abrogation.html (accessed 30 April 2010). David Bukay, "Peace or Jihad? Abrogation in Islam," *Middle East Quarterly* 14, no. 4 (Fall 2007): 3–11.

6. Muhammad Khalifa, *The Sublime Qur'an and Orientalism* (London: Longman, 1983).

regard abrogation. The doctrine of abrogation is based on Sura 2:106, which reads, "Such of Our revelations as We abrogate or cause to be forgotten, we bring (in place) one better or the like thereof. Knowest thou not that Allah is able to do all things?" Those Muslims who accept the doctrine of abrogation argue that it reflects the power and glory of God, who, in his wisdom, adapted his revelation to changing circumstances and the needs of both individuals and the community as a whole. They also argue that it helps believers explain apparent contradictions in the Qur'an.

For example, today Muslims are forbidden to drink alcohol. Yet in Sura 4:43 it says, "O ye who believed! Draw not near unto prayer when ye are drunken,..." This seems to imply that Muhammad's followers drank alcoholic drinks. Further, in Sura 47:15 we are told that in paradise there is "a similitude of the Garden which those who keep their duty (to Allah) are promised ... and rivers are wine delicious to the drinkers ..." According to this verse it seems that in heaven believers are allowed to enjoy wine. Similarly, in Sura 56:18–19 it again appears that in paradise believers will enjoy drinking wine. Again, this time explicitly, in Sura 83:25, the blessed are "given to drink of a pure wine." Yet Sura 5:90 clearly states, "Oh ye who believe! Strong

Photo 24.5 In this miniature it looks very much like the guests of an Arab doctor are drinking wine. This type of unorthodox scene is typical of many medieval miniatures from around the thirteenth century, when some Muslims justified drinking wine for medical purposes even though the orthodox condemned the practice. Pictures like this highlight the debate about abrogation and the importance of interpretation in the Islamic tradition.

drink and games of chance and idols and divining arrows are only an infamy of Satan's handiwork. Leave it aside in order that ye may succeed."

This last verse and many others clearly condemn the use of alcohol. How can anyone reconcile to these verses the fact that in Medina some of Muhammad's followers clearly got drunk and were only told that they must be sober when they approached God in prayer? Or that later alcohol was totally banned, although eventually it will be among the pleasures of paradise?

Although different Muslims give different answers to this question, one possible answer lies in the notion of abrogation. According to this view, Muhammad's followers were originally allowed alcoholic drinks, but because of drunkenness, alcohol was eventually banned with the promise that its use will be allowed in paradise.

Seen in this light, abrogation is a simple expedient by which God adapted his commands to Muhammad and the Muslim community in the light of changing circumstances.

Therefore, there is no contradiction in the Qur'an, because the revelations progressively adapted God's will to human needs, so that humans were able to become good Muslims despite their many failings.

THE MUSLIM STATE

Islam rejects the secular Western idea of the separation of religion and morality from the duties of the state. In traditional Muslim teaching there is no separation of church and state, nor is this idea even a remote possibility. The Muslim community is the community of the faithful that submits to God's law as revealed in the Qur'an, taught by the example of Muhammad, expounded by Muslim legal experts, and enforced by the state.

For example, Sayyid Abul A'la Mawdudi, whose book is published by the influential Islamic Foundation in Leicester, England, bluntly states, "If people are free to commit adultery, no amount of sermons will stop them. But if governments forbid adultery, people will find it easier to give up this evil practice ... So, I say to you: if you really want to root out corruption now so widespread on God's earth, stand up and fight against corrupt rule, take power and use it on God's behalf. It is useless to think that you can change things by preaching alone."[7]

He then explains that "No man should rule over another man; all men should live under God." This means, "Merely believing in God as God and in His law as the true law is not enough. As soon as you believe in these two things, a sacred duty devolves upon you: wherever you are, in whichever country you live, you must strive to change the wrong basis of government, and seize all powers to rule and make laws from those who do not fear God ... The name of this striving is Jihad."[8] To avoid any misunderstanding of his meaning, Mawdudi goes on to say, "So go forward and fight; dislodge the rebels of God from the government and take over the powers of caliphate ... Such a government will quickly be able to reform the people ..."[9]

The radical nature of this call for social revolution is made clear in a chapter on the "Central Importance of Jihad." Here he argues for the imposition of Sharia law based on the Qur'an and Hadith, claiming that no true Muslim can live content in a country where secular law prevails. Rejecting the political doctrine of

Photo 24.6 A sixteenth-century print of Süleyman, or Suleiman, the Magnificent (1494–1566), ruler of the Turkish Empire and one of the great Muslim rulers.

---

7. Sayyid Abul A'la Mawdudi, *Let Us Be Muslims* (Leicester, U.K.: Islamic Foundation, 1991), 287–88; first published 1985.

8. Ibid., 290.

9. Ibid., 292–93.

popular sovereignty, he writes, "If you submit to popular sovereignty, or to the Din (i.e., law) of Britons or Germans, or to your nation and motherland, then again Allah's Din will have no place in it. But if, in reality, you are adherents of Allah's Din, there will be no room for any other Din."[10] Consequently, he argues that Muslims must strive to establish the kingdom of God, where Muslim law prevails, and to do this, he tells them, "you have no alternative but to exert your utmost strength to make it prevail on earth: you must either establish it or give your lives in this struggle … If you passively accept to live under another Din, you are not a believer in the true sense of the term."[11]

Lest it be thought that this is an extreme example, it is important to note that Afif A. Tabbarah makes similar claims in his widely read *The Spirit of Islam*.[12] He too argues that "the Islamic nation is commanded to establish justice on earth, and … establish the Word of God on earth without doubtful intentions … The cause of God is the cause of justice … The *Qur'an* demands believers fight in the cause of God …"[13]

For Tabbarah, "Islam is a continuous strife to establish the Word of God on earth, to establish the proper system which brings content and bliss to mankind."[14] Accepting this goal, he argues that "the *Qur'an* uses various means to stimulate people to the war of *Jihad* in the cause of God [and] warns people against giving up the fight in His cause and of being content with mere worldly bliss …" Of course, most Muslims do not like fighting, but Tabbarah reminds them of Sura 2:216 in the Qur'an, which says, "Warfare is ordained for you, though it is hateful unto you; but it may happen that ye hate a thing which is good for you, and it may happen that ye love a thing which is bad for you. Allah knoweth, ye know not."

Photo 24.7 The Turkish siege of Vienna in 1529 by the army of Süleyman the Magnificent. Western Muslims and scholars, for example John Esposito, often accuse Europeans, such as the Austrians, and other critics of Islam, of "Islamophobia," forgetting that all phobias have deep psychological roots. Actually, Muslim armies besieged Vienna in 1529 and 1683, leaving deep scars on the public mind of Europe.

---

10. Ibid., 296–97.
11. Ibid., 300–301.
12. Afif A. Tabbarah, *The Spirit of Islam* (Beirut: Dar El-Ilm Lilmalayin, 1978).
13. Ibid., 282.
14. Ibid., 384.

Photo 24.8 The siege of Vienna in 1683.

THE MEANING OF JIHAD

Popular writers in Western societies often argue that the term *jihad* has been misinterpreted by Western writers as a result of what Edward Said called "Orientalism."[15] In their view *jihad* does not mean "holy war"; rather, it means a spiritual struggle. Attractive as this argument is, there appears to be little backing for it in either traditional Muslim texts or the work of more recent writers whose influence shapes modern Islam. For example, Sura 2:190–195 reads:

> 190 Fight in the way of Allah against those who fight against you, but begin not hostilities. Lo! Allah loveth not aggressors.
>
> 191 And slay them wherever ye find them, and drive them out of the places whence they drove you out, for persecution is worse than slaughter. And fight not with them at the Inviolable Place of Worship until they first attack you there, but if they attack you (there) then slay them. Such is the reward of disbelievers.
>
> 192 But if they desist, then lo! Allah is Forgiving, Merciful.
>
> 193 And fight them until persecution is no more, and religion is for Allah. But if they desist, then let there be no hostility except against wrong-doers.

15. Edward Said, *Orientalism* (New York: Vintage, 1979). For a critical discussion of this influential work, see Daniel Martin Varisco, *Reading Orientalism: Said and unSaid* (Seattle: Univ. of Washington Press, 2007).

Photo 24.9 The main square of Zwikau, Saxony, in Germany. In the seventeenth century this was a Protestant town. Notice the red building in the middle of the picture. On it is a small plaque, which is shown in **Photo 24.10**. The plaque thanks God for the defeat of the Turks by the armies of the Catholic prince Eugene of Savoy in 1683. Actually, Vienna was relieved by the army of the Polish king Jan Sobieski, or John III (1629–1696), reinforced by that of Prince Eugene, who then continued the war to drive the Turks out of Hungary, which they had successfully invaded in 1521. Taken together, the two prints help us begin to realize the depth of the European trauma created by Turkish invasions. These, more than anything since the Crusades of the eleventh century, shaped European attitudes toward Islam.

194 The forbidden month for the forbidden month, and forbidden things in retaliation. And one who attacketh you, attack him in like manner as he attacked you. Observe your duty to Allah, and know that Allah is with those who ward off (evil).

195 Spend your wealth for the cause of Allah, and be not cast by your own hands to ruin; and do good. Lo! Allah loveth the beneficent.

Sunni and Shiite Muslims share a similar outlook on the state. It is to be found in the works of Shiite writers, even though there are many practical and theoretical differences between these two traditions.

For example, Imam Khomeini, better known as Ayatollah Khomeini, holds essentially the same view of jihad in his book *Islam and Revolution*,[16] where the concept is contextualized in the situation of the exploitation of Iranian resources by large oil companies and foreign powers.[17] Thus he argues for the establishment of an Islamic government and for jihad as one of the means to bring this about. He also sees both jihad and the establishment of Sharia law as means of bringing freedom to all people, so that they are free to choose to serve God.[18]

16. Imam Khomeini, *Islam and Revolution* (Berkeley, Calif.: Mizan Press, 1981).

17. Ibid., 115–16.

18. Ibid., 40–149.

Following the assassination of Egyptian president Anwar el-Sadat on 6 October 1981, the soldiers who were his assassins issued a statement defending their actions. This was published as a booklet two months later, and eventually translated into English, with a long introduction, by Johannes J. G. Jansen as *The Neglected Duty*.[19] Couched in terms of traditional Muslim concepts, it presents a logical and clearly argued case based on accepted Muslim authorities, including the Qur'an and Hadith. Rejecting Western interpretations of Islam, the assassins boldly declared that jihad means holy war and that it is incumbent upon all good Muslims. Further, they argue that jihad must not be restricted to "defensive war," as most Western and many Muslim scholars claim on the basis of Sura 2:190. Rather, they assert, Muslims must recognize that Islam was "spread by the sword" and that to believe otherwise is to reject the clear teachings of Muhammad himself. Defending their case with verses from the Qur'an, particularly Sura 9, and the Hadith, they then appeal to traditional Muslim commentators on the Qur'an to justify their position.[20]

For many Muslims like them, "jihad by the sword" is not an embarrassing relic from the Middle Ages but a practical means to free humans from the demonic dominance of a corrupt society. Jihad provides Muslims with a practical way of imposing God's law, the Sharia, on society to free people from their own evil inclinations and the evils that are encouraged by rulers who do not acknowledge the true law of God. Thus jihad brings freedom through creating the conditions for the imposition of Islamic law on all people. This does not mean that everyone must become a Muslim, because the Qur'an clearly states, "There is no compulsion in religion" (Sura 2). Forced conversion is wrong. But so is anything that discourages conversion to Islam. Therefore, Sharia law is necessary to create the social conditions under which conversion to Islam becomes attractive. Jihad makes this possible.

This interpretation of jihad flies in the face of popular Western interpretations that seek to dismiss anyone who holds such a view as an "extremist." For example, in *World Religions Today*, by John L. Esposito, Darrell J. Fasching, and Todd Lewis,[21] students are told that "jihad, 'to strive or struggle,' is sometimes referred to as the sixth pillar of Islam, although it has no such official status. In its most general meaning, jihad refers to the obligation incumbent upon all Muslims, as individuals and as a community, to exert (jihad) themselves to realize God's will, to lead a virtuous life, to fulfil the universal mission of Islam, and to spread the Islamic community through preaching Islam to convert others" or writing religious tracts ("jihad of the tongue" and "jihad of the pen"). Although it is then explained that jihad "also includes the struggle for or defense of Islam," we are told "jihad is not supposed to include aggressive warfare."[22]

From this passage, which is similar to many others found in introductory textbooks, it can be seen that the role of war as a form of jihad is acknowledged today, but it is played

---

19. Johannes J. G. Jansen, ed. and trans., *The Neglected Duty* (New York: Macmillan, 1986).

20. Ibid., 193–96.

21. John L. Esposito, Darrell J. Fasching, and Todd Lewis, *World Religions Today* (New York: Oxford Univ. Press, 2002).

22. Ibid., 213.

down by many scholars, who describe it as a view held by "early extremists" and "contemporary extremists."[23] Similarly, jihad is said to primarily mean "struggle" in the widely used textbook *World Religions: Western Traditions*, edited by Willard G. Oxtoby.[24] Here students are told, "Disciplined reform is called in Islam *jihad*, or striving in the way of God. *Jihad*, too, becomes an obligation when social and religious reform is gravely hampered, or the community's integrity is threatened. It has found political and military expression over the centuries, but the greatest *jihad* is for every person to strive against his or her own carnal soul."[25]

The reference to "the greatest *jihad*" as a spiritual struggle appears to have been popularized through the pub-

Photo 24.11 A nineteenth-century artist's reconstruction of the fortress of the Hospitaller Knights at Kerak, south of the Dead Sea. This reminds us of the role the Crusades played in shaping Christian-Muslim relations from the tenth century onwards. Originally the Crusades were intended to defend Constantinople from Arab conquest and secure safe passage for Christian pilgrims to visit Jerusalem. Greatly outnumbered, the crusaders tended not to take prisoners, creating a well-earned reputation for barbarism. Eventually, after almost five centuries, the states the crusaders established around Palestine were overrun by Muslim armies. Today Muslims often regard the Crusades as an example of Western aggression and Muslim shame. Historically Muslim writers regarded the Crusades as a footnote to history in a long war that Christians were doomed to loose.

lication of Maulana Muhammad Ali's *A Manual of Hadith*[26] and is not to be found in any of the standard collections of the Hadith. Ironically, Ali is an Ahmadiyya Muslim whose version of Islam is not recognized by many Muslims and, in states like Pakistan, is officially declared a "non-Muslim" faith. Nevertheless, this work, which contains 690 of the thousands of different Hadith, has been taken up as a standard reference source by many scholars.[27]

---

23. Ibid., 213.

24. Willard G. Oxtoby, ed., *World Religions: Western Traditions* (Don Mills, Ont.:, Oxford Univ. Press, 2002).

25. Ibid., 368.

26. Maulana Muhammad Ali, *A Manual of Hadith* (Islamabad, Pakistan: Ahmadiyya Anjuman Ishaat Islam, 1944).

27. For example, it is used by Whitfield Foy in *Man's Religious Quest: A Reader* (London: Open Univ. Press, 1978), 512–16. Later Ali's work was reproduced in Ninian Smart and Richard D. Hecht, eds., *Sacred Tests of the World: A Universal Anthology* (New York: Crossroad, 1982). Both books were very popular. Since then their example of using Ali's *Manual* as a source for Hadith has been followed by many other compilers of religious texts.

Photo 24.12 The tomb of Muhammad Ahmad ibn As-sayyid Abd Allah (1844–1885), known as the Mahdi. In 1881 he launched a jihad against Egyptian rule in the Sudan. In 1885 his forces captured the capital, Khartoum, killing the British general Gordon (1833–1885), who was commanding the garrison. Six months later the Mahdi died of typhus, but the government he established continued until its army was defeated by General Kitchener (1850–1916) on 2 September 1898 at Omdurman, near Khartoum. After the battle, his troops desecrated the tomb of the Mahdi, exhumed his body, and, on Kitchener's orders, had his remains scattered as a lesson to all who opposed colonial rule. It is the brutality of Kitchener and other imperialists in the late nineteenth and early twentieth centuries that shape modern Muslim attitudes toward the West far more than the Crusades, which traditionally Muslims saw as a defeat for Christian forces and an ultimate Islamic victory.

The Ali collection states quite openly that "Islam's greatest jihad is, therefore, not by means of the sword, but by means of the Holy Qur'an, *i.e.*, a missionary effort to establish Islam."[28] According to Ali,

Jihad means the exerting of one's power in repelling the enemy or in contending with an object of disapprobation. It carries a twofold significance in Islam, being applied to both the purely missionary activities of a Muslim and his defense of the Faith. When necessary, in a physical sense. The first duty—the duty to invite people to Islam—is a permanent duty laid upon all Muslims of all ages; while the second is a duty which arises upon certain contingencies. The Holy Qur'an calls attention to both these duties in the clearest and most forceful words. In the first place, it speaks of a jihad to attain to Allah (v. 1). Then it speaks of carrying on a jihad against unbelievers by means of the Holy Qur'an, and this it calls *jihad-an kab r-an*, a very great jihad (v. 2). Islam's greatest jihad is, therefore, not by means of the sword, but by means of the Holy Qur'an, *i.e.*, a missionary effort to establish Islam. We are further told that there should always be among Muslims a party who invite people to Islam (v. 3). Thus the missionary jihad of Islam is to be carried on in all circumstances.[29]

The problem with this, as Rudolph Peters points out in his *Jihad in Classical and Modern Islam: A Reader*,[30] is that "Classical Muslim *Qur'an* interpretation ... regarded the Sword Verses, with the unconditional command to fight the unbelievers, as having abrogated all

28. Ali, *Manual*, 252–53.

29. Ibid.

30. Rudolph Peters, *Jihad in Classical and Modern Islam: A Reader* (Princeton, N.J.: Markus Wiener, 1996).

previous verses concerning the intercourse with non-Muslims."[31] These "Sword Verses" are found in Sura 9 of the Qur'an, which is traditionally understood as the last Sura to be revealed to Muhammad. Therefore, it is said to take precedence over all previous Suras. The key verses read as follows:

5 Then, when the sacred months have passed, slay the idolaters wherever ye find them, and take them (captive), and besiege them, and prepare for them each ambush. But if they repent and establish worship and pay the poor-due, then leave their way free. Lo! Allah is Forgiving, Merciful.

6 And if anyone of the idolaters seeketh thy protection (O Muhammad), then protect him so that he may hear the Word of Allah, and afterward convey him to his place of safety. That is because they are a folk who know not.

7 How can there be a treaty with Allah and with His messenger for the idolaters save those with whom ye made a treaty at the Inviolable Place of Worship? So long as they are true to you, be true to them. Lo! Allah loveth those who keep their duty.

8 How (can there be any treaty for the others) when, if they have the upper hand of you, they regard not pact nor honour in respect of you? They satisfy you with their mouths the while their hearts refuse. And most of them are wrongdoers.

9 They have purchased with the revelations of Allah a little gain, so they debar (men) from His way. Lo! evil is that which they are wont to do.

10 And they observe toward a believer neither pact nor honour. These are they who are transgressors.

11 But if they repent and establish worship and pay the poor-due, then are they your brethren in religion. We detail Our revelations for a people who have knowledge.

12 And if they break their pledges after their treaty (hath been made with you) and assail your religion, then fight the heads of disbelief—Lo! they have no binding oaths—in order that they may desist.

13 Will ye not fight a folk who broke their solemn pledges, and purposed to drive out the messenger and did attack you first? What! Fear ye them? Now Allah hath more right that ye should fear Him, if ye are believers.

14 Fight them! Allah will chastise them at your hands, and He will lay them low and give you victory over them, and He will heal the breasts of folk who are believers.

The Sura closes with the following words:

33 He it is Who hath sent His messenger with the guidance and the Religion of Truth, that He may cause it to prevail over all religion, however much the idolaters may be averse.

34 O ye who believe! Lo! many of the (Jewish) rabbis and the (Christian) monks devour the wealth of mankind wantonly and debar (men) from the way of

---

31. Ibid., 2.

Allah. They who hoard up gold and silver and spend it not in the way of Allah, unto them give tidings (O Muhammad) of a painful doom.

35 On the day when it will (all) be heated in the fire of hell, and their foreheads and their flanks and their backs will be branded therewith (and it will be said unto them): Here is that which ye hoarded for yourselves. Now taste of what ye used to hoard.

36 Lo! the number of the months with Allah is twelve months by Allah's ordinance in the day that He created the heavens and the earth. Four of them are sacred: that is the right religion. So wrong not yourselves in them. And wage war on all of the idolaters as they are waging war on all of you. And know that Allah is with those who keep their duty (unto Him).

After discussing classical interpretations of these and other Suras, Peters notes that it was not until the 1850s that questions were raised about the nature of jihad. One of the earliest Muslims to disagree with the classical interpretations was Sayyid Ahmad Khan (1817–1898), who lived in India under British rule. After the failure of the Indian Mutiny/First War of Independence, he argued for a more flexible interpretation of *jihad* that allowed Muslims to serve in the Indian army.

Peters's conclusions are supported by Reuven Firestone in his *Jihad: The Origin of Holy War in Islam*. He states that "the semantic meaning of the Arabic term *jihad* has no relation to holy war or even war in general ... There are, therefore, many different kinds of *jihad*, and most have nothing to do with warfare ... When the term is used without qualifiers such as 'of the heart' or 'of the tongue,' however, it is universally understood as war on behalf of Islam ..."[32]

Furthermore, Firestone points out that "according to the oft-cited *Hadith*, Muhammad, upon returning from battle, remarked: 'We have returned from the lesser *jihad* to the greater *jihad*.' When asked what he meant by that, he is said to have replied, 'The greater *jihad* is the struggle against the self.' Its source is not usually given, and it is in fact nowhere to be found in the canonical collections."[33]

Clearly, from these examples found in the writings of both Western scholars studying the term *jihad* and leading Muslims whose works are widely read today, the popular, milk-and-water version of Islam found in most religious studies texts is, to say the least, misleading. Jihad is indeed primarily a form of warfare waged in defense of Islam. This means that, however much one may disagree with the methods of people like Osama bin Laden, it is highly misleading to dismiss them as "extremists" or argue that they "don't understand Islam," as some writers suggest. The truth is, bin Laden and his followers have decided that Islam is under threat from the West and that Western values are undermining Muslim societies. Therefore, in their own eyes, they are fighting a legitimate war, or jihad, in defense of Islam. Unless North Americans recognize this fact, they will never understand the depth of Muslim feeling on this issue or why so many Muslims

32. Reuven Firestone, *Jihad: The Origin of Holy War in Islam* (New York: Oxford Univ. Press, 1999), 16–17.
33. Ibid., 139–40.

1000

1150

KINGDOM
OF SPAIN

Las Navas
de Tolosa

GRANADA — To Spain in 1492

1450

Spanish Christian states

Muslim states

Portugal

0   300 km.

0   300 miles

Map 24.1 The Christian reconquest, or liberation, of Spain. During the early Muslim invasions of the eighth century, the whole of North Africa and most of Spain were conquered by Muslim armies, who also made forays into France until they were defeated at the Battle of Tours in 732. From that time on, the remaining free Christian kingdoms of Spain began a long process of reconquest, which culminated in the victory of the armies of Ferdinand of Aragon (1452–1516) and Isabella of Castile (1451–1504) over the last remaining Muslim state of Granada in 1492. Shortly after this victory, Ferdinand was persuaded to embark on a policy of conversion or expulsion, first for Jews and later for Muslims. Scholars estimate that around 200,000 people left Spain at this time, with many Jews moving to places like Amsterdam and elsewhere in northern Europe. This policy had a long-term impact on Spain's economy and ultimately harmed the nation.

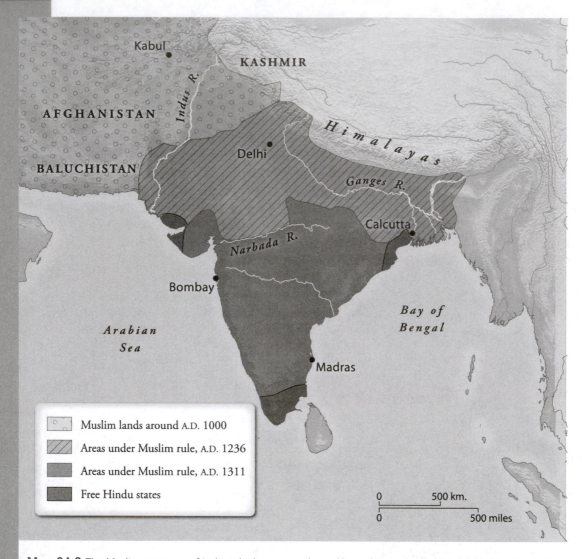

Map 24.2 The Muslim conquest of India, which continued steadily until it was brought to an end by the British East India Company, as shown in Map 10.1.

express sympathy for bin Laden while at the same time disassociating themselves from his attack on America.

While Americans have difficulty understanding how someone can condemn the actual attack on the World Trade Center while maintaining a grudging admiration for its perpetrators and the people who planned it, Muslims have difficulty understanding American attitudes toward Israel. How is it possible, Muslims ask, for people who loudly proclaim their Christianity to support a state that was created by displacing fellow Christians? How can Americans continue to support a Jewish state that continues to wage war

Photo 24.13 The Taj Mahal as seen from Agra's Red Fort. Scholars who downplay, or deny, the military aspects of jihad often do so from the best of motives: a desire to stress the positive aspects of Muslim culture and the beauty of its art and its architectural and literary traditions. The problem is that such an approach is contrary to what even today the majority of Muslims understand jihad to mean and generally creates skepticism among Westerners who know history. As a result, it fails to engage either Christians or Muslims in the type of open and honest dialogue that is needed to reach a lasting understanding between these two faiths and their peoples.

against indigenous Christians who are fighting to regain lands taken from them by an invading force?

No doubt the intent of writers who minimize the military aspects of jihad is to ameliorate criticism, correct the distorted views of Islam common in Western society, and attempt to help Muslim immigrants gain acceptance in places like western Europe and North America. Yet, to the extent that this distorts both traditional interpretations and current Muslim understandings of jihad, it appears misguided.

For example, in *Towards Understanding Islam*,[34] published by the Islamic Circle of North America, Abul A'la Mawdudi writes, "*Jihad* is part of this overall defence of Islam. Jihad means to struggle to the utmost of one's capacity. A man who exerts himself physically or mentally or spends his wealth in the cause of God is indeed engaged in jihad. But in the language of Divine Law, the word is used specifically for the war that is waged solely in the name of God against those who perpetrate oppression as enemies of Islam."[35]

For Muslims, Islam is a religion of peace, because the imposition of Islamic rule brings areas under Muslim control to peace and order in accordance with Islamic teachings about

---

34. Abul A'la Mawdudi, *Towards Understanding Islam* (New York: Islamic Circle of North American, 2002).
35. Ibid., 124–25.

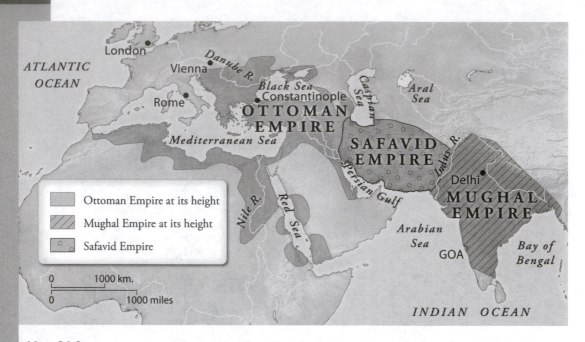

Map 24.3 Islamic empires of the seventeenth and eighteenth centuries. At this time the British Empire was just emerging as a network of trading companies, and there were no other European or "Christian" empires to challenge Islam. Further, in the Far East the Chinese Empire was weak. Islam was at its height in terms of world dominance, and was therefore feared in Europe and other non-Muslim areas.

the will of God. Thus it is a Pax Islamica, which imposes peace by dominating all opponents by force or arms. At the same time, areas remaining free from control by Muslim rulers are viewed as the "realm of war," awaiting subjection to Islamic rule and the administration of Sharia law.

This is why Muslims throughout history have regarded "the Conquests" of the first century of the Muslim era as the second great miracle of Islam, after the reception of the Qur'an. Islam proclaims submis-

Photo 24.14 The Wilmersdorfer Mosque, in Berlin, Germany, reminds viewers that, while in the past Islam was often spread as a result of military victories, thus justifying a military understanding of jihad, today Islam is rapidly spreading throughout Europe and other parts of the world through immigration and conversion without coercion. As a result, it now presents a far greater intellectual challenge to Christianity and other religions than when it was possible to explain away its success in terms of conquest.

Map 24.4 Muslim expansion into southeastern Europe from the twelfth to the seventeenth centuries, showing large Christian areas of Europe, such as Greece, Bulgaria, Romania, and Hungary coming under Muslim rule. This map explains to a large extent why many contemporary Europeans are uneasy about the admission of Turkey into the European Union and fear Islam.

sion through the acknowledgment of God's demands laid out in the Qur'an and interpreted by the Hadith. These demands are codified in Sharia law, which is believed to be applicable to all people because it enforces morality and God's will on errant humans.

This is why historically non-Muslims spoke of Islam as a religion of the sword and why many classical Muslim authors, like al-Ghazali, took pride in this claim. As Fazlur Rahman argues, "Whereas it is a travesty of the facts to insist that Islam was propagated 'by the sword,' it is also a distortion of the facts to say that Islam spread in the same way as, say, Buddhism or even Christianity ... The real explanation lies in the very structure of Islam as a religious and political complex. Whereas Muslims did not spread their faith through the sword ... Islam insisted on the assumption of political power ..."[36] Thus he argues that while Islam as a religion was not "spread by the sword," Islamic rule was spread in this way, and many people eventually converted as a result of Muslim conquests. Whether or not this is correct depends on what is meant by "spread by the sword." Conquest is conquest, and if the conquerors then make life difficult for all but people of their own faith, there is a strong incentive to convert. Nevertheless, Rahman agrees that to interpret *jihad* in "purely defensive terms" is "unacceptable on historical grounds."[37]

From this discussion of jihad, it seems clear that to say that "Islam is a religion of peace" is not the same thing as saying that "Islam is a peaceful religion." Nowhere in Islamic teachings do we find statements like "Love your neighbor as yourself" (Matthew 22:39) or "Love your enemies and pray for those who persecute you" (Matthew 5:44). Nor do we find the general proclamation, "Glory to God in the highest, and on earth peace, goodwill toward men" (Luke 2:14 NKJV).

Thus, for the majority of Muslims worldwide, jihad has the primary meaning of war on behalf of Islam. This means that for Christians to enter into meaningful discussions with Muslims, they must begin by recognizing that Muslims sincerely hold a belief very different from the beliefs of most North Americans. To say this is to respect Islam as a religion in its own right, recognizing its distinctive features, without imposing on it a liberal Christian interpretation of religion.

Yet pacifist movements do exist within Islam, and some Muslim writers work hard to genuinely present their religion as a religion of peace that has moved beyond its earlier military phase. Such authors as Maulana Wahiduddin Khan, who wrote *Islam Rediscovered*,[38] belong to this school. Therefore, although the primary understanding of jihad among most Muslims is war on behalf of Islam, which is often, but not always, interpreted as defensive war, a small minority see it as a spiritual struggle, as many Western writers like to emphasize.

---

36. Fazlur Rahman, *Islam* (London: Weidenfeld and Nicoloson, 1966), 2.
37. Ibid., 37.
38. Maulana Wahiduddin Khan, *Islam Rediscovered: Discovering Islam from Its Original Sources* (New Delhi, India: Goodword Books, 2001).

CHAPTER 25

MUSLIM PIETY

THE MUSLIM CALENDAR

To discuss Muslim piety, we must know something about the Islamic calendar. Although there are some variations, the standard Muslim calendar begins with the first day of the Hegira, the flight of Muhammad and his followers from Mecca to Medina in September 622. The Islamic calendar differs from Western calendars in that it follows the lunar year while the Western calendar follows the solar year. As a result, although there are twelve months in the Muslim year, an average year has 354 days, because the average interval between new moons is 29 days, 12 hours, 44 minutes, and 3 seconds, which means lunar months vary between 29 and 30 days in length. According to the Qur'an, Sura 10:5, the new moon marks the beginning of each new month: "He it is Who appointed the sun a splendour and the moon a light, and measured for her stages, that ye might know the number of the years, and the reckoning. Allah created not (all) that save in truth. He detaileth the revelations for people who have knowledge."

Because of differences between the solar and lunar years, and the prohibition against inserting what might be described as a thirteenth month to create a type of leap year at regular intervals, Muslim calendar months actually move backwards by eleven days each year. As a result the Muslim year works on a thirty-three-year cycle. The Muslim year contains the following months and holidays:

Months	Holidays
1: Muharram	1st, New Year's Day 10th, The Day of Ashrua, commemoration of assassination of Husayn, the grandson of Muhammad, celebrated by Shia
2: Safar	
3: Rab' I	12th, the Prophet Muhammad's birthday, celebrated in some Muslim countries but discouraged in some others, including Saudi Arabia

Months	Holidays
4: Rabi' II	
5: Jamadi I	
6: Jamadi II	
7: Rajab	27th, the night of the journey and ascension (Lailat al-Isra wa al-Mi'raj) of Muhammad
8: Sha'ban	14th, the night of repentance, important in India and Indonesia
9: Ramadan	All Muslims are required to fast during the hours of daylight throughout the ninth month of the lunar year. 27th, the last night of fasting, which commemorates the first revelation received by Muhammad and is a time of special prayer
10: Shawwal	1st, the breaking of the fast (Id al-Fitr), an obligatory feast day like Easter in the Christian calendar
11: Dhul-Qu'da	
12: Dhul-Hajja	1st–10th, the time of annual pilgrimage, when pious Muslims are encouraged to visit Mecca 10th, the feast of sacrifice (Id al-Adha), another great celebration, when gifts are exchanged, as at the Christian Christmas. The celebration can continue for several days, reminding us of the Christmas carol "The Twelve Days of Christmas."

Muslim piety begins with a confession, "Ilaha illa Alla. Muhammad rasul Allah," which is translated, "There is no God but God. Muhammad is his Prophet," and, as noted, is the basis for conversion to Islam. This confession is whispered into a child's ear when it is born. It forms part of Muslim prayer and is confessed daily. As such it is a basis of Islam.

Central to Muslim piety is the practice of what is usually called prayer by Muslims and non-Muslims alike. Yet Muslim prayer is very different from what most North American Christians and even non-Christians consider prayer. It is similar to acts of prayer found in liturgical Christian traditions such as Eastern Orthodoxy and Roman Catholicism. In other words, it is similar to what Christians consider worship.

DAILY PRAYER

Practicing Muslims are commanded to pray five times every day. The first prayer occurs when one wakes, sometime between the first light of dawn and sunrise. The second, between noon and the middle of the afternoon. The third, between midafternoon and sunset. The fourth, much like the first, between sunset and the onset of darkness. The last prayer takes place after dark, anytime before the dawn breaks.

Photo 25.1 A poster from a mosque instructs Muslims in the correct gestures to be made while standing at the beginning of their prayers.

At each of time of prayer, worshipers prepare by cleansing themselves through a series of carefully prescribed acts, called ablutions, that enable them to separate themselves from this profane world. First, particularly before praying in the mosque, they wash their bodies: hands, mouth, nostrils, faces and forehead, feet and ankles, each three times. Following these ablutions, they prepare a surface where they can kneel in prayer while facing the direction of Mecca. This is usually a prayer mat, but theoretically it can be anything—a piece of paper, a plastic bag—that separates them from the ordinary ground around them. Thus the use of a prayer mat separates worshipers from the world of everyday things and ritually sets them apart in a sacred realm. Muslims may pray anywhere except in cemeteries and places used as lavatories, which are considered ritually unclean.

Preparations over, worshipers perform a series of ritual actions known as *rakahs*: standing, kneeling, standing again, and falling down on one's face while reciting passages from the Qur'an that express praise and adoration of God and submission to him. As such, these prayers are ritual proclamations rather than the type of personal prayer usually found in Christian churches.

Within Islam, personal prayer as most Christians know it does exist in

Photo 25.2 This image shows the gestures to be made while kneeling in prayer. Unlike Christian prayer, Islamic prayer is essentially a ritual performance.

Photo 25.3 This photograph shows a prayer mat of the sort used by Muslims. The purpose of a prayer mat is to remind the worshiper that when they step onto the mat they are entering the world of the sacred. The mat separates them from the floor and all around them, thus creating a sacred space that helps the mind concentrate on God. This is a highly ritualized performance aimed at physically helping the worshiper to approach God. Although the mat in the photograph is highly decorated, anything that separates the believer from their surroundings, such as a piece of paper or even a sheet of newspaper, serves the same intellectual and ritual purpose.

terms of supplications, known as *du'a*, addressed to God. Consequently, many Muslims pray for help and guidance and thank God for personal things, following Sura 40:60 which says, "Pray unto Me and I will answer your supplications." But in terms of the great tradition of Islam, such prayers are essentially closer to the folk religion than to the formal expression of Islam. The required prayers of Islam, or daily prayers, form part of the central practice of all Muslims and are ritual acts of worship rather than acts expressing a personal relationship to God.

COMMUNAL PRAYER

It is thought best that a Muslim always pray with a group of other Muslims, as part of the Muslim community. The best place to pray is in a mosque. There worshipers are led in prayer while facing Mecca. Every Friday, known as the day of assembly and intended to bring God to remembrance, all male Muslims who are able are required to pray at noon in the mosque.

Women, the sick, the old and infirm, and travelers are excluded from this requirement, and even those under it are granted considerable leniency. For example, very bad weather and similar situations like illness are valid excuses for not attending Friday prayer. Similarly, anyone whose absence from or neglect of their work at the time of prayer might cause danger to others, such as an air traffic controller, doctor, or member of the armed forces, is excused. Those who miss Friday prayer are required to perform four ritual acts, or *rakahs*, as though they were participating in normal noontime prayer. In all these, the worshiper proclaims, "In the name of God. Most Gracious most Merciful. Praise be to God that Cherisher and Sustainer of all that is most Gracious, most Merciful King on the day of judgment." Thus, Muslims submit their lives to God, reflecting the very meaning of the word *Islam* itself, which is "submission." Further, they see failing to acknowledge God or ignoring him and his commands as a great sin.

A MUSLIM THEOLOGY OF PRAYER

For Muslims prayer is quite different from prayer in the average evangelical church in North America. When evangelical Christians pray, they talk to God as their loving, heavenly Father. Such a concept is virtually blasphemous to a pious Muslim. God is the creator and preserver, not Father. Therefore, the very idea of talking to God in a casual manner, as though we have an intimate relationship with him, is very strange.

For Muslims, as Sayyid Qutb explains, "Prayer, an act of total submission and dedication to God, epitomizes the entire Islamic outlook on life." Thus prayer is "an integrated act of worship dedicated completely to the adoration and glorification of God Almighty," because "maintaining this standard in the performance of prayer is a reminder and a fulfillment of the essence and purpose of Islam as a whole."[1]

Other Muslim writers view prayer in a similar way. For Afif A. Tabbarah, "prayer is an appeal we perform to gain God's Favor, entreat forgiveness for a misdeed we have committed, express gratitude for a grace bestowed upon us, ward off a possible calamity, and perform a religious duty."[2] He also notes that "prayer allows him to implore all that he wishes from God, and thus release his innermost feelings."[3] His entire chapter on prayer is devoted to the performance of ritual actions, without any hint that prayer is a conversation with God. Rather, the chapter closes by warning Muslims that if they do not perform prayer in the prescribed manner, their "prayer is said to be annulled."[4]

Photo 25.4 This nineteenth-century print shows three Muslims performing their prayers in the port city of Tyre, Lebanon.

Similarly, Maulana Abul A'la Mawdudi writes, "The basic and most important act of worship among those which Allah has taught us to perform is Salah, or the Prayer."[5] Prayer causes "us to be *constantly* aware that we are servants of God." This is why, "when you get up in the morning, the Prayer reminds you of this even before you start your day. When you are busy in your work during the day, it again reminds you of this fact three times. And when you are about to go to bed, you are reminded once again. This is the first blessing of the Prayer."[6]

1. Sayyid Qutb, *In The Shade of the Qur'an*, ed. and trans. Adil Salahi and Ashur Shamis (Leicester, U.K.: Islamic Foundation, 1999), 222–23.
2. Afifa. Tabbarah, *The Spirit of Islam* (Beirut: Dar El-Ilm Lilmalayin, 1978), 118.
3. Ibid., 119.
4. Ibid., 137.
5. Sayyid Abul A'la Mawdudi, *Let Us Be Muslims* (Leicester, U.K.: Islamic Foundation, 1991), 145.
6. Ibid., 147.

The second great purpose of prayer is to remind Muslims of their duty toward God; the third, to create in them a "consciousness of God" so that they may avoid "His punishments," because "Prayer evokes and sustains in the heart of man fear of God and the belief that he lives in His presence." Fourth, since Muslims recite verses from the Qur'an in their prayers, prayer constantly reminds them of God's law. Finally, the principle that prayer is best performed with other Muslims means it is essentially a communal act and therefore helps create a sense of community.[7]

Photo 25.5 Ritual cleanliness is another important aspect of Muslim prayer. Before praying, worshipers must clean their hands, feet, face, and mouth. The above photo shows the water fountain at the Grey Street Mosque in Durban, South Africa, where believers can cleanse themselves before prayer.

After discussing the value of prayer, Mawdudi explains how prayer is to be performed and discusses various verses from the Qur'an that should be recited during prayer. Yet, once again, there is no hint of the type of activity that most Christians consider the essence of prayer. For Muslims prayer has very different connotations and meanings than it does for Christians. The closest Christian prayer comes to what Muslims regard as the essence of prayer is in the Eastern Orthodox, Coptic, and Syriac prayer rituals performed by monks and members of religious orders. Like Muslims, and indeed long before the birth of Islam, Christian monasticism developed traditions of prayer that prescribed set times when set prayers were to be recited. But, even here, the content and tone of such prayer, as can be seen from something like the Anglican *Book of Common Prayer* or Roman Catholic missal, are quite different from the content and tone of Muslim prayers.

For example, Mawdudi provides the following example of a prayer for guidance: "O God! We seek help from Thou; we ask Thee for guidance; we seek forgiveness; we have faith in Thee; we put our trust in Thee; we give all good praises to Thee; we thank Thee, and do not commit ungratefulness; we abandon and leave everyone who disobeys Thee."[8]

Compare this prayer with that found in the Anglican service of morning prayer:

O Lord, our heavenly Father, almighty and everlasting God, who hast safely brought us to the beginning of this day: Defend us in the same with thy mighty power; and grant that this day we fall into no sin, neither run into any kind of danger; but that

---

7. Ibid., 148–51.
8. Ibid., 163.

we, being ordered by thy governance, may do always what is righteous in thy sight; through Jesus Christ our Lord.[9]

In many ways these two prayers are similar. Yet they are also very different in tone and content, reflecting a different understanding of prayer, of the relationship between humans and God, and of God's revelation to humans. Essentially, Muslim belief and practice, like that of Judaism, concerns obedience to God's revealed will.

SCRIPTURES AND SCRIPTURE READING

As already discussed in the previous chapter, from a Muslim viewpoint Christians confuse the idea of revelation with that of inspiration. Thus, for Muslims, while the Bible is an inspired book, it is not the revealed word of God. For Muslims only the Qur'an is the revealed word of God. It was given to mankind through the Prophet Muhammad, who recited it at the command of God. The words of the Qur'an are not the words of the Prophet but the words of God, and the original and uncreated Qur'an exists in heaven. This means that, unlike the Bible, the Qur'an is not a historical book in the sense that it originated in distinct historical settings, where it was written down by men who influenced its literary style.

This is not to say that there is no historical component to understanding the Qur'an. There is, but this is to be found in the interpretation of individual passages. To understand this, we need to look at the way in which the Qur'an was compiled. According to orthodox

Photo 25.6 The famed Grey Street Mosque in Durban, South Africa, which for many years was the largest mosque in the Southern Hemisphere. It was also the home of a major Islamic apologetics outreach headed up by Ahmed Deedat (1918–2005), a South African born in India who sought to engage Christians and others in intellectual dialogues about truth in religion. Deedat abandoned the use of Arabic as the prime language for communicating Islam in favor of English and emphasized peaceful and conciliatory aspects of Islam. In many ways he was like a Christian evangelist.

9. *The Book of Common Prayer* (Oxford: Oxford Univ. Press, 1957), 48.

Muslim belief, the Qur'an was recited, or dictated, by Muhammad, sometimes in a trance-like state. When he recited the Qur'an, his followers, especially the Companions, wrote down the words he spoke. These verses of the Qur'an, or Suras, were written on anything that came to hand: sometimes parchment, sometimes pieces of bone, often palm leaves. During Muhammad's lifetime these Suras were remembered and recited by his followers. Following his death, however, Muhammad's successor, Abu Bakr, was worried that with the deaths of Muhammad and his close followers, the words of the Qur'an might be forgotten. Therefore, he collected together as many of these writings as possible and from them compiled what today we know as the Qur'an.

In arranging the order of the Qur'an, Abu Bakr destroyed any variant readings and organized the text into 114 Suras, or chapters. These chapters are poetic in form and, according to Muslims, are the greatest example of poetry in existence. While Abu Bakr created a unified text, he also created a problem for scholars, who as a result have no manuscript history for the Qur'an and therefore cannot study the history of its transmission as they can that of the New Testament. Nor can anyone know what difference the variants might have made in interpretation and therefore in the history of Islamic society. Nevertheless, when Abu Bakr compiled the Qur'an in its present form, he did so in a manner on which all Muslims, even his enemies, could agree. He also had it arranged more or less so that the chapters occur in order of length, from the longest to the shortest.

Because the Qur'an relies upon poetic forms and is believed to be the actual words of God, it cannot be translated into any other language. Therefore, all so-called translations are more accurately described as renditions. As such, they can only convey something of the meaning of the Qur'an. This is why Marmaduke Pickthall (1875–1936) entitled his "translation" *The Meaning of the Glorious Koran*,[10] to make it quite clear to the reader that what they were reading was not the Qur'an itself.

Two other things need to be noted when interpreting the Qur'an. First, Muslims clearly distinguish between the early, or Meccan, and the late, or Medinan, Suras. In general, the Medinan Suras are far more inclusive and ecumenical than the Meccan, while the Meccan are viewed as more authoritative than the Medinan whenever the two appear to disagree. Also, for many Muslims, Sura 9, a Medinan Sura, represents the final revelation to Muhammad and abrogates all earlier revelations. This is important, because Sura 9 takes a far more critical view of other religious traditions, including Christianity and Judaism, than any of the earlier Medinan Suras.

Second, because the historical context of the verses is not clear from the text itself, the meaning of many verses has to be explained from other sources. The extrascriptural sources that are used are the traditions of the Prophet. In Islam these traditions are known as Hadith. Although all Muslims accept the importance of traditions about the Prophet, and therefore of some Hadith, not all Muslims accept the same Hadith. In general, Sunni Muslims have the largest Hadith collections, and until very recently few of these had been translated into English. The Shia accept a much smaller collection of Hadith. Indeed, some

---

10. Mohammed Marmaduke Pickthall, *The Meaning of the Glorious Koran* (New York: Dorset Press, n.d.). First published in London by George, Allen, and Unwin in 1930.

Photo 25.7 A group of students from Lancaster University, led by Dr. James Dickie (Yakub Zaki), visiting one of Britain's earliest mosques, the Raza Mosque, in the northern town of Wigan. Note how everyone has their head covered and the women are wearing trousers to cover their legs; the women were also asked to ensure that they were not menstruating when visiting the mosque. Ritual purity is an important aspect of Islam, training the worshiper to respect the holiness and purity of God.

Shia authors go so far as to claim that Sunni Muslims manufactured Hadith during the reigns of the first four caliphs to discredit the true claim that Ali, the son-in-law of the Prophet, was the rightful ruler of the Muslim community.

Considered another way, it is possible to say that there are four basic sources of authority in Islam for the development of Islamic law. This means that there are four ways of interpreting the Qur'an, or rather that four tools are used to reach an agreement about the meaning and implementation of the teachings of the Qur'an. The first, and ultimate, source of authority for interpretation is the Qur'an itself. If at all possible, verses in the Qur'an that appear unclear are to be interpreted by other verses in the Qur'an itself.

Second, there is the example of Muhammad, whose actions and sayings, how he lived and how he interpreted the Qur'an, are recorded in Hadith and are subject only to the Qur'an itself. Since there are thousands, if not hundreds of thousands, of Hadith, one task of Muslim scholarship is to determine which Hadith are spurious and which are genuine and can be traced back to Muhammad.

Third, there is the *Ijma*, or consensus, of the Muslim scholarly community and the Muslim community in general. In theory, at least, scholarly interpretations of both the Qur'an and the Hadith are weighed and carefully considered until the community arrives at a consensus in terms of the history of the interpretation of the Qur'an. In practice, since around the tenth century, these interpretations are fairly standardized.

Fourth, there is *Qiyas*, or analogical argument using deduction and induction based on the other three sources. Regarding *Qiyas*, there are four major schools, known as schools of law or jurisprudence: the Shafite school, the Hanafite school, the Malikite school, and the Hanbalite school. The Shafite school, founded by al-Shafir (d. 820), is the classical tool of Islamic interpretation. The Hanafite school, founded in Iran in the eighth century by Abu Hanafa, allows greater scope for personal interpretation and is relatively liberal. The Malikite school, founded in Mecca by Malik ibn Anas (d. 795), promotes what is probably an authentic Meccan interpretation of the Qur'an. The Hanbalite school, founded by Ahmad ibn Hanbal (d. 855), presents a highly literal and legalistic understanding of the Qur'an that may be seen as a forerunner of the Wahabbi interpretation of Islam, which is promoted by Saudi Arabia today.

SOME EXAMPLES OF QUR'ANIC INTERPRETATION

Michael Cook provides a number of examples of Muslim interpretations of the Qur'an in his concise study *The Qur'an: A Very Short Introduction*.[11] In chapter four of this highly readable work, he discusses three problematic issues and shows how Muslim commentators have dealt with them both historically and today. The first issue discussed is "the Qur'an and the scientific worldview." Here Cook examines the way many modern Muslim apologists attempt to read scientific discoveries back into the Qur'an and shows how difficult this actually is. In particular he focuses on Sura 7:166, which reads, "So when they took pride in that which they had been forbidden, We said unto them: Be ye apes despised and loathed!"

The problem with this verse, as Cook shows, is that traditional commentators, "with a single exception," have consistently maintained that these evildoers, who were Jewish fishermen who transgressed the Sabbath, actually turned into apes. Today, of course,

Photo 25.8 A modern mosque in a western city of North America, where Islam is a growing religion.

most modern readers see the verse as a metaphor and take it figuratively. Nevertheless, Cook points out that recently, "well known Syrian fundamentalist Sa'id Hawwa" attacked the view that this was a metaphor, arguing instead that it has to be taken literally, and that the Jews in question became apes.[12]

Far more problematic than whether or not some rebellious Jews were turned into apes by God is the difficulty of reconciling various verses in the Qur'an that discuss the appropriate treatment of nonbelievers. Sura 9:5,

11. Michael A. Cook, *The Qur'an: A Very Short Introduction* (Oxford: Oxford Univ. Press, 2000).
12. Ibid., 31–33.

known as "the sword" verse, is particularly important here. It reads, "Then, when the sacred months have passed, slay the idolaters wherever ye find them, and take them (captive), and besiege them, and prepare for them each ambush. But if they repent and establish worship and pay the poor-due, then leave their way free. Lo! Allah is Forgiving, Merciful."

Here, Cook points out, all the commentators are agreed that the reference to "idolaters" includes both Christians and Jews. Yet, later on in the same Sura, verse 29 allows unbelievers to pay tribute to Muslims instead of facing either conversion or death: "Fight against such of those who have been given the Scripture as believe not in Allah nor the Last Day, and forbid not that which Allah hath forbidden by His messenger, and follow not the Religion of Truth, until they pay the tribute readily, being brought low."

The impact of both of these verses is lessened somewhat by the much-cited Sura 2:256: "There is no compulsion in religion. The right direction is henceforth distinct from error. And he who rejecteth false deities and believeth in Allah hath grasped a firm handhold which will never break. Allah is Hearer, Knower."

Nevertheless, as Cook notes, other commentators are not so certain of the meaning of Sura 2:256, and many traditional commentators interpreted it in ways that restricted the religious freedom of nonbelievers. A few more recent writers, such as Sa'id Hawwa, however, say the verse must be read in light of traditional interpretations and that Muslims must renew the demand that nonbelievers in Islamic countries be excluded from government and pay taxes to Muslims.[13]

Perhaps the most difficult verse for modern Muslims to interpret is Sura 4:34: "Men are in charge of women, because Allah hath made the one of them to excel the other, and because they spend of their property (for the support of women). So good women are the obedient, guarding in secret that which Allah hath guarded. As for those from whom ye fear rebellion, admonish them and banish them to beds apart, and scourge them. Then if they obey you, seek not a way against them. Lo! Allah is ever High, Exalted, Great." Historically this was not a problem for Muslims, and the right of men to "scourge" or beat their wives went largely unquestioned, as it did in many other societies, including large parts of "Christian" Europe. Today, however, things are different, as a result of Western views about human rights. Therefore, modern Muslim commentators disagree about this verse. Some argue

Photo 25.9 An Islamic propagation center and bookstore in the downtown area of a large midwestern city in North America.

---

13. Ibid., 33–36.

Photo 25–10 Young Ismaili Muslims demonstrate their ability to integrate into North American society by participating in the Calgary Stampede. Note the cowboy hats and modern dress of the women, as well as the Canadian flag in the background. Events like this show that there is no necessary conflict between Muslims and their neighbors.

that it refers to hard cases and appears to confirm the property rights of women, which were often denied in supposedly Christian societies until quite recently. Others continue to interpret it more traditionally, though, as Cook notes, few modern commentators agree with Sa'id Hawwa in his view that men have a duty to rule, even dominate, their wives.[14] Nevertheless, all of the commentators lay down strict conditons to limit a husband's right to physically punish his wives, and, Qur'anic interpretation aside, there is general agreement that Muhammad never beat his wives and that his example ought to be followed by all true Muslims.

Perhaps even more problematic for modern Muslim interpreters of the Qur'an, and something that Cook does not discuss, is the fact that paradise appears to be a male domain. Contrary to the claims of some writers, the Qur'an teaches that women have souls and can go to paradise, but once they get there what will they do? The image of paradise in the Qur'an is very much a male paradise, where beautiful women serve men, who have numerous wives and lovers. Nothing is said about women except in connection with their relationship to their husbands or lovers.

All of these issues illustrate the complexity involved in reading the Qur'an and the questions modern Muslims have to deal with in Western society. They also raise questions about how secular law and believers in other religious traditions can interact with Muslims constructively.

14. Ibid., 37–41.

CHAPTER 26

SAYYID QUTB AND THE REBIRTH OF CONTEMPORARY ISLAM

INTRODUCTION

Although virtually unknown in the West, Sayyid Qutb (1906–1966) is widely recognized as the most influential Muslim writer of the twentieth century.[1] An Egyptian by birth, he came to see himself as a citizen of a new Islamic civilization, which, he argued, represented the wave of the future. His books and other writings are widely read throughout the Muslim world, from Morocco to Turkey to Pakistan, and are the most articulate statement of Sunni Islam in modern times. They are also widely read in places like Iran, among Shia Muslims and the members of smaller Islamic sects. Qutb's appeal is that he gives a vision of a new Islamic world that is within reach and quite distinct from what he sees as the corrupting influences of Western civilization.

SAYYID QUTB

Born in the small village of Musa in Upper Egypt, Qutb came from an old and pious Muslim family of landowners who were experiencing financial difficulties as a result of changing conditions at a time when Egypt was ruled by the British. His birth coincided with the stirring of Egyptian nationalism among educated elites and wealthy members of Egyptian society. It was a time when political parties were being founded, the most important of which was the National Party of Mustafa Kamil (1874–1908), to which Qutb's father apparently belonged.

Kamil was the son of an Egyptian army officer who had faithfully served the British. He was educated at the French school in Cairo and studied law at the University of Toulouse in France. Initially, his nationalism seems to have been supported by both the French and the Turks, but slowly he developed his own distinctive form of Egyptian nationalism that sought the complete independence of Egypt from foreign control and

---

1. Ibrahim M. Abu-Rabi, *Intellectual Origins of Islamic Resurgence in the Modern Arab World* (Albany, N.Y.: State University of New York Press, 1996), 93.

Photo 26.1 Sayyid Qutb, visiting Greeley, Colorado, during his trip to the United States in 1949, looks at a book with William R. Ross, the president of Colorado State College of Education.

influences, particularly that of the British, who controlled Egypt at the time. He became a journalist and popular speaker and founded his own school for boys in Cairo as well as the influential Egyptian newspaper *The Standard*, which first appeared in 1900. Two months before his death he founded the National Party, which became the leading organ of Egyptian nationalism.

It seems that initially Qutb was attracted by a secular form of nationalism similar to that of Kamil, based on the example of European nationalism and lacking direct religious motivations. Consequently, there was no direct link between his religious background and developing political ideas. At the age of thirteen he was sent to Cairo to complete his schooling, after which he went to the Dar al-Ulum, an institution of higher education much like a junior college. Dar al-Ulum was founded in 1871 to cater to students who wanted a traditional Islamic education while at the same time learning the skills acquired by students in Western-style universities. Initially it was headed by the French-educated Egyptian statesman Ali Pasha Mubarak (1824–1893), who had served as education minister in the Egyptian government and reformed Egyptian schools and universities.

Two of the most famous graduates of this institution were Qutb himself and Hasan al Banna (1906–1949), who, inspired by the Sufi movement, founded the Muslim Brotherhood in 1928. The Muslim Brotherhood was an anticolonial liberation movement that sought to restore Egypt's independence and the dignity of Islam by rooting its politics in Muslim tradition. So successful was this movement that in ten years it had over half a million members in Egypt alone, while its ideas spread far beyond Egypt's borders. After the establishment of the state of Israel in 1948, the brotherhood sent volunteers to fight in Palestine against the Israelis. It also agitated against the government of Mahmoud an-Nukrashi Pasha (1888–1948), who was assassinated three weeks after he ordered the disbanding of the brotherhood and the seizing of its assets in December 1948. Two months later Banna was also assassinated, apparently by a government agent.

What influence all of this had on Qutb is unclear. Although it is clear that while he did not directly identify himself with the Muslim Brotherhood, its ideas were beginning to penetrate his thinking. After completing his schooling, Qutb became a schoolteacher who devoted himself to writing poetry, novels, and works of literary criticism. One reason for his lack of involvement with the Muslim Brotherhood may be the fact that at this time, some reports claim that he described himself as an "unbeliever." Nevertheless, throughout his life he regularly read the Qur'an, but in his youth he was more attracted to its literary style and poetry than to its content and teaching.

Photo 26.2 Port Said, Egypt, in the 1920s. Looking at the various modes of dress in this picture, it is difficult to understand why a man like Qutb was so shocked by the ways Americans dressed in the 1940s. Egyptians had been exposed to European dress for a long time, and Qutb must surely have known all about European fashions long before he left Egypt.

QUTB'S TRANSFORMATION

Although he began with secular sympathies, over the years, both as a schoolteacher and then as an official in the education ministry, he was gradually drawn toward traditional forms of Islam. At the same time he developed a passionate interest in social justice that was intensified by the open corruption of the Egyptian government and the continuing legacy of British imperialism. Consequently, he wrote an increasing number of articles critical of both the West and Egyptian politicians. It appears that his thinking was affected profoundly by the creation of the state of Israel and the subsequent ethnic cleansing of Palestinians by Israeli forces, which he believed to be a gross injustice.

After completing work on a manuscript which became his first major work on Islamic politics, entitled *Social Justice in Islam* (1949),[2] Qutb accepted an American government scholarship to the United States, where he spent two years studying the American educational system. By all accounts, his visit to the U.S. brought him closer to the Muslim Brotherhood and confirmed his views about the West. Put bluntly, the U.S. repulsed him. Ironically, most of his time in the U.S. was spent in the small conservative town of Greeley, Colorado. Nevertheless, he was horrified by what he saw, which he described as a lawless society lacking civilization. As he was to write later in his book *Milestones*,[3] which some believe is one of the most influential statements of Muslim belief ever written, the U.S. was a doomed society: "Look at this capitalism with its monopolies, its usury and whatever else is unjust in it, at this individual freedom, devoid of human sympathy and responsibility for

---

2. William E. Shepard, ed. and trans., *Sayyid Qutb and Islamic Activism: A Translation and Critical Analysis of Social Justice in Islam* (Leiden: Brill, 1996).

3. Sayyid Qutb, *Milestones* (1964; Beirut: Holy Koran Publishing House, 1980); available on the internet as a downloadable pdf file at http://majalla.org/books/2005/qutb-nilestone.pdf.

relatives except under the force of law; at this materialistic attitude which deadens the spirit; at this behavior, like animals, which you call 'Free mixing of the sexes'; at this vulgarity which you call 'emancipation of women,' at these unfair and cumbersome laws of marriage and divorce, which are contrary to the demands of practical life."[4]

THE APOSTATE SOCIETY

According to Qutb, what was true of the U.S. was true of the rest of the Western world. In his view the Islamic world, and the world in general, had returned to a pre-Islamic state of ignorance. This he identified as *jahiliyyah*, an Arabic word that is used in the Qur'an to describe paganism and might well be translated "apostate." In Pickthall's translation of Sura 5:50 we read, "Is it a judgment of the time of (pagan) ignorance that they are seeking? Who is better than Allah for judgment to a people who have certainty (in their belief)?"

During the Middle Ages, Islamic scholar Taqi ad-Din Ahmad ibn Taymiyyah (1263–1328) took up this idea and used it to describe both backsliding among Muslims and the world in which he lived. Qutb writes of the U.S.,

> Among jahili societies, writers, journalists and editors advise both married and unmarried people that free sexual relationships are not immoral. However, it is immoral if a boy uses his partner, or a girl uses her partner, for sex, while feeling no love in his or her heart. It is bad if a wife continues to guard her chastity while her love for her husband has vanished; it is admirable if she finds another lover. Dozens of stories are written about this theme; many newspaper editorials, articles, cartoons, serious and lite columns all invite to this way of life. From the point of view of "human progress," all such societies are not civilized but are backward.[5]

Later, he explains the basis for his strong criticisms of the West when he writes, "These were the realities of Western life which we encountered. These facts, when seen in the light of Islam, made the American people blush ... this filth in which Jahiliyyah is steeped."[6] Consequently, for all good Muslims, "our first task is to replace this Jahiliyyah with Islamic ideas and traditions."[7]

Such a transformation, he recognized, would take time. Muslims therefore needed a strategy: "First we must be steadfast; next we must prevail upon it; then we must show Jahiliyyah the low state it is really in compared to the lofty and bright horizons of Islamic life which we wish to attain. This cannot come about by going along a few steps with Jahiliyyah, nor by now severing relations with it and removing ourselves to a separate corner; never. The correct procedure is to mix with discretion, give and take with dignity, speak the truth with love, and show the superiority of the Faith with humility."

---

4. Ibid., 185.
5. Ibid., 99.
6. Ibid., 261.
7. Ibid., 262.

Photo 26.3 In the above photograph from the Colorado State College Yearbook for 1950, Sayed Kotb (Qutb) is seen in the middle of page two.

CREATING A NEW ISLAM

In 1952, after returning to Egypt, Qutb joined the Muslim Brotherhood, becoming its most articulate spokesperson. His involvement with a politically oriented religious organization led to clashes with the government, and he spent over ten years in jail before being eventually executed in 1966, accused of attempting to overthrow the state. Whatever Qutb's involvement in the plot against President Nasser, it is clear both that he wanted to see the establishment of an Islamic state and that the Egyptian authorities used the occasion to stage a show trial in the hope of discrediting the Muslim Brotherhood. In the end all they did was create a martyr for Islam.

Qutb's literary output was enormous, particularly after he entered his Islamic phase. Apart from *Milestones*, his most important contribution from the early 1950s onwards was his enormous and erudite commentary on the Qur'an, *In the Shade of the Qur'an*,[8] much of which he wrote while in prison. This work, which is enormously popular in its English translation, systematically expounds Muslim doctrine in a style similar to that of Christian commentaries on

8. Sayyid Qutb, *In the Shade of the Qur'an*, vol. 1, ed. and trans. Adil Salahi and Ashur Shamis (Leicester, U.K.: Islamic Foundation, 1999).

Photo 26.4 Greeley, Colorado, in 1940. Although it was eight years later that Qutb stayed there, little had changed in this very conservative midwestern town.

the Bible or Christian systematic theology. Initially it was serialized in the magazine of the Muslim Brotherhood, and from 1953 onward it was published as a series of books. Later, Qutb repudiated many of his earlier writings and revised his early commentaries on the Qur'an, as well as writing a second edition of *Social Justice in Islam*. From these writings it is clear that his views about Islam became increasingly traditional and opposed to modernity.

For Qutb, Islam was a rational religion which, through the sheer force of its message, was eventually destined to rule the world. Nevertheless, he expressed a traditional Muslim view of religious tolerance. That is, he believed conversion ought not to be forced, although he did not believe Muslims and non-Muslims ought to have equal rights in society. In his view, "Islam looks at religious faith as a matter of conviction, once basic facts are provided and explained ... By the same token Islam never seeks converts through compulsion or threats or pressure of any kind. It deploys facts, reasoning, explanation and persuasion."[9]

Despite this commitment to tolerance, albeit limited within the confines of Islamic law, Qutb firmly believed in the necessity of creating a Muslim society dominated by devout Muslims who apply Islamic law to all of its citizens for their own good: "Islam cannot fulfil its role except by taking concrete form in a society, rather, in a nation; for man does not listen, especially in this age to an abstract theory which is not seen materialised in a living society."[10]

Comments like these reflect a belief that, for Muslims, there is no separation between church and state. Rather, all of life is to be governed by the divine law, the Sharia. Again: "The basis of the message is that one should accept the Shar'ah without any question and reject all other laws in any shape or form. This is Islam. There is no other meaning of Islam."[11]

THE DECLINE OF THE WEST

Viewing Western society from the perspective of Islamic thinking, Qutb's analysis goes as follows. Christianity arose in a colonial society dominated by Rome and Roman law.

---

9. Ibid., 412.
10. Qutb, *Milestones*, 11.
11. Ibid., 63.

As Christianity spread throughout the Roman Empire, largely as a result of the work of the apostle Paul, it was impossible for Christians to impose their own system of law on the empire. Consequently, under Paul's leadership, they turned inward, offering a spiritual solution to the problems of the world. The Romans were the heirs of a pagan culture, and their law was tainted with paganism, but Christians accommodated themselves to the situation by proclaiming the separation of church and state.

To Qutb the separation of church and state, or of religion from the state, was anathema. What it meant was an abdication of responsibility on the part of Christians that allowed paganism to remain triumphant throughout Christian society. As a result of the spread of western European colonialism, such attitudes and beliefs had penetrated the Muslim world, leading many Muslims to believe that it was "modern" and "scientific" to adopt ideas like the separation of society from its religious basis in the teachings of the Qur'an, Islamic law, and its interpreters, as well as in the influence of spiritual leaders in the mosque. Given this situation, Qutb believed an Islamic revolution was necessary to restore Islam to its rightful place in society.

For Qutb the modern world held little appeal, because it was a society based upon blind belief in science and a soul-destroying materialism. Instead of freeing humans to worship God, it enslaved them to worship mammon. Therefore, it was the duty of Muslims to preach the law of God and bring all humans into submission to him.

THE ISLAMIC REVIVAL

To do this, Muslims needed to return to God's one true revelation to humankind, the Qur'an, and the example of the Prophet contained in the record of his deeds, the Hadith. Only by doing this, and letting the Qur'an speak for itself, could a truly Muslim society be created.

Photo 26.5 Typical American college women in the 1940s and early 1950s. Today their dress looks very tame, but for Qutb it was licentious.

Aware of apparent contradictions and problematic verses in the Qur'an, Qutb appealed to the ancient doctrine of abrogation to explain key Qur'anic texts. For example, when Muhammad and his followers first arrived in Medina in 622, they were instructed to face Jerusalem while they prayed. Sixteen months later the Prophet received a revelation instructing Muslims to face Mecca while they prayed. Qutb explains to his readers that to many Jews of the time this appeared to be a contradiction. He states that they began to make "an issue of the modifications and amendments that had to be made to some Islamic rules and requirements during the formative years of Islam." Qutb then goes on to explain that the Jews did "this to raise doubts in Muslim minds, questioning the validity and veracity of their religion."[12] What the Jews

---

12. Qutb, *Shade of the Quran*, 135.

failed to understand, he argues, was "the principle and the wisdom" of abrogation, which allowed the "replacement or amendment of some rulings."[13] Some Muslim writers and websites rail against the idea of abrogation as a "Western" invention designed to discredit Islam, but, as can be seen, this view is definitely rejected by Sayyid Qutb and many other traditional Muslims.

In another place Qutb endorses the idea of jihad as holy war in his discussion of the state in relation to jihad. The discussion occurs in the context of his commentary on Sura 2:190–195:

190 Fight in the way of Allah against those who fight against you, but begin not hostilities. Lo! Allah loveth not aggressors.

191 And slay them wherever ye find them, and drive them out of the places whence they drove you out, for persecution is worse than slaughter. And fight not with them at the Inviolable Place of Worship until they first attack you there, but if they attack you (there) then slay them. Such is the reward of disbelievers.

192 But if they desist, then lo! Allah is Forgiving, Merciful.

193 And fight them until persecution is no more, and religion is for Allah. But if they desist, then let there be no hostility except against wrongdoers.

194 The forbidden month for the forbidden month, and forbidden things in retaliation. And one who attacketh you, attack him in like manner as he attacked you. Observe your duty to Allah, and know that Allah is with those who ward off (evil).

195 Spend your wealth for the cause of Allah, and be not cast by your own hands to ruin; and do good. Lo! Allah loveth the beneficent.

Qutb now summarizes his understanding of jihad: "The Muslim community must pursue this course of *jihad*, or struggle for God's cause until all threat of opposition is eliminated and people are free to believe in Islam and practice it. This does not imply any sense of compulsion, but it does mean allowing Islam to prevail."[14]

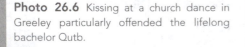

Photo 26.6 Kissing at a church dance in Greeley particularly offended the lifelong bachelor Qutb.

---

13. Ibid., 136.
14. Ibid., 268–69.

Later he explains, "The aim of war in Islam is to let people be free to uphold Islam and practice it ... *Jihad* is incumbent on Muslims until the end of time," because "Muslims everywhere continue to be the victims of aggression, oppression and religious intolerance as individuals and groups ..."[15]

As Qutb argues in his groundbreaking work *Milestones*, Islam is a creed that encompasses the whole of life. As such, it demands the imposition of Muslim law as a necessary step toward freeing men and women from the tyranny of other men and women so that they may freely obey God. Although there is "no compulsion in religion," the goal of all Muslims is to establish a state guided by God's law where people can freely choose to become Muslims because their natural tendencies toward disobeying God's laws are restrained by the state. Thus, "no compulsion" does not mean that Muslims cannot use force to establish Islamic rule; on the contrary, jihad is a legitimate means of extending Muslim domains and thus the rule of God's law.[16] Therefore, while forced "conversion is wrong," it is also true that "so is anything that discourages conversion to Islam. Therefore, Sharia Law, which is a universal Law applicable to all people, is necessary to create the social conditions under which conversion to Islam becomes attractive and *Jihad* makes this possible."[17]

Photo 26.7 Life in medieval Iran showing a party atmosphere and the type of behaviour that Qutb found totally un-Islamic. Yet the picture is a picture of Muslim life in a very different age. Painting by the Iranian artist Nasrin Elmi.

This understanding of Islam as total submission to the teachings of God through the Qur'an is closely related in Qutb's mind to the idea of prayer. For Muslims, he explains, "prayer, an act of total submission and dedication to God epitomizes the entire Islamic outlook on life."[18] This description of prayer provides vivid insight into the difference between Christian and Muslim ways of thinking about their faith. It also shows that, however much some people may question Qutb's political writings, those writings were motivated by a deep sense of personal piety and prayer.

ASSESSING QUTB

It is exceptionally difficult to assess the real impact of Qutb's thought. On the one hand, the Islamic Foundation[19] in Leicester, England, which publishes many of his works, including a

15. Ibid., 274–75.
16. Qutb, *Milestones*, 79–140.
17. Ibid., 162–70, 199–202, 139.
18. Qutb, *Shade of the Quran*, 222–23.
19. Found on the internet at http://www.islamic-foundation.org.uk/ (accessed 20 January 2008).

Photo 26.8 The main hall of Greeley College around 1950.

fourteen-volume translation of his commentary on the Qur'an,[20] strives "towards building bridges between the Muslim community and the rest of society."[21]

On the other hand, Ayman al-Zawahri (b. 1951), one of the cofounders of Al Qaeda and a close confidant of Osama bin Laden (b. 1957), sees himself as a disciple of Sayyid Qutb, and of his younger brother, Muhammad Qutb (b. 1919), whose combined vision al-Zawahri is seeking to implement. In particular, al-Zawahri bases his argument on those of Qutb's *Milestones*. After joining the Muslim Brotherhood at the age of fourteen, he has since worked tirelessly for the triumph of Islam as he understands it. Eventually, after a time in jail, he was forced to flee Egypt to take up the armed struggle against what he saw as imperialist aggression against Islamic states. It is easy to dismiss a man like al-Zawahri as a Muslim "fundamentalist fanatic." Such a reaction is understandable in the light of 9/11 and various other attacks that both al-Zawahri and his critics claim he has organized against American interests. Nevertheless, to see him only as a terrorist is to miss the depth of his religious devotion.

To suggest that the motivations of a man like al-Zawahri might arise from his personal piety will no doubt strike many people as totally absurd. Religion, they have been brought up to believe, is a good thing that promotes peace. Therefore, how can someone like al-Zawahri really be motivated by religion when he wages war against the West? Surely, it will be said, he uses religion for his own political ends. Such a response, while understandable, misses the point. Religion is a very serious affair that people are prepared to die and kill for. For centuries men have lived and died for their faith. In al-Zawahri's case, his

20. This and other publications of the foundation can be obtained from the foundation's bookstore: http://www .islamic-foundation.com (accessed 10 May 2010).
21. See http://www.islamic-foundation.org.uk/ under the tab "About Us" (accessed 10 May 2010).

crusade against the West has led to the death of both his wife Azza and his daughter Aisha as a result of an American bombing raid. Therefore, in the eyes of many Muslims, he is approaching the status of a martyr prepared to die for his faith. Unless this is recognized, it is impossible to understand the dynamics of militant Islam.

Equally important is the fact that however much Europeans, North Americans, and many other people throughout the world, including Indians and Chinese, deplore the tactics used by Al Qaeda, there is a logic to their actions that is rooted in their particular interpretation of the Qur'an. Further, this interpretation is solidly based in the work of Qutb and similar writers. In fact, Osama bin Laden, in his essay "Resist the New Rome," which appeared on 24 January 2004 in the form of an audiotape sent to the Al Jazeera television network, explicitly endorses Muhammad Qutb's work *Concepts That Should Be Corrected*,[22] which the younger brother and devoted disciple of Sayyid Qutb not only wrote but also published. It is also claimed by some sources that bin Laden attended lectures by Muhammad Qutb when he was a student in Egypt. Whatever the nature of this relationship, there can be no doubt of the influence of Qutb on the Al Qaeda movement.[23]

QUTB AND TRADITIONALISM

Finally, there are some curious similarities between the work of Sayyid Qutb and his brother Muhammad, on the one hand, and the works of the so-called Traditionalist School, on the other. The key figure in this movement is René Guénon (1886–1951), whose books *The Crisis of the Modern World*[24] and *Man and His Becoming* present an argument against modernity remarkably similar to that of Qutb.[25] Sometimes dubbed by its supporters "the perennial philosophy," this movement never gathered many followers, although it appears to have had an enormous influence among European intellectuals and some Americans. Edward Conze, for example, expressed his admiration for Guénon and saw himself as influenced by this perennial philosophy.

Guénon was converted sometime around 1911 under the influence of a Swedish Muslim, Ivan Aguéli (1869–1917), who also called himself Sheikh

Photo 26.9 Qutb as a student, from the Greeley College yearbook.

---

22. An alternate title for this work is *Understandings That Must be Corrected*. Although this book is quoted in various places it does not seem to be available in the West.

23. Osama bin Laden, *Messages to the World: The Statements of Osama bin Laden*, ed. Bruce Lawrence, trans. James Howarth (New York: Verso, 2005), 229.

24. René Guénon, *The Crisis of the Modern World* (London: Luzac, 1942; first published 1927); *Man and His Becoming* (London: Luzac, 1946).

25. See Mark Sedgwick, *Against the Modern World: Traditionalism and the Secret Intellectual History of the Twentieth Century* (Oxford: Oxford Univ. Press, 2004).

'Abd al-Hadi Aqhili and claimed to have founded the first Western Sufi order. After the death of his first wife, Guénon met a wealthy American woman, Diana Shillito, about whom little is known, and visited Egypt with her in 1929. Several months later Shillito returned to France, and Guénon married Fatima Muhammad Ibrahim, a devout Egyptian Muslim. Although it appears he originally intended a short stay in Egypt, he settled there, taking Egyptian citizenship in 1948. During this time he wrote profusely on what he termed traditionalism and attacked the modern Western world for what he saw as its lack of spiritual values. In Egypt he sometimes called himself Sheikh 'Abd al-Wahid Yahya, and over time he became increasingly reclusive, believing that his enemies were launching magical attacks against him.

The most prominent of Guénon's followers was the writer Frithjof Schuon (1907–1998), who converted to Islam after praying for God to guide him as to which religion he ought to embrace. Following his prayer, Schuon saw "a detachment of North African cavalry," which he believed meant he must become a Muslim. He became a Muslim in 1932. Eventually he too moved to Egypt, where he met Guénon, whose works had impressed him years earlier. For whatever reason, it seems the two men did not get along, and there was no continuing relationship between them. Nevertheless, Schuon was to remain in Egypt for the rest of his life.

Both Guénon and Schuon had an enormous influence, particularly among members of occult groups, the New Age movement, and Theosophy. After the counterculture of the 1960s, the popularity of these writers grew in the West, although few seem to have followed them into Islam. Nevertheless, the similarity between their analysis of the modern world and that of Qutb is quite remarkable. He echoes their sentiments and presents criticisms of the West that are indistinguishable from those the Traditionalists presented. The major difference between Qutb and most Traditionalists is that he remained free from the incipient racism, based on an admiration for the Indian caste system, which appears in their works.

Eventually, scholars may show a link between these two intellectual movements. Until they do, we can only comment on their similarities and ponder the implications that this type of reaction that rejects modernism in the West has for our understanding of religion.

Photo 26.10 Muslims in Iran celebrating the New Year in a traditional manner that goes back to the time when Zoroastrianism was the religion of the people. It was this type of blending of cultural traditions the Qutb sought to erase from Islamic thought and practice. Painting by the Iranian artist Nasrin Elmi.

CONCLUSION
WHITHER RELIGIOUS STUDIES?

INTRODUCTION

Religious studies is a challenging and relatively young academic field. Therefore, it is worth reflecting on its development and prospects for the future. When Eric Sharpe (1933–2000) sought to trace the history of religious studies in his book *Comparative Religion: A History* (1975),[1] he identified Max Müller as the key figure in the development of the field.[2] The "science of religion," he argued, began with Müller's insight, "He who knows one, knows none."[3] After lauding Müller's achievements, he observed that Müller "recruited an entire generation of scholars to his cause, as editors, translators, and commentators . . . ,"[4] thus firmly establishing the study of religion, as distinct from theology, in the Western academic tradition.

Sharpe then comments on the tensions between the academic study of religion and theology by comparing those tensions to the conflicts between *Religionsgeschichte,* or the history of religions, and theology in Germany. Although he acknowledges that at the time of those conflicts there were "over fifty chairs of Oriental studies in Germany," he laments that "there was no chair of comparative religion (under any name)." Then he singles out Adolf von Harnack's address "Die Aufgabe der theologischen Fakultäten und die allgemeine Religionsgeschichte" (The Task of Theological Faculties and the History of Religions, 1901) as indicative of the narrowly confessional attitude of theologians toward the study of religion.[5] Although Sharpe notes Harnack's concern that the comparative study of religion would likely lead to an "unhealthy dilettantism," he merely notes objections to this view without exploring Harnack's argument in any detail.

Yet, as Hans Rollmann has pointed out, Harnack's criticisms were far more profound and well based than Sharpe acknowledges.[6] Contrary to the impression created by Sharpe,

---

1. Eric J. Sharpe, *Comparative Religion: A History* (London: Duckworth, 1975).
2. In doing so, Sharpe dismissed Dutch scholar C. P. Tiele (1830–1902) as the "father of comparative religion" on the grounds that "Max Müller was the more universal figure" (ibid., 35).
3. Ibid., 31.
4. Ibid., 45.
5. Ibid., 126–27.
6. Hans Rollmann, "Adolf von Harnack and the 'History of Religious' as a University Discipline," in *Religious Studies: Issues, Prospects, and Proposals*, ed. Klaus K. Klostermaier and Larry W. Hurtado (Atlanta: Scholars Press, 1990), 85–103.

Photo 27.1 The stark reality of Berlin's Holocaust Memorial reminds visitors that ideas have consequences. Whatever his faults, Adolf von Harnack recognized the evils of the Nazi movement even though, ironically, his own liberal theology contributed to the development of Nazi ideology, according to both Nazi intellectuals and members of the German resistance. For more information on this, see Karla Poewe, *New Religions and the Nazis* (Oxford: Routledge, 2006).

it was not Harnack's intention to discourage the study of world religions. Rather, he believed that they needed to be studied in their entirety. That meant a thorough knowledge of such things as the languages involved as well as their historical and social contexts.[7] What he objected to was the study of religion as "comparative religion" within a faculty of theology. One might paraphrase his argument thus: "The study of religion is too important to be left to theologians."

Unfortunately, this message was lost on most Anglo-Saxon scholars, because in response to Müller's dictum, Harnack made the clever but ultimately unfortunate rhetorical quip that "anyone who does not know this religion, knows no religion, and anyone who knows Christianity, its history and development, knows all religions."[8] Good rhetoric can sometimes backfire, and backfire it did. Instead of asking why a liberal thinker like Harnack would object to comparative religion, other thinkers dismissed his argument as an example of theological bias. This discussion sets the stage for what follows.

RELIGIOUS STUDIES AS A MULTIDISCIPLINARY FIELD

When Ninian Smart (1927–2007) delivered his inaugural address at Lancaster University on 14 February 1968, it was a significant event in the development of what became religious studies. A year earlier Smart had founded Britain's first department of religious studies full of hope. Now he attempted to articulate his vision for the field by outlining both its scope and the methods he thought most appropriate for studying religion and religions.

Smart began by locating his new department in a historic and disciplinary context, as akin to both anthropology and history. The study of religion, he argued, requires that scholars describe religion in its historical and what he called its "structural" forms. By "historical" he meant its many manifestations through history. By "structural" he meant its social manifestations as observed by anthropologists and sociologists. To perform these tasks, Smart further argued, "the study of religion must be comparative."[9] That is, one must study religions, not simply one particular religion.

---

7. Adolf von Harnack, "Die Aufgabe der theologischen Fakultäten und die allgemeine Religionsgeschichte," in *Reden und Aufsätze*, 3rd edition, Zweiter Band, Erste Abteilung. Berliner Universität König Friedrich Wilhelms III gehalten in der Aula derselben am 3 Aug. (Giessen, 1901).

8. Ibid., 168.

9. Ninian Smart, *The Principles and Meaning in the Study of Religion* (Lancaster, U.K.: Lancaster University Department of Religious Studies, 1968), 3–4.

His next point was that to study religion involved understanding the discourse of religious people and texts. As a result, "It follows, therefore, that the logic of the study of religion itself impels one toward taking the philosophy of religion seriously."[10] Smart then shrewdly commented that "the understanding of others, whether in the past of one's own tradition or other cultures, requires self-understanding," because "the observer is not wholly detached."[11] Without an appreciation of the logic involved in studying religions, the exercise becomes meaningless.

After outlining his basic position, he summed up his views about the teaching of religion. Religion must be studied (1) historically; (2) phenomenologically; (3) sociologically, anthropologically, and psychologically; and (4) philosophically. It must also (5) engage modern atheistic thought and (6) engage other religious traditions, not simply Christianity.[12] "The pattern of religious studies," he concluded, "is determined by an inner logic. This pattern of a pluralistic, structural, ancient and modern study of religions suits all interests."[13]

Twenty-one years later, on 22 June 1989, Ninian Smart delivered his exaugural address shortly before leaving Lancaster to take up a full-time position at the University of Santa Barbara. In sharp contrast to his inaugural address, Smart's words were heavy with foreboding. The title "Religious Studies and Some Contradictions in Mrs. Thatcher's Policies" summed up his main concern that the educational "reforms" pushed through by Sir Keith Joseph were a step backwards and not reforms at all. The quest for "economic relevance," he argued, was a short-term expedient that failed to offer long-term solutions for Britain's future.[14]

He then restated his vision of religious studies as "an approach which is crosscultural, open,

Photo 27.2 The above plaque from the Oranienburg Street Synagogue in Berlin honors the local police commander who prevented Nazi mobs from setting fire to the synagogue on the notorious Night of Broken Glass, 9–10 November 1938. What this shows is that individuals can make a difference and what they believe shapes their lives.

---

10. Ibid., 6.

11. Ibid.

12. Ibid., 10–11.

13. Ibid., 14.

14. Smart, *Religious Studies and Some Contradictions in Mrs. Thatcher's Policies* (Lancaster, U.K.: Lancaster University Department of Religious Studies, 1989), 1–5.

empathetic, descriptive, theoretical and critical."[15] This led him to argue that "because the study of religion is crosscultural and plural it is transnational,"[16] and this is where it came into conflict with Thatcher's "strong nationalism."[17] Facing what he clearly saw as barbarians at the gate of higher education, Smart offered a defense of education as a good in itself. Education, he argued, "is more than a way into usefulness. It involves cultivation of human quests and interests," because, he argued, "direct relevance may tend to be self-defeating."[18] Apart from his criticisms of prevailing policies, Smart made several asides lamenting the failure of Britain's "new universities," built in the 1960s, to live up to their initial promise. All too often they had reverted to old ways and lacked imagination.[19]

A third theme that ran through this speech echoed a tone of disappointment with the way religious studies had developed. Smart found it necessary to define what he meant by a secular university. For him this did not mean a university that promoted, or was built on, secularism; rather, "Religious Studies is, as I have said, crosscultural. Its scope includes world religions. It is the logical way to explore religion in the secular university. By 'secular' here I mean 'pluralistic.' It is part of the logic of the university that it should be open to truth."[20] For Smart this meant that "the liberal cannot shut out non-liberal positions, but should preserve the plural milieu."[21]

Thus "all worldviews are open to question and debate," including "the evolutionary model ... We cannot dogmatically assert any one worldview to be established."[22] Asserting one of his basic educational principles, he argued, "It is I believe a principle of education that you should, where there is doubt, point out alternatives."[23] Praising both Gandhi and British philosopher Karl Popper (1909–1994) for their openness, Smart argued that what is needed is academic "openness," adding, "I count myself a glasnostic."[24] This led him to declare, "If we wish, therefore, to teach British history creatively, we should emphasize the progress toward openness, criticism and democracy which we have made: and indeed toward internationalism. We do not want to stick to utter tradition, but to find in tradition modern values."[25]

He wound up his paper by reasserting his views about the nature of religion and religious studies and about the value of religious studies to society. Then he compared the study of religion to the study of nationalism, urging that one enlightened the other. Finally, he declared that religious studies "is a wonderful subject."

---

15. Ibid., 1.
16. Ibid., 3.
17. Ibid., 1, 3.
18. Ibid., 4.
19. Ibid.
20. Ibid., 6.
21. Ibid., 7.
22. Ibid., 9.
23. Ibid., 10.
24. Ibid.
25. Ibid., 13.

Eight years later, in 1997, the Council of Societies for the Study of Religion published in its bulletin several papers on the relationship between religious studies and theology, including papers by Ninian Smart and his former colleague Eric J. Sharpe. Once again Smart displayed an almost missionary zeal by restating the aims outlined in his inaugural address. Although he made a strong plea for a "multidisciplinary" approach to the study of religion, which of necessity involved the interaction of several disciplines, he never really fully explained, here or elsewhere, how he saw this approach working in practice.

At the same time, he clearly recognized growing concerns about the development of religious studies restating that "religious studies is a field which is aspectual, crosscultural, multidisciplinary (polymethodic), and non-finite," a field, he argued, that is "an important social science and humanities subject."[26] The closest he came to addressing problems within the field was when he stated quite bluntly that "too much of academe is swayed by propaganda, notably in the humanities and social sciences," and asserted his belief in the importance of "professionalism."[27]

Three years later Smart took up the theme of professionalism once again in his article "Methods in My Life," where he provided the social and historical context for his inaugural address and defended his basic argument about the nature of religious studies. Yet again in this paper, he stressed the importance of empathy for understanding religions and the need for what he called a "plural, polymethodic, non-finite" approach to the subject.[28]

Then he outlined some dangers he believed were threatening the integrity of the field, in particular what he called "the trend to the particularization of cultures,"[29] based on "New Theories, such as deconstruction," that he saw as encouraging people with "ideological or spiritual axes to grind" to use religious studies for their own ends.[30] After spending considerable effort decrying "pseudo-specialization" and the growing influence of specialists who, in his view, threatened "the fragmentation and disintegration of

Photo 27.3 Anthropologist Karla Poewe working in German archives while researching her book *New Religions and the Nazis.* Her anthropological research led her into the study of history, demonstrating the value of a multidisciplinary approach to the study of religion.

26. Ninian Smart, "Religious Studies and Theology," in *The Council of Societies for the Study of Religion Bulletin* 26, no. 3 (1997): 68.

27. Ibid., 68.

28. Ninian Smart, "Methods in My Life," in *The Craft of Religious Studies*, ed. Jon R. Stone, (New York: Palgrave, 2000), 22.

29. Ibid., 30.

30. Ibid., 34.

Religious Studies,"[31] he concluded that "Religious Studies, provided it does not choke on specialism or commit methodological suicide, has a marvelous future."[32]

THE FUTURE OF RELIGIOUS STUDIES

The development of religious studies in Britain and North America from the 1960s to the present seems to confirm Harnack's forebodings about the dangers inherent in the new field. Indeed his comments appear prophetic. In Britain religious studies developed against the background of a growing wave of immigration from Africa, India, and Pakistan, and other parts of Asia. As a result, the growth of departments of religious studies had an immediate and very practical appeal in terms of helping the British understand their new neighbors.

In North America the decline of traditional churches seems to have created the motive force behind the growth of religious studies departments in the 1960s and 1970s. For example, the University of Alberta created its department after the number of theological students fell to below the number of tenured professors. Thus expediency and the need to attract students led to the rapid retooling of theologians as experts in world religions. Today, however, the situation has changed again with new waves of immigration into both Western Europe and North America.

Perhaps even more important than immigration is the globalization of economic life, with its social and political implications. We no longer live in religiously homogeneous societies; instead our emerging reality is that of a multicultural, multireligious world. Here the work of scholars like Kurt Rudolph is important.

Rudolph recognizes the weaknesses of existing programs in religious studies and points to an alternative future.[33] He begins by arguing that the big mistake scholars in this area have made is to attempt to study "religion" rather than "religions." This mistake was enshrined in Ninian Smart's conception of Lancaster University's department of religious studies when he argued in his inaugural address that "religion contains both an inward and an outer aspect both of which deserve equal attention," and in his insistence that scholars study not simply religions, as Rudolph argues, but "religion."[34] In his numerous writings he never fully explained what he meant by this "inner aspect."

One way to interpret Smart's comments about the "inner aspect" of "religion" is to see them in terms of his oft-repeated emphasis on the importance of empathy. Throughout his long career Smart was fond of saying that the study of religions involves "a kind of imaginative participation."[35] If by this he simply meant the sort of empathy both anthropologists and historians have traditionally brought to their studies, then there is no problem with his remarks, but Smart implies more, although he never fully articulates it, either in the papers discussed here or elsewhere.[36] This is one of the main weaknesses of his approach. We can-

---

31. Ibid., 31.
32. Ibid., 35.
33. Kurt Rudolph, *Historical Fundamentals and the Study of Religions* (New York: Univ. of Chicago Press, 2004).
34. Smart, *Principles and Meaning*, 1–3.
35. Ibid., 5.
36. Ibid., 3, 5.

not, as Rudolph observes, study religion in the abstract, and to attempt to do so is to invite disaster. What we can and must study are religions.[37] Yet many, if not most, religious studies departments in the English-speaking world have conveniently forgotten this lesson.

The second problem with Smart's basic approach is his enthusiastic commitment to making it "multidisciplinary," without adequately explaining what he understood by this term and how he thought it ought to work in practice.[38] What is clear is that in his thinking such an approach

Photo 27.4 Ninian Smart in casual conversation with a group of scholars during a conference in Washington, D.C.

involved history,[39] "the principle of inwardness,"[40] and what he called "structural explanations," which he identified with anthropology, psychology, and sociology.[41] In addition to these, he stressed the importance of philosophical analysis[42] and "multiplicity," or the use of comparisons between religious traditions.[43] Should anyone think Smart was asking too much of any one person, he came close to admitting this when he noted, "The student of religion thus needs to have historical knowledge and expertise, sensitivity and imagination in crossing cultures and time, and analytic grasp. He has to be a latter-day Leonardo."[44]

This emphasis on the multidisciplinary nature of religious studies runs through all of Smart's published works and the papers discussed here. Yet throughout his writings Smart never really explores the logic of multidisciplinary and interdisciplinary studies in great depth. The closest he comes to doing so is in places, such as in the inaugural and exaugural addresses, where he links history, anthropology, and philosophy as key disciplines for the study of religions. Paradoxically, a detailed examination of his own work reveals that essentially he was a philosopher who found history useful. This is something he comes close to admitting in various places.[45]

The problem with Smart's emphasis on a multidisciplinary, or, as he later came to call it, "polymethodic," approach to the study of religions is that it quickly embraces the jack-of-

---

37. Rudolph, *Historical Fundamentals*, 28–29.

38. Smart, *Principles and Meaning*, 1.

39. Ibid., 2.

40. Ibid., 3.

41. Ibid., 4.

42. Ibid., 6.

43. Ibid., 10.

44. Ibid., 11.

45. Ibid., 5–6; Smart, "Religious Studies and Theology," 67–68.

all-trades who is master of none.[46] As Adrian Cunningham, who with Robert Morgan and Smart founded the Lancaster department of religious studies in 1967, observed in 1989, the growth of religious studies was by any measure a success story. After a mere twenty years, more than sixty Lancaster graduates were employed in university departments of religious studies around the world. There were also fifteen distinct departments of religious studies, based on the Lancaster model, flourishing in Britain alone, not to mention their various clones throughout the commonwealth. Yet despite this success, the number of people who could really negotiate between religious traditions was, in Cunningham's words, "somewhat patchy due to the relatively small pool of qualified people to draw upon."[47]

If this situation has changed at all, it has gotten worse. Thus at the undergraduate level, people often teach a broad range of courses, which is acceptable as far as it goes. The problem is knowing where to set limits. For example, should specialists in Buddhism teach specialized courses on topics such as Christian church history if they have never taken a course in the area while they were students, or established their credentials through extensive reading followed by publications that prove their ability to move into such an area?

Photo 27.5 German scholar Dr. Ulrich van der Heyden, seen above at his office in Berlin's Humboldt University, is one of the world's leading experts on Christian missions in Africa. His work shows that even someone who was given an explicitly Marxist education, in this case in the former German Democratic Republic, where he grew up, can reach relatively "objective" conclusions when they seriously confront the available evidence. In his numerous and well researched books van der Heyden shows that Christian missions and missionaries have made a very positive impact on Africa.

At the graduate level the situation in many universities is serious. Here specialists in areas like classical Islam are allowed to accept MA and PhD students in areas where they have no expertise apart from some loose link to Islam. Thus one finds graduate students writing theses on topics like "Muslim Youth Programs in New York City," based on "social surveys" and "participant observation" supervised by people who are textual scholars with absolutely no experience or training in these research methods.

That universities allow such practices is astonishing and comes very close to academic fraud. No doubt, in time practices like these will return to haunt departments

46. Smart, "Religious Studies and Theology," 67.
47. Adrian Cunningham, "Religious Studies in the 1990s," in *Department of Religious Studies Report 1984–1989* (Lancaster, U.K.: Lancaster University, 1989), 5.

that allow them, through consumer-protection and similar law suits based on the concept of what lawyers call "educational neglect." Until this happens, many students will be trained by professors who lack the qualifications and training needed to adequately supervise such work at the graduate level.

If religious studies is to survive, a vigorous debate is needed about both its scope and its methods. As Smart noted in 1968, "The fundamental basis of the study of religion has scarcely been thought out."[48] Since he wrote these words, nothing has changed. This situation cannot go on much longer.

Eric Sharpe was correct when he observed that both the public and governments demand that surgeons, airline pilots, and other professionals meet and maintain high standards of training and competence. Such standards apply to a whole range of other professions and trades, from lawyers to plumbers. Only people who meet minimum standards are allowed to practice their craft. Yet in the humanities, including religious studies, it is often the case that anything goes.[49]

Why is this situation tolerated, either by members of the academic profession or by outsiders? One explanation is that neither the practitioners, that is, faculty members, nor university governors, nor government agencies, nor the public really consider fields like religious studies important. If they did, they would not tolerate such a lack of clearly defined and enforced standards. Only people who believe, at least subconsciously, that what they are doing and teaching has no real impact on daily life will tolerate such incompetence. Imagine a gas fitter, for example, being allowed to install a gas furnace without adequate ventilation. In a short time people would become ill and some might actually die. Therefore, the civic authorities insist on standards and on the need to inspect the workmanship. But in many academic fields, anything goes, which proves few people really take religious studies, and similar fields, such as history, seriously enough to care about what happens in it.

Yet the wars of the twenty-first century have shown beyond all doubt that an accurate knowledge of other cultures and religions is just as important as, perhaps more important than, ensuring that a heart surgeon is well trained. After all, the fraudulent surgeon is only going to kill a few dozen people before someone notices his or her incompetence. But, the ill-trained government adviser, politician, or journalist, who misinforms the public about the political implications of religious and cultural beliefs, has the power to condemn thousands of people to death through air strikes and a host of other indignities. Why, then, do we allow students, who may rise to important decision-making positions, to receive an inadequate education?

Clearly the only reason such a situation is tolerated is that most members of the public and many academics do not see the social implications of scholarship. If scholars really believe that in the course of an entire teaching career one of their graduates might become the chancellor of Germany, prime minister of Canada, or even president of the United States, surely they will be more careful about what they teach.

---

48. Smart, *Principles and Meaning*, 1.
49. Eric J. Sharpe, "The Compatibility of Theological and Religious Studies: Historical, Theoretical and Contemporary Perspectives," *Council of Societies for the Study of Religion Bulletin* 26, no. 3 (1997): 58.

If this sounds far-fetched, remember that Stephen Harper, the prime minister of Canada, is a graduate of the University of Calgary, where the author teaches. True, he did not take any religious studies courses, but he did study politics, economics, and a variety of other subjects. These studies left him with the distinct impression that his teachers in areas other than the more mathematical aspects of economics and political science were out of touch with everyday realities and played with theories without any concern for their social impact.[50] And he is probably correct in this conclusion. Therefore, it is legitimate to ask, What effect did the information, ideas, and experiences his professors imparted to him have on his thinking? And how does his education affect the lives of Canadians and many others, including people living in Afghanistan, today?

Another example is that of John Lee, who obtained his MA from the University of Manitoba, where he worked with the author, and his PhD from the University of Toronto in the mid–1980s. After completing his studies, he taught at a university in South Korea before becoming president of the Anglican University of Korea. Later he became a Korean senator and chairman of the South Korean Government Commission, which is charged with negotiating the future unification of the two Koreas. Just like Prime Minister Harper, Lee has helped shape the future of war and peace in Asia and perhaps the world. Surely, the things he learned, or failed to learn, when he studied in two Canadian religious studies departments are important and affect all of our lives.

The examples of these two men demonstrate the need for high standards in both research and teaching in all academic fields, not only in medicine or engineering.

Today most students have learned—indeed one might cynically reflect that university administrations encourage them to learn—to decry professors who, they believe, spend too much time on writing and research. Yet, short of instituting regular examinations and tests, or mandating compulsory upgrading of courses, all of which are impractical, the only guarantee that a student or the public can have that a professor continues to be productive and keep abreast of developments in their field is that they carry out their own research.

Yet research alone is insufficient. The results have to be made public so that they can be reviewed by peers and

Photo 27.6 During the Go-Fest Convention organized by Youth with a Mission in 1997, attendees were so moved by the reality of their situation, the injustices of apartheid, and the Bible's clear teachings about social justice that they spontaneously began to pray together, regardless of race, class, or color. This moving event shows the power of religion in shaping and reshaping social attitudes and why the study of religion can be an exciting and important topic that provides vivid insights into our world.

---

50. Conversation with Mr. Harper, February 2002.

anyone familiar with a field. Equally important is the publication of a graduate student's MA and PhD thesis, as happens for PhD theses in most European countries. Only if such theses are readily available to other scholars, and the public, is there any guarantee that a student has not fooled their examiners with fraudulent work. These things are self-evident in all other professions. Further, it is suggested that details of professors' careers, their curriculum vitae, and lists of publications are made available to the public, preferably through their publication on departmental websites. Students and all interested parties have a right to know what professors actually do and how they spend their time. Such steps should be taken to encourage good scholarship in an open academic environment. To that end, it is crucial that we begin a dialogue on how religious studies, and for that matter many other areas of study in the humanities and social sciences, can be rescued from constant criticism by outsiders, particularly anti-education journalists and politicians.

CONCLUSION

Ninian Smart was right to describe religious studies as an exciting field with great potential. His bold vision of a new multidisciplinary field inspired a whole generation of scholars and ought to inspire us all today. Where Smart erred was in the generosity of his understanding. A careful and gifted scholar who embraced the best in the liberal tradition, he naturally assumed that anyone embarking on a scholarly career would aspire to the highest ideals. To him, therefore, the sort of dilettantism feared by Harnack and the academic fraud that sometimes goes with it were all but unthinkable.

Harnack was also a great liberal, in the best sense of the word, whose theological liberalism was clearly tempered by the doctrine of original sin. However much he may have deviated from his pietistic upbringing or denied certain Christian traditions in theory, he retained a far more skeptical view of human nature than Smart. Therefore, he recognized the danger of removing traditional restraints on the activities of scholars, and he recognized the need to ensure that scholarship is rooted in the use of solid methods that can be checked and cross-checked by impartial observers.

Photo 27.7 The symbolism of two white doves of peace overlooking Lancaster University's Multi-Faith Chaplaincy Centre, which Ninian Smart helped design, is a fitting way to end a book on world religions. Although passionately interested in other religious traditions and a great practitioner of interreligious discussion and understanding, Smart was also a practicing Christian whose very real faith inspired all he wrote.

What remains for the next generation is to renew Smart's vision without the fatal flaw of an ill-defined multidisciplinary perspective. Here an interdisciplinary approach grounded in a limited number of distinct disciplines, one of them dominant but informed by a good grasp of a second and perhaps others, appears to offer the best hope for reforming religious studies and turning back the anything-goes attitude that prevails today.

Should this task appear too daunting, it is worth remembering that at the beginning of the nineteenth century, numerous universities, including those of Frankfurt/Oder and Wittenberg, were closed in Prussia because of their lax attitudes and low academic standards. Yet within a few years the University of Berlin was established, setting a standard for high-quality scholarship that changed the world. Today the university as an institution, not just the field of religious studies, is in crisis, yet all crises present new opportunities for reform and regeneration. This is that task that lies before us.

SUGGESTIONS FOR FURTHER READING

INTRODUCTION

Healthy academic disciplines are characterized by vigorous debate. Look up any reader in anthropology, history, psychology, sociology, or even zoology, and you will find conflicting theories and dissenting views. What is clear to one scholar is rubbish to another, and in academic journals people do not hesitate to criticize the folly of others. Indeed in some fields, such as history, entire libraries of books are devoted to such issues as problems in European civilization, presenting the student with a series of conflicting views that are expected to expose them to important academic debates with which any educated member of the profession ought to be familiar.

When one turns to religious studies, however, a very different picture emerges. With few exceptions, the writers of monographs and textbooks in religious studies are very nice people who want to give every possible viewpoint a fair hearing. Such liberality is commendable in situations of religious intolerance and dogmatism and was justified thirty-five years ago, when few Europeans or North Americans were familiar with religious traditions other than Christianity. At the time, against a background of a monopolistic Christianity, the need to develop sympathetic insight was essential.

But today we face a different situation. Many students know more about Buddhism than about Christianity, and even if they do not, they are certainly far more sympathetic to Eastern religions than they are to their own Western tradition. Therefore, the old liberal approach is obsolete. This bibliography aims to present controversial books which students might otherwise overlook. It is provided in the hope that it will provoke a stimulating academic debate.

INTERNET SOURCES

Resources for use with this book can be found at http://www.understandingworldreligions.com.

Many older texts may be found on J. B. Hare's excellent Internet Sacred Texts Archive: http://www.sacred-texts.com.

REFERENCE WORKS

The following are some standard dictionaries and encyclopedias on religion.

Crim, Keith, ed. *Abingdon Dictionary of Living Religions.* Nashville: Abingdon, 1981.

Eliade, Mircea, ed. *The Encyclopedia of Religion.* 16 vols. New York: Macmillan, 1987.

Gibb, H. A. R. *Encyclopedia of Islam.* Leiden: Brill, 1954.

Hastings, James, ed. *The Encyclopedia of Religion and Ethics.* 13 vols. Edinburgh: T&T Clark, 1908–1927.

Hexham, Irving. *Concise Dictionary of Religion.* Carol Stream, Ill.: InterVarsity Press, 1994.

Klostermaier, Klaus K. *A Concise Encyclopedia of Hinduism.* Oxford: Oneworld, 1998.

Malalasekara, Gunapala P. *Encyclopedia of Buddhism.* Colombo, Ceylon: Government Press, 1961.

McDonald, William J., ed. *New Catholic Encyclopedia.* 17 vols. New York: McGraw-Hill, 1967.

Roth, Cecil, and Geoffrey Wigoder, eds. *Encyclopaedia Judaica.* 16 vols. New York: Macmillan, 1972.

Walker, G. B. *Hindu World: An Encylopedic Survey of Hinduism.* New York: Praeger, 1968.

Zaehner, R. C., ed. *The Concise Encyclopedia of Living Faiths.* London: Hutchinson, 1959.

RESEARCHING WORLD RELIGIONS

Kippenberg, Hans G. *Discovering Religious History in the Modern Age.* Princeton: Princeton Univ. Press, 2002. An excellent introduction to the historical study of religion.

Popper, Karl R. *The Myth of the Framework: In Defence of Science and Rationality.* Edited by M. A. Notturno. London: Routledge, 1994. A valuable work that implicitly challenges many popular approaches to the study of religion.

Sharpe, Eric J. *Comparative Religion: A History.* La Salle, Ill.: Open Court, 1986.

Stone, Jon R. *The Craft of Religious Studies.* New York: Palgrave, 2000. This is one of the few texts that introduce various disciplinary approaches to the study of religion.

BASIC TEXTS—THE CLASSICS THAT OUGHT NOT TO BE FORGOTTEN

The following texts should be read by any student who wishes to master the field of religious studies. The list provided here is intended to introduce the reader to the field.

Basham, A. L. *The Wonder That Was India.* London: Collins, 1954. An essential and highly informative introduction to Indian religions and civilization.

Bauer, Yehuda *Rethinking the Holocaust.* New Haven: Yale Univ. Press, 2001. A refreshing survey of the current state of Holocaust scholarship, dispelling many popular myths and misunderstandings that trouble thinking Christians.

Bin Laden, Osama. *Messages to the World: The Statements of Osama Bin Laden.* Edited by Bruce Lawrence. Translated by James Howarth. New York: Verso, 2005. Too many people generalize about bin Laden and contemporary Islam. This book presents his views in his own words.

Candragomin. *Joy for the World: A Buddhist Play.* Translated by Michael Hahn. San Francisco, Calif.: Dharma, 1987. A delightful traditional Buddhist apologetic, translated by a scholar who is probably the leading Sanskritist in Germany.

Chaudhuri, Nirad C. *Hinduism: A Religion to Live By.* Delhi: Oxford Univ. Press, 1997. One of the best introductions to the religion of Hindus by a practitioner.

Conze, Edward *Buddhism: Its Essence and Development.* Oxford: Bruno Cassirer, 1957. No other work approaches Conze's genius for conveying the feel of Buddhism as well as the facts about the Buddhist tradition.

———. *Buddhist Thought in India.* London: Allen & Unwin, 1962. A much neglected work which Conze viewed as his greatest contribution to Buddhist studies.

Cook, Michael A. *The Qur'an: A Very Short Introduction.* Oxford: Oxford Univ. Press, 2000. The best introduction to the Qur'an for Western readers unfamiliar with Islam.

Cragg, Kenneth *The Event of the Qur'an: Islam in Its Scripture.* London: Allen & Unwin, 1971. A useful study which sets Islam firmly within its own scriptural tradition.

———. *The House of Islam.* Belmont, Calif.: Dickinson, 1969. A good popular introduction to Islam.

Earhart, H. Byron. *Japanese Religions: Unity and Diversity.* Belmont, Calif.: Dickinson, 1969. A good general survey.

Eliade, Mircea. *The Sacred and the Profane: The Nature of Religion.* New York: Harcourt, 1959. This book, like Eliade's many other works on mythology, does not show his vast scholarship at its best. Nevertheless, it ought to be read because your professors will want you to know about his ideas on the subject of myth.

———. *Yoga: Immortality and Freedom.* Translated by Willard R. Trask. London: Routledge, 1958. This is the classic introduction to Yoga. Critics may find fault, and some of the material may be outdated, but it is a must for anyone approaching the religions of India.

Gibb, H. A. R., and J. H. Kramers, eds. *Shorter Encyclopedia of Islam.* Leiden: Brill, 1953. An invaluable text for understanding Arabic concepts that shape Islamic theology. This is particularly important for anyone studying Islam, a religion that claims to be based on a sacred and untranslatable scripture.

Hopkins, Thomas J. *The Hindu Religious Tradition.* Belmont, Calif.: Dickinson, 1971. A good general introductory text.

Klostermaier, Klaus K. *Hindu Writings: A Short Introduction to the Major Sources.* Oxford: Oneworld, 2000. A valuable introduction to Hindu texts.

———. *Hinduism: A Short History.* Oxford: Oneworld, 2000. An excellent survey of modern views of the Hindu tradition and its development.

Moore, Charles A., and A. V. Morris, eds. *The Japanese Mind: Essentials of Japanese Philosophy and Culture.* Honolulu: East-West Center, 1967. A stimulating work which emphasizes the diversity of Japanese thought.

Nakamura, H. *Ways of Thinking of Eastern Peoples: India, China, Tibet, Japan.* Honolulu: East-West Center, 1964. A valuable introduction to non-Western ways of thought and action which provides an essential background to understanding religious behavior.

Poewe, Karla. *New Religions and the Nazis*. Oxford: Routledge, 2006. This disturbing work highlights the role of religious beliefs, liberal theology, and academics in the creation of German National Socialism.

Prebish, C. S., and D. Keown. *Buddhism: The eBook; An Online Introduction*. Providence, Utah: Journal of Buddhist Ethics Online Books, 2005. A fascinating text written by leading American Buddhists.

Qutb, Sayyid. *In the Shade of the Qur'an*. Edited and translated by Adil Salahi and Ashur Shamis. Leicester, U.K.: Islamic Foundation, 1999. This multivolume commentary on the Qur'an is now available in English and is indispensable for understanding how modern Muslims view their religion. Though disdained by some Western scholars, the work of Qutb is immensely popular in the Muslim world and among Muslim communities in the West.

———. *Milestones*. Indianapolis: American Trust Publications, 1990. First published 1964. Available online as a downloadable pdf file at http://majalla.org/books/2005/qutb-nilestone.pdf. This is arguably the foundation document of modern Islam.

Segal, Eliezer. *Introducing Judaism*. London: Routledge, 2009. Arguably the best introduction to Judaism available today.

———. *Why Didn't I Learn This in Hebrew School? Excursions through the Jewish Past and Present*. Northvale, N.J.: Jason Aronson, 1999. One of a series of popular books introducing Judaism for Jews who have lost their cultural roots. These books form a highly recommended and easily read guide to Judaism as a living religion.

Smart, Ninian. *Doctrine and Argument in Indian Philosophy*. London: Allen & Unwin, 1964. An excellent philosophical introduction to interreligious dialogue and understanding.

———. *Reasons and Faiths*. London: Routledge, 1958. A more popular version of *Doctrine and Argument*.

Smith, David Howard. *Chinese Religions*. London: Weidenfeld and Nicolson, 1968. This book is regarded by many as the best survey of Chinese religions available.

Spencer, Robert, ed. *The Myth of Islamic Tolerance: How Islamic Law Treats Non-Muslims*. Amherst, N.Y.: Prometheus, 2005. A highly disturbing book that deserves to be debated.

Van der Heyden, Ulrich, and Heike Liebau. Missionsgeschichte, Kirchengeschichte, Weltgeschichte: christliche Missionen im Kontext nationaler Entwicklungen in Afrika, Asien und Ozeanien [Mission History, Church History, World History: Christian Missions in the Context of National Development in Africa, Asia, and Oceania]. Missionsgeschichtliches Archiv. Bd. 1. Stuttgart: F. Steiner Verlag, 1996. The first of a series of excellent studies of Christian missions that overlap with the study of religion edited by Ulrich van der Heyden. What is remarkable about this and the subsequent books is that van der Heyden, the main editor, was educated in Communist East Germany, where he developed a thorough appreciation of Christian missions and the need to take them seriously intellectually. About half of the essays in this and the other books are in English.

Warraq, Ibn, ed. and trans. *The Quest for the Historical Muhammad*. Amherst, N.Y.: Prometheus, 2000. A challenging book of essays collected by a highly controversial writer.

———, ed. *The Origins of the Koran: Classic Essays on Islam's Holy Book*. Amherst, N.Y.: Prometheus, 1998. An important collection of historical essays compiled from various sources by an ex-Muslim and controversialist.

Welbourn, Fred B. *Atoms and Ancestors*. London: Edwin Arnold, 1968. The style of this short book easily misleads the uninitiated. Nevertheless, this is by far the best introduction to African religions.

———. *East African Rebels*. London: SCM Press, 1961. Essential reading for anyone who wants to understand interreligious contact, religious change, and the impact of missionaries on traditional religions.

Wiebe, Phillip H. *God and Other Spirits: Intimations of Transcendence in Christian Experience*. New York: Oxford Univ. Press, 2004. An important study of what are perhaps best called the primal dimensions of religious experience.

———. *Visions of Jesus: Direct Encounters from the New Testament to Today*. New York: Oxford University Press, 1997. A pioneering study of religious experience and the impact of visions on individuals.

Williams, Paul. *Buddhist Thought: A Complete Introduction to the Indian Tradition*. With contributions by Anthony Tribe. London: Routledge, 2000.

Zaehner, R. C., ed. *The Concise Encyclopedia of Living Faiths*. London: Hutchinson, 1959. An invaluable reference work with essays by leading scholars in all fields. First published in 1959, the book has gone through many editions and is still in print.

———. *Hinduism*. London: Oxford Univ. Press, 1968. An excellent, if philosophical, introduction to the religion we know as Hinduism.

CONTRARY WORKS

The following books present alternative points of view, and in one way or another should provoke thought and debate.

Davis, Winston. *Dojo: Magic and Exorcism in Modern Japan*. Stanford, Calif.: Stanford Univ. Press, 1980. A classic study of a new religion in Japan. Raises many problems of interpretation and questions about reliance on written texts.

Farmer, William R. *The Synoptic Problem*. London: Collier-Macmillan, 1964. Just as telling as Palmer's logical analysis is Farmer's introductory essay in this thought-provoking book, which deals with the social construction of the Synoptic Problem. A must for all students of the New Testament and anyone interested in the sociology of knowledge.

Greeley, Andrew M., and Michael Hout. *The Truth about Conservative Christians: What They Think and What They Believe*. Chicago: Univ. of Chicago Press, 2006. This book is a real eye-opener.

Kakar, Sudhir. *Shamans, Mystics and Doctors*. Boston: Beacon, 1982. Essential reading for anyone wanting to understand the social dynamics of Indian religion. A challenging and provocative book.

Kaufmann, Walter. *Critique of Religion and Philosophy*. London: Faber and Faber, 1958. This Princeton philosopher's work ought to be known by every religious studies student and read alongside other introductory texts. An iconoclast, of Jewish descent, he is a delight to anyone seeking a different perspective on religious issues. This book is a must for anyone interested in the philosophy of religion or biblical criticism. Kaufmann takes an uncomplimentary look at contemporary theological fads and makes some devastating criticisms.

———. *Religions in Four Dimensions: Existential and Aesthetic, Historical and Comparative.* New York: Reader's Digest Press, 1976. Instead of presenting the usual clone of other religious studies texts, Kaufmann has written a hard-hitting book which is highly critical of many religious traditions. Christian readers may have difficulty with some of his conclusions about Christianity, but, to be fair, he spares no one.

Koestler, Arthur. *The Lotus and the Robot.* London: Hutchinson, 1966. Don't mention this one to your Hinduism professor. Perhaps it's not the most reliable book on Indian religions. Nevertheless, it provokes thought and is worth reading for a view that is usually dismissed by academics.

Kramer, Martin S. *Ivory Towers on Sand: The Failure of Middle Eastern Studies in America.* Washington, D.C.: Washington Institute for Near East Policy. A contrarian work that questions much of modern scholarship in the area of Islamic studies.

Naipaul, V. S. *Among the Believers: An Islamic Journey.* Harmondsworth, U.K.: Penguin, 1981. A disquieting look at the Islamic world.

———. *India: A Wounded Civilization.* Harmondsworth, U.K.: Penguin, 1979. Like Koestler's work, this book is hated by many teachers of religious studies. Nevertheless, it presents a perspective which must be taken seriously.

Palmer, Humphrey. *The Logic of Gospel Criticism.* London: Macmillan, 1968. This book presents the reader with a logician's examination of the arguments used by biblical critics. The conclusions are devastating. No wonder it is ignored by biblical scholars, including many evangelicals.

Sankrityayan, Rahul, et al. *Buddhism: The Marxist Approach.* New Delhi: People's Publishing House, 1970. A very different and thought-provoking approach to Buddhism.

Sedgwick, Mark J. *Against the Modern World: Traditionalism and the Secret Intellectual History of the Twentieth Century.* Oxford: Oxford Univ. Press, 2004. A fascinating history of one of the intellectual currents that helped create modern religious studies.

Stark, Rodney. The Rise of Christianity: How the Obscure, Marginal Jesus Movement Became the Dominant Religious Force in the Western World in a Few Centuries. San Francisco: Harper, 1997. A challenge to rethink Christian origins by one of America's leading sociologists of religion.

Warraq, Ibn. *Why I Am Not a Muslim.* Amherst, N.Y.: Prometheus, 1995. A highly controversial work by an ex-Muslim who raises numerous objections to both Islam and popular perceptions of Islam.

SOME CHRISTIAN RESPONSES TO OTHER RELIGIOUS TRADITIONS

The following books offer a variety of Christian perspectives on religion and religions.

Bavinck, Herman. *The Philosophy of Revelation.* Grand Rapids: Baker, 1979. Another theological work with important implications for the study of religion, written in 1909 by Abraham Kuyper's colleague Herman Bavinck. Though dated, it is still a valuable resource for the Christian student.

Bavinck, Johan Herman. *The Church between Temple and Mosque*. Grand Rapids: Eerdmans, n.d. A stimulating and orthodox Christian attempt to interpret the reality of religious pluralism.

Benedict XVI. *Truth and Tolerance: Christian Belief and World Religions*. Translated by Henry Taylor. San Francisco: Ignatius, 2004. First published in German in 2003. Probably the most intelligent and well-argued book on the challenge of pluralism facing Christians today, written by the current pope.

Berkouwer, G. C. *General Revelation*. Grand Rapids: Eerdmans, 1955. This should be read alongside Berkouwer's book on theological anthropology (1962). It deals with biblical approaches to revelation outside the Bible.

———. *Man: The Image of God*. Grand Rapids: Eerdmans, 1962. Essential background thinking for a Christian interpretation of other religious traditions.

Callaway, Tucker N. *Zen Way–Jesus Way*. Tokyo: Tuttle, 1976. A remarkable book by a Southern Baptist missionary.

Carson, D. A. *The Gagging of God: Christianity Confronts Pluralism*. Grand Rapids: Zondervan, 1996. A strong defense of Christian uniqueness.

Cragg, Kenneth. *The Christ and the Faiths*. Philadelphia: Westminster, 1986. A modern Christian approach to other religious traditions.

Dawson, Christopher. *Religion and World History: A Selection from the Works of Christopher Dawson*. Edited by James Oliver and Christina Scott. New York: Image Books, 1973. An excellent introduction to religious history by an insightful Roman Catholic historian. This book is well worth reading.

Freeman, David Hugh, and David Freeman. *A Philosophical Study of Religion*. Nutley, N.J.: Craig, 1964. Written from a Reformed Christian viewpoint, this work raises many issues normally overlooked by more liberal scholars. It is therefore a good complement to Kaufmann's works.

Holmes, Arthur F. *Contours of a World View*. Grand Rapids: Eerdmans, 1983. It is important for Christians to have a broad vision of their own religion as well as of other traditions. This text provides such a vision and helps the reader find other sources of information on Christianity.

Hogg, Alfred George. *Karma and Redemption: An Essay toward the Interpretation of Hinduism and the Re-statement of Christianity*. Madras, India: Christian Literature Society, 1970. An old classic that bears rediscovery.

Kraemer, Hendrik. *Religion and the Christian Faith*. London: Lutterworth, 1956. An excellent survey of Christian approaches to non-Christian religions by an outstanding Dutch scholar.

———. *World Cultures and World Religions*. London: Lutterworth, 1960. A valuable work which places the study of religion within its social context.

Kuyper, Abraham. *Lectures on Calvinism*. Grand Rapids: Eerdmans, 1968. First published in 1931, and originally the text of a series of lectures delivered at Princeton University in

1898, these essays provide a framework within which Christian students can begin to tackle the immense problems of religious diversity and cultural pluralism.

———. *Principles of Sacred Theology*. Grand Rapids: Eerdmans, 1968. Although it is a theology text, many parts of this work apply to issues in religious studies, especially Kuyper's stimulating discussion about the meaning of "faith."

Lecerf, Auguste. *An Introduction to Reformed Dogmatics*. Grand Rapids: Baker, 1981. A French Calvinist's approach to the study of religion and theology which has stimulating discussions of Émile Durkheim and various other figures whose work affects our thinking about the nature of religion.

McDermott, Gerald R. *Jonathan Edwards Confronts the Gods: Christian Theology, Enlightenment Religion, and Non-Christian Faiths*. New York: Oxford Univ. Press, 2000. A must-read for anyone interested in knowing how an earlier generation of Christians approached the challenge of world religions.

Muck, Terry and Frances S. Adeney. *Christianity Encountering World Religions: The Practice of Mission in the Twenty-first Century*. Grand Rapids: Baker Academic, 2009. A fresh look at Christian encounters with non-Christian religions.

Newbigin, Lesslie. *The Gospel in a Pluralist Society*. London: SPCK, 1989. A classic discussion of the challenge of pluralism for Christians.

Orr, James. *The Christian View of God and the World*. Grand Rapids: Eerdmans, 1948. Though somewhat dated (1891), this work has many discussions—particularly those found in the extended footnotes—that apply directly to issues in religious studies.

Sharpe, Eric J. *Faith Meets Faith: Some Christian Attitudes to Hinduism in the Nineteenth and Twentieth Centuries*. London: SCM Press, 1977. A very useful survey which sets interreligious discussion in its historical context.

———. *Not to Destroy but to Fulfill: The Contribution of J. N. Farquhar to Protestant Missionary Thought in India before 1914*. Uppsala: Swedish Institute of Missionary Research, 1965. A valuable, in-depth study of one missionary's interaction with Hinduism.

Tennent, Timothy C. *Christianity at the Religious Roundtable: Evangelicalism in Conversation with Hinduism, Buddhism, and Islam*. Grand Rapids: Baker Academic, 2002.

Verkuyl, Johannes. *Contemporary Missiology*. Grand Rapids: Eerdmans, 1978. The value of this book lies in the wide range of topics it covers.

Williams, Paul. *The Unexpected Way: On Converting from Buddhism to Catholicism*. Edinburgh: T&T Clark, 2002. A Christian critique of Buddhism by a recent convert who was a practicing Buddhist for many years and is a leading scholar of Buddhism.

Yong, Amos. *Beyond the Impasse: Toward a Pneumatological Theology of Religions*. Grand Rapids: Baker Academic; Carlisle, Cumbria, U.K.: Paternoster, 2003. A uniquely Pentecostal approach to the issue of world religions and interreligious dialogue.

SCHOLARLY JOURNALS

For writing essays, one way the serious student gains command of their field is through using scholarly journals in addition to recommended books. In journals one finds the latest thinking in an area and many ideas which can take years to find their ways into books. The following journals will provide a basic introduction to this field.

Faith and Philosophy. An excellent Christian publication which often carries articles related to religious studies.

History of Religions. A good American journal with an emphasis on history and comparative studies.

Journal for the Scientific Study of Religion. Another excellent, if quantitative, sociological journal.

Journal of Contemporary Religion. A British journal that concentrates on new religious movements.

The Journal of Religion. One of the best American religious studies journals.

Journal of Religion in Africa. The major journal in this little-developed but important field.

The Journal of Religious Ethics. A useful comparative journal concentrating on ethical systems.

Journal of the American Academy of Religion. An important journal published by the leading American academic society in this field.

Man. This anthropological journal often has articles of a religious nature and is well worth looking at regularly.

Missionalia. A unique publication from the University of South Africa which, though intended for people interested in Christian missions, abstracts a large number of journal articles in religious studies and related fields. Very useful.

Nova Religio. The leading American journal for the study of new religions and new religious movements.

Numen. The journal of the International Association for the History of Religions. Very important.

Philosophy East and West. Important as a source for philosophical articles of a comparative nature.

Religion. The best British and probably the best all-around journal in religious studies.

Religious Studies Review. This excellent quarterly journal reviews current books in religious studies and related fields. Any serious student of religion ought to refer to it regularly.

The Skeptical Inquirer. Not strictly a religious studies journal, but rather, as the name suggests, a publication intended to debunk irrationalism. It is especially useful with regard to the apologetic claims of new religious movements and the New Age movement.

Sociology of Religion. The name speaks for itself. It tends toward qualitative research.

Studies in Religion. An excellent Canadian journal which presents a broad perspective in religious studies.

CREDITS

All of the maps were provided by Zondervan. The diagrams were created by Irving and Jeremy Hexham. Unless otherwise stated, all of the photographs were taken by Irving Hexham, Jeremy Hexham, or Karla Poewe. Where photographs and other illustrations are in the public domain, their source is clearly stated. All other photographs and pictures are appropriately credited. Special thanks go to Omar Kahn and the Harappa Bazaar (found on the internet at www.harappa.com) for helping me obtain pictures of the Indus Valley Civilization and India, and to Sandhya Mehta of the Mani Bhavan Gandhi Sangrahalaya, Gandhi Archive (found on the internet at www.gandhi-manibhavan.org), who provided me with pictures of Mahatma Gandhi. Caleb Nienkirchen is also to be thanked for some Indian photos. The staff at the German company Directmedia, who produce numerous excellent texts and collections of pictures on CD and DVD in their Digitale Bibliothek and Yorck Project *Meisterwerke* series, deserve special thanks for allowing me to reproduce various pictures. Although non-German-speaking people may find the CDs hard to work with, anyone who has a smattering of German and is interested in art is encouraged to explore their website, where their art CDs are offered at a very reasonable price. They are found on the internet at http://www.digitale-bibliothek.de or www.yorckproject.de. Other CDs available from this excellent German company in the *Digitale Bibliothek* series include the complete works of such important figures as Kant, all on searchable disks. I must also thank Ms. Jutta Kirsch for helping me obtain permission to use pictures from Directmedia's CDs.

All of the following people, and many others, gave me invaluable assistance in seeking suitable pictures for this book. Each of them deserves a mention and thanks: Daniel Scott-Davies, at the Archive & Heritage Manager of the the Scout Association of Great Britain; Mary Bergin-Cartwright and Ben Kennedy at the Oxford University Press; Gabrielle White at Random House; Stewart Wicker at the South American Missionary Society; Janet Kerschner, the Archivist for the Theosophical Society in America; Norbert Ludwig at the Berlin Museum; Dan Wright at Ares Publishing; Betsy Kohut, of the Freer Gallery of Art and Arthur M. Sackler Gallery; the Smithsonian Institution; Terren Wein, at the University of Chicago Divinity School; Ruth Tonkiss Cameron, Archivist for Union Theological Seminary & Burke Library Collections; and Gary Berton at the Tom Paine National Historical Association. I thank Peggy Ford Waldo of the Greeley Museum for her valuable help obtaining photographs of Sayyid Qutb. Judy P. Zhao and Saundra Lipton at the University of Calgary should not be forgotten. Thanks also need to go to impersonal sources like Project Gutenberg and the Internet Archive, which provide excellent textual sources that are in the public domain. Finally, I must thank Kim Tanner at Zondervan for her excellent help and advice. Hopefully this list includes everyone. If not, I sincerely apologize for my oversight.

CHAPTER 1: INTRODUCTORY ISSUES IN THE STUDY OF RELIGION

Photo 1.1 Buddhist temple. Photo 1.2 Max Müller. Georgina Adelaide Müller, *The Life and Letters of Max Müller* (London: Longmans, Green, 1902), in the public domain. Photo 1.3 Ninian Smart. Photo 1.4 Mircea Eliade. Romanian stamp in the public domain. Photo 1.5 Mircea Eliade. University of Chicago Divinity School. Photo 1.6 Paul Tillich. © Union Theological Seminary. Courtesy of Union Theological Seminary and the Burke Library collections. Photo 1.7 Fred Welbourn. © Hebe Welbourn. Photo 1.8 Herman Dooyeweerd, portrait by M. Verbrugge. © Dooyeweerd Centre for Christian Philosophy. Photo 1.9 Karl Marx and Friedrich Engels. Photo 1.10 Rodney Stark. © Rodney Stark.

CHAPTER 2: A BIASED CANON

Photo 2.1 Herbert Spencer. University of Texas portrait archive. Photo 2.2 Ethiopian Christian dancers. Mansfield Parkyns, *Life in Abyssinia* (London: J. Murray, 1853). Photo 2.3 Coptic ikon. Photo 2.4 Hindu temple. Photo 2.5 African Sacrifice. © Hennie Pretorius. Photo 2.6 Londa Shembe. Photo 2.7 St. Maurice. Photo 2.8 Voltaire. University of Texas portrait archive. Photo 2.9 David Hume. Photo 2.10 Hegel. Photo 2.11 World Congress of Religion. Photo 2.12 African healer. © Hennie Pretorius.

CHAPTER 3: AFRICAN RELIGIOUS TRADITIONS

Photo 3.1 *The Monk by the Sea*. Digitale Biblioteck. Photo 3.2 Zulu diviner. Photo 3.3 Traditional African life. Photo 3.4 Traditional African life II. Photo 3.5 Estelle Nxele. Photo 3.6 Émile Durkheim. Wikimedia Commons. Photo 3.7 Xhosa man and wife. Photo 3.8 *News World* newspaper. Photo 3.9 Baptism ceremony. Photo 3.10 Computer screen. Photo 3.11 Marley's ghost. Charles Dickens, *A Christmas Carol* (London: Chapman & Hall, 1843). Photo 3.12 African patient.

CHAPTER 4: WITCHCRAFT AND SORCERY

Photo 4.1 Traditional healer. Photo 4.2 South African Police Museum picture of a victim of witchcraft, photographed by Irving Hexham, 1987. Photo 4.3 A traditional Zulu. Henry Callaway, *The Religious System of the Amazulu* (Springvale, Natal, South Africa: J. A. Blair; London: Trübner, 1870). Photo 4.4 Traditional prophetess. Callaway, *Religious System of the Amazulu*. Photo 4.5 Christian prayer group. Photo 4.6 Ritual cure. © Hans-Jürgen Becken. Photo 4.7 Sick woman's companion. © Hans-Jürgen Becken. Photo 4.8 Healing dance. Photo 4.9 The dark side of traditional healing. Callaway, *Religious System of the Amazulu*. Photo 4.10 Reading the signs. © Hans-Jürgen Becken. Photo 4.11 Estelle Nxele in her consulting room. Photo 4.12 Dr. Hans-Jürgen Becken with two traditional healers.

© Hans-Jürgen Becken. Photo 4.13 Two traditional healers search for herbs in the forest. © Hans-Jürgen Becken.

CHAPTER 5: GOD IN ZULU RELIGION

Photo 5.1 British Anti-Slavery Society leaflet. Photo of original leaflet is in the office of Fred B. Welbourn. Photo 5.2 The Tugela River. Photo 5.3 Henry Callaway. From Marian S. Benham, *Henry Callaway, M.D., D.D., First Bishop of Kaffaria: His Life-History and Work; A Memoir* (London: Macmillan, 1896). Photo 5.4 The African plow. Photo 5.5 The Great Dance at Embellybelli. Allen Gardiner, *Narrative of a Journey to the Zoolu Country in South Africa* (London: William Crofts, 1836). Photo 5.6 Baptism as exorcism. Photo 5.7 Captain Allen Gardiner. South American Missionary Society. Used with permission. Photo 5.8 The Great Zulu king Shaka or Chaka. Potchefstroom University Archives. Used with permission. Photo 5.9 Initiation rites. Photo 5.10 Initiates leaving behind the initiation lodge. Photo 5.11 Burning the initiation lodge. Photo 5.12 Mariannhill Mission. Photo 5.13 Ekuphakameni. Photo 5.14 Professor Oosthuizen interviewing.

CHAPTER 6: THE CASE OF ISAIAH SHEMBE

Photo 6.1 Prayer counselor. Photo 6.2 Isaiah Shembe. Photo 6.3 John Buchan. National Archives of Canada. In the public domain. Photo 6.4 Fred Welbourn with the founder of the African Israel Church Nineveh. © Hebe Welbourn. Photo 6.5 Anthropologist Karla Poewe interviewing the Right Reverend Londa Shembe. Photo 6.6 AmaNazarite worship service in a South African shack area. Photo 6.7 Waiting to hear a sermon by Bishop Amos. Photo 6.8 The Reverend Petrus Dhlomo. Photo 6.9 Team of amaNazarites who collected the oral histories of their tradition. Photo 6.10 Bishop Johannes Galilee Shembe. © Hans-Jürgen Becken. Photo 6.11 The Right Reverend Londa Shembe and Irving Hexham. Photo 6.12 Bishop Amos Shembe. Photo 6.13 The followers of Bishop Amos Shembe dancing. Photo 6.14 Group of dancers belonging to the Right Reverend Londa Shembe's group. Photo 6.15 Young children wearing the traditional dancing attire of the amaNazarites. Photo 6.16 First volume of the amaNazarite oral histories.

CHAPTER 7: THE ORIGINS OF YOGIC RELIGIONS

Photo 7.1 Indus Valley site. Courtesy of the Harappa Bazaar. Photo 7.2 Indian holy man. Francis Younghusband, *Kashmir* (London: A. & C. Black, 1917). Reproduced with permission. Photo 7.3 Punjab fort. Lord Robert Baden-Powell, *Indian Memories* (London: Herbert Jenkins, 1915). Courtesy of the Scouting Association of the United Kingdom. Photo 7.4 Grave of an adult man from Harappa. Harappa Bazaar. Photo 7.5 The "Narrative seal" from Mohenjo-daro. Harappa Bazaar. Photo 7.6 Yoga Seal. Harappa Bazaar. Photo 7.7 The "Great Bath" at Mohenjo-daro. Harappa Bazaar. Photo 7.8 Priest King. Harappa Bazaar. Photo 7.9 Great bath at Madura. R. C. Dutt, *History of India* (London: Grolier Society, 1906). Photo 7.10 Ancient Indian reliquary. Vincent Smith, *Early History of India* (Oxford: Oxford Univ. Press, 1914); Mortimer Menpes, *India* (London: A. & C. Black, 1905). Photo 7.11 Potter with his pots. Smith, *Early History of India*; Menpes, *India*.

CHAPTER 8: THE RICHNESS OF THE HINDU TRADITION

Photo 8.1 *The Sacred Books of the East*. Photo 8.2 Oxen seal. Harappa Bazaar. Photo 8.3 The figure of Krishna. Harappa Bazaar. Photo 8.4 Small shrine in a Pietermaritzburg temple complex. Photo 8.5 Aryan horse sacrifice. Romesh Chunder Dutt and A. V. Williams Jackson, eds., *History of India*, vol. 1 (London: Grolier Society, 1906). Photo 8.6 Hindu Temple. Lord Robert Baden-Powell, *Indian Memories* (London: Herbert Jenkins, 1915). Scouting Association of Great Britain. Photo 8.7 Deities in a North American Hindu temple. Photo 8.8 Hindus sacrifice in North America. Photo 8.9 Bathing in Benares. Mortimer Menpes, *India* (London: A. & C. Black, 1905). Photo 8.10 Water ceremony on the Ganges. Menpes, *India*. Photo 8.11 South African Ramakrishna mission. Photo 8.12 Hare Krishnas in San Francisco.

CHAPTER 9: RETHINKING THE HINDU TRADITION

Photo 9.1 Alexander the Great. Vincent Arthur Smith, *The Early History of India: From 600 BC to the Muhammadan Conquest* (Oxford: Clarendon, 1914). Photo 9.2 Hindu sacrifice. C. P. Cape, *Benares* (London: Robert Culley, 1910). Photo 9.3 Martand Temple of the Sun. Sir Richard Temple, *Journals Kept in Hyderabad, Kashmir, Sikkim and Nepal* (London: W. H. Allen, 1887). Photo 9.4 Goddess Yaksi. Otto Fischer, *Die Kunst Indiens, Chinas und Japans* (Berlin: Propyläen-Verlag, 1928). Photo 9.5 Sculpture of a Naga king. Fischer, *Die Kunst*. Photo 9.6 Pickup truck blessed by a priest. Photo 9.7 Scene from the Bhagavad Gita. Freer Gallery of Art, Smithsonian Institution, Washington, D.C.; Gift of Charles Lang Freer, F1907.627 fol. 1. Photo 9.8 and Photo 9.9 The sacred lingam and yoni. Photo 9.10 Ram Mohan Roy. Photo 9.11 Suttee (sati). Robert W. Frazer, *British India* (London: T. Fisher Unwin, 1896). Photo 9.12 Modern Hindu temple in a large western city in North America. Photo 9.13 The stunningly beautiful Hare Krishna temple outside Durban, South Africa.

CHAPTER 10: GANDHI THE GREAT CONTRARIAN

Photo 10.1 The young Gandhi. Gandhi Archive. Photo 10.2 Rudyard Kipling. Francis Miltoun, *Kiplingiana: Biographical and Bibliographical Notes anent Rudyard Kipling* (New York: Mansfield and Wessels, 1899). Photo 10.3 Gandhi outside his law office. Gandhi Archive. Photo 10.4 Victoria Station in Bombay (now called Chhatrapati Shivaji Terminus). Alfred Comyn Lyall, *History of India*, vol. 8, ed. A. V. Williams Jackson (London: Grolier Society, 1907). Photo 10.5 Gandhi and Jinnah. Courtesy of the Gandhi Archive. Photo 10.6 "The Massacre at Cawpur." Lyall, *History of India*, vol. 8. Photo 10.7 Christian mission. John Peter Jones, *India's Problem: Krishna or Christ* (New York: Revell, 1903). Photo 10.8 Grave of John Bunyan. Photo 10.9 Count Lev (aka Leo) Nikolayevich Tolstoy. Russian book published in Moscow in 1911. Photo 10.10 Gandhi at his famous spinning wheel. Gandhi Archive. Picture provided by Ms. Sandhya Mehta. Photo 10.11 Gandhi with the Theosophical leader Annie Besant. Gandhi Archive.

CHAPTER 11: BUDDHISM

Photo 11.1 Sir Edwin Arnold. Edwin Arnold, *The Light of Asia* (Philadelphia: Henry Altemus, 1879). Photo 11.2 *The Light of Asia*. Arnold, *Light of Asia*. Photo 11.3 Bamiyan Buddha. Harappa Bazaar. Photo 11.4 Likr Buddha. Harappa Bazaar. Photo 11.5 The column of King Ashoka. Vincent A. Smith, *History of India*, vol. 2, ed. A. V. Williams Jackson (London: Grolier Society, 1906). Photo 11.6 Ancient statue of the Buddha. Otto Fischer, *Die Kunst Indiens, Chinas und Japans* (Berlin: Propyläen-Verlag, 1928). Photo 11.7 Modern representation of the Buddha on the altar of the Buddhist Centre in Möhra. Photo 11.8 *Tibetan Tripitaka*. Photo 11.9 Ancient Buddhist stupa. A. V. Williams Jackson, *History of India*, vol. 9, ed. A. V. Williams Jackson (London: Grolier Society, 1906). Photo 11.10 West coast North American Buddhist temple. Photo 11.11 Berlin's Buddha House. Photo 11.12 Buddha statue in the quiet garden of Berlin's Buddha House. Photo 11.13 Buddha House library. Photo 11.14 North American Buddhist temple. Photo 11.15 North American household shrine. Photo 11.16 The same shrine in the context of the living room where it is housed.

CHAPTER 12: THE DEVELOPMENT OF BUDDHIST BELIEF AND PRACTICE

Photo 12.1 Chinese Buddhist monastery in the nineteenth century. Emily G. Kemp, *The Face of China* (London: Chatto & Windus, 1909). Photo 12.2 Buddhist group in a large North American city. Photo 12.3 Buddha statues for sale. Photo 12.4 Current Tibetan Dalai Lama. Photo 12.5 Dalai Lama at Brandenburg Gate. Photo 12.6 The Girnar Rock. E. J. Rapson, *Ancient India* (Cambridge: Cambridge Univ. Press, 1914). Photo 12.7 A group of North American academics at a Buddhist center. Photo 12.8 Small personal shrine. Photo 12.9 Entrance to North American Buddhist temple. Photo 12.10 Chinese Buddhist pagoda. Kemp, *Face of China*. Photo 12.11 Inscription of Ashoka. Rapson, *Ancient India*. Photo 12.12 Nineteenth-century Buddhist monastery in China. Kemp, *Face of China*. Photo 12.13 A Buddhist priest delivers a homily. Photo 12.14 Buddhist school.

CHAPTER 13: THE MORAL QUEST OF EDWARD CONZE

Photo 13.1 Professor Conze. Courtesy of Herbert Elbrecht. Photo 13.2 Trafalgar Square. Photo 13.3 The Berlin Dom. Photo 13.4 Kathy Kolwitz war memorial. Magdeburg Dom. Photo 13.5 A street in central Hamburg. Photo 13.6 Topography of Terror Exhibition. Photo 13.7 Topography of Terror exhibit. Photo 13.8 Sachsenhausen. Photo 13.9 English woods. Photo 13.10 Glastonbury Tor. Photo 13.11 Ruins of St. Nicholas Church in Hamburg. Photo 13.12 Lancaster University. Photo 13.13 A statue of the Protestant Reformer Martin Luther. Photo 13.14 Astrological chart for Annie Besant.

CHAPTER 14: OTHER YOGIC-TYPE TRADITIONS

Photo 14.1 Tiger Gate in the Jain city of Palitana. Alfred Comyn Lyall, *History of India*, vol. 8, ed. A. V. Williams Jackson (London: Grolier Society, 1907; reprint, New York: Cosimo, 2008). Photo 14.2 Jain temple at Mount Abu-Dilwara. Lyall, *History of India*, vol. 8. Photo 14.3 Modern Jain temple in a midwestern North American city. Photo 14.4 Inside the Jain temple. Photo 14.5 Tower of Silence. Lyall, *History of India*, vol. 8. Photo 14.6 Holy mountain of Tai Shan. Emily G. Kemp, *The Face of China* (London: Chatto & Windus, 1909). Photo

14.7 The tomb of Confucius. Frank Brinkley, *China: Its History, Arts, and Literature* (Boston: J. B. Millet, 1902). Photo 14.8 Ancestral shrine. Kemp, *Face of China*. Photo 14.9 Confucian temple. Kemp, *Face of China*. Photo 14.10 The Golden Temple in Amritsar. Flora Annie Steel, Flora Annie Webster Steel, Mortimer Menpes, *India* (London, A. & C. Black, 1905). Photo 14.11 Modern Sikh temple in western North America. Photo 14.12 Ceremonial shields. Photo 14.13 Sikh wedding. Photo 14.14 Sikh wedding meal.

CHAPTER 15: EARLY JUDAISM

Photo 15.1 Jewish scriptures. Isidore Singer, *The Jewish Encyclopedia* (New York: Funk & Wagnalls, 1901 – 1906). Photo 15.2 African tapestry. Photo 15.3 Egyptian pharaoh. Anton Springer, *Handbuch der Kunstgeschichte* (Leipzig: Seemann, 1904). Photo 15.4 Hebrew slaves. John Wright, *A History of All Nations* (Philadelphia: Lea Brothers, 1905). Photo 15.5 Pharaoh Ramses. Springer, *Handbuch der Kunstgeschichte*. Photo 15.6 Lucas Cranch, *Crossing of the Red Sea*. Digitale Dibliothek, Yourk Project, *Meisterwerke*. Photo 15.7 Valley of Jericho, Richard Temple, *Palestine Illustrated* (London: Allen, 1888). Photo 15.8 *King Solomon*. Digitale Dibliothek, Yourk Project, *Mesiterwerke*. 15.9 *Nehemiah*, Digitale Dibliothek, Yourk Project, *Meisterwerke*. Photo 15.10 Emperor Claudius and General Vespasian. Richard Delbrück, *Bildnisse römischer Kaiser* (Berlin: Julius Bard, 1914). Photo 15.11 Mount Masada. Singer, *Jewish Encyclopedia*. Photo 15.12 Jewish captives. Singer, *Jewish Encyclopedia*. Photo 15.13 Ruins of the Kafr Bir'im. Singer, *Jewish Encyclopedia*. Photo 15.14 The Ark of the Law. Singer, *Jewish Encyclopedia*. Photo 15.15 Nineteenth-century impression of Jerusalem temple. Richard Temple, *Palestine Illustrated* (London: W. H. Allen, 1888).

CHAPTER 16: RABBINIC AND OTHER JUDAISMS

Photo 16.1 Traditional Jewish betrothal contract. Isidore Singer, *The Jewish Encyclopedia* (New York: Funk & Wagnalls, 1901 – 1906). Photo 16.2 Eighteenth-century Sephardic Jews. Singer, *Jewish Encyclopedia*. Photo 16.3 Jew arrested and burned at the stake. Photo 16.4 Clifford's Tower. Singer, *Jewish Encyclopedia*. Photo 16.5 Sabbatai Zevi. Singer, *Jewish Encyclopedia*. Photo 16.6 Oliver Cromwell. Photo 16.7 Menasseh ben Israel. Photo 16.8 Baruch Spinoza. Singer, *Jewish Encyclopedia*. Photo 16.9 Moses Mendelssohn's grave. Photo 16.10 Moses Mendelssohn. Photo 16.11 Felix Mendelssohn-Bartholdy (1809 – 1847). Singer, *Jewish Encyclopedia*. Photo 16.12 Jews' distinctive forms of dress. Singer, *Jewish Encyclopedia*. Photo 16.13 Captain Alfred Dreyfus. Singer, *Jewish Encyclopedia*. Photo 16.14 Jewish agricultural settlement. Singer, *Jewish Encyclopedia*. Photo 16.15 General Erich Ludendorff. Photo 16.16 The grim entrance to Sachsenhausen concentration camp. Photo 16.17 Budapest's Holocaust memorial.

CHAPTER 17: JEWISH FAITH AND PRACTICE

Photo 17.1 Manuscript of Maimonides. Isidore Singer, *The Jewish Encyclopedia* (New York: Funk & Wagnalls, 1901 – 1906). Photo 17.2 The Sefirot. Singer, *Jewish Encyclopedia*. Photo 17.3 Christian and Jewish scholars disputing. Singer, *Jewish Encyclopedia*. Photo 17.4 Rabbi Gamaliel instructing his students. Singer, *Jewish Encyclopedia*. Photo 17.5 Traditional penance. Singer, *Jewish Encyclopedia*. Photo 17.6 Ritual observance. John H. Adeney, *The Jews of Eastern Europe* (London: Central Board of Missions & Society for Promoting Christian Knowledge, 1921). Photo 17.7 Ancient boundary. Singer, *Jewish Encyclopedia*. Photo 17.8 Jewish lawyers argue the pros and cons of a divorce case. Singer, *Jewish Encyclopedia*. Photo 17.9 Amulets. Singer, *Jewish Encyclopedia*. Photo 17.10 Medieval Jews prepare the *matzot*. Singer, *Jewish Encyclopedia*. Photo 17.11 Erfurt's "Small Synagogue." Photo 17.12 Synagogue in Erfurt. Photo 17.13 Entrance to the ancient ritual bath. Photo 17.14 Feast of Tabernacles. Singer, *Jewish Encyclopedia*. Photo 17.15 Small prairie synagogue. Photo 17.16 Inside the pioneer synagogue. Photo 17.17 Bar Mitzvah. Singer, *Jewish Encyclopedia*.

CHAPTER 18: MARTIN BUBER'S ZIONIST SPIRITUALITY

Photo 18.1 Galicia religious festivals. Isidore Singer, *The Jewish Encyclopedia* (New York: Funk & Wagnalls, 1901–1906). Photo 18.2 The Second World Jewish Congress. Singer, *Jewish Encyclopedia*. Photo 18.3 The Mozart monument in Vienna. Photo 18.4 Henriette Hertz. Singer, *Jewish Encyclopedia*. Photo 18.5 Immanuel Kant. Eduard Engel, *Geschichte der deutschen Literatur von den Anfängen bis in die Gegenwart* (Leipzig: Koehler & Amelang, 1929). Photo 18.6 George Eliot. J. W. Cross, *George Eliot's Life* (London: William Blackwood and Sons, 1885). Photo 18.7 Friedrich Nietzsche. Elizabeth Förster-Nietzsche, *Wagner und Nietzsche* (München: Georg Müller, 1928). Photo 18.8 Martin Buber. Courtesy of the *Deutschen Literaturarchiv*, Marbach, Germany.

CHAPTER 19: CHRISTIANITY

Photo 19.1 Medieval Maddona. Anton Springer, *Handbuch der Kunstgeschichte* (Leipzig: Seemann, 1904). Photo 19.2 Thomas Paine. Thomas Paine, *The Life and Works of Thomas Paine*, ed. William M. Van der Weyde (New Rochelle, N.Y.: Thomas Paine National Historical Association, 1925). Photo 19.3 Johann Gottfried von Herder. Eduard Engel, *Geschichte der deutschen Literatur von den Anfängen bis in die Gegenwart* (Leipzig: Koehler & Amelang, 1929). Photo 19.4 The death of Jesus, from *The Rabbula Gospels*. Digitale Bibliothek. Photo 19.5 Rembrandt van Rijn's Homer. Digitale Bibliothek. Photo 19.6 Pietro Perugino's (1445–1523) fresco of Jesus giving Peter the key to heaven. Digitale Bibliothek. Photo 19.7 Giovanni Battista Cima da Conegliano's (1459–1517) *Presentation of the Baby Jesus at the Temple*. Charles Herbermann, ed., *The Catholic Encyclopaedia* (New York: Encyclopaedia Press, 1911). Photo 19.8 Adam and Eve's expulsion from paradise. Springer, *Handbuch der Kunstgeschichte*. Photo 19.9 God's covenant with Noah, by Anton Koch. Digitale Bibliothek. Photo 19.10 The Annunciation. P. L. Jacob, *The Arts of the Middle Ages and Renaissance Period* (London: Chapman and Hall, 1870). Photo 19.11 *The Resurrection of Christ*, by the Master of Hohenfurth. Digitale Bibliothek.

CHAPTER 20: CHRISTIAN HISTORY

Photo 20.1 *The Triumph of Constantine*. Digitale Bibliothek. Photo 20.2 Jesus in glory. Photo 20.3 Bethlehem. Richard Temple, *Palestine Illustrated* (London: W. H. Allen, 1888). Photo 20.4 Constantinople in 1481. George Young, *Constantinople* (London: Methuen; New

York: George H. Doran, 1926). Photo 20.5 The empty tomb. Anton Springer, *Handbuch der Kunstgeschichte* (Leipzig: Seemann, 1904). Photo 20.6 Abbey of Rievaulx. Photo 20.7 Exhibit in the abbey's Interpretive Centre. Photo 20.8 Abbey Church of Iona. Photo 20.9 Martyr's Bay, Iona. Photo 20.10 Martin Luther. Georg Buchwald, *Doktor Martin Luther: Ein Lebensbild für das deutsche Haus* (Leipzig: B. G. Teubner, 1914). Photo 20.11 Wartburg Castle. Photo 20.12 Portrait of John Calvin. John Wright, *A History of All Nations* (Philadelphia: Lea Brothers, 1905). Photo 20.13 Ignatius Loyola. James Gardner, *The Faiths of the World: A Dictionary of All Religions and Religious Sects* (Edinburgh: A. Fullarton, 1858). Photo 20.14 Statue of John Wesley. Photo 20.15 Friedrich Schleiermacher. Photo 20.16 *Oath of the Horatii*. Courtesy of Digitale Bibliothek, Yorck Project *Meisterwerke*. Photo 20.17 Jacob and Wilhelm Grimm. Eduard Engel, *Geschichte der deutschen Literatur von den Anfängen bis in die Gegenwart* (Leipzig: Koehler & Amelang, 1929). Photo 20.18 Grave of Adolf von Harnack. Photo 20.19 Memorial to Dietrich Bonhoeffer.

CHAPTER 21: CHRISTIAN FAITH AND PRACTICE

Photo 21.1 Title page of Martin Luther's catechism. Georg Buchwald, *Doktor Martin Luther: Ein Lebensbild für das deutsche Haus* (Leipzig: B. G. Teubner, 1914). Photo 21.2 Grabower Altar. Digitale Bibliothek. Photo 21.3 *Abraham and Melchizedek*. Digitale Bibliothek. Photo 21.4 *The Last Judgment*. Digitale Bibliothek. Photo 21.5 Pilgrim revival meeting. Wilhelm Oncken, *Allgemeine Geschicte in Einzeldarstellungen* (Berlin: Grote' Verlags, 1879–93). Photo 21.6 Thomas Müntzer. Photo 21.7 *Book of Kells*. Anton Springer, *Handbuch der Kunstgeschichte* (Leipzig: Seemann, 1904). Photo 21.8 Nativity. Digitale Bibliothek. Photo 21.9 The passion. Springer, *Handbuch der Kunstgeschichte*. Photo 21.10 *Evening Prayer*. Digitale Bibliothek. Photo 21.11 Basilica of St. Anne de Beaupré. Photo 21.12 African baptism. Photo 21.13 Confirmation. Photo 21.14 Homily in St. Martin's Cathedral, Bratislava, Slovakia.

CHAPTER 22: CHRISTIAN POLITICS ACCORDING TO ABRAHAM KUYPER

Photo 22.1 Abraham Kuyper. Anti-Revolutionary Party commemorative picture, 1920. Photo 22.2 Guillaume Groen van Prinsterer. Potchefstroom Archives. Photo 22.3 Willem Bilderdijk. Potchefstroom Archives. Photo 22.4 The 1920 Anti-Revolutionary Party commemorative picture. Photo 22.5 William Gladstone. Photo 22.6 Kuyper's study. Anti-Revolutionary Party commemorative picture. Photo 22.7 Coronation of Charles V. P. L. Jacob, *The Arts in the Middle Ages and the Period of the Renaissance* (London: Chapman and Hall, 1870). Photo 22.8 1971 election poster for the Anti-Revolutionary Party.

CHAPTER 23: THE CHALLENGE OF ISLAM

Photo 23.1 The holy city of Mecca. Wilhelm Oncken, ed., *Allgemeine Geschichte in Einzeldarstellungen* (Berlin: G. Grote Verlags, 1885). Photo 23.2 Page from an ancient Qur'an. Wilhelm Oncken, ed., *Allgemeinen Geschichte in Einzeldarstellungen* (Berlin: G. Grote'sche Verlagsbuchhandlung, 1885). Photo 23.3 Medieval Muslim pilgrim book. Oncken, ed., *Allgemeine Geschichte*. Photo 23.4 Western mosque. Photo 23.5 Syrian manuscript. Digitale Bibliothek. Photo 23.6 Written tradition. Photo

23.7 The shrine of Ali in Najaf, Iraq. Source: Wiki Commons, where it is said to be the work of a U.S. Navy employee while on official duty and therefore in the public domain. Available at http://commons.wikimedia.org/wiki/File:Meshed_ali_usnavy_(PD).jpg. Photo 23.8 Egypt's Al-Azhar University. Source: Wikimedia Commons, which states that the owner of this file has released it into the public domain without restriction. Available at http://commons.wikimedia.org/wiki/File:Al-Azhar_2006.jpg. Photo 23.9 The Al Askari Mosque in Samarra. Source: Wikimedia Commons, where the author, Toushiro, releases it into the public domain. Available at http://commons.wikimedia.org/wiki/File:Al_Askari_Mosque.jpg. Photo 23.10 Modern mosque. Photo 23.11 Sufi dervishes. James Gardner, *The Faiths of the World: A Dictionary of All Religions and Religious Sects* (Edinburgh: A. Fullarton, 1858).

CHAPTER 24: MUSLIM BELIEFS AND PRACTICES

Photo 24.1 Ancient Qur'an. August Müller, *Der Islam im Morgen- und Abendland*, in Wilhelm Oncken, ed., *Allgemeine Geschichte in Einzeldarstellungen* (Berlin: G. Grote'sche Verlagsbuchhandlung, 1885). Photo 24.2 Moses preaching to the Jews. Digitale Bibliothek. Photo 24.3 John the Evangelist dictating his gospel. Digitale Bibliothek. Photo 24.4 Fragments of the Decalogue. Isidore Singer, *The Jewish Encyclopedia* (New York: Funk & Wagnalls, 1901–1906). Photo 24.5 Guests of an Arab doctor drinking wine. Digitale Bibliothek. Photo 24.6 Süleyman the Magnificent. John Wright, *A History of All Nations* (Philadelphia: Lea Brothers, 1905). Photo 24.7 The Turkish siege of Vienna in 1529. Franz Tschischka, *Geschichte der Stadt Wien* (Stuttgart: A. Krabbe, 1847). Photo 24.8 Turkish invasion of Austria in 1683. Tschischka, *Geschichte der Stadt Wien*. Photo 24.9 Market square of Zwikau. Photo 24.10 The plaque thanking God. Photo 24.11 The fortress of the Hospitallers. Wright, *History of All Nations*. Photo 24.12 The tomb of Muhammad Ahmad ibn As-sayyid Abd Allah. Charles W. Domville-Fife, *The Encyclopedia of the British Empire* (London: Virtue and Co., 1925). Photo 24.13 The Taj Mahal. © Caleb Nienkirchen. Photo 24.14 The Wilmersdorfer Mosque. Wikimedia Commons.

CHAPTER 25: MUSLIM PIETY

Photo 25.1 Gestures for standing prayer. John Wright, *A History of All Nations* (Philadelphia: Lea Brothers, 1905). Photo 25.2 Gestures for kneeling in prayer. Wright, *A History of All Nations*. Photo 25.3 Prayer mat. Photo 25.4 Muslims performing their prayers. William M. Thomson, *The Land and the Book* (New York: Harper and Brothers, 1859). Photo 25.5 Water fountain for ritual cleansing. Photo 25.6 Grey Street Mosque. Photo 27.7 Raza Mosque, Wigan. Photo 25.8 Modern mosque in western North American city. Photo 25.9 Islamic propagation center. Photo 25.10 Young Ismaili Muslims.

CHAPTER 26: SAYYID QUTB AND THE REBIRTH OF CONTEMPORARY ISLAM

Photo 26.1 Sayyid Qutb and William R. Ross. Courtesy of Greeley Museum. Photo 26.2 Port Said, Egypt, in the 1920s. Charles W. Domville-Fife, *The Encyclopedia of the British Empire* (London: Virtue and Co., 1925). Photo 26.3 Sayed Kotb (Qutb) pictured in the Colorado State College yearbook. Courtesy of Greeley Museum. Photo 26.4 Greeley, Colorado, in 1940. Courtesy Greeley Museum. Photo 26.5 Typical American college women. Courtesy of Bentley Historical Library, University of Michigan (BL005669). Photo 26.6 Kissing at a church dance. Courtesy of Greeley Museum. Photo 26.7 Medieval Iran. Painting by Iranian artist Nasrin Elmi. Used by permission. Photo 26.8 Greeley College. Courtesy of Greeley Museum. Photo 26.9 Qutb as a student, pictured in the Greeley College yearbook. Courtesy of Greeley Museum. Photo 26.10 Muslim New Year. Painting by Iranian artist Nasrin Elmi. Used with permission.

CONCLUSION: WHITHER RELIGIOUS STUDIES?

Photo 27.1 Berlin's Holocaust Memorial. Photo 27.2 Oranienburg Street Synagogue. Photo 27.3 Anthropologist Karla Poewe. Photo 27.4 Ninian Smart. Photo 27.5 Dr. Ulrich van der Heyden. Photo 27.6 Go-Fest Convention. Photo 27.7 Doves of Peace.

INDEX
WRITTEN BY SHERRI LINSENBACH

Note: page numbers in italics refer to maps, photos, photo captions, and figures.